"Combining the breadth of a scho...
ist, and the open spirit of a radica........ Graham St John has written
the definitive cultural history of the weirdest molecule on the planet (and
in your body). *Mystery School in Hyperspace* tells amazing tales, sheds light
on the shadows, and brilliantly referees the ongoing psychoactive rumble
between the sacred and profane."

> —Erik Davis, author of *TechGnosis: Myth, Magic, and Mysticism
> in the Age of Information*

"Graham St John's tour de force through the tapestry of alchemists, hippies,
DJs, scientists, mystics, and seekers of the mystery that DMT
reveals is an exhilarating ride and a thoroughly researched achievement. St
John successfully builds up a historical profile of both dimethyltryptamine
and the quest to understand it, piercing the mystery to bring back translinguistic trip reports that illuminate the central gnosis of our time. As the
latest generation of psychonauts explores the invisible landscape of Terra
Incognita, *Mystery School in Hyperspace* could very well be the map that we
have all been looking for."

> —Rak Razam, director of *Aya: Awakenings*

"Boldly going where no one had gone before, Graham St John takes his
readers on a properly hallucinatory yet extremely well documented tour
through the history of DMT. Analyzing six decades of radical countercultural experimentation and exploration at the limits of human consciousness
and beyond, this is a significant contribution to the emerging study of
entheogenic religion"

> —Wouter J. Hanegraaff, University of Amsterdam

"Wrap your mind around the most ubiquitous and profound psychedelic
on the planet, DMT! A multidimensional journey that provides a smorgasbord of information, and will give seasoned psychonauts, dogmatic
academics, culture aficionados, and frankly any curious mind, plenty to
chew on."

> —Mitch Schultz, founder of MYTHAPHI and director
> of *DMT: The Spirit Molecule*

MYSTERY SCHOOL IN HYPERSPACE

A CULTURAL HISTORY OF
DMT

GRAHAM ST JOHN

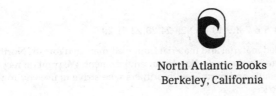

North Atlantic Books
Berkeley, California

Published by
North Atlantic Books
Berkeley, California

Cover art by Beau Deeley
Cover design by Daniel Tesser
Book design by Brad Greene

Printed in Canada

Mystery School in Hyperspace: A Cultural History of DMT is sponsored and published by the Society for the Study of Native Arts and Sciences (dba North Atlantic Books), an educational nonprofit based in Berkeley, California, that collaborates with partners to develop cross-cultural perspectives, nurture holistic views of art, science, the humanities, and healing, and seed personal and global transformation by publishing work on the relationship of body, spirit, and nature.

DISCLAIMER: The following information is intended for general information purposes only. The publisher does not advocate illegal activities but does believe in the right of individuals to have free access to information and ideas. Any application of the material set forth in the following pages is at the reader's discretion and is his or her sole responsibility.

North Atlantic Books' publications are available through most bookstores. For further information, visit our website at www.northatlanticbooks.com or call 800-733-3000.

Library of Congress Cataloging-in-Publication Data

St John, Graham, 1968–
    Mystery school in hyperspace : a cultural history of DMT / Graham St John.
        pages cm
    ISBN 978-1-58394-732-6 (paperback) — ISBN 978-1-58394-733-3 (e-book)
    1. Hallucinogenic drugs. 2. Dimethyltryptamine. 3. Fourth dimension (Parapsychology). 4. Hallucinogenic drugs and religious experience. 5. Shamanism. I. Title.
    BF209.H34S72 2015
    204.2—dc23   2015012875

3 4 5 6 7 8 9 10 MQ 25 24 23 22 21 20

This book includes recycled material and material from well-managed forests. North Atlantic Books is committed to the protection of our environment. We print on recycled paper whenever possible and partner with printers who strive to use environmentally responsible practices.

ACKNOWLEDGMENTS

A provocation of midwives encouraged this book into the world. Daniel Pinchbeck initially forwarded the idea to North Atlantic Books in 2012, where Doug Reil gave it a chance and with unswerving professionalism and a dedication to excellence, Louis Swaim later oversaw the editorial production, Adrienne Armstrong the copyediting, and Candace Hyatt, the index. Dennis McKenna kindly wrote the foreword and provided valuable feedback. Jon Hanna offered a thoroughgoing forensic assessment of Chapter Three along with various other leads and connections. Rick Watson was most accommodating with details and commentary concerning his material used in the book. Many others responded kindly and with many crucial details to my relentless inquiries, helping with the inclusion of original and interview material: Julian Palmer, Rick Strassman, Ralph Metzner, Mitch Schultz, Nen, Carey Thompson, Ray Thorpe, Gwyllm Llwydd, David Luke, Neil Pike, Raja Ram, Nik Sequenci, Youth, Simon Ghahary, Olli and Miki Wisdom, Des Tramacchi, Rak Razam, Ed Sanders, Tim Scully, Keeper Trout, Jonathan Taylor, Orryelle Defenestrate-Bascule, Milosz, Floyd Davis, Dennis Tapper (Hux Flux), Robin Graat, and Peter Hale. Many others remain nameless and blameless.

There are many artists whose marvelous artwork and photographs are reproduced in the book. I won't name them here, as they are in the List of Illustrations. A few artists warrant mention: Beau Deeley, whose *Divine Moments of Truth* graces the book's cover and who contributed another work to the project; Adam Scott Miller, whose piece *Condewsinc* was used on the first draft cover; and Cyb, whose epic oeuvre could fill a book (and who donated several works to the project).

Research and writing for the book was undertaken over a few years, with many friends contributing in unique ways to the project: nanobrain, Julian, Paris, Jules, Eric, Yoyo, Jay, Sean and Mish, Damo, Pascal and Lydia, Kathleen, Wolfgang, Mattias, Ian, Kurt, Rak, Alex, Chiara, Gen, Gwyllm,

Michael, Ted, Geert and Linda, and Csaba.

Most thanks go to the inspirational freakloriate himself, Terence McKenna; and not least of all, the Spice Queen.

I should point out that, while I received assistance from those mentioned above, I assume full responsibility for all content, including any errors, in this book.

CONTENTS

LIST OF ILLUSTRATIONS

Cover: *Divine Moments of Truth,* by Beau Deeley (2009),
www.beaudeeley.net.

Figure 1. *Dreamcatcher,* by Android Jones, www.androidjones.com.

Figure 2. *Burroughs.* Oil painting on canvas, by Jay Lincoln (2005).

Figure 3. *Felinus Holographicus,* by Cyb (2012).

Figure 4. Neal Cassady at Millbrook (1964). Allen Ginsberg LLC, 2015.

Figure 5. Jack Kerouac on a Visit to Manhattan (1964). Allen Ginsberg
LLC, 2015.

Figure 6. Dennis and Terence McKenna. The Brotherhood of the Screaming Abyss (1971). Photo: Dennis McKenna.

Figure 7. Terence McKenna. Photo by Kathleen Harrison (1976).

Figure 8. *Bushfire of Life,* by Shiptu Shaboo (2013).

Figure 9. *Curandera.* Oil on canvas, by Martina Hoffmann (2012).
48"× 42" / 122×107 cm.

Figure 10. *Divine Messenger of Truth,* by Randal Roberts.

Figure 11. *Contact,* by Cyb (2014).

Figure 12. *Hidoodlydo Neighbor,* by Art Van D'lay (2014).

Figure 13. *Vishvarupa,* by Luke Brown (2015).

Figure 14. *Condewsync: Transpiration of the Bose-Einstein Condensate.*
Oil paint, chalk pastel, pencil on 24"×18" bristol on board,
by Adam Scott Miller (2012).

Figure 15. *Transfiguration.* Oil on canvas with mixed-media frame,
by Alex Grey (1993).

Figure 16. *Beyond the Gate Keepers,* by Gwyllm Llwydd (2013).

Figure 17. *Soul Food from the Inner Sun.* Digital artwork,
by Jayarama Bryan (2014).

Figure 18. DiMethyl Temple at Burning Man 2005. Photo by Jesse Cohn.

Figure 19. *Diosa Madre Tierra.* Oil painting, by Carey Thompson (2002),
www.galactivation.com.

DMT (*N,N*-dimethyltryptamine) is, structurally, the least complex of the naturally occurring psychedelics, and yet it is the most enigmatic. In biology, it derives from tryptophan, one of the twenty amino acids that are coded by DNA as structural elements of proteins. Tryptophan is found universally in living systems, from the simplest bacteria to the most complex lifeforms. DMT originates from tryptophan via two utterly trivial enzymatic steps, the cleavage of the carboxylic acid group to yield tryptamine, and the addition of two methyl groups to the side-chain nitrogen. The enzymes that catalyze these reactions serve multiple functions in basic cellular metabolism, and thus, like tryptophan itself, are also universal components in living systems. Since tryptophan, the precursor to DMT, is present in every living thing, the implication is that DMT itself very likely occurs—albeit usually at vanishingly small levels—in every living organism on the planet. Nature, in other words, is drenched in DMT. Is this simply an accident of biochemistry or is it an indication of something more profound, an inherent "intelligence" that is built into nature? DMT invites us to look just a little more closely at the most fundamental levels of biological organization to perceive there a mystery, present since the origins of life and yet unsuspected until the vicissitudes of evolution granted a certain group of primates the neural complexity to apprehend its pharmacology, and the tools to isolate it, and the capacity for astonishment at the transcendent vistas it illuminates.

DMT was synthesized in the 1930s but was not recognized as a natural compound until 1946; and its psychedelic properties were not recognized until 1956, following the heroic self-experiments of Hungarian psychiatrist Stephen Szára. Of course, plant-based preparations containing DMT and other tryptamines as the active constituents were at the center of New World shamanic traditions for millennia before Western science turned its gaze in their direction. Unambiguous archaeological evidence, in the form of carved snuff trays and snuffing tubes, confirms that DMT-containing snuffs prepared from *Anadenanthera* species were in use in the pre-Incan Tiwanaku culture possibly as early as 1000 BCE. Snuff trays have also been recovered from the most ancient megalithic site of the New World, the five-thousand-year-old ancient city of Caral-Supe (also known as the Norte Chico civilization) of north-central coastal Peru. It is likely that the shamanic technologies utilizing *Anadenanthera* in these ancient civilizations predated the construction of these megalithic structures by centuries, if not millennia.

DMT can be viewed as a kind of molecular virus, permeating nature since earliest times, quietly awaiting discovery by neurologically complex, curious, tool-using, language-using primates. The human species has been learning from DMT ever since this coevolutionary partnership was forged. We have barely scratched the surface of what it has to teach us.

Graham St John's landmark work, *Mystery School in Hyperspace: A Cultural History of DMT,* should more properly be termed a "modern cultural history," because it focuses on the twentieth-century events that followed its discovery by science. The prehistoric and indigenous use of DMT in New World shamanism is a prequel to the story narrated here, which begins in the mid-twentieth century following its isolation in several plant species and Szára's self-experiments demonstrating its psychedelic properties. Although the decades discussed in this work encompass a relatively short time frame compared to the centuries of its indigenous usage, the story is nevertheless both rich, and dense. What St John's narrative makes clear is that DMT *has* a modern cultural history, a realization that comes as a bit of a surprise to those accustomed to thinking of it in the context of its ethnopharmacologic history. DMT came to the attention of science in the mid-1950s, in an era before "psychedelics" as a class had become vilified and marginalized, but also at a time when the newly minted discovery from Sandoz Laboratories, LSD-25, was creating most of the excitement and garnering all of the attention. By 1956, the year of Szára's self-experiments, the curious and fascinating properties of LSD had been known for some thirteen years, ever since Albert Hofmann's wild bicycle ride through the streets of Basel on April 19, 1943. Hofmann's discovery sparked great interest in the psychiatric and neuroscientific communities (such as they were at the time), especially when its structural resemblance to the recently discovered neurotransmitter, serotonin, was noted, and because its unique psychological effects appeared to be partly mediated by effects on serotonin. Speculation was rife that an endogenous metabolite resembling LSD might play some role in the etiology of mental illness, and the search for a possible "endogenous psychotogen" became a bit of a Holy Grail quest for the emerging science of biological psychiatry. Stephen Szára, at the time head of the Biochemistry program at Lipótmezõ, Budapest, was one of those questing scientists. Stymied by Sandoz's denial of his request for clinical samples of LSD (probably because he was working behind the Iron Curtain), Szára turned his attention to DMT, stimulated by recent reports of its isolation from samples of *cohoba*, a psychoactive snuff powder prepared from the seeds of *Anadenanthera peregrina* by the Taino Indians. With the help of his colleague, chemist Miomir Mészáros, Szára cooked up 20 g of DMT and after some animal experiments and a false start in which he discovered the oral inactivity of DMT, he injected 75 mg and thereby became what St John has termed "the Neil Armstrong of DMT." Thus began the scientific and cultural odyssey of DMT in modern times.

It is an odyssey that continues to unfold in the decades following. Unsurprisingly, William Burroughs was among the first of his countercultural generation to explore its properties, and pronounced it a "nightmare hallucinogen." Such a sinister compound could not and did not escape the attention of the CIA's MKUltra program in "mind control," sited in the VA Hospital in Menlo Park, California, and the nearby Stanford Research Institute. Some four years after Burroughs's experiments with a DMT-enriched extract that he called "Prestonia" triggered his nightmare trips, Terence McKenna's ontological reference frame was thoroughly shattered by his first encounter with DMT in his apartment in Berkeley in 1965; according to the apocryphal myth, the source of this material was boosted by an unknown "mole" at the SRI from a putative "fifty gallon drum" of military-grade DMT; more likely it found its way to Terence through the aegis of his high school friend, one William Patrick Watson, who was working on a summer organic chemistry project at the Stanford School of Medicine. In his unpublished account of the events leading up to Terence's encounter with DMT, Watson speculates that, rather than fencing government research chemicals as he thought, he (Watson) was an unwitting participant in a "controlled release program" in which these chemicals were selectively disseminated into civilian populations while maintaining plausible deniability for the agencies conducting this covert program.

Whatever the ultimate source of the catalytic chemical that Terence bio-assayed on that rainy night in Berkeley, there is no denying that it changed him, and everything, forever. Unlike Burroughs, who found a nightmare in DMT, Terence discovered the "Secret that cannot be told," and it was in quest of an understanding of this Secret that led us, as brothers, to undertake our journey to La Chorrera in Amazonian Colombia in 1971 and there to execute the now-famous "experiment at La Chorrera." For the next three decades, until his death in April 2000, Terence's life and career, as well as my own in part, unfolded in the light of the discoveries and revelations we stumbled upon together in the mist-shrouded pastures of that remote Colombian mission. I remained out of the public eye, by choice and inclination, focusing on my scientific endeavors; Terence, however, by choice and perhaps compelled by destiny, became the public spokesman for DMT and mushrooms. Our collaborations in developing and publishing the simple techniques for growing psilocybin mushrooms from spores collected at La Chorrera opened the visionary portals to the wider world. The methods for growing mushrooms, and eventually simple techniques for extracting DMT-rich fractions from numerous plant sources, have been developed and improved over the years by a new and younger generation of aspiring psychonauts, so that now the "tryptamine dimension"[1]—for that's really what it is—is accessible to anyone with the courage and motivation to visit its exotic shores. And yet it remains a Secret, and a Mystery; as fascinating and puzzling to twenty-first-century humans as it was to the first curious primate who ever munched mushrooms and closed their eyes in wonder.

As a species, and as a society, we are not done with DMT, or perhaps it is more accurate to say that DMT is not done with us. It continues to teach,

---

1 Psilocin—the physiologically active form of psilocybin—differs from DMT only in having a hydroxyl group in the indole ring. This trivial molecular difference is crucial pharmacologically since it is this structural feature that renders it orally active without the need for MAO inhibitors. Psilocin is the perfect orally active form of DMT that we sought at La Chorrera.

and we continue to learn from it. DMT has spawned entire movements of visionary art and mind-altering music. New psychedelic communities, committed to ritual and spiritual explorations, have coalesced around it. Some are even proposing to initiate formal diplomatic relations with the hyperdimensional entities they have encountered "beyond the chrysanthemum." Experimental ethnopharmacologists have developed new formulations of DMT-rich extracts generically known as "changa" that have made it more accessible, less "alien," and certainly more widespread. Building on the pioneering work of neuroscientists such as Szára, Julius Axelrod, and psychiatrist Rick Strassman, we now know that DMT is endogenous in the body and brain, that it is indeed a "spirit molecule" whose functions, while still poorly understood, must be profound, that must, in fact, lie at the heart of what it means to be conscious beings in a universe of life and mind and intelligence.

The cultural, historical, and evolutionary story of DMT is still being written. Graham St John's engaging and well-researched chronicle casts its gaze back on the recent past much as a traveler crossing a pass might pause to look back on a road hard traveled, and provides an important and much-needed narrative of the events that have transpired since science's discovery of the Spirit Molecule. The future of this ongoing relationship, as futures usually are, is a bit murkier but it is likely that we will be seeking to understand the Secret for some time to come. For anyone interested in that quest, this book is required reading.

I arrive at an oasis at a bend in the creek.

The gully rises to a stand of eucalypts on the far bank, as a perfect glade rolls out under my feet. An isolated campground, and in most circumstances it would be more than suitable. But this is no ordinary circumstance. Stumbling forward, I climb out of the gully and pick out a crest at the base of a ridge leading farther up the mountain. Here, a wide-branched *Acacia* sheds long, black seedpods on a green ledge overlooking the Goomburra Valley. After the recent rains, it's a luscious promontory about two clicks from the dancefloor, the bass emanating from somewhere below, an overture to a darkening mood.

As I scuttle to the deck, crows open up with a fusillade of invective. Blue patches flash through oppressive gray. Winds accelerate and recede, mirroring my internal undulations. Dried leaves on a fallen branch chatter uncertain tidings. Frequencies from a sound rig rise through the trees, sunlight and breeze remastering melodies en route to my ears on this solitary mount under a nonordinary tree. With its swollen trunk bearing unusual waistline markings, generous boughs offer its leaves all the sunlight they need on this day. But on this day, the clouds do not hang idle. Forming a restless roof, they offer protection from sun exposure and dehydration. And yet, blustery winds show me no quarter, scattering thoughts and voiding my stomach in accompaniment to the wind-warped bass. Carrot and chickpeas splutter forth in streaks of bitter fluid. Coughing up my spleen so close to the sky, I give thunderous applause to the performances in the valley below, even while I remain, myself, a pathetic spectacle to the birds.

It is February 2008, and I've ranged a long way upstream. This is Main Range National Park in South East Queensland at the end of a steamy subtropical summer. I am at the far boundary of Earth Frequency Festival. But how did I arrive in this valley, in this condition?

Several days before, I was in Melbourne, staying with my old friend Callum at his rented haven in Keele Street, Collingwood. But a storm had been brewing. For two weeks I threw lines at the bollards, sleeping no more than four or five hours a night in a bedroom empty except for an old mattress. In that time, I imagined the room a cabin balanced on an unstable pier, lashed by howling winds, threatened by breakers. I also imagined one of the tenants, Kevin, a stealthy Korean IT worker who rarely left his room, performing a perverse sorcery deep into the night. I became engulfed by a high-pressure system, sweeping me off deck, setting me adrift.

Daily, I cut the narrows of nearby Smith Street, an inner-city underworld. With its treacherous reefs, Smith Street offered uncertain waters for the inspirited voyager. One week passed into the next. Sometimes running errands, more frequently knowing no purpose, I crossed into a subterranean delirium inhabited by dark archetypes. The charts had blown overboard. The needles in the systems gauges whirred. What spirit was abroad? What had gotten into my hold?

I must trace my wake back to late January, to Rainbow Serpent Festival, Melbourne's psychedelic carnival. I'd caught a ride in back of a white Defender with John-Paris and tall outrider Jules, neither of whom short of a smile and good humor, Paris a bloke George Johnston might have known as an "eternal bartender," Jules drawing back on a well-crafted tube of Heavenly Music. A seasonal congress of knowing nods, smiles, and infectious gestures, Rainbow had an avuncular topography, familiar but rarely short of surprises. I'd traveled widely in the previous years, and as a scout I'd learned to "be prepared," but I was ill-equipped for the foreign Jamboree I was about to enter.

Martin was demolishing a single cone at a Mr Whippy van in the market. A few yards away, three thousand souls were throwing down on the dancefloor, where my friend Shane was cutting shapes in the turf, a ribbon of his great-grandfather's service medals pinned to his jacket. It was Australia Day weekend, and, surrendering to the rhythms performed by local legend Andrew Till, a legion of baked and bronzed diggers of dance were earning their decorations. Over this reverie, I was invited to a small ayahuasca circle Martin planned to hold at my old friend Phil's place in Keilor East.

Two days after the festival, I find Martin grinning mischievously over the stove in Phil's kitchen under a flight path of Tullamarine airport. Shredded pieces of a fat *Banisteriopsis caapi* vine are boiling in a pot. The vine is so thick my thumb and index finger do not touch when I clutch it. Decorated with statues, hand paintings, and woodcarvings of varying spiritual traditions, the house is a suburban temple, the scene of an unconventional experiment. The mood is calm. Soon we are boarding, and taxiing for departure, the climb angle and destination unknown. Cushions, blankets, jugs of water, candles, and buckets . . . deep buckets . . . line the apron.

Having observed a diet for a few days, that night I drain off a cup of freshly prepared tea. It's nauseatingly bitter. Now night, the door to the backyard open, I lie back into the cushions and close my eyes. Over the next hour or so, foregrounding the ambient notes of Pete Namlook, in the periphery of my vision there appear bust-like forms, some strangely familiar, glissading to meet my gaze, then vanishing as my mind pursues them. About an hour later, the potion is chased down with 200 mg of N,N-dimethyltryptamine extracted from *Acacia courtii*, a rare tree that I was informed primarily grows on "one small hill in NSW" and should not be harvested wild. Several years later, Martin clarified that this was, to his knowledge, the first time DMT extracted from *A. courtii* had been used with *B. caapi*. "When we first used it, it didn't know how to work with us or what to do. I had to call it in." It was "like welcoming a very shy person into your house for a cup of tea."

Sometime afterward, I sense liquids snaking about my stomach and intestines, scanning my internal architecture. A sinuous sentience coursing through my body, hairline cracks forming on the lining of my guts. I form a sensation that wisdom, a perennial gnosis, is available, though remains occulted, locked in an impenetrable black box. What was this device? And, more to the point, what lay inside? Could it be cranked like a phonograph? Would I perceive its frequencies? I seem to have become a caricature grinding this esoteric hardware. Sometime later, staggering with uncanny precision, I find the toilet. Rushing to unbuckle my belt, my backside smacks the seat and I perform a powerful liquid evacuation.

The others present vomit throughout the night, some spectacularly, poking fingers back to force the purge, upending to the accompaniment of Adham Shaikh. It was a savage soundbath. And amid the chorus, I detect Martin whispering to someone/something. Was he in dialogue with the flight controller? While not joining the spontaneous acoustic bucket band, I'd overseen the spirit's discharge astern. An end to the occupation. Anchorage in a calm harbor. Touch down . . . or so I imagined. I was unaware that the incursion was far from over and I was to remain at sea for weeks to come.

That morning, I departed the western suburbs for Collingwood . . . drifting, into a hypnagogic fugue. Afflicted by abdominal pressure, broadsided by dark influences, nauseated in the inner suburbs, I was directed by a power stranger than fiction. I developed an acute awareness of a hinge complaining ceaselessly on the door to the otherworld. At once, a dark recess formerly unobserved, and an arc from a lantern swinging there. A warning? A beckoning? I couldn't be certain.

One afternoon in the narrows of Smith, my prow broke the surface and made toward anchorage. Churning in the shallows on an uneven keel, during a partial solar eclipse I made interception with the Kent Street pub, a perfect bucket shop for a disembodied seaman. Seated alfresco with ChaOrder Magician Orryelle Defenestrate-Bascule, I poured over hir esoterotic sketches, a magickal union of opposites sprouting from a sketchpad, reproduced in hir then-forthcoming graphic grimoire *Conjunctio*. I had met Orryelle in 1995 on a bank of the wide, brown Murray River at Australia's alternative-lifestyle festival ConFest, back when s/he and the Metamorphic Ritual Theatre Company had mounted an unforgettable interactive Labyrinth installation. Drawing on Greek and other mythologies, the ritual theater had Theseus slaying the Minotaur, the beast within. It struck me that my reconvergence with this alchemical mutant trickster was no small coincidence.

A dark cloud shadowed me, as my weary rig plowed into a swell twelve nights from drinking. I'd spent several hours that day seeking refuge in Northcote's Edinburgh Gardens. But the winds were picking up, the seas had grown menacing, and shadow bands raced toward the horizon. Earlier that evening, in despair, I phoned friends seeking solutions to worsening spells of nausea, and imagined organ failure. I was vacillating. The pier had collapsed. Memories drowned in rapid review as I plunged into darkness. Dragged by turbulence along the seabed, disturbed sediment rose in clouds. The waters turned overcast, and . . . I . . . needed . . . to . . . vomit. I opened my eyes, lifted my head above the surface, and sucked in a deep breath. I began heaving.

And so, it commenced. That night, I floated subsurface, convulsed by wave upon wave of warm light—a light that could be *felt* by all of my senses. I was saturated to the bone by an iridescence unlooked for, my jaw dropping so low that it may well have fallen from my face. These convulsions triggered euphoric surges through my systems equipment. The floodgates opened, the flight data had been accessed, and although I did not have a processor capable of handling this raw information deluge, these were the most astounding readouts in my records. Surfacing repeatedly, I found myself blowing like a whale. Washed over with an electric charge, I was immobilized as one who has just bodysurfed a tsunami inland. Only upon much later reflection did it occur to me that the event will have registered on the Shulgin scale, approximating a "Plus-four."[1] Android Jones has offered a visual approximation of a resonant peak episode in his work *Dreamcatcher* (see Figure 1).

In the calm waters of the next day, questions mounted. Had I located my Kurtz, and taken him out, before becoming him? Had I defeated the Minotaur? Captain Willard had hacked down the Colonel with a machete. Theseus finished the beast with Ariadne's sword, and returned using a ball of thread. I hadn't even a pocketknife. A miraculous reversal had occurred, a tidal transit from deep despair to dumbfound relief. And yet, like buckled flotsam, I lay ashore, foundering, with neither definition nor clarity. Loading my backpack, I knew I had to leave these metropolitan shores and make the journey upriver. To the headwaters, if necessary.

It was necessary. And so, two days later, I found myself 2,000 km north, up the Goomburra Valley. It was Sunday, the final day of Earth Frequency. The day held much promise, buoyed by a false suspicion that I had performed the psychic equivalent of rounding Cape Horn on a windjammer. But there's nothing like well-made plans gone south. And magnetic south they went. Around midmorning, I wandered to the floor, greeting old friends en route, accepting treats offered without much thought. On the dancefloor, brothers Tetrameth and Shadow Fx were collaborating in the mix, with dancefloor denizens performing vertical reentries on the lip of a fierce rhythm. But I was floored by the vocal sample amplified at the moment I entered the dancescape—"ayaaaa . . . huasca . . ."—which in that moment evoked an extreme state of *duende*. It struck me as ominous, a perceptual cue hailing me like a harbor beacon rocking in a gale, a signal becoming visceral as my guts churned, ears thumped, and the music grew inaudible. I was stranded beachside on a sea of nausea. And it was King Tide.

Agoraphobic on the dancefloor, I had to evacuate myself from the area. Taking to the valley, I traced the winding creek-bed away from the party. And so it was, meandering, in search of elevation, that I found the promontory and its tree, under which I'd collapsed. The handle had been wound to its limit. Jeers erupted from the bush balconies. And my terrible cache would finally exhaust. If *La Purga* is a one-man circus staged above the headwaters, this may have been its dismal finale. A murder of critics hectoring the clown to the death, as rain squalls over a distant range.

Hours pass . . . and at some point the tide turned. The pall lifted, the winds softened, and a new light angled through the branches. The show over, the crows had grown satisfied, and the tree bore a curious elegance. This was no ordinary tree, and I felt sheepish in its presence. I stepped gingerly about my ridgeline station absorbing surrounding views through the eyes of a neophyte. It was as if I'd dwelled there for years, committing minute details to memory.

As distant kookaburras broke their silence, I descended my mount through the long incline of sclerophyll. Upon the final approach to the gully at the familiar bend in the creek, lurching sideways to avoid a large orb spider's web, a commotion froze me in my tracks. I turned to look. A eucalypt was set in the gully wall. Like an angled chimney, its thick roots were visible as the wall drops to a serene rock pool and a green glade beyond. On the tree's trunk in full repose and with neck and chest flared, there emerged the finest goanna I'd ever set eyes upon. Having jumped from its blocks farther up the tree, its bulk progressed in slow motion with the thinnest of heads falling slowly in my direction. It was an enormous Lace Monitor, maybe 1.3 m in length. The guardian of the gully. And it seemed to be communicating: "Go now . . . but remember, you are not alone."

I understood, stepping across the creek to the glade beyond. I moved to the bank opposite the serpent, its elevated eyes tracking every step. Forming an S on the trunk above, it reversed and gradually reassimilated into the tree. Crouching, I plunged a head cloth in the pool to wash my face and neck. Glancing about the glade, I felt like I'd been leveled by a cosmic steamroller. It was more than two weeks since the intervention in Keilor East. I'd skippered my rig round the Horn in violent seas, emerging, finally, under watchful eyes. Out there, at the farthest edge of the dance-floor, I'd given my black box a crank. Kurtz had received a decent hiding, though I knew implicitly that he lurks, still, in the hinterlands. And so, as the sun met the horizon, awakening from this trance, I wandered back to face the music.

CHAPTER 1

DMT

An Enigma Wrapped in a Mystery

This is not the mercurial world of the UFO, to be invoked from lonely hilltops; this is not the siren song of lost Atlantis wailing through the trailer courts of crack-crazed America. DMT is not one of our irrational illusions. What we experience in the presence of DMT is real news. It is a nearby dimension—frightening, transformative, and beyond our powers to imagine, and yet to be explored in the usual way. We must send fearless experts, whatever that may come to mean, to explore and to report on what they find.[1]

Since the mid-1950s, when its effects became known to science, *N,N*-dimethyltryptamine (DMT) has had a turbulent career. While a clandestine compound for decades, knowledge about DMT has accumulated in recent years. The simplest of tryptamine derivatives—others include 5-MeO-DMT, bufotenin, and psilocybin—DMT is found throughout world flora and is naturally present in the human brain. Created in small amounts by the body during normal metabolism, DMT possesses affinity with various (principally serotonin-family) receptor "gateways" in the brain, where it may even function as a neurotransmitter. But while data on DMT gathers apace, its ubiquitous presence throughout nature, and its occurrence within the brain, remain a mystery—an enigmatic status that appears to have strengthened its own appeal. Compared to LSD, with which DMT has been classified as an illegal drug since the 1960s, and which was abruptly dropped into the popular imagination between 1965 and 1968, DMT has accomplished a long, slow release into the cultural bloodstream. This book offers a detailed exposé on the strange and perplexing career of DMT, documenting developments in the arts, religion, and sciences, both official and underground, that have given shape to its identity.[2]

Hardly figured beyond scientific agendas in the 1960s, DMT's dramatic effect on perception commanded reverential attitudes among small cohorts, a circumstance inhibiting popular use. Largely as a result of the disparate efforts of Terence McKenna, Rick Strassman, Alex Grey, among others, coupled with the availability of new botanical sources, extraction techniques, improved methods of use, and the advent of the internet, DMT achieved something of a "coming out" in the 1990s and early 2000s. The U.S. National Survey on Drug Use and Health has shown the lifetime use of DMT in any form to have increased twofold, from an estimated 688,000 in 2006 to 1,475,000 in 2012.[3] At the same time, a study based on data obtained from the 2012 Global Drug Survey yielded significant details on what for decades had been an obscure compound that served as a magnet for misinformation. DMT was found to have "offered a strong, intense, short-lived psychedelic high with relatively few negative effects or 'come down.'" In this, the largest global study of DMT users to date, it was found that DMT is typically smoked and was seen to attract a larger proportion of new users (24 percent) compared with other substances, including LSD, psilocybin-containing mushrooms, and ketamine, suggesting that its popularity is likely to increase. Overall, DMT was stated to possess "a very desirable effect profile indicating a high abuse liability that may be offset by a low urge to use more." The researchers found that the new-user subpopulation was more likely to be younger, male, and currently in education, and, not unlike other psychedelic substances, "DMT's profound effects on consciousness" were stated to potentially "limit its appeal to the wider population and likely prevent habitual use, except in those who use it in a religious context."[4] Under such sketchwork, DMT has been identified as an emerging phenomenon of note.

Mystery School in Hyperspace grows flesh on these skeleton notes. DMT is probably most known for its role as an ingredient integral to the visionary Amazonian drink ayahuasca, a practice that today flourishes outside of forest traditions and around the globe, via syncretic churches, in visionary art, in tourism, in neoshamanic practices, and in experiments with "ayahuasca analogues."[5] But while the psychoactive properties of DMT have been most commonly experienced as part of the synergistic, shamanic, and purgative ayahuasca-delivery mechanism, as this book illustrates, DMT is a phenomenon unto itself. Not only a unique story in the history of psychedelics, DMT holds a secret that, according to a great many who've been charmed by its extraordinary influence, may prise ajar the Pandora's box of consciousness—illuminating, perhaps, what it means to be human. The "secret," the "key," the "grail," DMT is a story as compelling as its denouement is uncertain. But what struck my curiosity from the outset was that this story had gone largely untold—surprising given the many comparable histories of, for example, LSD, hallucinogenic mushrooms, cannabis, and MDMA, among other survivors of the War on Drugs.[6]

With its psychopharmacology known to science since the mid-1950s, and with subsequent discoveries and advances in methods of synthesis, extraction, and techniques of use, between the 1960s and 1990s, DMT has made an unassuming entry upon the cultural stage. Leading roles have been performed by Beat pioneer William Burroughs, psychedelic dramaturge Timothy Leary, alchemist Nick Sand, tryptamine hyperspace philosopher Terence McKenna, ethnopharmacologist Dennis McKenna, visionary artist Alex Grey, and not least of all clinical psychiatrist Rick Strassman, whose early-1990s research conducted at the University of New Mexico was received with popular critical acclaim. Documenting trials in which sixty healthy volunteers were injected with DMT and then observed for immediate phenomenological outcomes, Strassman's *DMT: The Spirit Molecule* became a best seller, with its speculations rippling throughout the underground and solidifying as folk knowledge. The book inspired filmmaker Mitch Schultz to produce a documentary film with the same title. If the Facebook page for Schultz's *DMT: The Spirit Molecule* is a measure of its celebrity stature—flying past the 500,000 "likes" milestone in January 2015—DMT is currently undergoing cultural elevation. And yet, while ayahuasca has become a target of interest among anthropologists, historians, and celebrity watchers, and a variety of psychedelic compounds have received thoroughgoing documentation, DMT has flown under the radar, even while it has inspired a prolific underground research culture, and has had a shaping impact on visual and sonic arts. While writing this book, and becoming familiar with the enigmatic nature of its subject, I grew less surprised by the lacunae.

Several reasons could be fielded to explain why DMT remains mysterious. In this introduction, I outline five interrelated reasons. First, the science of consciousness remains in its infancy. Our grasp of the purpose of DMT (and other psychoactive tryptamine derivatives) remains sketchwork since we have a limited understanding of the neurology of consciousness. Simply, we don't yet have an accurate picture of the purpose of DMT in the human organism. This is no revelation for researchers of psychedelics. While compounds like LSD, psilocybin, mescaline, and DMT have been rated as valuable tools in negotiating the vexing relationship between mind (i.e., consciousness) and the brain (its physical matter—neurochemistry), their potential remains neglected, despite the "renaissance" of psychedelic research in recent years. We are doubtlessly in the midst of exciting developments. While DMT, remarkably similar in its molecular structure to the neurotransmitter serotonin, is a known agonist at serotonin 2A ($5\text{-}HT_{2A}$) receptors, it also expresses at other brain sites, including G-protein-coupled trace amine (TA) receptors, and at the ubiquitous sigma-1 receptors, where it is known to be the first endogenous ligand.[7] With growing awareness of the profusion of possible signals communicated by way of DMT and other psychedelics within the brain, its action has been likened to "a chord played upon a musical instrument."[8] But we remain in the infancy of our understanding of the pathways and signatures of this "symphonic effect" in human subjects, let alone laboratory animals. While this effect may be considered "psychedelic," the dimensions of this quality continue to elude science because research on nonhuman animals—i.e., most of the clinical research on DMT and other psychedelics—cannot meaningfully determine the subjective human nuances of the psychedelic state. The inroads paved by Strassman have not been advanced substantively since the 1990s.

Second, DMT is more than a drug. While DMT is taken into the human body for psychoactive effects—normally smoked or vaporized, but also injected, insufflated, and taken orally (as with ayahuasca)—the tryptamine derivative is already naturally present in the body. A series of breakthroughs have shed light on the neurobiological provenance of DMT. Tryptamine and its derivatives (including DMT, but also serotonin, 5-MeO-DMT, bufotenin, and psilocybin) are simple indole alkaloids derived biosynthetically from tryptophan, an essential amino acid present in all plants and animals. DMT is the simplest of the psychedelic tryptamines, formed from a chemical modification of tryptamine by way of the simple addition of two methyl groups

(CH$_3$) to the side chain nitrogen.[9] Since Julius Axelrod's early 1960s report on its production in rabbit lung, this simple compound, known to be present in at least 150 species of higher plants, has been found in the urine, blood, brain, and cerebrospinal fluid of humans.[10] Neurobiologists subsequently discovered the gene that codes for the enzyme (INMT) that catalyzes the synthesis of DMT from tryptamine, with INMT discovered in the lungs, retina, and pineal gland of primates and rats.[11] More recently, DMT was detected in the pineal gland of rats.[12] DMT (and 5-MeO-DMT and bufotenin) is permitted to pass the blood-brain barrier, a unique privilege leading to speculation about its role in normal human perception, physiological functioning, and perhaps neuroprotective functioning.[13] But, as stated, our understanding of this functioning is cursory. While often celebrated (along with functional analogues) as "the brain's own psychedelic," these discoveries illustrate that DMT cannot be fairly circumscribed, or dismissed, as a "drug." While the compound's celebrated endogenous status has spawned theories about its role as a gateway to "hyperspace," a "spirit molecule" produced in the pineal gland, or a compound that mimics the function of an "ancestral neuromodulator," the further in we go, the bigger the mystery becomes. When asked about the inspiration for his art, Alex Grey once made a nod toward such revelatory speculation.

> Quite frankly, many of my images come to me unbidden at odd times having nothing to do with intake of exogenous entheogens. But since DMT is a naturally occurring neurotransmitter, there are always bio-chemical correlations to vision states, that is, as long as you are trapped in a skin bag. I think the pineal gland, the ol' melatonin pumping third eye, is the brain's illicit drug factory. Big brother arrest yourself for your own naughty visionary neurons. It's the stuff dreams are made of.[14]

Third, language fails. With a rapid onset and notoriously brief duration (its effects typically last about fifteen minutes, compared with LSD's eight hours), the effects of DMT are truly astonishing. The visible language it reveals is unspeakable, words barely adequate to convey the experience. Magister Ludi of the spoken word, Terence McKenna, would do more to articulate the experience and popularize the compound than any other, his rare genius leaving his audience spellbound. McKenna's long-practiced oratory on "machine elves," for instance, seemingly preempted their proclivity in the cultural imaginary. Within a few seconds, users may "break through" into a state of unheralded awe. While the experience is completed within minutes, it is typically felt to be epic in character. And while the impossible ontology of the event does not translate well in language, in decades of accumulated experiential journaling and tripping reports posted at virtual locations like the Vaults of Erowid and the DMT-Nexus, a user community has commonly reported accessing a visionary "space" that is higher dimensional in character, and where disincarnate entities or sentient beings encountered appear "realer than real." But if this were all, the goal of this book would be relatively simple. Geometric patterns, distortions in space and time, synesthesia, out-of-body states, near-death experiences, and exposure to "truths" about the universe and one's self are all associated with the "DMT flash"—an event far from uniform. While the essential phenomenological features of DMT-induced experiences are varied,[15] experients are typically overwhelmed by a strange familiarity. And while the event may be ineffable, the beholden are commonly compelled to communicate their experience. Here is one ebullient attempt to describe the indescribable.

> A gooey liquid of phosphorescent brilliance knits itself into neon lattices of emerald green and iridescent blue against a molten gold background. Always changing, always new, always novel, these geometric storms of shape and color never cease to amaze me with their beauty and intricacy; something one can FEEL as well as see. Clouds of molten gold liquid, boiling, seethe into arabesques and chainwork networks. Each node of each net and lattice form a jeweled point of incredible pure color, all rotating and pulsating through the eyes, brain, and stomach, as one becomes a transparent electric ghost deciphering mysto-glyphs for eternity![16]

Rupert Sheldrake once suggested to McKenna that DMT be dubbed a "necrotogen," since it offers sharp focus on the condition of one's mortality, and may even offer a "dry run"—a *little death*. For the curious seeker, DMT offers insight on the greatest of mysteries, that which lies beyond life, and before birth. This is the fourth explanation of why DMT is suffused with mystery. As we'll see, Terence and his brother Dennis McKenna regarded DMT as "the key." But while many have subsequently unlocked the gateway to the otherworld, and returned like heroes bearing gifts, are we any closer to mapping the dimensions beyond the here and now? Taken to the edge of the known universe, where users are often challenged without adequate means to communicate what they "saw" there, more questions seem to issue from the experience than answers.

Fifth, it is forbidden fruit. Besides Strassman's ambitious trials, clinical research on the effects and role of DMT within the human brain has been denied and obstructed for fifty years as a result of the drug war embargo that threw an iron blanket over a range of substances classified as drugs possessing "significant potential for abuse." Since the 1960s, first in the United States and then in most other countries, DMT has not only been classed together with LSD, mescaline, psilocybin, and other nonaddictive psychedelic compounds, it is typically classed alongside heroin and cocaine as a "dangerous drug" with "no recognized medicinal value." That said, within the United States, members of syncretic churches União do Vegetal and Santo Daime—both originating in Brazil, where ayahuasca has been legal for religious purposes since 1992—are permitted to import, distribute, and consume DMT-containing ayahuasca teas, the sacramental use of which is protected under the Religious Freedom Restoration Act.

Outside such small pockets of sanctioned use, DMT users and researchers face severe penalties, a circumstance breeding secrecy and silence. The silencing of research on the effects of DMT on humans perpetuates official misinformation regarding its value and status, and promulgates conspiracy theories concerning its origins and destiny. In the dark age of the War on Drugs, in the absence of sanctioned rituals of use, and amid a knowledge aporia on the purpose of the neurotransmitter, DMT obtains chimerical status. The forbidden status of DMT returns us to explanation number one: our virtual ignorance of DMT, enshrined in legislation.

If DMT is present in the human body in trace amounts and synthesized in our brains, but is at the same time an illicit substance, does this mean all humans are natural-born criminals? Such does appear to be the implication of the United Nations Convention on Psychotropic Substances, 1971, where DMT was scheduled under the most restrictive classification (i.e.,

Schedule I). The implication was recognized by ethnobotanist Jonathan Ott, who, in relation to Public Law 91-513 of the U.S. Controlled Substances Act, 1970, pointed out that the law "specifically proscribes unauthorized possession of any material which contains DMT in any quantity," and that under this law, "any individual human being is guilty of such possession."[17] The ambiguous status of humans in such laws and conventions is an absurd circumstance bearing heavily on DMT's taboo status, prompting users to pose the question—as found in the title of a popular YouTube video—"Why is DMT illegal if it occurs naturally in everyone's brain?"[18] An update on this inquiry could be "Why is DMT illegal if it occurs in citrus plants and fruits?" It's a question arising in the wake of research that has indeed found lemons and orange trees (and their fruit) to contain minute traces of DMT. Since a scheduled drug is illicit in any quantity (according to the U.S. Controlled Substances Act), as one commentator was driven to remark: "Every orange in your local grocery store is a Schedule I compound."[19]

So where does this research vacuum and forbidden status leave us today? Not unlike that evident in the career of other illicit substances, the forbidden is alluring, offering an (un)holy grail for the contemporary seeker, a clandestine appeal that, as we'll see, drew William Burroughs to yagé (ayahuasca) in the early 1950s. But while Burroughs may purge a black river to learn that ayahuasca is today promoted in *Elle* and *Marie Claire* as the key to success in love and business,[20] its tryptamine ingredient, often known today as "spice,"[21] garners cachet as a kind of gnostic bullet, a hit-and-run ritual for spiritual outlaws, the prestige of which is drawn not from ceremony and the authority of tradition (or Madre Ayahuasca), but from the defiance of authority, where the most revered shaman is one's self—the quest(ion)ing subject whose path was blazed by romantics, transcendentalists, surrealists, and psychedelicists.

And yet, we are not on the edge of a spiritual free-for-all, since repeat exposure to spice space, its "entities," and the associated dalliance with the *little death* has instilled in users respect for the compound, its botanical sources, and its conjectured role in consciousness. While dogma and inflexibility are déclassé in neotribal milieus, the search for self-knowledge and flirtation with "death" have led seekers to revere "spirit molecules," "shamanic herbs," and "teacher plants." Over generations of private teachings and hard-earned insights, users have learned to navigate worlds with abilities dependent on experience, discipline, and commitment. Codes of conduct evolve and are exchanged among the virtually networked who build guidelines for safe practices and enable the dissemination of practical information that, in its entirety, maintains a bulwark against the carnival of transgression that might otherwise transpire under the aegis of the ongoing drug war. At the Entheogenic University, for instance, the self-enrolled may take the Open Hyperspace Traveler Course, a guide for the safe and responsible handling of DMT, among a variety of other "entheogens."[22] The research vacuum appears to have been occupied, at least in part, by a vibrant networked underground research community.

As a result of the contest over meaning, disparate theories explain the function of DMT, seen variously as a "psychotomimetic," "hallucinogen," "psychedelic," or "entheogen," among other designations. This spectrum is addressed in these pages, but the view most common among users is that, as an "entheogen," DMT *awakens the divine within,* a view in stark contrast to the official position that it not only possesses little or no value to medical science, but that its theological merit is negligible. But while societies set injunctions against research that may contradict these evaluations, the divinity of the DMT event makes itself known in visionary and sonic arts, in neognostic media that gives expression to the desire to awaken from a lifeless malaise, which illuminate lessons about life (and death), perhaps even serving to highlight the nature of mystery itself. In the wake of empirical experience, users may regard dimethyltryptamine as a sacrament. It commands respect and seeds the crystallization of user communities whose participants are fellow travelers who know and share in its mystery, are devotees to its chemistry, cultivate its botanical sources, augment its effects, optimize methods of use and techniques of administration. Amid a pharmacognostic compendium of compounds, the effects of DMT and 5-MeO-DMT are today championed in narratives of conversion, initiation, and transformation documented in a vast library of online personalized "tripping" reports.

While this book charts the literature, art, and science that cast light on the mystery of DMT, its chief purpose is to document the cultural ambivalence that continues to characterize the phenomenon—an ambivalence communicated in views that cast DMT as a symbol of fear or hope. The former can be felt in media reports where the specter of innocence lost to the scourge of drugs is a long-favored tactic of stoking fears that serve religious and political campaigns. The new menace was, for instance, reported to the Australian public in May 1998 in the *Sydney Morning Herald*. While in the Northern Rivers area of New South Wales, "teachers and police had reported frightened teenagers on DMT running through fields," Paul Dillon, a spokesperson for the National Drug and Alcohol Research Centre, is stated to claim that these teenagers "tend to use it in ceremonial situations, much like young people play with ouija boards."[23] The implication was that unchurched ceremony could only amount to no good at all. And yet, the powerfully transformative implications of naturally sourced DMT, and other entheogens used within appropriate conditions, was soon to receive positive attention.

In the last decade, enthusiastic students have gravitated to "teacher plants" like iboga, ayahuasca, and DMT, with many cramming *Breaking Open the Head: A Psychedelic Journey into the Heart of Contemporary Shamanism*, the book that established Daniel Pinchbeck as the poster boy for entheogens.[24] In a 2006 *Rolling Stone* report on Pinchbeck, alt.cult commentator Erik Davis was afforded the opportunity to remark on a subject he'd been regaling crowded domes of dusty denizens at Burning Man about for years— namely, that "there's something about the televisual, hyperdimensional, data-dense grandiosity of the DMT flash that seems to resonate with today's globalized, hyperreal culture."[25] It would certainly resonate with *Fear Factor* host Joe Rogan, who began proclaiming the virtues of DMT in 2006, and whose pronouncements would circulate rapidly on YouTube, where millions of viewers were ravenous for the breaking news. For Rogan, with profound implications for users and the world in which they live, DMT was far from a recreational drug. By 2009, interested readers of the Denver-based internet news site Examiner.com were informed that DMT was "not for the bong and pizza crowd," but for the serious psychotropic explorer.[26]

That it commanded respect was more than apparent in the opening sequence of Gaspar Noé's 2009 film *Enter the Void*, where viewers would embark on an epic life/death, time/space-distorting journey after Oscar took a hit of DMT from a pipe in the opening sequence. The effects of that hit, and others like it, seemed to have made a deep cultural impression. On his talk show *BrandX,* in 2012 Russell Brand opined that "by taking DMT our consciousnesses would expand and we wouldn't live in such an impulse-based culture."[27] Participants in the impulse-based culture were seeking not only a powerful, short-duration trip, but quick downloads on the character of use and effect. The popularity of Dexthepole's YouTube video "What a DMT Trip Is Like" (with, at the time of writing, more than 860K views and more than 4,000 comments) is indicative of a trending desire to know the answer. Dexthepole submitted a candid report on his "ego-death" from his bedroom, encouraging others to do the same.[28] In 2012, *VICE* magazine chased this action by vox-popping several young people who "just smoked DMT."[29] That year, an episode of National Geographic's *Drugs, Inc.* featured a young man named Nation who smoked DMT, labeling it the "God agent."[30] By 2013, news about the "illegal psychedelic drug that you've probably never heard of that's produced by your own body" surfaced on Australia's government-funded broadcasting service, SBS, even if for only three and a half minutes, via online news program *The Feed.*[31]

Inquisitive Googlers could get a range of returns. At Cracked.com, young readers were introduced to the contrivance that "if travelling to another dimension and shooting the breeze with some aliens is what peaks your interest, then DMT is the way to go."[32] Over on *London Real,* six-time Mr. Olympia Dorian Yates announced that he had smoked pure DMT powder and took "a direct route straight to the spirit world." The professional bodybuilder stated that "you go to a place that's full of energy and colors, and geometric shapes, and what you realize is that everything is connected, everything is one and one is everything, and we're all part of it." Yates claims he was "spoken to, if you want, by God. . . . It was like the higher me talking to me and telling me that the biggest problem we have on this planet, on this plane, is the ego."[33] In recent times, more explorers have gone public. Interviewed by journalist Amber Lyon on podcast *Reset.me* in 2014, neuroscientist Michele Ross, for example, described her first DMT experience, stating, among other things, that it affected in her an overwhelming compulsion to help others.[34]

This rolling snowball of mediations demonstrates that DMT is a complex and ambiguous subject, with documentation posing a challenge for historians. This complexity is in particular due to its dual status as an exogenous and endogenous compound, the character and function of which remain (by fiat of law) underresearched. It is also significant that the effects of DMT vary considerably, with a diversity of reported experiences, from hellish nightmare to transfiguring dream. Such are conditioned by what is conventionally referred to as the user conditions of "set" (i.e., a user's psychological state, their experience, and their expectations) and "setting" (i.e., the physical environment and social context of use), with outcomes further determined by dose, techniques of administration and synthesis, methods of extraction, and source phenotypes, which, like many plants of the genus *Acacia,* are known to contain multiple tryptamines. All of these factors complicate the very idea of "DMT," as well as the "DMT user," given that combined variables will determine that both DMT and user are different each time.

A further reason why DMT presents such a recondite subject matter is that multiple disciplines stake a claim on definition, giving over to disparate theories about function, origin, effects, and value. As a vehicle for various knowledge claims, the compound carries a heavy metaphysical burden. For instance, while there are those who have hypothesized the religious function of the psychedelic effects of DMT in the brain, and specifically the purpose of its activity in the pineal gland, others build arguments for its bioadaptive role. As a result, DMT possesses a powerful ambiguity at the crossroads of science and religion, provoking conjecture on its neurochemical function, and its role in dream states, religious experience, and the origins of human consciousness. For six decades, DMT has been living out multiple identities. Venerated as "the key," or condemned as a "clear and present danger," it has circulated within psychiatric, recreational, spiritual, and law enforcement contexts with distinct profiles. And yet, despite all the hats it wears, and perhaps because of them, DMT remains a mystery most mysterious.

In the chapters that follow, I address this ambivalence, beginning in Chapter Two with the specter of DMT as the "nightmare hallucinogen," the position adopted by trailblazer William Burroughs in the early 1960s. This perspective was countered by Timothy Leary, whose embrace of the "transcendental trigger" is covered in Chapter Three, along with the emergence of the recreational use of DMT, an occurrence with its diverse outcomes. Chapter Four unfurls the integral story of DMT heralds, the brothers McKenna, before introducing the work of Rick Strassman and the enigmatic pineal gland, in Chapter Five. We then embark upon a journey into the DMT research underground, with attention to the smoking blend "changa," in Chapter Six. Two chapters then address the impact of DMT in electronica, with Chapter Seven exploring DMT and the arts of media shamanism, and Chapter Eight charting its influence in psychedelic electronica and other music. The book's remaining chapters chart the cultural impact of DMT by way of deeper explorations. Whereas Chapter Nine addresses how "DMT space" is interpolated by way of hyperspace philosophy, and Chapter Ten compares the diverse breakthrough experiences of numerous key figures, Chapter Eleven investigates the liminal aesthetics of DMT and the way the experience is countenanced across a spectrum of visionary arts. By way of various models offered to explain DMT entities, Chapter Twelve encapsulates the complex legacy of the phenomenon. Finally, Chapter Thirteen offers a concluding roundup, in advance of substantive sources listed in the References, Discography, and Filmography.

CHAPTER 2

Nightmare Hallucinogen?

> The mask-like mysteriousness of the objects in the room gave me the feeling that I had arrived in another world, entirely different and queer and full of secrecy and mystery.... There was a peculiar double orientation in space and time: I knew where I was, but I was inclined to accept this strange world as a reality, too.... [It] seemed to me as if this period might be an entire epoch, filled with events and happenings, but at the same time I knew that only several minutes had passed.[1]

It was April 1956, and Stephen Szára was reoriented in space-time. With the compound administered via intramuscular injection, the Hungarian psychopharmacologist discovered what had until then been pure speculation—the psychoactive effects of DMT.[2] These were exciting times, given the newly minted theory of "schizotoxins," chemical agents with a structure similar to serotonin that were thought responsible for schizophrenia. In the 1950s, the search was on for drugs, so-called "psychotomimetics" or "psychotogenics," that modeled mental illness in normal volunteers. Within psychiatric circles, LSD, mescaline, and other psychoactive compounds were championed as psychosis-mimicking chemical agents.[3] If a "model psychosis" in normal volunteers could be blockaded or reversed with drugs, those drugs may also be effective in treating endogenous psychotic conditions. The rigorous testing of these psychotogenic agents had far-reaching implications. Could humanity be on the brink of discovering a chemical panacea for madness? Might not sovereign states have at their disposal the maddest of chemical weapons?

Head of the Laboratory of Biochemistry at Lipótmezõ, Budapest, Szára was in the former camp. Believing it essential to personally experience the effects of a known hallucinogen before he could consider doing research with the substance, he strode a path blazed by predecessors, notably German chemist Arthur Heffter, who in 1897 experimented with pure mescaline. Szára had himself bioassayed mescaline in 1955 after reading *The Doors of Perception,* in which Aldous Huxley articulated his envisioned state under an experimental dose. But Szára was unconvinced that mescaline (or LSD) possessed the significance—a quality subsequently defined as "psychedelic"—championed by Huxley. "About 90 percent of the content of the book," he later claimed, "can be attributed to Aldous Huxley as a writer, and only 10 per cent to the drug, mescaline."[4] Determined also to lay his hands on LSD, Szára sent a request to Sandoz Pharmaceuticals in Basel—a company supplying LSD to chemists for research purposes—but his request was denied, presumably because he was working behind the Iron Curtain. With this option closed to him, Szára turned to DMT, a decision that appears to have been motivated by the recent discovery that DMT (and bufotenin, among other constituents) was present in *cohoba,* a psychoactive snuff-powder prepared from the seeds of *Anadenanthera peregrina* by Taino Indians (of what is now Haiti), although its precise psychopharmacological properties remained unidentified.[5]

The Neil Armstrong of DMT

Hatching a plan for clinical studies, with the help of colleague Miomir Mészáros, Szára prepared 20 g of DMT. A full battery of tests was performed on animals, with Szára noting the effects on a cat that had been initially very afraid. "But when I injected the drug it became quiet and very friendly. This behavior lasted maybe for half an hour or so and then he started to be afraid again and ran away."[6] The results were curious. But as Szára knew that the real science lay in human trials, he prepped himself for beta testing. Having ramped up oral doses (to 150 mg) without effect, he opted for intramuscular injections. Within three or four minutes on 75 mg, tingling sensations and trembling were noted, along with slight nausea, mydriasis (dilation of the pupils), elevated blood pressure, and an increased pulse rate, in addition to "optical illusions." Szára reported his discovery of DMT's psychoactive properties in Milan in May 1957 at the International Symposium on Psychotropic Drugs.

The hallucinations consisted of moving, brilliantly coloured oriental motifs, and later I saw wonderful scenes altering very rapidly. The faces of the people seemed to be masks. My emotional state was elevated sometimes up to euphoria. I had compulsive athetoid movements in my left hand. My consciousness was completely filled by hallucinations, and my attention was firmly bound to them.[7]

Hitting upon what he later called "the secret"—i.e., that DMT was active when injected into the bloodstream—Szára and his colleagues recruited thirty volunteers to receive doses intramuscularly at the Central State Institute for Nervous and Mental Diseases, Budapest.[8] In articles written over the ensuing years, including a preliminary report published in the Swiss journal *Experientia*, Szára claimed the "psychotic" effects of tryptamine derivatives supported "the aminotoxic and indole theory of schizophrenia."[9] Szára was in the possession of a rapid, psychosis-inducing drug that made LSD seem like weak beer, developments influencing reports on the apparent psychopathology of DMT. In this climate, researchers were determined to make a name for themselves by characterizing DMT as "ein neues Psychoticum," which was an attempt to add a new class to the system Louis Lewin developed in his 1924 volume *Phantastica: Narcotic and Stimulating Drugs* to describe the effects of psychoactive drugs based on their pharmacological action: *Phantastica, Euphorica, Hypnotica, Inebriantia,* and *Excitantia.*[10]

It is more than likely this field of research was monitored with great interest by the architects of Project MKUltra, the Central Intelligence Agency's mind- and behavior-control program, which coordinated with the Special Operations Division of the U.S. Army Chemical Corps, and involved research of interrogation drugs and psychochemical-warfare agents. Since its formation in the late 1940s, the CIA had taken a keen interest in brain warfare, with the phantasm of Soviet and Chinese brainwashing tactics imagined to jeopardize free thought everywhere, and fueling sinister home-baked programs in the battle for the mind. In the United States between the 1950s and mid-1960s, volunteers and unwitting subjects—including military personnel, those incarcerated in federal prisons, opiate addicts, and patients in mental health institutions—were subject to tests using a plethora of chemicals, including LSD, but also DMT, among other tryptamines embraced for their ostensible capacity to exploit personalities, to coerce and cause suggestibility, if not to effect the strategic discombobulation of targets, from select individuals to entire populations. In the paranoid climate of the 1950s, psychotogens were a Cold Warrior's wet dream, a chemical gateway to the realization of dark fantasies. With a healthy budget and top-level directives to secure state interests, the CIA bought the cooperation of doctors and scientists from across the United States and Canada, many among them champions of the psychotomimetic paradigm. Often working independently from one another and oblivious to CIA designs, this well-oiled research network gathered intelligence, often using unethical methods, on the effects of a veritable pharmacopoeia on human subjects. In one case, the lives of "mental patients" in a New York institution were threatened with near-lethal injections of bufotenin and DMT combined with electroshock and "insulin coma."[11]

Since CIA Director Richard Helms ordered the obliteration of MKUltra documents in 1973, the full extent to which the U.S. government researched DMT and other substances throughout this period is unknown. Recruiting "chemical agents" in the service of state security and public health, it *is* known that the Agency was interested in developing behavioral products and poisons from exotic botanicals collected through almost any means possible: "a leaf that killed cattle, several plants deadly to fish, another leaf that caused hair to fall out, sap that caused temporary blindness, and a host of other natural products that could alter moods, dull or stimulate nerves, or generally disorient people," as John Marks noted in *The Search for the Manchurian Candidate: The CIA and Mind Control*. Among the CIA's agents was chemist James Moore, who infiltrated an expedition of mycologist Gordon Wasson to the Sierra Mazateca, Mexico, in 1956 to procure "God's flesh."[12] Samples of the mushroom *teonanácatl* duplicitously collected from its source would lead, the Agency hoped, to the identification of its psychoactive properties, presumably to be locked away and deployed in the service of state interests. While unsuccessful in isolating and sequestering the mushroom's magic,[13] among a vast network of private contractors on the payroll, Moore collected and eventually synthesized a range of "natural products" for the CIA. As Marks noted from his research of materials made public following a Freedom of Information Act lawsuit, Moore became "a kind of short-order cook" for what CIA documents identified as "offensive CW, BW" (i.e., chemical warfare, biological warfare) weapons at "very low cost and in a few days' time." If operational needs called for it, Agency-backed chemist Henry Bortner "had only to call in the order, and Moore would whip up a batch of a 'reputed depilatory' or hallucinogens like DMT or the incredibly potent [incapacitating agent] BZ."[14]

In 1957, shortly after the Hungarian Revolution, Szára emigrated to the United States—where he worked at the National Institute of Mental Health (NIMH), and eventually became Chief of the Biomedical Branch, Division of Preclinical Research, at the National Institute on Drug Abuse, where he continued his research over subsequent decades, working on the metabolism of DMT and its homologues in healthy and schizophrenic volunteers with Julius Axelrod, among others. Following these studies until the early 1970s, many academic papers were published in leading journals on the chemistry, pharmacology, and psychedelic actions of DMT. By the mid-1960s, DMT had been identified—alongside two of its analogues (5-MeO-DMT and bufotenin)—as endogenous to humans, and later recognized to possess a molecular structure with actions similar to those of the neurotransmitter serotonin.[15] And yet, while the era saw research leading to the discovery of DMT's endogenicity, it also marked the inception of a scientific dark age, stifling research efforts to this day. In 1966, all civilian clinical programs of research using DMT (along with LSD and other psychedelics) were shut down, and further research into the effectiveness of DMT was restricted, whether as a psychotomimetic or as a psychedelic used in drug-assisted therapy.

With its possession and distribution subject to prohibitions across the United States beginning in California in 1966, by 1970, DMT and analogues DET (*N,N*-diethyltryptamine) and bufotenin were included in the Controlled Substances Act of 1970, which was followed closely by the United Nations' Convention on Psychotropic Substances of 1971, putting pressure on foreign governments to follow suit.[16] As researchers were confirming the natural occurrence of DMT in human metabolism by the mid-1970s, the absurdity of this scheduling and the severity of its penalties were not lost on commentators. With regard to these laws, Terence McKenna rapped:

"This is the Catch 22 that they hold in reserve if they ever have to come after us—you are holding, and you can't stop yourself."[17] Classified in the United States as a "Schedule I substance" (and, for instance, in the United Kingdom as a "Class A" controlled substance under the Misuse of Drugs Act 1971), with ostensibly "no recognized medicinal value" and possessing "significant potential for abuse," all but unsanctioned research into DMT's effects on humans ceased thereafter.[18] That is, until Rick Strassman's FDA-approved clinical trials at the University of New Mexico from 1990 to 1995.

For now, we return to the contested terrain of DMT in the pre-prohibition era.

"The Man Who Can Dig It"

Identifying tryptamines as "psychotogens" hardly commended DMT to laypersons. That is, if you weren't William Seward Burroughs. How one of the most influential artists of the twentieth century came to experiment with DMT is a story as fabulous as it is harrowing. It's a tale worth chasing given that the implications are as sweeping as the man's legacy. In 1953, writing as William Lee, Burroughs published his first novel, *Junkie*, the final passages of which signaled the author's compass direction. "I read about a drug called *yagé*, used by Indians in the headwaters of the Amazon. Yagé is supposed to increase telepathic sensitivity. A Colombian scientist isolated from yagé a drug he called *telepathine*. . . . I decided to go down to Colombia and score for yagé. . . . I am ready to move on south and look for the uncut kick that opens out instead of narrowing down like junk." An opiate addict who had tried every drug under the sun, Burroughs was on a quest for the brew ayahuasca. "Yagé may be the final fix" was the last line in *Junkie*.[19] The allure of the purported telepathic properties[20] of yagé was central to a modern-day Grail story starring a source of fascination for which there was very little reliable information in the early 1950s. "Grail" is most fitting given chalice-like vessels and magic cauldrons have been thought to bestow unusual powers on questing adventurers since at least the Celts, and as drinking vessels would become somewhat iconic of the then highly mysterious ayahuasca.

But while ayahuasca tourism has become a popular industry in the Amazon, with prospective drinkers today finding a wealth of information at their fingertips, sixty years ago there was a scarcity of information beyond specialized collections like that housed in the Botanical Museum at Harvard University. While British explorer and botanist Richard Spruce had observed and experienced the use of yagé among Tukano Indians in the upper Rio Negro of the Brazilian Amazon in 1851—exactly one hundred years before Burroughs first traveled in the region—until the 1960s, little was known about the psychopharmacology of this "magic" brew, the mysterious practice of which had been diffused throughout the Amazon with scattered observations dating back to the sixteenth century.[21] Burroughs may have gained awareness of yagé as an anthropology student—he flirted with the subject at Harvard and Columbia in the late 1930s, and then at Mexico City College in 1956—but in the "Yagé Article" he was concocting for a popular audience throughout the early 1950s, he led with the perception that he'd first learned about it waiting for a train at Grand Central Station. "I bought one of those he-man *True* magazines, and read an article about a lurid narcotic known as *yagé*, or *ayahuasca* used by Indians of the Amazon."[22]

A dense ecology of motives appeared to be pulling Burroughs toward yagé. While his "*Yagé* Article" was never published, an early manuscript offers two interwoven interests driving the search—drugs and the paranormal—the combination of which revealed an extraordinary skill-set, for which there were surely few, if any, rivals. The document reads like an application for a position for which there could be no competitors. "I have a special interest in narcotics," he explained. "I have taken Peyote with Indians in Mexico, I have smoked hashish in Morocco, used cocaine, opiates, barbiturates, benzedrine, and known the horrors of drug psychosis from an overdose of hyocine. I have the subjective cellular knowledge of drugs that would enable me to compare, evaluate and classify a narcotic that I had not already experienced." This résumé, as incomplete as it was, and laying out a brazen willingness to trek the pharmanautical frontier, is complemented with an expressed passion for "telepathy, foresight and clairvoyance, the ESP phenomenon."[23] These pursuits form a uniquely potent combination. If his article had seen print, it would have surely made Huxley's mescaline-inspired intervention appear comparatively mundane. Permutations of this manuscript promised an exotic-occult adventure, mixing dry quirkiness with ethnological detail, as readers were to be exposed to yagé, or *nateema*, as used among "the Jivaro head hunters of Peru and Ecuador."[24] Interest in the ethnology of yagé soon found its way into a letter published in the *British Journal of Addiction:* "Among the Jivaro young men take Yagé to contact the spirits of their ancestors and get a briefing for their future life. It is used during initiations to anaesthetize the initiates for painful ordeals. All Medicine Men use it in their practice to foretell the future, locate lost or stolen objects, name the perpetrator of a crime, to diagnose and treat illness."[25]

Anesthetizing, divinizing, crime solving, communing with the dead, yagé was the ultimate addition to any sorcerer's kit, an all-purpose key all the more intriguing given the next act in the Burroughsian drama. As is well known, Burroughs shot and killed wife Joan Vollmer supposedly during a drunken game of William Tell at a party above a bar in Mexico City on September 6, 1951. "I live with the constant threat," he later reflected, "of possession, and a constant need to escape from possession, from Control. So the death of Joan brought me into contact with the invader, the Ugly Spirit, and maneuvered me into a lifelong struggle, in which I have had no choice except to write my way out."[26] Burroughs was on the yagé trail before he shot Joan, but this notorious incident was integral to an obsession mobilizing efforts to "write his way out" by way of the Amazon and the secret it harbored.

A complete archaeology of Burroughs's motives would reveal that yagé also represented an opportunity—a story from which he could derive sorely needed funds. As a scoop appropriate for *Time* or similar venue, in the early 1950s Burroughs believed both the United States and Russia were scrambling to locate, retrieve, and weaponize yagé. The perception that the superpowers were scouring the Amazon for the stuff is evident in a letter to legendary Beat poet and longtime friend Allen Ginsberg on May 15, 1952. Based on feedback from one of Burroughs's former psychiatrists, Dr. Lewis Wolberg, he surmised that "the U.S. Army is conducting secret experiments with this drug. Next thing will be armies of telepathy controlled zombies marching around. No doubt about it. Yagé is a deal of tremendous implications, and I'm the man who can dig it."[27] Yagé was becoming the ultimate mystery, the quest promising multiple rewards.

Written in 1952, partly as a sequel to *Junkie* (but unpublished until 1985), *Queer* is inscribed with the possibility Burroughs entertained of unearthing an enigma in the Amazonas.[28] The autobiographical protagonist Lee, in his "routines" to gain the attentions of the indifferent Eugene Allerton in bars and steak houses across Mexico City, drops reference to the "telepathic sensitivity"[29] that yagé is supposed to affect in the user. "We must find the scientist," Lee tells Allerton, the one who "isolated Telepathine from Yagé." The objective comes to light. Lee describes an article he had read about the Russians using yagé in experiments to "induce states of automatic obedience" and ultimately "thought control." "The Basic con. No build up, no spiel, no routine, just move in on someone's psyche and give orders."[30] Burroughs may have been privy to fears motivating the Special Operations Division of the U.S. Army Chemical Corps, but stitched into a narrative threaded with "routines" deployed to keep the young Allerton under his spell is a homespun fix on yagé as a means to command obedience in others, like a secret weapon stockpiled in an interpersonal Cold War. As a device in the story's background, yagé functions as a kind of covert superweapon that could be exploited to the benefit of interests that are by their nature geopolitical ("armies of telepathy controlled zombies") or sexual/ interpersonal (at one point Lee asserts, half-jokingly, the psychoactivity of yagé might render Allerton a virtual slave to his desires). For Burroughs, the draw of yagé was that it could enable him to *be in control*—implying the presence of controlling forces he sought to overpower. But we might ask, from what or whom was he seeking to wrest control? A dire financial situation? Addiction? Ego? The Ugly Spirit? Conflated in *Queer*, these narratives line the path to the Amazonian interior, where the most elusive and mysterious of drugs could facilitate access to the dark interior of the mind.

Letters from the Psychotropics

The July–August 1951 search for yagé with Adelbert Marker (the inspiration for *Queer*'s Allerton) came to a dead end near Puyo, Equador. But in January 1953, still obsessed with yagé, and following the death of Joan, Burroughs, at thirty-nine, embarked on a seven-month quest through Panama, Colombia, and Peru to find "the secret." The journey was partly documented in epistolatory narrative ten years later in *The Yagé Letters*. I first read *The Yagé Letters* in March 2008. It was the 1975 edition, with no contextual introduction, nor appendices, just a perplexing series of "letters" between Burroughs and Ginsberg exchanged as Burroughs searched for yagé in 1953, and Ginsberg followed suit seven years later. While this extraordinary little book began with Burroughs writing to Ginsberg from the Hotel Colón on January 15 ("Dear Allen, I stopped off here to have my piles out"), it ended back in Panama with the epilogue "Am I Dying, Meester?," a flickering collage of memories sampled from earlier letters.[31]

While this text may be noted more for the letters that were unpublished,[32] *The Yagé Letters*, in any case, documents key junctures on the path to Burroughs's Grail. Traveling to the Instituto de Ciencias Naturales in the Colombian capital, Bogotá, he found ethnobotanist and fellow Harvard man Richard Evans Schultes. Bearing "a thin refined face, steel rimmed glasses, tweed coat and dark flannel trousers," Schultes was named "Dr. Schindler" in the book. While apparently never having himself experienced a full-blown ayahuascan event, Schultes had, by then, taken yagé on various occasions, and was also familiar with psychoactive snuff deriving from the bark of species of the *Virola* genus—in preparations that were common among tribes of the northwest Amazonias.[33] On Schultes's advice, Burroughs traveled to the Putumayo region. Following a series of misadventures in which he was jailed, was robbed, and contracted malaria, he returned to Bogotá, where in early March he blagged his way onto an expedition to Puerto Leguizamo from which he netted some 20 pounds of the ayahuasca vine, *B. caapi*. As described in letters to Ginsberg, he located a *brujo* to prepare the yagé. However, Burroughs was impatient, distrustful, and paranoid. On his first exposure, he grew nauseated and powerless, convinced that the "witch doctor" and his assistant were conspiring to murder him—a crime he averted by knocking back barbiturate. In his letter to Ginsberg on April 12, he conveyed the "sheer horror" of the experience. As he reported, "I was completely delirious for four hours and vomiting at 10 minute intervals. As to telepathy I don't know. All I received were waves of nausea."[34]

Reading this story, I gained the impression that, for Burroughs, yagé was mostly ineffectual, his expectations unmet. This set a contrast to Ginsberg, who, reporting his yagé experience to Burroughs from the region seven years later, depicted merger with "the Great Being" and his realization of the illusion of separate consciousness. That the Amazon was a failed mission for Burroughs has been a view popular among commentators who, like John Lardas in *The Bop Apocalypse: The Religious Visions of Kerouac, Ginsberg, and Burroughs,* remark on Burroughs's "disappointing experience with the yagé elixir,"[35] or who have found in the text a confirmation that "hallucinogens"—whether yagé, DMT, mescaline, or psilocybin—were not his poison.

But these views are inaccurate since Burroughs *did* have a breakthrough with yagé. And it was an experience that, in the wake of earlier attempts, caught him by surprise. Soon after drinking yagé with a *brujo* at Pucallpa, Peru, he wrote Ginsberg on June 18, 1953 (an account that did *not* appear in *The Yagé Letters*): "What followed was indescribable. It was like possession by a blue spirit. . . . Blue purple. And definitely South Pacific, like Easter Island or Maori designs, a blue substance throughout my body, and an archaic grinning face." He was compelled to describe this encounter with the primitive smiley face, confirming (on July 8) that he had taken "the most powerful drug I have ever experienced." Alluding to Rimbaud, he experienced "the most complete derangement of the senses. You see everything from a special hallucinated viewpoint. If I was a painter I could paint it." In the same correspondence, he expressed a conviction that "Yagé is it," and there was no comparison. "It is like nothing else. This is not the chemical lift of C, the sexless, horrible sane stasis of junk, the vegetable nightmare of peyote, or the humorous silliness of weed. This is insane overwhelming rape of the senses."[36]

The initial reactions were revelatory, even game changing. "Yagé is the final kick and you are not the same after you have taken it. I mean literally."[37] Despite the absence of these direct sentiments, *The Yagé Letters* nevertheless illustrate the impact of yagé on Burroughs's style—that he was indeed "not the same."

> Yagé is space time travel. The room seems to shake and vibrate with motion. The blood and substance of many races, Negro, Polynesian, Mountain Mongol, Desert Nomad, Polyglot Near East, Indian—new races as yet unconceived and unborn, combinations not yet realized

passes through your body. Migrations, incredible journeys through deserts and jungles and mountains (stasis and death in closed mountain valleys where plants sprout out of your cock and vast crustaceans hatch inside and break the shell of the body), across the Pacific in an outrigger canoe to Easter Island. The Composite City where all human potentials are spread out in a vast silent market.[38]

As this text held flashbacks of memories and motifs from previous letters, it demonstrated the effect on Burroughs's writing of the "space time travel" induced by yagé, anticipating his assault on "the Word." Here, as Harris noted, we find perhaps the earliest example of Burroughsian "travel writing," in which the technique is designed to replicate the experience of traveling outside of familiar temporality and cartography, a technique that would grow more advanced by the time he composed the book's epilogue, an illustration of the "cut-up" method deployed by the turn of the 1960s.[39] As Richard Doyle confirms in *Darwin's Pharmacy*, "as the cadences and gaps between segments of coherence engage the reader with their rhythm," as they do in "Am I Dying, Meester?," they "transmit something of the paratactic 'travel' sometimes induced by the drinking of yagé."[40] By the turn of the 1960s, no longer was Burroughs concerned with describing the effects of yagé (and, implicitly, DMT), but with simulating its effects in his art. And by the time *The Yagé Letters* was published, Burroughs's art was no longer strictly found in the format of the novel, or even in the written word, but in a profusion of multimedia happenings and cut-up techniques. While impossible to measure accurately, or completely isolate from other influences, Burroughs's entire collage of multimedia activities has been shown to demonstrate what has been called his *"yagé* aesthetic." Since "cut-up" techniques inspired by collaborations with Dreamachine inventor Brion Gysin are an art form that could induce altered states of consciousness in the participating audience much like those of yagé/ DMT, they are a "perfect vehicle," argues Joanna Harrop, "to develop an aesthetic of space-time travel."[41] A technique that you could "try," not unlike a drug, art was not so much representation as *what happens to you*. By the late 1950s, Burroughs had abandoned the yagé project, just as he had replaced chemical-derived alterations of consciousness with forensic textual juxtapositions, audio-video tape editing, photomontage, and collaborative endeavors. While we might question the effectiveness of such drugless strategies vis-à-vis the appropriate use of ayahuasca/DMT, enabling users to break from the straitjacket of language, and exposing the conditioning power of cultural media through their *détournement*, these methods pervade popular cultural criticism.

It is in Burroughs's most celebrated work, *Naked Lunch*, written in Tangier, Morocco, following his South American travels and first published in 1959, where the world first glimpsed his excursions into the psychotropics. Contrary to popular opinion, shaped by a censorship trial in which Grove Press successfully defended the book as a legitimate expression of heroin addiction, the nauseating mosaic of The Interzone is informed by Burroughs's experiences with yagé as much as if not more than with opiates. In *Naked Lunch*, we learn that "a haze of opium, hashish, the resinous red smoke of yagé" hangs over the city, infused with the "smell of the jungle and salt water and the rotting river and dried excrement and sweat and genitals."[42] Readers wander a city "visited by epidemics of violence, and the untended dead are eaten by vultures in the streets. Albinos blink in the sun. Boys sit in trees, languidly masturbate. People eaten by unknown diseases watch the passerby with evil, knowing eyes." And as for the scene at The Interzone's Meet Café:

> Followers of obsolete, unthinkable trades doodling in Etruscan, addicts of drugs not yet synthesized, pushers of souped-up Harmine, junk reduced to pure habit offering precarious vegetable serenity, liquids to induce Latah, Tithonian longevity serums, black marketeers of World War III, excusers of telepathic sensitivity, osteopaths of the spirit . . . doctors skilled in the treatment of diseases dormant in the black dust of ruined cities, gathering virulence in the white blood of eyeless worms feeling slowly to the surface and the human host, maladies of the ocean floor and the stratosphere, maladies of the laboratory and atomic war . . . A place where the unknown past and the emergent future meet in a vibrating soundless hum . . . Larval entities waiting for a Live One.[43]

For most readers in the early decades of this text's circulation, the effects of yagé will have been as fanciful as Xiucutl, a grasshopper-like bug that, as Lee learned from a German prospector dying in Pasto, Colombia, was a powerful, sometimes life-threatening, aphrodisiac. As readers were not apprised of Burroughs's personal experience with yagé—his unabridged letters to Ginsberg weren't published until 1993—its fictitious aura is enhanced. And yet, like a "sketchbook" of many different altered states of mind, *Naked Lunch* is an early carrier of the *"yagé* aesthetic."[44] Implicitly this means that, given its synergistic role in yagé, the text is, in part, a transposition of the DMT effect. But since ayahuasca's synergistic mechanism—i.e., that ß-carbolines from the ayahuasca vine potentiate the actions of orally consumed tryptamine alkaloids[45]—was not yet understood, DMT is never mentioned in *Naked Lunch*. It is harmine that is listed among a pharmacopoeia (including "mescaline, LSD6 and deteriorated adrenaline") abused by the Director of the Reconditioning Center of Freeland, the notorious Dr. Benway, the archetypically unprincipled medico persistent through Burroughs's work. And consistent with the psychotomimetic paradigm of 1950s psychiatry, harmine is noted to "produce an approximate schizophrenia" with "the best stuff extracted from the blood of schizos."[46]

While "telepathine" is no longer parlayed by the time of *Naked Lunch,* Burroughs writes on the prevailing assumption that harmala alkaloids were the psychoactive agents in yagé. And yet, in his formative experience with ayahuasca, as reported to Ginsberg on June 18, 1953, Burroughs *had* been exposed to a "secret" known to few Westerners: that shamans mix the vine with boiled leaves from an additional botanical source. "Hold the press," he'd written. "Everything I wrote about Yagé subject to revision in the light of subsequent experience. It is *not* like weed, nor anything else I have ever experienced. I am now prepared to believe the *Brujos* do have secrets and that Yagé alone is quite different from the Yagé prepared with the leaves and the plants the *Brujos* add to it."[47] In the manuscript of his *"Yagé* Article," Burroughs had referred to these leaves as *"essential* for the full hallucinating effect" of yagé, identifying the plant (with the help of an unidentified Peruvian botanist) as *Palicourea sp. Rubiaceae.* With this unpublished discovery, states Harris, Burroughs was the first to identify the genus of the plant now known as *Psychotria viridis,* which is called *chacruna* in the Quechua languages and is a chief source of DMT used in ayahuasca in South and Central America.[48] While Burroughs had dried specimens of the admixture plant identified, this discovery was curiously unacknowledged by Schultes. But with this fix on what is among the most synergistic wonders of ethnobotany, connoted in *Naked Lunch* as "souped-up Harmine," Burroughs went on to infuse his life and artistic output with a resonant mystery, cutting up source materials, mixing media, decocting language, extracting new thought forms, and trying them. Referring to Burroughs's photomontages, Leary had the measure of this process: "cut up pictures. Boil out the essence of the pictures. And then shoot it."[49]

Dim-N in Tangier

In the wake of the breakthrough in Peru, Burroughs was convinced the pharmacology of yagé required further research. "Since the crude extract is such a powerful, hallucinating narcotic," he knew "even more spectacular results could be obtained with stronger, synthetic variations."[50] Reckoning the matter warranted laboratory research, he preempted Szára's experiments that same year. While there is no evidence that Burroughs had known at the time that it came from the admixture plant used in the very brew that he had trekked into the heart of the Amazon to drink, and the genus of which he apparently had identified in 1953,[51] Burroughs would eventually try DMT in Tangier. This was at the end of a period (1959–61) in which he also used mescaline and psilocybin, in addition to hashish. This new period of experimentation coincided with the beginnings of the "cut-up" development in October 1959 delivering derangements of the senses reminiscent of yagé's effect. DMT was received in Tangier in March 1961 as a powder called "Prestonia."[52]

The "Prestonia" had been synthesized and presumably labeled by Dennis Evans, whom Burroughs had befriended in either Tangier or Paris. Most known for his work with a nuclear magnetic resonance spectrometer, a keeper of exotic pets, Evans also pursued "the recreational aspects of organic chemistry." In his basement lab at Imperial College, London, where he was a reader in organic chemistry, Evans, according to Burroughs biographer Barry Miles, is said to have synthesized compounds such as "diethyltryptamine" (DET), which he would "first test on himself to discover their effects." With Miles writing that Burroughs visited Evans in his lab on a weekly basis while living in London at the turn of the 1960s, it is likely that Burroughs was soon testing it also (along with other compounds Evans apparently synthesized, such as bulbocapnine). In Tangier in 1961, Burroughs appears to have first taken "Prestonia" with friend and author of *The Sheltering Sky,* Paul Bowles, who after snorting it reported "a vision of his head blown open, as in a comic strip."[53] Burroughs continued experimenting with "Prestonia" in Tangier until May '61.

Experiences injecting "Prestonia" were reported in letters to Gysin during this period. In the published letters, it is first mentioned on April 8, 1961, where Burroughs appears to have been summoned directly to the "Prestonia Ovens," likening the experience to a mental holocaust. "Trip to the ovens like white hot bees through your flesh and bones and everything, but I was only in the ovens for thirty seconds."[54] While initial reports sounded out warnings, it wasn't all sinister. The synesthetic quality of the experience appears to have been implicated in ongoing experiments where the "synaesthetic cross-activation" of text, image, and audio potentiated radical shifts in perception.[55] One such experiment was the "color alphabet." At this time, Burroughs was interested in exchanging letters of the alphabet for distinct colors, and performing walks through Tangier using a color map, with these alternative associations bringing attention to the language-based associations normally directing thoughts and actions. "Burroughs was interested in how the synaesthetic experience could be adopted as a deconditioning tool for the habits of thinking that circumscribe and limit understanding and action. Like psychoactive substances, these walks induce a heightened awareness of non-linguistic relationships, in this case the relationship and associations between colors: 'And very soon you flash along on color lines without words moving through the streets like a fish. Try it.'"[56]

In Harrop's reading, Burroughs navigated his way through the DMT experience by color, lessons brought back to modify "color walks" through the streets of Tangier. But this was no candy-coated Kodak moment. In a letter to Gysin, on April 20, 1961, Burroughs describes how he

[t]ook again of dim-N and stood in front of the Mirror waiting for the Attack that always comes when the dim-N hits. The attack came from the left side of the mirror—Blue eyed red haired Russians in Tunics and Chinese Partisans among the marchers many women as they advanced towards me to the sound of gongs all chanted "we'll show you something show you something Johnny Come Lately WAR"—Tracer bullets and shells and flame throwers threw me back onto the bed groaning in the torn flesh of a million battle fields.[57]

A series of experimental sessions culminated in an "overdose" on about 100 mg in his room at the Villa Muniria, an experience said to have caused *"unimaginable* pain," an event that appears to have precipitated experiments in photomontage. Allegorizing this episode in an article for *Evergreen Review* as an experiment of Dr. Benway gone south, we gain the impression that Burroughs had plunged into a most disturbing place.

Fire through the blood: photo falling—word falling—breakthrough in gray room—towers open fire. A blast of pain and hate shook the room as the shot of Dim-N hit and I was captured in enemy territory Power of Sammy the Butcher. The Ovens closed around me glowing metal lattice in purple and blue and pink screening burning flash flesh under meat cleaver of Sammy the Butcher and pitiless insect eyes of white hot crab creatures of the ovens.[58]

The imprint of this brutal exposure flickers in subsequent work. A clawed insectoidal menace known in *Nova Express* as the "Minraud," behind enemy lines in the perma-war, the unbearable fact of the ovens—this was "strictly the nightmare hallucinogen."[59] And as Gysin, who was apparently also in possession of the stuff, probably given to him by Burroughs, was warned: "For Allah's sake Brion be careful with that fucking Prestonia."[60] Escaping the ovens by taking "twelve twentieth-grade tablets," Burroughs advised his friend to keep the apomorphine—a morphine derivative used in treating heroin addiction—handy. The measure was an echo of the approach earlier adopted with yagé, which required "barbiturate or other strong anti-convulsant sedative" on hand as an "antidote."[61] "Prestonia" tested Burroughs's limits—an exposure to the hell-realm. After all, "dim-N" is a deliberate twist on "demon." "I really shrink from taking it and you know what a glutton I am for kicks but not that hard," he wrote Gysin subsequently.[62]

Biographers have tended to dismiss, if not simply overlook, the effects of DMT on Burroughs. In *Literary Outlaw: The Life and Times of William S. Burroughs*, Ted Morgan wrote that Burroughs, like Bowles, didn't like the stuff, "and was increasingly sure that hallucinogenic drugs were not for him."[63] Burroughs certainly made his public reprovals. In 1961 he presented a paper (under Leary's auspices) to a symposium of the American Psychological Association, warning that "dimethyltryptamine and bufotenine seem to produce in many subjects alarming and disagreeable symptoms," concluding that an overdose of these and other consciousness-expanding drugs "can be a nightmare experience owing to the increased awareness of unpleasant or dangerous symptoms."[64] And yet, Burroughs's bioassaying events were absorbed into his work. Nightmares were the stuff dreams are made of. Still, his were no suburban "nightmares," as "Prestonia" seems to have triggered a dark vision leaking into the present—an association, one could guess, with the early-1960s perception that one was only minutes away from nuclear Armageddon. Although impossible to separate from multiple influences, these brief experiments with DMT inspired copy on the coming apocalypse that, in truth, had already commenced. Searing impressions from the 1961 "Prestonia" sessions are diffused in the Nova Trilogy, where the "Green Octopus" and "the ovens," with its cruel "white-hot metal lattice," are recurrent themes of control and punishment.[65] The opening lines from "Overdose of Synthesized Prestonia" ("Photo falling—Word Falling—Break Through in Gray Room—Towers, Open Fire") appear in various permutations. In *Nova Express*, "Slight overdose of dimethyltryptamine" precedes "Your cities are ovens where South American narcotic plants brought total disposal."[66] If *Nova Express* displays a DMT aesthetic, it holds a paranoid attitude toward "the new hallucinogens." Burroughs's traumatic DMT experiences amplified his long-held fears that mind-altering substances were being developed by the military. In his broader opinion, hallucinogens were chemical "agents" to be kept under the highest suspicion, with cut-up a means to kick all forms of addiction—drugs, the written word, the media.

We know more about Burroughs's fears regarding DMT in correspondence with Leary on May 6, 1961, when he reported his overdose event, which was "completely and horribly real and involved unendurable pain."[67] As with Gysin, he urged Leary to "proceed with caution" and to familiarize himself with apomorphine, which should be kept on hand as a "metabolic regulator." He allegorized this experience for a report submitted to *Encounter*, the magazine later known to have been funded by the CIA. While the report did not appear to have been published there or elsewhere, Leary, who received from Burroughs "pertinent sections" of this manuscript, relayed the following story.

> Burroughs told a gripping tale about a psychiatrist in London who had taken DMT with a friend. After a few minutes the frightened friend began requesting help. The psychiatrist, himself being spun through a universe of shuttling, vibratory pigments, reached for his hypodermic needle (which had been fragmented into a shimmering assemblage of wave mosaics) and bent over to administer an antidote. Much to his dismay his friend, twisting in panic, was suddenly transformed into a writhing, wiggling reptile, jewel-encrusted and sparkling. The doctor's dilemma: where to make an intravenous injection in a squirming, oriental-martian snake?[68]

One wonders if the panicked friend requesting the "antidote" wasn't Burroughs himself. These reported forays with DMT are among the earliest accounts of private, experimental DMT use, a circumstance that, according to James Oroc, merits Burroughs the title "the Godfather of recreational DMT."[69] And yet one could question the valence of this mantle on several grounds. Burroughs was partly motivated by the therapeutic potential of the active constituents in yagé. While formative, subsequent experiments with DMT and other psychoactives at the turn of the 1960s were abruptly terminated in the tireless quest to formulate cross-media attacks on the word virus, Burroughs never promoted DMT, recreational or otherwise. If anything, his approach was, in spite of himself, scientific. In what may have been a response to "the antipodes of the Mind" staked out by Huxley, Burroughs was working on "a theory of neurological geography" by the early

1960s. In the contrivance of Burroughs, by way of Leary, "certain cortical areas were heavenly, other areas were diabolical. Like explorers moving into a new continent, it was important to map out the friendly areas and the hostile. In Burroughs' pharmacological cartography, DMT propelled the voyager into strange and decidedly unfriendly territory."[70]

Sinister Compound

If misinformation parading as "news" is anything to go by, half a century from prohibition the "nightmare hallucinogen" remains at large. The "scourge of drugs" has long been a profitable fear stoked by tabloid news media. Take, for example, the *The Sun* reporting to readers in the United Kingdom in 2010 that smokers of DMT "almost immediately suffer intense and often terrifying visions," with "side-effects" including "paranoia and flashbacks weeks or months later." Reporting a police haul of an alleged 126 kg of DMT—an absurd figure possibly conflated with the weight of the alleged DMT-containing plants—the article deploys standard moral panic triggers, with an exotic twist. "A brain-bending jungle drug is set to become a bigger menace than crystal meth on Britain's streets." Not only is DMT "linked to schizophrenia," and is "deadlier than meth," it's associated with "deaths across the world." However, the only death summoned to support this extravagant claim was that of seventeen-year-old Danielle Jacobsen, who had drowned in a pond in Connecticut earlier that year in an incident where "a coroner cited DMT as a contributory factor to her death."[71] That the cause of death in that case was asphyxia from drowning, and beyond that, irresponsible conditions of use—and not DMT itself—are boring details that stand in the way of a good demonization.

While the tabloid media has painted the portrait of a sinister compound, filmmakers have also joined the fray. Despite its focus on the effects of a fictional drug named "DMT-19," Blair Erickson's 2013 cult horror film *Banshee Chapter* is hardly good copy for DMT (from which "DMT-19" is barely distinguished). Adopting a "found footage" approach, the film weaves the shadowy legacy of state-funded "mind-control" research, and popular suspicions of DMT's production in the human pineal gland, into a story inspired by H. P. Lovecraft—i.e., "From Beyond," and its 1986 film adaptation, *From Beyond* (directed by Stuart Gordon). *Banshee Chapter* opens with stock footage of President Clinton in a televised apology to the families of American citizens subjected to MKUltra experiments. The opening is sutured with clips of shady scientists, news journalists, test-subject testimonies, and spooked commentators building the fiction of the tragic effects of "DMT-19" on volunteers who've all apparently been witness to "malignant and threatening" entities. Following this opening montage, the film's missing investigator, James Hirsch, appears on "discovered film" that had been shot by a friend. He is at his house slugging a vial of blue liquid described to the camera as "150 milligrams of specially enhanced dimethyltryptamine," or "DMT-19." Sometime afterward, Hirsch grows unsettled by a phantom radio broadcast, eventually announcing to a shaking camera that "it's coming towards the house." And as a shadow appears at the window, the film breaks into a sequence of flash fragments, terminating with a disfigured Hirsch, who vanishes. Like a tune from a creepy ice-cream truck overlaid with dissociated words spoken in multiple languages, and destined to be sampled more than Dutch Vermeer at a cheese-tasting party, the broadcast increases in frequency and intensity throughout the film.

Hirsch's college friend, investigative journalist Anne, discovers the broadcasts to be associated with the appearance of long-clawed, ashen-faced entities who appear to own their victims. The signal and its associated malevolence is found to emanate from the Black Rock Desert, Nevada—and more specifically Chamber 5, a disused fallout shelter repurposed in the 1960s as an MKUltra laboratory. Anne learns that the entities were unleashed as a result of experiments gone awry—CIA scientists struck the "primary source" (DMT-19 tapped directly from the pineal gland of newly deceased test subjects). The plot infers that U.S. government experiments with DMT on live test subjects produced a concentrated hybrid ("DMT-19") extracted from the brains (pineal gland) of their cadavers and then administered into further live subjects, who were then terminated and harvested for their postmortem pineal-extract, and so on, and on. The murkiness of this story is, of course, consistent with the cloaked nature of MKUltra, lending a weird plausibility to the narrative. Whatever the background to these experiments, it appears from the "discovered" film fragments that a nightmare was unleashed—i.e., malevolent entities from another dimension wearing their human hosts.

As it turns out, the most significant of these hosts is the film's Ted Levine character, Thomas "buy-the-ticket-take-the-ride" Blackburn, a rogue literary figure bearing an obvious hint of Hunter S. Thompson. Blackburn provides Anne with the pay dirt: "the government turned something beautiful, something transcendent and powerful like pure dimethyltryptamine and fucked it up, turned it into something dark, something ugly." He informs Anne that "the chemical is like a catalyst, it turns your mind into a receiver, it lets them in." Toward the film's conclusion, we learn how Blackburn came to possess such knowledge. Uncovered footage of the experiments in Chamber 5 reveal that, as a college student, Blackburn was among the original test subjects, and over subsequent decades became host to nasty interdimensional entities. This background resonates somewhat with the activities of Ken Kesey, who was given LSD-25, mescaline, psilocybin, a synthetic relative of belladonna, Ditran, the superamphetamine IT-290, and various other drugs (although apparently not DMT) as a volunteer in a (MKUltra-backed) research program at the Veterans Administration Hospital in Menlo Park, California, in 1960.[72] This exposure, and later work as an intern in the hospital's mental ward, provided inspiration for Kesey's debut novel *One Flew Over the Cuckoo's Nest*. But while Blackburn shares status with Kesey as an unwitting CIA guinea pig, unlike the psychedelic pied-piper who liberated LSD from the hospital and shared it among his friends—a beneficence that gave birth to the Merry Pranksters and an underground movement whose participants embraced psychedelics not as weapons but as instruments of liberty—Blackburn plays unwitting accomplice to a growing Cthulhuian menace in which DMT (or "DMT-19") is deeply implicated.

Where for Burroughs, DMT (in the form of "Prestonia") was the "nightmare hallucinogen" precipitating personal horrors, in *Banshee Chapter* (care of Lovecraft) the stygian world of dreams and the quotidian enjoy a fantastic merger. *Banshee Chapter* develops faint plausibility by exploiting two themes: the clandestinity of the CIA's MKUltra program, especially in relation to DMT research, and the debated significance of the pineal gland, which I will return to in Chapter Five. While it may have demonstrated that

MKUltra architects and apologists were criminal in their neglect of human ethical standards, the film is crudely disinformational, given the key plot device, "DMT-19," is hardly differentiated from a prohibited compound (indeed, "DMT-19" is depicted as a form of concentrated pineal DMT), and does little to challenge perceptions that uphold the law.[73] As subsequent chapters show, the "nightmare" characterization of DMT is in the minority. *Banshee Chapter* is fiction. But while few might take the film's complex plot seriously, one thing remains tangible—in the United States and elsewhere globally, DMT is a tightly controlled substance.

The "found" scientific footage in *Banshee Chapter,* revealing as it does the horrors of secret medical research, gestures toward Burroughs, himself most comfortable blending fact with fiction. Uncovered flashes of Dr. Kessel, who in the film appears to mastermind the exhumation of the "primary source" from human pineal postmortem, may have a pedigree in Nazi doctors as much as in the villainous Dr. Benway, whose character serves to expose the myth of objectivity in medical science—a perspective informed by Burroughs's relationship with the medical profession as a (queer) junkie, and as a medical student in Vienna. In his oeuvre, Burroughs is as contemptuous of the medical profession as much as he is of politicians, war hawks, and advertising execs. His fears about the ends to which the "nightmare hallucinogen" DMT and other hallucinogens might serve in the hands of scientists help explain his ambivalence toward Leary and the psychedelic club in the early 1960s.

While Burroughs may have had an overactive paranoia, given the information that has come to light on MKUltra, his concerns were hardly ill-founded. His ideas, and those animating films like *Banshee Chapter,* illustrate how classified research can exert a strong influence on the imagination. The public fascination with Cold War–era experiments involving "research chemicals" tested on unsuspecting minds seems directly proportional to the covert nature of the operations. In any case, if there are further disclosures of MKUltra-era initiatives—including those that may have involved DMT research—it seems likely they will be more mundane in character than experimental research facilities naturally scripted for suspenseful horror films, such as circumstances where unsuspecting targets are found in the community at large. And yet, perhaps no less creepy. In fact, we already know of such programs—like the CIA-backed "secret acid tests" of the 1950s and '60s in which U.S. citizens were given LSD in real-life situations—programs that, while inherently dubious, were driven by fears that the Soviets were outrunning the United States in their capacity to produce terrifying incapacitants. In 1964, Richard Helms, the prime instigator for MKUltra, warned that the CIA's "positive operational capacity to use drugs is diminished owing to a lack of realistic testing."[74]

This is indeed the premise of a remarkable short story penned by Rick Watson in 1993. Watson was a first-class chemistry student who, in the mid-1960s, worked during summers at the Stanford University School of Medicine as an organic chemist. An experimentalist, he took his first LSD care of Ken Kesey. It was in 1964 or 1965 that Watson first tried DMT, which looked like earwax and, he recalled, probably came from "someone in Kesey's circle."[75] By the mid-1960s, the shadows cast by MKUltra fed rumors about the provenance of the research chemicals used in experiments at the VA Hospital and other research centers. The Stanford Research Institute, in Menlo Park, was not beyond reproach as, among the many other research programs accommodated at the SRI, were classified U.S. Army Chemical Corps contracted experiments with psychoactive compounds that had long been earmarked as potentially useful chemical agents. Watson already knew biochemists who were working at the SRI, and who were "doing research on psychedelics, psychic communications, all kinds of strange stuff." As he related to me, he had himself visited the SRI and "learned something of the research being done there on psychedelics. I know they had a purer form of DMT."[76]

In his short story, Watson imagines intriguing events inside the SRI in the mid-1960s, where chemists were commissioned to "search every cerebral metabolic pathway, investigate every serotonin analogue in the hopes that they might be able to deliver some mind-incapacitating agent, some soul-destroying drug that would be operationally effective in the tool-kit of ultra-espionage and Psychowar." The story offers sharp detail on experimental activities, like the "large aquaria filled with LSD-saturated water" that were monitored by strobe-flash cameras "recording the erratic, Brownian movement of stoned carp." And the chemistry, Watson observed, was advanced. "They were synthesizing compounds that were close mimics of neuro-metabolites." On one of his visits, he was shown "a molecular structure he recognized as a link in the brain serotonin-metabolism cycle." Then, his biochemist friend, "John," announces:

> This is it, I think we've found the Holy Grail, you see it's a serotonin metabolite, so it's endogenous in us, but is metabolized so quickly none of it stays around, you give the brain this stuff and it immediately recognizes it and knows what to do, it eats it like candy, put this into the body and it vanishes! No waste product, no trace left, it's like it just disappears into the void, into a biological Black Hole, but what a Vanishing Act! This is the strangest drug we've come across, the strongest psychedelic any of us has had in our heads, it's acid to the power of you name it, and yet it's perfectly safe.
>
> Perfectly? How many people have tried this?
>
> Well, there's me, and you've met Tim, let's just say you are about to join a circle of the elect, you can be a founding father, one of the signatories on the Declaration of Human Consciousness, but it will cost you.[77]

Watson was then shown "several canisters, approximately six-inch-high cylindrical metallic containers with adhesive labels and handwritten identification codes." When John opened one up, it reeked of camphor and looked like "earwax, an orange semi-crystalline solid of low melting point." It was offered to him at $100 a gram—enough for ten hits—with half paid in advance and the promise to pay the balance if "the road test lived up to the sales pitch." This was twice the expense of good LSD, but the young Watson was, he confesses, incited by the "lure of the esoteric, the snob appeal of being there at the birth of a new drug."

The key revelation in the story is when the author realizes he was a research guinea pig. Watson—i.e., his fictional self—surmises years later that the transaction was no simple racket involving the fencing of government research chemicals. Instead, he was likely part of the military research. He was, he surmises, on the end of "a short-circuit of deniability," whereby overseers can deny culpability if outcomes are adverse. If a blind eye is turned toward chemists dispensing product to civilians, in the event of something going wrong—like kids nuking their minds—overseers could claim that the material had been stolen from stockpiles, and was thereby out of their control. The plot highlights a process where, rather than becoming ex-government black-market commodities, research chemicals are subject to controlled release, like a controlled burn. As advanced as the chemistry was at the SRI—and here is the point where fact and fiction are difficult to pry apart—in the desperate stages of the Cold War then heating up in Vietnam, such progress amounted to little without human test subjects.

> They were synthesizing compounds that were close mimics of neuro-metabolites left and right, but what they lacked, what they required, were human guinea pigs; fish were fine for checking out gross disturbances of neuro-muscular behavior, rats pretty good at testing for psychotomimesis, but for the high-resolution shot, they needed humans, and the project was so secret, and the consequences so dangerous, they could find no appropriate audience.[78]

It is doubtful that the Neil Armstrong of DMT, who eventually became director of the Biomedical Branch of the National Institute on Drug Abuse, could escape from the bite of Bill's routines.[79] In 1968, Stephen Szára penned a report for his superiors at the National Institute of Mental Health, Washington, DC, titled "A Scientist Looks at the Hippies." Unpublished until it was partly reproduced thirty years later, the revealingly titled document offered a study on the role of hallucinogens among "hippie" scenes based on Szára's travels to psychedelic shops, coffeehouses, theaters, and meditation rooms across America, from Haight Street to the East Village, at the height of the 1960s counterculture. It is not known what motivated the NIMH, who presumably sponsored this study of what was, by then, criminal behavior. It occurred to me that Dr. Szára, in producing this report, may well have embodied the authoritative all-seeing eye fueling Burroughs's parodic imagination.

Lest exigent categories developed to understand and control the psychopharmacology of various compounds, especially DMT, run amok, Szára kept up appearances into the 1990s, when he submitted a new label:

"psychoheuristic." To regard these compounds as "psychoheuristics" and not "psychotogens" (his original perception) or "psychedelics," "mysticomimetics," etc., was an exercise in remembering that "the physician is in control" (and not the drug). The 1990s was the Decade of the Brain, and it wasn't just the brains of individual patients that stood to benefit from the application of specific drugs, but the very definition of *the brain* was at stake. As Szára put it, DMT and other "drugs" serve "as keys to unlock the mysteries of the brain/mind relationship." And he postulated his freshly minted label to "emphasize the potentially immense heuristic value of these drugs in helping to explore the neurobiological bases of some fundamental dimensions of psychic functions."[80] But one could reasonably ask, what "mysteries" might the controlling physician be open to in a model where all but the neurobiological bases of psychic functions are dismissed—where consciousness is simply the end result of physical brain processes. In any case, it is no coincidence that Szára was minting nomenclature around the time Rick Strassman's research program at the University of New Mexico was, as we'll discover, throwing up challenges to neurobiological reductionism. The lines in the DMT turf war were being drawn. While I have in this chapter offered background to this developing drama, in the next I'll cover approaches within scientific and artistic communities from the 1960s that offer alternative perspectives.

CHAPTER 3

Transcendental Trigger
The Keys to the Cosmic Hard Drive

Before Burroughs was hammering "Prestonia" in Tangier, Beverly Hills psychiatrist Oscar Janiger had undertaken an experiment of his own. Among the first to try DMT in North America, outside of CIA and U.S. Army directed interests at any rate, Janiger is renowned for conducting LSD therapy with some nine hundred clients between 1954 and 1962, during which period he investigated its influence on creativity. Curious if DMT might perform the role of a psychotogen, Janiger learned of Szára's work and decided to try the drug himself. Alone in his office one night at the turn of the 1960s, he self-administered an intramuscular injection that was, as it turned out, a massive dose. In an interview more than three decades later, Janiger recollects his powerful experience:

> Man, I was in a strange place, the strangest. I was in a world that was like being inside of a pinball machine. The only thing like it, oddly enough, was in a movie called *Zardoz*, where a man is trapped inside of a crystal. It was angular, electronic, filled with all kinds of strange over-beats and electronic circuits, flashes and movements. It looked like an ultra souped-up disco, where lights are coming from every direction. Just extra-ordinary.... I went through this dance of the molecules and electrons inside of my head and I, for all the world, felt like a television set looks when on between pictures.

Janiger met with an overwhelming "sense of terror," blacking out repeatedly, and was made aware on every occasion of the certainty of his pending death. Out for forty-five minutes, he thought he'd been gone for two hundred years. Believing that he'd been exposed to "the architectonics of the brain itself,"[1] Janiger called up his friend Alan Watts, wagering he was in possession of "a drug that could finally shut him up." Open to the challenge, the loquacious popularizer of Eastern philosophy and psychedelics took the DMT and for thirty minutes stared at Janiger, who kept repeating, "Alan, Alan, please say something. Talk to me. Your reputation is at stake."[2] Tim Leary later empathized with Watts and the impossibility of giving "a moment-to-moment description of one's reactions while being fired out of the muzzle of an atomic cannon with neon-byzantine barreling."[3] Still, other than noting that he found DMT to be "amusing but relatively uninteresting," Watts rarely uttered a word of the experience for the remainder of his life.[4]

Another figure Janiger loaded up at the time was Captain Alfred M. Hubbard, widely regarded as the Johnny Appleseed of LSD. In psychedelic folklore, Hubbard is a legendary anomaly. Kentucky-born inventor of a mysterious power generator, Prohibition bootlegger, covert munitions runner for the Office of Strategic Services (predecessor to the CIA) with ongoing connections in the intelligence community, millionaire by the 1950s, acid apostle through the 1960s, he cut a most perplexing figure. As Lee and Shlain note in their classic social history of LSD, *Acid Dreams,* the thickset, rum-drinking "Cappy" was widely credited as "the first person to emphasize LSD's potential as a visionary or transcendental drug."[5] Hubbard appears to have been guided by beatific visions at crucial life junctures, including on one occasion hiking in the woods near Spokane, Washington, when an angel descended in a clearing and called on him to take part in significant, albeit obscure, near-future events. When he first took LSD in 1951—with the help of British psychiatrist Ronald Sandison, who pioneered "psycholytic" ("mind-loosening") psychotherapy using low and medium doses of psychedelics—and witnessed his own conception, Hubbard realized what his role was going to be. He would be a facilitator of divine inspiration c/o LSD.[6]

Hubbard was so convinced of the therapeutic potential of the LSD-induced mystical experience that he purchased large quantities from Sandoz and Spofa, ferrying himself across North American and European airspace through the 1950s and 1960s, dropping the drug like acid rain on thousands of willing recipients: scientists, politicians, intelligence officials, diplomats, church figures, and others (notably, Aldous Huxley). It has never been settled as to whether or not the man from Kentucky was a CIA player, nor exactly how he was funded, but it is clear that he was an arch-conservative. In addition to a background in the OSS, Hubbard ostensibly worked for several U.S. and Canadian government agencies, including the U.S. Bureau of Alcohol, Tobacco, Firearms and Explosives,[7] and, as "special investigative agent" at the Stanford Research Institute, he traveled in later years in full uniform, with badge and sidearm like a caricatured Southern sheriff.

Cappy was known to carry a variety of experimental psychedelics in his leather pouch "full of wampum," and Janiger's place was among his many ports of call. "We waited for him like the little old lady on the prairie waiting for a copy of the Sears Roebuck catalogue."[8] On one visit, Hubbard didn't leave empty-handed. As Janiger tucked some of his DMT into Cappy's pouch, he explained, "This isn't a gift. I want reports back." Apparently the feedback wasn't good. According to Janiger, "everyone who took DMT agreed it was a hellish half hour, with absolutely no redeeming qualities," a view that seemed to support the endogenous psychotogen thesis.[9]

And yet Hubbard's own recorded experience with DMT does not match this assessment. On the afternoon of March 23, 1961, at Hollywood Hospital, Vancouver, Hubbard responded to a series of DMT injections (from 0.5 mL to 1.0 mL), reporting on experiences that were unmistakably "Wonderful! Wonderful! Wonderful!" Hollywood Hospital housed a psychedelic therapy clinic specializing in the use of LSD and mescaline in the treatment of alcoholics. The clinic had been established in 1958 by Hubbard himself, or rather "Dr. Hubbard," given his acquisition of a "doctorate" in biopsychology from a Tennessee diploma mill. The high-dose "psychedelic" therapy model employed by Hubbard—who helped turn Humphry Osmond (the pioneering psychiatrist who coined the term "psychedelic") away from his psychotomimetic approach to treating alcoholism—had proved remarkably successful in stripping away old habits and facilitating new self-concepts, altered forms of reference, and even conversion-like transformations. On March 23, Hubbard was lying on the chesterfield in the specially designed room at the clinic featuring a state-of-the-art stereo system and a strobe light. Prints of Salvador Dalí's *Christ of Saint John of the Cross* and Gauguin's *Buddha,* along with a crucifix, a statue of the Virgin Mary, and a small altar with burning candles, were prominent among the religious iconography assembled in the Hubbard Room (also dubbed the Acid Room), an aesthetic bearing strong hints of Hubbard's Catholic faith and found to be effective in more than 1,600 LSD sessions Hubbard had conducted over the previous decade.[10] It's likely that Bach provided the overture to this pioneering odyssey.

At T minus eleven minutes into the first phase of his journey, Hubbard observed Dalí's depiction of Christ on the wall opposite, a figure at the helm of a star-bound vessel. "You can walk into it with great ease," he said, meditating upon an image that may have mirrored his own triumph against adversity. "The man on the Cross is completely at peace with himself. He wasn't afraid to begin with." The courageous Captain (and dubious Doctor) was in the departure lounge of a vessel of his own making, surrounded by the accoutrements of a carefully constructed tripping apparatus. Within the in-flight commentary recorded by psychiatrist Donald C. MacDonald, Hubbard—the man who might have amassed the largest stockpile of acid outside of Sandoz—announced that this was the "most intense experience" he'd ever had. Around the time Burroughs was jacking the juice in Tangier, Hubbard's DMT trip was no hellish odyssey, but an exercise in "the soul expressing itself." In low orbit, there were enchanting visions. "Flashing stars and a deep network of blue—very intricate design, spirals interwoven with spirals. A complete LSD world as we normally visualize it. . . . The designs resemble Aztec designs—beautiful fish but without any flesh on them—a fish skeleton. Beautiful streams of colour, very friendly." At the higher dose, he passed far beyond the standard LSD experience, and perhaps no one was more qualified to make that assessment. "This throws you physically into it—you are ripped to your essential self—you can't resist it—a maniacal force. I saw great stars turning in their courses . . . Even your bones feel good."[11]

While no unpleasant physiological symptoms were reported during these tests, a caution sounded repeatedly from the cockpit of this most seasoned of flyboys: "If one resisted it it could be extremely vicious. . . . More powerful than LSD, any resistance would be like fighting a monster." Flight-mode commentary on therapeutic potential is also recorded: DMT could be a tool of great value in psychotherapy, a natural for meditation, and would serve as a good introduction to psychedelic mental spaces before dosing someone on LSD. In the immediacy of these statements, Hubbard is among the earliest researchers to endorse the psychotherapeutic potential of DMT, although there appears to be no evidence of him or his associates using DMT in psychedelic therapy. One holds the impression that Captain Al's life, especially the ten years immediately following his first LSD experience, had passed in preparation for this day. He is ambassadorial in his recorded breviloquence, feeling "A sense of gratitude—a big wonderful responsibility regarding being able to use these materials." But while beta testing for the coming generations, he was clear that "the masses have to learn it slowly."[12]

The Time Chamber and the Key to Eternity

While reports of its irredeemability marked DMT and its analogues virtually taboo within the psychiatric community, Leary and his colleagues in the Harvard Psychedelic Research Project had other ideas. Leary was motivated, not unlike Hubbard, by a primary mystical experience, when on August 9, 1960, he consumed psilocybin-containing mushrooms in the garden of a Cuernavaca villa, in Mexico. "Awakened from a long ontological sleep" at the ripe age of thirty-nine, he had witnessed the Divine Process at the molecular level and sought to make his insights available to others. In 1962, the Harvard group moved into a large communal house in Newton, Massachusetts, where they set about optimizing the setting for psychedelic journeys remote from Hubbard's guardian-angel-with-a-gun approach. Indeed, studies with psilocybin, mescaline, and LSD would demonstrate that, as Leary outlined, if the "expectation, preparation, and setting are spiritual, an intense mystical or revelatory experience can be expected in from 40 to 90 percent of subjects ingesting psychedelic drugs."[13] An embryonic setting, the Newton Center commune had a secret room accessible by ladder from the basement. With its ceiling and walls softened by paisley prints, with red velvet cushions, candles in ornate holders, and a large bronze Buddha seated at one end, the Time Chamber was used for DMT and other intensive exploration sessions. One of the founding editors of *The Psychedelic Review,* Paul Lee recalls one such session in the chamber. Leary's then-girlfriend Marsha Pressman—according to Lee, a vision of

Sophia Loren—"lay down next to me and caressed me as Tim shot me up with DMT and I watched amoeba film loops projected on a screen while Miles Davis was playing *Sketches of Spain*."[14]

Before dosing up friends in their superbasement launching pad, Leary and Richard Alpert had, of course, taken experimental doses themselves, later reporting their findings in *The Psychedelic Review*.[15] Demonstrating that personal and environmental factors were integral to meaningful therapeutic outcomes, the conclusions in this benchmark report posed a challenge to the "terror drug"[16] characterization, and to the reports of an unnamed psychiatrist—possibly Janiger—whom Leary spoke with in November 1962, at a Southern California meeting of clinical psychologists. Conferring with Leary, this researcher mentioned that he had given DMT to more than one hundred subjects, among whom "only four had reported pleasant experiences,"[17] suggesting that the compound had limited therapeutic value compared to LSD. Convinced that "elaborate clinical differences allegedly found in reactions to different drugs were psychedelic folk tales," Leary and his colleagues were committed to determine if "set and setting" variables like expectation, preparation, emotional climate, and the relationship between the drug provider/sitter and the user accounted for these variations.

While evidence for the unidentified research with more than a hundred test subjects never emerged, researchers *were* fielding negative reports of DMT that did support Leary's conviction that set and setting were determining the outcomes. One notable incidence was reported by Robert E. L. Masters and Jean Houston in their classic study of the effects of psychedelics on the human psyche, *The Varieties of Psychedelic Experience*, first published in 1966. Of the more than two hundred sessions reported by Houston and Masters in their fifteen years of research, there were only three with DMT; however, one of those three sessions offers an outstanding portrait of a trip gone pear-shaped. The subject is reported to be "a young woman in her mid-twenties" who experienced "the most terrifying three minutes" of her life on DMT. Several factors shaped her adverse experience: she had "been up for three days and two nights working on a manuscript," the experiment took place in a room that was "a dirty, dingy, insanely cluttered pesthole," and the investigator pre-warned the subject that she would "see God" and "know the meaning of the universe."

Something, coming at me from a distant and empty horizon. At first it was a pinpoint, then it was a smudge, and then—a formless growing Shape. A sound accompanied its progress towards me—a rising, rhythmic, metallic whine; a staccato meeyow that was issuing from a diamond larynx. And then, there it loomed before me, a devastating horror, a cosmic diamond cat. It filled the sky, it filled all space. There was nowhere to go. It was all that was. There was no place for me in this—*Its* universe. I felt leveled under the cruel glare of its crystalline brilliance. My mind, my body, my vestige of self-esteem perished in the hard glint of its diamond cells.

It moved in rhythmic spasms like some demonic toy; and always there was its voice—a steely, shrill monotony that put an end to hope. There should not be such a voice! It ravaged the nerves and passed its spasms into my head to echo insanely from one dark corridor of my mind to another. Me-e-e-e-yow-ow-ow-ow me-e-e-e-yow-ow-ow-ow me-e-e-e-yow-ow-ow-ow—the incessant, insatiable staccato went on. It would not have been so bad if it had just been diabolical noise. The chilling thing was that I knew what it was saying! It told me that I was a wretched, pulpy, flaccid thing; a squishy-squashy worm. I was a thing of soft entrails and slimy fluids and was abhorrent to the calcified God.

Describing her experience as akin to being trapped in "Euclidian nausea," the subject reported that, while she attempted to resist, even demanding an "antidote" (there was none), "it seemed to me that this was the only reality I had ever known, the one I was born with and the one I would die with."[18]

Although the work of Leary and his colleagues would, not unlike that of Masters and Houston, be disrupted by the War on Drugs, their preliminary research offered a remarkable contrast. The primary session was in the home of "Dr. X" on December 10, 1962, when Alpert, Leary, and former World War II U.S. Air Force major and Vedanta monk Fred Swain were each, in turn, administered 60 mg of DMT intramuscularly. Here's Alpert's subsequent report.

The faces in the room had become billion-faceted mosaics of rich and vibrant hues. The facial characteristics of each of the observers, sur-rounding the bed, were the keys to their genetic heritage. Dr. X (the psy-chiatrist) was a bronzed American Indian with full ceremonial paint; the Hindu monk was a deep soulful middle-easterner with eyes which were at once reflecting animal cunning and the sadness of centuries; Leary was a roguish Irishman, a sea captain with weathered skin and creases at the corners of eyes which had looked long and hard into the unsee-able, an adventurous skipper of a three-masted schooner eager to chart new waters, to explore the continent just beyond, exuding a confidence that comes from a humorous cosmic awareness of his predicament—genetic and immediate. And next to me, or rather on me, or rather in me, or rather more of me—Billy. Her body was vibrating in such harmony with mine that each ripple of muscle, the very coursing of blood through her veins was a matter of absolute intimacy . . . body messages of a subtlety and tenderness both exotically strange and deliciously familiar. Deep within, a point of heat in my groin slowly but powerfully and inevitably radiated throughout my body until every cell became a sun emanating its own life-giving fire. My body was an energy field, a set of vibrations with each cell pulsing in phase with every other. And Billy, whose cells now danced the same tune, was no longer a discrete entity but a resonat-ing part of the single set of vibrations. The energy was love.[19]

The experience as reported in such detail describes an exposure at dra-matic variance to that of Burroughs, or for that matter, of Masters and Houston's research subject who was hunted by a big cat with "a staccato meeyow." Leary reported that at exactly twenty-five minutes from launch, Alpert smiled, sighed, sat up swinging his legs over the side of the couch, and said, "It lasted for a million years and for a split-second." Leary then assumed the position. Not long into his first dose:

Suddenly I opened my eyes and sat up . . . the room was celestial, glow-ing with radiant illumination . . . light, light, light . . . the people present were transfigured . . . godlike creatures . . . we were all united as one organism. Beneath the radiant surface I could see the delicate, wondrous body machinery of each person, the network of muscle and vein and bone—exquisitely beautiful and all joined, all part of the same process. Our group was sharing a paradisial experience—each one in turn was to be given the key to eternity—now it was my turn, I was experiencing this ecstasy for the group. Later the others would voyage. We were members of a transcendent collectivity.[20]

The mood was not dissimilar to Hubbard's account—radiance, an uplifting sensation, clarity of vision, a pioneering spirit, a sense of responsibility and belonging. But while the Captain cut himself as a uniformed cosmic enforcer, Leary's transit to a "transcendent collectivity," as utopian as it was, marked the direction in which the Harvard group would tack. And yet not all secured membership in this cosmic club, as indicated by Swain's experience. "Catapulted into a sudden ego-loss," his reaction was confusing and unpleasant. The monk "struggled to rationalize his experience in terms of classic Hindu techniques. He kept looking up at the group in puzzled helplessness. Promptly at twenty-five minutes he sat up, laughed, and said, 'What a trip that was. I really got trapped in karmic hallucinations!'" The lesson seemed clear—set, setting, suggestibility, and temperamental background were filters to the experience.[21]

Enthusiasm prompted numerous (Leary claimed more than one hundred) DMT sessions in the Time Chamber in subsequent months: "at first training exercises for experienced researchers and then later trials with subjects completely inexperienced in psychedelic matters." Although unclear how they were measured, and himself prone to exaggeration, Leary asserted "ecstatic" and "positive" outcomes in more than 90 percent of the sessions.[22] The article notably included reflections on a separate DMT hit (60 mg) Leary underwent for a programmed session in which he would man the "experiential typewriter." A curious piece of equipment built before the end of the state-funded spaced race, this device was designed, at Leary's behest, by behavioral psychologist Ogden Lindsley (an associate of B. F. Skinner) and electrical engineer William Getzinger. It featured two keyboards with ten buttons for each hand for optimal use in situations where the subject is reclining. Each button corresponded to an experiential category (like "cognitive" and "hallucination") ostensibly learned by the experient during flight training. The device's twenty keys, illuminated by a lamp for operation in darkened spaces, were connected to a twenty-pen polygraph that registered an ink mark on a flowing roll of paper each time a key was struck.

Designed to facilitate nonverbal communication during psychedelic sessions, the experiential typewriter was an ambitious interface for transcribing the psychedelic experience *in situ*. The device might be compared with techniques used by spiritualists at the turn of the twentieth century. But whereas Ouija boards were used to interface with *spirits* (from the afterlife), the experiential typewriter was designed to interface with *energies* (cellular, atomic, molecular). Retrieving information not from beyond the *grave*, it was proposed that the machine could receive measurable data from beyond the *game*, of the self and its social constructs. It was intended to assist the formulation of a language of the psychedelic state expounded at that time in *The Psychedelic Experience*, a manual for using psychedelics to obtain transcendent states that adopted the *Tibetan Book of the Dead* as a practical resource and programming language.[23] In a report on the experiential typewriter, a genuine problem was identified: the incommunicability of the ecstatic experience.[24] Experiments with psilocybin, mescaline, and LSD had shown that reporting intelligible accounts of the psychedelic experience midflight proved as feasible as offering meaningful feedback while pulling Gs on a roller coaster. Complete with accelerated sensory inputs, the hypercoaster of DMT appeared to magnify the problem. What was needed was an "experiential language," a shorthand that would enhance perception of the energy fields—plasmic, atomic, molecular, electrical—in which humans are constantly immersed but are unable to perceive outside of unique experiences.

If this language was to derive from experience, a set of protocols programmed to elicit outcomes for each "raid into the uncharted" was necessary. In the programming session at the Newton Center, Leary was directed by "ground controller" Ralph Metzner to press a key every two minutes in response to the inquiry "Where are you now?" Here is Leary's retroactive account of where he was at T minus four minutes.

> WHERE ARE YOU NOW? Spinning out in the tapestry of space comes the voice from down below ... dear kindly earth-voice ... earth-station

calling ... where are you?... what a joke ... how to answer ... I am in the bubbling beaker of the cosmic alchemist... no, now softly falling star dust exploding in the branches of the stellar ivory birch tree ... what?... open eyes ... oh dear lapidary insect friends ... Ralph and Susan beautiful orange lobsters watching me gently... faces shattered into stained-glass mosaic ... Dr. Tiffany Lobster holds out the casket of trapezoidal sections ... look at glowing key... where is Venutian ecstasy key?... where is key for the stellar explosion of the year 3000?... EXTERNAL PROCESS IMAGES ... yes ... hit the key.[25]

The history of science reveals some rather kooky endeavors performed under its aegis, and here was no exception. But while Dr. Leary was at this moment launching himself into uncharted terrain, he became acutely aware of his project's limitations. Repeated interruptions from ground control caused him to continually pull out of hyperdrive and "grind the ship to a slow stall." The entire process proved to be a "continual serial 'come-down,'" with effective translation impossible.[26] It is, then, unsurprising that the circumspect raw data—the mission readouts—weren't even offered up for analysis. Leary suggested that future navigators using similar or improved devices ought to be trained with "flight plans" and be cognizant of the "temporal sequence of his visionary voyage" in advance. And rather than disrupt the mission with pointless inquiries, ground control ought to guide subjects on predetermined flight paths, with the task of the voyager to somehow communicate compliance with, or deviation from, the flight plan.

How this could be achieved was not clarified. At any rate, an even ruder disruption was coming, as Harvard dismissed Leary and Alpert the year following their first DMT experiments. It appeared that psychonauts weren't going to be trained with the "automatic proficiency of the touch typist." The experiential typewriter and its protocols were consigned to history, and its experiential language abandoned.[27] But was it? Reflecting upon the rupturing controller-command phases of his flight, Leary passed comment on the drawbacks of the technique while at the same time providing rhetorical evocation of DMT space.

MINUTE 2. TIM: WHERE ARE YOU NOW? Ralph's voice, stately, kind
... what? where? You?... open eyes ... there squatting next to me are
two magnificent insects ... skin burnished, glowing metallic, with ham-
mered jewels inlaid ... richly costumed, they looked at me sweetly...
dear, radiant Venutian crickets ... one has a pad in his lap and is holding
out a gem-encrusted box with undulating trapezoidal glowing sections
... questioning look ... incredible ... and next to him Mrs. Diamond
Cricket softly slides into a lattice-work of vibrations ... Dr. Ruby-emerald
Cricket smiles ...[28]

The approach undertaken to evoke this experience illustrates the psychedelic recognition that, rather than an object to be measured, the mind
was a process to be experienced empirically. The evocative rhetoric spilled
clearly was of far greater value than polygraphic ink patterns. Also evident in this report is an insectoidal theme the benevolence of which is
in sharp contrast to that encountered by Burroughs the year before. The
comparison with the cartographer of the unknown is pertinent since, in
the summer of 1961, Burroughs had "taken up resistance" in the third-floor
room of the Newton House, where his presence had been a far cry from
Leary's original desire to have "the great novelist running precise-con-
trolled research sessions."[29] Burroughs loathed the Harvard Psychedelic
Club, caring for neither psilocybin nor LSD. He was the "all-time All-Star
in the wrong tribe," according to Leary,[30] who was himself an admirer all
the same, adopting cut-up methods in an attempt to evoke the psychedelic
experience. The influence appears in Leary's autobiography *High Priest*,
which uses double-column texts with interwoven narratives, and where
a chapter on Burroughs lifts keywords from his paranoid DMT urtext
("Overdose") and samples caustic statements from *Nova Express* directed
at Leary and colleagues "poisoning and monopolizing the hallucinogenic
drugs."[31] More generally, according to "ecodelic" scholar Richard Doyle,
by adopting a cut-up and mixed-media approach of his own, Leary hoped
to "interrupt the grip of the authorial ego" interfering with the direct
recording of the psychedelic experience.[32] How successful that was is left
to speculation, but in his DMT article, Leary offered a retroactive poetics
that ruptured the control tower's commands. Leary may have been less

an agent of Burroughsian "travel writing" than a game show host for the word virus. But then, unlike Burroughs, who armed himself with chemical "antidotes" to protect his controlling ego from capitulation—which most commentators reckon essential to the psychedelic process—there was no kill switch, emergency control lever, or ejector seat on the Leary machine.

The "antidote," according to Leary, was the psychedelic itself, and his trajectory was toward the clear light, conveying a Jungian and transhumanist disposition to transformation that could not have been more remote from Burroughs. As Leary re-reconstructed his divine joyride, we're privileged to the forward thrust, a rapturous barreling toward the primal source. With eyes closed,

> eyeballs trapped in orbit around internal light center . . . celestial radiance from the light center . . . light of sun . . . all light is sun . . . light is life . . . live, lux, luce, life . . . all is a dance of light-life . . . all life is the wire . . . carrying light . . . all light is the frail filament of the light . . . solar silent sound . . . beamed out from sun-flare . . . light-life . . . MINUTE 8. TIM, WHERE ARE YOU NOW? In the heart of the sun's hydrogen explosion . . . our globe is light's globe . . . open eyes drape curtain over sun flare . . . open eyes bring blindness . . . shut off internal radiance . . . see chiaroscuro God holding shadow box . . . where is life? . . . press WHITE LIGHT KEY.[33]

Leary returned to report a stunning "world" that was molecular and yet somewhere else entirely. The DMT experience is "a sub-cellular cloud-ride into a world of ordered, moving beauty which defies external metaphor." It is a *world* to which one is transported. The otherness of this space is illuminated in the detailed mechanical quality of organic forms. Hurtling inward with eyes closed, our navigator observed the "lightning fast, whirling dance of incredible cellular forms—acre upon acre, mile upon mile of softly-spinning organic forms." Hardly the trigger for a "neurological horror show," in echoes of Hubbard, and without "a second of fear or negative emotion," DMT acted as the catalyst that transported him into a mind state similar "to the highest point of LSD illumination—a jewel-like satori."[34] This firm symbol of individuation puts Leary squarely in the terrain of the mystical experience, as is evident from readouts about being "in the heart of the sun's hydrogen explosion," the source of all life. On "Prestonia," Burroughs's mystical experience (if one could call it that) was polar. In a response revealing the effect of exposure to an unbearably painful light source, he *felt* its heat, and it radiated death. Participant observer to a cosmic holocaust downwind from a thousand Nagasakis, nowhere near "the source," Burroughs was caught in an infernal compression at the end of the world.[35]

Not least of all, Leary was impressed with the remarkably brief duration of DMT, perhaps thirty minutes, by contrast with the eight-hour odyssey of LSD. DMT's brevity of effect had a great many advantages. It provided the user a comforting security that the experience would be over in a half hour, which "should make possible precise exploration of specific transcendental areas." The conclusion was to be influential, among both underground experimentalists and law enforcement: "I am left with the conviction that DMT offers great promise as a transcendental trigger."[36] Although the term was not yet in use, Leary's efforts were formative to the future *entheogenic* profile of DMT (alongside, or indeed in the shadow of, other psychedelics). Far from a psychotogen, given the personal and environmental conditions of use, DMT inaugurated a religious experience.

As a testament to his ability to court staggeringly diverse audiences, in the same year that his report was published in *The Psychedelic Review*, Leary was cheerleading for DMT in an entirely different venue. Still promoting the comparative brevity of the experience, "in years to come," he forecast in an interview for the September 1966 issue of *Playboy*, "it will be possible to have a lunch-hour psychedelic session; in a limited way, that can be done now with DMT, which has a very fast action, lasting perhaps a half hour."[37] These were the only comments about DMT in the feature, but they occasioned an unprecedented public outing, birthing a meme that DMT was the "businessman's trip."[38] Oddly enough, Leary may have had an ally in Hubbard, who sought to introduce Fortune 500 club members to LSD (and I imagine, given the chance, DMT). However, Leary's stated view that LSD is "the most powerful aphrodisiac ever discovered," which could potentially give a woman "several hundred orgasms," would have doubtlessly triggered a red flag from the Captain.[39] Spilling neon light on the future of psychedelics, the *Playboy* interview was, wrote Jonathan Ott, a "major stimuli to widespread ludible use of entheogens in the United States and other countries."[40]

And yet, DMT did not make the menu on the businessman's lunch—naked or pin-striped. It was spare, even among the underground. Despite Leary's efforts to rebrand the experience, DMT remained "the nuclear bomb of the psychedelic family."[41] The fallout from this was that its circulation was limited, its use exclusive. Histories of psychedelia, even those focusing on Leary, whose own report on DMT (the "transcendental trigger") was glaringly positive, hardly broach DMT, if at all. There is little mention of DMT, for instance, in Don Lattin's *The Harvard Psychedelic Club*.[42] At the consumer end, the needleworks required for use before the mid-1960s also proved a turnoff for those other than dedicated psychonauts. LSD was remarkably invisible by contrast. It was convenient and transportable. And from a production standpoint, it made economic sense to manufacture LSD before DMT since while 1 g of the latter might allow up to forty doses (with a 15–30-minute trip), 1 g of LSD could make twenty thousand doses (with an average experience up to eight hours or more). For these reasons, DMT was as rare as moon rock, retaining a deep underground status for decades, a circumstance of course compounded by its prohibited status established between 1966 and 1971.

The Castalians versus the Pranksters

The notoriety of DMT as a perilously mad trip was amplified in *The Electric Kool-Aid Acid Test*, as author Tom Wolfe related an episode where troubled Prankster Sandy Lehmann-Haupt (a.k.a. dis-MOUNT) was administered DMT by "a Main Guru" during the Pranksters' drive-through visitation at Leary's expansive new digs in Millbrook, New York. It was the summer of 1964, and Ken Kesey and his band of Merry Pranksters, having been set alight by LSD liberated from a federally funded research program at the VA Hospital in Menlo Park, and having sailed across the United States in their reenvisioned school bus "Furthur," docked at the Big House. They'd parked, that is, in the shadows of a mansion on the 2,500-acre estate. Thanks to wealthy patron Peggy Hitchcock and her brothers, Leary and followers had called the forested wonderland home in 1963, following their expulsion from Harvard (and subsequently, from Mexico and Dominica). The ultimate setting for the psychedelic experience, Millbrook was the center for the diverse activities of the Castalia Foundation, named after the fictional province in Hermann Hesse's *The Glass Bead Game*. It would be the first time Leary and Kesey had met. But in Wolfe's account, Millbrook was an anticlimax to Kesey's rollicking day-glo American movie, the division between the aloof, academic Castalians and the "fierce roan-mad" Pranksters, a serviceable fiction for the author, which is amplified in the unhinging of dis-MOUNT, who was one of Wolfe's primary sources.

> Sandy had a mad sense of the world torn apart into stained-glass shards behind his eyelids. No matter what he did, eyes open, eyes shut, the world erupted into electric splinters and the Main Guru said, "I wish to enter your metaphysical soul." But to Sandy—paranoia!—he seemed like a randy-painted lulu bent on his rectococcygeal shoals, a randy boy-enjoyer, while the world exploded and there was no antidote for this rocketing, rocketing, rocketing, rocketing....[43]

Widely circulating accounts of the "East versus West" Coast congress portray a cool parlay between alien tribes, a countercultural myth originating in Wolfe's story. It's true Kesey and Leary pursued unique pathways into the coming concrescence of psychedelia. Juxtaposed to the scientific research community of the mind that Leary and his colleagues were pioneering, the Prankster approach was protean punk. Kesey's position vis-à-vis Leary is well stated by Lee and Shlain. "Why did acid require picturesque countryside or a fancy apartment with objets d'art to groove on and Bach's Suite in B Minor playing on the stereo? A psychedelic adventure on the bus needed no preconceived spiritual overtones; it could be experienced in the context of a family scene, a musical jam, or a plain old party." And for a mutant "guinea pig" like Kesey who had escaped the laboratory, any "medically sanitized or controlled psychedelic experience was abhorrent."[44] He and the Pranksters were disinterested in guided therapy or structured routes to transformation, for as Jay Stevens noted, "the true test of psychedelic selfhood was one's ability to plunge into the whitewater of this new experience."[45] Further than that, programming the psychedelic experience to

Eastern religious texts amounted to turning one's back on what was immediately available in American popular culture. But while one can build distinct and contrastive biographies of these charismatic icons, in a world of hypermediated experience refracted through the prism of psychedelics themselves, coherence is a convenient luxury. By the time Kesey met Leary at Millbrook, Leary's scene had become unhitched from its academic moorings, and was mutating on a day-to-day basis. Millbrook displayed the symptoms of a kaleidoscopic cultural movement in formation. "That place changed every 72 hours," Leary had once stated. "You'd be there one weekend and we would be doing tai chi and the next weekend we would be following [Aleister] Crowley."[46] But despite the disparity there remained a common cause—psychedelics, for which Leary and Kesey were freedom fighters. From the *Bardo Thodol* to *Captain Marvel*, from the experiential typewriter to the acid tests, from enhanced psychotherapy to the cosmic carnival, psychedelics were championed for their potential to affect transformation of psyche, culture, and world.

In Wolfe's warp and weft, Leary snubbed Kesey. But accounts from those present set the record straight. The Pranksters arrived at Millbrook unannounced, the night after an acid party. As Ram Dass (then Alpert) recalled, if they "had come the night before, it would have been an entirely different story for all of us for the rest of our lives."[47] A candidate, perhaps, for the greatest party that never happened. But Dass, Metzner, Leary, and others *did* enter the Prankster movie as chaperones and cameos. The inspiration for Dean Moriarty in Jack Kerouac's *On the Road* (the reading of which had been an inspiration for Kesey's cross-continental odyssey), Furthur driver Neal Cassady was led up into the Big House, where he was welcomed with a shot of DMT in the attic—with views overlooking the grounds of Castalia. Photographs captured the moment. In one, Cassady is lying on the bed, shorts down, with backside offered to administering "nurse" Susan Metzner.[48] In an after capture, Cassady hovers on the attic bed, which seems to be positioned in relation to the adjacent window as a space capsule is to the outer void. Metzner is lying at his side (see Figure 4).

If only Wolfe had captured Cassady's impressions from his vantage. The photographs were taken by none other than cultural mediary Allen Ginsberg, who had arrived on the bus with Cassady and Kesey, and who had in fact brokered the Millbrook mission. Ginsberg was a renowned envoy of experience; he was, for instance, responsible for introducing mushrooms to pianist Thelonious Monk and trumpeter Dizzy Gillespie. And Ginsberg, having returned from Millbrook with some DMT, made sure that the next time Kerouac visited him at his Lower East Side apartment, the Beat pioneer found himself cranked up on the stuff. To document that experience, Ginsberg took a snapshot, journaling how Kerouac "looked like his father, corpulent red-faced W. C. Fields yawning with mortal horror" (see Figure 5).

Another account of the Millbrook meeting, however, offers insights at odds with the impression Wolfe left on his readers. *Mondo 2000* cofounder R. U. Sirius provides a new reading in his recent book *Timothy Leary's Trip Thru Time.* "Wolfe dramatized the scene, depicting the pranksters sneering at Millbrook's 'crypt trip'… but it wasn't all quite the mano a mano standoff

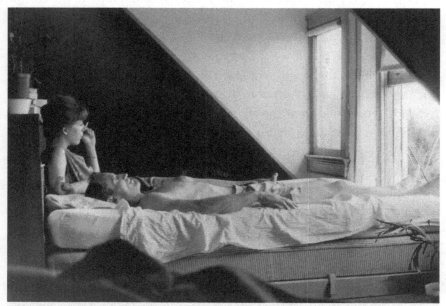

Figure 4. Neal Cassady at Millbrook (1964). Allen Ginsberg LLC, 2015.

that legend has it. Eventually, Leary came out of hiding. He and Babbs and Kesey injected DMT together and formed a long lasting friendship."[49] It is an extraordinary revision of this critical moment in '60s counterculture, with the unfortunate anticlimax at the hand of Wolfe rewoven as a magical powwow, where DMT performs a tribal reconciliatory function. Since the incident neither arises in the autobiographies of Kesey and Leary, nor in any of the many biographies of these and other period figures, and since Sirius has himself been unable to identify his source as he presents it, it appears that his version may have resulted from a misreading and conflation of historical records.[50] As Sirius was a close friend of Leary's, it's also not beyond probability that this revisionism reflects an unconscious riposte to Robert Greenfield's biographical "hatchet job" on Leary.

As far as I know, there is no evidence of DMT use among Pranksters before the Millbrook meeting. It is plausible that Kesey & Co. departed Millbrook with a special gift. We know Ginsberg did, as he noted on his photo of Kerouac, stating: "I'd brought some back from Millbrook where I'd recently been with Neal Cassady in Kesey's bus." Any road, the Pranksters soon returned west to Kesey's place in La Honda. The next mention of DMT use among the Pranksters comes more than a year later, as reported by Wolfe. Following Hunter S. Thompson's introduction of the Hells Angels to the Pranksters at an epic party in August 1965, iron-steed riders became frequent attendees at regular throwdowns. Occasionally, a Prankster would take one of the Angels up into their tree house and dose him on DMT. In Wolfe's saga, Mountain Girl informs Kesey that a good dose rendered Freewheelin Frank "as naked as an Angel is ever gonna git."[51] In Thompson's classic biker gonzography, *Hell's Angels,* gang members are observed to "gobble drugs like victims of famine turned loose on a rare *smörgåsbord,*" and DMT is prized among the spectrum of ways to get wasted. Accordingly, "a few will go the whole route and on top of everything else shoot some methydrine or DMT and turn into total zombies for hours at a time."[52]

Wolfe also paraphrased Jefferson Airplane's Grace Slick, that if "LSD is a long strange journey; DMT is like being shot out of a cannon."[53] It was another legendary band from that era that was responsible for firing off what was likely the first lyrical allusion to DMT. A self-satirical Lower East Side folk-rock band founded by Ed Sanders and Tuli Kupferberg, The

Jack Kerouac on visit to Manhattan, last time he stopped at my apartment 704 East 5th Street Lower East Side; he then looked like his father, Corpulent red-faced W.C. Fields yawning with mortal horror, eyes closed a moment on D.M.T. visions — I'd brought some back from Millbrook where I'd recently been with Neal Cassady in Kesey's bus, Pre-election 1964 Fall.

Allen Ginsberg

Figure 5. Jack Kerouac on a Visit to Manhattan (1964). Allen Ginsberg LLC, 2015.

Fugs, wrote a song referring to DMT amid other drug, sex, and anti-war messages. "We're the Fugs" was performed at the Peace Eye Bookstore on East Tenth Street in February 1965.

O we hate war
We love sex
Twos or threes
Fours or fives
L.S.D.
Di-methyl-tript'
Grope for peace
Naked & ready
Poets & freaks
Mad motherfugs

O East Side
We're on the East Side
And we're the Fugs![54]

Sanders recalls having it "sprayed on parsley flakes and wrapped in aluminum foil in the desk drawer at Peace Eye Bookstore." That was early 1965, during their first rehearsals. "When it was smoked, it gave everything a kind of blue haze."[55]

While these lyrics offer little more than a brief allusion, one of the earliest psychedelic rock bands, 13th Floor Elevators from Austin, Texas, was specifically fueled by a range of psychedelics, including DMT. Most significant was "Fire Engine" from debut album *The Psychedelic Sounds of The 13th Floor Elevators* (August 1966). It was the second song guitarist/vocalist Roky Erickson and electric jug player Tommy Hall wrote together. The song's lyrics not only make allusion to DMT (in the words "the empty"), but give expression to procedure and effect.

Let me take you to the empty place in my fire engine
Let me take you to the empty place in my fire engine
It can drive you out of your mind
Climb the ladder of your own design in my fire engine

Don't you tell it to go slow or stop
You've got to work it right up to the top
A piercing bolt of neon red
Explodes on fire inside your head

Let me take you to the empty place in my fire engine
Let me take you to the empty place in my fire engine
Boiling rhythms making your ears sting
Rounding the corner you can feel the ring of my fire engine

Close your eyes and you erase
Your image you no longer chase
A fiery flood engulfs your brain
And drowns your thoughts with scarlet rain

Let me take you to the empty place in my fire engine
Let me take you to the empty place in my fire engine
It can drive you out of your mind
Climb the ladder of your own design in my fire engine[56]

According to Elevators' biographer Paul Drummond, Erickson and Hall "likened the rush experience of DMT to rushing upward in an out-of-control elevator, or to the excitement of riding a fire engine rushing through the streets with the sirens blazing."[57] The experience was clarified by Erickson, who has stated that on DMT, "everything is spinning like fire engine wheels. So we said, 'Let me take you to DMT place.'" While for other band members the "blazing sirens" may have signaled an emergency response to the sudden erasure of all that one's ever known, DMT was a source of inspiration for Erickson. "It was like a fire engine ride without the calamity of a fire, as if all the negativity could be taken away from the fire itself."[58]

DMT had begun filtering through to a network of artists and experimentalists where the drug's high gained a reputation as slapstick as it was terrifying. Regaling an audience at UCLA on February 9, 1966, comedian Lenny Bruce related an occasion of smoking DMT after having taken LSD. In the off-the-cuff story recounted, Bruce had been struck by a desire to defy the rules—of gravity, propriety, you name it—promptly leaping through his San Francisco hotel window and grabbing the genitals of the first cop to arrive. Fortunately for Bruce, his room was on the first floor,[59] although he did end up with both legs in casts.[60] Sadly, only a few months later he was found dead on the floor of his bathroom from a morphine overdose.

DMT was gathering notoriety as an epic rocket fuel, a chemical lever that could plunge its operator into another world, a world where "everything is spinning like fire engine wheels." It was the ultimate liminal drug, and the most daring of adventurers were reserving its use for epic moments. In *The Man Who Turned on the World,* Michael Hollingshead—who introduced Leary and many others to LSD by way of his infamous mayonnaise jar filled with acid paste—includes a narrative journaled by famed bebop sax player, racecar driver, and heroin user Allen Eager, who was at one time engaged to the heiress of the Mellon fortune (including the Millbrook estate), Peggy Hitchcock. Eager wrote about a 1964 road trip from New York to Charleston, West Virginia. While it may be among the world's first DMT road trips, that influence is not exclusive, as Eager's custom was to mix it up.

> We decided to take a trip. It was very cold in New York. I was shooting a lot of DMT... at that time a smoking form had not been discovered. Arnie, Cathy, Simba the Siamese cat and me, plus guitar, soprano sax, pocket coronet, phono, records, psychedelic magic kit and a suitcase of drugs piled in the white Alfa and headed for warmer territory. The *I Ching* might have suggested it, I think.
>
> The total picture we gave freaked out every cop south of the Mason-Dixon line and we were busted every time Arnie drove.... Arnie and I were in costume, he looking like Jesus, but in baseball pants, high sneakers, beads, etc., which is quite the mode now... Our clothing was a time trip and it caused short circuits in robot people.[61]

Leakage from Millbrook or otherwise, only three years after Burroughs's aborted missions, we have a sighting on the early recreational use of DMT. The Eager party eventually landed in the bridal suite of the Charleston Holiday Inn, unloading "incense, candles, bottles, India prints, mirrors, toys, comics, phonograph, musical instruments, movie camera, fireworks, magic kit and the drugs." After chasing down caps of beige acid with three-quarters of a bottle of JB118 (purportedly NASA's "space drug"), and with DMT ever present, the Holiday Inn became the scene of a drug ordeal fit for Dr. Gonzo.

> Suddenly, violently, and with a sickening lurch we were moving faster than light. I fell back on the bed and had a vision of a Roman or Etruscan warrior holding a sword to my stomach. It was no vision. I knew it was real. We had poisoned ourselves. Death was here. Real Death. I remembered and gave in surrendering to it. A pain lanced through my right side and my convulsive gasps stopped. BLACKNESS. And then pinpoints of light in the stygian dark. I realised the lights were stars and we were moving through the very edge of our solar system at some unknown speed, but without the feeling of movement. Then to the front of my mind, I sensed an alien intelligence.[62]

Eager felt a mind probe that "tripped every alarm in my nervous system and body. I could feel my body on earth panicking, ready to explode with terror." He eventually returned to the room in the Holiday Inn, where his friend Arnie was "moaning and flickering in and out of reality, sanity pain and dimension." After a visit from a disapproving hotel physician, and a notice to vacate, the Eager party left Charleston "through spiral type buildings, heading south, the top down. By the time we were out of the DMT-coloured city-limits and on the open road, we were feeling normally glorious. The car purred, the cat slept, and overhead the most tremendous, white thunderhead in a purple-rose sky formed a glorious paean to earth and the future and we sped into the technicolour southern dusk."[63]

Fit for fools, madmen, Hells Angels, and for almost checking out at the Holiday Inn, DMT gained notoriety as the cultural outlaw's weapon of choice: a crystallization of transgression, a shot in the arm for the defiance of authority, with its clandestinity soon enshrined by state, federal, and international edicts. Journalist Joe Bageant recalled the showdown in which Leary, "the most dangerous man in America" (according to Nixon), was the target of a raid by the Dutchess County Assistant DA, G. Gordon Liddy. Later gaining fame as a convicted Watergate burglar, Liddy led a swarm of state troopers into the Millbrook Big House in May 1966. Here is Liddy's raid from Leary's perspective, recounted in 1982 to Bageant in Boulder, Colorado.

It was a Saturday night and we had already been tipped off by all the deputy sheriffs' teenaged kids, who acted as informants for us. We had extraterrestrial company at the time, all sorts of Buddhists, yogis, scientists, light artists, psychedelic cannibals.... The light artists had it all set up to greet the cops with a 40-foot rainbow-colored pulsating vagina over the lawn. But the cops got hung up, and things dragged on, so we all called it a night and went into the bedrooms to smoke a strong hallucinogenic drug called DMT. After a few puffs the room was a glowing and hissing molecular time-space warp.

But soon thereafter, "James Bond Liddy" stormed forth, leading twenty-four armed officers through the door. "Gordon was just beatific. His face was every color of the rainbow, his eyes shot out laser beams, and he had this powerful halo around him. And I cannot even describe what the 24 dinosaurs in trooper uniforms looked like! Whew! Meanwhile, the dope pipe laid there on the bed screaming 'HERE I AM! HERE I AM!' My wife immediately covered it with a blanket, then pointed across the room and yelled, 'Don't you dare touch my pot!' In typical knee-jerk storm trooper fashion, 24 cops and Gordon himself stomped across the room and seized a pound of peat moss, and off we all merrily went to jail."[64] You can sense the alien olfactory sting inciting the hunt as the cops, in orange flak jackets, holding rifles and clipboards, made their way up to the third floor and into the bedroom. Rosemary Woodruff diverted police from the smoking gun—the DMT pipe. Although neither DMT nor LSD were yet prohibited, marijuana was: hence the cops falling for Woodruff's ruse. The charges were dropped when a judge ruled the raid improperly conducted, although Leary would eventually see the inside of almost thirty prisons. Most notable for us, the "smoking gun" reveals that, by May 1966, DMT was being smoked.

Chief Alchemist

Millbrook *would* be shut down following a second raid mounted by Liddy in December 1967, events presaging an era of prohibition that remains in effect (and ineffective) to this day. Nick Sand remembers how the magic was replaced with fear overnight: "the reign of terror had begun. The Inquisition had arrived."[65] Among the citizens of New Castalia, Sand would later become most known for his production (with Tim Scully) of the legendary Orange Sunshine LSD, which was distributed via the smuggling/surfing network the Brotherhood of Eternal Love. He was also the first underground chemist on record to synthesize DMT, probably manufacturing more than anyone else in history. Sand has estimated that over the course of his career he manufactured between 20 and 30 kg of DMT.[66] Sand's father, a chemist, worked on the Manhattan Project, a circumstance crucial to Nick's decision to make the purported antidote to the hydrogen bomb: LSD-25. A yogi from the age of fifteen, a devotee of Gurdjieff, and student of anthropology, Sand's interest in cultural revitalization movements (and an experience with mescaline in 1962) drew him to Mexico, where he met the Mazatec curandera María Sabina, returning home with the intent to make psilocybin.

While that project failed, in 1963 Sand did successfully synthesize DMT in a lab he had set up in his mother's Brooklyn home. Within a year or so, Sand had attracted the attention of Richard Alpert, who was impressed with Sand's experiments. Alpert had visited Sand's home after a lecture he gave at Brooklyn College, where Sand had been taking classes. Back at Sand's home lab they'd taken some DMT together. Alpert reciprocated the hospitality, inviting Sand to visit Millbrook, which he did in early 1965. Of course, Sand brought some DMT with him, with which he began turning on the residents of Millbrook. After their first meeting at Millbrook in June of '65, Leary encouraged Sand to learn more chemistry and expand his production of the sacraments for this new spiritual movement. Sand eventually became "chief alchemist" and trip-sitter for the League for Spiritual Discovery, the legally incorporated religion whose charter included the use of psychedelics. But Sand was no acolyte of Leary, and he would blaze a lifelong departure from psychotherapeutic models. His attitude was "not about curing ill people but about making well people weller.... We're not just beasts brought to walk in one path all of our lives: we are here to fly."[67]

It was also at Millbrook in the summer of '65 that Sand first met Owsley "Bear" Stanley. It was a powerful juncture—a dyadic mini-summit of kindred spirits, the impressionable yet ambitious young Sand, and the cantankerous but wise, older Bear. This quiet convergence had a profound bearing on the psychedelic zeitgeist that was just then set to concatenate, ignited not in small part by the fuels concocted by these men, alongside a handful of others in the underground flight club. At this time Sand had moved out of his mother's house after a fire in his basement lab, but he continued operating a lab set up behind front company Bell Perfume Company, established with childhood friend and lab assistant Alan Bell. Their lab was originally installed in a loft in South Brooklyn, but after a sulfuric acid spill they moved the lab to a location downtown, where they cooked DMT at a top-floor site near Court Street "just below Police headquarters."[68] Early in his career, Sand's experiments were primitive compared with the gold standard later achieved. According to one unkind assessment, Sand was "not particular about the purity he achieved." In this view (perhaps informed by Stanley), as a yellowish-orange product, rather than a white salt-like crystal, "Sand's DMT stank."[69] While this may have been true, Sand eventually became a stickler for perfection, a circumstance fired by his meeting with Stanley. In a recent interview with producer of the Mind States conferences, Jon Hanna, Sand expressed how grateful he is for Stanley's guidance. "He had really kicked me in the ass about DMT purity and LSD purity. LSD purity, I never did wrong, because I learned it from him. DMT purity, I got together a *lot* because of his inspiration and reasoning and criticism. He was very scornful of my first DMT because it was just kind of this orangish-yellow paste, and he said it should be white crystals. And so I figured out how to make it white crystals."[70] By the winter of 1966/1967, Sand finally achieved the "breakthrough in purifying his DMT."[71]

The convergence had a reciprocal effect on Stanley. It is likely that Sand introduced Stanley to the smoking method of ingesting DMT at their meeting in 1965. It was the same year that Owsley appears to have made a small quantity of DMT himself, which he began circulating on the West Coast. In late 1965, one person on the receiving end was electronics technician and future LSD alchemist Tim Scully. When Stanley first visited Scully at his Berkeley home in '65, Scully had wanted to learn how to make LSD. It appears Bear was unprepared to endow this virtual stranger with such an early apprenticeship, and proceeded to smoke-out Scully and his friend Don Douglas with DMT (material Scully believes had been made by Stanley).

> [Stanley] had a small glass pipe and a bag of fine English mint leaves. He scattered a few sparkling white crystals of DMT over the mint leaves and told me to take the pipe. He held a match over the bowl and instructed me to toke deeply as many times as I could. Even though his DMT was pure and the fine English mint leaves helped mitigate the chemical taste and odor of the vaporized DMT base, it still wasn't very palatable. Of course that almost instantly ceased to be important as the world vanished and I found myself moving through a space filled with multidimensional brightly colored geometric figures.[72]

Scully wasn't terribly impressed. He found DMT "cold, geometrical and mathematical or machinelike" next to the "warmer, softer edged, more empathic" LSD.[73] By the summer of 1966, Stanley and Scully had produced small quantities of DMT and mescaline together—alongside about a million doses of While Lightening LSD—in a laboratory at Point Richmond in the San Francisco Bay Area.[74] Looking to get in on the action, Sand visited Stanley in California that year, gifting Stanley with a ¼ lb of his home-baked crystal.[75] Ultimately, Sand relocated to the San Francisco Bay Area in 1967, where he went on to make STP and LSD.

By the mid-1960s, experimentalists who had a nose for the grail, and others who just happened to be in the right (or wrong) place at the right (or wrong) time, were finding themselves in "DMT place." Rick Watson paints an episode involving himself and three friends—"Doug," "Sophia," and "Jerry"—who'd gathered in a living room in Palo Alto shortly before the summer of 1965 to smoke DMT. While the names of his fellow travelers that day are pseudonyms, as Watson briefed me, the people are real, as was his experience. Watson, who was the only one in the group who'd had any experience with DMT, arrived with two joints, and would be the first to take the payload. He describes the scene unfolding even before he passed the joint to Jerry.

> The Cosmos exploded, and suddenly the four of us became a hyperdimensional molecule, we were the four atoms at the corners of this

structure, joined by neuro-magnetic bonds. Each of us, our body-mind-being, was an intricate organism of concentric vitreous transparent spheres or nested Platonic diaphanous solids like Kepler's diagram in the *Mysterium cosmographicum,* all spinning inside each other on axes impossible to imagine in Euclidean space, creating topologies beyond the dreams of Gauss or Escher, joined by tubes through which flowed in pulsating rippling pink and green neon a strange opalescent superfluid that was thought and feeling and love and language, colour and sound all together, the primordial stuff that everything is made of, some archetypal wave matter.[76]

Watson describes how he felt profoundly connected to the others present, who had transmogrified into one radiant creature "scintillating beyond space and time." While individual identities remained intact, they had become "some kind of glowing resurrection body, a field of pure and blissful energy." And yet "the fourth quarter of this tesseract was dark." Jerry, it seems, was not getting off, a spectacular circumstance in its own right.

He appeared to me as some demonic monster, a Wrathful Deity from the Tibetan pantheon, totally black, a dozen ogling eyes protruding on stalks, horns sprouting from his skull, a tongue like an enormous serpent coiled around a flayed, struggling human about to be swallowed into Tantric Hell, a necklace of severed heads strung around his neck on a rope of intestines, and he is standing on the back of a fiery bull who is sodomising a corpse which he prods with his trident, while breathing fire and pouring out soul-eclipsing smoke.[77]

Jerry was now starting up the second joint Watson had prepared as a backup. "I looked again, my God, he *was* breathing fire, he was bending over the candle and inhaling an inferno, but the darkness was impenetrable, he was not getting off, roiling clouds of smoke surrounded him like a macabre aureole. This was impossible, no brain could resist such an onslaught." But this was to be Jerry's fate, with Watson reminding us of Burroughs in his reflections that the reason why Jerry had grown "convulsed with a violent, wrenching headache" was due to "the Herculean effort he had made to resist" the DMT's effects.

Obviously on some deeply primal level that first taste of metallic fear had set off such an alarm signal that all his body's defences were mobilised to resist this attack, and they had succeeded, but at what cost. They had shut down the reaction, contained the explosion, but also had shut down all possibility of awareness of any level higher than the carnal, a No Man's Land had been declared in the country of his consciousness and into which he would never venture again.[78]

While the material in Watson's payload likely came from "Kesey's circle"—that is, from material made by Owsley—the method of ingestion seems to have originated on the East Coast with Nick Sand. A distinguished serviceman of the underground flight club, among Sand's remarkable achievements, before transiting to the Bay Area and producing Orange Sunshine LSD with Tim Scully, was his chance discovery that DMT could be volatilized for consumption: the vapor from freebase DMT could be inhaled, with effects lasting 5–20 minutes. This discovery came about serendipitously sometime around 1964/65 when crystal DMT had fallen onto a hotplate, turning into vapor (leaving almost no residue), and inspiring Sand to try freebasing it. Raised under the shadow of the mushroom cloud, and haunted by nightmares of vaporized cities, Sand had discovered a new way to get vaporized. Ralph Metzner recalls the situation. "As far as Nick Sand is concerned, it was thanks to him that we learned that DMT could be smoked, which was much more controllable and thus useful experience than the very tricky injecting method (unappealing to non-medical folks)."[79] But while its short duration made DMT more appealing to "the casual street user," the demand for DMT remained low. Although users no longer needed syringes, they now faced the unfavorable circumstances associated with vaporizing DMT. Jonathan Ott has explained the problem that became apparent when the substance was vaporized. "Because of its noxious smell of 'burning plastic'... DMT came to epitomize the 'plastic,' 'synthetic,' 'chemical.'" Despite being a natural product, DMT's reputation was somewhat tarnished. "Black-market supplies were clearly synthetic, and DMT was characterized alongside LSD as a 'chemical' when members of the drug scene began to express a preference for so-called 'organic' (that is, plant-derived) entheogens."[80] With the superior demand for LSD, which was also more profitable to manufacture than DMT, by the late 1960s the limited supply of DMT crystal did not justify freebasing. By then, it would typically arrive to the consumer in little squares of aluminum-foil packets containing crystal infused onto parsley, mint, or other herbs as a smokable product. This method was observed by Stephen Szára in 1968. In his document "A Scientist Looks at the Hippies," Szára reported that DMT was more expensive than LSD and hardly available to "hippies" across the scene to which he paid visits. That said, Szára did observe the smoking of a parsley-"soaked" DMT blend. And, as relayed by Cheryl Pellerin, author of *Trips: How Hallucinogens Work in Your Brain*, it seemed significant to the Hungarian that the grocery store in Topanga Canyon near Los Angeles "was doing a brisk business in dried parsley leaves."[81]

Such brisk trade was several years after the pioneering efforts of Sand, who knew he had "discovered something so deep, so magnificent, so profound, that it blew away everything I had ever experienced before. Period."[82] The eureka moment triggered a dedication to manufacturing entheogens. In a biographical description of his life as a devoted alchemist of these sacraments, for which he spent time in fifteen jails and prisons, Sand became, as Jon Hanna related, "a criminal as a matter of principle and as an act of civil disobedience, because he believed he was working for a higher good."[83] This dedication resulted in the arrest of Sand, as well as Scully, in 1974. Scully did his time, while Sand jumped bail and moved to Canada, where he set up another lab. Under the radar for more than twenty years, Sand was again arrested in 1996 in Port Coquitlam, British Columbia: the bust hauling, among other things, 4 kg of DMT. After serving time in Canada and the United States, Sand was released in 2000, receiving a standing ovation soon afterward at a Mind States conference in Berkeley, California, stating in his speech that "we are all doing time in the jail of life for as long as we don't stay completely present, responding to each situation as it arises."[84]

Sand had a cautious attitude toward Leary, whom he regarded as somewhat of a "snake oil salesman."[85] And yet, while Leary hailed from the "beer and baseball" tradition and received the calling at thirty-nine, and Sand had been a yogi from the age of fifteen, they shared the objective of self-realization, and in particular that which could be achieved through an optimized set and setting. Millbrook was clearly *that* setting. In an article with the unassuming title "Just a Wee Bit More about DMT" published in *The Entheogen Review* only months after his release from prison, Sand wrote a concise missive on the healing and transformative power of DMT, all dependent upon set/setting. "Having set up one's space as aesthetically as possible (eliminating the possibility of any interruptions), one readies one's self for a DMT trip. Having followed the peaceful set and setting, sensible diet, and totally supportive companions, one sits down and ingests the DMT."[86] With an unpublished, six-hundred-page guide to tripping he'd written in prison called *Psychedelic Secrets*, Sand explained that "DMT is the touchstone of the psychedelics." "The visions it produces," he continued, "are here and gone in a matter of minutes by clock time, but by our existential clock, time has been transformed—by the concentrated and incredible fullness of the experience—into eons. All this and only 15 minutes have passed? Wow!"[87] Expressing a view that was not unlike Leary's, he wrote, "We create our own reality."

> We are all individually responsible to ourselves for the reality we create, whether we are miserable or joyous, this is our choice—our design. We are not alone; we exist as an integral part of all life, breathing, pulsating, vibrating, giving off plant food, absorbing animal food, in a multi-level fabric of incredibly beautiful designs and patterns. This is what DMT shows us—those patterns, as much as we can absorb at one time—to realign us to the sacred design of which we are a part. DMT works with the energy that surrounds and enters you.[88]

Recognizing that DMT and other psychedelics are sacraments, Sand translated his entheogenic experiences through the interpretative lenses of the world's spiritual traditions. Over the course of his life, including while in prison, Sand has practiced a variety of teachings and disciplines: "Kabballah, meditation, Krishna consciousness, Sufism, aikido, taiji, Zen, and Tantra, as well as having studied the teachings of Krishnamurti, Milarepa, Ramakrishna, Rajneesh, and other philosophers."[89] In a synopsis of these traditions, he related that dimethyltryptamine is, among all the compounds, "unique and extremely powerful," essentially because, under the right conditions, it can facilitate a mystical-visionary state of consciousness. "It is the doorway to the intensely personal temple of our own sacredness."

> It opens the doorway to the vastness of the soul; this is at once our own personal soul, and its intrinsic connection to the universal soul. When the underlying unity of this fictional duality is seen and felt, one experiences a completeness and interconnection with all things. This experience, when we attain it, is extremely beautiful and good. It is a song that rings and reverberates through the lens of God. Now we know why we were born; to have this intense experience of the sacred, the joyous, the beauty, and the blessing of just being alive in the arms of God.[90]

Beyond misguided *Fear and Loathing*-esque adventures, DMT could enable users to "access the cosmic hard-drive and find some answers."[91] But whether vision quest or oracle, intention was everything. "This is your uniqueness, your inner journey, your own quest for truth or answers that you have hidden away inside you. Everyone has those answers inside, but only those truly seeking self realization will have the courage to go beyond the veils to the center." Here DMT becomes a unique tool for the post-1960s spiritual seeker to achieve that which new spiritualist practitioners—adapting Gurdjieff here and adopting transcendental psychology there—had been promoting since that time, albeit typically loath to acknowledge the role that psychoactive drugs play in one's quest for wholeness, unity, and awakening.

> This quest then, is about re-emerging from the swamp of forgetfulness and distraction in which we live, and being reborn in consciousness. Here there are no landmarks, no limits, no boundaries, no road signs. We progress in this nether landscape, this cosmic interiority, by accessing intuition, by observing carefully all that happens, and by following penetrating vision. And above all, by following the heart. Intently, we listen for the single true voice that sings out from a unified heart and mind, beyond the infernal chorus of conditioned commands and conflicting directives.[92]

As a means of accessing truth or uncovering lost or forgotten parts of ourselves, this compound could be adopted as a technique, among many.

For Sand, it is the most powerful technique and therefore requires discipline, respect, and preparation. In a statement that is not dissimilar to that of a yogi endorsing the effectiveness of his or her tradition, he stated, "Properly prepared, we enter into a fluid multi-dimensional field of interpenetrating realities, which are all things to all people. On this path, when we are ready, we meet the Gods that live deep within all of us. In that meeting we experience intense recognition of the oneness of all things. We receive true and simple instructions. We experience such poignant realizations that we are swept away by the exquisite beauty and truth of this inner knowing, which is utterly undeniable."[93] With Sand, we have arrived at a place that is about as far from Burroughs, and Janiger, as we could travel. If DMT is to be used, it is to be adopted as an entheogen, not exploited for its assumed psychotogenic properties. The "secret" wasn't down in the Amazon; it's right here, right now.

The Loud Fumes of the Dead

Sand's carefully crafted statements arrived four decades after the alchemical initiation in New York. There is a striking comment made by Sand in a candid online interview by Daniel Williams for *The Opium Den Talk Show*.[94] Since Sand worked for so long as an underground alchemist, isolated and perfecting his craft, he hadn't been much aware of the extent of his chief product's impact on the world, an extraordinary circumstance given the deep and lasting groove Orange Sunshine left on millions of minds. While DMT was never produced on an industrious par with LSD, nor invested with comparable brand energy, it too would have an impact, drifting like its vapor far from the pipe. But in the mid-1960s, the impact could be observed in relatively tight circles of use and experimentation. On the West Coast in particular, DMT circulated among communities of artists closest to the source of production. And at this time and place, there was no community of artists more *connected* than the Grateful Dead.

The principal locale in the emergence of the Dead (or the Warlocks, as they were then known) as a scene phenomenon was Ken Kesey's ranch in La Honda, the location of the early acid tests. And among the principal figures was Owsley Bear Stanley, who has claimed that he introduced Kesey to DMT during his initial visit to La Honda, sometime in late November or early December 1965, just before the first acid test.[95] Stanley's visit with Kesey was also just before Stanley met Phil Lesh, who was himself no stranger to the drug. Dennis McNally's book *A Long Strange Trip* relates an account of Lesh injecting DMT on the day he moved to Palo Alto, California: June 7, 1965. It was a significant moment for Lesh, who had recently acquired his first electric bass guitar. "It was perfect, too perfect," he later recalled. "There's that core of perfection that runs through the whole thing, that thread, we're still sliding along it."[96] At that stage, Lesh hadn't played his first gig with the liquefied electric blues band. There are variations on this story, but as reported by Blair Jackson in *Grateful Dead: The Music Never Stopped,* with the band in a quandary, having discovered that the name "Warlocks" was already in use by another band, members gathered at Lesh's place on High Street, Palo Alto, in November 1965. The band had rejected a thousand possibilities. Jerry Garcia, who had smoked DMT before coming over, opened a dictionary. "Everything else on the page went blank . . . diffuse just sorta *oozed* away, and there was GRATE-FUL DEAD, *big* black letters *edged* all around in gold, blasting out at me, such a stunning combination."[97] It's not clear for how long Garcia had been using DMT at this point, but it appears that DMT was active at the inception of the most significant psychedelic rock band to have emerged from the '60s West Coast scene. From then on, when DMT traveled with the Dead, it tended to stay within the inner circles. One didn't often find it for sale in concert parking lots, which became integral to the Deadhead scene over the next thirty years. Covert use, of course, solidified once psychedelics were illicit, and the loud perfume—i.e., the characteristic smell of burning plastic asshole when smoked—may have mitigated against public use.

In any case, band members were using DMT for inspiration, and more than likely in conjunction with their tonic of choice: LSD. The impact of LSD on their live performances is well documented, but far less is known about the impact of DMT on the life and times of the Grateful Dead. Bear Stanley was not only a prolific LSD manufacturer, he also designed the Dead's earliest sound systems. Stanley related on one occasion how "some of the psychedelics seemed to affect our ability to interact with inanimate equipment. Specifically, when someone at a show or in a room where someone was playing music was to take some DMT... the music would immediately become louder and more strident. It has a certain tonality to it, a certain quality to it, which is very distinctive."[98] Stanley hadn't paid this mystery much heed, but upon further observation he noticed that DMT smoked in the vicinity of sound equipment was capable of increasing the decibel levels considerably. Not only was Stanley able to measure an increase in decibels, but "the tubes would get red hot and burn out half the time and it would tear the voice coils out of the speakers." If the amplifier was maxing at 127 dB, when somebody smoked DMT it would increase to 132 dB. Stanley even postulated a theory about how the DMT user whose consciousness has been altered when smoking DMT could affect the configuration of electrons in the guitar.

If there's any credence to the observation that smoking DMT can affect amplified sound, the Dead's lyricist Robert Hunter may have been the chief culprit effecting these reconfigurations. Between 1967 and 1969, Hunter had taken DMT—or it him—about one thousand times. That is, before "the Boss of that place" served him eviction notices on three separate occasions. He eventually took heed. Commenting thirty years later, "I was informed that I'd been shown all that was mine to know, to use that, and not try to extract more."[99] Hunter was the Dead's psychedelic trailblazer. In 1962, like Kesey before him, Hunter volunteered to participate in federally funded research at the Menlo Park VA Hospital, covertly sponsored by the CIA's MKUltra program. He was paid $140 to take LSD the first week, psilocybin the second week, and mescaline the third week, and all three combined in a final session the fourth week. Served up this psychedelic cocktail by the government at the age of twenty-one, "all I wanted in 1967 was MORE consciousness!" Having gone "xing" (his word for the DMT experience) possibly more times than he'd had sex by his early twenties, Hunter sounded a note of caution when reflecting on his youthful DMT experiences in the approach to his fifty-fifth birthday. "Anyone who has been surprised by heavy surf, whirled helplessly and slammed on the sand, has a reasonable metaphor for the power of DMT. Control isn't even in question here. Who controlling what? Caveat emptor is the byword for this empress of psychotropic substances." Terence McKenna agreed, replying that while "consciousness expansion" may be the ultimate gift provided by DMT, it will nevertheless "turn your blood to ice water."

Hunter's public email exchange with McKenna in 1996—published on the web as a five-part series titled *Orfeo*—was significant in DMT's history. With countless online readers "looking over their shoulders," what was sometimes known as "the secret" in the 1960s was out of the bag thirty years later. Yet early in the exchange, Hunter inveighed that he didn't want his public discussion with McKenna to be read as advocacy.

> I don't want to sell this stuff, DMT. It's damned well not for everybody. Fortunately, its abuse potential is rock bottom. I, who loved it, have only taken it twice in the last 20 years and that was too much. It's like jumping on or off a speeding train. Omni-dimensional fact finding is not a very high priority among the "kicks" crowd; they're better off with gas and its infinite fractals of memory, or airplane glue. DMT is for those with a desperate need to know, and, among those, for only a small percentage whose neural wiring happens to be heavy gauge with appropriate sheathing. Nobody ever got rich peddling DMT. It was only always passed from hand to hand outside normal "drug ring" circles. It is, to LSD, as 198 proof rum is to hot milk with a few drops of brandy.

But he qualified, "nor do I say it shouldn't be tried." The preferred route was intravenous, and he wrote that upon his first hit, "I X'd growing out of a flowerpot on Venus beneath a great dome." The Grateful Dead's master lyricist evokes the protean language that he believed was necessary to capture the condition of being in DMT space.

> A lot of DMT lore can't be expounded because our verbs and prepositions correspond to realities of four dimensions or less, gainsaid. To catalogue conditions where one accelerates at warp speed to stand still in one place . . . we must understand the nature and limitations of our grammar and be self-motivated to think beyond it. To avoid the condition of pathological meme-ing, we must not over-state our experiences, or mis-state them for easier referentiality. We may, however, talk around them and establish communication based on mutual recognitions. A language begins in this manner.

Hunter addresses the futility of languaging the condition of "being/ non-being" in DMT space, a dilemma that Leary had confronted, and one that McKenna was himself facing in the 1990s. Back in the 1960s, artists were experimenting with music and visual arts, and forging nonsymbolic "languages" to express their intimacy with the infinite. Leary called this "tranart" ("transcendental art"), a communication that bypasses symbols and uses "direct energy to 'turn on' the receiver of the message." He claimed "the symbolic mind of the artist is not active" here. "The artist is an energy transformer and his artistic instruments are energy transforming machines, projectors, polarizing and diffracting lenses, sound recorders and transformers."[100]

The description is fitting for the Grateful Dead and other artists, like Jimi Hendrix, who were "energy transformers" adapting tools at their disposal (including psychedelics), to communicate their message (i.e., love). In his account of the Brotherhood of Eternal Love, *Orange Sunshine,* Nicholas Schou recounts the influence of DMT on one of Hendrix's finest live performances—a "series of beautifully melodic, spaced-out jams," including "Hey Baby (Land of the New Rising Sun)" played in the second set of his gig at Rainbow Bridge, a free concert on the slopes of Haleakalā, Maui, on July 30, 1970. Apparently Eddie Padilla gave Hendrix a hit from one of his "Lightning Bolt joints laced with DMT." "As the tent filled with smoke, Hendrix, who seemed tired, suddenly came to life. 'Yeah, I feel like playing some more music' he announced." According to Padilla, Hendrix "got up, and played for a couple of hours without a break and no teeth. It was just incredible."[101] We will encounter more contemporary "energy transformers" later in the book, but it is intriguing to learn that—utterly flabbergasted by his first experience with DMT—and unable to find the words to capture it, Simon Posford came out of the experience thinking "we need to design a new typewriter with a few extra keys to help describe this extraordinary, totally real Universe."[102] As we'll see, Posford would devise a means to translate the extraordinary, not with a new typewriter, but via Shpongle, whose debut album *Are You Shpongled?* (1998) offers a titular update on the encounter sonified on Hendrix's *Are You Experienced* (1967).

DMT and Early Visionary Art

What Leary called an "experiential language" became manifest in psyche-delia starting in the mid-1960s. It wasn't expressed in the arcane readouts of a polygraph machine connected to custom-built keyboards, but in the aesthetic practices of the nascent psychedelic movement, mediated by an assemblage of sensory technologies. It would be mediated by guitars and keyboards, amplifiers and mixing consoles, by synthesizers, samplers, and computers, as well as in graphic arts. Given its small circles of use and below-the-radar experimentations, DMT played a minor role in '60s psy-chedelia: LSD was clearly the most important influence on this art move-ment. Most accounts of psychedelic art history do not even broach DMT, despite the impact that DMT had on 1960s visual art. The visionary states induced by DMT were often so rapid and astounding that they rendered the experient without words. And yet these events are recalled many years later as if they'd happened only yesterday. Consider Iggy Pop's recollection of his experience smoking DMT just before the first performance of The Psychedelic Stooges (later just The Stooges) at a house party on Halloween night (October 31), 1967.

> You'd inhale it. And then when you'd exhale—poof, you'd be high. I saw Buddha, man. I know that sounds like no big deal. But I saw a gigantic holographic Buddha—correct in every way! Buddhas can be very intri-cate—these drawings that you see in books. Thousands of details were included in this Buddha. Where did they come from? I didn't make them up. I can't even draw, you know. I could barely spell cat, you know. And there it was. And I thought, Wow—the power of the mind, you know.[103]

Eventually this stuff was finding its way into the hands of those who *could* draw, and whose hands were impelled to depict the worlds to which users were being transported. Starting in the 1990s, DMT-inspired art would begin to flourish in league with the prevalence of DMT, which was being embraced as an entheogen, not only due to its relationship with aya-huasca, but also as an independent compound. The growth in interactions with DMT and the "worlds" with which users were being made familiar is clearly significant. During the 1960s, the South American botanical sources of DMT were little known, and otherwise difficult to obtain or transport. Synthesis was also not particularly attractive from an economic viewpoint. But as travelers and practitioners gained familiarity with the ethnobotanical background of DMT as an integral component of the ayahuasca brew, as its synergistic mechanism was confirmed and tinkered with in "ayahuasca analogues," as seekers sourced and cultivated DMT from a diversity of local species easier to obtain within Australia, North America, and elsewhere (e.g., sourced from *Acacia* species, *Desmanthus* species, *Mimosa hostilis*, and various *Phalaris* grasses), and as bioassayists, explorers, and cowboys developed and circulated (with the aid of the internet) recipes for extraction and synthesis, DMT "moved to center-stage as one of the entheogens of choice of the late eighties and early nineties."[104] In the next chapter, I explore the figure who would inspire this flourishing.

CHAPTER 4

La Chorrera

Jungle Alchemy and the Consciousness (R)evolution

When in 1967, aged sixteen, Dennis visited his older brother in Berkeley, California, Terence stated that he knew what the philosopher's stone was. "It's sitting in that jar right there on the bookshelf."[1] Earlier, in the fall of 1965, Terence McKenna had been visited one night in his rented room at 2894 Telegraph Avenue by "a very strange friend who lived in Palo Alto." By then, Terence, who had commenced studies at UC Berkeley, had been familiar with the psychedelic effects of morning glory seeds, and had sampled Sandoz LSD by way of his neighbor, lead guitarist of Country Joe and the Fish, Barry Melton. But those exposures afforded him little preparation for what transpired that night. Wearing a little black suit buttoned up to the throat, his friend—whom Terence referred to as "kind of a social menace and intellectual criminal," whom he held as his "great inspiration," and who was always the one "to get there first, whatever it was, to do it, to reject it, and to be absolutely contemptuous of it by the time anybody else even arrived at the scene of the crime"—came over with a little glass pipe and stuff that looked like orange mothballs. "Something you might be interested in." Regaling those gathered at California's Ojai Foundation with information he might never have publicly stated before or since, Terence indicated that his friend had imparted to him that the material had been boosted from a U.S. Army chemical-research operation down at the Stanford Research Institute in Menlo Park. "Someone managed to get a fifty gallon drum of this material out of the inventory without anybody knowing." Terence wanted to know what it was. His friend, who only months before had announced that "we must live as if the apocalypse has already happened," said "It's called DMT."[2]

The friend visiting Terence was none other than Rick Watson, whom we've met in previous chapters. Along with John Parker, Watson was among Terence's closest friends from Awalt High School in Mountain View, California, since 1963. Terence appears to have minced facts, since the provenance of the material he smoked at Telegraph Avenue was not Army-sourced, but, according to Watson himself, from "Kesey's circle"[3]—and thus likely the work of Bear Stanley. Furthermore, the reference to a "fifty gallon drum" is a spectacular embellishment on the "six-inch-high cylindrical metallic containers" that, in Watson's imagination, may or may not have housed DMT at the SRI.

Regardless of the provenance of the material smoked, Terence McKenna's world was turned inside out on that night in the fall of '65. Taking hits from a "mothball," he was immediately transported into another dimension: "a brightly lit, non-three-dimensional, self-contorting, linguistically intending modality that couldn't be denied."

> I sank to the floor. I had this hallucination of tumbling forward into these fractal geometric spaces made of light and then I found myself in the equivalent of the Pope's private chapel and there were insect elf machines proffering strange little tablets with strange writing on them, and I was aghast, completely appalled, because in a matter of seconds... my entire expectation of the nature of the world was just being shredded in front of me. I've never actually gotten over it. These self-transforming machine elf creatures were speaking in a colored language which condensed into rotating machines that were like Fabergé eggs but crafted out of luminescent superconducting ceramics and liquid crystal gels. All this stuff was just so weird and so alien and so un-English-able that it was a complete shock—I mean, the literal turning inside out of my intellectual universe...! It's like being struck by noetic lightning.[4]

The double Scorpio in his late teens had considered himself intellectually prepared for pretty much anything. He was an art history major, a Hieronymus Bosch fan, read *Moby-Dick*, William Burroughs, all the works of Huxley. But the experience was so "un-English-able" it cast him into a state of shock.[5] Rocked by the impossible, he would later tour the globe to enunciate how "the ordinary world is almost instantaneously replaced, not only with a hallucination, but a hallucination whose alien character is its utter alienness." There was "nothing in this world," he cautioned, that "can prepare one for the impressions that fill your mind when you enter the DMT sensorium."[6] Not unlike Burroughs, who had declared to Ginsberg in 1953 "Yagé is it," McKenna understood that he had been exposed to *the* secret. "There is a secret and this is it," he remarked to the folks gathered at Ojai. "It is the secret that the world is not only not the way you think it is, it's that the world is a way that you can't think it is." And further, this secret was not "something untold," but that which "can't be told." While convinced that he'd discovered the most powerful of all hallucinogens—unlike Burroughs, who, having summoned the "dim-N" genie in 1961, concluded that he'd been exposed to "the nightmare hallucinogen"— armed with the knowledge of its endogenous status, McKenna promulgated the "paradox that DMT is the most powerful yet most harmless" of all substances.[7] While he may have lived his own paradox throughout the 1980s and 1990s communicating that which can't be told, his speaking tours were not so much miraculous feats of transposing the ineffable than spells cast through an idiomatic word contagion. If ultimately, "the house of constipated reason must be infiltrated by art, by dreamers, by vision,"[8] he was a lightning rod for a visionary arts and a neo-hermetic dance movement. What was at stake was "nothing less than the redemption of fallen humanity through the respiritualization of matter,"[9] and DMT was the spiritual agent.

Meanwhile, returning at the end of the Summer of Love from Berkeley to Paonia, Colorado, where he lived with their parents, Dennis carried a couple of lids of cannabis, half an ounce of hash, a few hits of acid, something he thought was mescaline, and "the Holy Grail—half a gram of DMT." Following his debut with DMT in 1967, Dennis recounted in his diary visions "of a bizarre and otherworldly beauty, so alien and yet so beautiful. The human mind cannot endure that much beauty, and that kind of beauty, without losing its conception of what reality is."

Though I could not myself speak, I heard, felt, saw, listened to, perhaps communicated with, a sound that was not a sound, a voice that was more than a voice. I encountered other creatures whose environment was this alien universe that I had broken through to. I became aware of, perhaps entered into communication with, actual distinct and separate consciousnesses, members of a race of beings that live in that place, wherever that place may be. These beings appeared to be made of part thought, part linguistic expression, part abstract concept made concrete, part energy. I can say no more as to the nature of these beings except that they do exist.[10]

Dennis's dance with dimethyltryptamine marked a profound life transition, as he eventually became an ethnopharmacologist whose romance with ayahuasca saw him embrace the visionary brew as the key to averting global ecological catastrophe.[11] While destined for dramatically varied careers—one a loquacious frontman for the machine elves of hyperspace, the other a renowned scientist—each of the McKenna brothers was profoundly impacted by their experiences with DMT between 1965 and '67. And four years hence, they were drawn toward a momentous frontier: the Amazon.

E@LC

At the turn of the 1970s, devouring existing ethnobotanical knowledge on DMT and other tryptamines, the brothers were keeping tabs on the research of ethnobotanist Richard Evans Schultes in the northwestern Amazon. Attention was directed to the intoxication said to be produced by an oral preparation known among the Witoto of the Putumayo region of the Colombian Amazon as *oo-koo-hé*, made from the ground bark of *Virola theiodora* and the ashes of admixture plants.[12] They knew that *Virola* was a genus of trees in the *Myristicaceae*, or nutmeg, family, containing tryptamines, with their curiosity building around a remark from Schultes that the Witoto used the substance to see and speak with the "little people." By the 1970s, Schultes was familiar with the mind-altering effects produced from the insufflation and oral ingestion of prepared resin from the bark of species of the genus *Virola* among several groups, including the Witoto and Waiká. As reported in his field diary on May 31, 1942, walking from El Encanto to La

Chorrera in the Putumayo, Schultes collected a specimen from an unidentified tree that was apparently responsible for an intoxicating effect.[13] It
was not until June 26, 1951, that a likely candidate for this effect came into
view, when informed by a shaman's son assisting his survey of the forest on
the Apaporis River in the Colombian Amazon that a flowering tree they'd
come across, *Virola calophylla,* was "the tree that gives *yá-kee*" (also called
oo-koo-hé). "My father," the young assistant continued, "uses it when he
wants to talk with the little people." Although insufflating the dried and
pulverized extract through a V-shaped bird-bone tube—which from his
account was most discomforting—and experiencing its "narcotic effects,"
Schultes was not himself treated to a visit from the little ones.[14]

The picture was becoming clearer for Schultes. In February 1969, commissioned by pharmaceutical companies to gather *Virola* bark, Schultes
made another important discovery in the Karaparaná-Igaraparaná region
of the Colombian Amazonas. When stripping the bark from *Virola theiodora*
on the banks of the Rio Loreto Yacu near Leticia, Schultes's assistant, a
native of El Encanto, informed him that the tree was the one from which
his father made little pellets. "He ate them when he wanted to speak with
the little people."[15] The boy was referring to a practice, then disappearing,
of ingesting *Virola* resin coated with the ashes of a variety of plants and
consumed orally with inebriating effect. Since the psychoactive principle in
species of *Virola* was known to be tryptamine (especially 5-MeO-DMT), and
the stomach enzyme monoamine oxidase (MAO) inhibited the effects of
tryptamine, this surprising discovery fueled speculations about Amazonian
alchemies that rippled out of the forest to fire the imaginations of amateur
ethnobotanists. Excited about the mechanism producing what would later
be referred to as the "ayahuasca effect," "this is it," declared Dennis, "the
orally active form of DMT we theorized must exist!"[16] And it was no small
beer that the trail left by Schultes had a scent of the diminutive tykes who'd
curried such favor with Terence.

But we must pause to take in the panorama at this historic juncture.
Trekking to the Amazon, the McKennas were animated, at least partially,
by the need, confirmed by Schultes, for ethnobotanical studies consequent
to the rapid disappearance of subsistence inhabitants and rainforest ecology. And they were pressed too by the acceleration of events back in "the

world"—the escalating conflict in Southeast Asia and the reaction at home. Nuclear détente. The Apollo landings. And given the recent death of their mother, this was also a critical plateau in their own lives. And so while the disappearance of botanical heritage and the mounting historical drama at the turn of the 1970s colored their journey, this was also the plight of young men in mourning for, and even seeking dialogue with, their recently departed mother. Added to that, Terence had, only months prior, lost his library and art in a brushfire in the Berkeley hills. It didn't help that he was also at this time a fugitive, wanted by U.S. Customs authorities for hashish smuggling after a shipment had been intercepted. He'd been wandering in India and Southeast Asia for three years. In a moment out of time potent with crises, exile, endings, contact, and renewal, Terence (aged twenty-four), Dennis (twenty), and three friends landed in the Putumayo in February 1971, an expedition that led to the celebrated experiment at La Chorrera (the E@LC).

"The experiment" first came to public attention in 1975, in the coauthored work of the McKenna brothers, *The Invisible Landscape,* which related an epic series of anomalous occurrences in the Putumayo during February and March 1971.[17] Amid brilliant speculations, poetic genius, and wild science, the book documented a freak expedition tasked with purposes alchemical, divinatory, utopian, and millenarian. Originally published as a "talking book" in 1984, and recognizable as a counterpart to Joseph Conrad's *Heart of Darkness,* Terence's *True Hallucinations* offered detailed background to the "experiment," beating a wickedly erudite path into the heart of the Putumayo. The region through which the McKenna party traveled was, not unlike the Congo, subject to colonial interest in rubber extraction with similar outcomes for the indigenous population: slavery, brutality, terror. The "pilgrimage of the McKenna brothers into 'the heart of darkness,'" observed Wouter Hanegraaff, "was inspired by utopian hopes of restoring paradise."[18] "How small we were," wrote Terence, "knowing little, yet fiercely proud of what we knew, and feeling ourselves somehow the representatives of humanity meeting something strange and Other, something at the edge of human experience since the very beginning."[19] These were, he claimed, near-perfect conditions for unraveling "the secret." In this classic unsurpassed in entheography, McKenna wrote that as its "strangeness and

PART THREE

INVISIBLE LANDSCAPES

Figure 6. Dennis and Terence McKenna. The Brotherhood of the Screaming Abyss (1971).
Photo: Dennis McKenna.

89

power so exceeded that of other hallucinogens, dimethyltryptamine and its chemical relatives seemed finally to define, for our little circle at any rate, maximum exfoliation—the most radical and flowery unfolding—of the hallucinogenic dimension that can occur without serious risk to psychic and bodily integrity."[20] And yet, in its manifestation as "the *lux natura*, the spiritual radiance behind organic nature," they had, by the time of their journey into the Putumayo, achieved only brief flashes of their objective. "We were in that moment the fans of the goddess, not yet her lovers."[21]

Beating a trail blazed by Burroughs back in 1953, their hunt for *the key* in the resinous form of *oo-koo-hé* expanded once Terence stumbled across *Psilocybe cubensis* (then classified as *Stropharia cubensis*), a hallucinogenic mushroom in bounteous supply in the region's cow pies.[22] They gathered mushrooms in Puerto Leguízamo on February 6, the day after Apollo 14 landed on the moon. "We felt an affinity for the astronauts on their journey into the unknown," Dennis recalled. "Drifting downriver, we, too, were impelled by the call of a mystery we felt to be no less worthy of pursuit."[23] Among the chief reasons why *oo-koo-hé* was de-prioritized was because Horacio Calle, the "paranoid" Colombian coca-chewing anthropologist named Alfredo Guzman in *True Hallucinations*, who years earlier informed Schultes about the orally active preparation, and whom the McKenna expedition located at the Witoto village El Encanto, was appalled at the sudden arrival of a troupe of freaks in loose white garb and apparently insensitive to local cultural practice, and yet who sought access to its most cherished alchemy. Referring to one of his companions, a crazed fruititarian who bailed soon afterward, Dennis recalled the anthropologist's "dismay when we showed up in our white linens, long hair, beards, bells, and beads, accompanied by Solo's menagerie of sickly dogs, cats, monkeys, and birds. We could have stepped into his scene directly off the streets of Haight Ashbury."[24]

The party rolled on to La Chorrera, where they did what freaks do under adverse conditions. They improvised. And in doing so, they abandoned all remaining charts. The resulting experiment was a dog's breakfast of high esoterica: ayahuasca analoguing, telepathy, telekinesis, channeling, and a presumed transdimensional alteration whereby one of them was to be transformed into "a DNA radio transmitting the collective knowledge of all earthly life, all the time."[25] Dennis, who appears to have become Terence's very own experiment, and who went without sleep for days, passed into a reverie somewhere between psychosis and prophet. They had arrived, according to Terence, at "the history defining moment when humanity would march into the higher dimension,"[26] a cosmic venture culminating with Dennis tolling the village church bell and Terence encountering a flying saucer.

One of the more curious aspects of this shamozzle was the insectoidal buzz emitting from Dennis during the "experiment at La Chorrera." Among the writings that had appealed to them was an article by anthropologist Michael Harner describing the magic darts used by ayahuasca-drinking shamans among the Jivaro (now Untsuri Shuar) of eastern Equador to cause or cure illness. Harner had outlined the sound of the "supernatural" to which he was himself exposed, having been served a strong dose by a Conibo ayahuasquero in the Peruvian Amazon in 1961: "I met bird-headed people, as well as dragon-like creatures who explained that they were the true gods of this world. I enlisted the services of other spirit helpers in attempting to fly through the far reaches of the Galaxy."[27]

The brothers independently knew this sound, or something they imagined very much like it. Dennis had reported in his diary in 1967 that, smoking DMT, he had encountered "a sound that was not a sound, a voice that was more than a voice." Commenting on his freshman experience, Terence stated, "and then there's a sound, like a piece of bread wrapper or cellophane being scrunched up and thrown away. . . . A membrane is being ripped; something is being torn . . . that's like a hit and run accident except the car came from hyperspace." And deferring to Eliade, it was "a complete rupture of the mundane plane," a rising humming like "the flying saucer tone of Hollywood B movies."[28] The audio rupture is also implicit to the effect of a hit of DMT Terence had taken on a rooftop in Boudhanath, Nepal, in 1969:

> I immediately had a sense of entering a high vacuum. I heard a high-pitched whine and the sound of cellophane ripping as I was transformed into the ultra-high-frequency orgasmic goblin that is a human being in DMT ecstasy. I was surrounded by the chattering of elf

machines and the more-than-Arabian vaulted spaces that would shame a Bibiena. Manifestations of a power both alien and bizarrely beautiful raged around me.[29]

And the sounds emanating from the elven mascots to Terence's trans-dimensional travails grew intriguing as they made themselves heard in spontaneous glossolalia, and as they became associated with extraordinary visualizations. From these experiments, the McKennas knew that trypt-amines could precipitate "a kind of seizure of synesthesia in which syn-tactical structures, spoken language, actually became visible."[30] As Dennis recalled, "the sound doesn't lend itself well to imitation, but if one tries, the voice eventually seems to lock on to the inner buzz, which then pours out of one's mouth in a long, powerful ululation that is quite alarming and unlike any sound one would ordinarily utter."[31] Curiously, these sonics might have had a resonant visual cue in what has been referred to as "Kirby Krackle," the "unique field of black, blobby dots" representing metaphys-ical energy and radioactive "body electricity" drawn in the *Fourth World* metaseries of comics created by Jack Kirby between 1970 and 1973.[32] Ter-ence himself describes in graphic detail a body energy (like mercury) expe-rienced on that rooftop in Boudhanath, the elevated site for a sensational liaison in which *violet psychofluid,* a "living opalescent excrescence," was seen to emanate from his sexual partner, a woman who had ingested the ground seed of a Himalayan datura while Terence himself had dosed on a "treasured tab" of Orange Sunshine, the foundations for the DMT that was then inhaled deeply from his glass pipe. This was no "Coca Cola Douche" as The Fugs might have had it. "There was flowing, out of her, over me, over the floor of the roof, flowing everywhere, some sort of obsidian liquid, something dark and glittering, with color and lights within it."[33]

At La Chorrera, when DMT did not become available as hoped, the brothers deduced that high doses of psilocybin would achieve similar results. Gulping down copious amounts of mushrooms bioassayed with cannabis smoked with locally procured *B. caapi* shavings (containing the MAO-inhibiting harmala alkaloids), they confabulated the idea that these tone vibrations would enable a fusing of their DNA transdimensionally with that of the metabolizing psilocybin, from which there would emerge a genetically altered human. Dennis, apparently, was to be this star-child. In his diary from February 21, 1971, he reported

> a sound almost like a signal, or very, very faint transmissions of radio buzzing from somewhere, something like tingling chimes at first, but gradually becoming amplified into a snapping, popping, gurgling, cracking electrical sound. I tried to imitate these noises with my vocal chords, just experimenting with a kind of humming, buzzing vocal sound made deep in the throat. Suddenly, it was as if the sound and my voice locked into each other and the sound was my voice—but coming out of me in such a way that no human voice could possibly distort itself the way mine was doing. The sound was suddenly much intensified in energy and was like the sound of a giant insect.[34]

The loud, dry, machine-like buzz emanating from Dennis was self-identified in his notes from the time to be "vocally generating a specific kind of energy field which can rupture three dimensional space." He remained uncertain if the field was electromagnetic, though it seemed to "bend space in such a way as to turn it upon itself through a higher dimension."[35] Over two weeks, Dennis underwent a profound unraveling and re-coalescence, a "long voyage of self-discovery and return" in which, according to Terence, he embodied the alchemical equation "lapis = self = UFO."[36]

Although an actual key was said to have manifested, for Terence, the "philosopher's stone" lay in the future as a "transcendental object" or event. Emerging from the contact zone, the calling was clear: "our destiny was apparently to be the human atoms critical to the transformation of *Homo sapiens* into galaxy-roving bodhisattvas, the culmination and quintessence of the highest aspirations of star-coveting humanity."[37] With its inception in the Amazon and in tryptamine journeys over subsequent years, he determined that the *I-Ching*'s King Wen sequence could be used as a thirteen-month lunar calendar, and he believed that he was channeling a predictive paradigm (as found in the fractalized structure of time in his "Timewave Zero" model) that could, with the help of Alfred North Whitehead's novelty theory, explain when this ultra-novel phenomenon would manifest (i.e., December 21, 2012).[38]

Forty years after the events at La Chorrera, Dennis painted a perplexing if somewhat sobering picture of the experiments, undecided as to whether in his weeks-long episode he'd entered "hyperspace" or "psychosis." He is ultimately as ambivalent about the experience as he is about his brother. In an interview, he concluded that he and Terence had undergone "a simultaneous shamanic initiation" in the Amazon. "We crossed this threshold into this place, and what we had predicted didn't happen but we had definitely crossed some kind of threshold, where I became, in my experience, spread across spacetime."[39] Distancing himself from the content of the threshold, while writing about the significance of the sound he emitted, he would settle on the idea that DMT orchestrates a "pharmacokinetic symphony." The inert tryptamine molecule, in a bottle on a shelf, is reckoned to be like "the 3-D score of the molecule's 4-D potential." Inferencing the affinity it is now known to possess with multiple brain receptors, "only when that mundane crystalline substance is combined with a complex mammalian nervous system does the pharmacokinetic symphony—the trip—unfold."[40]

I will take up the sensory experience of DMT in subsequent chapters. For now, as vexing a task as this may be, I will describe the busy nest of ideas from which Terence McKenna was able to communicate his tryptamine encounters. This necessarily returns us to Berkeley and takes us on the road as Terence belted out the neognostic shamanic revival reckoned essential for modern times.

Jungle Alchemy and the Shamanarchy

Recalling the "epiphany" that Terence articulated moments after coming down on that fateful night in the fall of '65, gift-bearer Rick Watson observed that Terence "announced that he would devote his life to seeking out the origins and meaning of this experience."[41] Seized by the "DMT flash," Terence sought to uncover its traces in history, philosophy, psychology, and ethnography. He searched, in vain, for it in Jung. "The dominant motif is a flood of visual imagery that, try as one might," he once stated to Nevill Drury, "one cannot recognize as the contents of either the personal or the collective unconscious."

Figure 7. Terence McKenna. Photo by Kathleen Harrison (1976).

I had made a thorough study of Jung and therefore had the expectation that motifs and idea systems from the unconscious mind would prove to be reasonably homogeneous worldwide. What I found, instead, with the peak intoxication from these plants, was a world of ideas, visual images, and noetic insight that really could not be co-mapped on any tradition—even the esoteric tradition.[42]

He pursued it in the art world. "Verrocchio never saw it. Michelangelo didn't anticipate it. Yates didn't know. Blake hadn't a clue. Melville wasn't briefed. And yet, there it is," he informed his audience.[43] There was no wrinkle, "not an *atom* of the presence of this thing . . . in the carpets of Central Asia, in the myths of the Maya, in the visions of an Arcimboldo or a Fra Angelico or a Bosch."[44] And he plunged into the history of shamanism, where clues were to be unearthed, even while traditional studies of shamanism and religion were largely found wanting.

It is pivotal that Terence was exposed to the flash at the beginning of his college education—at UC Berkeley between 1966 and 1968—at the epicenter of the counterculture, undertaking a self-directed study in the history and philosophy of shamanism. This extraordinary research, coupled with a radical extracurricular empiricism, facilitated what was, to say the least, an unorthodox understanding of shamanism. Compared with Mircea Eliade, whose ideas about shamanism were modeled on northern Eurasian ritual specialists and who earlier regarded shamanic ecstasies induced by inebriants as inauthentic and degenerate, Terence observed psychoactive compounds to be "a primary requirement for all true shamanism."[45] And, what's more, as Terence declared, "a shaman is a true anarchist."[46] That deemed *shamanic* was unlike anything taught in Anthropology 101, but was an approach combining natural history, gnosticism, millenarianism, science fiction, and more, to forge insights on the power of tryptamines to enable a "dissolution of boundaries" necessitated by these historical conditions—a dissolution deemed essential in an era in which humanity faces its greatest challenges. Involving a profound personal break with the known, psychedelic shamanic practice was not merely for the benefit of the individual.

Every one of us when we go into the psychedelic state, this is what we should be looking for. It's not for *your* elucidation, it's not part of *your* self-directed psychotherapy; you are an explorer and you represent our species and the greatest good we can do is to bring back a new idea because our world is endangered by the absence of good ideas. Our world is in crisis because of the absence of consciousness. To whatever degree any one of us can bring back a small piece of the picture and contribute it to the building of the new paradigm, then we participate in the redemption of the human spirit.[47]

The 1971 expedition into the Amazon was hewn with this perspective, commissioned as it was with the beguiling pretension that history was being made, and indeed revitalized, through personal experience. It was the kind of precocious post-1960s attitude that gave way to brazen disregard for native practice, already apparent in the tidal wave of enthusiasm breaking upon the Little Ones That Spring Forth, following ethnomycologist Robert Gordon Wasson's 1957 *LIFE* magazine article "Seeking the Magic Mushroom," triggering hippie gravitation en masse to the Oaxacan mountain village of Huautla de Jiménez, where an ancient Mazatec ceremony was rapidly despoiled and Wise One María Sabina transformed into a local pariah.[48]

McKenna had surmised that the closest approximation to the DMT flash was to be found in Amazonian ayahuasca and snuff traditions, as hinted at in the writings of Schultes. And yet he found there no description of accounts matching his own experience, leading him to conclude that these shamanic practitioners utilizing DMT had no awareness of its impact "when concentrated through modern analytical and chemical laboratory techniques."[49] It was a perception that would magnify in encounters with ayahuasqueros and their "jungle alchemy." Together with wife Kathleen Harrison—an artist and ethnobotanist with whom he would have two children, Finn and Klea—a field trip was undertaken to Peru in 1976 expressly to drink ayahuasca. The three-week journey was not regarded as "fieldwork" in the conventional sense. "In Peru we lived the life, saw the plants, met the people, and shared all the joys and discomforts—but this, however it may seem, was not fieldwork. True fieldwork for us meant being psychedelically ecstatic and at play in the fields of the lord in search of the shamanic dimensions where UFO contact is likely." Finding themselves in Pucallpa, Terence found himself irritated as "a mere spectator to the drug experience" that he had traveled so far to obtain.[50] The journey confirmed that native use was generally too weak for an appetite whetted by concentrated doses from which curanderos were apparently shrinking. At least that was Terence's conclusion. As for Dennis, comparable levels of DMT intoxication can be achieved through ayahuasca. "Terence was a bit too quick to dismiss the curanderos' knowledge by assuming that they did not know," he comments. "I think they did know but had little reason to let him in on this."[51]

The skills and knowledge of ayahuasqueros were found to vary considerably, but there was a niggling frustration with, and distrust of, specialists who appear to have been removed from their roots, which is an attitude echoing the weary eye trained on charlatan *brujos* implicit to the work of Burroughs and later traveler-writers. And while such attitudes may echo a nostalgia for an authentic tradition that exposes a primitivist sensibility, i.e., of the untouched noble shaman who still dwells deep in the forest, Terence McKenna exposed a fault-line dividing the western shamanarchist—the shaman anarchist on the quest for a "mind-expanding" and consciousness-evolving gnosis who may have grown accustomed to an increasingly complex pharmacopoeia—and the ayahuasquero who is trained in curative techniques and who sings icaros attached to long traditions of medicine and sorcery.

Expressing the view that the hyperdimensional experience is "too numinous and energy-laden to be accessible through a tradition," McKenna held that the gnosis should not be governed by administrators of the divine, but "must be personally discovered in the depths of the psychedelically intoxicated soul." Further, his ambivalence toward shamanic traditions is clear: "immense novelty is not something guarded by a shamanic brotherhood that understands what it guards. Rather, all brotherhoods that claim certain knowledge of anything are shams."[52] The possibility of direct, unmediated gnosis was declared to be a human right, an idea striking appeal among his audience. UK band The Shamen were among the earliest artists to amplify McKenna's shamanarchic millenarianism, wearing it on the sleeve of 1992 platinum album *Boss Drum*. Album track "Re: Evolution" featured Terence rapping on the significance of the breakthrough experience, in which one ·typically "cannot continue to close one's eyes to the ruination of the earth, the poisoning of the seas, and the consequences of two thousand years of unchallenged dominator culture, based on monotheism, hatred of nature, suppression of the female, and so forth. So, what shamans have to do is act as exemplars, by making this cosmic journey to the domain of the Gaian ideas, and then bringing them back in the form of art in the struggle to save the world."[53]

Shamanism was, then, not simply redressive psychotherapy for afflicted (post)moderns, but integral to a revitalization movement. There are parallels here with what Jonathan Ott has identified as the Entheogenic Reformation, even though McKenna himself balked at using the term "entheogen," which he thought "a clumsy word freighted with theological baggage."[54] The dialogue he conducted between alchemy and shamanism remains a unique legacy. It was his abiding contention that a renewed shamanism was at the same time a revived alchemy. He admired the work of hermetic magician and adviser to Queen Elizabeth I, John Dee, whose influence on the failed alchemical reformation is celebrated in the documentary *The Alchemical Dream: Rebirth of the Great Work,* which was filmed in Prague and Heidelberg in the mid-1990s, and on which McKenna was a chief collaborator.[55] The thwarted efforts of Frederick V of Bohemia to establish a new alchemical kingdom under the guidance of Dee in the early 1600s is compared to the psychedelic revolution of the 1960s, where the alchemy of LSD and rock 'n' roll failed to bring about a radically transformed society. What is recognized between these utopian instances is a perennial esoteric undercurrent that erupts periodically in novel forms, such as that which he observed at the end of the third millennium CE. Essentially, alchemy provides a stealthy heuristic and mythopoetic strategy in response to the historical crisis. "The entire global civilization is undergoing some kind of meltdown," McKenna announces in this extraordinary film. "The planet itself is now to be seen as a kind of alchemical retort. The *prima materia* to be transformed are the nuclear stockpiles, the toxic waste dumps, the industrial wastelands."

The clue had been discovered in the Amazon, where in their decoctions, snuffs, and other preparations, ayahuasqueros and vegetalismos had been perfecting a jungle alchemy for thousands of years of unwritten trials and tribulations. But while native and mestizo methods opened up a path to the *lapis philosophorum*, if not the "philosopher's stone" itself, the onus was on the modern user—i.e., those whose consumer lifestyles are connected with the despoliation of the Amazon itself—to adopt and optimize the use of ayahuasca and its analogues for purposes at variance to traditional curative uses. It was his view that "it almost requires a modern mentality, or great courage alone, to probe this area unflinchingly, for it is the bedrock of being." "We have reached the point," McKenna motioned, "where we must accept all responsibility for the direction we follow and then go alone without the comforting delusion that what we are trying to define is not unique and unprecedented."[56] In this shamanic-inspired renewal, we have remembered, he continues in *Alchemical Dream*, "what was forgotten during the reductionist centuries of modern science. We have re-understood that the world is one thing, and it's a living thing, with an intent and a spirit." Implicit to this psychedelic shamanism was not a dedication to self-transformation as an end in itself—technique-as-therapy—but a demand for the *(r)evolution of consciousness*. And DMT was the principal weapon in the (r)evolutionary's arsenal.

Shamanic Revival

From the outset, McKenna's formative DMT experiences were interpolated by way of the literary and philosophical frameworks in which he was schooling himself (at that time, formally at UC Berkeley). Arriving in San Francisco during the chill of the Cold War, at the peak of the lunar space quest, and at the height of the era's experimentalism in consciousness expansion, he enrolled in the short-lived Experimental College Program founded by philosopher Joseph Tussman. Bestowed the rare distinction of graduating with a DIY major in "shamanic studies," the experience was formative. This self-directed program that replaced the first two years of normal undergraduate curriculum saw the young McKenna schooled in Eliade, the process theory of Whitehead, phenomenology via a course offered by Hubert Dreyfus, Jungian psychology, and Western esoteric traditions, including hermetic philosophy, gnosticism, and alchemy, adding to this an interest in Renaissance art and modernist literature, whereupon he acquired a cache of tropes with which to translate in rare eloquence his navigations of the mind.

At this critical juncture, shamanism was among the most *outré* subjects in the curriculum of any would-be entheographer, and McKenna seemed well equipped to traverse the natural history of the mind. Not to be armchair-bound like Eliade, he would become a psychedelic renaissance man sampling from organic exotica obtained while trekking far from the ordinary, forging an outlook appealing to those embracing a neoshamanic approach in response to the modern crisis of alienation. He was already an admirer of Huxley, who painted a portrait of what modern shamanism might appear like when the Palanese, the fictional inhabitants in his final novel *Island*, consumed locally harvested medicine (*moksha*) enabling profound insights during their coming-of-age rituals. The fascination with shamanism gained momentum among youth at the turn of the 1970s via Carlos Castaneda, whose works were responsible, despite Castaneda's reputedly fictitious portrayal of Yaqui Don Juan Matus, for popularizing the self-empowering figure of the shaman. These books encouraged the disenchanted that they, through apprenticeship to the Indian Man of Knowledge, and through travels in the otherworld, could become shamanized. Shamanic states of consciousness would later be popularized by Michael Harner in *The Way of the Shaman*, but although Harner himself had a formative near-death experience drinking ayahuasca with the Conibo of the Peruvian Amazon in the early 1960s, his "Core Shamanism" approach essentially excised psychoactive substances from the experience of shamanism made available to "neoshamans."[57] But this was the 1970s/1980s. In the decades prior to prohibition, writers appear to have had fewer inhibitions. In *The Doors of Perception*, Huxley endorsed mescaline and LSD as means by which to cleanse the "filters" ordinarily protecting humans from the infinite, practices previously the domain of saints, seers, mystics, and prophets, but perhaps more essential than ever in the mid-twentieth century, in the shadow of the mushroom cloud. Huxley, and later psychedelic chemists Owsley Stanley and Nick Sand, recognized the urgency of an atomic blast of consciousness in an Atomic Age.

The mounting crisis of the late 1960s demanded that the envelope be blown out on standard consciousness. The times demanded an uncommon courage in the human interfacing with psychoactive compounds—although whether it was courageous or simply folly is a moot point repeatedly recognized in McKenna's unflagging humor. The crisis, which he knew to be a crisis of consciousness, called for an "archaic revival" modeled on pre-Enlightenment hermeticism, and inspired by psychoactives (especially tryptamines). When announcing that "the last best hope for dissolving the steep walls of cultural inflexibility that appear to be channeling us toward true ruin is a renewed shamanism,"[58] McKenna wasn't simply backing a shamanic revival, he was propagating gnosis-enabling tools for the modern age. You don't need to go "five hundred miles up a jungle river and live with primitive peoples and study techniques for thirty years," an eager audience was informed. "If I had a pipe loaded with it in my hand, each one of you would be thirty seconds away from . . . this absolutely reality-dissolving, category-reconstructing, mind-boggling possibility."[59] By virtue of possessing a set of lungs, the secret was only seconds away.

Alien Gnosis

The DMT flash was championed by Terence as nothing short of a human "birthright"—as much, or so he thought, as "our sexuality, our language, our eyesight, our appreciation of music."[60] It is a crucial point since the effects of DMT were, given its endogenous status, signs of the natural human propensity toward becoming shamanic. That said, while a sufficient dose of tryptamine could expose one to the mysteries, it wasn't meant for everyone. If he shared with Huxley the notion that successes with psychedelics could be obtained through turning on engineers, artists, and diplomats, as opposed to the messianic tendency that counted success in the millions of followers, perhaps even more selectively these things were meant for proven psychedelic experimentalists committed to take it to the next level. Given an appropriate psychological condition, with careful attention to context, dose, and delivery technique, DMT was a gnosis-bearing compound, affording exposure to parallel universes, other worlds, or higher dimensions, revealing the provisional characteristics of the user's lifeworld and what one knows as one's "self." Further still, tryptamine derivatives could lift the veils on oppressive systems that conspire to suppress the "truth."

But *the truth* revealed by tryptamines is that *it* is stranger than you *can* imagine. McKenna often quoted British evolutionary biologist J. B. S. Haldane: "My own suspicion is that the universe is not only queerer than we suppose, but queerer than we can suppose."[61] Even if *the truth* were wholly transparent via some enchantment or gnosis, one has no adequate means to express it. This was his dilemma. No matter how scintillating the language manipulated in the service of beguiling his audience, he was acutely aware of forever falling short of the goal—that the transmissions remained oblique.

Another way of stating this conundrum is that mystery is not that which *can* be unveiled, as a puzzle solved, but that which remains essentially mysterious. If there is any final truth, it is that the world needs mystery, as it is the source of enchantment that animates human being. And those who, in the history of religions, politics, and science, proclaim their authority as keepers of ontological certainty defended by doctrine, ideology, and method should be recognized as charlatans and propagators of intolerance. This is where McKenna is in dialogue with fellow iconoclast Argentine writer and poet Jorge Luis Borges, whom he read. The influence was recognized by John Horgan in *Rational Mysticism,* and is further clarified by scholar of Borges and Swedenborg, William Rowlandson.[62] In his quest to comprehend modern mysticism, Horgan interviewed McKenna less than a year before his death, receiving him as a "holy fool," "the crazy wisdom adept" whose task it was to shake us from our perceptual torpor.[63] To the end, Terence McKenna's fascination with novelty, with adventure, alchemy, the quest, placed him in an ambivalent position vis-à-vis gnosis (or knowledge arrived at by personal experience), which while impossible to articulate, provided a persistent charm, much like a calling to a poet, or a vision to a prophet, the *prima materia* to the alchemist. This is precisely the kind of ambivalence operating in the work of Borges. Both men were intently aware of the paradox by which mystery is ultimately... well... mysterious, unspeakable, and the perilous implications of believing otherwise. As Rowlandson observes, the conundrum identified by both figures is that ordered human systems such as politics and institutionalized religions "provide ontological security only through nullifying the sense of ineffable mystery. One is given sanctuary only at the expense of freedom."[64] What seemed to be confirmed to Borges through his recognition of the value of dreams, and to McKenna through his encounters triggered by tryptamines, was the ontological value of nonordinary states of consciousness. What is lost in systems that devalue these states is a confounding astonishment that ought to be relished on an everyday basis. "Interest, curiosity, amazement" were the chief attributes of both Borges and McKenna, and as Rowland-son maintains, effecting delight in the place of despair in the absence of concrete answers.[65]

McKenna himself delighted to share the notion that mystery is integral to being human, a gnosis that he maintained had been all but eroded by a *culture* that had stolen our birthright. He was dedicated to promoting a kind of *psychedelic habitus* consisting of ethnobotanical knowledge, tools, and techniques by which explorers could interface with this revelation, and directly observe the powerfully manipulative artifice and veneer of culture. It was during the Q&A sessions toward the end of his performances, often continuing far longer than the official talk itself, as well as in private interactions afterward, that he responded to the question that burned the lips of many—i.e., "Where can we get some?"—by providing guidance on sources of regional DMT-containing plants, MAO-inhibition techniques, the details of suppliers of seeds, and so forth. Short of actually supplying his audience, he was a tireless fount of information for explorers, both nascent and advanced, of the inner-outer dimensions. Suitably equipped, travelers could be awakened to an understanding that, as believers, patriots, and consumers, they surrender their sovereignty as artists, as seekers, as free-willed beings, to those who consensually maintain power as guardians of the truth and certainty.

Now, if it weren't for culture, media, and language, McKenna could hardly have communicated his views, a high irony that appears to have grown in magnitude as the McKenna machine proliferated in his wake. In countless public lectures delivered throughout the 1980s and 1990s, he became the loquacious celebrity of the psychedelic community, whose participants would digest his hypermediated monologues and alt-pop koans like digital fast food. In his speaking tours, the recordings of which now permeate the internet, the man who had seen the curtain raised on the otherworld and was capable of translating these breakthroughs in effortless eloquence, dispensed the gnosis. Making outrageous ideas fly with ease, and never giving the same lecture twice, he attracted a large following by the time he died in 2000 at the age of fifty-three from a rare form of brain cancer.

Although exiting these dimensions in 2000, today Terence McKenna is more animated than ever. The following is such that fans crowdfunded Dennis $85,750 in a 2011 Kickstarter campaign to complete a book on his life experiences with his brother. *The Brotherhood of the Screaming Abyss: My Life with Terence McKenna* confirms key influences shaping these children of the Space Age. "We were enthralled," writes Dennis, "by the idea that mankind's unknown destiny lay far beyond this planet. Years before *Star Trek* mass-marketed our mix of optimism and yearning, we were certain that humans were bound to explore the trackless reaches of outer space, and that we'd be among those who would go."[66] Science fiction had a lasting influence on the McKennas, especially the 1953 first-contact classic *Childhood's End* and other novels by Arthur C. Clarke. For Terence, human evolution had an off-planetary trajectory. "The transformation of humanity into a spacefaring, perhaps timefaring, race is, on a biological scale, the great goal of history." The entire solar system was perceived as habitable real estate, "but only if we can transform the human imagination to realize that getting high is not a metaphor; getting high is what the whole human enterprise is about. It's true that the earth is the cradle of mankind, but one cannot remain in the cradle forever. The universe beckons."[67]

This star-bound philosophy was countenanced with a Jungian perspective. Jung provided a hermeneutic highly suited to the explorer who recognized that the outer journey mirrors the inner pilgrimage. Here, outer space and its assumed others are allegories, magnifications, of the workings of the unconscious, refractive expressions of the self, such that the farther one journeys beyond the exosphere (e.g., in the narratives of science fiction) the further inward one treks. Such journeys were, from the 1960s, propelled by the chemical fuels of underground pharmacology. "If cosmology was the lens through which we learned to view the universe at large," stated Dennis, "Jungian psychology became our cosmology for the universe within.

Buried in every person's neural tissue was a dimension at least as vast and fascinating as that of the stars and galaxies. We knew the cosmic frontier would, for now, remain beyond our reach; humanity had to contemplate and construct its models of that from afar. The universe of the unconscious was different, being right there for exploration; and psychedelics were the chemical starships for bearing us inward."[68]

While Jung didn't dwell in the psychedelic era, turned-on Jungians adapted his charts of the unconscious as a guide to negotiate the psychedelic experience. Archetypes were clarified and integrated with the assistance of psychedelics, which, if used appropriately, were instrumental to the project of individuation, illuminating the "philosopher's stone," arriving at what Terence understood as the *alien within*. Among Jung's final projects, the work on the mythology of "flying saucers" was influential. In *Flying Saucers: A Modern Myth of Things Seen in the Skies,* Jung proposed that, circular and mandalic, UFOs were symbols of wholeness thrown up from the collective unconscious that, in a world on the brink of nuclear catastrophe, were desperate to rise to the surface, and gain conscious attention.[69] If this model provided an explanation for the popular form of alien contact in the United States in the 1940s and 1950s, and if psychedelics subsequently enabled direct exposure to the collective unconscious, to access truths potentiating the avoidance of catastrophe in a period of escalating crisis, then resolving to become a contactee, an explorer of extreme states, a charter of new worlds, taking DMT and mushrooms at concentrated doses appeared to be an appropriate expression of free will. As Terence announced in 1990 on PBS TV's *Thinking Allowed with Jeffery Mishlove,* "the psychedelic experience is like a UFO encounter on demand,"[70] an encounter that, given the repression of research into consciousness exploration, was a necessary step in resolving the condition the human condition was in. And this was believed momentous since humanity had grown so alienated from the collective unconscious and its Others, that humankind searches the outer universe for anthropomorphized "aliens" while at the same time criminalizing the means by which we encounter the mysteries back here on Earth, inside our own minds. The absurdity of sanctioning efforts to communicate with extraterrestrial lifeforms—with, for instance, the images, sounds, and technology of the 1970s penetrating interstellar space onboard the Voyager space probes—while prohibiting compounds that expose private users to the mysteries of the Other/the UFO was made abundantly clear. As Terence once noted, in a slow and deliberate delivery: "Psychedelic drugs are as important to the study of UFOs as the telescope was to the redefining of astronomy. *You can meet the alien.*" And the "alien" to be encountered was expected to be more bizarre than one could possibly imagine. "It's so counterintuitive, it's so unexpected," he stated in his "Psychedelics Before and After History" lecture at the California Institute of Integral Studies in 1987, "but if ships from Zeta Reticuli were to arrive tomorrow and land on the South Lawn of the White House, it would not change the fact that the DMT flash is the weirdest thing that you can experience this side of the yawning grave."[71]

The Quintessential Hallucinogen

Speaking off-the-cuff toward the end of a five-hour engagement at the Esalen Institute in 1984, McKenna reflected on how he came to be standing there before his audience, remarking that when trekking to La Chorrera he'd been on the run from the Feds, his resources depleted, "and then THEY recruited me and said, 'you know, with a mouth like yours there's a place for you in our organization.'... THEY shifted me into public relations and I've been there to the present."[72] The choice analogy served to bring the house down. Since stumbling upon it in Colombia, the mushroom would speak to Terence throughout his life, with psilocybin inspiring his conjecture that language-using *Homo sapiens* descended from hallucinogenic mushroom (and DMT and harmaline)–eating hominids, with exposure to such compounds later catalyzing language and religion, as proposed in his manifesto *Food of the Gods*. Whether or not we are to swallow the notion of a psychedelic Golden Age implicit to the freewheeling historiography and archaeology presented in that book, the mushroom was the "urplant" that endowed him with his gift of gab, reconfabulating him as an impresario for the psychedelic community.[73] But while psilocybin was ostensibly authorizing McKenna's actions, undertaking intensely critical reflections upon his own experiences, DMT earned his imprimatur as "the quintessential hallucinogen, and consequently the quintessential spiritual and magical tool of this dimension."[74] His lecture "Tryptamine Hallucinogens and Consciousness" delivered at the Lilly/Goswami Conference on Consciousness and Quantum Physics at Esalen in December 1983 remains among his best formulations on what may occur when hitting the "bull's-eye." Indeed, Esalen would become a key venue, with McKenna speaking there on multiple occasions in the summers at the turn of the 1990s. Identifying with the role of "explorer" more than "scientist," in his inaugural Esalen appearance, intriguing digressions were offered on the DMT state visited that night in '65 on Telegraph Avenue.

> I was appalled. Until then I had thought that I had my ontological categories intact. I had taken LSD before, yet this thing came upon me like a bolt from the blue. I came down and said (and I said it many times), "I cannot believe this; this is impossible, this is completely impossible." There was a declension of gnosis that proved to me in a moment that right here and now, one quanta away, there is raging a universe of active intelligence that is transhuman, hyperdimensional, and extremely alien. I call it the Logos, and I make no judgments about it. I constantly engage it in dialogue, saying, "Well, what are you? Are you some kind of diffuse consciousness that is in the ecosystem of the Earth? Are you a god or an extraterrestrial? Show me what you know."[75]

The Esalen lecture illustrated how literary and film sources were adopted to paint a canvas charged with insights from Plato, Heraclitus, Joyce, and alchemist John Dee. The "space" into which he was propelled is mapped by way of *Finnegans Wake*, where such a place is dubbed the "merry go raum." "The room is actually going around, and in that space one feels like a child, though one has come out somewhere in eternity." In this cosmic playground, "one discovers one can make the extra-dimensional objects—the feeling-toned, meaning-toned, three-dimensional rotating complexes of transforming light and color. To know this is to feel like a child." And in deference to Heraclitus, "one is playing with colored balls; one has become the Aeon."[76] This state of consciousness defied temporality.

> The tryptamine state seems to be in one sense transtemporal; it is an anticipation of the future. It is as though Plato's metaphor were true—that

time is the moving image of eternity. The tryptamine ecstasy is a stepping out of the moving image and into eternity, the eternity of the standing now, the nunc stans ["everlasting now"] of Thomas Aquinas. In that state, all of human history is seen to lead toward this culminating moment.

And the entities making themselves known in this everlasting now were reminiscent to him of a scene from *The Wizard of Oz*, "after the Munchkins come with a death certificate for the Witch of the East. They all have very squeaky voices and they sing a little song about being 'absolutely and completely dead.' The tryptamine Munchkins come, these hyperdimensional machine-elf entities, and they bathe one in love. It's not erotic but it is open-hearted. It certainly feels good." And "like fractal reflections of some previously hidden and suddenly autonomous part of one's own psyche," these beings are reassuring: "'Don't be alarmed. Remember, and do what we are doing.'" And so it was that Terence had been summoned to become a traveling medium of a secret that could not be told, to reorient the modern world toward the "Gaian Supermind," to channel a fractalized model of time, and to be a near-messianic advocate of DMT. He couldn't have been further removed from Burroughs. Driven by the synesthetic materiality of language in the DMT experience, tinkering with the wiring underneath the culture machine, the McKenna road show held a likeness to that of "the man who can dig it." But rather than guide users toward Dreamachines and "nonchemical" multimedia aesthetics, McKenna implored anyone lending an ear to position themselves in the blast zone.

As this book illustrates, McKenna's cheerleading for tryptamines inspired a generation of seekers to chase the alkaloid rabbit deep into the warren. Transfixing the habitués of alternative communities, psychedelic salons, weekend workshops, and outdoor festivals with synergistic linguistics cutting across alchemy, mycology, UFOs, comparative religions, and art history, he became a many-pointed arrowhead for neopsychedelia, his profusion of spoken-word performances permeating cyberspace,[77] setting the stage for his resurrection, recomposition, and reanimation in graphic, digital, and electrosonic media.

Despite such venerated virtualization, religious studies academics, scholars of shamanism, and officers of ideas have had little rapport with McKenna. He loathed academic and scientific careerism as much as dogma and doctrine, and preferred radical psychedelic empiricism before the labors of treatises. And as an entertaining orator he encouraged listeners to question everything he said. For these reasons, it has not been easy for scholars (of religion or otherwise) to comprehend or pigeonhole McKenna. Additionally, not unlike William James, he recognized that *all* human experience is open to examination, and that no experience is too strange for intellectual inquiry, even if inquiry is incapable of containing such experience. But unlike James, whose experimentations with nitrous oxide were legal practices, McKenna advocated psychoactive compounds the research and use of which are subject to prohibition, ensuring a marginal stature within academia. This situation made him something of a confounding UFO buzzing the minds of academics, especially in U.S. airspace. In *Esalen: America and the Religion of No Religion,* a study of the American human potential movement and its embrace of "the Tantric transmission," professor of religion at Rice University Jeffrey Kripal reports a sighting of the anomaly, hedging "it is difficult to know what to do with McKenna today."[78] The reaction is unsurprising, given the prophecy delivered in McKenna's 1983 Esalen debut:

> My vision of the final human future is an effort to exteriorize the soul and internalize the body, so that the exterior soul will exist as a superconducting lens of translinguistic matter generated out of the body of each of us at a critical juncture at our psychedelic *Bar Mitzvah.* From that point on, we will be eternal somewhere in the solid-state matrix of the translinguistic lens we have become. One's body image will exist as a holographic wave transform while one is at play in the fields of the Lord and living in Elysium.[79]

While McKenna's mystic-like characteristics are noted and admired, Kripal is careful to distance himself from the source of the mysticism. He reports a "patently erotic" mystical experience in Calcutta that he says "bears all the hallmarks of a tryptamine-catalyzed ecstasy as studied by Strassman," but lest you conflate Kripal's gnosis with an illicit practice, the strategic declaration arrives in an endnote: "I have never taken a psychedelic substance."[80]

You can almost hear the resonant nasal song whipping out remarks about the professor "holding," not unlike the rest of us, all along.

The attitude within academia is unsurprising in an age when drug prohibition has cauterized research. The problem is not simply that scientists and scholars refuse to look through "Galileo's telescope," but that even if they do, they risk losing access to the udders of the ruling paradigm once proclaiming what they've "seen." It's a form of intellectual lobotomization to which the academe is implicit. And yet, signs of life have grown apparent in recent years. In a new climate of thinking, religious studies scholars outside the United States recognize the importance of McKenna's work. For scholar of "rejected knowledge" Christopher Partridge, McKenna's eclectic brand of shamanism performs like a supernova for the "psychedelic occulture"—where psychedelics are reckoned integral to the historical reenchantment he identifies as "popular occulturation."[81] Professor of history of hermetic philosophy at the University of Amsterdam, Wouter Hanegraaff, has also taken steps to recognize the role of McKenna in the history of esoteric religion in the West. In reference to Eranos, the intellectual discussion group gathering annually near Ascona, Switzerland, since 1933, Hanegraaff regarded McKenna as an exemplar of Eranos religionism. It's possible to imagine Terence nestled among illustrious scholars like Eranos participants Jung, Eliade, Erich Neumann, D. T. Suzuki, and others adapting psychology, quantum physics, and world religions to forge scholarship on human universalisms.[82] Still, one wonders how Eranos founder, and teetotaler, Olga Fröbe, will have countenanced the man who once told an audience that, having swallowed 9g of dried mushrooms, he'd been visited by a woman in bondage gear who leaned into his face inquiring: "Is it strong enough for you, asshole?"[83] In a revision of his tome *New Age Religion and Western Culture*,[84] in which the role of psychedelics as gnostic technologies had been overlooked within an otherwise-thorough investigation of modern esoteric practices, Hanegraaff now acknowledges psychoactive compounds to be "catalysts of new spiritual revelations," and sees McKenna as the figurehead of what he calls "entheogenic esotericism."[85] But while psychedelic shamanism may now have a recognizable place in the history of Western esotericism, which is no small advent in religious studies, bioassaying essayists, home-baked tinkerers in the natural history of ideas, and adjunct scholars on radical sabbatical have known as much for decades.

Invisible College

In his decades-long reflections, Terence McKenna knew that DMT was the key to a secret that could not be communicated, a mystery with which one could flirt, but never go all the way (at least not on this side of the yawning grave). Dues were paid to Borges, who refers in the short story "The Sect of the Phoenix" to a mysterious rite performed throughout all history and all societies by participants in a secret society.

> The rite is the only religious practice observed by the sectarians. The rite constitutes the Secret. This Secret ... is transmitted from generation to generation. The act in itself is trivial, momentary, and requires no description. The Secret is sacred, but is always somewhat ridiculous; its performance is furtive and the adept do not speak of it. There are no decent words to name it, but it is understood that all words name it or rather inevitably allude to it.

Read by McKenna at Esalen in 1983, the passage opens a door on the furtive and undefined milieu to which he had grown accustomed, following his initial episodes with DMT. Until then and long afterward, the rites of DMT use were crude, clandestine, and yes, ridiculous. Its shadowy status was quite clearly consequent to repressive laws and its renown as an atomic bullet, its ludicrous characteristics noticeable to anyone entering, as McKenna called it, "the elf dome." The audience at Esalen was presented with the news that shamans are universal outsiders, survivors of adverse conditions. In possession of a piercing vision, they are "true phenomenologists of this world."[86] And the calling arrives unexpectedly. At La Chorrera, when incredulous about why he and Dennis were seemingly called "to be the ambassadors of an alien species into human culture," the mushroom itself responded: "Because you did not believe in anything. Because you have never given yourself over to belief in anyone."[87] McKenna hereby places his chronicles with tryptamines in a lineage that has few spokespeople, with the experiments reported in *The Invisible Landscape*, *True Hallucinations*, and a vast online repository of spoken-word material popular among a psychedelic milieu whose participants bear the hallmarks of a mystic collectivity. In the parlance of sociologist of religion Colin Campbell, this diffuse "cultic milieu" is "the cultural underground of society."[88] Further, practitioners behave like adepts, those initiated into an amorphous secret society whose silent actions are somewhat coterminous with the mythology of the Rosicrucians, who, from the seventeenth century, and with the assistance of "intermediary" beings, are purported to have worked covertly to "perform benevolent acts to the transformation of the world and the salvation of humanity."[89] While few DMT practitioners would make such claims, the empowering and transformative character of the "DMT entity" (i.e., intermediary) phenomenon illuminates the connections between practitioners and secret societies in Western esoteric history. Initiates of an amorphous secret society, practitioners of abominable knowledge, spiritual technicians, and hyperspace farers populate this entheogenic esoteric milieu, a network nurtured by and sustaining the DMT underground.

In Santa Fe in 1990, Terence recalled how astounded he was when first smoking DMT that its status remained subterranean. "How do they keep the lid on this? Why isn't it 4-inch-high headlines? I mean, we live in a culture where people jump out of airplanes for the fun of it! And yet, there aren't DMT societies, nobody is talking about this, and it makes jumping out of an airplane look like peanuts in terms of 'If you want Thrills, This is THRILLS.'"[90] And later, at Ojai, his amazement had grown. "I couldn't understand why there weren't 11-inch-high headlines on the front page of every newspaper on the planet saying something like 'Doorway to Hyperspace Discovered . . . elf negotiations proceeding.'"[91] But while the quintessential hallucinogen was not getting the headlines it deserved, an excavation of DMT history might unearth participants who will find strange communion in the "black hole effect" typical to its use. In part answering his own inquiry, Terence wrote that "DMT is like an intellectual black hole in that once one knows about it, it is very hard for others to understand what one is talking about. One cannot be heard. The more one is able to articulate what it is, the less others are able to understand. This is why I think people who are able to attain enlightenment, if we may for a moment comap these two things, are silent. They are silent because we cannot understand them."[92] The ineffability of this experience is naturally due to the normal human inability to describe the experience of the higher dimensions, which defy the properties of our spatial, three-dimensional world and for which lower-dimensional "language" falls short. Of course, this makes McKenna all the more remarkable, since, far from silent, he was a loquacious genius on these matters.

But while language falls short, and clandestine behavior is felicitous in an era of prohibition, there has proliferated a net-enabled community of seekers, ontological skydivers, and hyperspatial bungee jumpers who have ranged deep into the invisible wilderness and who have returned to express the inexpressible, transmit the unrepeatable, and exchange zero-point fieldnotes on the ineffable. And while it remains that the "secret," the mystery—death—cannot possibly be divulged, the means of translation in literature, music, visionary media, and science have evolved since Terence McKenna's passing. Appearing among this milieu was a clinical psychiatrist by the name of Rick Strassman. Referring to a visit with McKenna in Sebastopol in 1988, Strassman recalled that "if it weren't for my friendship with Terence, it's unlikely I ever would have studied DMT. Nor would the form of my research be the same without a particularly memorable brainstorming session in his library in the Summer of 1988."[93] It is to this research and its legacy that I now turn.

CHAPTER 5

Room 531
The Pineal Enigma

Even Dr. Gonzo wouldn't touch "extract of pineal." It was the limit. "One *whiff* of that shit would turn you into something out of a goddamn medical encyclopedia! Man, your head would swell up like a watermelon, you'd probably gain about a hundred pounds in two hours . . . claws, bleeding warts, then you'd notice about six huge hairy tits swelling up on your back . . ." He shook his head emphatically. "Man, I'll try just about anything; but I'd never in hell touch a pineal gland."[1] While Raoul Duke's Samoan attorney in *Fear and Loathing in Las Vegas* respectfully avoided the pineal, others have made this enigmatic gland, and all that it excretes, a *cause célèbre*. Remote from the misshapen grotesqueries conjured by Hunter S. Thompson, in the enthusiasm of Rick Strassman, the "blinding light of pineal DMT" enables transit of the life-force from this life to the next. With his ideas received more often as declarations of truth than speculation, the following passage encapsulates the mood of discovery in the clinical psychiatrist's (and, at the time, Zen Buddhist's) best-selling *DMT: The Spirit Molecule*.

> The consequence of this flood of DMT upon our dying brain-based mind is a pulling back of the veils normally hiding what Tibetan Buddhists call the bardo, or intermediary states between this life and the next. DMT opens our inner senses to these betwixt states with their myriad visions, thoughts, sounds, and feelings. As the body becomes totally inert, consciousness has completely left the body and now exists as a field among many fields of manifest things.[2]

Subtitled *A Doctor's Revolutionary Research into the Biology of Near-Death and Mystical Experiences*, Strassman's landmark study raised the profile of DMT, and represents a milestone in the history covered in this book. Triggering a tidal wave of interest in the pineal gland—seen more as a "lightning rod of the soul" than the brain's laboratory for hellish hallucinations—*DMT: The Spirit Molecule* shone a light on the profound implications of DMT's endogenicity (that is, its natural structure and function in humans)—all deriving from Strassman's observations of goings-on in Room 531 of the University of New Mexico Hospital Clinical Research Center, Albuquerque, between 1990 and 1995. It was in Room 531 that Strassman conducted trials administering more than four hundred IV doses of DMT into the forearm veins of sixty healthy volunteers. His groundbreaking observations of the subjective effects of DMT on these volunteers was the first sanctioned research on the clinical application of psychedelics in the United States for a generation.[3]

The Spirit Molecule

As painfully recounted in *DMT: The Spirit Molecule,* Strassman cut through a mountain of red tape for two years before gaining approvals to conduct his trials.[4] While this hardly makes for riveting reading, the edge-of-seat action derives from watching the hermeneutic Trojan Horse wheeled inside the walls of the Academy. If the DEA, FDA, or NIDA had been alert to the deeper motivations underlying Strassman's project, it seems unlikely he would have been given the green light. But we need to backtrack somewhat to the time before Strassman became a sanctioned spokesperson for the pineal gland. Not unlike colleagues across numerous disciplines drawn to DMT and its functional analogues, Strassman was intrigued with their status native to humans, and their possible role. From the mid-1950s, a series of discoveries demonstrated that DMT and its close relatives 5-hydroxy-DMT (bufotenin) and 5-methoxy-DMT (5-MeO-DMT) are compounds naturally occurring in humans and other mammals, as detected in urine, blood, and cerebrospinal fluids.[5] Starting in the early 1960s, after Julius Axelrod published in *Science* findings of the enzyme capable of producing DMT in rabbit lung, interest in endogenous DMT in humans and other mammals grew.[6] Tryptamine was subsequently known to be produced in the human body via a biosynthetic pathway that originates with the essential dietary amino acid tryptophan, and a second enzyme, INMT. With growing evidence of DMT's endogenous activity, it was observed that DMT may function as a neurotransmitter or a neuromodulator.[7] Other researchers speculated that DMT may be involved in the production of dream visions experienced during REM sleep.[8] That DMT was among the select compounds admitted passage across the blood-brain barrier spurred Strassman's imagination as to its purpose. Not least of all, he was driven by the awareness that precursors and enzymes necessary for DMT synthesis occur in the pineal, the mysterious gland around which he would orbit.

Impressed by this catalog of discoveries, Strassman was dissatisfied with prevailing research prerogatives. While the reasons motivating his research became evident in *DMT: The Spirit Molecule,* he later clarified how his project objectives "cut both ways."[9] On the surface, the project was rolled out with all the trimmings of a traditional psychiatric research framework operating under the premise that DMT remained the most suitable candidate for an endogenous psychotomimetic compound—where the study of the mechanisms by which it exerts its effects was proposed to shed light on the etiology of endogenous psychoses, such as schizophrenia. As we already know, since the 1950s and 1960s, DMT had been most recognizable to science as a possible "schitzotoxin." But while this was the convention driving much research, such as that motivating Szára, Strassman had his reservations. The circumstance by which DMT's endogenicity was limited to a possible cause of psychoses was deeply dissatisfying since its role in human consciousness, especially through its involvement in non-psychotic altered states of consciousness, was being neglected. The limited research undertaken before federal and international restrictions took effect determined no significant differences in the levels of endogenous DMT in the body fluids of normal volunteers and those with psychotic illnesses, a result prompting science to blanch, effecting a research lacunae that would show little sign of improvement in the wake of the Controlled Substances Act of 1970. As a result of this inactivity, psychiatry was said to have "lost a unique opportunity to probe deeper into the mysteries of consciousness."[10] Consequently, upon prohibition, DMT would suffer a fate perhaps even more tragic than that befalling LSD. Confronting this depressing situation, Strassman worked against the grain to consider the possibility that "the body synthesized a compound with psychedelic properties that produced highly prized spiritual experiences, rather than highly maladaptive psychotic episodes."[11]

This then reveals what Strassman identified as the "deeper reasons" for his investigation of DMT: "an interest in the biological bases of naturally occurring psychedelic experiences, such as mystical and near-death states." If exogenous DMT reliably replicated these experiences as reported in civilizations and cultures throughout world history, such research could open the door to an investigation of the function and significance of tryptamines endogenous to humans. Going further, and now wearing his psychotherapist's hat, Strassman clarified that "straddling the more or less overt reasons for my work with DMT" was an effort to revive research considering "the therapeutic properties of DMT in particular and psychedelics in general."[12]

Strassman's Horse was crafted from scratch from elements of science and religion to illuminate the effects, experience, and purpose of DMT. Among the virtues of this approach was the role he performed as faithful scribe to his hyperspace-faring volunteers. Drawing on copious notes of each volunteer's post-event commentary, as well as their journaled reports, Strassman provided for readers in sometimes enthralling detail the exploits of traveler-volunteers and their encounters with a range of entities. A diligent transcriber, he formulated telling comparisons with near-death experiences and alien-abduction reports leading to further speculation testing the limits of science. Increasingly dissatisfied with biochemical and psychological models that served to explain away the experiences, reflecting upon the trials in which volunteers were frequently encountering beings that appeared "more real than real," Strassman was urged to take these occurrences seriously as phenomenological events.[13] What appeared compelling to his mind was that the effects of introduced DMT in a significant proportion of his volunteers—categorized in "clinical clusters," including somatic effects, affect, perception, cognition, and volition—were not dissimilar to what are universally reported as "spiritual," "enlightenment," or "mystical" experiences, complete with blinding white light, timelessness, contact with omniscient beings, and the sensation of having died and been reborn. Strassman was compelled to find a new hermeneutic. Labeled the "spirit molecule," DMT may lead us to "an acceptance of the coexistence of opposites, such as life and death, good and evil; a knowledge that consciousness continues after death; a deep understanding of the basic unity of all phenomena; and a sense of wisdom or love pervading all existence."[14] If this was the effect of administered DMT, could this same compound produced endogenously be the physical media for mystical experience? Positioning a wedge into the tight opening on the Pandora's box of consciousness, Strassman took to transcribing the infinite in the empiricist dicta of science, albeit in language suffused with a Buddhist worldview.

The Pineal Enigma

Back in 1974, Strassman had taken a year's leave of absence from medical school to participate in a series of retreats at a Midwestern Zen monastery. The connection with Zen Buddhism would continue for the next twenty years, principally through his ordainment as a lay member of a monastic community in Sacramento, California. Contemplating the likeness that the psychedelic experience induced by LSD and other substances had with *bodhicitta*—what many Buddhists understand to be the most important step on the road to enlightenment—it became evident to Strassman in the 1970s that up to three-quarters of the monks at his monastery were not only experienced with LSD, but that psychedelics had been "their first entry into the enlightenment stream of life." To explain the apparent proximation, at least in some cases, of experiences occasioned by psychedelics and meditational states, it was deduced that "there must be something going on in the brain." The seeds were sown for the search for "a biological basis for mystical experience."[15]

Buddhism had a shaping influence on Strassman's DMT project. He had modeled his Hallucinogenic Rating Scale—an instrument enabling the psychopharmacological characterization of DMT's effects in humans—on the Buddhist psychological system Abhidharma, and he employed the Zen technique of "just sitting" with his volunteers.[16] Perhaps most importantly, his relationship with Tibetan Buddhism guided speculation concerning the very purpose of DMT (i.e., its purported role in death/rebirth). That DMT effects a near-death experience was intuited from a telling synchronicity that bridged Strassman's spiritual and medical science training. He'd learned that the forty-nine-day transit in which the soul reincarnates—as taught in the *Tibetan Book of the Dead*—is exactly the interval from conception to the first signs of pineal formation in the human embryo, and nearly exactly the same moment that the fetus's gender can be determined. This understanding triggered speculations concerning the hidden role of the pineal gland—what René Descartes called "the seat of the soul"—in death and rebirth.

It seemed less hypothesis than conviction that Strassman's "spirit gland" was "the intermediary between the physical and the spiritual."[17] With the proposition that the organ excretes large quantities of DMT at the moments of birth and death—i.e., at either end of this cosmic interval— the pineal is reckoned to be the "lightning rod of the soul." The pea-sized organ's central position in the epithalamus, between the two hemispheres, could allow DMT synthesized in the pineal to be secreted directly into the cerebrospinal fluid and affect visual and auditory pathways. When we die (or indeed, have near-death experiences), it was supposed, "the life force leaves the body through the pineal gland," where a DMT release is speculated to be like the floodwaters carrying the soul into the liminal phase (or bardo) between life and life, as depicted in the *Tibetan Book of the Dead*. And functioning as a kind of spirit antenna, "pineal DMT release at forty-nine days after conception marks the entrance of the spirit into the fetus." Although the burden of proof remains, Strassman conjectured that "pineal tissue in the dying or recently dead may produce DMT for a few hours, and perhaps longer, and could affect our lingering consciousness. While our 'dead' brain wave readings are 'flat,' who knows about our inner mental state at this time?"[18] The proposal that the soul is released at death from the region of the pineal is indeed depicted in Alex Grey's painting *Dying*, reproduced on the cover of Strassman's book, a painting depicting a deceased human with vapor rising from the crown, all overseen by a spiraling pattern of multiple, disembodied, wide-open eyes.

The pineal gland possesses vital functionality recognized by science. It regulates the hormone melatonin, which it converts from serotonin, with a balanced melatonin cycle being essential for sleep, reproduction, motor activity, blood pressure, the immune system, cellular growth, and body temperature, among other vital functions. While Strassman's early research had investigated the role of melatonin in depression, it seemed depressing for a man who intuited the hidden function and purpose of the pineal that the more critical questions weren't being asked. If the pineal gland was found to secrete DMT at certain times, couldn't its proximity to crucial sensory-relay stations in the brain "explain the highly visual and auditory nature of many mystical and other endogenous psychedelic experiences"?[19] Interest in the "psychedelic pineal gland" was evident in 1986 when Strassman was invited to speak at Esalen, meeting Terence McKenna and Rupert Sheldrake. The hidden function of the pineal was then hypothesized in a 1991 issue of *Psychedelic Monographs and Essays,* where Strassman identified the pineal as an "enigmatic organ" shrouded in mystery. Alongside a discussion of its role in converting melatonin from serotonin, Strassman proposed that the tiny endocrine gland in the vertebrate brain has a secret psychedelic function. Drawing inspiration from Descartes's meditations on this pinecone-shaped, nonpaired organ's role as a conduit for the soul, he proposed that the pineal "mediates the psychophysiological actions of what might be referred to as the consciousness-bearing life force of an individual." Amid detailed speculation on the mechanisms by which endogenous psychoactive tryptamines may be synthesized in the pineal, Strassman introduced his metaphysical hunch regarding the forty-nine-day embryonic pineal formation coinciding with the reincarnation of the life-force according to the *Bardo Thodol.*[20] It soon became an underground truism that, as D. M. Turner wrote in *The Essential Psychedelic Guide,* "DMT is produced in the human pineal gland which is correlated to the '3rd eye' or Ajna Chakra in the Indian spiritual system." By meditating, yogis could, for instance, increase their DMT levels.[21]

News of the psychedelic function of the pineal provided an update on a gland that has exerted a magnetic influence on esotericists who've long extolled its spiritual and paranormal propensities—in particular, the pineal's capacity, once activated, to enable previously dormant powers of perception, especially those associated with vision: clairvoyance, seeing auras, and being awakened to information from other dimensions. Within the esoteric milieu, the visionary capacity of the pineal has been elucidated via interwoven trajectories. The all-seeing eye can be traced to the ancient Egyptian symbol of the Eye of Horus, recognized among occult historians as a precise graphic depiction of a cross section of the pineal gland. The light-transducing ability of the pineal gland has led to its reception as the "third eye," whose activation unleashes extrasensory powers, an idea traced to Hindu traditions from which practices of meditation and yoga have derived, and through which the activation of the crown chakra is thought to activate psychic powers. Strassman's research quickly proved important among those seeking neurochemical explanations for such extrasensory abilities and psi phenomena. For instance, his conjecture that pinoline (a ß-carboline and MAO inhibitor present in the pineal) could be involved in converting serotonin into DMT led parapsychologist Serena Roney-Dougal to the proposition that "our pineal gland makes our own endogenous Ayahuasca every night of our lives!"[22]

As the pineal's latest champion, Strassman's speculations in *DMT: The Spirit Molecule* were readily absorbed within an occult science milieu where the spiritual function of the pineal was a foregone conclusion, now enjoying the support of a formal scientific investigation. "A resonance process may occur in the pineal similar to that of shattering glass," wrote Strassman. "The pineal begins to 'vibrate' at frequencies that weaken its multiple barriers to DMT formation: the pineal cellular shield, enzyme levels, and quantities of anti-DMT. The end result is a psychedelic surge of the pineal spirit molecule, resulting in the subjective states of mystical consciousness."[23] Such artful speculation met with the approval of those seeking to hitch a ride on the coattails of science, a practice evident throughout modern esoteric thought stretching back to the theosophists and beyond. As Helena Blavatsky had popularized the idea that an actual "third eye" belonging to the ancients had atrophied through the course of evolution into the pineal—a faint reminder of "the early spiritual and purely psychic characteristics in man"[24]—contemporary esotericists celebrate the means by which, like an opened third eye, the (re)activation of the pineal gland enables lucid dreaming, out-of-body experiences, hypnagogic imagery, near-death experiences, astral travel, and ultimately, as Anthony Peake conveys in *The Infinite Mindfield*, the evolution of consciousness.[25] These ideas are also an echo of Blavatsky, who observed that the pineal is the key to higher consciousness. "This seemingly useless appendage is the pendulum which, once the clock-work of the inner man is wound up, carries the spiritual vision of the EGO to the highest planes of perception, where the horizon open before it becomes almost infinite."[26]

The breaking news on endogenous DMT becomes a golden arrow in the quiver of spiritual warriors like "Hippie Jedi" and "Freedom-Preneur" Justin Verrengia, who is on a mission to change the world one person (and one sale) at a time. Through practice and development, Verrengia claims that pineal activation can produce natural DMT, allowing individuals to access "extrasensory superpowers you never knew existed." Psychic abilities like astral travel, exploring other dimensions, and even foreseeing the future are at your fingertips. Moreover, when the pineal is fully operational, the individual can be, or so Verrengia ostentates, "in a constant visionary state most of the time." For writer and hypnotherapist Iona Miller, the "master gland," implicated in the production of DMT, is responsible for "the internal perception of Light, the raising of Kundalini the serpent power, and for awakening inner sight or in-sight." For author of *Modern Esoteric: Beyond Our Senses,* Brad Olsen, mass pineal activation amounts to an awakened population, which is revolutionary, given that the "current control group" retards pineal function through contaminating public water supplies with sodium fluoride, a practice reckoned to intentionally calcify the pineal.[27]

At a time when life coaches promote meditation, yoga, qigong, taiji, and other practices to activate the brain's "spiritual gateway" and open up "the line of communication with the higher planes," when wellness instructors endorse dietary supplements—like neem and organic blue ice skate fish oil—that will decalcify your pineal gland and enable you to "exploit your full spiritual capabilities,"[28] when "solar gazing" is reckoned to be an ancient activity converting solar energy into physical nourishment by way of the light-sensitive pineal,[29] when Dark Room techniques have been developed to stimulate the production of "Pineal Soma and DMT" or "Endohuasca,"[30] or when the Lucia N3 Hypnagogic Light Machine is conjectured to stimulate DMT release, Strassman's ideas flow like quicksilver. With mounting speculation concerning the role of DMT and the pineal, those seeking to maximize their human potential and ability to access transpersonal states of consciousness could ostensibly activate, or reactivate, their third eye, through life practices designed to optimize the pineal and to ensure DMT synthesis or release. Included among these life practices is the art of taking exogenous DMT.

The Life and Times of the DMT Gland

Strassman's propositions would develop a life of their own. You could find elements of the theory inspiring "new paradigm" science. Linked to other lifestyle practices—i.e., raw foods, tantric sexuality, and shamanic practices—DMT activation could reverse the degeneration from paradise, returning humanity to an "Eden-like consciousness." Such is the position of *Left in the Dark* authors Tony Wright and Graham Gynn, who have hypothesized that a progressive neurodegenerative condition associated with hormonal alterations and left-brain-hemisphere domination some two hundred thousand years ago—a condition echoed in universal myths of the fall from paradise—distorted human perception toward "fear, mistrust and craving." In the struggle to save the world through checking our devolution to a "fear-based age of plastic and prozac," endogenous DMT release is postulated to be among the solutions to regaining "our lost perceptual heritage."[31] It's a small leap to making forecasts on the role of external electromagnetic fields and radio waves in this new awakening, a thesis implicit to biophysician Dieter Broers's film *Solar Revolution*. In the 2012 documentary, Broers postulates that electromagnetism possesses the capacity to activate DMT release, "weakening the limitations on our perception or even dissolve them altogether," potentiating transpersonal experience, consciousness expansion, and specieswide changes (like the acquisition of language). The pineal is singled out as the hypersensitive brain organ that could act "as a transmitter or receiver of cosmic signals." Cut to Strassman seated cross-legged on the edge of a cliff overlooking a vast canyon, meditating on the notion of "spirituality being the science of invisible things." Strassman presides over the view that, as a result of a possible grand celestial event, "if every organism which contains the DMT-synthesizing gene were flooded with high levels of DMT, the implication is that all those organisms would be entering into the DMT state."[32]

The pineal theory has animated revisions of history. For instance, the newly proposed properties of the pineal have been adapted to illuminate the frequency of the third-eye symbology in the temples of ancient Egypt and the preparative treatment of pharaohs (including the removal of the brain). During an episode of the series *Magical Egypt*, following a long interview with Strassman, the viewer is informed that "in strange and unexpected ways," the temples of ancient Egypt "demonstrate a special emphasis on the pineal gland and its role as the intermediary between mind and body, the seat of consciousness, and possibly the gateway into and out of life."[33]

The pineal meme is alive in popular culture, with Strassman's ideas filtering into, for instance, Gaspar Noé's provocative *Enter the Void*. Smoking DMT in the opening point-of-view sequence—itself offering homage to the transdimensional voyage of space avatar Dave Bowman at the closing of Kubrick's *2001: A Space Odyssey*—young American drug dealer Oscar is informed by friend Alex that DMT exists in the brain and is released at the time of death to give you the "hardest trip" you'll ever get. Oscar is also made familiar with the *Tibetan Book of the Dead*, which offers a guiding narrative on the death/rebirth experience, portrayed after Oscar is suddenly gunned down by police in the bathroom of seedy Tokyo bar The Void. His soul departs on a terrifying ride down through his past and up above the Toyko underground, a bardoic journey amplifying in death the little bardo of his earlier exogenous DMT experience. The presumed role of DMT is further exploited in the 2014 supernatural horror film *The Possession of Michael King*, where, following the tragic death of his wife, aggrieved atheist Michael King sets out to make a film disproving the existence of God, the Devil, and life after death. In one scenario, King finds himself in a graveyard at night smoking DMT given to him by a necromancer who earlier explained that DMT is "released when we die. It helps us pass to the other side, but taking it while we're still living simulates a near-death experience." It's a deeply disturbing experience for King, the skeptic, who appears to have contact with his recently departed wife during the episode, becoming possessed soon after.

That pineal-gland-produced DMT appeals to writers of science-fiction horror, among others who seek new devices to dissolve the boundary between life and death, is evident in David Gelb's *The Lazarus Effect* (2015). In the film, pineal DMT is "the base compound" for "Lazarus," a serum that, no prizes for guessing, brings back the dead. "The moment you die, right then, your brain just floods your system with a massive blast of DMT, which is the most potent psychedelic on the planet." Such is the matter-of-fact assertion of serum inventor Frank (Mark Duplass), who early in the film engages in a friendly debate with his coresearcher (and girlfriend) Zoe (Olivia Wilde). While they disagree about what transpires when pineal DMT floods the brain—Frank: "It's just a big trip" / Zoe: "It helps souls get to where they're supposed to be"—there appears to be no argument that something happens when you die, and DMT is there to lubricate the event. When the research team, who are based at a California university, find success with the DMT serum, first reviving a dog named Rocky, and then Zoe herself, who was killed in an electrical accident in the laboratory, we learn that things might have been better off if the dead weren't tampered with. With Zoe resurrected into a nightmarish hell-realm and endowed with dark paranormal abilities (which she exploits to slay the other members of the research team along with a student documentary filmmaker), pineal DMT offers a fresh means of replaying, in a rather lifeless and confusing story, the tragic consequences of attempts to conquer mortality (and "play God") that have been a staple of science-fiction horror since Frankenstein.

In a remotely different context, the meme has reached into children's animated television, with adult themes. Here's dialogue between the adventurous Finn and Princess Bubblegum from the American series *Adventure Time*, created by Pendleton Ward.

PRINCESS BUBBLEGUM: *"My guests are terrified!!"*

FINN: *"Yes!! And their brains are releasing adrenaline! Dopamine! Even dimethyltryptamine from the pineal gland! This has serious educational value!! Thanatophobia and this NDE is giving us euphoric altered awareness!! Don't you see, princess?!? We were all born to die!!"*[34]

Strassman's ideas have also been adopted by representatives of a variety of religious practices. To begin with, they have fueled interest in the neurochemical basis of Left Hand Path magical workings. Promoted as "a collection of occult prose-poems which attempts to convey the ecstatic states that allow one access to hyper-dimensions of consciousness and encounters with transmundane entities," Blair MacKenzie Blake's grimoire *IJYNX* is exemplary. In the foreword, Blake, who also maintains the official website of rock band *Tool*, conveys that Aleister Crowley's abstruse short story "Atlantis: The Lost Continent (Liber LI)" is not simply a veiled treatise on OTO (Ordo Templi Orientis) sex magick, a view widely received, but conceals a "higher Arcanum involving a highly-specialized form of esoteric cannibalism practiced by a necrophagous cult older than the earliest dynasties of ancient Egypt (Khem)." Blake informs readers that "the valuable orichalcum dug out of the 'earth' by the Atlanteans was in reality a mysterious post-mortem endogenous substance" with a variety of names: "Occultum of Harlequin," "The Residuum of Paradise," "The Glitter of the Sleepers," "The Dream of the Dreamless," and among latter-day alchemists "The Philosopher's Stone."[35]

Blake clarified the situation in an article for the journal of esoteric science *Dark Lore*. The endogenous substance in question is, naturally, DMT. While it is known to be released in significant quantities at the time of death, with appropriate ritual, skilled practitioners can, meanwhile, access the motherlode and harness it to magical ends.[36] Psychonautical descriptions of DMT realms share much in common with Crowley's encounters with transdimensional phenomena, including strange, nonhuman lifeforms like Lam and the "mighty concourse of angels" and their appearance within "the rapidly-changing kaleidoscopic ballet of intensely colorful geometric patterns." Such were among the finer points Blake observed in the "new paradigm" magazine *Sub Rosa*, where it was further explained that Crowley was himself consciously unaware of the higher Arcanum alluded to in "Liber LI." While Crowley was not in possession of "real knowledge of the precise neurochemical basis of a successful magical operation," it seems that, at least according to Blake, ritual activation of neurochemical pathways enabled his contact with "trans-mundane entities," like the angelic constructs invoked through the language of Enochian Magick.[37] It is Strassman's propositions that enable the inside scoop on Magick, with the DMT-releasing pineal venerated as the mother of occult organs, the "higher Arcanum."

If we can agree that there are striking similarities in the descriptions of those who are launched into what could amount to a parallel universe via exogenous DMT (such as ayahuasca) with the diary entries of Crowley and other serious occultists, then is it not reasonable to conclude, or, at least to suggest . . . that the seemingly magical phenomena experienced and recorded was actually the direct result of a release of varying levels of endogenous DMT (which Strassman hypothesizes is synthesized by the pineal gland and perhaps enhanced by beta-carbolines) that occurred once the protective barrier which normally prevents high levels of pineal DMT activation in humans is "shattered" by a certain resonance or vibration triggered by meditative disciplines and/or visualization techniques? In occult terminology, this could be seen as the opening of the "third" eye.[38]

While Strassman's speculations have provided key-like insights unlocking the mystery of magical workings, they have also shed light on a mystery encoded in the Talmud, Midrash, and Zohar. Downloading what he takes to be the full implications of the pineal-DMT model, Rabbi Joel David Bakst seems to have found himself in possession of the Kabbalah's equivalent of the "higher Arcanum." In *The Jerusalem Stone of Consciousness: DMT, Kabbalah and the Pineal Gland,* Bakst contends that the new science on the pineal illuminates the significance of the Foundation Stone, the holiest site in Judaism. For Bakst, pilgrimage to the Jerusalem of the Mind (or "JeM"), the "holiest site in the *inner* world of every man, woman, and child," begins, unexpectedly, "within the smallest and most mysterious organ in the human body—the pineal gland sequestered away in the middle of the cranium." This pilgrimage ends with "a small but the most controversial piece of property on the planet," the Foundation Stone, also known as the "Peniel" or "Face of God," located in the middle of a large "cranium-like" site called the Dome of the Rock in the middle of Jerusalem. While a perplexing array of information now exists on the mystery of DMT, now, for the first time, Bakst claims, a coherent explanation exists for "the higher-dimensional roots of DMT." Having scoured the Torah for forty years, Bakst reassembled Talmudic and Kabbalistic formulas with the assistance of the "template" provided by Strassman to unearth the "JeM," which he offers as an "updated application of an ancient, unbroken transmission." This uncovered spiritual technology is found in the "operating system" referred to as the "P2P principle," or

"Pineal (gland) to Peniel (the Foundation Stone)." The P2P is Bakst's way of stating how the foundations of Judaism are confirmed by the revealed implications of Strassman's ideas, that cosmic process is mirrored in neurochemistry, "as above so below." Will you get with the program and join the P2P network?[39]

Rabbi Bakst, who runs a small yeshiva in Colorado Springs called City of Luz, teaches his P2P meditation methods to awaken the pineal gland, and, at the same time, traditional Kabbalistic teachings. His meditational methods and spiritual exercises are designed to permit access to transcendent states of being. But while the P2P state "can produce bliss, inner visions, encounters with benevolent entities, and endless cascading levels of God-consciousness," these nonordinary states do not only benefit one's own enlightenment, but have a messianic role. "The sacred work of P2P is also a momentous responsibility," he states. "This work is true *tikun olam*—rectification of one's personal world within, and rectification of our global world without."[40] The goal appears to be that of awakening "the cosmic pineal gland of the world," a prerequisite, he claims, for world peace.[41] So while *The Jerusalem Stone of Consciousness* is offered as an instruction manual enabling one to "stimulate endogenous DMT within one's own brain and body," it is far from a manual for the use of psychedelics. JeM is designed to "stimulate the *spiritual root* of the molecular and material-based DMT," which is the "divine substance" he calls "M-DMT," or "*Messianic* DMT." M-DMT is elucidated as

> the renewed "Living Liquid" (*Mayim Chayim*) foretold by the Hebrew prophets from ancient times. If there was a Jewish equivalent of a Holy Grail, a Fountain of Life, an Elixir of Eternal Youth, or the Divine Light at the end of the cosmic tunnel, Jerusalem of the Mind would be it. . . . Within the soul of the mysterious little pineal organ there lies the hidden portal to *Derech Aitz Chayim*—the path leading back to the original higher dimensional Tree of Life at the very center of the Garden of Eden.[42]

In triggering endogenous DMT release, and opening up the portal between this world and the other, as the Rabbi has it, the seeker embarks on a long journey of spiritual discovery. And the end goal? "You can't hate, you don't want to do war anymore.... The veil is lifted between this reality and the hidden dimension. All the spiritual truths are revealed to you at once."[43]

While Blair MacKenzie Blake and Joel David Bakst explore the implications of pineal-DMT release, and explain how spiritual practice—from the magical to the messianic—is mediated in neurochemical pathways, both avoid advocating the introduction of DMT into the body. In fact, Bakst is careful to disclaim that "no external drugs are necessary" in the purifying pilgrimage to the Jerusalem of the Mind. By contrast, pastor and coke dealer Gabriel D. Roberts smoked a bowl and was floored by a genuine religious experience. Raised in Salt Lake City to dedicate his life to preach the Gospel, by the time Roberts graduated with a degree in theology he had crossed a hollow threshold. Something was terribly amiss with the fundamentalist Christian path, the promise of holiness not delivered. Full realization of this deception came to Roberts when first smoking DMT. For the first time in his life, he made direct contact with the Divine, or as he put it, "a telephone line to transdimensional beings, to the mind of God, to the limitless sea of knowledge, all in 15 minutes." Roberts's first DMT experience was "by far the most powerful thing I've experienced in my life." Stammering out the following words on the ineffable, he would be informed telepathically: "... don't worry about your body. Your body isn't you. You're gonna be old one day. This thing that you are wearing is not you." The revelation "crushed 27 years of devotion," since for the first time Roberts achieved genuine gnosis. He beheld an intrinsic understanding of the nature of reality, which—as is internal to the logic of gnosis—he arrived at himself, unmediated. Almost paraphrasing McKenna, as he stated in a 2014 podcast interview, "religions are built on someone else's trip report ... and if you don't have the trip yourself, then you are buying someone else's experience."[44] Roberts's experience appears to have exemplified the full implications of entheogenesis, here described by Jonathan Ott:

> Since these drugs tend to open people's eyes and hearts to an experience of the holiness of the universe ... yes, enable people to have personal religious experiences without the intercession of a priesthood or the preconditioning of a liturgy, some psychonauts or *epoptai* will perceive the emptiness and shallowness of the Judeo-Christian religious tradition;

even begin to see through the secular governments which use religious symbols to manipulate people; begin to see that by so ruthlessly subduing the Earth we are killing the planet and destroying ourselves.[45]

But it was Strassman who delivered the Word oiling the machinery of Roberts's new mission. An interview with Strassman from Roberts's book *The Quest for Gnosis* was reproduced in *VICE* magazine as "Blasting Off with Dr. DMT."[46] Referencing *DMT: The Spirit Molecule*, "it's actually in our brains right now. . . . It's in your pineal gland. It's possible for you to have an endogenous . . . internal burst of DMT and this will produce a vision that is among the most powerful things you can experience in your life." And, as he continued, "I believe there is conclusive evidence that an endogenous burst of DMT occurs when you are born, and it occurs when you die. We know that because the pineal gland, after your body is cold, your pineal gland is working six to eight hours after your body is dead. It's still transmitting, so to speak."[47]

Unflagging believers smell the danger. That Strassman's ideas should take hold is disquieting for the Church, whose vigilant representatives are forewarned by scripture of the interventions of Dr. DMT and his ilk. This is the impression of Dr. Future, a biblical warrior who, in even-voiced hysteria, concerns himself with a near-future spiritual rumble consistent with the end-times prophesied in Revelation. DMT appears to perform a leading role in this apocalyptic eschatology for the Future Quake radio show host. In a disinformative diatribe where tryptamines, GMO foods, and school shootings are interwoven threats, and in a rant where "entheogen" is identified as the practice of allowing Satan in, DMT becomes a chemical malfeasance that must be *inhibited*. In a lecture, "Sorcery and Drugs in Opening the Last Days Spirit Portal," delivered at the 2010 Last Days Conference in Nashville, Dr. Future distorted Strassman's ideas, even misnaming his book "DMT: The Spirit Drug," to postulate the *real* function of the pineal gland: a portal through which malice and evil break into our world. The implication is that the unguarded pineal is a swinging gate on hell. As "Article A" in support of this accusation, take the stand Adolf Hitler, whom Dr. Future invokes care of Hermann Rauschning's biography *The Voice of Destruction: Conversations with Hitler 1940*, in which Hitler is reported to state: "Some men can already activate their pineal glands to give a limited vision into the secrets of time." Apparently Hitler also informed Rauschning that a "New Man" would be "created using the visions and scientific knowledge already being transmitted through these men's pineal glands."[48]

But Hitler is only the most overt manifestation of an omnipresent danger. Crowley, Kenneth Anger, and Hollywood film and computer game industries are among the legions of the fallen, forerunners to a premeditated "mass evocation event," a "black awakening" in which the pineal gland may be the final battleground—unless this sorcery is first suppressed. For Dr. Future, the pineal is less spirit gland than a sorcerous organ, and the brain a neurochemical battlefield interpreted anew from scripture. Deciphering biblical allusions to "inhibit" contact with the spirit world and "protect" humankind from evil, Dr. Future finds it curious that the "flaming sword" in Genesis holds neurological symmetry with the protective actions of body enzymes (e.g., MAOs) that naturally hose down the flames of DMT licking at your soul, and protecting one from "using the pineal gland to contact the spirit world"—unless, as he says, these enzymes are themselves neutralized by other compounds (e.g., MAO inhibitors). Dr. Future refers to sorcerous "roots," which would presumably include *B. caapi* and other DMT activators growing wild on "the Tree of Life" in the Garden of Eden, temptations for humankind, who must be protected from our own nature. While I may be translating Dr. Future's ideas with greater coherence than originally articulated, this is the gist of his gab—at some remove, I might add, from Rabbi Bakst, who, embracing the speculative insights of "Dr. DMT," has it that Jews and Gentiles alike can make the pilgrimage back to the Garden, with a little help from an activated "Messianic DMT."

Moral guardians of the Christian right who make their living protecting humanity in free-fall from Eden, aren't the only ones who've applied their active imaginations to the possibilities inhering in an unchecked pineal. In the fiction of H. P. Lovecraft, the pineal was an antenna that not only detects signals from the cosmic horror show beyond, but, as evident in the 1920 short story "From Beyond," effectively ushers malevolence into our world.[49] In this and later stories like "The Shunned House" (1924), "The Colour Out of Space" (1927), and "The Dreams in the Witch House" (1933), Lovecraft developed his non-Euclidean supernatural horror. Not the "seat of the soul," the "third eye," the gateway to higher consciousness, or the source of "M-DMT," a stimulated pineal gland is a portal to the dimension favored by the Great Old Ones of the nihilistic Cthulhu Mythos, including The Dread Ones Cthulhu and Azathoth—who make Satan, rule bound by Christian demonology, comparatively homely.

The narrator in "From Beyond" recounts a gripping tale of his friend, the estranged scientist Crawford Tillinghast, who has discovered in the dark confines of his attic in a house set back from Benevolent Street the true function of that "great sense organ of organs." It's a revelation that had apparently rendered Tillinghast a "shivering gargoyle." The story has at its center an essentially malevolent pineal gland, the atrophied status of which is reversed by an electrical machine "glowing with a sickly, sinister violet luminosity" that generates "waves" stimulating the dormant gland, making transparent to the senses properties of a dimension overlapping with our own. "Those waves will open up to us many vistas unknown to man and several unknown to anything we consider organic life," announces an excited Tillinghast. "We shall see that at which dogs howl in the dark, and that at which cats prick up their ears after midnight. We shall see these things, and other things which no breathing creature has yet seen. We shall overleap time, space, and dimensions, and without bodily motion peer to the bottom of creation."

Making "the beyond" available to the senses, the unspeakable horror of Tillinghast's machine is that, according to Lovecraft, *It* exists in the here and now, all the time, albeit outside normal awareness. Not only are humans newly sensitive to an alternate dimension in which entities dwell, but these entities see humans, who are now susceptible to their interventions. After causing the disappearance of Tillinghast's servants before he himself succumbs to their sinister manipulations, in the presence of the machine's ultraviolet glow, the narrator recounts a psychedelic horror show.

The scene was almost wholly kaleidoscopic, and in the jumble of sights, sounds, and unidentified sense-impressions I felt that I was about to dissolve or in some way lose the solid form.... From some point in space there seemed to be pouring a seething column of unrecognizable shapes or clouds, penetrating the solid roof at a point ahead and to the right of me. . . . Indescribable shapes both alive and otherwise were mixed in disgusting disarray. . . . inky, jellyfish monstrosities which flabbily quivered in harmony with the vibrations from the machine. They were present in loathsome profusion, and I saw to my horror that they over-lapped; that they were semi-fluid and capable of passing through one another and through what we know as solids. . . . I felt the huge animate things brushing past me and occasionally walking or drifting through my supposedly solid body.

In *From Beyond*, the 1986 film adaptation directed by Stuart Gordon, Tillinghast is the assistant to S&M kinkster Dr. Pretorius—although the lead role is performed by an electromagnetic machine with a large tuning fork. Lovecraft's swinging door is now a truly animated sci-fi novum. Awaken-ing the "sixth sense" (i.e., the pineal, which literally expands), the machine causes the abduction and disfigurement of Drs. Tillinghast and Pretorius, and then enables their return with an apparent appetite for brains. But if this story isn't complex enough, there's an added twist. The resonator's vibrations not only increase the visions of and interaction with a parallel dimension (including wriggling, worm-like creatures), they stimulate erotic sensations within anyone possessing a pineal gland inside the widening energy field. This circumstance apparently transforms Pretorius into a sadist, and what's more—having had his head ignominiously chewed off by an interdimensional monster—into a gelatinous blob with pincers and talons. An aroused pineal, unbridled lust, increased temptation. Crusaders defending morality at the gates of the pineal would have a field day. And the swelling of the pineal attains a phallic turn, as glands emerge from foreheads like engorged third-eye snakes, all the better to locate the human brains they crave. In league with the Lovecraftian reversal of the pineal's role as a trigger for spiritual evolution, albeit adopting an erotic subtext foreign to Lovecraft, when the gland is aroused it activates not higher con-sciousness but an inhuman specter, sadistic and all consuming.[50]

The activated pineal as a source of chaos and confusion is a theme developed in *Banshee Chapter,* the film, introduced in Chapter Two, that pays heavy dues to "From Beyond" (and its film adaptation). As a con-temporary vehicle for the enigmatic gland and the mysteries it leaks, *Banshee Chapter* fictionalizes the abominable outcomes of exploiting the pineal gland. In faintly plausible experiments that yield a sinister strain of DMT, extract of pineal does more than cause tits to grow on your back. While *Banshee Chapter* exposed the CIA's MKUltra program, which *did* fund unethical human experiments involving DMT along with other psychoactive compounds, the filmmakers sired a monster of their own—the malevolent endogenous compound DMT-19. Like an evil sister to the heavily restricted "spirit molecule," and possessing no virtue next to Bakst's M-DMT, this fiction may, oddly enough, serve the interests of guardians of morality, upholders of prohibition, and defenders of the boundary that separates the material and spirit worlds.

Intention Is All

"There's nothing you can read that will prepare you for what it feels like to go from zero to 100 Mph in 1.3 seconds," warned Jim DeKorne, who was "catapulted from 'normal' consensus reality one moment into a totally bizarre, profoundly alien space the next!" Among Strassman's sixty volunteers, founder of *The Entheogen Review* DeKorne reported "alien contact" following administration of the maximum approved dose (i.e., 0.4 mg per kg = 26.56 mg DMT IV) on January 14, 1993. DeKorne's beings had awaited him inside a "space station" with other android-like creatures performing "some kind of routine technological work" who "paid no attention to me." He noted that "the imagery was pouring in too rapidly to process and integrate," an experience not unfamiliar to the DMT user. But then, ambushed upon reentry from hyperdrive, DeKorne met with terror: "In a state of overwhelmed shock and confusion, I opened my eyes to see the doctor's nurse-assistant horribly transformed into a grotesque 'clown,' with huge, protuberant red lips maybe 20-times enlarged from normal."[51] The transformation of the nurse—typically a benevolent figure—evokes the horrifying scene in Room 237 of *The Shining*'s Overlook Hotel, where a disrobed young beauty transforms into a suppurating hag in the arms of Jack Torrance.

But DeKorne had not been cast in a Kubrick film. He was a volunteer lying in a hospital bed in Room 531 at the UNM Clinical Research Center, where, seated bedside, Dr. Strassman was monitoring his condition and taking notes. DeKorne's example offers clear evidence of the problems facing Strassman when administering DMT in a clinical setting. And it offers graphic illustration of the concerns raised by Nick Sand, who having read "Contact through the Veil: 1," a pre-release chapter excerpted from *DMT: The Spirit Molecule* and published in *The Entheogen Review* in 2000, was prompted to break his silence.[52] A fugitive for twenty years and imprisoned between 1996 and 2000 after a raid on his lab near Port Coquitlam, British Columbia, in 1996 (where he had overseen one of the largest psychedelic labs in North American history, producing LSD, DMT, and MDMA), Sand was at this time a spiritual prisoner newly released. *TER* became a vehicle for Sand's weathered perspective on DMT as a powerful sacrament necessitating a highly optimal set and setting. Imagined quite unfairly as an example of "the ambience of government terrorism against psychedelics,"[53] Strassman's project was deemed to violate these requirements. Harboring deep distrust for DEA-"authorized" DMT research, Sand's first article for *TER* launched into a scathing rebuke of Strassman and his project. Claiming to have used DMT more than one thousand times, "I have been making, using, and initiating people into DMT use, for around 40 years," Sand announced under the pen name ∞Ayes. By comparison, Strassman's approach was plagued by a "fundamental misunderstanding" of DMT, a failing that was amplified in the experiences of many volunteers.

> Over and over, Strassman's subjects describe being examined by numerous strange beings in highly technical environments during the visual phase of their DMT experience. They are being examined, discussed, measured, probed, and observed. They are in high-tech nurseries and alien laboratories. There are 3–4 people moving around operating machinery according to some design or agenda.... There are a number of people in attendance, helping the one who is in charge, Dr. Strassman.[54]

Indeed, there are a few accounts fitting this description. Take for instance Aaron, who, after his first high dose, reported "an insectlike thing got right into my face, hovering over me as the drug was going in." He was then taken to "a very large waiting room, or something. It was very long. I felt observed by the insect-thing and others like it." Aaron referred to the "sinister backdrop, an alien-type, insectoid, not-quite-pleasant side" of the event. "It's like they have an agenda. It's like walking into a different neighborhood. You're really not quite sure what the culture is. It's got such a distinct flavor, the reptilian being or beings that are present."[55]

In an article in the subsequent edition of *TER*, Sand elaborated on the importance of setting and context. "Whatever you give DMT, it weaves this into patterns," he cautioned. "If you are a doctor sitting in a hospital room filled with people watching a 'subject' and injecting said subject with DMT while people are acting out their roles of nurse, doctor, researcher, government representative, etc., and your subjects have little alien robots, insects, reptiles or what have you, crawling all over them, probing and examining, is this really so strange? You are just seeing a DMT woven projection of the very environment you have created."[56]

Administering DMT within regulated biomedical parameters amounted to a total perversion of the "true potential" of DMT, identified as a "very profound multileveled experience." If DMT "is about the beyond, . . . beyond the intellect, beyond the senses, beyond any devices and biological instruments for dealing with the external world," efforts to measure, rate, and quantify the experience are flawed from the outset. Influenced by Leary's school of psychedelic spirituality, Sand ultimately questioned the "authority" of the researcher while at the same time elevating the "authority" of the questing individual and his or her relationship with one's higher self (or God) mediated by DMT. "Holistic, deep spiritual research cannot be authorized by its very nature. Authority does not command God." It was Sand's view that it is "only in a free and supportive environment of grace and love, aesthetic and compassionate caring, can this sacrament be used to attain the highest."[57] Not privy to Strassman's complete work—his book would not be published until the following year—and thereby holding a misunderstanding of its design parameters, Sand imagined the worst in Room 531: "human beings being used as experimental lab animals."[58] It's not impossible that Sand had conjured the scene from Ken Russell's *Altered States*, the film inspired by John C. Lilly's sensory deprivation research conducted in isolation tanks under the influence of psychoactive substances. Released in 1980, and possibly the first movie to refer to the compound, among the film's early scenes is an experimental research facility in New York Hospital, 1967. Seated upright in a wheelchair is a schizophrenic patient who is administered "dimethyltryptamine" in an observation room populated by five white-coated scientists with a one-way glass mirror wall enabling the covert observation and recording of behavior. It's a scenario that would doubtlessly disturb both Sand and Strassman.

Fitted out with the trappings of absent imperatives and official agendas, occupied by human lab animals manipulated to ends remote from their own welfare, for Sand, Room 531 was chock-full of wrongful intent. It was Sand's contention that DMT ought not be administered to the benefit of an inquiry other than the pursuit of inner truth and self-discovery. As an adjunct to other psychedelics, tantra, meditation, and/or yoga, it ought to potentiate the empowerment of the seeker of self-truth, and not be a means to enhance the status and power of knowledge claimants. While ill-informed about the project, Sand was nevertheless expressing views that may be among the reasons why no further clinical research with DMT has been carried out in the twenty years since Strassman's study. By constrast, Sand outlined what was imagined as an ideal setting.

> Suppose now, that instead of a hospital room with beepers and weird electromagnetic currents in the subliminal environment and medical personnel with odd motivations and curiosities, you were in a beautiful wooden house in the woods with a stream outside making gurgling and tinkling sounds. Inside there are friends in casual clothing—soft, tastefully-colored robes. Men and women dressed for a celebration, seated on velvet cushions on oriental carpets with candles and flowers, and beautiful music. Flowers in vases, mandalas, and wondrous paint-ings on the walls, aesthetically lit by natural and traditional lights, not fluorescents. A fire glowing in the hearth, multicolored fish swimming in an aquarium. Before you is a teacher who has decades of personal DMT experiences who is serving as your travel facilitator. You've prepared for days with yoga, meditation, and pure food. . . . Instead of reptiles, aliens, and robot doctors, you have Gods, magicians, celestial and magical beings—intimating, winking, indicating, and even speaking to your inner being with lessons of love, healing, inspiration, and creation. . . . Your heart and mind fuse in loving understanding that heals the rifts in your heart. Tears of gratitude stream down your face, joy lights in your being.[59]

The description evokes the ceremonial communities that have evolved in the ayahuasca diaspora. Sand offered an optimal experience of his own according to the fundamentals of set and setting, which is worth quoting at length.

One of my many memorable DMT trips (at about 0.9 mg per kg of body weight, intramuscular of the HCl) was sitting on a Persian carpet listening to a recording of Sharan Rani playing a love raga on a sarod. I had my two trip buddies with me. There were candles and incense. The room was set up as a temple space for tripping. As I arrived at my internal trip space, I was filled with overwhelming feelings of womanly love and sensuality. I looked down and was very surprised to see myself dressed in filmy harem pants and no shirt on. I had a beautiful copper-colored female body—breasts and all. I had many bangles on my arms, and ankle bells on my legs. I looked around and found that I was dancing a seductive love raga to the two musicians facing me playing sarod and tabla. We were performing in the courtyard of a beautiful Indian temple similar to Bubhaneshwar Temple, famed for its erotic sculpture and soaring towers. My dancing was an exact counterpart in rhythmic motion to the melodies and rhythms of the music. It was an exquisite act of love. It was so beautiful that when I came down, I declared that if I died right at that moment, I would regret nothing as I had experienced beauty more exquisite than I could ever imagine. Perfect love and unity. As I came down, I saw my beautiful breasts shimmer away and the bangles slide off my arms twinkling into nothing. There was a momentary ache in my heart as all of this love withdrew. As the room reappeared around me, I experienced a confusion; I could not remember if I was a sacred temple dancer dreaming I was a man, or if I was a man dreaming I was a female dancer. This was obviously a very touching and profound trip that infused my being with a new appreciation of love and harmony, something I carry as a memory and a perspective on life to this day. Obviously, I am not a woman, but I was so profoundly influenced by a woman playing a love raga that I created myself in accordance to what was entering into me from my environment.[60]

Since DMT is venerated as a "magnifying, creative, and sensitizing medium," set and setting are regarded as extremely influential. But to be fair to Strassman, environmental design was among his chief concerns. He was familiar with at least some of the problems incensing Sand. Suspicions about the inadequacies of the biomedical model and the clinical research environment contributed to the decision to discontinue the research. As *DMT: The Spirit Molecule* details, Strassman minimized the limitations of the clinical setting as best he could in the circumstances. The bodies granting approvals had not done so for a generation, and there was no chance that the research could have been undertaken in "a beautiful wooden house in the woods." Strassman's group were volunteers, many apparently with an advanced comprehension of what they'd signed up to participate in. They were carefully screened, with many experienced in psychedelics, including DMT. And Strassman was acutely aware that God is immeasurable. He recorded in detail a diversity of subjective experiences, including personal, and transpersonal, eventually holding an open mind with regard to explanatory models. It also seems disingenuous to launch an attack without reading the book, and consequentially without full comprehension of the thrust and implications of the research. As both book and subsequent film documentary *DMT: The Spirit Molecule* directed by Mitch Schultz demonstrate, a great many of the volunteers receiving high-dose injections had significant and positive outcomes, demonstrating that the clinical context and official agenda may have had little impact on their events. A story related by Sand himself reveals that transformative experiences are possible within total institutions. It was in the penitentiary on McNeil Island, Washington, where his eight-man cell was occupied by mostly psychedelic prisoners.

> Every Saturday night we would sit together in a circle around a little makeshift shrine, and take LSD, as well as smoke DMT. One of our cell mates, whom we could not dislodge from the cell, was an exception. He was a Mafia hitman. Sick as he was, he eventually gave it a try. The night he smoked DMT he came out of it with a look of astonishment and awe, and he said, "That's the first time I've gone to church in 30 years." Even this stone-cold killer could recognize the sacred.[61]

While the Clinical Research Center, Albuquerque, was a long way from McNeil Island, the sacred repeatedly broke through the clinical veneer of Room 531. Take, for instance, Marsha, an African American woman in her mid-forties who on her initial high dose found herself in "a beautiful domed structure, a virtual Taj Mahal." "I don't know what happened. All of a sudden, BAM!, there I was. It was the most beautiful thing I've ever seen." Many accounts shared a similar qualitative fulfillment. For Gabe, a thirty-three-year-old physician, "there was an initial sense of panic. Then the most beautiful colors coalesced into beings. There were lots of beings. They were talking to me but they weren't making a sound. It was more as if they were blessing me, the spirits of life were blessing me. They were saying that life was good."[62] Other accounts will be offered later in this book, but it is also important to note that Strassman breaks the mold of the detached observer, occasionally breaking into the patois of an adept. "There is a searing sense of the sacred and the holy. It is a personal encounter with the 'Big Bang,' God, Cosmic Consciousness, the source of all being. Whatever we call it, we know we have met the fundamental bedrock and fountainhead of existence, one that emanates love, wisdom, and power on an unimaginable scale."[63] With such language, it is easy to understand how Strassman gained the trust and confidence of his volunteers, and indeed how the folk theory implicit to *DMT: The Spirit Molecule* would achieve such amplitude.

As Sand came in from the cold, applying the heat on the only research project involving DMT and human subjects in the United States since prohibition, he was setting fire to a straw man. While Strassman was rebuked for exploiting DMT in the interests of building status and power, given the prohibited stature of DMT, and his underlying agendas for conducting the research, such reprobation seems undeserving. Strassman doubtlessly surrendered a successful career in paradigmatic acquiescence and status building standard to academic science when he sought (and was granted) approvals for his project. Furthermore, toward the conclusion of his project he suffered the condemnation of his religious community, a circumstance that, in addition to other mounting pressures, forced his resignation and a premature termination of the project. In the chapter "Stepping on Holy Toes," Strassman conveys how he was rebuked in a letter from a monk-informer that his research "constitutes wrong livelihood according to the Buddha's teachings" and that "hallucinogens disorder and confuse the mind, impede religious training, and can be a cause of rebirth into realms of confusion and suffering."[64] Around this time, an article he published in *Tricycle: The Buddhist Review* sealed his fate, with his religious order demanding the cessation of his research. The article related how impressed Strassman had been when joining his community by "the 'psychedelic' descriptions of intensive meditation practice within Buddhist traditions." And since the scriptures made no mention of drugs, even while the meditative states sounded similar to those resulting from psychedelic drug use, he "suspected there might be a naturally occurring psychedelic molecule in the brain that was triggered by deep meditation."[65] While it had been far from Strassman's agenda to advocate drug use as a spiritual practice or to raise DMT to the status of a sacrament—a position closer to Sand's—taking umbrage with the uncomfortable implications of a compound outlawed as a "dangerous drug" being associated with the path to enlightenment, his community associates and supporters closed ranks. He was forced to leave the community in 1996.

"Now Do You See?"

In concluding *DMT: The Spirit Molecule,* Rick Strassman conveyed that the research he had performed was "opening a door that had remained tightly locked for a generation." But lifting the lid on Pandora's box "let out its own agenda and language." It unleashed a power that had startlingly diverse and unpredictable effects. And while it appeared to "call out in a voice that was tender, challenging, engaging, and frightening," he says "the question never changed." He then explained that this question had been put to volunteer Saul, whose contact report was kept until the final pages of the book. "Out of the raging colossal waterfall of flaming color expanding into my visual field, the roaring silence, and an unspeakable joy, they stepped, or rather, emerged. Welcoming, curious, they almost sang, 'Now do you see?' I felt their question pour into and fill every possible corner of my awareness: 'Now do you see? Now do you see?'"[66]

The visitation upon Saul seemed like a powerful confirmation of Strassman's project hypothesis: i.e., that "outside-administered DMT elicits altered states of consciousness similar to those that people report during spontaneous psychedelic experiences: near-death and mystical states and the phenomenon we call alien abduction," an overlap supporting a role for endogenous DMT in the production of these spontaneous psychedelic experiences.[67] I will explore the role performed by entities, and the clamor of theories they have been recruited to support, in Chapter Twelve. For now, the words *"Now do you see?"* appear to form more the shape of an acclamation than an inquiry, gnosis that the kingdom lies within, that endogenous DMT mediates mystical experience, that the pineal is the spirit gland—that *you are the alien*. It is as if Saul's beings were pointing to him, toward the human subject, as a reminder to him, and to us, that *they* are *right here*, and have been all along. In a multitude of apparitions each as veridical as the last, interactions with "others," and indeed the "Other," have inspired, enchanted, and haunted contactees, returnees, and the envisioned throughout history. While another kind of gnosis elicited by a different form of Other, the response from the tormented Dr. Tillinghast in Lovecraft's "From Beyond" offers a variation on the same theme, i.e., an awareness that *this* is not all there is: "You see them? You see them? You see the things that float and flop about you and through you every moment of your life?"

Spirit's gland, sorcerer's portal, or something decidedly more mundane, the pineal gland is a most curiously contested organ. At the center of the brain, the pineal also lies at the center of contested imaginative, epistemological, and theological campaigns that will not abate anytime soon. The threshold separating the material from the spirit world, the biological interface secreting the soul from the body and even enabling the living to contact the dead, and complete with a venerated substance that fuels the entire mechanism, the pineal gland has been evaluated, circumscribed, and defended in accordance with a variety of intellectual, spiritual, and theological perspectives, each claiming definitive rights over its terrain. There is clearly much at stake, although exactly what is *seen* in the light of Strassman's revelatory speculations flooding out of Room 531 is open to dispute.

DMT: The Spirit Molecule has been welcome news for those building a neurological platform on the human propensity for religious experience as evident among shamans, mystics, prophets, and spiritualists the world over and throughout history. It is a platform that could link visionary, hallucinatory, and dream states common to human being, and, furthermore, explain alien-contact and near-death experiences. Over at the *Ultraculture* blog, for instance, we're assured that "religion is a naturalistic phenomenon, and like all of nature, it may be interpreted scientifically."[68] Such pop-science formats graft the implications of Strassman's findings on the role of endogenous DMT release to the objective of uncovering the physiological mechanisms for spiritual experience, and bolster the neurotheological position that spirituality provides an evolutionary advantage to the human species. And yet this misconstrues Strassman's own views, since for him DMT is heralded as "the mechanism of action by which [our] spiritual nature is manifest." In other words, in a mechanism that bridges matter and spirit, divinity does not *seem* to be possible, but *is* possible. Interviewed by Graham Hancock in 2005, he stated, "God wants us to be godly. So, by being close to God, we can learn to emulate God. Perhaps DMT is one of the ways in which we are able to communicate with God that much more intensely—for better or worse." It is the near-death experience that offers glimpses of this process. "It is on DMT's wings, so to speak, that consciousness takes flight from the body on its way towards death. . . . The NDE is not a hallucination—it is what happens as we die. It's what our consciousness experiences. How else could there be such an astonishingly consistent reporting of such experiences throughout time and cultures?"[69] With a genealogy traceable to William James, Strassman has clarified the position in his recent book *DMT and the Soul of Prophecy*. The compelling comparisons between events resulting from the modern administration of DMT and those experiences native to humanity throughout history have triggered a research model counterposed to the prevailing model of neurotheology, which proposes that the brain *generates* spiritual experience. Instead, "theoneurology" asserts that "the brain is the agent through which God communicates with humans."[70]

We'll later learn what life after Buddhism was like for Rick Strassman, and where he finds evidence of "theoneurology." For now, what of the pineal gland, the ostensible bridge between spirit and matter? A recent report that DMT was found in the pineal gland microdialysate of rats demonstrates that we are now closer to confirming Strassman's proposition.[71] And yet, even if it were confirmed that the human pineal gland produces DMT in "halluci-nogenic" quantities—what then? It would be fanciful to conclude that such a confirmation would lead to universal acceptance of Strassman's metaphys-ical claims regarding the spiritual function of the pineal/DMT. It is more reasonable to assume that the usual suspects will rally to well-rehearsed, and in some cases, entrenched, positions on the nature of consciousness. But then, given the wide-reaching impact of and popular engagement with Strassman's ideas, it does appear we are today witness to the opening of an epistemological can of worms. While the outcomes are unpredictable, it does appear that we are in the preliminary phase of a significant debate. The aftermath of *DMT: The Spirit Molecule* saw the groundwork laid for the coming debate, with members of the reigning neurotheology team and the upstarts who represent what Strassman calls "entheoneurology" positioned at opposing ends of a court, with players volleying the pineal gland back and forth. The signs are that competing players in this game—and the para-digms they represent—are in training for the tournaments. Will entheoneu-rologists soon have a powerful new serve up their sleeve? Either way, it will be difficult to ignore the theological implications of this unique research, for while his own approach—i.e., his science and indeed his faith—would be altered subsequent to the UNM project, Strassman's legacy is to have made the inquiry on DMT an investigation into the human nature of spirituality.

CHAPTER 6

Entheogenic Culture and the Research Underground

Interviewed in 2014, Rick Strassman made a point of distinguishing sanctioned scientific from underground psychedelic research. Using double-blind experiments, hypotheses based on previous research with animals and humans, and rigorous statistical analyses, the virtues of legitimate research were extolled above the "self-experimentations" of the underground, where "the pursuit of pleasure as well as self-understanding through chemically enhanced introspection" thrives. Believing the latter does not amount to "research," Strassman had some advice for the underground, including members of the DMT-Nexus community, who formulated his interview questions and published his answers in *The Nexian:* "Go back to school, get the requisite training, and then start breaking new ground in a publishable manner."[1]

Sans an exhortation to "get a haircut," Strassman's critique of the absence of rigor and sound methodology in underground research appeared to be dismissive of the grassroots research culture whose experiments have, nevertheless, advanced understanding of DMT and other tryptamines over the decades since prohibition. Since he is among very few individuals to have been licensed to conduct clinical trials with DMT on human subjects in half a century, you could be excused for being deflated by his counsel. Indeed, disappointment could be felt down at the DMT-Nexus, the virtual research hub of entheogenic culture, a community whose e-zine *The Nexian* is a standard-bearer for underground research. *The Nexian* coeditor David Nickles countered, "claims of hedonism masquerading as research do not hold up when the body of underground research is examined." In an article in *The Nexian* published hard on the heels of Strassman's interview, Nickles made a strong case for the necessity and merits of underground research, assessing how sanctioned research opportunities are only available to the socioeconomically privileged, that institutions operating within the confines of a prohibitionist paradigm have seriously limiting agendas, that scientific knowledge produced within the academy tends to become privatized and unavailable to the community, and that research conducted within academia is no guarantee of meritorious outcomes. Nickles additionally expressed concern about the dominant trend of limiting research in accordance with disease-prevention/treatment models at the expense of acknowledging the potentials for psychedelics to enrich the whole person, and cause "prolonged feelings of well-being and openness to direct participation in the divine mystery of being." Strassman would doubtlessly share the position that, as stated by Nickles, "psychedelics also challenge many of the ontological models and assumptions we hold about the very nature of reality and existence."[2]

This wasn't ill-informed upbraiding in the style of Nick Sand. Calling for a "discreet partnership" between sanctioned and underground research, and citing advances made by numerous online research communities, including Bluelight, The Corroboree, The Shroomery, Mycotopia, ICMag, and the now-defunct The Hive, Nickles highlighted the exemplary output of the collaborative research community at the DMT-Nexus in the fields of extraction methodologies, phytochemical and ethnobotanical research, sustainable plant propagation methodologies, harm reduction, and measuring/classifying subjective experiences.[3] The DMT-Nexus, along with other online research communities, builds and distributes knowledge otherwise unavailable in a climate where DMT and other compounds are classified as dangerous with no merits to humanity, and with no sanctioned means to prove otherwise. As haphazard and piecemeal as the results often are, under the oppressive weight of iron-blanket criminalization, the entheogenic underground is a popular movement furthering knowledge and awareness at the nexus of science and religion.

It is worth recognizing that, with regard to DMT, the "underground research community" is *almost everyone*, since projects are not typically conducted under the auspices of government-funded directives, but are initiatives of marginal, and marginalized, researchers. It would be more accurate to acknowledge that this community is a folk movement where for decades participants have not only made remarkable botanical discoveries and advances in the fields of cultivation, extraction, and synthesis, but have advanced understanding of the phenomenological characteristics of use. This makes Strassman's research career all the more intriguing, since he has himself turned to the theological and metaphysical study of the DMT experience, first care of Buddhism and then as a returnee to Judaism. But since Strassman does not himself possess credentials as a theologian or as a religious studies professional, it could be proposed that his claims concerning the phenomenology, spirituality, and divinity of DMT are those of an amateur researcher occupying a marginal or "underground" position.

Whether Rick Strassman populates it or not, the *underground* has been a dynamic field of activity since prohibition, where the results of self-experimentation are extraordinary and self-evident. In support of Nickles's claims concerning the merits of underground research, among the most significant conceptual advances is the idea of the "entheogen"—a substance said to *awaken the divine within*. Emerging from research conducted largely outside or at the periphery of academia, this concept—which many advocates today use in the place of, or interchangeably with, "psychedelic"—is the result of commitments by scholars to recognize the spiritual significance, ontological import, and metaphysical function of DMT, ayahuasca, psilocybin, *Salvia divinorum,* iboga, and other psychoactive compounds, blends, and decoctions. It's worth our while discussing entheogens before diving deeper into the DMT underground.

Entheogenesis

"Entheogen" is a concept introduced in the late 1970s and later popularized by natural-products chemist Jonathan Ott in his compendium *Pharmacotheon: Entheogenic Drugs, Their Plant Sources and History,* a treatise on entheogens amid a thoroughgoing excoriation of the absurdities, inequities, and incongruities of their prohibition in the United States. It was Ott's conviction that a *pharmacotheon* of botanicals played a kind of messianic role for a "hypermaterialistic humankind on the threshold of a new millennium." The experience of ecstasy conferred by these "wondrous medicaments" could inaugurate, he averred, "the start of a new Golden Age," thereby constituting "humankind's brightest hopes for overcoming the ecological crisis with which we threaten the biosphere and jeopardize our own survival." In his evaluation, "when people have direct, personal access to entheogenic, religious experiences, they never conceive of humankind as a separate creation, apart from the rest of the universe."[4] It was Ott's belief that amateur ethnomycologist (and professional banker) Robert Gordon Wasson's rediscovery of the shamanic cult of *teonanácatl* presaged the modern advent of the entheogen and the revival of ecstatic religion.[5]

The word "entheogen," and the adjective "entheogenic," arose from dissatisfaction with existing terms. Given its association with mental illness, "psychotomimetic" connoted psychosis and sickness, "psychedelic" evoked prejudice and suspicion through the behavior of "deviant" subcultures with which it had been associated since the 1960s, and "hallucinogen" intimated drugs that inaugurate deception, false notions, or outright delirium. Describing psychoactive plants and their effects used within indigenous and other traditional contexts with any of these labels was recognizably fraught with ethnocentrism. The proposed alternative was deemed appropriate for "describing states of shamanic and ecstatic possession induced by ingestion of mind-altering drugs." *Entheos*—literally "god within"—had been used by the Greeks to denote "prophetic seizures, erotic passion and artistic creation," and to refer to "those religious rites in which mystical states were experienced through the ingestion of substances that were transubstantial with the deity."[6] By adding the root *gen*—denoting the action of "becoming"—the new term evoked a substance that could generate or awaken divinity. The newly minted terminology, then, highlighted the therapeutic and spiritually transformative potential associated with a variety of plants and compounds as they are adopted in nontraditional contexts, and where they are typically subject to prohibition.

The concept would take root, striking appeal during a period in which humanity is implored to awaken from ignorance and fear, a pall responsible for pathologizing, criminalizing, and suppressing the very tools that pry open and pave independent pathways to divinity. There is growing recognition that a range of natural and artificial substances are "entheogens," and that entheogenic effects then compare favorably to the outcomes of other (initially marginal) practices of self-divinity proliferating in the West, like meditation, yoga, and other holistic healing modalities and techniques such as rhythmic drumming, trance dance, ritual prayer, and incantations. Wouter Hanegraaff has, for instance, clarified that what he calls "entheogenic religion," if taken literally, does not strictly imply psychoactive "substances," since many other factors can generate "unusual states of consciousness in which those who use them are believed to be 'filled,' 'possessed' or 'inspired' by some kind of divine entity, presence or force," among which we might include many shaping factors that are often found under the umbrella of "set and setting." In this broader definition, Hanegraaff makes the distinction between "entheogenic religion in a *narrow* and in a *wide* sense."[7] Whereas scholars of religion have typically neglected the role that psychoactive plants may have had in "neoshamanism," let alone the "spiritual revolution," Hanegraaff tears through institutional veils impeding research and that have otherwise shaped Christian-theologically biased claims to the human experience. By way of preliminary research on a network of Dutch ayahuasca-drinking groups, he has opened up entheogens to legitimate scrutiny within academic studies of religion.[8]

Over the last two decades, and generally within the "narrow" sense outlined by Hanegraaff, entheogenic practices have been explored within experimental, therapeutic, and academic circles. Since the early 1990s, bioassayists, transpersonal psychologists, theologians, and entheologians, within and outside academia, have contributed to a growing database on the significance of entheogens for mental health and well-being.[9] Huston Smith has been a persistent voice of wisdom, stating that "nonaddictive mind-altering substances that are approached seriously and reverently" can enhance a religious life, even though they do not themselves facilitate *the* religious life.[10] While this period saw a growth in studies focusing on the significance of unique compounds and practices, notably the ayahuasca brew and its diasporic proliferation beyond the Amazon, studies of the "wider" implications of the use of entheogens and what Thomas Roberts calls "mindapps" have contributed to paradigm-changing insights on the nature of the mind—e.g., Grof's "holotropic mind" and Roberts's "multistate" theory—in which psychedelics/entheogens are recognized among many psychotechnologies that not only possess therapeutic benefits but augment human potential: optimized mind/body states, aesthetic developments, enhanced cognition, scientific innovation.[11]

Signaling this paradigm shift, the concept of "entheogen" has today gained wider appeal among research scientists and theologians.[12] Staking down a position appearing to be at a sharp remove from Terence McKenna's, while at the same time seeking to appeal to theologians, psychiatrist William A. Richards encourages the association of entheogens with "the reality that theologians call grace." This is because, he claims, "profound revelatory experiences almost always are experienced as gifts received, not as feats of heroic egos." In the wake of the psilocybin research initiative led by Roland Griffiths at Johns Hopkins University School of Medicine conducted with the support of the Council on Spiritual Practices, in which psilocybin was found to reliably occasion mystical experiences among research volunteers, Richards states that not only are scientists encountering the sacred, "we now know how to facilitate the occurrence of mystical forms of consciousness with maximum safety for many, if not most persons who desire them."[13]

Almost anyone who has ingested *Psilocybe cubensis* needs no verification from scientists nor theologians that it has occasioned in them a *mystical experience.* As sovereign persons, users are at liberty to privately interpret these occasionings by whatever framework they choose. And yet cognitive liberty is not a given, since ingestion, more often than not, also occasions an *illicit experience,* punishable by law. The "teachings" associated with entheogens—or what has been recognized as *entheogenesis*—are by association ambiguous in relation to the law that identifies these compounds as "dangerous drugs." At the same time, academies, churches, and their official representatives censor and suppress the pedagogies of entheogenesis—effectively forbidden knowledge. In the case of DMT, the folly is magnified when, under prohibition, everyone is born criminal. In an era when DMT and other entheogenic tryptamines are deemed to have "no recognized medicinal value" but with science effectively obstructed from finding otherwise, and when religious institutions are typically hostile toward entheogenic pathways to spiritual life, researchers and experients must cultivate knowledge in the cultural laboratory of the underground.

DIY DMT and Anahuasca

At a time when minds and bodies are criminalized with impunity, those who are dedicated to modifying and optimizing their neurocognitive processes rally in opposition. Gaining control over the means of perception is championed at a juncture at which the disingenuous implications of prohibiting that which is, as Alexander Shulgin once observed, "everywhere," are recognized with telling clarity. Shulgin was alert to the extraordinary reality that while DMT had been discovered in dozens of plants, it is potentially present in thousands of plant species. As Dennis McKenna has stated, "Nature is drenched in DMT," further speculating that "DMT could be found in all plants, at tiny but detectable levels if anyone bothered to look."[14] Committed to the synthesis and assaying of hundreds of new compounds, Shulgin was himself dedicated to the public dissemination of potential psychotherapeutic aids—most notably MDMA—as published in the classic usertomes *TiHKAL* and *PiHKAL*.[15] Though exemplary, this desire to uncover and share forbidden knowledge—what Shulgin has referred to as "dirty pictures"—was not new. Methods describing DMT synthesis have been in circulation since the 1960s, when *The Turn On Book* of 1967 and in the following year *The Psychedelic Guide to Preparation of the Eucharist in a Few of Its Many Guises* were available.[16] Probably the most widely known handbook encouraging the cultivation of tryptamines was *Psilocybin: Magic Mushroom Grower's Guide*, first published in 1976 by O. T. Oss and O. N. Oeric (i.e., the McKennas, with Jeremy Bigwood and Kathleen Harrison). In 1986, Gracie and Zarkov published their popular *Notes from Underground*, which offered the first details on the potentiation of DMT using *Peganum harmala* (Syrian rue) extract—producing what Ott has called the "ayahuasca effect."[17]

Integral to the story of DMT are practices invested in knowledge of ayahuasca's unique alchemy. As Ott has commented, the "ingenious discovery by South American Indians of the ayahuasca effect—conceivably the most sophisticated pharmacognostical discovery ever made in the archaic world—bids fair to revolutionize contemporary, nontraditional entheobotany of visionary shamanic inebriants."[18] While plant synergies have been implicitly understood among Amazonian ayahuasqueros for millennia, it was not until the late 1960s that ethnobotanists hypothesized that MAO-inhibiting[19] ß-carboline alkaloids were effecting the activity of

DMT in snuffs and ayahuasca.[20] Even then, it wasn't until a series of experiments with rats, human bioassays, and systematic psychonautical experiments with "pharmahuasca"—precise measurements of pure DMT and ß-carbolines—that this hypothesis was confirmed.[21] For his experience on a threshold dose of 120 mg of harmine combined with 30 mg of DMT, Ott found that "effects were quite similar to what I have enjoyed with genuine Amazonian ayahuasca potions in Brasil, Ecuador and Peru."[22] Once the "ayahuasca effect" had been discovered, analogues were experimented with using non-Amazonian botanical and chemical sources referred to as "ayahuasca analogues." Underground flagship journal *The Entheogen Review* (1992–2008) was renowned for promoting ayahuasca analogues, especially those found and cultivated in temperate zones. Approximating "ayahuasca" by using analogue plants was, for readers, "as simple as making a pot of coffee." While a few plants were recognized as "potent enough to simply run through a wheatgrass juicer, dry, and smoke," the *TER* published "acid–base extraction procedures geared toward enthusiasts with no chemistry background." Furthermore, "Most chemicals needed to perform extractions were available at hardware stores."[23]

These practices weren't being promoted as recreational pursuits. In early issues of *TER*, founding editor Jim DeKorne cultivated a reactionary approach consistent with his dire pre-millennial prognostications. As was announced in the second issue, entheogens "may be the only realistic chance we have to make such an unlikely quantum leap of consciousness in the brief time remaining. While we definitely run the risk of opening up another wave of drug excesses in furthering this work, I believe the extreme gravity of our situation makes that risk irrelevant."[24] A weatherman serving up the pre-apocalyptic forecast, DeKorne was blunt. "Our survival prognosis is grim; barbarous abuses of power escalate unchecked while social structures developed over long centuries disintegrate within decades, years, even weeks and days, with nothing to replace them except generic forebodings about our destiny." He demonstrated an indebtedness to McKenna by suggesting that, in these forbidding times, anything that could "alter the reality-perception of a significant mass of humanity" should be investigated. And showing familiarity with Huxley, what was required was a "catalyst to blast us out of our material myopia."

To be effective, this catalyst must be available to the widest possible number of people at little or no cost—something so common that it would be impossible for the entrenched power structure to control or destroy. It must be easy to use, requiring minimal preparation. And it must be potent, even psychologically dangerous, for nothing less will open our awareness to the encompassing Mystery.[25]

DeKorne already had the answer: the tryptamine-containing species within the *Phalaris* genus of grasses. In an early report in *TER*, DeKorne related a threshold bioassay he had with DMT he believed he had extracted from the *Phalaris arundinacea*, a perennial bunchgrass with wide distribution in North America (and Europe, Asia, and northern Africa). The main active alkaloid was actually 5-MeO-DMT, which would have been mixed with DMT, and ß-carboline alkaloids.[26] DeKorne regarded *Phalaris* as the "catalyst" that, unlike LSD—"a drug presently obtainable only from a complex technology via an underground hierarchy of dealers" and an "example par excellence of a contemporary consumer-culture psychedelic"—just might "transform our world." It might not have been delivered in eleven-inch headlines, and *TER* had limited circulation among fellow explorers, but as an enthusiastic promoter of a solution near the end-times coming, DeKorne was publishing the "news" the absence of which was decried by McKenna. "Here for the first time—untainted by high technology, drug dealer capitalism, cultural unfamiliarity, or somatic malaise—is an extremely powerful entheogen potentially available to anyone who wants it." In another report, it was announced that "it is as if a 'trans-personal intelligence' is revealing data deliberately designed to create the widest possible opportunity for the mass expansion of consciousness."[27] If DeKorne sometimes came across like the Jim Jones of the entheogen revolution, salvation would not derive from the physical deaths of those so exposed to the tryptamine kool-aid, but from something far more significant—an ego-death precipitating an expanded and evolved consciousness.

In *TER*, psychonauts of the courageous and crazed kind were sharing the outcomes of novel adventures with combinations of tryptamine-containing plants grown or found wild in temperate regions. Prized among these were the powerful and qualitatively different experiences enjoyed when inhaling *Peganum harmala* extract prior to smoking DMT and/or 5-MeO-DMT extracted from *Phalaris arundinacea,* a combo also promoted by DeKorne in his *Psychedelic Shamanism.* A collection of ill-tended ramblings and far-reaching insights, *Psychedelic Shamanism* championed the potency of the shaman as rebel, the mind-tinkering outcast who, by way of ethnobotanical experimentation, can heal the "planetary disease caused by human refusal to acknowledge whole systems."[28] Also important at this time was *The Essential Psychedelic Guide* by D. M. Turner, who tested and advised on various combinations, including taking harmala alkaloids with DMT in smoking blends that prolonged the effects by thirty to forty minutes. In this duration, he reported, "I often feel that my body and Being are 'embraced' by an ancient earth spirit. And this earth spirit is instructing me to become aware of, and open up, many lines of communication that exist between my mind, body and the external world."[29] Temperate-zone analogues supplying sources of DMT and MAOIs were referred to by Dennis McKenna as "ayahuasca borealis," while Ott has used "anahuasca," or analogues of ayahuasca.[30] By 1999, Ott claimed that since there were more than seventy each of MAOI- and DMT-containing plants known at that time, there were several thousand possible combinations, each yielding a unique psychedelic profile, and each compounded by a variety of social, environmental, and personal factors.[31]

Forty years downstream from pioneering dispensations, cyberspace became the natural platform for facilitating and democratizing DMT hyperspace. Published originally in *TER* and then going viral online, Noman's tek for dummies "DMT for the Masses" simplified extraction methods (from *Mimosa tenuiflora* root bark).[32] With the advent of the World Wide Web and its expanding mycelia of webfora, the lines of communication were opening up. With its stated mission to "document the complex relationship between humans and psychoactives," the colossal psychoactive information source Erowid.org had been in operation since the mid-1990s. The Lycaeum's DMT World provided the earliest DMT hub: a chat room, message board, and archive of trip reports, as well as information on synthesis and extraction procedures. In the early 2000s, the DMT-Nexus became the chief collaborative educational resource and cultural commons for the DMT research community, exemplified by an eighty-plus-page forum thread featuring an indexed list of worldwide *Acacias* facilitating phytochemical identification, encouraging sustainable use, discouraging commercialization, and enabling "an understanding and caring for these lifeforms."[33]

With the internet, McKenna's proselytizing, and the appeal of shamanic traditions, there came a steady growth in experimentation. Users became dedicated to maximizing well-being, augmenting creativity, and fomenting independence, where psychoactive compounds are embraced as "mindapps" applied to hack one's self, and enhance one's relationships, including the relationship one has with one's self, or one's other self. While the complex historical interplay of cybernetics and psychedelics remains largely untold, DMT (along with LSD) is implicated in the DIY movement, which, as Fred Turner demonstrated in his landmark study *From Counterculture to Cyberculture,* was a Do It Ourselves movement.[34] As Richard Doyle has argued in *Darwin's Pharmacy,* the commitment to open-source operating systems (e.g., Linux) demonstrates a radical discontentment with privatization also evident in the dissemination of patent-free synthesis and extraction methodologies. Not only that, not unlike the "strong belief in the right to tinker . . . the right to alter one's tools" evident in the digital commons, in the psychedelic commons there exists "an extraordinary desire to alter and test diverse cognitive tools," which Doyle argues are rhetorical as well as molecular practices.[35] Therefore, rhetorical practices that permeate "trip reports" distributed across a labyrinth of webfora are themselves "open-source" technologies—evolving readouts on the commitment to experiment with, and report on, alternative modalities of consciousness.

Aussiewaska

Terence McKenna's visit to Australia in 1997 would be among his last international adventures, a fitting locale for his psychedelic mission given that Australia's European descendants possess a self-entitled commitment to leisure, pleasure, and mobility seemingly unparalleled among the planet's populations. By the time he stepped from the airplane, an underground milieu with an evolved leisure apparatus of its own greeted the man whose message was to open one's life to chaos and become part of the "will of the world soul." In his raps at the Beyond the Brain club at the Epicentre in Byron Bay, and the Trancelements Festival in Apollo Bay, McKenna shared the wisdom that DMT can be extracted from species of local *Acacia,* referred to colloquially as "wattle." As McKenna commented at the time, "the national symbol of Australia is the wattle. It's an *Acacia.* The *Acacia* ecology of Australia is jammed with DMT." These lines were deployed as a voice sample on "Geometric Patterns" by Dark Nebula & Scatterbrain, a psytrance production that also clarified the outcome of ingestion with an Australian accent: "Everything sounds really loud and alive. I'm seeing iridescent rainbow spirals and complex geometric patterns. Feels like I'm being bombarded by some sort of ancient knowledge or universal consciousness."[36] It's possible McKenna had been reading a review copy of *TiHKAL: The Continuation* prior to arrival. In that tome, Shulgin digresses "into a bit of 'Down-Under' history," fascinated as he was with the identification among Australians with the genus *Acacia* (there are more than seven hundred species of *Acacia* native to Australia).

The first Wattle Club was formed in 1899, and in 1910 the first national Wattle day was celebrated in Sydney, Adelaide and Melbourne on September 1. Songs and poems were written, and sprigs of Wattle were worn on lapels. The movement grew like topsy. It was used for fundraising for charities and for public morale connected with the World War I war efforts. There were Wattle queens elected and crowned, Wattle Day badges were worn, and every one pinned on a small sprig of it to wear to school. On the first of September, 1988, at a ceremony in Canberra, the Golden Wattle was officially proclaimed Australia's national floral emblem, exactly 75 years after the idea had been first proposed. Just recently I had the pleasure of being in Sydney, and heard from my Sydneysider host a nursery rhyme he had learned as a child:

This is the Wattle.
The emblem of our land.
You can stick it in a bottle
Or hold it in your hand.[37]

This slice of history had already been remixed by local psychonauts, as apparent in the opening lines of "The Pipe Song" written in 1996 by Neil Pike for the band The Pagan Love Cult:

> *This is the wattle*
> *symbol of our scene*
> *you can smoke it in a bottle*
> *or eat with harmaline.*

These repurposed lines blink in sharp-hued neon at a critical juncture in the formation of an Australian ethnobotanical synergy, sometimes referred to as an "ayahuasca analogue," but also sometimes designated colloquially, and less contentiously, as "aussiehuasca," or "aussiewaska." These designations refer to brews and smoking blends where the DMT is sourced from local *Acacias*, with the harmalas sourced typically, but not exclusively, from *B. caapi*. As the historical detail above implies, *Acacia* is iconically Australian, a circumstance relished by those who cultivate alternative—and sometimes more ancient—visions of "country." While the "golden wattle" (*Acacia pycnantha*) is not itself a widely used source of DMT, phytochemical analyses have identified DMT in its phyllodes.[38]

While the idea that DMT could be sourced from the Australian floral emblem delighted McKenna, locals had been bioassaying *Acacias* prior to his arrival. Recognizing that harmalas inhibited MAO, and thereby potentiated DMT when taken orally (or smoked), they had been discovering botanical sources and combining alkaloids to this end since at least the early 1990s. Entheocognoscenti were already aware of what they might stumble across in their own backyard—i.e., more DMT-bearing plants (at least 150 species) than anywhere else on the planet. For those purists bent on herbal-sourced DMT, thought to be more organic than the sci-fi hyperspace of synthetic derivations, this was like striking gold, or at least its precursors, on your claim. That alchemists had been successful at refining the eureka moment from native botanicals was something you could feel in the air on the night of Beyond the Brain. Space Tree (a.k.a. Nen, who we meet below), who DJed at the event, performed his "Cetus 5," an unreleased track produced in 1994 and inspired by the ayahuascan use of *Acacia*. Furthermore,

Neil Pike recalled "big joints of wattle were being passed around the audience" during McKenna's appearance.[39] With the band The Pagan Love Cult, Pike had been smoking joints of *Acacia*-sourced DMT on stage during their final piece of music since the mid-1990s, a variation on performance practices using DMT going back to the late 1970s. With the advent of *Acacia* extractions in the mid-1990s, Pike observed how "a rare treat for the entheogenic cognoscenti" in Australia since the late 1970s became "a staple part of the local psychedelic arsenal" prior to McKenna's arrival.[40]

The protean culture hero in this story is a brilliant, experimental, and anonymous University of Sydney chemistry student who uncovered crucial botanical information, guiding him to northeastern New South Wales (NSW), where he extracted DMT from locally sourced *Acacia maidenii*.[41] The budding chemist reported bioassays in an article published in the student newspaper *Honi Soit* in 1992, with extraction methodology subsequently leaked to the internet via the alt.drugs newsgroup, visionary plants forum The Lycaeum, and later Erowid.[42] Australia's first DMT trip report is exemplary frontier beta testing.

> Preliminary attempts at smoking small amounts of the alkaloids gave varying mild effects, and a friend and I decided to try a larger dose. He took a cone in one toke, and was immediately on the ground, making strange sounds and looking odd. He hugged me and told me to meet him in that place, and said it was very strong. I managed to finish a large cone in 3 tokes, and was instantly blown apart as if by a large brick through the head. I think I was temporarily blinded, and found myself on the ground grasping my friend, and coughing for air, as I watched all of my surroundings fragment into small pieces divided by lightning bolts, and feeling all the air in the universe escape through the holes. We were both totally astounded and scared shitless. Two minutes later, the intense part was over. We staggered out into the open, and walked in the park until we calmed down. Pleasant mild visions continued for about half an hour, and there were no after-effects whatsoever.

In a subsequent trial, a vaporizing method was used. After small tokes at long intervals led to "an extremely pleasant trip," drawing two large tokes turned the world inside out. "Without warning, I was blown apart. I was walking, but staggered and choked, gasping for air. The effects were totally overwhelming, like being thrown out of the universe, and I watched my visual sphere being pixelated at successively lower resolutions, until I could see merely individual elements of color. The intensity was such as to make it very unpleasant." Notably, the author also reported "an intense incredible rush of physical pleasure" after taking sixty tablets (500 mg each) of *Passiflora incarnata* extract (a source of a variety of ß-carbolines) forty minutes prior to smoking DMT.

> Within seconds, I was riding on the most intense unimaginable pure total body orgasm. I was unable to control myself, and I was screaming at the top of my voice until the effects subsided. The visual and auditory enhancements were mild, but the physical hallucination was by far the most enjoyable thing I have ever experienced. Observers, who were taken aback by my behaviour, claim that I was in this state for about 10 minutes. Afterwards, I felt intensely euphoric, and both very excited and very relaxed.[43]

Among those exposed to these reports in *Honi Soit* was Nen, a then recent graduate in Psychology and Ancient History at U Sydney, who befriended the chemist and learned his extraction method. Highly motivated, in December 1992 Nen set out on a journey to locate the DMT tree (i.e., *A. maidenii*). Scouring the scrub for days, he intuited that he was "on the edge of something massive and unprecedented." Then, "one day a beautiful tree just shone and whispered to me." Small branches were pruned and he returned home to perform the extraction. "My first experience was more profoundly spiritual and enchanting than I could ever have imagined, including a direct addressing by the spirit of the tree, to which I have felt allied with ever since."[44]

As it turned out, the tree Nen located was not *A. maidenii* as initially believed, but *Acacia obtusifolia*, previously unrecognized as a DMT-bearing species of the genus. *A. obtusifolia* was found to contain multiple alkaloids: i.e., two-thirds NMT (*N*-methyltryptamine), one-third DMT, and a small amount of ß-carboline. The effects of the "full spectrum extracts" cooked up from this tree had a profound impact on a small cohort of pioneers, included among them a humble ethnobotanist, Mulga, who in 1996 compiled "Australian Acacias and Entheogenic Tryptamines," a privately circulated document with details on cultivating, preparing, and self-experimenting with local *Acacias* and Syrian rue. Nen found the effects of pure synthetic DMT lackluster compared with those of *obtusifolia*. "The synthetic DMT was to me like 'virtual reality' while the plant extract was like 'reality.'" The "full spectrum plant extract," he recalled, "just did more, had more directions and depth." Nen realized that he and his friends were undergoing a kind of self-induced initiation. In a culture where traditional rites of passage like coming-of-age rituals had been reduced to getting wasted on alcohol at the age of twenty-one (the gateway to adulthood), it was a "profound and rare gift from the bush" that marked a beneficent transit into a whole new way of being human. "You die shamanically, you reconnect to the ancestors and the spirit world, you see the existence of more than the material, you have a profound mystical vision which makes you see that there's more beyond death."[45] Since this and other *Acacias* possessed a wide variation of alkaloids (and not simply DMT), there was a perception that they supplied a next-level DMT experience. "A few who saw the acacias as a unique tryptamine gateway developed a folklore of deep respect for the plants and, echoing animist traditions, they accepted the alkaloid variations . . . as a 'teaching' of the plant."[46]

The tree (i.e., *A. obtusifolia*) commanded Nen's respect, and with a dedication to plumbing its depth, in 2001 he began orchestrating bioassays of pure NMT (*N*-methyltryptamine or methyltryptamine), its primary alkaloid, and a compound generally considered "inactive." But this compound—which, like DMT, is a naturally occurring component of human blood/cerebrospinal fluid—first synthesized by Shulgin, was found to be active at larger vaporized doses (90–120 mg). Separating and vaporizing the pure material, NMT yielded "entheogenic effects, becoming noticeable after 3–5 minutes, attaining full strength for 30–45 seconds, and gradually disappearing over 45–70 minutes. No negative or lingering side effects were noted. It was roughly estimated at 1/3 the potency of DMT." In a thread on DMT-Nexus, Nen conveyed how one volunteer reported that rather than being a visual or auditory entheogen, it was a "Spatial hallucinogen" where one could, for example, feel, and not see, "an Escher world."[47] This sensibility encouraged the phrase "spatial entheogen," used to describe the compound in subsequent lectures. At the Entheogenesis Australis conference in December 2011, Nen concluded that "a little NMT may go a long way toward expanding the 'vocabulary' of the tryptamine experience. It may be a subtler compound than dimethyltryptamine, but its unknown full potential in neurophysiological, medical and consciousness research remains tantalizing and mysterious."[48]

As is the case, then, for *Acacia* and other popular sources of DMT like jurema (*Mimosa tenuiflora*), many botanical sources contain a variety of tryptamines and even MAO inhibitors, making "DMT use" a complicated matter, simply because "DMT" in many cases is not just DMT. The frequency with which *Acacia* and other botanical extracts are smoked in Australia and elsewhere—and thus where DMT is likely to be taken in synergistic combination with other entheogenic tryptamines, including 5-MeO-DMT, bufotenin, and NMT, the frequency and potency of which depend on a host of seasonal and environmental factors—underlines the difficulties in performing questionnaire-oriented analyses that seek to offer meaningful conclusions about "DMT users."[49]

While the discovery that *A. obtusifolia* had entheogenic properties drew greater numbers of initiates, with the tree promoted in the mid-1990s as a source of DMT, commercial exploitation soon followed. "A number of large-scale European drug dealers arrived in Australia, specifically hunting the DMT source," Nen reported in *TER* in 1996. He reported witnessing the sacrilege in national parks "untouched for thousands of years, not for medicine or growth, but to make money," declaring that a "successful long term shamanic use of these plants involves forming a relationship with the plant by growing it and protecting it." Against the advice of sensitively removing bark strips or single branches from *A. obtusifolia* to guarantee a tree's survival, perpetrators "ripped hundreds of trees out, started selling to the rave party set, and encouraged people to smoke it in joints at parties (which has led to some pretty extreme psychological disturbances). They shipped several hundred grams to places like Goa, India."[50] Over the subsequent decades, as the market for DMT grew, Nen became distraught by the impact of larger-scale harvesting and trade. That intimate connections with the natural world potentiated by DMT could be enabled by extracts from source trees devastated through unsustainable harvesting practices was a painful irony.[51]

The damage wasn't only being done to the trees. Wild harvesting of trees for recreational purposes was deplored because it maximized the chances for inappropriate use, especially in a time when few knew about DMT. In the Goa scene—in Goa, India, and within its global sites of efflorescence, including that in northeastern NSW—DMT was initially "shared as a gift by seasoned travellers to others." Because *Mimosa hostilis* sources hadn't yet taken on in the United States and Europe, in its formative years, the global Goatrance scene's DMT was derived in large part from Australian *Acacia*. This had a direct impact on the Australian scene from the mid- to late 1990s. "It was like the 60s again on a smaller scale, an era which set many precedents and styles continuing today. Inspiration of re-understanding various spiritual traditions. And highly experimental."[52] But some in the scene began commodifying DMT, and transported it to Europe. While the scale of these operations was small, the situation was harmful, as the farther the plant sources were removed from origins the more likely knowledge of sources was lost on end users. What's more, while some treated the *Acacia*-sourced DMT with reverence, approaching it as a "teacher," others weren't so respectful. Nen refers to "horror stories" of people being introduced to DMT in inappropriate sets and settings. He conveyed reports of uninformed users being given DMT to smoke at dance parties.

> One person described immediately feeling "this is wrong! I don't want to be doing this here."... they felt psychically raped as strangers gawked at them ... they fell to the ground and curled into fetal position, feeling violated ... they were still in trauma weeks later ... for a few people exposed to DMT in this way, they were disturbed that something which felt so personal had been put on display in a public environment with strangers, where not everyone felt friendly or sympathetic ... "attacked by psychic vampires" was another person's description.[53]

With the consequences of recreational use borne out in unfortunate incidents, Nen felt that the "DMT revolution" was being undermined. In response, he undertook to educate people that *Acacia*-sourced DMT "is a very special gift from nature, and that DMT in an appropriate set and setting could be like communion with the divine." He added that "I think it takes more than simply taking DMT to derive lasting beneficial change."[54]

Meanwhile in North America, *P. arundinacea* would become recognized as a "unique plant entheogen unto itself" and not simply a source of DMT (and more often 5-MeO-DMT). It is a conclusion deriving from an understanding that a wide variety of chemical phenotypes exist within the species, presenting different alkaloid profiles among different populations of grass. According to DMT-Nexian jamie, *P. arundinacea* are "power plants." They are not seen as "one single teacher, but as a family of allies, each with their own respective voices."[55] Determined by phenotypes and cycles of alkaloid production shaped by seasonal and environmental factors, not to mention extraction and user techniques, these "voices" have varying intonations. Just as *A. obtusifolia* had provided effects beyond DMT, *P. arundinacea* offered a curious variation on the experience.

> An unknown amount of the extract was carefully vaporized in a glass pipe. Effects began instantly upon inhalation, and by the time the remaining vapor was exhaled, I encountered an extremely powerful tryptamine body-rush. Within moments, I felt an odd pressure in the pineal region, which increased until I both felt and heard a "pop," at which point the pressure was released, bathing my body in an energetic experience so powerful that I fell back, out of my seated position, and was forced to endure the experience lying down. The main effect was very powerful and psychedelic, but without any significant visual activity, instead presenting a state of profound mental expansion. There was a faint visual shimmer with my eyes closed, however, no geometry or complex forms were noted.[56]

Backyard Alchemists and Changaleros

Downstream from the early wattle research and in the wake of McKenna's visit, there emerged a vibrant ethnobotanical scene in Australia. Torsten Wiedemann, operator of Shaman Australis Botanicals, recalls the "talking point" at Ethnobotanica III, the 2003 Australian Ethnobotany Conference:

the hallucinogenic snuff yopo. Doctoral student in anthropology at James
Cook University Robin Rodd introduced participants to the practices of the
Piaroa of southern Venezuela.[57] The Piaroa traditionally insufflate *Anadenanthera peregrina* seeds (a source of many compounds, including DMT
and 5-MeO-DMT) after chewing the bark of *B. caapi,* and a small group of
psychonauts later simulated this technique. "The effects blew us all away,"
said Wiedemann. "Rather than the manic 60 seconds of crystal space that
we were used to there was this calm trip that was still quite overwhelming, but several minutes long. It seemed much more manageable and at
first actually more productive . . . in terms of 'bringing back' visions."[58] It
was a pivotal year. Through the efforts of freelance writer Kate Hamilton
and Fairfax Media, Melbourne's *The Age* and the *Sydney Morning Herald*
published in their *Good Weekend* supplement a hysteria-free synopsis on
the subject of DMT and its growing popularity connected to *Acacia* in the
NSW Northern Rivers region. "The Freakiest Trip" served up DMT 101 for
the adventurous intrigued about how it, according to one commentator,
enabled access to an "intergalactic telepathic gateway, through which I
could commune with 'higher' alien life forms."[59]

In the years prior to this period, there had emerged a vibrant outdoor
arts and dance culture nourished by the plants. As a "shy little wattle tree
turned out to be the key to multidimensional knowledge," as Floyd Davis
reported, in northeastern NSW in the mid-1990s this discovery saw the
flourishing of an alternative culture that "began to gel once more into a
coherent tribal underground."

> A fledgling shamanism stirred within the land of love, re-initiating the
> ever-evolving process of awakening. . . . There was immense joy as the
> awakening continued to spread, such was the magic of these plants, with
> legendary psychedelic parties and wild visions and successful healing
> with plant medicines all working their way into the everyday fabric of
> life. Shamanic houses materialised and tremendous rivalries grew as
> markets opened up for all things herbal.[60]

Davis was the creative force behind the DMT-inspired publication *Illuminated
Adventures,* an early collection of visionary works with accompanying words.

"Yes, I am Mantis. Behold the keys to search you inside and out. I express you. I open the mantle to extend your transcendental horizons. I see you for your true self."[61] Among the flowering buds of this culture was Happy People Productions' Exodus Cybertribal Festival held at Bald Rock Bush Retreat near Tenterfield, NSW. Exodus accommodated the Intra-Cortex zone, an education hub for entheogenistas. The event also showcased local expressions of visionary art inspired by seekers helping themselves to "wattle" and other entheogenic plants like San Pedro. Among such artists is Hayden Peters (Shiptu Shaboo), whose work depicts tryptaminal mysteries in the flavor of Aussie hypnagogia not dissimilar to that printed on functional domestic linens. Within this DMTea towel tradition is Peters's emblematic *Bushfire of Life* (see Figure 8), a montage teeming with native birdlife, insects, and spiders standing out upon an undergrowth of brilliant colors.

The early 2000s saw the emergence of an ethnobotanical solution with a unique symbiosis—changa (pronounced CHĀNG-uh). A story of homegrown alchemistry, changa is a smoking blend involving a variable synergy of DMT and harmala alkaloids often identified, sometimes rather speciously, as a "smokable ayahuasca." Typically extracted from *Acacia* (and originally *A. obtusifolia*), in changa DMT is combined with harmala (traditionally from *B. caapi*) via customized infusion and blending techniques to create a smoking mix at a range of ratios normally between 20 and 50 percent DMT by weight. Changa was fashioned by Australian Julian Palmer as an alternative to smoking or vaporizing DMT crystal. Practical endeavors to regulate intake had inspired innovation since the mid-1960s, following the advent of the freebase vaporizing method. But while underground users invented smoking blends using synthetic varieties of DMT with a variety of herbs, including cannabis and parsley, in practices that surfaced in Australia by the early 1970s, the *Acacia*-sourced DMT plus harmalas combination markedly augmented the delivery and the experience. Flying countless sorties into the ineffable, beta testing techniques of extraction, Palmer and compatriot bioneers became thoroughly convinced by the transformative power of the botanical synergetics they were working with.

Over a few years, through trial and error, with the aid of willing accomplices, lab rats, and crash dummies, Palmer learned how to extract alkaloids, optimize blends, and undertake better living through alchemy, as explained in his book *Articulations: On the Utilisation and Meanings of Psychedelics*. DMT-containing Australian *Acacias* are among the chief plants covered in the work of this bold entheo-explorer. As he writes, "modern day researchers have only scratched the surface of this mysterious genus of tree and why and when it secretes DMT." Palmer fields the view that the *Acacias* are sentient and that they are communicating by way of their neurotransmitter alkaloids. "The trees create a kind of metaphysical field of intelligence through these neurotransmitters via the evident nervous system of veins and nerves in their phyllodes, which appear to receive, transmit and even process information." The trees are in dialogue with seekers, and not only are they communicating with Palmer, they have apparently granted him permission to harvest their tryptamine alkaloids, using appropriate sustainable methods. And lest one hold the opinion that he and other recent-settler alchemists believe themselves to be the first humans to whom these trees have chosen to express themselves, there are curious signals otherwise. "I have seen *Acacia obtusifolia* trees right on the edge of rock formations considered very sacred to aboriginals," he writes. "And yet nowhere else in the area will these trees be found." But while *Acacia* and other indigenous biota may have borne fruits to the benefit of the indigenous human population for millennia, the new fruit of the harvest is changa, promoted as "a valid medicine and agent of awakening."[62] An "intelligent" blend, Palmer's innovation responded to several inter-related concerns: the harrowing effects of smoking, as Leary had it, "the nuclear bomb of the psychedelic family," which initiates typically show little desire to repeat;[63] the impracticalities associated with smoking crystal DMT; and elitism characterizing the use of DMT and ayahuasca before changa's emergence.

Prior to the original changa mixes of mid-2003, regional experimentalists were smoking what they called "luxury joints"—*Acacia*-sourced DMT sprinkled in cannabis joints or mixed with popular herbs like passionflower and damiana, accessible in dried form from herb shops and at festivals. The most popular of these experimental smoking mixes was commercially available as Dreamtime, labeled as "an exotic mix of Wattle leaf, mullein, and *Passiflora* for insight and meditation." This mix was sold under the counter at some Happy High Herb shops where it was endorsed by franchise founder Ray Thorpe. Herb crusader and drug law reformer, Thorpe held DMT in high regard, not least of all given its origins in the "wattle," the nation's own herb. In naming this mix Dreamtime, besides the significance of the letters "d," "m," and "t" in the word, Thorpe entertained the idea that Aboriginal Australians, whose animist religion is known as the Dreamtime, were familiar with the secrets of *Acacia* to which settler Australians had been recently introduced. "They used to smoke themselves in the wattle branch and that's what they would smudge themselves in," he surmised. "They would have gone into dreamtime with trance dancing, possibly using something like pituri and the smoke from acacia leaf and branches."[64] Thorpe was given to dispense DMT mixes that were less potent than crystal and more appropriate for social-festive contexts. There were concerns that individuals with a history of psychological disturbance and instability could be handed joints or cones of DMT crystal in inappropriate social settings without preparation or warning. He recalled an extreme case of someone he knew fitting that description who was once "passed a cone of DMT pure crystal, unknowingly sucked it all down, lost it completely, lost his job, lost his kids, never really recovered and eventually took his own life."[65] Thorpe stressed that there was no clear link between the use of crystal DMT and that tragedy, but this and other incidents highlighted the need for appropriate herb technologies.

When Palmer and his friends decided to sprinkle DMT onto an "ayahuasca vine joint" (20 percent DMT), the effects were remarkable. It was the makings for what would become changa, a blend originally including passionflower, peppermint, mullein, and blue lotus. When reports came in of users "giving up decades-old meth or coke addictions," Palmer had it confirmed that he was onto something. The harmala alkaloids present, typically shaved *B. caapi* bark or leaves, but also Syrian rue (a less effective MAO inhibitor when smoked), were enabling an experience longer in duration—sometimes up to forty minutes—than DMT, yet softer and with a more "pleasant afterglow." This was essential for Palmer, an advocate of the "sub-breakthrough" experience as a necessary modification on the sometimes-brutal impact of DMT. While users had been regulating doses with smoking blends since the 1960s and 1970s, the new blends were an advancement in optimization. Not typically facilitating the visionary, out-of-body impact of DMT, changa's medicinal effects are purported to be consistent with the function of ayahuasca. With a therapeutic agenda underlying this approach, changa is designed to transport users "to places of grace (universal love, total peace) to catharsis, where old patterns, emotions and beliefs can come up to be released."[66]

The innovation assisted users to overcome a set of anxiety-inducing impracticalities typically confronting the DMT smoker. As one convert explained, users "go through incredible lengths and spend countless dollars on methods and devices to administer their precisely weighed doses of beautiful white and orange crystals in a timely manner." This preparation can build apprehension at the point of contact, where the traveler must "juggle the logistics of a torch lighter, the flame distance, inhalation timing, etc.—all while knowing you need to get it just right! It's no wonder some people have a hard time relaxing once they put the pipe down—they feel like they just raced through a timed challenge on a game show!"[67] By varying blends and ratios, users could effect smoother entries and prolong selected states of intensity by periodically taking more hits, effectively personalizing their experience. "You have the ability to fully customize your blend to fit your exact preferences. You can create a harmala-heavy blend, a one-hit breakthrough blend, or anything in between, with various aromas and flavors infused."[68] As knowledge of potentizing, flavoring, and coloring DMT expanded, herbal mixologists experimented with aromatic bouquets by dissolving blends in solvent-soaked herbal infusions using lemon balm, spearmint, and lavender, among other herbs. With the results more like a boutique boost (with herbal flavors) than a businessman's trip (with the taste of burning plastic), the blends effected a slower onset with a longer duration of effects, with users better able to navigate the experience.

The accessibility of the experience contrasts with ayahuasca ceremonies toward which Palmer and others have expressed their reservations. Involving expensive fees and what is perceived to be a constricting, even oppressive, ritual format, often held in big cities with growing numbers of participants crowded into single sessions, the value of these ceremonies has been challenged. Cheap, shorter in duration, without heavily structured ceremonial reliant on a shaman or guide, changa had advantages over ayahuasca. These differences are considered advantageous and empowering in a culture where many "are afraid of facing themselves, their own soul, intelligence and shadow nakedly." Responding to typical ayahuasca rituals, Palmer expresses a spiritual anarchist sensibility that insists upon the opportunity afforded to individual drinkers to lose control of their minds, "to really face their fears and go into the multitude of so many different levels of reality that can be very confronting to an individual's cultural programming."[69] But while loosening the reins on the mind is reckoned essential to the work of healing, to surrender control (and one's mind) to others is troubling within scenes where independence and self-responsibility are vaunted as the ultimate goals of growth and development—a paradox signaling the ambivalence toward conventional forms of shamanism expressed by the likes of Burroughs and Terence McKenna. All this said, Palmer conveys how "changa circles" have sprung up in Australia, South Africa, Norway, and elsewhere. "Swiss people are doing big circles of 100 people in Chile," he claimed.[70]

While ayahuasca rituals provided a point of departure, the association with ayahuasca and its purported "effect" was pivotal to the identity of changa from the outset. It was during a mid-2004 ayahuasca session that Palmer facilitated that the "changa" name "came through" to him. He clarified to me that "the Ayahuasca spirit is engaging with the human organism and doing what is essential healing work on different layers of the human bio-electrical system—which can often be clearly experienced by those attuned to this experience. You simply will not have this same feeling when smoking DMT crystal—the experience will perhaps feel more empty and less integrated."[71] Over the last decade, changa may well have become the most widely traveled route to an effect debatably analogous to "ayahuasca." It would inspire a pharmacopoeia of custom smoking blends, including those in Australia like the stronger "nanga" (Acacia-sourced DMT 50 percent and matured B. caapi vine shavings 45 percent by weight), "zanga," or the variety of blends known on DMT-Nexus as "enhanced leaf," or "10× changa," with users extolling the efficacy of B. caapi (i.e., its ability to inhibit MAO) and its therapeutic "afterglow" effects. Blends are also sometimes reported to be smoked after ayahuasca ceremonies to enhance the experience, circumstances that appear to dissolve boundaries between "recreational" and "ceremonial" use.

With entheo-missionary zeal, Palmer and his friends initiated changa directly to hundreds of people over a few years after 2004. "We learnt a lot about how to make sure that people smoked it properly, how to support people to be in the most conducive mindset, to ensure the best physical environment for them to go deep, present to them in a space of witnessing and also, after they had smoked the DMT, listen to their debriefing." Over ten years, Palmer and various international traveler acquaintances, who gifted changa and modified variations in private rituals, were responsible for changing the DMT playing field. "It was a kind of rebranding of DMT away from being this super monstrously intense 'death drug,' to a form where people often found in it, a kind of a graceful, herbal benediction."[72]

Smoked in bongs, pipes, and joints in living rooms, by rivers, on mountaintops, under wattle trees, and at festivals around the globe, changa use has proliferated. With Australia's Exodus Festival, Rainbow Serpent Festival, and Entheogenesis Australis event-plateaus of exchange and experimentation, psychedelic dance, visionary arts festivals, and entheobotanical symposia have been primary vehicles of transmission. In 2006, changa entered the slipstream for inner circles at Portugal's Boom Festival, after which it took root in far-flung locations, including Brazil, where DMT has been extracted from *Mimosa hostilis* to make changa, quickly gaining appeal in that country. According to Palmer, since the ambient heat in the region melts DMT crystal, Brazilians developed a preference for changa over DMT (although he added that Brazilians often do not use *B. caapi*, or other sources of harmalas, in their changa).[73] Intriguingly, many Brazilians think changa is an "ancient indigenous traditional blend." Given that *Anadenanthera peregrina* (or "yopo") beans (a source of DMT) are known to have been smoked in Jujuy Province, Argentina, some four thousand years ago—based on the discovery and analysis of smoking pipes made of puma bone at Inca Cueva—this belief might be based on conflation with historical practices.[74]

Among the chief crossroads of distribution was Holland, where twenty-three Conscious Dreams smart shops were raided by Dutch police in January 2007. Dutch authorities were chiefly concerned with the new "hallucinogen," and it is believed that an Interpol alert urged Australian

Federal Police to respond to the threat of dimethyltryptamine coming from Australia. Subsequently, Australian authorities took action, mounting a coordinated raid on twenty Happy High Herb shops in July 2008. It was DMT (i.e., in Dreamtime and changa) that Ray Thorpe believes was the chief cause for the raid. Many shopkeepers, along with Thorpe himself, were summoned into a "star chamber," the Australian Crime Commission's secret court set up under the Howard government to combat organized crime and terrorism. In this case, the ACC's ample resources were expended to terrorize wattle smokers, a circumstance known since at least 2006, when "shamanism became the new secret enemy."[75] In the dark, silent heart of the star chamber, those summoned were compelled to answer all questions, and were prohibited from communicating with anyone about the summons for five years, the punishment being two years' imprisonment. Disallowed legal representation, with lie detectors and cameras on him at all times, Thorpe was heavily grilled by the ACC, but was convinced his products were lawful. The DMT blends sold in his shops derived from Australian native flora—the nation's floral symbol no less. "They were trying to prosecute us for DMT," recalls Thorpe. But he surmised that if word escaped about the compound and where it is sourced, the drug laws would be under threat. "It would mean that every teenager would know that our revered wattle tree is a drug tree ... the drug laws would be blown apart ... I would bring publicity to all of that."[76] Would the authorities disclose the secret power of plants flowering in the national imaginary, flourishing in backyards, school yards, church grounds, and on government-owned land, and potentially triggering an entheogenic efflorescence? Apparently they weren't up to the challenge, as neither Thorpe nor any of his shopkeepers were charged. And although authorities have attempted to bring him down by other means—i.e., crackdowns on ephedra, kava, and even apricot kernels—what is now trading as Happy Herb Co. remains proudly in business.

And wattle trees remain legal, at the time of this writing. While DMT, and preparations containing it, is classified as a "controlled drug" by the Australian Therapeutic Goods Administration (TGA), there have been recent efforts to extend powers of control over its herbal sources. In the wake of recommendations from the International Narcotics Control Board, the fundamental shortcomings of which have been challenged by critics,[77] in 2013 the TGA launched a campaign to extend current law to enact comprehensive bans on all natural sources of psychoactives, including plants known to contain DMT. This effort failed following industry lobbying and public backlash voicing the ubiquity of *Acacias* and the absurdity of rendering citizens criminally responsible by fiat for owning property upon which native plants grow. It seems that, if passed, such laws would cast a bizarre shadow over domestic gardeners and government agencies alike—the latter using, for example, *Acacia longifolia* (a DMT source) extensively as a highway planting.

While Australian police were coordinating raids upon the Dreamtime, Jon Hanna was introducing Erowid to changa, and one could buy it or "xanga"—sometimes pronounced "CHAN-gah"—in Camden headshops for around £20–30 ($30–$45) a gram.[78] Changa developed commercial appeal from this period, a circumstance apparent at psychedelic festivals in Europe. In July 2013, I attended VIBE, a psytrance festival in the Czech Republic. Near the main dancefloor, I fell into conversation with DJs billed at the event, one of whom acquired a bag of changa from a passing dealer offering "acid, MDMA, and changa." The Russian novice lunged at the opportunity and bought half a gram for 50€ ($50) (the regular price for a gram). "This is one of the things I really want to do right now." As we'll see in the following chapters, in the world of psychedelic electronica, changa is a *now* phenomenon. It even motivated a short-lived commitment to establish psytrance as a "religion." The initiator of that idea was inspired by an experience at the United Kingdom's Glade Festival in 2009 where he smoked changa and saw "the most amazing alien beings dancing, flirting at me, a couple kissing and exploding in to a flood of multicoloured tesselated tiled fragments, the egyptian sun god Horus erupting from a foam of seething fractals. I saw homer simpson eating a doughnut and cathedrals of extreme beauty and colour. It was the most amazing 15 minutes of my life! Far better than any CGI visuals or computer graphics could generate ..."[79]

Reports like this read like advertisements for a temporary religious experience, with such conversions oiling the conversion of DMT into a commodifiable product. While its advent may facilitate an unprecedented desire for repeat DMT experiences, as Huston Smith has long observed, "religious experiences" (e.g., the "psychedelic theophany") do not amount to a "religious life."[80] Changa appears to offer an optimizable spiritual technology—a "smokable ayahuasca" no less—without the cumbersome weight, and obligations, of religion. And yet, lest this entire enterprise be dismissed as pure entheotainment, Erik Davis offered another view upon his exposure to "smokable ayahuasca." At Boom Festival 2008, up on a hill facing across Lake Idanha-a-Nova toward the ancient town of Monsanto, Portugal, he wrote:

> The smoke was sweet, and the entrance into the vestibule of the tryptamine palace was smooth but strong, and I slid gently along DMT's inside-outside Mobius strips of sentient energy with more clarity and with less anxiety than usual. My fingers folded into spontaneous mudras and the breath of fire sparked without will. Then the vibrating weave of nature's alien mind fluttered and unfolded us and set us gently back on the scraggly hillside, where the crickets and their ambient chirp-track trumped the distant thump of machines. Boom![81]

While this description evokes the gnostic potential of DMT and other entheogens, the apparent Disneyfication of hyperspace worries those lamenting changa as a front for the recreationalizing (and commercializing) of DMT (as "smokable ayahuasca"). The mood was forecast by DeKorne, for whom DMT is a molecule to be revered and respected. "I can't imagine it ever becoming a recreational drug—its nature is to sear away our illusions down to the core of being—a process few would describe as 'recreational.'"[82] And as for Nen, while the advent of changa changed the DMT playing field, it was not necessarily for the better. "The level and degree of ceremonial setting changed," as did the apprehensiveness and careful technique pivotal to the initiation. "In the early 90s it was with acacia DMT in glass pipes, in silent darkness, solo, one-on-one, or with as few people present as possible, with a lot of serious thought beforehand." With changa, what he calls "DMT-lite," "the full, pure breakthrough, which is what McKenna had inspired a generation to try," is dissipating like vapors on the wind.[83]

Out of the Jungle

While the advent of changa triggered dissension among acaciaphiles, its status as a "smokable ayahuasca" ignited debate between ayahuasqueros and changaleros. An article published in 2010 on *Reality Sandwich*, "Changa: The Evolution of Ayahuasca,"[84] fueled the controversy, with changa convert Chen Cho Dorge implying that ayahuasca had "evolved" into the smoking blend—a position he later retracted. For Dorge, the blends exemplified the way psychointegrator plants can "aid in human synergistic relationships with place just as these plants have done for the peoples of the Amazon." As ayahuasca and its effect have migrated "out of the jungle," changa was lauded as the "next evolutionary step for the synergistic shamanic technology." Dorge claimed that changa smoking shows influences from South American vegetalismo and curanderismo practices. "A new form of shamanry" was said to have emerged from practicing with these plant teachers. "A new entheogenic healing modality, new rituals, new ways of relating to ceremonial structure and the role of the healer as well are beginning to shift and transform—each adapting to the authentic needs of those working with this medicine."

But while ayahuasca was purportedly enjoying a facelift, the natives were getting restless over at Ayahuasca.com. Aya purists have typically been suspicious of spice users—who lack a certain legitimacy, if not virtue, so far removed from the cultural and theologically sanctioned traditions of brews and snuffs. In debates on Ayahuasca.com, defenders have voiced claims that DMT is "the crack of Ayahausca," that the beings it summons are "Mickey Mouse spirits," and that its users are little more than reckless cowboys. Ayahuasqueros adopt stances long taken against abuses (and abusers) of psychedelics, especially those who measure their experience in acts of psychedelic bravado and fleeting moments of tryptamine tourism. The accumulation of religious experience and spiritual capital without entering a religious life is disquieting for those whose use of ayahuasca is characterized by a commitment to ceremony, community, and ethos—and not simply "effect." Among committed ayahuasqueros and daimistas, those who smoke for "effect" and promote their practice or liken the experience to ayahuasca are appropriating and even expropriating tradition. Eyebrows are raised when practices appear directed more toward peak experience than integrative returns, when experience is not adequately integrated within an ethos by which one lives and acts in the world, when deep insights do not become the basis for the transformation of self, relationships, and the world. Psychologist Jorge Ferrer has identified processes by which such integrative work is arrested, with his observations inadvertently shedding light on the troubling appeal of the "ayahuasca effect." In his criticism of "intrasubjective reductionism," Ferrer observes how, in the modern obsession with inner experience to the exclusion of ethical commitments, community life, relationships with teachers, serious study of scripture, and other elements of traditional spiritual paths, peak experiences become little more than "temporary gratifications for an always hungry-for-heights Cartesian ego."[85] A consequence of objectifying spiritual phenomena and collecting peak experiences is that these experiences are more than often designed to maintain one's stature than to inaugurate realizations and transformations in one's lifeworld. Whether the significance of the DMT flash or the changa trance is to be rebuked in this way would require an in-depth study.

Responding to Dorge, visionary artist Daniel Mirante got down to brass tacks: "Ayahuasca is the indigenous Amazonian name for the Banisteriopsis caapi vine, where it has been used for thousands upon thousands of years in healing, sorcery, and cleansing. The vine is used as a gatekeeper to the realm of a myriad of medicinal plants, such as Ajo Sacha and Tobacco, which are 'dieted' in close proximity to the Vine." Furthermore, Mirante stated that "Ayahuasca lives within a unique complex of customs, traditions, knowledge and wisdom which are strong to this day, and continue to develop within syncretic communities and movements." While Mirante consented that analogues have facilitated profound healing and visionary states not unlike those associated with traditional ayahuasca brews, they should be respected as unique ethnobotanical phenomena. Furthermore, and this underlines the insult felt by many an ayahuascuero, "the Ayahuasca vine is not merely a facilitator for a DMT experience. It is a profound entheogenic plant teacher in its own right." The status of the ayahuasca vine as "an ambassador of the plant kingdom" is corroded when it becomes little more than "a delivery system for DMT."[86]

The advent of changa forced to the surface underlying resentment over claims that DMT is the active component of ayahuasca, the result of, according to Mirante, a wave of "DMT-centric" entheogenic literature in the early 1990s. By staking claims to the "ayahuasca effect," users were effectively lauding the "DMT effect," and the implication that changa was an *evolutionary* improvement upon, or successor to, ayahuasca was like pouring gasoline on the fire. Critics like Mirante were concerned that the champions of changa and other custom products with an ostensible "ayahuasca effect" were usurping the cultural power of ayahuasca. "To claim any plant combination that enables DMT to become orally active is 'Ayahuasca,' or more, that the DMT effect = 'Ayahuasca effect' = Ayahuasca itself, is trouble on grounds of cultural appropriation, because it ignores a living indigenous tradition, language, etymology, folklore, taxonomy." The threat posed by DMT-centric sensibilities in the time of ayahuasca analogues is then reminiscent of the threat to "tradition" imagined to follow the advent of *ayahuasca affectations* more generally, including "drug tourism" in the Amazonas,[87] or post-traditional urban, neoshamanic, and New Age ayahuasca practices that were allegedly "inauthentic."

For Julian Palmer, it is unnecessary to validate changa through an association with ayahuasca-using traditions. In a response to Dorge and Mirante, Palmer argues that changa is primarily an augmentation of DMT. It is an optimal vehicle for an "analogue" experience that not only makes DMT accessible, but facilitates the DMT/MAOI mechanism for more users worldwide than ayahuasca.[88] Referring to changa as a "mini-ayahuasca" experience, Palmer stated that ayahuasca "is not always readily available in every country. Good luck finding ayahuasca in Skopje, Macedonia! However, you may well be able to find people there smoking changa." Furthermore, once adapted to changa, smokers often elect to "go deeper with the brew." Neither constituting an evolution from ayahuasca, nor serving as a substitute for it, changa and its own proliferating analogues would then seem to grease the mechanisms of use, perhaps even becoming an accessory of the ayahuasca experience. As Palmer notes, changa "is already its own tradition."[89] As a fully customizable tradition suited to the contemporary entheogen user, and with variations of its aromatic vapors recognizable in locations worldwide, it appears that, with changa and its variations, the DMT/ayahuasca effect will continue to evolve.

The "ayahuasca effect" is a conceit received with reservation at the DMT-Nexus. Given that many plants substituted as "ayahuasca analogues" are known to contain a variety of alkaloids other than the DMT/harmalas synergy, not only are they recognized to possess varying modes of action, but a respect for the unique "signature, spirit, or energy" of each plant is cultivated in a way not dissimilar to that of the animistic traditions of world plant medicine systems. In an agenda-setting pace adopted in *The Nexian*, changa and other practices involving DMT and the extracts of a variety of admixture plants are thought to be more closely associated with the probably much older Amazonian traditions utilizing tryptamine-containing snuffs and smoking mixtures than with the Amazonian ayahuasca traditions. Embracing contemporary smoking and insufflating practices as "entheogenic folk medicine" characterized as innovative rediscoveries, for Nexians jamie and nen888 these forms of administration "present fertile ground for new modes of personal healing, reflection, and insight, beyond just ayahuasca and the curandero—the 'warrior-explorer,' as McKenna put it." While ayahuasca has become the paragon of entheogenic tryptamine folkways in the West, the discussion at the DMT-Nexus serves to uncover a world of folk DMT and tryptamine use that existed before ayahuasca and that continues in a myriad of evolving forms. Changa is then symptomatic of an entheogenic efflorescence that better approximates these "other traditional practices" than it does ayahuasca, while at the same time embodying "a sovereign, grassroots, neo-folk approach as a living, evolving Western tradition."[90] By "other traditional practices," the authors refer not only to South American traditions of using DMT, 5-MeO-DMT, and bufotenin-containing snuffs and smoking mixtures, but to the adoption of tryptamine-containing plants since antiquity. What was the significance of *Acacia* trees for ancient Egyptians, in Africa, the Middle East, India, China/East Asia, and the Pacific/Oceania? Did the ancient Greeks use *Phalaris* grasses?[91] Was the harmala alkaloid–containing plant *Peganum harmala* integral to the soma/haoma of the Indian Vedas and the ancient Persian Avesta?[92] This is to ask nothing about the historical usage and significance of psilocybin, which has fueled an industry of speculation. There appears

to be enough speculation on the ancient history of DMT and related entheogenic tryptamine use, and their possible remnants, to fill volumes.

As for Australia, with the knowledge that there are 150 species of
DMT-containing plants on the continent, Nen became drawn toward their
ostensible use by those who have inhabited the continent for more than
sixty thousand years.[93] In a series of "DreaMTime Invasion" lectures in
the United Kingdom in 2013, Nen proposed that the indigenous Australian philosophy of the "Dreamtime"—which refers to neither the past nor
the future, but an "eternal creation out of pattern in the Now," and which
teaches that the living are "shadow beings" cast by higher or ancestral
beings—resonates with the experience of DMT "hyperspace." More than
that, with the emergence of "plant teachers" through which growing numbers of nonindigenous peoples access indigenous wisdom, he envisions "a
reverse colonization of the modern world—the Dreamtime Invasion."[94]

With the aim to "empower individuals, while still honoring the intact traditions of indigenous peoples," jamie and nen888 echo the views of the
underground research community flourishing at the DMT-Nexus. "As we
watch the collective flames engulf our dying world," they write, "we have
a chance at remediation, at the cultivation of a seed that can begin mending
our broken culture and transforming the traumas of this world." Not the
commercialized and packaged "empty vessel of appropriated cultural ide-
ologies," but the folk traditions of the "entheogenic revival" are perceived
to embody this opportunity.[95] The DMT-Nexus and the *pièce de résistance* of
its research culture apparatus, *The Nexian*, illustrate how, as David Nickles
put it, "the underground is active, regardless of the desires of sanctioned
researchers." And it will, he added, "continue to engage in research and
will continue to present results and information to the public."[96] Many
advances in our comprehension of DMT, its composition, effects, sources,
and the mechanisms of its augmentation, are attestations of the underground research culture that dialogues, collaborates, and disseminates
at the DMT-Nexus, and flourishes within the wider cyber-undergrowth.
Receiving the baton from *The Entheogen Review,* and evolving from small
circles to a community of users whose veneration for "teacher plants"

(perhaps more than "spirit molecules") is expressed in the awareness of diverse plant sources grown from seed and nurtured, the DMT-Nexus is an interactive resource whose participants build databases, share knowledge, compare techniques, crack botanical codes, and even formulate courses in an "Entheogenic University." This and other independent, net-enabled communities, forums, and portals constitute the variegated research arm of a grassroots entheogenic movement whose collective output may help illuminate the way out of the dark age of prohibition.

CHAPTER 7

Remixticism
Media Shamans and Entheonica

"Heavy doses of dimethyltryptamine." The string of words passes over the dancefloor like a concord . . . and we're all ablaze . . . driven beyond fatigue into a transfiguring grace. It's the last day of the festival. Or is it the second to last? Who cares, for at this moment the founder of California's Moontribe, DJ Treavor, is at the helm of the Dance Temple, at the 2010 edition of Portugal's Boom Festival, where twenty-five thousand freaks from more than seventy countries have disassembled. We're inside the Mothership, and right now, we are its abductees, getting pasted to the firmament by way of a digital, chemical, and cyber artifice, an optimized multisensorial tsunami that sweeps all before it. And our date with the cosmos has a hypnotic rhythm, complete with backing vocals. The songline—on this occasion a vocal sample programmed into a track produced by Israeli duo Quantize and played by Treavor, who performs within a stellated dodecahedron DJ portal before a cast of thousands—is a superliminal suggestion both echoing and amplifying the desirable altered state, quantized into the rhythm as the indole vapor of a fresh spice blend hangs pungent in the air.

You could feel the news in the music and greet its bouquet on the breeze. I bump into nanobrain, who is presiding over an expertly hewn doof bong and a potent changa derivative he styled "nanga." He's sporting a surgeon's smock and a cap that says "Head Turkey." An animated ghettoscientist known for experiments reversing the Coriolis effect, nanobrain collapses the boundaries on standard procedure. He is the lost captain of soul, a genuine duck-steppa, and right now he's deep inside his element. His blend contains Peruvian *Banisteriopsis caapi* vine shavings and DMT, proudly announced to have been "coaxed from Aussie *acacialoids* by alchemical maestros." And then the bass drops: "50/50 percentage ratio by weight, mixed with intent and charged with love . . . vibrate to integrate,

BOOM!" Inside the Dance Temple under a light sun-drenched misting system, there is no formal ritual, nor formal lessons, but as of this inhalation, I'm getting an education on the blending of form and perception. As I exhale, everything starts making sense as every sense dissolves in definition. Amid a fractalized task force of subwoofer worshippers, my fingers are drawn to outline the frequencies that grow visible before me. And as I wheel on a 360 degree axis of smiling, high-definition vibe pilgrims, and my bare feet go subterranean like worms in the sand, I commence shaking hands with god at 148 bpm.

Digital Media Techgnosis

At Boom, I had arrived at the crucible of the visionary arts dance movement, a place where all of one's senses are accounted for and rearranged. Like passengers aboard a transdimensional lightship, participants behave as altered sensory lifeforms. And inside the interactive theater of Boom's Dance Temple, I was exposed to ways DMT has shaped the sonic mythography and visionary artistry of natives of the digital age. I became witness to a *remixtical* artifice in which media and molecules are remixed and sampled to fashion a vibrant mystique shared by dancefloor participants. By *remixticism,* I mean the practice by which producers of electronic music and visual arts evoke nonordinary states of consciousness augmented by audio/video detritus sampled and repurposed from disparate un/popular cultural resources. In the repurposing of source materials, DJ/producers are medianauts cobbling together story-lines of dream travel, soul flight, and cosmic transit using materials ripped from the worldwide datasphere. While it is standard procedure that in programming and DJ/VJ techniques, artists recycle existing recordings to compose new works, as digital alchemists they will ransack films, TV documentaries, game software, radio shows, podcasts, and other sources for choice material. In multiple electronic dance music genres, scripted syntax from science-fiction cinema, sound bites from political speeches, counsel from religious figures, the routines of comedians, and the extemporizations of altered statesmen are sampled in koan-like epigrams, repeated like chorus lines, reassembled as audio-bombs detonating at the breakdown. Via electrosonic techniques, this repurposed media ecology provides the sonic decor to the ecstatic experience, decaling the soundscape, and augmenting the vibe, on dancefloors planetwide. Since the late 1990s within the psychedelic electronic milieu, "DMT" would resound like a mantra in the chaos.

The roots of this media shamanism can be found in an esoteric cut-up heritage including Dadaists, Surrealists, Burroughsians, and Discordians alike. It is steeped in Jamaican dub, hip-hop, breakbeat science, house, techno, and chill DJs who've broken down, re-versioned, and synthesized existing works to birth new form. This refinement is notable in techno-shamanic traditions and is overt in psy-electronica, where media content is intentionally strip-mined and reprogrammed to spiritual endeavors—to augment, parrot, and burlesque *spirit*. This milieu is drenched in an unmistakable penchant for "shamanism," a sensibility that reveals dedication toward vision and gnosis over the healing and catharsis of traditional curanderos, commitments that place this development in the vanguard of contemporary Western esoteric religion. Newly promulgated through popular culture, or as alternative religions scholar Christopher Partridge might have it, "popular occulture," sonic murals of alien gurus, ancient astronauts, superheroes, spirit familiars, DMT entities, and other in-between figures communicate a desire for *being liminal,* a transitional experience marking passage beyond the ordinary, potentiating exposure to *the way*.[1] As a carrier-wave of the counterculture, one part genuine, another hubristic, and other parts immeasurable, from its inception, *liminal experience* became a preoccupation of Goatrance producers who plundered the global media database to capture the essence of the Goa "state of mind" and project their intimacy with the *project* of transition.[2] Among the first Goatrance acts, The Infinity Project amplified the condition for those greeting a new day: "Seven AM, as the day begins, the drug is inhaled to introduce the strange language of the initiation rites."[3] Later, on another dancefloor in another decade ambient/dub project Blue Lunar Monkey (Mexican Daniel Gradilla) takes up the fate of the initiates. "The peyote takes hold ... the senses send them on a journey, not across the land, but inside their heads. Guided by the shaman they enter the spirit world and encounter their own god."[4]

Dicing and splicing media content to evoke the sensation of altered time-space, DJ/producers like Gradilla offer repeated commentary on themes linked by their association with altered states of consciousness—shamanism, astral traveling, out-of-body experiences, near-death experiences, alien abductions, hypnosis, dreaming, chemically enhanced hallucinations. A veritable pharmacopoeia has been mixed into the jam with sounds becoming carriers of bioassaying audio alchemists journaling their experience in sound productions, lightwork, and visionary art. In 1997, the legendary Danish mind experimentalists Koxbox went "Searching for Psychoactive Herbs," the ultimate track on Blue Room Released classic *Dragon Tales,* an inspired album cleaving away from the astral-planes drifters hallmarking the Goa tradition. While psychoactive compounds are especially common in sampledelic tactics within the psychedelic electronic continuum, there is no definitive narrative, as aptitudes can be transgressive or progressive, the heroes outlaw or folklore, psychedelic fictions noisy or gnostic, the carnival zany or dark. Enabling dialogue with states of consciousness beyond the ordinary, chosen content may hold the uncanny familiarity of an inner voice. "As your attorney I advise you to take a hit out of the little brown bottle in my shaving kit. You won't need much, just a tiny taste." As the pace builds to a consistent thud, and as effects are used with an impact not unlike that of a slowly tightening head clamp, a sonic billboard lights up: "That stuff makes pure mescaline seem like ginger beer, man." These samples are found on Hungarian Para Halu's "Adrenochrome,"[5] a track named after a questionably psychoactive compound the use of which was mythologized in the fiction of H. S. Thompson. But while some texts, such as the familiar voice of Dr. Gonzo from *Fear and Loathing in Las Vegas,* are exploited to connote mythically transgressive states, others are deployed to invoke neognostic quests aided by compounds and decoctions revered as "entheogens." Visionary artist Alex Grey, for example, recalls "a kind of taunting voice in the back of my mind that was saying to me, 'get in touch with the ayahuasca.'"[6] In Serbian act Sideform's progressive "Santo Daime," audio graffiti effectively promotes the mystical experience commonly associated with the Amazonian brew. Switching floors and venues, Grey's voice appears again and again. Amid exotic wildlife and shamans' song backed by a slow-burning arrangement care of Merkaba, he whispers in the ear of the entranced: "the plants are talking to us, we need to listen."[7]

186

The yagé aesthetic has grown louder in recent times, wrapping itself around psychedelica like thick coils of *B. caapi*. The growth evokes an *entheonic* sensibility curated by a transnational milieu of DJs, promoters, and converts. The entheo-electronic mission was abroad in the work of Ayahuasca, the name adopted in 1994 for a short-lived collaboration between Joti Sidhu, Dino Psaras, and Steve Ronan. Sampling and mixing techniques sometimes allegorize the synergistic techniques of vegetalismo, notably that evident in ayahuasca shamanism. Decades downwind from Burroughs, the title of Ayahuasca's compilation *Digital Alchemy* seemed to resound with exactitude given the jungle alchemy required to produce ayahuasca. Labels like TIP World became clearinghouses for this kind of alchemy, distributing their new mixes to be cut, boiled down, and infused worldwide. Try this!

Around the turn of the millennium, artists were seeking to diversify their audio stashbag, perhaps none more so than 1200 Mics, formed by Raja Ram, Chicago, Shajahan Matkin, and Joe Quinteros (the latter two being Riktam and Bansi of Spanish outfit GMS). The act's name seemed to illustrate that, far from being psycholytic sissies, band members and their fanbase were prepping to ramp up the doses in the tradition of the psychedelic warrior. Closing track "DMT" followed a smorgasbord of sonic anthems on debut album *1200 Micrograms*, serving up an entheonic feast for the *flâneurs* of altered mind states. On the opener, "Ayahuasca," exotic birdlife explodes in the canopy and there's a voice: "A thousand years ago deep in the darkest jungles of the Amazon, the ancient Incas discovered the mystical vine to brew up the sacred psychoactive hallucinogenic drink, the holy *ayahuasca* . . . you enter a special magical dimension, the dimension of the spirit world." A polyrhythm builds with the faint suggestion of a liquid growl repeated behind the pace. With the purging having begun, the session is in full swing as 1200 Mics guide their listeners through a substance-induced odyssey, via "Hashish," "Mescaline," "LSD," "Marijuana," "Ecstasy," "Magic Mushrooms," and "Salvia Divinorum," before "DMT" is dropped into the mix.[8] In this fashion, 1200 Mics have distributed their product to DJs who've mixed from this entheonic smorgasbord for dance-floors around the world.[9]

Through the first decade of the twenty-first century, the allusion to ayahuasca multiplied as artists guided enthusiasts deeper into the forest to source the ingredients needed to concoct the visionary brew. A commentator on Swiss Ralph Knobloch's (a.k.a. Braincell's) "Psychoactive Plants" promotes a concoction "made by the Indians of the Amazon from a congregation of jungle vines and leaves that is brewed into a purple tea that produces a psychedelic experience."[10] Someone aboard Tron's (Mexican Patricio Pinero) "Amasonic" tells rumor of a "psychoactive beverage" called "ayahuasca," the word regurgitated amid spindly electric vines and satisfying purges that erupt throughout its sonic jungle.[11] Deeper in the forest the sounds metamorphose into a seething undergrowth of fractal insects and scandent vines. Locating the ingredients, Australians Dark Nebula & Scatterbrain saddled up to neck the potion: "Everything sounds really loud and alive. I'm seeing iridescent rainbow spirals and complex geometric patterns. Feels like I'm being bombarded by some sort of ancient knowledge or universal consciousness."[12] A few years later, the remediated fragment "complex geometric patterns" resonates at the heart of "Aya," the centerpiece of Canadian Ekoplex's (Ray Vincent's) mesmerizing *Discovering the Ancient*. And icaros echo throughout these soundscapes, as is amplified in Fragletrollet's forest trance release "Shamanizer," or Merkaba's "Icaro," released on the entheonic masterwork *Language of Light*.[13] Having climbed the jungle vine and seen the visions, a female convert is frank about her mission aboard SiLo and Humerous's "New Path." Having done "two ayahuasca ceremonies," she announces with conviction: "I have to teach people about it."[14] If the reputation of Darpan, leader of Australian ayahuasca ceremonies, is any measure, the icaros have floated out of the Amazon and around the world. Darpan's work shows that *la purga* can be performed closer to home (than the Amazon) for Western drinkers, as illustrated by his popular ceremonies. And why is this significant? "It's a holographic library. It speaks to you in visions. It communicates through pictures. You're also very sensitive to sound. Sounds can influence wherever you go, so we use sounds as a navigator. We use intent, and we use sound. Ayahuasca can be seen as a doorway, a link between the dimensions."[15]

Among the many who've faced the music and heard the calling, Brazilian psy-prog artist Rafael Corrales (Via Axis) celebrates excursions into the "Tryptamine Dimensions."[16] With its passage to the brain protected by the harmalas (notably from *B. caapi* bark) in the ayahuasca brew, it is

DMT that has given specific shape, color, and form to entheonica. Since the mid-1990s, electrosonic productions in the psychedelic diaspora, and, by implication, dancefloor habitués themselves, have been smudged with DMT. If we listen to sound bites broadcast in a host of productions, it's like tuning in to an underground radio show, where the news is delivered in cut-up. On the cutting-room floor, event-goers are exposed to important announcements. "I remember the very, very first time I smoked DMT." This is Terence McKenna reminiscing at a 1993 Parallel YOUniversity lecture at London's Megatripolis about his life-changing experience in 1965, as sampled on "DMT" by 1200 Mics.[17] In other news, Alex Grey reports "DMT is one of the most potent hallucinogens known to humanity. Most often it's smoked and when you do that you break through very rapidly within thirty seconds to, say, a peak of an LSD experience and so alternative realities come up very fast."[18] Onboard "Baraka," included on their 2006 self-titled debut album, F.F.T. (a.k.a. Future Frequency Technology) transmit the news in brief, which is repeated in the breakdown: "for the vast majority of people, DMT was the most powerful psychedelic experience of their entire lives." Later, author Graham Hancock does the journaling: "DMT is astonishingly widely available in plants and animals all around the world and so far nobody really knows why it's there or what its function is."[19] With these select editorials, digital media techgnosticians program the news, with tracks serving as media of transmission for DMT consciousness.

The Red Pill

DMT is a megatonnage hallucinogen. It occurs naturally in the metabolism of every single one of us. At this moment you're holding a schedule one drug and are subject to immediate arrest and trial.[20]

Listening to electronica programmed with the lexicon of an altered statesman is like attending a symposium in which delegates on the dancefloor are chewing the perforated CliffsNotes. And if dancefloors like Boom's Dance Temple are like symposia, then Terence McKenna delivers the keynote address, in endless permutations and filtered reiterations. McKenna is clearly the voice most heard in this movement, if the frequency of track samples is anything to go by. While Leary's voice was solicited ad nauseam in early Goa productions, the new mood was captured by UK legends Eat Static, reusing McKenna's voice on "Prana" on 1993 release *Abduction:* "we're not dropping out here, we're infiltrating and taking over."[21] This preference belies a penchant for gnosis, for, as we've seen, McKenna was an advocate of tryptamine-derived gnosis. And yet if the seeker cutting sick on the floor intends to depart with lecture notes bristling in sacred formulas delivered unto them by the anointed ones inside the Divine Disco, should we be surprised if their notepads are blank in the light of day? Perhaps they are not unlike the *mystai,* who, having drunk the *kykeon* inside the Telesterion, the main temple at Eleusis in ancient Greece, could not communicate the *aporrheta*—the unrepeatables—to the uninitiated after the rites of passage into the cult of Demeter and Persephone; not only because they were prohibited to do so upon pain of death, but because they actually *could not*—their shared experiences essentially unGreekable outside the grounds of the Festival of Eleusis. Perhaps the primary *knowledge* to be had in the Telesterions of electronica is the *experience of unknowing,* a noetic experience that may well be the secret held close by the architects of a visionary apparatus cultivated in events like Boom, Burning Man, and other cocreated events. Despite efforts among modern-day *mystai* to blog, tweet, and text-message their revelations, their experiences are essentially incomprehensible beyond the precincts of the vibe itself.

As made manifest in their visionary assemblages and in the craft of remediation, sensory engineers conspire to enhance the experience of the unknown on dancefloors planetwide. They manipulate media to unsettle and confound the senses, effecting exposure to the anomalous, that which defies logic, disobeys physics, is nonsensical—conditions causing stupefaction. In short bursts, sample-smiths find the words to explicate what words can't explain. Liquid on Safi channel McKenna: "I go to a place where language finds it very hard to pull over, look around. It's almost as though it takes you to a world that is not English."[22] Deploying the *words* of McKenna to convey this *world* would become a commonplace technique, faithful to revelations concerning language deriving from sufficient doses of tryptamines. "What the alien voice in the psychedelic experience wants to reveal is the syntactical nature of reality," McKenna had stated in 1993 in

Alien Dreamtime. "That the real secret of magic is that the world is made of words, and that if you know the words that the world is made of, you make of it whatever you wish."[23] Audio/visual media hackers subsequently re-sutured and synthesized the syntax of the wizard of words himself to express the notion of the world made manifest through sound. This is not to suggest, as might be inferred, that the artifice of psychedelic electronica has been swamped by McKennaesque audio-koans to the point of saturation and suffocation, but that his ranging across multiple fields at the nexus of technology and spirituality has provided a catacomb of reference points for artists themselves seeking to project sound that can be seen, read, or felt.

In psychedelic electronica with a distinctly progressive accent, unsettling the senses is harnessed to the goal of *self-discovery.* Transiting through extremes, meeting challenges, the synthesis of opposites, becoming familiar with the unknown, the process of self-becoming is deeply layered in the soundscape, which shows the influence of transpersonal psychology and possesses hints of Gurdjieff, Jung, and Eckhart Tolle. Digital natives poach a variety of religious traditions whose symbolic heritage offers passports to the truth from which humanity has deviated, and from which the individual has been separated. Their efforts offer support to the perception that an awakening to this separation will precede a return. Others are more committed to the view that momentum builds not from reawakening, but in the dawning of a new consciousness. Others still, pass between these romantic and ascensionist becomings. But whether primal return or posthuman evolution, the trigger is a eureka moment, a detonation that blasts away that which shrouds the truth. In sampledelic transmissions, the answers are to be found within the vast, undiscovered landscape of the interior, the locked hard-drive of the mind, accessible with the right keys, or combinations, a view consistent with current knowledge of the neuropharmacology of DMT, that it functions in ways analogous to a neurotransmitter, that it acts on brain receptor sites like chords struck in a symphony. "The real information is locked within ourselves," Merkaba reminds the meditative massive. "The point is to open up the potential that we have."[24] The payload here is heavy on the theme of possibility, the potency of the threshold, the moment of transmission. In a virtual library of transmissions, producers are giving voice to the perception that it is possible to discover *things as they really are;* that the truth is available to habitués who can taste the bass, see the frequencies, smell the color, feel that they know, a synestheticized techno-etics shared with compatriots, right here, right now. As Captain Morpheus declared, by way of Astral Projection, "I believe this night holds for each and every one of us the very meaning of our lives."[25]

The Matrix series has indeed been a popular resource in the awakening, where sampled dialogue speaks to the effects of entheogens—i.e., triggering an awakening to truths previously hidden. Conjuring the image of a shaman offering a vessel of dirty brown liquid, or a seasoned purveyor of DMT crystal, a voice (that of Captain Morpheus) communicates to the questing neophyte via 9West: "Do you want to know what it is? It's all around us, here even in this room. You can see it out your window, or on your television. You feel it when you go to work, or go to church or pay your taxes. It is the world that has been pulled over your eyes to blind you from the truth."[26] The familiar narrative is not uncommonly interposed with McKenna, who stands astride an invisible podium championing the "light-filled vegetable" illuminating the darkness.

> We have no idea what it would mean in our own lives if we could throw off the notion of ourselves as fallen beings. We are not fallen beings. When you take into your life the gnosis of the light-filled vegetable . . . the first thing that comes to you is: you are a divine being. You matter. You count. You come from realms of unimaginable power and light, and you will return to those realms.[27]

A decade earlier, Morpheus had dropped the pharmacological payload on 1200 Mics's "DMT": "This is your last chance. After this, there is no turning back. You take the blue pill—the story ends. You wake up in your bed and believe whatever you want to believe. You take the red pill—you stay in Wonderland and I show you how deep the rabbit hole goes."[28]

These lines were spoken in almost the same breath that Terence is heard to recall his first experience smoking DMT. Consonant with DMT or other tryptamines, the red pill confirms the gnostic theodicy that all is not right in the world, whereas the "blue pill" may represent prescription suppressants that generally *blind you from the truth,* or other substances of addiction, principally alcohol, but also methamphetamine and cocaine, that make escape from the Matrix illusory. The red pill is the ultimate solution for the shamanarchist, the antidote to oppression, the key to the gates of the New Jerusalem, a subterranean city down the rabbit hole named "Zion," depicted in *The Matrix Reloaded* as a cavernous dance club. The distinction between Morpheus, captain of the *Nebuchadnezzar,* and McKenna, the loquacious linguist—or for that matter, between DMT and the "red pill"—appears to have dissipated on "The Exorcism of the Spirit" by Romanian Andrei Oliver Braşovean (a.k.a. Atma): "The morphogenetic field, the invisible world that holds it all together, the knit of it all.... It's been hidden from us for centuries because of the exorcism of the spirit that took place in order to allow science to do business."[29]

Since the release of both *The Matrix* into the popular imagination and Terence McKenna into the afterlife, spores, vapors, and vines would infiltrate the sonics and optics of psychedelic electronica and its many afterparties. Sometimes artists have projected McKenna as a seer; other times he materializes like a specter in a séance. In 2001, Avihen Livne saddled up with Jörg Kessler, legendary manager of label Shiva Space Technology, and, as Cosma Shiva, they produced "In Memory of Terence McKenna." The track features instructions from the beyond from you know who: "vaporize it in a small glass pipe.... A shaman is someone who has been to the end, is someone who knows how the world really works.... What the alien voice in the psychedelic experience wants to reveal is ..." And later Terence's ghost speaks in the unintelligible alien tongue he sometimes delivered in his lectures. With their material saturated in the effects of DMT and ayahuasca, the ethnodelic outfit Entheogenic (Helmut Glavar and Piers Oak-Rhind) offered a sounding board for McKenna. The opening track on *Spontaneous Illumination,* "Ground Luminosity," heads off into a deep jungle vibe, with birdcalls, insects buzzing, and water flowing over rocks, all nurtured by flute and warm percussive lines. And the epigrammatic voice of McKenna: "The search for a doorway out of mundane experience ... Nature is the great visible engine of creativity."[30] An apparent tribute to the work coauthored by the brothers McKenna, "Invisible Landscapes" begins with the bard: "life is a problem to be solved ... it's a conundrum. It's not what it appears to be. There are doors. There are locks and keys.

There are levels. And if you get it right, somehow it will give way to something extremely unexpected." The keys are subsequently jingled before listeners in the echoing chant of "ayahuasca." "Twilight Eyes" has a classic orchestral feel, with Terence averring that "shamans in times and places gained their power through relationships with helping-spirits." And with the line—from *I, Claudius*—"I promise you, you'll dream a different story altogether," the dancer is set adrift with McKenna standing on a ceaseless shoreline proclaiming "imagination, really, is the last frontier," while waving the wayfarer off into deep dreamspace.

Complex Geometric Patterns

But just where was all this digital regurgitation heading as the first decade of the new millennium ground on? Apparently, deeper inside the carnival of experience. In the '60s, Leary recognized that to convey one's current status on a high-dose psychedelic compound was as futile as communicating one's status while pulling Gs on a roller coaster. An "experiential language" was required, a set of protocols established through repeated testing. By the end of the century, through years of experimentation, a multimediated sensory apparatus—i.e., *the dancefloor*—appears to have evolved to form an experiential language that was being repeated back to its habitués. There was no need for words from occupants defying gravity on the dancefloor, that kinetic machine operated by the arms and legs of its passengers. The Learyesque "readouts" were now washing over one's sensorium inside the vibe: "I saw what life is really about. . . . imagining a supergalactic roller-coaster, and you just have to hold on."[31]

If the dancefloor was becoming a psychedelic amusement park, then repurposed voices were sounding much like barkers on a fairground midway coaxing the ambulatory raver to become disoriented in the Scrambler, take a plunge on the Megadrop, or ride the Mysterious Experience. "It starts quite quickly and there's quite a strong rush . . . and there's quite a display of geometric, kaleidoscopic visual imagery," announces the barker on Blue Lunar Monkey's "Mysterious Xperience," before becoming circumspect: "I think what may occur with DMT is that it opens specific doorways, which are otherwise closed, and through those doorways it is possible to make contact with external freestanding kinds of real experiences."[32] By 2009, the door to eternity seems to have been left ajar. Israeli Hujaboy's formulaic "Liquifried" offers American comedian and host of game show *Fear Factor* Joe Rogan's digest of McKenna and Strassman: "it's called dimethyltryptamine. It's produced by your pineal gland. It's actually a gland that's in the center of your brain. It's the craziest drug ever. It's the most potent psychedelic known to man, literally. But the craziest thing about it is it's natural and your brain produces it every night as you sleep. You know, when you sleep, during the time you're in heavy REM sleep and right before death your brain pumps out heavy doses of dimethyltryptamine."[33]

In 2006 Rogan had become a convert, even acquiring for himself a full-sleeve tattoo depicting his breakthrough experience in which he had witnessed a "Thai Buddha entirely made of energy" warning him "not to give in to astonishment." After this time, his radio podcasts became highly sampleable resources. At this juncture, Rogan's rants were upgraded to high-frequency replay. "Life is a massive fucking mystery. And there's only a few different ways to really crack below the surface of that mystery. And the best way is psychedelics."[34] The same bark had been used by Hujaboy, except he decided to include "and the heavier the psychedelic, the better." Mood Deluxe permitted Rogan another breath: "And guess what? No one's dying from psychedelics. All our thoughts on psychedelics are all based on bullshit propaganda, that you heard about people, you know, going crazy and losing their minds. You're not gonna go crazy, you're gonna go fucking sane."[35] The audio billboard for the red pill was earlier projected by darkpsy act Polyphonia vs. Zik: "you take this shit and literally you are transformed into another fucking dimension," with Mister Black subsequently plagiarizing the same monologue: "you should all smoke DMT and join my cult mother fucker!"[36] This radio recording is then intercepted by Fobi vs Mr. Madness, who fuses Rogan's cheerleading with the equivalent of psychedelic marching music, a.k.a. "full-on": "If you don't dream you'll go fucking crazy and you die. While you're in heavy rhapsody you are going through a psychedelic trip, and very few people know about this."[37] And by the time Israeli duo Reshef Harari and Adi Ashkenazi (a.k.a. Quantize) arrived on the scene, any subtlety appears to have vaporized.

Their "Dymethyltryptamine" [sic] begins with the filtered voice of McKenna repeating "DMT," which quickens next to the pulse before Rogan bursts through with the new black: "heavy doses of dimethyltryptamine."[38]

In response to Rogan's pied-piperesque screed, on "Join My Cult," Swede Wizack Twizack (Tommy Axelsson) is unequivocal: "I'm in."[39] It's difficult to measure the impact of these remediations that I am selectively sampling, in turn. For Milosz Zielinski, a psychedelic DJ from Bern, Switzerland, while it's possible that exposure to this kiosk of samples led him to try DMT in 2008,[40] he can't be certain about where he first caught the meme. With electric black frizzy hair, looking like a character from the pen of Robert Crumb, Milosz is an avid reader of books like Narby's *Cosmic Serpent*. He's also been a darkpsy/forest DJ for fifteen years. DJ Milosz specifically recalls laying down the digital billboard that is Polyphonia vs. Zik's "Fucking Dimensions" where Rogan announces "you should all smoke DMT and join my cult mother fucker!" But the effect of the sound bite on the audience is as wide as there are listeners, whose interpretations are influenced by many factors, including simple misrecognition. After all, Milosz had misread the above line as "smoke DMT and suck my cock mother fucker!" It's an irreverent attitude entirely consistent with the mood of fast-paced psychedelic night music, neurotrance, or hi-tech in the vein of Psykovsky, Fatal Discord, or Jesus Raves, masters of the unrelenting scatological cartoonscape that tends to warp meaning beyond recognition. This is not straightforward psychedelic marching music in the vein of Astral Projection, or an expression of a desire to Return to the Source, but the sonic architectonics to going out of your mind. That said, the out-of-body states, astral traveling, and consciousness research resonant with the Goatrance legacy remain key interests for Milosz as a DJ and independent researcher who investigates the relationship between DNA and consciousness by way of a study of DMT experiences, offering a lecture on the subject at Breaking Convention in London in 2013.

While it may be impossible to measure the reception of nanomediations, dancefloor occupants are blanketed by a blizzard of samples. In the formula-driven universe of psytrance, artist monikers, track names, and samples become earnest indexes of spiritual capital, as appears to be presented by Spirit Molecule's "Psychedelic Journey," layered ad nauseam with vocal hooks: "DMT," "LSD," "mescaline," and "psychedelic drugs."[41] Similarly, Therange Freak breaks into a dark, moody forest trance with tribal drums before sledgehammering the floor with "ayahuasca," "DMT," and "the full range of human consciousness."[42] By 2009, even progressive house fans were being audio-banner dropped with the stuff, care of Dutch producer Exoplanet by way of the oft-repeated sample phrases "a compound called DMT" and "DMT stands for Dimethyltryptamine" on the track called, no prizes for guessing, "Dimethyltryptamine."[43] But back in the psychedelic playground proper, Serbian Nikola Gasic, as Sonic Entity, was smearing "DMT," Rogan, and Grey all over his "Spirit Molecule," while Mexican Dr. Hoffman (Cristhian Robles) wasn't to be denied his very own "Spirit Molecules."[44] Other tracks have served as intrascene commentaries, like private memos with amusing punch lines recognizable to insiders. With its pound and drill action, Mexican Xikwri Neyrra's "Knockin' on Matrix Door" features Loud's overworked "DMT" sample with a slow, demented version of "knock knock knockin' on heaven's door." Meanwhile, Rogan is heard pointing up the condition your condition is in: "not like you feel like you are in another dimension, you *are* in another dimension."[45] And the effect of the condition is laid down by Wizack Twizack on his "Spirit Molecule," dropping reference in the mix to a "strange chemical" with a capacity to replicate an experience identical "to events to come after life"—all the more curious given, as the Swede told me himself, he hadn't actually ever tried DMT.[46]

But while I could keep amassing evidence of entheo-machismo and scrapbook braggadocio where competing DJ/producers name-drop substances and show-and-tell their exposure to "Dymethyltryptamine" [sic] without ever having "sampled" it themselves—symptoms of a psychedelic arms war in which increased and varied doses are the coin of the realm—other artists express a serious commitment to entheogens. Take, for instance, Dennis Tapper (a.k.a. Hux Flux), who at one time was smoking material he himself extracted from *Mimosa hostilis* and *Acacia* every second day. The spice has a strong presence in Tapper's sound; he also adopts Rogan to convey the experience of "complex geometric patterns moving in synchronous order" (e.g., on "Finite Automata"), demonstrating that artists not only are experienced with sufficient doses but have been returning to the source.[47] Tapper and many other artists will express their conviction that DMT visions are comparable to those associated with near-death experiences, or the continuity of spirit beyond the mortal body. This popularity evokes a yearning for the mystical experience, the desire to trespass across unnatural barriers that separate life from death, consciousness and unconsciousness, achieved, for better or worse, without a lifetime of meditational training.

These are among the themes preoccupying Mitch Schultz in his documentary *DMT: The Spirit Molecule*. Inspired by Strassman's book, Schultz interviewed original volunteers in the trial, along with numerous other prominent spokespeople.[48] With its Facebook page attracting more than 650,000 "likes" five years from its launch, the film's popularity is a testament to the growing appeal of the compound, a veneration projected onto the storyboards of entheonica. Spanish outfit Hypnoise, for instance, recycles Chris Mueli, MD, among Strassman's sixty, who tells his story. "And then I noticed there is this woman off to my right with a real long nose, green skin. She was turning this dial and I realized she was turning the volume of lights up and down on the city in the distance. And as soon as I looked at her she noticed I was watching her and she said, 'What else do you want?' I said, 'What else do you have?'"[49] Just as Schultz transcribed themes, people, and stories from text into screen format, entheonic musicians remix film into audio narratives impregnating tracks delivered to and performed for the interactive theater of the dancefloor. This remixology is precisely the practice Schultz endorses, as he turned his film into an open-source smorgasbord. Via a Creative Commons license, the DMTRMX project offered its media library of interviews, B-roll, visual effects, music, and sound files used in the making of the film as a resource for the global community. Apparently a vehicle of the DMT experience itself, which typically saturates the mind with a vast metalinguistic intelligence, the DMTRMX project sought collaborations to visually depict the experience with inspiration from "phantasmagoric codification systems" deriving from all religions and esoteric traditions with the objective of creating a "multi-dimensional language system."

With the DMTRMX, and a consequential effort to formulate a "metamythology" dubbed the MYTHAPHI Manifesto, we obtain further levels of complexity in the evolution of "experiential language." This "multi-dimensional language system," or "codex," is an ambitious endeavor. According to Schultz, the benchmark model is nothing less than the "blueprint of Western culture," Hesiod's "Theogony," "the first mythological remix" in 800 BC. "Hesiod's Divine remix rearranged many traditions into one myth for societal transformation through Pattern Alignment / Focus, which we aim to mimic on a much broader scale."[50] Whether a new codex on a scale of Hesiod's "Theogony" will emerge is to be determined, and it is unclear what form it could take. What is apparent is that while this transdimensional language is a synesthetic transmediated phenomenon that is as impossible to transcribe as the DMT experience itself, the closest formulation may actually be the visionary dance event cultivated within the entheonic milieu. As theaters for contagious memes and embodied experiences, superliminal events like Boom provide dynamic platforms for DMT (among other entheogenic compounds). In a dense jungle of beats and loops animating and entrancing the experienced on global dancefloors, McKenna has been the headline DJ. In the next chapter we'll find out more about how that came to pass.

Figure 1. *Dreamcatcher,* by Android Jones.

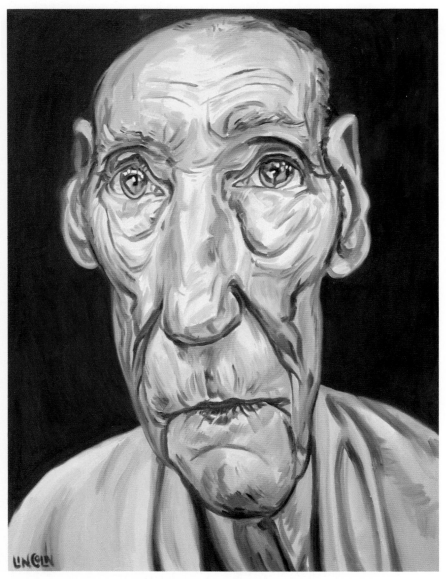

Figure 2. *Burroughs,* by Jay Lincoln.

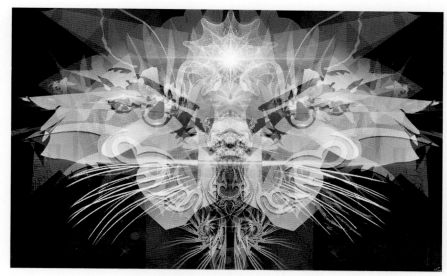

Figure 3. *Felinus Holographicus,* by Cyb.

Figure 8. *Bushfire of Life,* by Shiptu Shaboo.

Figure 9. *Curandera*, by Martina Hoffmann.

Figure 10. *Divine Messenger of Truth*, by Randal Roberts.

Figure 11. *Contact,* by Cyb.

Figure 12. *Hidoodlydo Neighbor,* by Art Van D'lay.

Figure 13. *Vishvarupa*, by Luke Brown.

Figure 14. *Condewsync: Transpiration of the Bose-Einstein Condensate,*
by Adam Scott Miller.

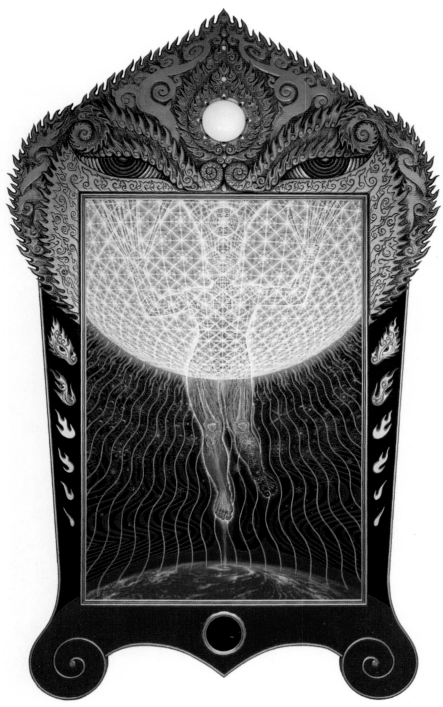

Figure 15. *Transfiguration*, by Alex Grey.

Figure 16. *Beyond the Gate Keepers*, by Gwyllm Llwydd.

Figure 17. *Soul Food from the Inner Sun,*
by Jayarama Bryan.

Figure 18. DiMethyl Temple at Burning Man 2005, photo by Jesse Cohn.

Figure 19. *Diosa Madre Tierra,*
by Carey Thompson.

Figure 20. Dance Temple, Boom Festival, photo by Jakob Kolar.

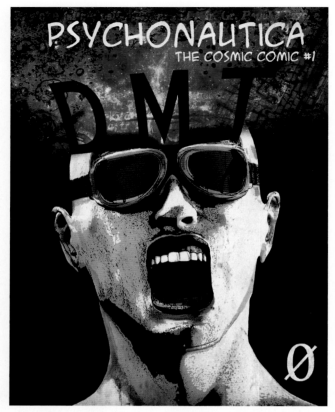

Figure 21. *Psychonautica,* vol. 1, cover design, by Mister Strange.

Figure 22. *Forward Escape,* by Android Jones.

Figure 23. *Metamorph,* by Cyb.

Figure 26. *Four Legged Myrtle, in Contemplation of
That Which Is Not Yet Revealed,* by Art Van D'lay.

Figure 24. *Intentionality: Dimensions of Manifestation,* by Beau Deeley.

Figure 25. *Melek Taus and the Path of Venus,*
by Orryelle Defenestrate-Bascule.

Figure 27. *Panspermia,* by Stuart Griggs.

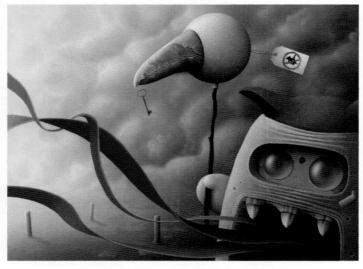

Figure 28. *Languages,* by Marianna Stelmach.

Divine Moments of Truth

It's midsummer 2011. The festival expands around me like an inflatable tropical aquarium, relieving parched hills between the towns of Beaufort and Lexton. At moonrise, I float at the perimeter of the main dancefloor, now bobbing with ten thousand souls. Piping magic through a flute, the figure up on stage is a psychedelic troubadour marshaling the charge across generations. Seventy years young, Raja Ram (Ron Rothfield) is cofounder of Shpongle, the most renowned act in the psychedelic diaspora, headlining here with full accompaniment at Australia's Rainbow Serpent Festival. As I weave closer, a loud aroma with a strong hint of changa rolls off a dancefloor that earlier featured a "welcome to country" where indigenous custodians led a "smoking ceremony." Gundidgundjundmara man Uncle Ted Lovett had burned green eucalyptus leaves here, cleansing the space, and permitting the boogying to commence. Between dense bushland and Granite Hill, these paddocks of pizzazz are likely inhabited by greater numbers of spice smokers than any other locale countrywide, and perhaps globally. From my position midfloor, turning my glasses forward, I see a figure in a familiar orange bodysuit up ahead. Up in the conning tower, Robin Cooke, cofounder of legendary industrial-sculpture outfit Mutoid Waste Co., is a step above the tumult. Edging closer, I note he's on a stepladder, adjusting his latest device. Soon, the tinkering complete, remote-controlled, rainbow-colored jet-flames frame Raja Ram and the band. Nudging closer to the front, I find Alex and Allyson Grey stage right, performing live brush-strokes, separated from their audience by an iron-mesh fence. Like caged artists under lights, their labors are iterations on earlier patterns, just as Shpongle, up on stage, are mutating their epic arrangement "... And the Day Turned to Night."

Australian expat Rothfield is a seasoned traveler. He had roomed in Greenwich Village in '59, dropping acid and playing guitar in the coffee lounges, before living in Ibiza and later taking up flute with improv master Lennie Tristano and fronting cosmic jazz outfit Quintessence. It was in 1988/89 that the man who would become known as Raja Ram first landed in Goa, that psychedelic interzone for freak travelers and cosmic refugees since the 1960s. Full-moon parties on Goa's Anjuna beach had become the prized destination for freaks through the 1970s cosmo-rock scene to the 1980s DJ-led electronic era. While that scene had arguably peaked by the time he arrived, Rothfield would become instrumental in capturing the Goa "state of mind" and amplifying it abroad. Forming The Infinity Project with Graham Wood and cofounding TIP Records (later TIP.World), with which he has produced more than one hundred releases, he effectively bridged the Summers of Love and stood hard on the pedal upon reaching the other side. And just as acid fueled earlier endeavors, two months before the Rainbow Serpent performance Raja Ram informed me that Shpongle was a love child of DMT. "Acid never went that far," he explained, "that internal . . . that BIZARRE AND STRANGE . . . dmt . . . it was the most amazing experience ever." Making season after season in Goa, by the mid-1990s, "a new world full of entities and spirits that were benign . . . guided me . . . spoke to me . . . took me . . . to shpongle land . . . and it was directly because of the dmt . . . that Shpongle and the word Shpongle was given to me through channeling and vision/what a blast . . . what a revelation."[1]

The Pink Packet

True enough, Shpongle's debut release *Are You Shpongled?* (1998) is infused with the spice. The midsection of album track "Divine Moments of Truth"—where it goes "DMT, DeeMT, DMT, DeeMT LSD do DMT, LSD do DMT . . ."—may be as recognizable among enthusiasts as the Coca-Cola symbol is for the rest of the world. Printed on the CD of 2000 album *Divine Moments of Truth* it is explained that "Shpongle is a state of being and experiencing," and later it is clarified that for those entering "Room 23" from the 2001 release *Tales of the Inexpressible:* "to be Shpongled is to be kippered, mashed, smashed, destroyed. Completely geschtonkenflapped!" The condition of *enshponglement,* and indeed one's journey to "Outer Shpongolia"—a track on 2005 album *Nothing Lasts . . . But Nothing Is Lost*—where psychonauts can be assured that "Shpongelese Is Spoken Here" (*Ineffable Mysteries from Shpongleland*, 2009), has become a conspiratorial nodding and winking experience for trance travelers, psychonauts, and entheonic emissaries worldwide.

The name "Shpongle" was a direct outcome of the compelling desire to formulate a lexicon for an experience for which existing language proved inadequate. The chief medium for the articulation was, of course, music, with Shpongle commissioned as DMT's emissary-class starship. I was unsurprised that being *shpongled* connoted DMT space, but it was what Raj said next that caused my eyebrows to elevate. A "pink packet" containing approximately 3 or 4 g of pink DMT crystal came into his guardianship in 1992/93, the contents of which were farmed out to numerous acquaintances over subsequent years. He claims he must have turned on more than a hundred people on the beach or in his house in Anjuna, where "people came and were transported into a fabulous new realm." "DIVINE MOMENTS of TRUTH" was painted across the entrance archway, with every pillar and wall in the house painted with DMT-inspired art.[2] What's more, the bag of "amazing pink power" had apparently not been exhausted by the time we communicated in November 2010.

I grew curiouser, and then, curiouser. Raj indicated that if I wanted the background story I needed to talk to Nik Sequenci, an English DJ who played ambient backing music on McKenna's UK lecture tours in the early 1990s. Surfing his own novelty wave, McKenna captivated crowds at that time with tales of stoned apes, machine elves, and Gaian entelechy. And Sequenci, whom I tracked down in 2012, recalled an afterparty for a *Food of the Gods* book launch where he had "envisioned a new shamanic dance scene."[3] In the wake of the rave-olution, it was a scene endorsed by McKenna himself, who was proposing that, sufficiently intimate with tryptamines, the emergent youth culture of the 1990s was going to manifest the "transcendent object at the end of time in 3-dimensional space," and bring about a tech-savvy "archaic revival." Or at least this was the rave implicit to his Alchemical Youth on the Edge of the World talk at the Camden Centre on June 15, 1992, where the audience learned how Terence had been "an intellectual of the Hegel/Camus crowd before I went through that violet scintillating doorway, and I came out a true believer."

The stand-up philosopher related how occasionally he was asked if DMT is dangerous. "I think the honest answer is—only if you fear death by astonishment."

Intrigued, Sequenci was impelled to climb aboard the novelty wave. Soon after, a friend returned from Hawaii with 11 g of the transdimensional board wax. During his first smoke in 1992, Sequenci "had elves and fairies playing music to me, which was psychedelic trance, and they were saying 'go back to Earth and make this music.'" Unable to transpose these visions into music himself, he found someone who could—in Martin Glover. By the early 1990s, the man Jamaicans in his squat dubbed "Yoot" (he was the youngest) had already gained notoriety as an alchemist of underground psychedelic electronica. But it was a long road to Goa. In 1976, at the age of fifteen, Glover had been accepted into Chelsea Art School, three years before most other students, and by '79, he formed industrial metal punk outfit Killing Joke, a band including members of The Hermetic Order of the Golden Dawn. Excesses, depression, and the absence of a spiritual anchor culminated in a major breakdown by the early 1980s, when Glover ended up "burning money on King's Rd in a kimono and a swimming costume."[4] Squatting in Ladbroke Grove, Notting Hill Gate, all but forgotten as mad and hopeless, he was introduced to "English Timothy Leary" Brian Barritt, who would become his mentor and father figure. In 1982, it was Barritt who, with the assistance of Lee Harris—who ran London's first headshop Alchemy and edited *Homegrown* magazine—was instrumental to Glover's flowering as a new-generation psychedelic emissary. He reflects upon the period as a "shamanic initiation" that amounted to a psychedelic rite of passage. The period would mark the advent of Youth, who would also take up membership in a Druid Order, as a studio production dynamo and a largely unsung pioneer of British dance music. If psychedelics effect the dissolution of boundaries, then this holds true for Youth's career since he would consistently defy and remix categories in the forging of new aesthetics. Early working with Brilliant, Ben Watkins, The Orb, and The KLF, among other acts, he became a highly sought-after producer and remixer for dozens of artists, from The Drum Club to Spiral Tribe to Crowded House, with many acts signed to his labels Wau! Mr. Modo Recordings (set up with The Orb's Alex Paterson) and later Butterfly Records. He himself became a member of more than thirty groups representing a full spectrum of electronic soundscapes from electro, to ambient house, to dub and psychedelic trance.

When he arrived in Goa for the first time in 1988/89, Glover was received like freak royalty. Traveler-DJs had been mixing and playing versions of his productions on DAT for years in the seasonal interzone. Music that was little known in the United Kingdom became proto-trance anthems on the beaches of Anjuna. "We've been waiting for you," was the reception in Goa. Among those awaiting him was Nik Sequenci, custodian of the pink power, who says of Glover, "I had an inner smile 'cause I knew he was the man." The connection with Sequenci (and through him, McKenna) established, Youth hosted Terence at Butterfly Records in Brixton in 1992. About four hundred people received McKenna that night, with the afterparty swelling to double that number. Jerry Dammers DJed, and partygoers enjoyed MDMA punch ladled from a pink bucket furnished with a crystal ball. Subsequently, Youth invited Raja Ram, Graham Wood, Greg Hunter, Johann Bley, and Brian Barritt to a ceremonial smoke-out with the pink crystal in the back garden at Butterfly. Raj acted as shaman, and recollecting this momentous occasion, Glover says he smoked the pipe, lay back, and closed his eyes.

> What I could feel was the very fast beating of hundreds of dragonfly wings on my eyelids, and I felt like I was strapped to the back of a dragracer-car-meets-a-spaceshuttle, and I was being thrust forward. I mean it was the most incredible kick I've ever had from a psychedelic experience. . . . All I could hear was the fluttering of butterfly and dragonfly wings. And then suddenly I was cast up, catapulted into the sky. And like the fuselage from a spaceship falling away, I could see these faces falling away, and it was everyone I'd ever loved, and yet there were these faces in there of people I thought I didn't love at all. It was quite shocking. It reminded me of someone telling me it's like a death trip; it was supposed to simulate death on a certain level. It was very real.

With Raj and Barritt also buzzing, the group piled straight into the studio, where they sculpted the track "DMT." As Glover explained, "We did something radical on that track where we put the kick drum on the wrong beat, and for some reason it sounded right." Despite his experience being disrupted by Ben Watkins's (of Juno Reactor) Jack Russell, Bley recalls being blasted into a "cyberceltic landscape of polished chrome columns." Retaining the breakthrough beat, he cooked up a tribal version of "DMT" on DAT and gave it to Masaray (Ray Castle), who played it in Goa that year.[5] Other versions featured the voice of Barritt in takes that were recorded soon after the ceremony for a remix Glover did for David Bowie, which Bowie rejected. According to Glover, a mix of "DMT" gaining notoriety in the early Goatrance scene featured the treated and delayed voice of Barritt that some people received as "the same language that the aliens were communicating to them while on DMT." Despite marking the territory with the track's release on Dragonfly in 1998 (as a collaboration of Glover, Barritt, Wood, Hunter, Rothfield, and Bley), as a mirror to the relative fates of the compounds, "DMT" remained in near complete obscurity compared with Hallucinogen's (Posford's) classic underground hit "LSD."[6]

Much more than the birthplace of one track, the potent pipe ritual in the backyard of Butterfly was pivotal to the birth of the psychedelic trance movement, whose original vehicle was sublabel Dragonfly Records, the first Goatrance label, newly born that day in Brixton. "That one ceremony was the genesis of what became psytrance today, as we know it. That was the moment of creation," recalls Glover. The garden at Butterfly was the context for many subsequent DMT ceremonies, which took place at an Arthurian style roundtable that Glover designed and built, at the center of which stood a sentient Earthkeeper quartz crystal. Many other productions were directly inspired by these early ceremonies. Among the immediate projects influenced, Glover listed the remarkable album *Hicksville*, which was the result of his collaboration with Simon Posford (Celtic Cross), with Killing Joke's *Pandemonium* (recorded inside the King's Chamber of the Great Pyramid in Giza), Crowded House's *Together Alone*, and The String Cheese Incident's *Untying the Not* among the diverse projects benefiting from the inspiration. The track "Mountain Girl" on *Untying the Not* possesses a distinct DMT vibe. There, Carolyn Garcia (a.k.a. Mountain Girl) herself recounts an episode of travelling to "a very far away place" and at some point needing to "make a decision to come back." It "felt like I could have been free, I could have gone and not come back."[7] Additionally,

Glover named material on the early Dragonfly compilation series *Order Odonata* and future work on his LSD—Liquid Sound Design label, such as Dub Trees' *Nature Never Did Betray the Heart That Loved Her* and the compilation *Butterfly Dawn* as specifically DMT-informed.[8] Regarding this sonic efflorescence, Glover commented that "What we represent is in essence the antidote to the collective corporate takeover of our consciousness," with the endeavors at Dragonfly intended to enable the further penetration of the psychedelic legacy, already passed on to him by Brian Barritt, through music, dance, and ecstatic trance. This endeavor extended to the formation, in 1997, of a covert Druid Order that Glover called the Society for the Reformation of Ancient Enchantment, of which Nik Sequenci, Jaz Coleman, Raja Ram, Brian Barritt, and Jimmy Cauty were founding members, alongside Glover.

Exposed to this sonic avalanche, Nik Sequenci says that he recognized the music "that the elves and fairies and pixies played." It was an exhilarating experience for Sequenci who, in Youth, found the one who could convert his vision into a dance movement. With numerous beneficiaries between 1992 and 1995, Sequenci was himself a midwife to the Goatrance sound, which would evolve into psytrance and numerous substyles from full-on to forest music. He approached candidates with care. "Has their music got the spiritual opening?" "Is this person open-minded enough to hear this story?" Beneficence is not unique in the history of psychedelia—think Captain Hubbard's "bag of wampum," Hollingshead's "mayonnaise jar" of LSD paste, or psychiatrist Leo "Adam" Zeff's magic MDMA therapy[9]—*but* in this case selectivity seems to have had a direct bearing on a cultural formation. While Sequenci would humbly shrink from such grand claims, it is through his efforts in the early 1990s that psytrance—and visionary psyculture more widely—became a multimediated vehicle for spice consciousness. There were many recipients he did not mention, but among those Sequenci did feel were ready were Mr. C, who emceed for The Shamen and later managed labels Plink Plonk and End Recordings. And as we already know, Raja Ram was making beneficent gestures of his own. Raj's bottomless pink packet colored the lives of many, among them Space Tribe founder Olli Wisdom and his brother Miki, chief designer of Space Tribe clothing and CD artwork. Miki received a "blast of inspiration" in Anjuna in 1995. "It was definitely one of the highest, most wonderful points of my life. I never felt more alive than after that first ego-peeling, moment stretching, visually exhilarating step through the whirling mandala gateway to the land of the crinkle-cut synapse, & life has never been the same."[10] Breakthroughs with the aid of DMT, LSD, and magic mushrooms are evident in the soundcraft and album artwork on Space Tribe releases like the EP *Ultrasonic Heartbeat* featuring "Cicadas on DMT" (2006), *Sonic Mandala* (1996), *Ultraviolet Catastrophe* (1997), *Religious Experience* (2000), and *Thru the Looking Glass* (2005). Rothfield recalls the period as a moment of "exploding pyramids and sacred geometry," layered into the sonic and visual arts of numerous acts. Among others who received sacrament from Raj's divine stashbag were Frank É Madsen (Koxbox). Rothfield recalls Madsen later giving him a "very cool" T-shirt bearing the letters "DMT" on the front.[11]

Most notably, Rothfield initiated Simon Posford, among the most respected artists in the psychedelic diaspora. Sound engineer at Butterfly, founder of Twisted Records, producing as Hallucinogen (and numerous other acts), and later cofounder of Shpongle, Posford is unequivocal about the impact of DMT. Meditating on his first smoke with Raj, which he was told came from "Terence McKenna's personal stash," Posford has stated that DMT provided him "with the most inspirational, life-changing, religious, mystical experience I've ever had. . . . You could do yoga and meditation for a hundred years and maybe not get to the place you get to with thirty seconds on a pipe."[12] The experience affected him so deeply it took a long time to assimilate. "Initially when I came down I thought I would never speak again. What's the point? Words . . . they are so inadequate, lifeless and stultifying. I spent a day in silence, before admitting that I have to try and express myself and share these experiences." Among the most significant experiences in that place was an unexpected encounter with entities.

> I sort of plunged into this portal, about where my 3rd Eye was, and yet out in deep space, where I was met by these entities. I can only describe these beings as "entities"—they were without bodies or physical features, more like a collection of intelligent energy continually shapeshifting that

communicated with me through a variety of mediums, not all of them language, sometimes color, sound, or a form of telepathy that I cannot describe with mere words. One of the things they said to me was, "Oh, we're so glad to see you! You made it! You're here."[13]

It was a momentous transaction. "I could see the music we had been working on leaving my head as a flowing liquid mercurial stream of holographic colored symbols, and these 'machine elves,' as Terence McKenna calls them, appeared to be getting off on it. They were dancing, laughing and enjoying it. There was a little flute riff in there, that we could all see, it was red and blue and melting like one of Dalí's clocks." Then these entities instructed him: "You have to go back and find this particular flute riff. It is the divine riff, and this is the one that you have to use."

While they could not replicate it exactly to spec based on Posford's transdimensional trip, an imitation of that riff was used in the track "Behind Closed Eyelids" from debut album *Are You Shpongled?* That track clarifies the effect of his experience, with the most proper accent of Aldous Huxley announcing: "Behind closed eyelids, in very many cases, the visionary quality, the quality of the visions so to say spills over into the external world, so that the experiencer, when he opens his eyes, sees the outer world transfigured." As a prelude to the transfiguration, preceding track "Monster Hit" sequences an inhalation and spluttering cough with the declaration: "That was a monster hit!" At the same time, Rothfield would have a gargantuan hit of his own. In the "Shpongle Trance Remix" version of "Divine Moments of Truth" later released on *Divine Moments of Truth* (2000), he divulged that "it was like a gigantic creature, which kept changing shape." His intent was clarified toward the end of the track: "I want to try it again real soon, and take more."

Rothfield stated to me that these sampled statements were inspired by a session shared with Posford where a giant octopus "put its tentacles into my third eye and pumped the information directly into my brain." He counted his blessings to have received such visitation repeatedly over his career. "I met a lot of aliens and they did speak to me.... Quintessence came as a vision and so did Infinity Project and Shpongle ... it just came into my brain delivered by aliens with blue auras ... it was a gift."[14] And it was a gift landing in his hands care of Sequenci, who recalled subsequently meeting Raj on Portobello Road on Notting Hill Gate. "[Raj] actually got down on his hands and knees and kissed my feet. And he said 'Nik, thank you so much. You have totally changed my life and given me a whole new reason to be working in music.' I was completely taken back by this, 'cause it was . . . just so moving, it was unbelievable that this guy who I looked up to as this brilliant musician was so humbled by this experience, and it was very, very moving . . ."[15]

If Shpongle is a Star Class lightship appearing out of hyperspace, navigating from the flight deck, Simon Posford laid out the mission. "I've only done DMT three times in my life, but if listening to the music could achieve the same effect as a chemical hallucinogen it would be a powerful thing and something worth striving for."[16] For more than fifteen years following his first encounter with DMT, Posford seemed committed to perfecting the sensory impact of DMT (and LSD, among other psychoactives) through music production and DJ performance. By 2011, the possibility seemed evident in Shpongle's "The God Particle" (from the self-titled 2011 EP), sonifying the impact of spirit molecules falling like an upturned crate of Ping-Pong balls on geometric surfaces. It may have been accomplished in the Shpongletron, a DJ booth covered with custom screens for 3-D video-mapped projections designed by Zebbler and used by Posford in Shpongle's tour of North America that year. And there were signs of it on the main floor at Rainbow Serpent 2011. With eyelids wide open, "The God Particle" in full spin, and visionary duo Alex and Allyson Grey syncing brushstrokes with the melody lines traced by ten thousand pairs of arms and legs, I became entangled in a transdimensional tango.

By 2011, the crystal contents of the "pink packet" and its aromatic successors had snaked their way around the planet by way of the Goa-trance scene and its many afterparties. The impact could be felt in locations worldwide, typically animating psychedelic electronica wherever its vapors drifted. It found its way, for instance, to Russia. One Muscovite label-head related to me a story of a Moscow company that had manufactured poisons to control parasites, rats, cockroaches, etc. I'm not sure if the storyteller had conflated reality with the film version of *Naked Lunch*, but as he told the story:

It had a lab and a dozen chemist specialists. Some of them started to use the abilities to make DMT and later involved all the rest, including the owner, who was impressed by DMT effects. They also discovered Castaneda's books and became an absolutely crazy team. They became bankrupt, labs were sold out, but guys really enjoyed themselves and made DMT and MDMA sessions, sharing the substances with friends. They had no idea how to sell it so mostly they just shared everything they made for free. And they considered injection as the most proper way to use any substances.

Spirit Molecular Sonics

In the 1990s, the impact of DMT was heard across a spectrum of experimental music. With influences that include The 13th Floor Elevators and electronic composer Morton Subotnick, UK artist Pete Kember (a.k.a. Sonic Boom) has displayed a serious commitment to "taking drugs to make music to take drugs to," spanning psychedelic styles from the 1980s' minimalist indie-rock of Spacemen 3 to the 1990s' experimental soundscapes of Experimental Audio Research (E.A.R.). From 1994 album *Mesmerised*, E.A.R.'s "D.M.T. Symphony (Overture to an Inhabited Zone)" is advanced hyperspace opera forging test tones for interdimensional encounters of the Nth kind.[17] Such commitments are further evident in Kember's act, Spectrum. In regard to Spectrum's dark experimental drone album *Forever Alien*, Kember is reported to have later stated to *The Guardian* that when he made that album "we were hitting DMT so we could check the music out. It's a 15-minute trip with no real comedown so it's easy to use in the studio. You have to be a bit of a psychedelic stormtrooper, because it takes you straight into the deep end of the trip within the first minute. And then you get the most intensely sublime and beautiful experience I've ever had through drugs. It's an awe-inspiring rush of psychedelia."[18] Other experimentalists were inspired by these realms, and sought to replicate the transitional sonics of the breakthrough experience. I'm thinking here specifically of European experimental band Coil. Formed in 1983 by John Balance as a solo side project to Psychic TV, and later joined by Throbbing Gristle's Peter "Sleazy" Christopherson, Coil gave voice to psychoactivating substances through drone effects. At 36:43 minutes, "5-Methoxy-N,N-Dimethyl: (5-MeO-DMT)" from 1998 EP *Time Machines* manipulates synthesizers and samplers to create these effects in the effort to "displace or 'slide' time." Sonic evidence perhaps of what Leary called "Tranart," besides the absence of symbolism, the monophonic drone is without melody, beat, or obvious structure.[19]

While DMT and its analogues—daubed from a palette of psychoactive tryptamine derivatives—were inspiring diverse sound-art aesthetics by the late 1990s, it was in the sonic architecture of the post-Goa psychedelic milieu where DMT would make itself most visible and audible. But it was not only the contents of the "pink packet" that was triggering divine mystical transmissions. As we already know, local artists had been aware since the mid-1990s that the native ecology of Australia is "jammed with DMT." Laying down an early impression of this alkaloidal gnosis was Insectoid, the post-Goa act formed by Ray Castle, with Nick Spacetree and Mark Turner. The release notes for debut twelve-inch album *New Vistas / Shamantec Images* (1996) had it that "the INSECTOID technicians of the sacred puree a truly tribeadelic trance euphoria with their cyborganic tunes which are totally idiosyncratic to the timeless wilderness of the land of oz. Expect didgeridoos, elephants and the stretching vortex sounds of DMT hyperspace. INSECTOID is ritualistic sonic shankar to transport you onto the supramental plane."[20] If Huxley had expressed how mescaline afforded the trek from the Old World of everyday consciousness into the Antipodes of the mind, the "psychological equivalent of Australia," where "we discover the equivalents of kangaroos, wallabies, and duck-billed platypuses—a whole host of extremely improbable animals,"[21] replete with kookaburras, insects, didgeridoo, and Aboriginal songlines, "Insecticide" and "Tribedelic Nomads (Animistic Mix)" from Insectoid's 1998 album *Groovology of the Metaverse* might have provided the soundtrack to this antipodean adventure. Album track "The Web" is driving electronicacacia and "New Vistas" offers the pertinent sample to this remote viewing (by way of Alex Grey): "I feel that I am merely an agent, giving you some keys, which have been given to me, to pass on to you. These keys are to unlock doors out of your present prison. Doors opening in on new vistas. Doors beyond where you are now."[22] Nick Spacetree (a.k.a. Nen) was a driving force in this development, with unreleased material under his solo project Space Tree evoking the DMT state on the dancefloor. Space Tree, he held, "was the really DMT music . . . the 'holographic' sound."[23] As possibly the first DMT-inspired electronic composition, featuring a soaring acid-chirp-pulse and melodic lines, Space Tree's "Eternal Staircases" was written soon after his meeting with *A. obtusifolia* in late 1992.[24] While the native ecology of Australia was being amplified, and the keys to an antipodean wonderland handed over, further work, such as the various artists producing on the Demon Tea label, whose catalog includes compilation titles like *Oozie Goodness—The Eye Opening Elixir* (1998) and *Not My Cup of Tea* (2001), offers insights on this development.

Spice sourced from Australian *Acacia* would have a shaping influence on the emergence of the full-spectrum Goa sound, notably through the conduit of Englishman and Blue Room Released founder Simon Ghahary. Designer of the "pod" loudspeaker series and architect of envelope-pushing event soundscapes, with the help of solid financial backing from British loudspeaker company B&W, Ghahary oversaw the release of an extraordinary procession of nonformulaic material (150 albums) with leanings toward ambient and dub between 1994 and 1999. The likes of Total Eclipse, Juno Reactor, Etnica, Koxbox, and X-Dream, among many others, were signed to Blue Room. And, according to Ghahary, DMT had a profound impact. Having come of age during a gargantuan psychedelic experience at eighteen, Ghahary sought to push the door wide open on the hypersensory realms with which he was already intimate. In 1996, he achieved this objective during a life-changing DMT episode in Goa. It was a moment for which he had long prepared. He'd been intrigued by word of spectacular sessions at Butterfly involving Ben Watkins of Juno Reactor and the guys from Total Eclipse. And, as an avid collector of DAT "holy relics," he specifically recalls one DAT labeled "DMT" given to him by Steph Holweck of Total Eclipse, which featured early versions of material later recorded on the ambient masterwork *The Mystery of the Yeti*. By the time he took part in a sacred DMT ritual in a house in Anjuna, Ghahary was mentally and physically prepared for an experience that he claims "finally found me." Wearing earplugs during the session enabled his total absorption into the experience. The result was "the most unforgettable musical moment of my life." But it wasn't a terrestrial music. "Every vision that I saw was connected to a sound."

I shut my eyes. Oh my god. My body fizzed. I heard this ferocious sort of fizzing sound, and as it was fizzing it literally split me in half, and I fizzed away. . . . It was so loud in my eardrums. I could hear bubbles popping. It felt like each one of my molecules was bursting and as it was bursting I was breaking like a fruit torn in half. It was ever so slow, but ever so fast. A gentle tear that ripped open my material self and pushed me forward.

Recalling the event as if it had happened just yesterday, he described the sensation of hurtling forward along colored bands of light, each color possessing its own sound at the "border of hearing," 16,000–20,000 hertz, maybe more. Like a "probe soaking up as much information as possible," he finally broke through to crash a party of dark-blue humanoids. They were elegant, nonthreatening beings intrigued by his appearance among them. One among them wore a headdress and after some shared moments of mutual wonder produced a bowl of "fluorescent pink cheesy-puffs." At the moment he accepted one of these strange offerings, Ghahary returned to the room in Goa, with a mile-wide grin. Aglow, he returned to the United Kingdom and inspired some Blue Room label artists to experience the transformative ritual, with full respect shown to the spice. A few among their number would forge influential sounds in the world of psychedelic and ambient electronica.[25]

In the latter half of the 1990s, the spice worked its way into the hearts and minds of DJ/producers seasoning in the interzone of Goa and at the borderlands of consciousness. By 1998, Japanese Goa freak Takeshi Isogai (a.k.a. Ubar Tmar) wore his heart on his sleeve, with "DMT," "entheogen," and "shamanism" coded on the cover art of album *True*, an eclectic aural masterpiece whose final track "Rhythmism 7" transported listeners into the presence of an insectoid intelligence. This piece is reminiscent of the high-pitched choral ululations frequently emitted among the entryptamined and reported at the foundations of psychedelic millenarianism (i.e., at the E@ LC). Obtaining parallel experiences, electronic musicians have attempted to replicate this very "contact" using strange buzzing sounds, especially the sonorous chirping of insects, as was notable on Space Tribe's "Cicadas on DMT" and Insectoid's *Groovology of the Metaverse*.[26]

And over in chillouts worldwide, ambient, dub, and downtempo developments were amplifying this influence. Not all acts will make their influence overt in telltale track names, samples, or name-dropping, but the name for Stephane Holweck's (cocreator of Juno Reactor and Total Eclipse) chillout collective formed in 2001—Digital Mystery Tour—offers a dead giveaway.

It makes sense that psychedelic electronica would be the springboard for DMT, given its placement at the crossroads of physical and psychical travels. Psychedelic arts and dance events worldwide, like those promoted in *Mushroom Magazine, Psychedelic Traveler,* and the *Trancer's Guide to the Galaxy,* are festivals at which travelers converge in body to disassemble their minds. At these locales downstream from Goa, travelers will trade details on means to navigate between known geophysical locations, at the same time exchanging and perfecting the artifice for transiting into uncharted regions of psychic space. On this subject, Posford clarified why Shpongle has had such a large following among travelers (across space and within the imagination).

> Our music creates a common thread and instant bond of alliance to other people who have had a psychedelic experience, in the same way that, say, traveling might. I think that I get on better with people if they've done psychedelics and traveled, because it opens your mind up in a way that is unequivocal. It makes one adept at relating and interacting in a playful, intangible, broadminded way that perhaps you don't have with people that maybe haven't had those experiences.[27]

And as explorers converge in these altered gatherings and mind spaces, they may be greeted with strange bouquets that drift through events like mysterious mists. The source of alkaloidal incense, principally changa, has shaped creative attitudes. Such is the case, for example, for Robin Graat (who with Adomas Juozapavicius is Gaiana), among many young artists who have adopted the changa blend to enhance creativity. While strong experiences with DMT and LSD had been formative to Graat's creative process, as he told me, with changa, he can interact with sound on a deep and direct, real-time level. A low dose heightens sensitivity to a frequency's effect, making it easier for him to find the right sounds. "It's so much more manageable and effective even in minute doses, just enough to slightly tweak your senses, without going full power into its dimension."[28] With background whisps hinting at the presence of a fractal wormhole, Gaiana's "Deep Blue Skies" is one such blend-inspired track.[29]

In the sampledelic world of psychedelic electronica, the elf spice illuminates the dancefloor, which lights up in turn. And perhaps there is no better place to go optimal than Boom's Dance Temple, the global intersection of physical/psychical travels for pilgrims of the mind and body.

In comes the incense—dry like hot air but softer—
I hold it in my lungs and it starts to blossom . . .
I perceive everything with absolute detail, down
to the quivering possibilities of entire universes
in the atomic fractaline edges of this shifting tesseract
vibrating intensively and pushing the consciousness from me
until it is everywhere and I am with it. . . .
It's dark now, the moon is sailing from the hills behind us
out over the lake, hovering above the huge growling UFO
of the dance temple, multi-layered melodies climaxing
and dropping into wugachook-wugachook-wugachook,
people running in wild orbits around the edges,
luminous sticks being swirled by psychedelic sylphs,
animated fractal universes projected onto hexagon screens
evoking the hive, the perfect tough utility of the stacks
of funktion-one, the body of sound marching from them,
the solid waves rotating through the crowd, the entrained
entertaining each other, a multi-dimensional interaction,
one high-vibration family feedback-looping love.[30]

While psychedelic trance has been the vehicle for self-experimentation with cutting-edge smoking blends—as illustrated by the "incense" burned at its global sites of worship—different music genres and their scenes show evidence of the impact of DMT, largely through the interdimensional travels of inspired artists whose output may yet demonstrate influences comparable to that found in the post-Goa psychedelic milieu. In dubstep, for instance, there have been signs of an expanding psychedelic aesthetic.

Founder of Austin, Texas, act Run DMT, John D. Robbins, has explained how his musical journey was inspired by a hit of DMT while listening to Shpongle's *Nothing Lasts . . . But Nothing Is Lost*. "I immediately saw my living room broken down into fractal, kaleidoscopic wheels spinning at different intervals," he recalled.

> In an instant, the time signature of the song that was playing shifted from a 4/4 beat to a 3/4 beat. Essentially, it's like going from a march to a waltz. In that moment, my floor started developing topography. I saw hills and valleys, then roads. There was one road amongst the nest of highways that seemed illuminated bright orange. This road extended beyond the confines of my living room into the other room, where my music studio was set up.[31]

Robbins followed the lighted path and created sounds consistent with his time-signature-shifted experience, as evident on debut album *Union of Opposites*. San Jose–based dubstep artist NiT GriT (Danny Beall) has built a bridge between trance and dubstep. NiT GriT's "Dimethyltryptamine" and other work like "The Awakening" transport a rare epic sound into dubstep.[32] According to one reviewer, Beall "stretches the traditional whomp bass lines out further than one could possibly imagine, turning deep synth into an almost metallic, otherworldly riff."[33] Many other artists who import psychedelia into dubstep bend genres and intentionally court the unclassifiable—artists like Mimosa (Tigran Mimosa), whose EP *Hostilis* features influences from dubstep, hip-hop, glitch, and drum 'n' bass.[34] And while dub-inspired music is traditionally dipped in "the herb" (i.e., ganja), other herbal materials and their extracts animate the music over at Sangita Sounds, like the unmistakable "Chacruna Dub" by ESP.[35]

Circulating memes on "the spirit molecule" and the assumed role of the pineal have inspired artists to vent their passion in a variety of musical styles and media. Having broken through, one such experimentalist is New York rapper Ben Zen, whose "Dimethyltryptamine" tells it like it is (well, almost) with smatterings of Strassman, the third eye, and astral traveling. "Listen: dimethyltryptamine, the chemical that breeds from deep inside the brain of everything that breathes, is a molecule within every single

living being, from the humans to the birds, and the fish and the trees." Ben
Zen's lyrics merge the DMT experience with dream states. "I wake up to
see that things ain't what they seem, breaking through to the other side
by blazin' DMT. . . . I pity you if you're fearing death, as we're all spirits
having a human experience. So every single thing that we've seemingly
seen is nothing but a dream within a dream."[36]

Chief among the diverse vehicles of the DMT breakthrough experience
is Los Angeles rock band Tool, who formed in 1990, later becoming a car-
rierwave for entheogens, including DMT. The influence is most evident
in the band's visual art. Alex Grey's painting *Net of Being* was featured on
2006 album *10,000 Days*, and Grey's animated art was used in music videos and in onstage sets. Another among these emissaries is Los Angeles's
DMT, a heavy-metal outfit formed in 2009 whose album cover art features
a visionary aesthetic unusual to this genre. The band creates music that
they say "pulses with the human energy field, and empowers people to
awaken the spirit." And "powered by the use of psychoactive drugs," they
claim to be "tapping into the source of energy to bring you music straight
from the gods themselves." Bass player and founding DMT member Alistar
Valadez acknowledges the influence of Strassman in his public statements,
and reveals that DMT is "a gateway to higher dimensions or astral realms."
Valadez's position is that "until one can know and understand the forces
that lie within us, and embrace the polar spectrum of being, they will never
understand the forces in nature, for they are one and the same. The world
and people are lost in a battle of dualism; the key to attaining wisdom in
life is to live a life known as being NON-DUAL." Valadez would have
a steering influence on fellow band members and, through the music of
DMT, open up a "gateway" to consciousness for fans. Featuring the line
"we will destroy what we create," early song "13" is a cry for cognitive
liberty, and was inspired by Terence McKenna, whom Valadez cites as his
greatest influence. "This is a good example of a multi-dimensional song,"
he stipulates. "On the surface it is a warlike anthem, taking back our rights
from the oppressive government. But on a deeper level it is about the battle
of ego, or the unconscious vs. the conscious mind. So when we say 'We
will destroy what we create' this goes back to the idea of destroying the
illusion of the ego and taking back our consciousness." Fighting for your

rights, not to party, but to "explore your own consciousness on a spiritual level," is the band's stated anthem.[37]

While some may wind themselves into a furor, others, like great-nephew of John and Alice Coltrane, Steven Ellison (a.k.a. Flying Lotus), raise the profile without raising the temperature—or the decibels. Impressed by the idea that DMT can enable a "near-death" experience, following the death of his mother in 2010, Ellison took DMT and produced one of its most popular evocations—"DMT Song"—released on the 2012 abstract, future jazz, hip-hop album *Until the Quiet Comes*.[38] Yet the spectrum of genres impacted by DMT widens even further, as is evidenced by country singer Sturgill Simpson's "Turtles All the Way Down." Released in 2014 with a psychedelic music video, the song displays the Kentucky singer's indebtedness to DMT (and Strassman) in a struggle with faith reminiscent of Johnny Cash.

> *There's a gateway in our mind that leads somewhere out there beyond*
> *   this plane*
> *Where reptile aliens made of light cut you open and pull out all your pain*
> *Tell me how you make illegal something that we all make in our brain*
> *Some say you might go crazy but then again it might make you go sane*
>
> *Every time I take a look inside that old and fabled book*
> *I'm blinded and reminded of the pain caused by some old man in the sky*
> *Marijuana, LSD, psilocybin, and DMT they all changed the way I see*
> *But love's the only thing that ever saved my life.*[39]

Getting back down to brass tacks, or spirit molecules, in the business of charting molecular sonics, there is no greater authority than Swiss mathematician and musicologist Hans Cousto. Some thirty-five years since his discovery, in 1978, of the "Cosmic Octave" found occurring in the orbit of the planets, the weather, colors, rhythms, and tones, Cousto calculated the octave-tone (frequency) of the DMT molecule. I knew about this circumstance after he sent me a complex table with calculations in 2013. Cousto's "octavation process" inspired multidimensional sound artists Star Sound Orchestra (Germans Steve Schroyder and Jens Zygar), renowned for their "cosmically tuned" productions and concerts using the Planetary Gongs.

Starting in the mid-1990s, Cousto worked with Barmin Schulze of the Akasha Project composing music inspired by the frequencies of psychoactive molecules (including MDMA, THC, and LSD-25). Intending to determine whether the octave-analogous sounds of psychedelic substances are similar in their effect on the mind as the substances themselves, the Akasha Project had an ambitious objective. "The effect of acoustic vibrations with its emotional consequences is based on the phenomena of resonances, and this moves against the key-lock principle of chemical materials and substances. . . . It may be possible in the near future to create spaces with sound and color based on molecular-analogue tones which surpass the intake of psychedelic substances."[40] How this logic could apply to DMT, the psychoactive we're all "holding," is yet to be determined. While the conception of a form of drugless-high soundscape infused with "molecular-analogue tones" may be one future for DMT-influenced sonic architecture, the jury is still out concerning its appeal among participants in entheoniculture.

Returning to the quantum enabler himself, Nik Sequenci, in 2012 he explained to me his vision of holographic sonic architecture called the "Magic Circle." Arranging a circle of speakers below and laser lighting above in a dome-shaped room, he envisions a space allowing the dancer on the floor to "see sound" in ways orchestrated by audiovisual jockeys.

> You'll be standing in a vortex where you'll see sound and you'll be inside a kaleidoscope that will be spinning clockwise and anticlockwise at the same time. Now in your brain and in your body, your DNA spirals, we spiral forward in time just like the planet does. But now that you are in this Magic Circle, in this vortex, the sound and the lights spinning clockwise and anticlockwise should send your DNA spiralling into both directions, so that while you're inside this circle, time stands still because you're getting younger and older at the same time, and this should create the DMT outer body experience using sound and light and nothing else.[41]

Sequenci clarified further that, with the Magic Circle, "we're playing with the whole of time that hasn't happened yet and the whole of time that has happened, and bringing them into the now," which he suggests has tremendous applications as a shamanic technology. Whatever its applications, and regardless of whether Sequenci will secure the funding to get his idea off the ground, with the Magic Circle, we've returned full circle to the Camden Centre in 1992, where Sequenci was DJing for McKenna. Terence had conveyed to his audience that what had given him cause for excitement about the native use of psychedelic plants in the Amazon and elsewhere was that "they seem to be on the brink of evolving forms of communication which move out of the realm of acoustical neurological processing and into the realm of visual acoustical processing." And, he'd conjectured, this is what twentieth-century art was striving for, new ways of "visually processing what is heard." "Ever since jazz and cubism and throughout the evolution of 12-tone row, abstract expressionism, rock 'n' roll, pop-up virtual reality," he stated, "all of these schools of art and technological innovations in the art-making process are setting us up to be able to see what we mean at some point in the future. And this will deliver us essentially into the equivalent of a telepathic society." And tryptamines, notably DMT, were presaged as the chief tool by which meaning could be made manifest—a process that escalated as the "pink power" endowed untold recipients with astonishment. As a spiritual technology channeling experiential language in the coming visionary-arts movement, starting in the mid-1990s the artifice of entheonica enabled sound to be seen and pictures to be heard in unprecedented detail.

CHAPTER 9

The Hyper Space Age

Checkerboard Beach

July 11, 2011, Checkerboard Beach, Rarotonga, Cook Islands. I had joined the Black Pearl Eclipse adventure, arriving on the island with an oddly familiar crew of Aussie explorers who converged to witness a total solar eclipse. Fifty eclipse chasers occupied the Rarotonga Backpackers on a beach next to the Pacific Ocean. By the day of the eclipse, with my fellow intrepids I had steamed overnight 100 nautical miles southeast of Rarotonga on the island trader *Tekou Maru II* to intercept the line of totality arching across the South Pacific. A dancefloor with sound system had been fashioned on the freight deck, but overnight, as the trader plowed choppy seas, most passengers clung (successfully) to the deck and (unsuccessfully) to their lunches. At 8:20 a.m., with the ship's engines and music switched off, inside 360° of ocean horizon, and with our prow in direct alignment with the Sun occluding Moon, the *Tekou Maru II* sailed into the cosmic singularity.

But now, back on Raro, it's after dusk and the moon waxes over a tranquil shore. I'm in an unusually receptive mood. Basking in the afterglow of the eclipse, I take several deep hits of DMT from a small pipe, and sink like a starfish into the beach, a space neither land nor ocean. Immediately, a white-noise generator switches on, and I'm swimming in the currents of an unmistakable buzz, an unrelenting and iridescent blue hummm, out of which I locate *the* frequency. It's showtime, and I'm on. The familiarity of the setting is uncanny. But look now, out of the noise, unidentifiable agents present me with puzzling objects . . . each more elaborate, more impossible, than the last. Rubik's Cubesques rigged out with a vexing panoply of moving components . . . nasal tubes, intravenous syringes, enemas, crystalline pipes of impossible design, contrivances of inconceivable geometricality, all apparently dedicated to the ministration of holiness, proffered like libations for my delectation, and yet each dissolving upon closer inspection. Conflations of ambassador, dealer, croupier, vicar, and something else besides, more and more agents herald contraptions of sensory augmentation... astonishing telescopic devices, earscopes, nosephones, and more preposterous doohickeys for the perception of the invisible than I could possibly count. Like representatives of competing guilds of the impossible, traffickers of non-sense knowware, and exporters of extrasensory exhibits, each agent outclasses the next in efforts to goad my inspection of their distinctly accessorized tek. Drawn to these outlandish contrivances, I remain guarded all the same.

The background to this visual cacophony is a blue-and-white checkerboard with shifting tiles. Each tile, if I look close enough, gives way to terraced depths that fall beyond comprehension. Across this checkered landscape, tiles open out to reveal distinct universes from which flower fractaline galaxies. Even closer inspection reveals these worlds to be contrived from a symphony of symbols, an unrelenting datastream of alien glyphs, each wrought from an impossible geometry. I do not possess the means to hack the stream, to transpose what is happening "there" to "here." But what I do know is that, in the foreground, the troupe of exhibitionists peddle their captivating cavalcade of impossibilities. It's like walking the aisles of a hallucinogenic haberdashery and having an untold number of Mrs. Slocombes jonesing to catch my eye—a cosmic bazaar, like the markets of Marrakesh if operated by alien snake charmers. But, if there is anything defining the character of these beings, it's their nonchalance. They appear to operate sans enthusiasm, performing their roles with professional detachment, like bored buskers relying on their tricks, their disinterested decorum a contrast to the objects they brandish. Soon enough, I sink farther into the beach.

Subsequent reflection gave me to consider the predicament of being marooned between these and other dimensions, beached in a place between the known and that which lies beyond. Were the agents intermediaries deigned to lure me beyond the reef, or diversions preventing departure from these shores? Was I drawn into an oceanic embrace with the Other, or held captive by trinkets? Some time after I abandoned my starfish pose on the beach, I entertained a loose comparison of the objects that transfixed me on Raro with those offered to Polynesians of the Cook Islands, and indeed all native peoples contacted and colonized by Europeans, seduced, cajoled, and persuaded by technologies advanced and captivating. Written language, the Bible foremost, has been the principal technology of colonization, the most powerful tool wielded by missionaries. So too, a visible language—or at least what appears to be "language," although not typically transmutable by way of the five senses—is among the principal means by which habitués of hyperspace communicate with DMT intrepids. Only now, in this higher-dimensional contact zone, the Captain Cooks of hyperspace persuade the islanders of Euclidean space to become dimensional nomads. As many thousands of returnees indicate by way of an efflorescence of user experiences now shimmering in cyberspace, emissaries entice locals to travel outside recognizable properties of time and space. Sail beyond the frontiers of the known. Compel natives to go alien.

As a broker of the impossible, Terence McKenna's insights spill light on my experience on Rarotonga. In his 1990 workshop in New Mexico, McKenna spoke of experiences in which he was presented with gifts that were "like something falling out of the mind of God." They were objects that could not exist in this universe but were nevertheless right before his eyes. While the beings were clamoring, "Look at this! Look at This! Look at THIS!," he was compelled to pull away from the things offered, to resist the temptations. "You say, 'No, don't look at it, look AWAY from it!' because it's so wonderful that it's swamping my objectivity and destroying my ability to function in this space." McKenna recognized where he'd had this feeling before. It was down in Crawford Market in Bombay with "a kilo of Gold" in his pocket that he sought to trade for hashish. "I was surrounded by all these Arab hash traders, and they were saying, 'We're your friend, just wait, don't worry ... How about thissss! How about This!'"[1] He later concluded that the entities in the DMT flash were traders, and the hyperdimensional objects trade goods.

Far from holding parity with McKenna and his advanced meme trading in hyperspace—apparently he traded everything he knew about the *I Ching* for the model of time (i.e., Timewave Zero) that he would spend his life promoting—I simply suggest that his interpretation of his penetrative ventures casts light on my floundering movements in the shallows of that realm. More to the point, his meditations offer navigational guidance for future entheographers. In the history of psychonautica, the tripper conventionally self-identifies as a courageous traveler, exploring the otherworld and returning with the mana, often imagined as a one-way process. The perspective is difficult to dislodge. While, as shown later in the book, Rick Strassman has recently adopted an "interactive-relational" model allowing a comparison of prophetic states in the Hebrew Bible and DMT experiences, since the divine efflux moves from God and his intermediaries to the experient, this remains a top-down relationship. For McKenna, interdimensional travelers are like cosmic fishermen whose "creative act is to let down the net of human imagination into the ocean of chaos on which we are suspended and attempt to bring out ideas."[2] But these travelers aren't simply netting the Other or mirroring the Divine, they are in direct dialogue with it. This is a theme to which I will return, but not before exploring the exploits of psychonauts and the evolving philosophy of hyperspace.

Magellans of the Interior

Psychonauts have long imagined themselves navigators of uncharted terrain, explorers plumbing the depths of the psyche, scaling the heights of consciousness, and mapping new regions of the mind. Carrying forward enlightenment objectives, narrating their exploits using geospatial and travel metaphors, they embark on journeys under the aegis of discovery, not of untouched frontiers of the globe, but of consciousness. If a "naut" is a person engaged in the operation of a vehicle, especially one used for scientific investigation, then the *vehicle* commanded by the psychonaut is the *psyche* itself, which starting in the 1950s and 1960s was operated using the keys and manuals of psychiatric science. Just as William James's earlier experiments with nitrous oxide had convinced him of the psychological significance of forms of consciousness beyond ordinary experience, the loquacious Aldous Huxley was compelled to report on the landscape of the visionary realm to which he was transported upon his debut with mescaline in 1953.

To convey his experience, and to present it as a landscape, or "space," Huxley developed the literary device of the geo-exploratory metaphor best illustrated in his essay "Heaven and Hell," which employed imperialist cartography to penetrate the mind. "Like the earth of a hundred years ago, our mind still has its darkest Africas, its unmapped Borneos and Amazonian basins," he conjectured. "A man consists," he continued, "of what I may call an Old World of personal consciousness and, beyond a dividing sea, a series of New Worlds—the not too distant Virginias and Carolinas of the personal subconscious and the vegetative soul; the Far West of the collective unconscious, with its flora of symbols, its tribes of aboriginal archetypes; and, across another, vaster ocean, at the antipodes of everyday consciousness, the world of Visionary Experience."[3] Onboard Huxley's literary *Beagle,* the surveying techniques of the naturalist, botanist, or collector provided fertile allegories for discoveries awaiting the traveler-visionary who, electing to depart the known world and taking leave from their everyday senses, becomes exposed to untold vistas.

> In relation to the fauna of these regions we are not yet zoologists, we are mere naturalists and collectors of the specimens.... Like the giraffe and the duckbilled platypus, the creatures inhabiting these remoter regions of the mind are exceedingly improbable. Nevertheless they exist, they are facts of observation; and as such, they cannot be ignored by anyone who is honestly trying to understand the world in which he lives.[4]

Huxley's psychedelic pharmacography demonstrated a curious mix of colonialist and psychiatric influences. In the colonial antipodes—the geophysical opposite to England (i.e., Australia)—exoteric wildlife connotes the untouched wilds of the mind. The shaping influence of psychiatric science on Huxley is more than evident in the concern, as *Psychedelic Press* editor Rob Dickins notes, for mapping and exploring the invisible landscape of mind in the service of ameliorating medical and social pathologies identified by psychiatric science.[5] Huxley was himself a literary trailblazer who laid the groundwork for Leary, and for McKenna (among many others), who, lecturing in Berkeley in 1987, stated that, in the confines of their own apartments, intrepids are becoming "Magellans of the interior world," bringing back tales of "insect gods, starships, unfathomable wisdom, endless realities."[6]

For Huxley, and the explorers who surfed his wake, the risks and challenges associated with geophysical exploration were transferred to the voyager of inner space. These wayfarers confronted challenges not in the imperial service of king and country, but in the quest for an evolved consciousness. As a plethora of male avatars have penetrated to the heart of the mystery, commanding new technologies in the quest to open up the mind, this risk-laden narrative of adventure and discovery has been a decidedly masculine story: Mad Max's of the mind, resourceful and daring, stepping out on the precipice, penetrating the psychic interior, and leaving evidence of their feats in literature and science. At least that is the phallocentric mythology. In the anthology *Sisters of the Extreme: Women Writing on the Drug Experience*, Cynthia Palmer and Michael Horowitz set the record straight. And yet, the narratives that have come down to us are decidedly masculine, penned by men, hailed as courageous explorers of consciousness. While it was Huxley who was most known at the turn of the 1960s, compared to him, Leary and Alpert noted that Alan Watts, for whom psychedelic tools offered results not unlike those achieved after years of training in Taoist or Zen disciplines, was "more daring" and "pushes beyond."[7] But the pioneering edgeworker and Beat scientist was Burroughs, who trekked upriver to the source. By the early 1960s, Burroughs had even tried his hand at a theory of "neurological geography," entertaining the notion that certain cortical areas were heavenly, others diabolical.[8]

It took eloquent and brazen practitioners of language to strike out into the unconscious, to trek the backwaters, badlands, and prohibited zones of the mind, that final frontier, where known spatial metaphors lacked meaning and valence—for, in what Huxley identified as "Mind at Large," space and time were no longer sensible. After all, how does one describe *eternity*? How could one command language to provide an adequate description of what was un-English-able? While the appeal of *The Doors of Perception* was founded on its noted author's eloquent translations of his own neurochemically charged visionary experiences, as psychedelics and notably LSD gained circulation in the late 1950s and in the 1960s, psychonauts sought to improve and refine psychedelic linguistics, a practice that was compelling.

As Richard Doyle conveys in *Darwin's Pharmacy*, the psychonaut is compelled to breathe life into the psychedelic experience through trip reportage that manifests as rhetorical programs of, and for, the initiated. We have a term for novel and alien "languages" downloaded in psychedelic states. In her semiautobiographical account of the practice of psychonautics, *Xenolinguistics: Psychedelics, Language, and the Evolution of Consciousness*, "soul sailer" Diana Reed Slattery introduces "xenolinguistics" as the study of unnatural and unspeakable languages.[9]

In the history of psychedelic pharmacography, in just a few short years we travel from Huxley quietly transfixed by his trouser-folds to Leary's resonant return to the source vibrations and subsequent freak assemblies where psychedelic synesthesia was no longer the lone pursuit of clinical scientists and learned gentlemen. By the mid-1960s, authorship of the psychoactivated Other was no longer in the hands of a few, as a veritable carnival of tropes, formulas, and idioms flourished to furnish the realms beyond and within with meaning. But the question might be asked: Who or what is speaking? As Leary's early-1960s experiments with DMT on the experiential typewriter illustrated, controlled experiments have a way of veering off course, with the "results" emerging in expressive forms unparalleled in the lives of experimentalists. It seemed apparent that one isn't necessarily *using* language, in the way a writer like Huxley was disciplined to perform, but that one is being acted upon, dictated to, written by, the Other. Among the great literary examples is evident in the divine pink light that bathed Philip K. Dick in a compelling life gnosis in February–March 1974, directing the writing of his *Exegesis* and the *VALIS* trilogy. Rather than an author in command of language (and of consciousness), the trip reporter, the xenolinguist, becomes a medium of consciousness, not dissimilar to the way a clairvoyant mediates the otherworld, a prophet proclaims divine transmissions, or, for that matter, the mad claim to have been furnished with the "truth" by the voices inside their head. McKenna inferred that he channeled the Logos, that *it* was speaking through him. He knew that these practices weren't meant just for elites, as he committed to a psychedelic pedagogy in which multitudes became exposed to techniques for accessing and channeling the Other. But this was not the mass exposure, the "psychedelic revolution," advocated by Leary. McKenna knew that alternative social havens, clubs, and dance festivals provided the optimum conditions for experimentation, the assembly grounds of the neopsychedelic movement where today his own words, the sampled distillations of a revered alt.cult hero, stand out among the nanomediated deluge that caresses the minds of floor-bound psychonauts surfing the lip of the novelty wave long after The Big One was scheduled to hit.

The Spaced Age

According to Leary and Alpert, Alan Watts's *The Joyous Cosmology* was "the best statement on the subject of space-age mysticism."[10] The observation was poignant. Not long after Huxley's "Heaven and Hell" began circulating, the trope of terrestrial (antipodean) otherness had grown outmoded, as the Space Age officially commenced on October 4, 1957, with the launch of *Sputnik 1*. At this time, the cosmos was celebrated as a source of potential, especially now that humankind had penetrated beyond Earth's atmosphere. And this was, as it turns out, the period in which the psychopharmacological effects of DMT were discovered. Following Hungarian Stephen Szára's pioneering bioassay in 1956, one volunteer recruited to receive an injection in Szára's first trial made the following report. "The whole world is brilliant. ... The whole room is filled with spirits. It makes me dizzy. ... Now it is too much! ... I feel exactly as if I were flying. ... I have the feeling this is above everything, above the earth." And as the effects wore off: "It is comforting to know I am back on earth again. ... Everything has a spiritual tinge to it, but it is so real. ... I feel that I have landed."[11]

It's not difficult to imagine the choice of metaphors influenced by fresh images of *Sputnik 1* (Russian) or *Juno I* (American) satellite launches (in 1957 and 1958). Over the next decade, the sequence of events from launch into space → orbit → return to Earth were analogous to the sequence involved in a psychedelic trip (i.e., intake → high → landing), which explains why, during this period, space programs, the activities of astronauts and cosmonauts, and NASA radio dialogue, in particular, provided immediate allegorical resources for those undergoing psychoactivated rites of passage. The tripper could express their progress by sampling this language, a circumstance with an ongoing legacy amplified by the possibilities enabled by the advent of mass digitalization and the internet, and psychedelic electronica whose DJ/producers have employed technologies at their disposal to evoke and facilitate the journey in inner space by sampling material from agencies whose mission has been to launch humankind beyond the exosphere. To note one example, the title track on French outfit Tikal's *Cosmic Dragon* (2008) deploys some of the most significant dialogue in the history of NASA's Apollo space program—Neil Armstrong from the moon's Sea of Tranquility: "Houston, Tranquility Base here. The Eagle has landed." While this vocal sample evokes the cosmic paydirt, the highest point of the mission/trip, the same track is equally evocative of the safe return to Earth—and the implications of, for instance, post-DMT inhalations—in the response of the Mission Control Center crew in Houston to the Apollo 11 astronauts (and the world): "Roger, Tranquility. We copy you on the ground. You've got a bunch of guys about to turn blue. We're breathing again."[12]

Throughout recorded history, space has been a source of awe, its depths occulting mysteries of origin and destination, genesis, and apocalypse. The mid-twentieth-century penetration of space became a rich allegorical resource for percipience, the penetration of the "final frontier," the journey into the mind. By the 1960s, the space beyond Earth's atmosphere had become a cosmic stage for the journey within—for the drama of self-discovery. This was not simply metaphorical, since, for Arthur C. Clarke, Carl Sagan, and other proponents of space flight, outer space was a cosmic theater essential to the advancement of the human condition. On the cosmic frontier, pathologies of the self and of society were reckoned to be conditions from which humanity could evolve. Fueled by science-fiction narratives and space exploration, potential contact with the extraterrestrial Other provided promise for human evolution—otherwise fated to self-destruction under the mushroom cloud.

Such progressive-reactionary eschatologies permeate psychedelic philosophy, as found in Leary's approach to space exploration being pivotal to human-consciousness evolution. The migration into space was implicit to the "Eighth Circuit Model of Consciousness," with Leary's agenda boiling down to the acronym SMILE: SM (Space Migration) + I^2 (Intelligence Increase) + LE (Life Extension).[13] Tools developed for mind exploration are devised not for the sole objective of improving the health and well-being of the individual, nor even simply improving species evolution, but reenchanting the "world soul." This echoes the ends to which McKenna pursued the millennium, since in his approach, the space race, the starship, space colonies, and other ingressions of novelty betraying the long-held species' desire to exit the planet, to become the alien, were among the last "shockwaves of eschatology" mirroring the coming cosmic metamorphosis when "in the final moment the Unspeakable stands revealed." For McKenna, this coming juncture was to be "the entry of our species into hyperspace," perceived, at the same time, to be the release of the mind into the imagination.[14] Regardless of how we appraise this notion, especially after humanity was fated to have been released into the imagination in 2012, the familiarity with the other-dimensional that is ancillary to the Spaced Age retains a compelling flavor.

According to McKenna, it wasn't to the unconscious, in its Freudian or Jungian variations, that we should be turning to understand this phenomenon. "The main event folks, doesn't even have anything to do with the psychology of human beings," moved the stand-up philosopher. "The main event is another dimension, a dimension so bizarre, so titanically peculiar, so strange, unanticipated by our language, our history, our literature, that it is literally like the discovery of another world."[15] Certain plants were identified to be pivotal to obtaining this plateau in the psychedelic age of discovery. And if plant-sourced psychedelics are to consciousness exploration as the telescope was to astronomy, as McKenna often proclaimed, DMT offered the intrepid explorer tickets to the main event. This is the case, since DMT has "the unique property of releasing the structured ego into the Overself. Each person who has that experience undergoes a mini-apocalypse, a mini-entry and mapping into hyperspace. For society to focus in this direction, nothing is necessary except for this experience to become an object of general concern."[16]

Hyperspace Philosophy

When McKenna became the main protagonist of psychedelic hyperspace philosophy, he entered a field with a convoluted history shaped by developments in geometry, spiritualism, science fiction, and the art world. The term "hyperspace" emerged in the mid-1800s among geometers as the designation for space other than Euclidean (i.e., space greater than the three dimensions of length, width, and height).[17] That this "hyperspace" was inconceivable beyond Nth-dimensional geometry and linear algebra was of little concern to philosophers, theosophists, and other esotericists breathing life into the fourth spatial dimension in the late nineteenth century, when the trope afforded legitimacy to spiritualist claims and mystical insights. This career path was stimulated by French mathematician Henri Poincaré, for whom four-dimensional space was not geometric but a perceptual "inner space." Believing that the three dimensions of space are an illusory property of normal brain consciousness, Poincaré proposed that "the dimensionality of space was a *subjective* property."[18]

Hyperspace gained publicity in the late nineteenth century, with the fourth dimension making its literary debut in 1884 in Anglican clergyman Edwin A. Abbott's satirical novel *Flatland: A Romance of Many Dimensions*. In *Flatland*, the growing fascination with higher dimensions was tapped to make a withering statement on inequality in Victorian England. In the novel, Mr Square lives comfortably in a two-dimensional universe stratified according to one's angularity. Priestly circles are at the apex of power, men are a variety of polygons, women are shrill line-segments, and others are untouchables of "irregular" shape. One day, Mr Square receives an unexpected visit from the mysterious Lord Sphere, a 3-D entity who takes him on a journey to Spaceland, a confounding three-dimensional universe where he is introduced to, among other things, 3-D squares (i.e., Cubes). Returning with an expanded dimensional awareness, Mr Square is eventually imprisoned for committing heresy by speaking out on the forbidden subject of higher dimensions.

In *Flatland*, Lord Sphere is as dismissive of the prospect of a fourth dimension—i.e., another mode of being—as the bidimensionals are of a third (i.e., depth). British mathematician Charles H. Hinton was not blinded with such assuredness. In *A New Era of Thought* (1888) and *The Fourth Dimension* (1904), Hinton developed his views on the mystical and evolutionary significance of four-dimensional space. The fourth dimension was perceived to be the source of alternative modes of consciousness like those experienced by mystics, psychics, mediums, and others with evolved means of perception. For Hinton, the fourth dimension was not a mathematical abstraction, but a mode of perception integral to the development of human consciousness. Believing four-dimensional mental vision could be acquired with sufficient effort, he devised a complex system of mental exercises—known as "Hinton cubes"—that enabled popular visualization of a four-dimensional "hypercube" he called the "tesseract."

Such speculations and exercises were good news for spiritualists, occultists, and others taking liberty with geometry to authorize their practices. Among these enthusiasts, a four-dimensional universe explained a host of paranormal phenomena, like ghosts haunting our three-dimensional consciousness or the practice of gifted mediums soaring into "higher planes of consciousness" and channeling entities from those realms. Theosophists like author of *The Astral Plane* (1895) and *The Other Side of Death* (1903), Charles W. Leadbeater, found Hinton's exercises of potential use in the quest for "astral vision," presaging a surge of declarations in this field pre–World War I, as evident, for example, in M. Gifford Shine's 1911 account of life on "the psychic plane" in *Little Journeys into the Invisible: A Woman's Actual Experiences in the Fourth Dimension*. And yet others were dissatisfied with Hinton's perspective. According to Russian esotericist P. D. Ouspensky, Hinton's attempt to deduce features of four-dimensional awareness by using lower-dimensional analogies and mathematical parlor games did not enable his audience to directly experience this higher state of consciousness. What Ouspensky called the "noumenal" were the occurrences of the *miraculous* that each and every one of us has known. "There is no side of life," he wrote in his opus *Tertium Organum*, "which does not reveal to us an infinity of the new and unexpected if we approach it with the knowledge that it is not exhausted by its visible side, that behind this visible side there lies a whole world of the 'invisible,' a whole world of the new and incomprehensible forces and relations."[19]

The title *Tertium Organum* meant "third instrument," or a new system of higher logic capable of understanding the noumenal world, which, as the fourth dimension, was neither an unsensed extension of physical matter (Hinton), nor a dubious realm of spirits (as many spiritualists and theosophists would have it), but our own consciousness. Ouspensky was determined to overcome positivist and dualistic logic preventing access to the transcendental order. Accessing the noumenal through experiments in dreams, yoga, prayer, fasting, breathing, and nitrous oxide, Ouspensky developed a philosophy of consciousness inspired by the enigmatic flashes of insight such methods afford. If, as he believed, the fourth dimension was the realm of the psyche—of consciousness—then art more than science would be the means to understand and translate the noumenal. "The artist must be a clairvoyant: he must see that which others do not see; he must be a magician: must possess the power to make others see that which they do not themselves see, but which he does."[20] We are not so remote from McKenna—who championed the active role of the artist and, more to the point, the imagination—in the evolution of consciousness. Not unlike McKenna, who mounted offensives on celebrity "culture," Ouspensky railed against what he saw as the philistinism and barbarism of his time, and argued that an evolution in human consciousness was not an inevitable outcome, as was the belief, for example, of author of *Cosmic Consciousness* Richard Bucke. For Ouspensky, the evolution in consciousness was to be achieved through the development of a culture that augments the new consciousness and causes it to flourish.

Among Ouspensky's chief insights was that time is a movement in the fourth dimension. As he declared, "Time is the *fourth dimension of space*."[21] Whereas physicists, following Minkowski and Einstein, regarded time as a dimension that is perpendicular to the three dimensions of space, and H. G. Wells imagined "time" or duration as the fourth dimension in *The Time Machine* (1895), Ouspensky saw our three-dimensional phenomenal world intersecting with the four-dimensional, noumenal world. In modified states of consciousness aided by experiments with nitrous oxide and hashish in early-twentieth-century Saint Petersburg, he had a vision of the *Linga Sharira*. A theme lifted from Blavatsky's *The Secret Doctrine*—itself adopting Hindu philosophy, where this idea infers *the form on which our physical body is molded*—this referred to a four-dimensional "temporal body." Gary Lachman summarized the position in *The Secret History of Consciousness*. "Beneath the visible alteration of our physical body, there remains something that endures: the image, the form of the person. That image and form is the *Linga Sharira*, which, Ouspensky believed, exists in a kind of Eternal Now. The key to higher consciousness, Ouspensky understood, lay in a changed perception of time, in an ability to escape the limitations of the present moment and see deeper into the past and future."[22] As Lachman pointed out, Ouspensky appears to have pursued a version of "the powerful sense of being above space and time" that editor of magazine *The New Age* Alfred Richard Orage knew as "ecstasy."[23] Ultimately, the direct perception of higher-dimensional space-time will inaugurate new categories with which to think, new concepts, and a new language with which to communicate reality. This was essentially what McKenna was offering with regard to tryptamines. Under his guidance, DMT surfaced as something of a pharmacological Hinton cube, only now the tryptamine-derived "tesseract," or something like it, could be experienced directly, as Ouspensky might have approved. Of course, in our time, the neo-"hypercube" is subject to prohibition, with the Mr Squares of the present risking the heavy hand of the state and public opprobrium by testing the boundaries of 3-D reality with outrageous claims on the New Jerusalems of hyperspace. In a time when "psychedelics remain the discourse of the unmentionable by the disreputable about the unspeakable,"[24] McKenna himself didn't live by the rule of the Circle priests that—as stated in *Flatland: The Movie*—"a still tongue makes a happy life."

It was in the first decades of the twentieth century that the idea of four- or higher-dimensional space gained widespread momentum. Whereas popular science, spiritual, and art movements had filtered the ideas of Poincaré, Hinton, the Theosophical Society, and the Cubists one hundred years ago, *hyperspace* received a popular makeover in the 1990s as the concept grew interchangeable with "cyberspace." Chiefly through the work of William Gibson, notably *Neuromancer*, what became recognized as "cyberspace" was animated in discourse used formerly to map terrestrial, outer, and inner space. A virtual reality came into existence, and, like avatars exploring new worlds, "cybernauts" were now uploading to, exploring, and inhabiting the furthest reaches of an out-of-body, net-enabled virtuality, tasked to retrieve—download—insights, wisdom, gnosis. In her cultural history of space, *The Pearly Gates of Cyberspace: A History of Space from Dante to the Internet*, Margaret Wertheim traced the quasi-religious idea of cyberspace to the Christian concept of heaven, that postmortem paradise for the disembodied souls of the righteous to exist for all eternity, a theme reanimated at the end of the last millennium, when the Empire once again faltered and its citizens sought salvation, only now in virtual reality, the new Empyrean "soul-space" outside of physical space.[25] From the vantage of its earliest utopian proponents who were repurposing the tools of the military-industrial-academic complex to alternate ends, cyberspace became a "space," not within which to wage war, commit institutionalized violence, or undertake surveillance and other infringements upon liberty, with which it has grown synonymous, but to enable contact with other "users," as evidenced, for example, by one of the oldest virtual communities, The WELL.[26] But something else was at play in this virtual communitas, for cybernauts were dissolving boundaries and transcending routine selfhood in ways that seemed to model the psychedelic experience itself—known to have had a formative influence on the personal-computer industry.[27]

Popular explorations in virtual reality have provided a generation of users with a language of the kind envisioned by Ouspensky, with post-VR psychonauts heir to an evolving technical repertoire with which to articulate their journeys. Longtime Burner and founder of Los Angeles's Flow Temple fire arts center, Teafaerie provides an intriguing commentary on this development. She explained that what she would normally identify as "the plant spirit" appeared to her during an ayahuasca ceremony in 2011 in the guise of a "sentient browser program."

> She didn't exactly talk to me, but she nevertheless conveyed that she was scanning me for viruses and installing all of the necessary protections, updates, protocols, patches, and cookies, as well as defragging my hard drive before logging me on to hyperspace proper. After a few minutes she announced that she had found a bunch of malware that I had picked up while cruising the Net on some of those "other" browsers, which she seemed to regard with something very much like professional contempt. She then, ah, purged all of the bad code from my system, along with the remains of my late lunch. After that happened, the Maestra came over and sang me a song, which installed something that I took to be analogous to a security update. I could actually see this being done, because this little old South American lady was apparently making alterations to my source code by using sound to manipulate a graphical user interface. Which also explained how she could keep all of the energetic spectators

out of the ceremony space just by blowing smoke at them. This woman was some kind of a hacker, and she could redefine the room's permissions with a simple gesture in the same way that you or I might change a program's settings by dragging and dropping a few icons.

While the digital revolution and computer programming have sown a rich vein of metaphors for travelers, as most DMT users have discovered, the veridicality of the experience demands more than metaphor. To clarify her suspicion that the experience resembles a computer processor, a system that processes information specific to her own needs and requirements, Teafaerie recalled a formative DMT experience in which she was abducted by "a fully immersive spaceship, lovingly rendered in exquisite and ostentatiously elaborate detail," complete with convincing interactive crew members. It was gobsmacking for her to find that the mind "can instantly generate a full scale masterwork alien spaceship from scratch, complete with all the trimmings ... and it can do it without any awareness or deliberation on the part of the hopelessly unsophisticated frontman program that plays the role of the astonished psychonaut." Imagining DMT and other psychoactives as technologies that augment the human OS is a corollary to the perception that they improve "processing power" and enable a "better connection." They "soup-up your 3-D card." They are "keys that activate download codes." In a speculation that has her proposing that the mind downloads information from a cosmic network in loose comparison with the apparent function of the Akashic Record, the brain "stores data locally but also connects you to the larger network ... and it then winnows through all of the raging chaos and (ideally) delivers you up a manageable sampling of the data that is most relevant to you."[28]

Teafaerie emphasizes the "mind manifesting" qualities of the internet, which, if nothing else, has provided a generation of users with tools to contemplate the nature of mind and consciousness—users like Rak Razam, who has grown familiar with what he calls the "vegetal internet," to which he has been uploaded and from which he's retrieved the divine data. "Because most DMT that we're using in the west is extracted from plants and we're adding it to our own endogenous levels of DMT," Razam imagines that when the traveler passes through the initial visual layers and geodesic patterns, "it's like the portal or the gateway or the wireless network point to log into the vegetal internet." Pursuing this metaphor, a "DMT connection" establishes a potential uplink "with all the other entities containing DMT on that frequency or that bandwidth."[29] And with the technologies enabling the internet, according to Razam, "we are almost being groomed for this return to nature, a return to an awareness of what nature really is. The consciousness behind nature that we're embedded in." In these brief asides, we find traces of the language of "moistmedia," championed by "technoetics" pioneer and visionary pragmatist Roy Ascott, for whom the digital, biological, and spiritual are the perfect combination for consciousness exploration—the goal of the artist. Ascott promoted a kind of cyberbotany in which the interplay of cybertechnology and psychoactivity, especially that associated with ayahuasca, encourages the sundering of established categories, potentiating novel language and new realities. The prediction that "vegetal reality and virtual reality will combine to create a new ontology, just as our notions of outer space and inner space will coalesce into another order of cosmography" appears to have found its voice in the likes of Teafaerie and Razam, among many other twenty-first-century cyberbotanists.[30]

Science Fiction and Imaginary Space

In the late nineteenth century, with the idea of the "supernatural" challenged by modernism, the concept of "hyperspace" had, with a legitimacy wrought by association with geometry, grown into an articulation of *transcendence* received within widening circles. The metaphor's power to evoke transcendence is a chief reason for its return in late-twentieth-century cyberculture. But while hyperspace achieved popular reanimation in the 1980s–1990s, it had by that time enjoyed an illustrious career in science fiction. Between the 1930s and the 1950s, sci-fi authors circumvented the relativistic prohibition against faster-than-light (FTL) travel in "ordinary" space, and overcame the problem (or "impossibility" in three spatial dimensions) of interstellar travel by developing the idea that human and other-than-human entities could travel by FTL speeds (sometimes known as "hyperdrive" or "warpdrive") in accordance with the mysterious laws of hyperspace, whose logic followed the metaphysics behind four spatial dimensions and up.

While hyperspace achieved notoriety as a means of interstellar mobility in *Star Trek,* and later in *Dune, Star Wars,* and *Babylon 5,* the trope was evident in early pulp science fiction. A reference can be found, for example, in John Campbell's "Islands of Space," first appearing in *Amazing Stories Quarterly* in 1931. A "5th order drive" allows travel anywhere in the universe in E. E. Smith's *Gray Lensman,* first serialized in *Astounding Magazine* in 1939. Isaac Asimov's *Foundation* series, first published between 1942 and 1944 in *Astounding,* is among the most influential. "Gravitic propulsion" across the twenty-five million worlds of the Galactic Empire relied upon entry into and exit from hyperspace. In the *Foundation* series and later Asimov stories like *Nemesis* (1989), which tells of the exploits of explorers aboard the spacecraft *Superluminal,* hyperspace is more than a space or location—it is a condition. This condition would grow somewhat elaborate, like the alternate universe developed in Iain Banks's *The Culture* series, in which "induced singularity" enables transfer to "infra" or "ultra" space from real space, as transpires in *Excession* (1996).

The fiction of hyperspace matured as it developed as a means of transit throughout the universe, *and* as an ontological condition. It could refer to the space or space-time through which one travels to arrive at A from B, or a space that is neither a space nor time, that is outside of space-time. Hyperspace was developed to signify the most advanced means of mobility and the means of interacting with worlds considered to be "other," "higher," or "parallel." Nelson Bond gave the game away in his 1940 story "The Scientific Pioneer Returns," where, using a "velocity intensifier" powered by hypatomic motors, a ship accelerates into a parallel universe called "imaginary space." Where mysterious Nth-dimensional laws allow for commuting between planets and galaxies (physical space), and for human communication with other worlds and beings (metaphysical space), hyperspace became a powerful literary device—the source of energetic powers and capabilities that enhance and transform normal human abilities.

In popular culture there is probably no imaginative source more powerfully representative of this complex liminality than Stanley Kubrick's *2001: A Space Odyssey,* based on Arthur C. Clarke's 1968 novel, where toward the film's end the viewer is shown both the passage *and* the evolved condition. The mysterious black monolith that appears before Dave Bowman is a gateway through which the astronaut passes. Beyond that, passage is depicted as a cosmic tunnel of lights. And beyond that, Bowman appears to enter Nth-dimensional space-time. Dennis McKenna has commented on this film.

> . . . the "light show" at the climax, as David Bowman's module is sucked into the hyperspatial portal, is close enough to the DMT "light show" that many of us assumed the film sequence had been modeled after it. . . . Like Bowman's hyperspatial plunge into the monolith/portal, DMT brings with it a sense of rapid acceleration, of diving headlong into an overwhelmingly bizarre abyss, freighted with portentousness and hints of insect-like metamorphosis.[31]

Curiously, the monolith from *2001* also appeared before Nick Sand after an intramuscular injection of 60 mg of DMT, following "a bit of Cannabis use, overeating junk food, and an inappropriate setting," where it seemed to be anything but a portal to the next level.

> It put me right into a field of pretty cartoon flowers, with little faces waving their petals and leaves in unison, singing together, "You know that this is not the way to use DMT." I looked up and saw the monolith from *2001* hovering above me, massive and dark; then instantly it came crashing down on me again and again, beating me down and spasming my whole body with cramps. I crawled to the toilet to puke huge amounts of vomit. The toilet bowl was crawling with mysterious interlocking hieroglyphs that seemed to be the keys to the universe. This was a clear message to enter into the DMT space with my system clean and no hectic social scene going on around me.[32]

But in the early 1970s, only a privileged few were accessing their inner fictional realms via DMT. Meanwhile, hyperspace, as a cardinal inter- or transdimensional threshold in the sci-fi imaginary, was pregnant with the possibility of contact with other worlds and their inhabitants. As raw potential, this transdimensionality was essentially indeterminate: a dangerous juncture and an evolutionary threshold.

In science fiction, entry into hyperspace can be acknowledged through such occurrences as a sudden unleashing of natural forces, the application of a powerful magnetic field, traveling to places in space where natural "incongruities" exist, or "the application of the emanations of mysterious new elements."[33] The last cause appears to involve "alien" technologies, perhaps not unlike the "quadridimensional drive" invented by the Jovians (nonhuman inhabitants of Jupiter) in Bond's "That Worlds May Live" (1943), the technology behind an artificial space warp into the fourth dimension. Resulting from the alteration of the geometry of space-time, the discovery of strange yet powerful anomalies, travels into the unknown, or alien interventions, sci-fi hyperspace is fraught with peril, and humans must take precautions. In *Gray Lensman*, the Boskonians attack the Lensman ship *Dauntless* with a weapon that made the crew feel as though they "were being compressed, not as a whole, but atom by atom ... twisted ... extruded ... in an unknowable and non-existent direction." Hyperspace is horrifying and dangerous, as was evident in Donald Wandrei's story "The Blinding Shadows," where Rhillium lenses open up a doorway to the fourth dimension, from which black shadows emerge to consume the inhabitants of New York City. In Milton Smith's "The Mystery of Element 117" (1949), the titular element is fashioned into an optical lens, opening a window into another dimension, a world inhabited by the dead. Hyperspace travel is hazardous. Asimov's short story "Little Lost Robot" (1947) features a "Hyperatomic Drive" and observes that "fooling around with hyper-space isn't fun. We run the risk of blowing a hole in normal space-time fabric and dropping right out of the universe." The lesson seemed clear in Milton Lesser's 1950 short story "All Heroes Are Hated." Set in 2900 CE, the interstellar spaceship *Deneb* went nova, incinerating all inhabitants of the planetary system Fomalhaunt as it exited hyperspace, its drive still on.

Despite such perils, in science fiction, hyperspace is not universally unpleasant or psychologically upsetting for travelers, nor is its condition necessarily disastrous. To the contrary, it may inaugurate something wonderful. While users of hyperspace are exposed to dangers, this imaginary space potentiates so much more. As the sci-fi imaginary illustrates, hyperspace is cast to the brim with potential. While the above narratives apply the twentieth-century imagination to the perils of transdimensional travel and contact, hyperspace has also been adopted as a vehicle of hope, a liminal technology integral to the evolution of the human condition. The theme was implicit to Carl Sagan's 1985 best seller, *Contact,* which positioned a woman—played by Jodie Foster in the 1997 film version directed by Robert Zemeckis—in the breakthrough chair. Transluscent wormholes are traversed by the astronomer and SETI scientist Dr. Eleanor "Ellie" Arroway, seated in a transdimensional pod integral to a machine built by humans according to designs sent to Earth from a civilization from the star Vega. Based on a screenplay first developed in 1979 by Sagan and wife Ann Druyan, the film offers a remarkable story of Ellie's conversion from rational skeptic to believer, where the embrace of other intelligence in the universe is a process of monumental capitulation to the greater mystery in which humanity participates. I say "monumental" here since her conversion is a global media event on a scale far greater than that associated with the first lunar landing. Here is a fragment of Ellie's speech (from the film):

> I had an experience. I can't prove it, I can't even explain it, but everything that I know as a human being, everything that I am tells me that it was real. I was given something wonderful, something that changed me forever, a vision of the universe that tells us undeniably how tiny and insignificant and how rare and precious we all are. A vision that tells us that we belong to something that is greater than ourselves, that we are not, that none of us are alone. I wish I could share that. I wish that everyone, if even for one moment, could feel that awe and humility and the hope, but ... that continues to be my wish.

There is a remarkable resonance between this story and an experience not uncommon to the DMT breakthrough. Take the report of Sara, among Strassman's sixty. A mother, freelance writer, and member of the Wiccan community, Sara had one of the strongest contact events among volunteers in the New Mexico study. Here is how her experience commenced.

> There was a sound, like a hum that turned into a whoosh, and then I was blasted out of my body at such speed, with such force, as if it were the speed of light. The colors were aggressive, terrifying; I felt as if they would consume me, as if I were on a warp-speed conveyer belt heading

straight into the cosmic psychedelic buzzsaw. I was terrified. I felt abandoned. I'm completely and totally lost. I have never been so alone. How can you describe what it feels like to be the only entity in the universe?[34]

Sara undertook a role equivalent to an "earthly spiritual emissary" who appears to have shouldered the responsibility of introducing these aliens to the human experience. It appears to have been a pivotal moment.

I always knew we weren't alone in the universe. I thought that the only way to encounter them is with bright lights and flying saucers in outer space. It never occurred to me to actually encounter them in our own inner space. I thought the only things we could encounter were things in our own personal sphere of archetypes and mythology. I expected spirit guides and angels, not alien life-forms.[35]

I am struck by the concordance of these encounters. Even though the pressure, in Ellie's case, is of a magnitude far beyond Sara's, she and Sara are both invested with self-awareness of participation in an event of great import, a potential watershed in human history. Both projects are funded at least partially by governments. They are monitored and observed by scientists. Either traveler "disappears" for a short duration. Falling through the machine, Ellie's pod disappears for an apparent nanosecond (which she claims was eighteen hours). The common experience with DMT is that those who partake sense they are "away" longer than the duration measured on the clock. Contact with discarnate beings is central to both narratives, beings that share cryptic messages possessing remarkable valence. In either case, the contactees are made aware that they are at an early state of contact and knowledge transfer. In the case of Ellie, the being explains that her journey is humanity's first step to joining other space-faring species. As Sara states, "They told me there were many things they could share with us when we learn how to make more extended contact."[36] Despite the apparent diversity of material (i.e., a fictional narrative on the one hand and a high-dose DMT experience on the other), the question of what these "beings" are, or perhaps where they come from, is a mutually applicable inquiry. The idea that "inner space" is the context for "contact" is implicit to Sagan's work. Mind expansion and space migration were integral processes. The Vegan "machine" can be interpreted as a device enabling portage to the inner landscape, as much as to the outer universe, and this is precisely Sagan's intent, given that Ellie's experience was flush with childhood and life memories, and indeed the figure she encounters takes the form of her deceased father. It is never quite clear if her contact experience is then real or imaginary. This is the very same quandary we have with the DMT and alien-abduction experience. Although psychoanalysts and neuroscientists will stake their claims, it's realer than real for the contactee. Furthermore, in *Contact* and with DMT the interpretation of the messages is the subject of mounting controversies. Ultimately, Ellie faces official skepticism on the one hand and a groundswell of believers on the other—not unlike the predicament in DMT research.

Rather than suggesting that Sara modeled herself on Ellie, both narratives are cut from the same cloth—i.e., a progressive cosmic-contact model implicit to many Space Age sci-fi narratives and the esoteric agendas upon which they rest. The idea of contact as an essential, albeit potentially perilous, step in human evolution comes to life among some DMT experients.

As DMT surfaced in the late 1950s amid the Space Age and a blooming sci-fi imaginary, the DMT user-to-come would be thrown into a world permeated with the hyperspace imaginary. Hitched to earlier promotions of the fourth dimension, astral planes, the miracle-causing world of the "noumenal," and to the imagination itself, sci-fi adopted hyperspace as a convenient and increasingly elaborate device to explain transcendent events at a truly cosmic scale. As a mode of transport and an ontology of being-altered enabling contact with the Other, this novum offers a powerful language for the experient. The relationship hyperspace has with travel and contact offers an idiom and a metaphysics through which DMT events can be owned and articulated. The grafting of the discourse and the visual aesthetics of sci-fi to render events expressible does not imply that the experience is inauthentic and illusory, or merely preempted by popular culture, only that circulating narratives become media of articulation. To ask where these narratives come from and what use they serve would be to undertake an inquiry not dissimilar to that performed by Jeffrey Kripal in his study of the superhero phenomenon, *Mutants and Mystics*, demonstrating that real-life paranormal events are at the root of that phenomenon and that "there is no way to disentangle the very public pop-cultural products from the very private paranormal experiences."[37] While further studies are needed to bear this relationship out, on the back of esoteric and occult developments, sci-fi may have provided an interpretative framework and discursive repertoire that gives expression to the perils and promises of the unknown, a language that communicates the DMT event.

Dimensional Frontiers

With the advent of experimental psychedelics, the concept of hyperspace would undergo portability, as artists and scientists could now undertake personal explorations of a space-time the hermeneutics for which had long been fictionalized in popular culture, where esoteric and science-fiction narratives have been fertile sources for interpretative frameworks suited to the experiential traveler. Consider the following report.[38]

> The vaults seemed to zoom explosively outward then and the gallery expanded ad infinitum into a gargantuan, labyrinthine, almost interstellar space, and through every vault poured the miraculous and zany imps who make the tryptamine hyperdimension their home. The tentacles of lapis lazuli gathered these capricious, multi-colored enigmas in towards the center, and became the architectonic scaffolding of their new multi-dimensional reality, a world which I found myself dab smack in the middle of. It was like a liquid mind ecology of staggering and alien complexity, the mind as it crosses over into quantum warpdrive and migrates ever further out into the oceanic beyond. At this point the glorious geometries transcended what is even vaguely feasible in this three-dimensional mundane world, constantly concrescing into new and variegated permutations, exfoliating out of themselves what might be called hyperspherologies of the divine, and to look anywhere was to be shot clean through with scintillating amazement. Crowding and cramming themselves into my field of vision were thousands upon thousands of beings of every imaginable sort and many that were completely unimaginable.

246

As can be read from this and many other reports of the DMT event, the user could literally jump into hyperspace, a realm complete with features familiar to a sci-fi contact zone, by smoking the compound. Electronic musicians have been keen to amplify this idea, sampling from science-fiction narratives to press their point. Shpongle remains exemplary. "It's three o'clock on what may well be the most important afternoon of the history of this world—humanity's first contact with an extra-terrestrial species." The sample is used in "Vapour Rumours" from *Are You Shpongled?*, where the *extraterrestrial-contact* narrative prevalent within Space Age psychedelia (and the cosmic trajectory of Goatrance) is remixed to evoke the *interdimensional contact* frequent to the DMT event. "Vapour Rumours" also adopts a line stripped from an episode of the 1995 revival of TV series *The Outer Limits*: "We're receiving the transmission. We're seeing some sort of vapour. I don't know, some sort of gas or something. Wait, something's happening." In this sci-fi audio hack, the extraterrestrial-alien gnosis is repurposed for the Hyper Space Age. The vapor drifting through this repurposed dialogue and introduced in the track title is a thinly veiled reference to what is produced when freebase DMT (i.e., its pure alkaloidal form) is heated to the point of vaporization (e.g., using a chillum) and its vapor inhaled.

Entering hyperspace with DMT was a revelation earlier suggested by *Mondo 2000* contributors Gracie and Zarkov in their instruction notes for the psychonautical engineer, "DMT: How and Why to Get Off."[39] In this manual, would-be psychedelic Gagarins were instructed on vaporizing techniques, "freebasing" using a glass pipe with a reaction chamber heatable from below.[40] With the correct method of inhalation, the voyager could "break through into DMT hyperspace." Between 1 and 2.5 minutes from launch, "for all practical purposes, you will no longer be embodied. You will be part of the intergalactic information network. You may experience any of the following: Sense of transcending time and space; Strange plants or plantlike creatures; The universe of formless vibration; Strange machines; Alien music; Alien languages, understandable or not; Intelligent entities in a variety of forms."[41]

Gracie and Zarkov enjoyed cameos in *Cyberia: Life in the Trenches of Hyperspace*, Douglas Rushkoff's optimistic take on the premillennial psyberdelic rave-o-lution.[42] Early 1990s rave was a kind of cultural crossroads for hallucinatory and cybernetic experiences, where, in small circles, DMT was confirming the perception that "reality itself is up for grabs."[43] Transcribing the experiences of scene participants who believed that "the age is upon us now that might take the form of categorical upscaling of the human experience onto uncharted, hyperdimensional turf,"[44] Rushkoff introduced the pseudonymous duo who "sometimes like to think of themselves as anthropologists from another dimension, merely observing the interactions and concerns of human beings." But if Gracie and Zarkov were like anthropologists, they were participant-observers describing to Rushkoff their ability to apply their DMT experiences in their lives. "Zarkov makes practical use out of the sublime DMT state to redesign the personality he uses in real life. He enjoys his DMT experience, then downloads it in order to devise new business strategies or even new sexual techniques." But, he added, "he does not take any of it too seriously."

This contrasts somewhat with the noetic archaeologist of psychedelic hyperspace. With McKenna, hyperspace was adapted to illuminate the experiential qualities of the Nth-dimensional space accessed with the assistance of tryptamines; and throughout the 1990s the effects of DMT would prompt a new experiential language of hyperspace widely adopted by voyagers, contactees, and returnees. Audiences were prepped in the 1980s with an insight bearing the stamps of Hinton and Ouspensky. "The way I think of the mind is as a fourth dimensional organ of your body. You can't see it because it is in the fourth dimension, but you experience a lower dimensional sectioning of it in the phenomenon of consciousness. But it is only a partial sectioning of it."[45] While Ouspensky's experiments with nitrous oxide aided his perception that time as he knew it did not exist, the Russian grew disenchanted with a tool that opened up an empty, lifeless, and extraordinarily oppressive world. On N_2O, it was as though everything in this world was wooden, "as if it was an enormous wooden machine, with creaking wooden wheels, wooden thoughts, wooden sensations; everything was terribly slow, scarcely moved or moved with a melancholy wooden creaking."[46] The experience was heavy and colorless, weighted down by three-dimensional objects. Ouspensky had, of course, experimented with what was available to him at the time. Having been in the right place at the right time, with DMT, McKenna clutched a lightning rod to the higher dimensions, where far from wooden sensations, the topography was scintillating. With this substance, one became a transdimensional emissary. Specialists were required to commit to becoming exposed to higher-dimensional events, and capable of retrieving all they could muster from the experience. By repeated expeditions into DMT-induced space, one could overcome the difficulties posed by the normal human incapacity of adequately transposing phenomena occurring in dimensions above three. Such would enable the forging of a language to express the inexpressible, dramatically surpassing Huxley's lower-dimensional colonialist metaphors.

As a skilled orator of the inexpressible, McKenna believed in the power of the imagination. Following Blake, he thought artists could become exposed to the Divine Imagination. At Esalen in 1983 he alluded to Borges's short story "The Aleph," where the protagonist unexpectedly gazes into a "small iridescent sphere, of almost intolerable brilliance," which turns out to be Cosmic Space, a space in time that appears to contain all other points. "In that gigantic instant, I saw millions of delightful and atrocious acts; none astonished me more than the fact that all of them together occupied the same point, without superposition and without transparency."[47] "The Aleph" was recognized to be Borges's articulation on the infinite and ineffable nature of the Secret, the kind of transposition that may lead to one's condemnation as a lunatic, or celebration as a great artist.

But for McKenna, the Aleph, if you will, is language itself. Tryptamine states were imbricated in the formation of language, and in these states the experient becomes a medium of the otherworld, an emissary of hyperspace, brokering its dialects in the form of novel syntax, visionary art, and occultural insights. The hyperspace farer is a message-bearer who seeks to transmit the content of their revelations. A primal mode of transmission is heard in the immediate outpourings and feral extemporizations of those returning from these realms. Such rare emissions are speculated to have been "the expression of the assembly language that lies behind language," a "primal language" like the Kabbalistic language described in the Zohar, "a primal 'Ursprache' that comes out of oneself."[48] For McKenna, this primary argot was commonly identified as the Logos, described as "an informing voice" that guided Western civilization for about 1,700 years. "All ancient philosophers strove to invoke it. It was a voice that told self-evident truth. With the passing of the Aeon and death of the pagan gods, this phenomenon faded. However, it is still available through the mediation of the plant teachers."[49] He further held that, with tryptamines, the teachings are not that which are heard, so much as seen—a *visible language*. It is a higher-dimensional language that "condenses as a visible syntax."[50] Often breaking out on stage with simulations of the noises emitting from his mouth during his DMT trance states, the ultimate xenolinguist explained during a session at Esalen that "the incoming sensory data can be recombined in such a way that no trace of the portal of entry is left upon it. And in that case, you get this freely evolving topology of light and sound that is translinguistic. It has a grammar of form if you will. So that it is not shorn of meaning, it is simply shorn of the kind of particularized meaning that logical necessity imposes on language. Instead, it has an emotional richness, a kind of poetic depth that is not like ordinary language at all."[51]

The visibility of language was a noted feature of the DMT trance as reported by Gracie in the mid-1980s in *Notes from Underground*. The "elf" beings visiting Gracie, who had on this occasion smoked 40 mg of DMT in addition to taking 150 mg of the entactogenic MDA, were comprised of an extraordinarily "visible language" that she "saw/read/felt/heard" all at once. The beings were entreating her to the message: "Strong, safe, strong, safe; help, ok, ok, help; safe, safe, alright!," which was conveyed in several simultaneous sensory modalities. "Vision, heard speech, read language, music, song, images and pictures all happen at once, so that the meaning is multi-dimensional."[52] The experience of a multisensual "language" is a common occurrence for those entering these realms. Take Binkie2000's extraordinary visitation in a Hollywood Hills bungalow in 1991. Within a short space of time from smoking DMT, Binkie2000 was greeted enthusiastically by beings that appeared to be unfolding themselves from all-pervasive geometric light patterns. "It was as if they pulled them selves out of 3-dimensional envelopes that were laid flat within the walls of the now living chamber of electric colour and light that now surrounded me." With a now-familiar ring, the "energy creatures" vied for attention. These beings:

> seemed to clamber over each other towards me, each wanting desperately to share his/her/its magical abilities with me. . . . They pulled

things into existence, as if from pockets of vacuum space within themselves, like beautifully jeweled liquid light revolving eggs, that transformed into and out of themselves like rolling smoke infused with layer after layer of brightly coloured electrical information. Hieroglyphics, fractal in nature, unfolded endlessly from everything, pouring into my view with beautiful sounds and vibratory waves.

Privy to information made of "pure light wave vibrations," an "energy" that could be simultaneously thought, seen, smelled, touched, and tasted, it was concluded that the language was nothing less than the "whirring, buzzing particles and waves of energy quantum physicists describe to us."[53]

Such wayfarers understand "time" as fundamentally altered in the DMT trance. According to Gracie, in a "space" where one's perceptions are enhanced, "the linear temporal order of ordinary reality is shattered." But while Gracie grappled with the personal significance of her encounters, traced to childhood memories where the elves appeared just as they do in the DMT trance "shifting, folding, multidimensional, multicolored ... always laughing, weaving/waving, showing me things, displaying the visible language of which they were created, teaching me to speak and to read," McKenna's attention was directed to the future, which was reckoned to be casting its dark shadow over the present. This perception was integral to the inverted telos in McKenna's cosmogony and central to the teachings he claimed to have received in tryptamine consciousness. Displaying a debt to Teilhard de Chardin, whose Omega Point is the attractor in the evolutionary process, history is not that which blunders along blindly but is being pulled by a "transcendental object," a force otherwise referred to as "the great attractor." It was apparently a force that can never be fully revealed, although its shadow could be intuited under the right conditions. In such states, one could multisense this attractor "throwing out images of itself that filter down through lower dimensional matrixes. These shadow images are the basis of nature's appetite for greater expression of form, the human soul's appetite for greater immersion in beauty, and human history's appetite for greater expression of complexity." History was considered to be an endless round of anticipation, with the entire historical catalog of apocalyptic and millenarian movements amounting to the "shockwave of the eschaton."[54]

In the vision of that which might have been designated *hypertime*, the whole of history "appears to be some kind of strategy for the conquest of dimensionality." In the eschaton forecast, humanity was to be released from three-dimensional space to literally enter hyperspace, with the transit from one dimension to another a "continuation of a universal program of self-extension and transcendence that can be traced back to the earliest and most primitive kind of protoplasm."[55] The ongoing pronouncements on this phenomenon amounted to a spinning vortex of speculation the accumulation of which seemed to echo the accelerating advent of novelty implicit to the Timewave Zero theory itself. If you peel away the layers of intellectual hubris, the pivotal revelation was that humanity was destined to depart 3-D reality for the next level.

> It's a Gnostic return, an idea of alchemical sublimation and rarefaction. I see the cosmos as a distillery for novelty, and the transcendental object as the novelty of novelties. When we formally refine that, we discover something like a Liebnizian planet; a monad of some sort; a tiny thing which has everything enfolded within it. This takes us to another dimension, where all points in this universe have been collapsed into cotangency. It's an apotheosis. The Earth is giving birth to a hyperdimensional being.[56]

And what's more, the cosmic birth was "coming soon"—i.e., 2012. The above statements derive from the "trialogues" conducted between McKenna, Rupert Sheldrake, and Ralph H. Abraham in the 1980s and 1990s at a variety of locations, including Esalen. Cofounder of chaos theory, Abraham wasn't swallowing the apocalyptic overtures and Judeo-Christian end-times trajectory of McKenna's speculations. While he would have doubtlessly reminded Terence that we're still here, Terence played truant by himself departing for the next level in 2000.

A critical link between the mathematicians of the nineteenth century and late twentieth century, and friends with McKenna since the early 1970s, Abraham is among the principal figures with whom he exchanged thoughts on these matters. The DMT/hyperspace connection was fueled by their dialogue. Holding a keen interest in using computers and staged performances to generate visual and aural expressions of math, Abraham was inspired by what we might call veridical space. He has recalled a formative life moment (outside of his first experience with LSD in 1967) when, in 1969, he "smoked up a large bottle" of DMT with a doctoral chemistry student working on the synthesis of DMT at UC Santa Cruz, where he taught in the mathematics department. As Abraham explained, following this incident and over the course of the next twenty years, he resolved to explore the connection between mathematics and the Logos. "This is a hyperdimensional space full of meaning and wisdom and beauty, which feels more real than ordinary reality, and to which we have returned many times over the years, for instruction and pleasure." Echoing his interests in Hindu philosophy, in the late 1970s Abraham built a "vibrating fluid machine to visualize vibrations in transparent media." In the 1980s, he simulated the mathematical models for neurophysiology and for vibrating fluids using computer programs with computer graphic displays, a project that led to a new class of mathematical models called "cellular dynamata." Eventually, he constructed machines simulating these models at increasingly faster speeds. In 1989, twenty years after his debut with DMT, Abraham was given access to the world's fastest supercomputer at the time, the Massively Parallel Processor at NASA's Goddard Space Flight Center in Maryland, into which his model for the visual cortex had been programmed. The result was, he explained, a "fantastic experience." Staring at the color screen of the MPP "was like looking through the window at the future, and seeing an excellent memory of a DMT vision, not only proceeding apace on the screen, but also going about 100 times faster than a human experience."[57]

As growing numbers became familiar with DMT hyperspace in the 1990s, the effort to map its terrain expanded. Dimensional psychonaut D. M. Turner adopted "CydelikSpace" to capture a higher-dimensional spacetime that he had frequented. "I could view my life through four dimensions," he journaled, "easily recalling in full detail perspectives and perceptions back through early childhood. I could see the development throughout my life, of ideas, identity, beliefs, coincidences, relations, and limitations. These were seen with the precision of someone analyzing graph charts displaying data, yet with full emotional connection."[58] While Turner, whom we'll learn more about in the next chapter, navigated "CydelikSpace," Des Tramacchi preferred the phrase "DMT Umwelt" when referring to the extended sensory environment enabled by DMT ingestion; and author of *Surfing through Hyperspace* Clifford A. Pickover adopted "DMTverse," which, in support of both McKenna's and Strassman's speculations, "seems to exist independently of our ordinary flow of time."[59] An armchair dimensionologist, Pickover proposed the development of "neurodelic" technologies, powerful neuro-imaging techniques that would yield data on brain function during travels in the DMTverse, comparing these to dream states.

Strassman would himself contrast the dream state with the DMT state through reference to a volunteer report. It had been conveyed that, when dreaming, one drifts from one dream to the next without any perception that the dreamworld one has left is still taking place without one being there to dream it. But with the DMT state, "that level of existence was going on all the while, even when you weren't in it, and you were just kind of dipping into it at the point where it was just happening. If it was a month between trip to trip, then a month of time, in some form or another, had elapsed in the DMT realms."[60] While nomenclature for this experience may not yet exist, the charting of hyperspacetime has inspired a Hyperspace Lexicon wiki created by psychonauts at the DMT-Nexus, where one can stumble across terms like "eschatothesia," a contraction of "eschaton" (end-time) and "esthesia" (sensitivity). The word refers to "the sensing of a future attractor towards which the dynamic system evolves over time. The future event casts its shadows backwards in time where the shockwaves of the eschaton can be perceived as sensations, feelings, visions." The Lexicon adopts a list of intriguing jargon for hyperspacejunk like *jimjam*, the "squishy, goopy, sticky, stringy matter of hyperspace that anything can be created from," and *plasmatis*, the "multicolored constantly shifting gel-goo of amazement which decorates the space around everything in the land of the elves."[61]

While some forge lexicon from their neo-antipodean adventures, others fall back on the advance survey-work of McKenna, who continues to chart the terrain from the beyond. As Terence McKenna made public the private communiqués he received from the "Logos," shaped as it was with its own translinguistic grammar, those communiqués have received high-profile posthumous transmissions. In one exemplar of digital alchemy, *Imaginatrix: The Terence McKenna Experience*, thousands of layered images, motion graphics, and private video recordings made with McKenna between 1989 and 1994 are used to map the unchartable, mediate the immediate, convey the unspeakable, and lift the veils on language itself. Filmmaker Ken Adams, creator of *Alien DreamTime* and *Strange Attractor,* adopts the concept of the "Imaginatrix" to describe—sampling McKenna—"a universe inside the human mind" and a "place that shamans have known of for millennia."[62]

Mapping these travels, and describing what's "X'd" there, presents the cartographer with challenges, perhaps the greatest of all being that the map is not the territory. No amount of intellectual prestidigitation, nor vocal sampling, nor pixelated surfacing, can stand in for experience. Who are the proud settlers of suburban geometries, not to mention tryptamine travelers marooned on the dimensional interstices, compared to those who blaze the frontiers of consciousness? A trailblazer driven to storytelling, McKenna's psychedelic empiricism plays heir to a frontier mentality integral to the American character. If LSD had lubricated the expansion of consciousness for Leary, who, like Huxley and many other forebears, trekked east following the conquest of the West, DMT constituted the new "fall line." The new frontier was dimensional, a *promised land* informed by an odd mix of New World shamanism and Western esotericism. As a frontiersman of consciousness, McKenna courted "reality's edges, and the edges of biology" in interventions that were "not for sissies."[63] Voicing the courageous spirit behind the breakthrough into new frontiers, he may well have been the Daniel Boone, perhaps more than the Galileo, of consciousness exploration. Riding high and saddled up on optimal techniques of synthesis, cultivation, extraction, and administration, the higher-dimensional plateau is in some measure a mythic place of absolute freedom not unlike the colonial frontier. Like a terrestrial frontier, the psychedelic frontier is an outlaw(ed) zone, where rugged individuals, passionate experimentalists, and reagent provocateurs find refuge, stake claims to impossible psychic terrain, and broker deals with undiscovered "populations" as strangely familiar as they're profoundly incongruous. But while the dimensional *other* may be as confronting as that encountered on the colonial frontier, rather than the alien other against which travelers, settlers, and their "civilization" are measured, the *alien* encountered in the hinterlands becomes cognate with the becoming of the human *self.*

Ranging the trailhead of psychedelic hyperspace, Jim DeKorne recognized that beings from higher dimensions can perceive lower dimensionals with far greater ease than the reverse. While the sense organs are unsuited to perceiving these entities, such can be achieved within what DeKorne called "mind-space." Stringing together elements of Jung, Western esotericism, and shamanic traditions, he argued that psychedelics enable access to a multidimensional reality ("mind-space") perpendicular to the three-dimensional one ("space-mind") we all know. Given our dimensional limitations, for humans this multidimensional reality can only be perceived as an internal condition, which was felt to be a transcultural and religious phenomenon identified as a transcendent hyperspatial Pleroma.

> The inner dimensions remain largely *terra incognita,* despite a million descriptions of them by a cross-cultural spectrum of observers throughout history. In addition to constituting the Upper and Lower Worlds of shamanism, this realm is the Pleroma of the gnostics, the Astral Plane of occultism, the Bardo realm of Tibetan Buddhism, the Eternal Dreamtime of the Australian aborigines, the Unconscious Psyche of modern psychology, and the Heavens and Hells of fundamentalist sects worldwide.[64]

While the modern world dismisses the Pleroma of "mind-space" as fantasy or "epiphenomena of the subjective imagination," the psychedelic shaman learns to trek deep into this inner-outer wilderness. Given the need for the reconnected to intervene in and redress the crises of the modern world, this was good news for DeKorne, for whom relationships forged in higher dimensions should serve to maintain equilibrium in our world. McKenna was less inclined to this strategy. The evolved human capacity to enter hyperspace was less a means to improve our lot in the world of the here and now than a preparation for the next. Hyperspace amounted to a cosmic wilderness experience allowing the intrepid to dissolve the illusion of separateness, the "perspective from which we recognize ourselves as gnats caught in the lens of eternity. Death reminds us of this. And so too, but by a different route, does DMT."[65] However we regard this quest for the hyperspatial promised land, McKenna was always the first to make himself the butt of the cosmic joke. He was intensely aware that, while a lived experience, the transdimensional could not be represented as unalloyed fact—which is simply to acknowledge the paradox of mystery itself (the mystery behind mystery). The epicurean appetite for the fruits of the hunt could never be fully satiated. And since *the mystery* could not be caught as such, any attempt to serve it for consumption ought to be disputed no matter how exquisite the presentation or appetizing the flavors. The experient must probe the hinterlands themselves. And so, with poetic license and multimedia techniques, the brazen dimensionologist and comically loquacious entheographer was essentially daring the world to *try this at home*.

CHAPTER 10

Breaking Through
Heroic Doses and Little Deaths

The Ontoseismic Event

For Terence McKenna, the crisis of history required a mythology born from the psychedelic empiricism inhering in, for example, three successive inhalations on a DMT pipe or the ingestion of five dried grams of psilocybin mushrooms. Such was the "heroic dose," the alkaloidal powder-keg fueling expeditions from which returnees gift their self, kin, and community with otherworldly beneficence. The evolution of consciousness was reliant on this intentional hyperspace odyssey, a journey not dissimilar to that observed by Joseph Campbell in world mythology. In *The Hero with a Thousand Faces,* Campbell articulated a panmythical—masculine—narrative: "A hero ventures forth from the world of common day into a region of supernatural wonder: fabulous forces are there encountered and a decisive victory is won: the hero comes back from this mysterious adventure with the power to bestow boons on his fellow man."[1] As illustrated in the exploits of figures I'll explore in this chapter, and today found in vast online repositories recording the experiences of anonymous psychonauts, the psychedelic odyssey retains core elements of Campbell's monomyth, a circumstance amplified by the fact that most of the celebrated storytellers are male, some with a penchant to champion their experiences as more heroic than the next guy's.

Significant nonordinary states of consciousness triggered by psychedelics are pivotal to these mythopoetics, and no one has contributed more to this field than holotropic-therapy pioneer Stanislav Grof, who has recounted the significance of a range of psychoactive compounds in his life, beginning with a spiritual awakening with LSD-25 in Prague in 1956. Among other significant transit points, in his autobiography *When the Impossible Happens: Adventures in Non-Ordinary Reality,* Grof describes a momentous death/rebirth experience on 5-MeO-DMT, which is approximately ten times more potent on a per-weight basis than DMT.[2] While lasting more than twenty minutes on the clock, the experience was immeasurable by any standards of reckoning time and space. On an unspecified date, he took about 25 mg of 5-MeO—i.e., up to four times the average effective dose. The onset was sudden.

> My only reality was a mass of radiant swirling energy of immense proportions that seemed to contain all of existence in a condensed and entirely abstract form. I became Consciousness facing the Absolute. It had the brightness of myriad suns. . . . It seemed to be pure consciousness, intelligence, and creative energy transcending all polarities. It was infinite and finite, divine and demonic, terrifying and ecstatic, creative and destructive—all that and much more. I had no concept, no categories for what I was witnessing. I could not maintain a sense of separate existence in the face of such a force. My ordinary identity was shattered and dissolved; I became one with the Source.[3]

Gradually emerging from this state—later interpreted as the Dharmakaya, the Primary Clear Light that, according to the *Bardo Thodol,* the *Tibetan Book of the Dead,* appears at the moment of death—Grof visualized returning to our solar system, then Earth, the United States, California, and finally his identity and present life. In this archetypal there-and-back-again journey, Grof had the deep impression that he was dying, his return coinciding with a flood of memories of his lives present and past.

> For some time, I believed I was experiencing the bardo, the intermediate state between my present life and my birth in the next incarnation, as it is described in the Tibetan texts. As I was regaining more solid contact with reality, I reached a point where I knew that I was coming down from a psychedelic session and that I would survive this experiment. I was lying there, still experiencing myself as dying, but now without the sense that my present life was threatened. My dying seemed to be related to scenes from my previous incarnations. I found myself in many dramatic situations happening in different parts of the world throughout the

centuries, all of them dangerous and painful. Various groups of muscles in my body were twitching and shaking, as my body was hurting and dying in these different contexts. However, as my karmic history played out in my body, I was in a state of profound bliss, completely detached from all these dramas, which persisted even after all the specific content disappeared from my experience.[4]

In a tradition inspired by Huxley, and adopted by Leary and colleagues, the *Bardo Thodol* provides the guiding idiom. Not unlike Leary, Grof wasn't simply adopting an existing framework to process the incoming data, but developing practices to assist others to access these states, and consequently repair and improve their lives. This is the measure of the psychedelic hero's journey—bringing back methods and formulating protocols to augment the experience. In Grof's case, his experiences were pivotal to an understanding of the perinatal and transpersonal domains of the psyche, and were formative to the holotropic breathwork practice developed with Christina Grof.[5]

Whether through alternate or parallel universes, other dimensions or unconscious psychic domains, the sensation of *travel* is implicit to tryptamine consciousness, which has its phenomenologically peak moment in the *breakthrough* experience. With the "heroic dose," which is simply an *effective* dose, users pass into realms thoroughly alien or uncannily familiar, yet typically received as veridical, even possessing an independent existence. Travelers may encounter improbable entities and ontological anomalies. They may become exposed to an all-pervasive light source or energy to which they feel intimately connected. The experience may be disturbing, or it may be exhilarating, it may trigger alarm, induce a state of grace, challenge one's beliefs, inspire reevaluation of one's motives, incite a sense of responsibility. Receiving crystal-clear visions, flushed by noetic torrents, and endowed with peaceful afterglows, wayfarers return to their everyday lives bearing "gifts" manifesting in a song, a piece of music, novel theories, engineering designs, visionary art, and countless other boons concretized and distributed as techniques and protocols through which the experience finds continuity.

The breakthrough event may shatter the world-image and preconceptions of first-time users, a circumstance for which the word "ontoseismic"—a portmanteau of *ontos* (Greek for "being") and *seismos* (earthquake, from *seiein*, meaning "to shake," in Greek)—was added to the Hyperspace Lexicon at the DMT-Nexus. The term is quite specific. Whereas it is more intense and deeper than "mindblowing," "disturbing" lacks the insight and beauty accompanying the experience. While the "ontoseismic" state may be traumatic and overwhelming, it is stated that "when the traveler can reach a certain inner concentration, a firmness, while being and experiencing these newer and deeper levels of truth, the psychedelic shock turns out to be utterly freeing. The paradox is that the experience has the disturbing effect of a trauma, yet the cause of the trauma is a Platonic experience of total truth, beauty and love." Grof's 5-MeO-DMT encounter offered evidence for this type of event. Further terms in the Hyperspace Lexicon include those identifying advanced powers of perception, such as the ability to "see" light with all of one's senses. Thus "kinesioöptic" refers to a state where "the body can dissolve in the experience and be left with just the sensing of light."[6]

Regardless of lexicon, a faculty of being empowered with enhanced visual perception is common during the DMT trance, of being fated with *presque vu*, an ability to see, or almost see, through a reality filter previously unnoticed. While launched through alien cities at such a lightning speed that content retention was virtually impossible, smoking DMT at the Chan Koh Hotel, Palenque, gave Daniel Pinchbeck an awareness of the realm "next door." As he wrote in *Breaking Open the Head*, "behind every billowing curtain, hidden inside the dark matter of consciousness, now playing every night in disguised form in our dreams. It is so close to us, adjacent or perpendicular to this reality. It is a soft shadow, a candle flicker, away." It was in this realm that those Pinchbeck referred to as the "cosmic supervisors" had repeated to him: "This is it. Now you know. This is it. Now you know."[7] In his collated reports on DMT ventures, prolific author and science columnist Clifford A. Pickover has commented that most users feel "as if a veil has been lifted, allowing them to view events that have been continuously transpiring in the DMTverse with an existence independent of the psychonaut." Accessing this divine universe, explorers are accessing another reality "mere millimeters away from our own." Pickover refers to the "feeling of enchantment, of sanctity, of beauty, a sense of gaining privileged access to knowledge and intelligence" among travelers in this space, for whom the world "appears to be 'constructed,' composed with care like a work of art or an intricate hand-spun fabric."[8] Such an ability may be identified in another term indexed in the Hyperspace Lexicon, "kalonkinesioöptic," which prefixes "kinesioöptic" with *kalon,* a Greek term referring to the Platonic idea of transcendental beauty, thereby referring to an immersion in astonishing beauty.[9]

Such depictions are removed from the revelatory gnosis reported by other avatars, and for whom the "cosmic supervisors" aren't necessarily benign. DeKorne's early-1990s 50 mg breakthrough on an extract—which he thought was DMT but whose main active alkaloid was 5-MeO-DMT— of *Phalaris arundinacea* is a case in point. Using metaphors reminiscent of Burroughs, he reported an experience "analogous to having a psychic hydrogen bomb go off" in his brain. But unlike Burroughs, who kept an antidote handy as a virtual sidearm to guard against complete psychic capitulation, DeKorne's attitude was to "resist any impulse to resist: flow with it, breathe with it. Imagine a Zen meditation at Hiroshima ground-zero." While DeKorne was at ground zero consumed by "an atomic fireball at the instant of detonation," his ontoseismic flash receded, allowing him to receive the breaking news, related by way of verses from the *Bhaga-vad Gita,* where Krishna gives Arjuna "divine eyes" through which he is able to behold Krishna's "mystic opulence."[10] In *Psychedelic Shamanism* DeKorne described the realm behind "the veils" visible to the psychedelic shaman with "divine eyes" as the Pleroma, an unconscious or imaginal realm transit to which should be undertaken by those suitably equipped for cosmic battle. Visionary artist Luke Brown seems suitably endowed, his own "divine eyes" gazing upon Krishna's multidimensional form in *Vishvarupa* (see Figure 13).

A Greek word meaning "fullness" or "plenitude," Pleroma is a term borrowed from Jung, who took it from the gnostics, who knew of a hidden kingdom inhabited by gods and demons, among them the Archons—entities that are, according to DeKorne, "cruel, unfeeling and dictatorial in their relationship with humans," and who are otherwise "dissociated intelligences who feed off of human belief systems the way that we eat hamburger."[11] What is at stake is liberation from the coercive power of these invisible rulers. In this view, DMT and other psychoactives enable modern explorers to recognize the otherwise-hidden agendas of the gods, and further to convert their coercive powers into those at one's own disposal. This process of empowerment is no simple procedure. "Obviously it behooves all psychedelic explorers to prudently evaluate the kinds of 'allies' they choose to integrate into their psyches in this way," DeKorne cautions. "The higher the level of unification the better; otherwise it is seductively easy to become entrapped within dimensional resonances of dubious ultimate value." It is repeatedly announced by DeKorne, care of the Upanishads, that "it is not pleasant to the Devas that men should know this."[12]

Compared with the saccharine depiction of the DMTverse in Pickover's assessments, DeKorne offers a radical vision of the reality construction to which the wayfarer is exposed. Seeing through the veils renders transparent the agendas of the Archons. Other explorers have noted enhanced powers of observation consistent with this form of "divine vision." Here, for instance, is Robert Augustus Masters in Tahiti in 1995 in the period following a notorious hit of 5-MeO-DMT.

> Without any warning, a tsunami of terror roared through me in the middle of a silky feast of a dinner, while a troupe of aggressively smiling, neonesque dancers moved through their nightly repertoire right in front of us—an overcolored, surrealistic soup of shrinkwrapped culture and amazingly meaty tourists both feeding and inundating my horrified, pseudoanthropological fascination with the whole indigestible scene.[13]

In the year following his experience, more of which will be described later in this chapter, Masters seems to have been overtaken by an extraordinary ability to penetrate the mundane. This magnified capacity to perceive the wonder-horrors of reality connotes the abilities of shamans as much as superheroes, whose powers are the manifest expression of real-life paranormal experiences visited upon a host of artists, including editor of *Amazing Stories* and *Fate Magazine* Ray Palmer (who didn't like psychedelics), and Scottish writer Grant Morrison (who did). Morrison may have been "straight edge" until the age of thirty-one, but in the 1990s he developed a penchant for psychedelic compounds that could "open up my subconscious and turn my brain into a super-conductor." *The Invisibles, Flex Mentallo,* and other renowned comic book work "emerged from the cockpit of a rocket-driven rollercoaster of LSD, cannabis, mushrooms, DMT, 2CB, ecstasy and champagne."[14] That psychedelics bestow supranormal powers of perception is made available in telling clarity in the work of Morrison, known for breathing life into serials and creating his own superheroes, fictional characters possessing magical and occult powers. Morrison's self-reflexivity in these matters has deep roots, and can be observed, for instance, in the unlikely person of Stephen Gaskin, who, before founding The Farm in 1971, experienced a series of superpsychedelic episodes through the Summer of Love, later recounted in *Haight Ashbury Flashbacks: Amazing Dope Tales of the Sixties*. In the style of a comic book hippie crusader, Gaskin recounts a series of magical feats, among them the time he fell in love with future wife Ina May. "We all toked up on DMT, and I looked at her and just fell telepathically into her, and saw that we just matched up to many decimal places, and were really as telepathic as we could be."[15]

"It Seemed an Awfully Lot Like Death"

Analogous to the initiatory ordeals of shamans and alien-abduction narratives, the effect of DMT is not uncommonly reported to resemble a near-death experience (NDE). "It seemed an awfully lot like death," Hubbard announced in the aftermath of his flight test in 1961. "Old Al. Hubbard was gone," Cappy reported. "This thing reminds you of something maniacal the way it strips it from you. You're almost dead to yourself."[16] It was a theme to which McKenna returned time and again, i.e., that intimations of immortality are vouchsafed by tryptamines, and that DMT offered a glimpse across the yawning abyss. "It now seems possible," clarified Peter Meyer, "by the use of the psychedelic tryptamines, to venture into the death state before we die and to accustom ourselves to that state. This is the path of the shaman and the spiritual warrior. At death, when the transition is finally and irrevocably made, the psychedelic explorer will enter a realm he or she knows from previous experience, and will, hopefully, not be swept away by fear and ignorance."[17] McKenna was driven to reflect on the peculiar "chemistry of dying" associated with DMT. Using language attributed to Rupert Sheldrake, DMT was regarded—in the period just before McKenna was himself destined to experience the final chemistry lesson—as a "necrotic substance." Also regarded as a "necrotogen," it is a substance that anticipates the death state.[18] Such a substance is figured to potentiate a state of grace in which one may become reconciled to the inseparability of death and life. Ministers of the psychedelic séance, Shpongle transmitted spectral enunciations on this theme on their 2005 album *Nothing Lasts . . . But Nothing Is Lost*. The album track ". . . But Nothing Is Lost" is a dirge to McKenna, whose voice is channeled to explain the essential value of impermanence: "Nothing lasts . . . nothing lasts. Everything is changing into something else. Nothing's wrong. Nothing is wrong. Everything is on track. William Blake said nothing is lost and I believe that we all move on." While under conditions of revelation, ecodelic neophytes may grow discontent with received truths, entheo-initiates are challenged to accept their complicity in the cycle of life/death. "Life must be the preparation for the transition to another dimension," explained Terence on "Molecular Superstructure," from the same release. On "Exhalation" there's a break in Raj's flute, and Terence eventually exhales: "Nothing is lost . . ."[19]

While the term "necrotogen" designates DMT's role in anticipating the death state, terminology appears to be lacking for its possible role in eliciting recall of pre-birth states. Having tracked down a "DMT cult" in early-1990s Oakland called Horizon, Douglas Rushkoff observed a ritual in which a young musician smoked 5-MeO-DMT and had a memory of what he'd lost during his own birth. Jonathan's shocking revelation was that he was not who he'd been raised to think he was. It was as if he'd received the news: "We're sorry you had to find out this way. Such a shock to you. But now you know . . . you're not Jonathan." For someone who was raised "Jonathan," the shocking download was perceived to serve "a smoother eventual transit from this life."[20]

As the examples in this chapter will demonstrate, the "DMT flash" exposes one to an experience very much like dying. Inaugurating "test runs of the inevitable fear and phantasmagoria, as well as avenues towards acceptance and integral insight," as Erik Davis has clarified, used within appropriate set and setting, psychedelics can serve a unique purpose. "Having died, even in hallucination, one can no longer quite live the same way."[21] And yet, "having died" in such fashion is, as McKenna would also remind us, "not death." The near-death experiences that may be associated with psychedelics or other life experiences "are not *death* experiences."[22] To the contrary, the user is exposed to the genuine parameters of being truly alive. Such may be accomplished through a psychedelic process that triggers real anxieties about the imminent conclusion of one's biographical and physical existence, followed by a rebirth experience that may be accompanied by feelings of grief—i.e., a therapeutic means of separating from one's death-denying self. In this way, the little death of tryptamine liminality offers a dose of authenticity, enhancing the perception that what is transpiring is *real*. Perhaps *too* real. So real that one will not readily seek to repeat the occasion. "If one is not terrified," McKenna counseled, "either one is a fool or one has taken a compound that paralyzes the ability to be terrified. . . . The experience must move one's heart, and it will not move the heart unless it deals with the issues of life and death. If it deals with life and death it will move one to fear, it will move one to tears, it will move one to laughter."[23]

While DMT may precipitate an NDE, the experiential parameters "near death" are wide. Horrific or sublime, grievous or joyous, suffocating or breathtaking, the event is dependent on complex variables. At one extreme, the event may be accompanied by profound dread, not unlike that reported by a member of The L.A.B. ("Large Animal Bioassay")—the psychonautical group of friend-volunteers of chemist Alexander Shulgin who bioassayed newly discovered molecules—after smoking 100 mg of DMT.

> As I exhaled I became terribly afraid, my heart very rapid and strong, palms sweating. A terrible sense of dread and doom filled me—I knew what was happening, I knew I couldn't stop it, but it was so devastating; I was being destroyed—all that was familiar, all reference points, all identity—all viciously shattered in a few seconds. I couldn't even mourn the loss—there was no one left to do the mourning. Up, up, out, out, eyes closed, I am at the speed of light, expanding, expanding, expanding, faster and faster until I have become so large that I no longer exist—my speed is so great that everything has come to a stop—here I gaze upon the entire universe.[24]

In this epic moment, self-implosion seems to have coincided with a centripetal expansion, with the bioassayer obtaining unmitigated cosmic terror.

On the other hand, a great many more reports offer variations on a theme eloquently expressed by Nick Sand.

> [DMT] opens the doorway to the vastness of the soul; this is at once our own personal soul, and its intrinsic connection to the universal soul. When the underlying unity of this fictional duality is seen and felt, one experiences a completeness and interconnection with all things. This experience, when we attain it, is extremely beautiful and good. It is a song that rings and reverberates through the lens of God. Now we know why we were born; to have this intense experience of the sacred, the joyous, the beauty, and the blessing of just being alive in the arms of God.[25]

Rick Strassman has similarly described the experience as a merger with "an indescribably loving and powerful white light that emanates from the divine, holy, and sacred." Not unlike those having an NDE event, the DMT experient is "embraced by something much greater than themselves, or anything they previously could have imagined: the 'source of all existence.'" Those who attain this experience "emerge with a greater appreciation for life, less fear of death, and a reorientation of their priorities to less material and more spiritual pursuits."[26]

With love/fear, wonder/dread, rapture/despair as possible themes and outcomes for the traveler, the DMTverse truly is an experiential multiverse. Travelers may declare with absolute newfound conviction that "This is it!," or they may be compelled to ask, "What the fuck was that?" In the former affirmational mood, the psychonaut may be overawed by the sensation that *All is One*, a revelatory panspiritual perspective for converts, mystics, and emissaries. In the latter, they are haunted by the uncertainties of existence, by the intuition that *All is not right*, that something wicked this way comes, that disharmony or imbalance prevails. And since such moods lead travelers to challenge worldviews, reassess relationships, and modify consumption practices, these are revelations equally affective and deeply transformative. The several cases that follow—which also document the interest in 5-MeO-DMT—span this experiential terrain.

Meme Trading in Hyperspace

For the first account, we return to Telegraph Avenue, Berkeley, on an evening in the fall of 1965, when future transdimensional freakloriate Terence McKenna was visited by the "machine elves of hyperspace." The ontoseismic event was captured by Shpongle on "A New Way to Say Hooray."

> So, you take, let us assume, a third toke, long and slow. You vaporize.
> And you take it, in, and in and in, and there's a sound like the crumpling
> of a plastic bread wrapper, or the crackling of a flame. And a tone. A
> hummmmmmmmmmmmmmmmm.... And there is a cheer. The gnomes
> have learned a new way to say hoooooooooooraaaay.[27]

McKenna recounts how he was mobbed by these beings, "babbling in a visible and five-dimensional form of Ecstatic Nostratic." Utterly perplexed, there were "mirror-surfaced tumbling rivers of melted meaning" gurgling all around him.[28] Invoking Syd Barrett's lyrics from "The Gnome," a song from Pink Floyd's 1967 debut album *The Piper at the Gates of Dawn*,[29] McKenna was himself sampling from the era's psychedelic rock to sing his spice fairies into form. Still listening to Shpongle's "A New Way to Say Hooray," McKenna is heard to marvel "what arrests my attention is the fact that this space is inhabited ... And so, like dual self-dribbling basketballs, these things come running forward, and what they are doing with this visible language that they create, is that they are making gifts, making gifts for you."

Rushed by the little people who tried to teach him "the lost language of true poetry," McKenna spent the rest of his life firing his public's imagination with startling propositions on these entities and their "gifts," well before an elven-tide rippled through the cultural underground. Cribbing from Jung's "collective unconscious" and author of *The Invisible College* Jacques Vallée, McKenna gained notoriety in the 1980s for his position that the "machine elves" were—in a logic not dissimilar to that of "flying saucers" and the messianic mythos—an expression of the Overmind (other times "Oversoul," or "Gaia"), the objective of which was to confound science at a time when the existence of the human species and the ecosystem of the planet came under serious threat. Following this interpretation, tryptamine-induced entities are as challenging to us as was the idea of the

Resurrection to the Roman Empire or a U.S. Air Force jet transport landing among precontact tribes in New Guinea. By the early 1990s, McKenna had grown attracted to the view that his entities bore resemblance to fairies, the sídhe, and specifically the Tuatha Dé Danann, a race of supernaturally gifted people in Irish mythology who are thought to represent the main deities of pre-Christian Gaelic Ireland. The revelation came upon a reading of Evans-Wentz's *The Fairy Faith in Celtic Countries,* for which McKenna wrote the reprint's introduction.[30] The understated implication was that the dead were making themselves known to McKenna in DMT space, and that their elven form was an expression of his Irish roots. In one of the best summaries of his views on elves from around the turn of the 1990s, he entertains the idea that these entities "have something to do with the dead."

> If you were to ask a shaman what these entities were, he would just say that these are the ancestors. These are spirits of the ancestors. There is a hair-raising quality to contacting these things. They are both very familiar and yet somehow freakishly bizarre. And the presence of the familiar with bizarre creates a kind of cognitive dissonance and there is nothing else that feels quite like that.[31]

In *The Fairy Faith,* McKenna learned that the doctrine of purgatory—the intermediate state after physical death in which those destined for heaven undergo purification before entering heaven—was used by St. Patrick when converting the Irish and thus Catholicizing Fae, or Fairyland. "The Celtic pure belief is that the dead go to a realm that is co-present all around us, we can't see them but that all around us is just jammed with souls in wild states of activity, and that if you have the eye, you know, a certain talent, you can see these things." To appeal to Celtic peasants, Fae was upgraded to the status of purgatory. The implication was that when smoking the spiritual technology of DMT, you explode the doctrine of purgatory and Catholic cosmogony and break through into Fairyland, a world that resembles Fae. And not only that, you access the "gnosis of elves." They may be humorous, unpredictable, somewhat cruel, and boisterous, but these elves are archetypal artificers. "They make things in metal and jewels and glass ... they are underground craftsman." And here we approach McKenna's gnostic kernel: the true artifice of elves. "The secret of the elves, what they really fabricate, is language. This is why in Irish mythology if you can get elves on your side you can make great poetry, because they are the keepers of linguistic artifice, and getting elves on your side makes you into a master poet." Terence did not make this claim to explain his own skills and status as an oratory genius, which may be a viable argument. Rather, his concern was to draw the connection with the Amazonas, and its traditions of DMT use, and where

> there are these things called *oo-koo-hé* and they are actually described as "bouncing demons" and they come into being when you're stoned, and you are supposed to invite them into your chest somehow. Well then the number of these things you have inside of you determines what kind of a *real man* you are.... And all the time they're saying "make these objects, do what we are doing." Well then you go down to the Amazon, to the icaro-singing ayahuasqueros and they are using voice to make objects. So what we are on the track of here is a pharmic-driven physiological ability to transduce language as something seen.[32]

Terence was on the scent of the magical foundation of the tryptamine-influenced hyperspatial encounter to which he and Dennis had been exposed in 1965–67. While apparitions have appeared before humans for millennia, McKenna recognized that we lack the conceptual tools to make adequate use of the incoming data, and in times when the West is deluded enough to believe it is "advanced." Whatever the hyperspace entities are—the unconscious, the Overmind, the Logos, ancestors, travelers from the future, etc.—McKenna believed that a relationship should be formed, and that their language be studied and analyzed, with a hyperspace lexicon forged through continued exploration of this "space." This was not the terrain of involuntary "abduction" by aliens, or the chance or accidental NDE. Our recourse, he argued, was to uncover language by voluntarily transporting one's self beyond the veil through the ingestion of tryptamines, principally DMT.[33]

McKenna's chief hyperspatial boon was his "Timewave Zero" model, relayed to him in a series of tryptamine states through the 1970s. He would explain how his journeying inaugurated an exchange relationship he entered with the habitués of hyperspace whom he recognized as "meme traders"—

those who "trade hyperspatial notions from across the cosmos." Apparently these entities courted him like "primitive art collectors," and in exchange for what he knew about the *I Ching*, they gave him "their model of time," the closest thing to a hyperdimensional object, clarifying that while such objects themselves cannot exist in this world, "blueprints of them can."[34] The outlandishness of this meme humped back from the other side is that it appeared to offer a mathematical model of death. With humanity apparently breaking through to the other side of history in 2012, the then-coming "end-time" was in its conception a magnificent projection of the "mini-apocalypse" inaugurated by DMT and psilocybin. While ego-dissolution is endogenous to the tryptamine encounter, McKenna's exploits demonstrated that a robust ego was mandatory to wax forth on the global stage about ego-dissolution. What has been identified as "psychedelic millenarianism" hitched to José Argüelles's ancient-Maya-calendar-inspired Dreamspell movement, and an apocalypticism with Judeo-Christian hallmarks similar to that identified by Norman Cohn in *The Pursuit of the Millennium*,[35] may have been an aggran-dization of McKenna's victory over mortality commencing with his DMT inauguration on that rainy night in 1965. With its impending culmination in 2012, the Timewave Zero model offered a vision of a cosmic rebirth that appears to have reified his tryptamine-inspired experience of immortality. "Each one of us is going to die, rather soon," he informed those gathered at the Camden Centre, London, in 1992.

> So why not assume that whatever that transformation is it will be gen-eral, and then prepare to meet it as a collectivity, not the death of the rationalist and the reductionists where we return to worms, but, you know, the death of Blake and of Revelations and of the *Tao Te Ching* and the *Tibetan Book of the Dead*—the death that is victory, the transcendence of matter. That's what death is, and what we need now for the good of the planet and for ourselves is to somehow find a doorway into the imagination, that's where the future lies. Our powers have grown too great to be unleashed on the surface of a fragile planet.[36]

If the cosmic congrescence—the "transcendental object at the end of time"—was simply a refracted projection of McKenna's personal ontos-eismic novelty event, his model of time may have been little more than a gratuitous inflection of his ego, in spite of his committed challenge to the ego and the reemergence of "masculine dominator culture." There are many who have regarded the McKenna road show as a danger to rational thinkers and the vulnerable everywhere, as is the measure of the accusation generally leveled at cults. Some critics may have been right. And yet, if nothing else, McKenna was self-aware of just how ludicrous his pronouncements were. "I find myself," he replied, under fire from Ralph Abraham and Rupert Sheldrake, "in the predicament of leading the charge into the greatest unanchored speculation in the history of crackpot thinking."[37] Already scornful of anything smelling like a religious movement, had he lived the final twelve years counting down to the 2012 "event," McKenna may have grown to become his own biggest critic.[38] And yet, he may have continued to buttress his hunch with further intellectual legerdemain to support his one-man road show. Regardless, cultic behavior seems a laughable prospect given that Terence McKenna offered no real teaching or system, and perfected a self-satirical attitude before audiences of hyper-reflexive individuals who responded to his ideas with equal measures of enthrallment, mirth, and skepticism.

CydelikSpace

Known as "the Chuck Yeager of psychonauts," Joseph Vivian (a.k.a. D. M. Turner) was a psychedelic shaman who did not seek the limelight, prophesy the world's end-times, nor offer an enthralling hermeneutics on the nature of death. Comparing and contrasting the effects of different compounds, often in multiple combinations, Vivian was a pioneer of comparative psychedelics. As reported in his 1994 underground classic *The Essential Psychedelic Guide*, he made repeated forays into the otherworld next door, providing vivid accounts of his experiments with a variety of then lesser known compounds like DMT, ketamine, the psychedelic 2C-B, and the harmala alkaloids. As his chosen pseudonym conveyed, DMT (and 5-MeO-DMT) was among his favored tools, as was, tragically, ketamine.[39] Having been raised in a "fairly strict" Roman Catholic family, psychedelics admitted Vivian into "a world of compassion and beauty and creativity."[40] It was a world in which he was a noted explorer. On one of his favored combinations—potentiating ingested DMT (160 to 200 mg), with the har-mala source Syrian rue (4 g) enhancing and prolonged the effect by three to four hours—the following reads like a passage from the field diaries of a surveyor of unexplored country.

> The scenes are rich, vivid, emotionally charged, and filled with sym-bols and archetypal images that feel imbued with deep meaning and significance. The speed at which visual images develop is slower than with those that accompany the "flash" of smoked DMT. I've found that this allows me to absorb the content of the images more fully. These DMT visuals had a degree of realism I've never before encountered. The images were so real, so alive, palpable, and tangible that I could almost taste them. And I nearly felt that I could reach into their dimension and physically touch them.[41]

Vivian reported communications with ancient entities that were vastly superior in intelligence to humans and that manifested in different forms. In one form, they were "elfin" or "leprechaun," in another, they approx-imated "God." Most unlike the Archons reported by DeKorne, Vivian's entities appeared omniscient and benevolent, akin to spirit guides or guardians. "They are able to tailor the whole contact experience in such a way that they move you through different levels of relevance and meaning at a very particular rate."[42]

In the 1995 winter edition of *The Entheogen Review,* writing as D. M. Turner, Vivian reported a startling breakthrough experience. Piggyback-ing the potent active chemical in *Salvia divinorum* (salvinorin-A) with three tokes on 30 mg of DMT, he seems to have caught the "guardians" off guard. Having been greeted by the standard welcoming committee of "children, elves, Cheshire cats, and intricate geometric objects," and gaining passage to a realm of guardians "busy watching over everything that happens in our space-time dimension and occasionally making minor adjustments to keep everything on track," he suddenly burst backstage into the important business.

> The place I entered was some type of research center, and my attention was on some large metallic pods that were being moved in and out of

racks by elaborate robotic arms. Each of these pods was something like an isolation chamber. They were shaped like large coffins, although with rounded edges. The oval cross-section was about three feet wide, the length about eight feet. The beings who used these pods looked exactly like humans. The pods were filled with a foam type material with a cutout for a person to lie down. The foam was connected to the sides of the pod and also contacted the entire skin surface area of the person inside the pod. The foam was serrated, and I understood that it served as a conductor of food, water, heat, medicines, etc. between the pods' technical systems and the person resting in it. These pods were also cold chambers. They were not for cryogenically freezing a person, but put them into some type of suspended animation. Anyhow, the whole purpose of these pods and this research center, was to increase the level of DMT in the brains of the pod sleepers. This was the only method the people of this planet knew of for obtaining the experience imparted by DMT. These people would basically go into a pod for weeks or months at a time. The DMT levels in their brain would be significantly increased, and they would spend their time having the most fascinating dreams! This research was considered the most important and serious aspect of this society's evolution.[43]

At this interdimensional nexus, there occurred an exchange among equally startled travelers. At the instant Vivian entered the mind of a "woman" inside one of the pods, and gained access to the "DMT dream" she was experiencing, she became aware of him and his world. "This was the first time her society had ever had contact with an Earthling," he wrote. It was a shock and an embarrassment for his contactee from the other side to discover that "there were other people who didn't need to go through the elaborate technological process of increasing DMT levels through suspended animation, but simply smoked the stuff, and could collect it from any of several plants." He gauged that she instantly wanted to "announce her discovery to the rest of the research team."[44] In this mutual discovery and extraordinary knowledge transfer with the alien natives, Vivian, the Marco Polo of DMT explorations, seemed to be extending the hyperspace transactions initiated by McKenna.

Clocking up countless hours on a variety of compound fuels, Vivian charted a region he called CydelikSpace, a labyrinthine field of power that was a variation on DeKorne's Pleroma.

> It appears to contain all matter and energy in all of its manifestations since the beginning of time. . . . While in this state I have experienced in lucid detail, what seems to be every thought that has been formulated in my mind throughout my entire lifetime, as well as each perspective through which I've viewed life, and each experience I have had. I have seen my entire life laid out in suspension before me, and I could wander through my previous perspectives as a detached observer. . . . It is said that when one is about to die, their entire life flashes before their eyes. While under the influence of psychedelics this flash has lasted for hours.[45]

While alluding to the digital world of "cyberspace" described in William Gibson's novels, the word "CydelikSpace" does not infer a fictive or allegorical world. "It is accessible now, and even appears to be the underlying reality behind all existence," Vivian claimed. "It is of this state that one becomes aware, to a greater or lesser degree, during deep psychedelic experiences, and any other mystical or spiritual experience."

Not only is CydelikSpace a repository of all of one's own life perceptions, like the Akashic Record it contains "all thoughts and experiences of every human, animal, plant, and molecular life form that has existed in the universe since time began, including the life experience of individual cells and galactic star systems."

> Other lives can be experienced with almost as much detail as one's own, down to a child's wonder upon first feeling dew on the morning grass, the trace of lipstick left on your lips after kissing a lover whom you've never before met, or a child's first impression of a pattern on clothing, seen while playing at nursery school, in a building too modern to have existed during your own childhood.

The experience could confer even more vivid impressions, such as "being in an extraterrestrial body while making love" and thereby enjoying sensations "perceived through a much finer tactile sense than exists in humans," or "the experience of a planet's soul over millions of years as different groups of plants evolve, flourish, and give way to their successors upon its surface." CydelikSpace is conveyed to be a domain of suprasensory perceptions, with Vivian claiming he experienced events that later manifested in consensus reality, and was sometimes able to view real-time events at a distance (not unlike as reported for dream states). He also reported an astral-traveling capability, usually when combining 2C-B with ketamine. When the conditions were right, he claimed an effortless ability to ride the cosmic wind through CydelikSpace at otherwise-impossible speeds. "Once in this Jet-Stream I am carried along with no effort of my own, and virtually locked onto a path headed to the most sublime dimensions."[46]

Since it produced more "kaleidoscopic universes per square millimeter of visual space than on anything else," with an unsurpassable detail in the patterns and brilliance in the colors, Vivian regarded DMT with great reverence.[47] But as his ego remained relatively unaffected when exploring "realms of discarnate entities and awesomely powerful psychic energies," his psychedelic safaris proved ontologically challenging. As he noted, "almost everyone I've known who has used N,N-DMT repeatedly, eventually encounters deeper fear than they've ever felt before." It may be somewhat ironic then, that the compound that didn't leave his ego intact (ketamine)—potentiating a habit-forming, oceanic, ego-dissolving sense of immortality, earning its reputation as the "heroin of psychedelics"—appears to have been incidental to his death, a circumstance all the more tragic since Vivian felt that DMT was the superior ally in the human quest to becoming "more evolved, and more knowledgeable."[48]

Comparing the "sheer perfection" of DMT with the "sheer force" of 5-MeO-DMT, Vivian also noted in the widely read *Essential Psychedelic Guide* 5-MeO's relative potency in terms of size of dose, its speed of effect, and "how forcefully it blows apart my universe." Offering an account that reads like a synopsis of Grof's experience, he wrote that in fifteen seconds on 5-MeO, "I can literally feel my mind exploding and expanding outward to encompass first the area near me, then the planet, and eventually the cosmos." If this didn't generate enough intrigue among readers, he added, "I've found taking a hit of 5-MeO just before having an orgasm to be most enjoyable, and this often makes the visuals abundantly colorful. However, getting the timing right on this can take some practice."[49]

The Toad, the Crystal, and the Palace

D. M. Turner was among the earliest popularizers of 5-MeO. Tracking down this compound became a hunting ritual for trekkers in the physical and hyperspatial realms—especially given its venerated source in *Bufo alvarius*, a toad native to the Sonoran Desert stretching from southern Arizona to Sonora, Mexico. The *Bufo* toad made a storied entry into popular culture, due in large part to a rampant urban legend that licking species of the toad induces psychoactivity.[50] Additionally, prior to the 1990s there were scattered reports on the practice of sourcing, harvesting, extracting, and inhaling 5-MeO from the venom of *B. alvarius*, with early explorers cautioning subsequent travelers on the unnerving character of the accompanying experience. One early explorer compared the effects to "having a large elephant sit on one's head."[51] In their report, Wade Davis and Andrew Weil relate a user describing the inhalation of 5-MeO vapor as "a rocket ship into the Void," while another commented: "If most hallucinogens, including LSD, merely distort reality, however bizarrely, 5-MeO-DMT completely dissolves reality as we know it, leaving neither hallucinations nor anyone to watch them. The experience need not be negative, but it is not for the novice."[52] Commenting that adherents to the "Church of the Toad of Light collect and dry the venom of this toad for inhaling its vapor as a sacrament," Jonathan Ott reported "a modern ritual cult" associated with *B. alvarius*.[53]

Cautionary tales and reports of mysterious user cults proved magnetic for some, like extreme-sports enthusiast James Oroc, for whom the visual effects of DMT were child's play compared with 5-MeO, which he lauded for its role in "temporarily erasing the interface between mind and matter," and enabling consciousness to "return to Mind as light." In July 2003, Oroc underwent a conversion from atheist to gobsmacked believer, "a powerful lesson," he recalled in *Tryptamine Palace: 5-MeO-DMT and the Sonoran Desert Toad*, "for someone who has never feared authority, the ridicule of my peers, loneliness, or the possibility of physical injury." Smoking 5-MeO on his thirty-sixth birthday on a "mattress in a nondescript suburban home in

Portland, Oregon," this self-confessed "hardheaded motherfucker" found "G/d." That's "G (over) d," his formula developed to distance himself from the Christian deity, and to "express the source of the universal energy that we collectively as a species have named God."[54] Naming "G/d," and fearing it too, Oroc rebranded the infinite and went in search of the source. As told in *Tryptamine Palace*, Oroc's subsequent toading adventure with friends to the Sonoran Desert has the hallmarks of a classic hero's journey. A trek to a remote location, an ordeal, the discovery of a sacred object—referred to as the "ultimate organic enteogenic prize"—and the gift (the onward journey to Burning Man in Nevada's Black Rock Desert to share the prize). Oroc's entourage traveled in an olive-green biofueled bus from Los Angeles to Paradise, a hot mineral springs in Southern California. The going wasn't easy in Paradise. They "scoured" the desert for a week in "a fruitless search," until they were "forced to think like toads—become toads—lying for hours at night in the hot mineral springs of Paradise." Doubtlessly traumatic! The seekers having virtually abandoned their quest, a *Bufo alvarius* appeared before them, and was promptly caught and milked. Harvesting several, Oroc netted about 3 g of crystallized venom, "enough so that we could sit down by the pool and smoke something sacred, something that had not been bought from any dealer, nor isolated by any chemist, something sought after and hard-earned, one of the rarest treasures known to humanity. We had milked an ancient and carefully scraped up crystals more precious than diamonds: our chemical white gold." While already a convert, Oroc's interest was in the gnosis unique to toading.

> When you smoke the venom of the Sonoran Desert toad, you enter a realm beyond the limitations of any human language, a place where even the wildest ranting of an afflicted mystic or the maddest fantasies of a theoretical physicist both fall universes short of describing the knowledge implicit in that omniscient tryptamine zone. In this place, all the words in the world are like a desperate message in a solitary bottle, thrown into an endless sea.[55]

Common to the 5-MeO encounter is a comparison users make with other (less heroic) journeys, and the rare encounter with the "white gold" milked from a toad simply amplifies the comparative hubris. "Our society has spent so much time trying to squash the production and sale of LSD," states Oroc, "yet all the while, sitting in the mud on the side of the road, there is a natural tryptamine that makes acid look like training wheels."[56] By comparison to DMT (and LSD), it was as if 5-MeO could better enhance one's latent psychic powers. And the superliminal landscape of Burning Man was pivotal to Oroc's mission. For nouveau psychedelic pilgrims, Black Rock City had become a desirable locale of experimentation, and yet that and other festival contexts offer little certainty for travelers of the DMTverse, especially since the festal setting is already chaotic and unequivocally altered. Smoking DMT on the desert *playa* is like throwing rocket fuel on a wildfire, or jaywalking across a twelve-lane superhighway, as DJ Spooky's experience at Burning Man seemed to attest. Interviewed by Erik Davis, Spooky addressed his "psychologically corrosive" episode in 2002. "I actually felt like my brain had gone past the point of no return. I mean, everything's already fragmented, but it feels like if I touch this stuff ever again, my brain will just fly to pieces. . . . I felt like my brain became Times Square, a kind of boring, rushing collage of conflicting images and ideas, each one demanding its own time and space in my brain."[57] While the demanding physical and random social character of Burning Man may put a wrench in the works, travel to and sharing "white gold" harvested from the Sonoran Desert toad among his "tribe" in the Black Rock Desert seemed pivotal to Oroc's claims to "modern mystic" status. Finding "G/d," Oroc delivered the word, first in the form of a manuscript gifted to his Burning Man tribe, then as a book and a website.[58]

In these metaphysical boons, James Oroc samples from contemporary quantum physics and Tibetan Buddhism to explain the brilliant white light he experiences on 5-MeO. These experiences, he writes, "have led me to believe that when our consciousness is freed of the constraints of matter and mass," as it is on 5-MeO, "it spontaneously returns to the universal ground state of light, where it ultimately recognizes the true nature of reality in union with light: union with G/d." The "true nature of reality" is serious business made simple with a hit of this stuff, and Oroc believes that the light encountered is "a highly coherent light emitted via the neurons in my brain and my DNA, which originates from the other side, from the quantum vacuum, the void."[59] Basically within seconds, one gains access to the "light of creation," which is the Tibetan light of Rigpa as outlined in the *Bardo Thodol*, as well as "the tunnel of light" in NDEs. Here, the Tibetan concept of the "bardos" or "intermediary states" remains important since, in these, "one possesses a body of light that is capable of crossing into universes existing in far-away dimensions at the speed of thought." While the *Tibetan Book of the Dead* had been adopted, as we know, by Leary to formulate a guide for the psychedelic experience and a manual for psychotherapeutic development, Oroc appears concerned more with epistemological claims, since he has been freed, after all, from illusion to observe the "true nature of reality," an authoritative stance grounded in modern quantum physics. Freed from its three-dimensional limitations, consciousness "is able to resonate in coherence with the zero-point field as a form of light."[60]

A quantum-entheogenic adaptation of the perennial philosophy is offered here, with Oroc holding that what has been identified by mystics throughout the ages is being rediscovered by physicists and cosmologists, and identified as the "zero-point field," which is "the true underlying reality of our universe." Since 5-MeO provides access to this underlying reality, which Oroc calls the "Akashic Field" by way of Ervin László, it offers a simultaneous mystical and quantum experience.

> Coherent nonlocal resonance with the standing ground-wave of all reality—the zero-point field—would give access to all knowledge in the universe, at once. And from this comes the recognition of self as a microcosm and reflection of the ultimate coherent state of the zero-point field—the Akashic Field—the conscious wave that we all came out of, and the wave to which we will return.[61]

If we compare the Akashic Field with CydelikSpace, there is much that resonates between the experience of enlightenment or satori entailed in the Akashic Field and the field of possibility endogenous to CydelikSpace. Vivian was clear that it is impossible for any human to comprehend all of CydelikSpace. He held that while the experience sought by many who practice Eastern religions closely resembles CydelikSpace, those who've claimed to achieve enlightenment "seldom describe vast and detailed perceptions, such as the infinite variety of life forms that have existed throughout time and space, and in the nonmanifest realms."[62] This "field" variation may aid understanding of experiential variances triggered by DMT and 5-MeO, which may also teach us something about the differences between shamanism and mysticism. Like hyperspace, Vivian's CydelikSpace features strong elements of the otherworld to which shamans are accustomed, where the entranced traveler receives messages and manipulates the world to varying degrees. In the Akashic Field, Oroc's consciousness and the zero-point field are reported as becoming One. While DMT may empower one to *Just Do It* (i.e., interact in an alternate topology jammed with moving geometric shapes and entities), 5-MeO submits one to *Just Be in the Presence of It* (i.e., dwell in a place in which one feels one has merged). The traveler on this royal road who returns to the light, and is freed of mass, may be "guided to the supreme realization of wholeness and Oneness that is at the center of existence."[63] This for Oroc was a genuine mystical experience, the burden of proof for which is evident in the tremendous responsibility it dealt him. *Tryptamine Palace* amasses details on a world in humanitarian and ecological crisis, and sounds an urgent need for a solution—involving some combination of the intentional ritual use of 5-MeO and Burning Man–type communities. Among the red tape one would need to cut through on the road to this utopian dream is the fact that 5-MeO-DMT was effectively added to Schedule I in the United States on January 19, 2011.

Discovering the Light in the Black Hole of Being

Where a divine beneficence persists among zero-point field workers, a dark mood abides in the accounts of others. Psychologist and psychospiritual guide Robert Augustus Masters did not return to the light in a supreme realization of Oneness, nor undergo a conventional entheogenesis. Recounting a three-month ordeal after smoking 5-MeO-DMT, in *Darkness Shining Wild: An Odyssey to the Heart of Hell and Beyond* Masters elucidates his agonizing estrangement from divinity in exquisite detail. Shortly after 3 p.m. on February 19, 1994, in a sun-drenched living room not far from San Luis Obispo, California, Masters became completely unconscious of waking/physical reality, finding himself out of body and falling into "a horizonless horror that was madly and monstrously pulsating, moving far too fast, in all directions at once."[64] Incredulously, Masters claimed to have smoked "about thirty grams," an amount that stood uncorrected in the reprint. Given that it would be impossible to smoke that amount in one sitting, upon my questioning Masters revised this to 30 mg, still about five times the average effective dose of 5-MeO. Whatever the precise quantity or provenance of the compound Masters smoked, almost succumbing to respiratory failure and seizures, and subsequently swamped by a cosmic fear marking the suspicion that existence is overshadowed by an unbearable truth, it appears he took a king hit.

Striking to this account is how, in rare poetics, the author journals his ontological nightmare, offering a skilled articulation of the trauma of being alive, the terror of eternity, and the cold comfort in knowing that death is merely a breath away. Like a news anchor reporting from the scene of his own derailment, Masters observes "a dimensionless black pit of primal panic" that "pulls at me, pulls and pulls, eerily sentient and far too close, its jagged electricity worming through me." The vivid hopelessness of this account would not be out of place in the work of H. P. Lovecraft.

> No limits, no edges, no exit. It was a timeless, boundless Chaos, continuously creating and consuming itself on every sort of scale with unimaginable power and ease and significance. . . . Everything was constantly dying and morphing into everything else in endless and impossible-to-anticipate ways, conveying to "me" with overpowering conviction that this was, and would forever be, my—and our and everything else's—fate, beyond every possibility of form or individuation. Evolution without end. No exit—nothing existed apart from or outside of this. I was in hyperterror, seeing without eyes, hearing without ears, desperately not wanting to die—or live—in such a condition. While this was occurring, my body was, unknown to me, rigidly locked as if in rigor mortis, purple-faced and unbreathing.[65]

Not a witness to his own conception, which had been Hubbard's awakening experience, Masters was a primary witness to death—his own and that of the cosmos, magnified as an ongoing ordeal.

I could not shut off my multisensory feeling-visions of endless recurrence, regardless of how much novelty was factored into it. My death, your death, our death, humankind's death, planetary death, solar death, death of the whole cosmos, would unfold before me with nauseating intensity, making a mockery out of human achievement and evolution, and then, worse of all, it—the entire fucking universe— would somehow start up again, then once more extinguish itself, over and over and over, ad infinitum. No beginning, no end. The entire universe less than a breath in the eternal, self-aware, boundless continuum of Is-ness.[66]

In an awesome revelation that might have engendered wonderment in others, in Masters's cosmic Groundhog Day, *Is-ness* is not wrapped in an ontological security blanket, but is a "madly pulsating, sentient Wonder-Horror," and "a shiveringly creepy transpersonal paranoia" from which there was no escape. Masters was apprentice to an experience of non-duality that was more cosmic Horrorshow than joyous Homecoming. "That everything appeared to be arising and passing in the same inexplicable moment—which I had meditatively intuited for years—brought me no comfort whatsoever, no warm and fuzzy sense of sacred time, no celebratory feeling of arrival or oneness, but instead only an ominous, sickeningly brilliant, omnipresent dread."[67] The dreadful shining darkness into which Masters plunged lies at a remarkable remove from Oroc's total dissolution into the light radiation of the Akashic Field, or the cosmic rebirth implicit to Grof's experience. While Oroc explained that "our atoms are resonating with the vibration of the quantum vacuum," and that 5-MeO enables merger with the "coherent cogent standing wave that is the universe,"[68] Masters's "standing wave" better approximated a tsunami that demolished him over and over again. It was a fall into an abyss Sartre or Camus couldn't have dreamed up. "I felt trapped 'in' primordial Being itself, as if doomed to exist 'there' in—and, worse, even *as*—an infinite variety of forms, forever and ever. No escape—just endless incarnation hand in transparent hand with the formless, unimaginable enormity of beginningless Is-ness. This was a Freedom from which there was no freedom."[69] At this point I am drawn to find parallels with the mad visionary for whom, as

Huxley conveyed, everything in the universe is transfigured "but for the worse." Everything, "from the stars in the sky to the dust under their feet, is unspeakably sinister or disgusting," for those so afflicted. "Every event is charged with a hateful significance; every object manifests the presence of an Indwelling Horror, infinite, all-powerful, eternal."[70]

Immediately liberating for Grof and Oroc and terrifying for Masters, these explorers had starkly disparate reactions, illustrating the diversity of the NDE terrain with 5-MeO. Masters's extreme response was likely due to a combination of factors, including excessive dose and a reckless ill-preparedness. Even with lifelong training in Buddhist meditation and yoga techniques, he appeared unable to relinquish attachment to his material identity and body. But while riding the cosmic horror train, and clutching the Jesus Strap all the way around the Big Bend, the ordeal was ultimately transformative for Masters, demonstrating that a total confrontation with dread may be integral to an NDE. Emerging from his experience like a humbled newborn, it was Masters's claim that dread—the "openly felt presence of Death"—was the gift he received from this journey, a dread that mutated into a "mind-shattering grief, a grief that gradually became suffused with awe and, finally, love." And he clarified that this love "was not the love of personal attraction or desire." It was, rather, the feeling of "primordial Being, overflowing with both compassion and openness, making the innate insubstantiality or 'void nature' of objects, perceptions, emotions, and identity nakedly obvious to me." This "holy poetic" gift appears to have exposed the fundamentally illusory nature of Robert Masters as a separate identity—the one he had clung to so desperately—the realization of which he claims catalyzed a transition from "egocentered selfhood to soul-centered selfhood and beyond."[71] In embracing his dread of nonbeing, Masters seems to have added weight to the significance of certain compounds as necrotogenic.

To truly prepare for our death is not an exercise in morbidity or despair, but rather a wholehearted entry into a fuller, more awakened and caring life, a life made more precious, vivid, and authentic by its ongoing intimacy with Death and dying. Such preparation is an excuse to at last go more fully into our life, an opportunity to journey into and through the very heart of suffering, until we emerge more whole, more alive, more and more intimate both with what dies and with what does not die.[72]

Not the meaninglessness and despair of Sartre's *Nausea,* but a lesson serving psychospiritual development, *Darkness Shining Wild* is a meditation on near death, which appears to have had a significant impact on the life of the author. The experience apparently served to identify Masters's crippling status as an "iconoclastic guru" who, as he wrote in his 2009 afterword, was "deluded enough to have made a virtue out of my multiple-partnering/polyamory." He also became resolved to dissolve his status as a "cult leader" of the alternative community he founded. The chief gnosis for Masters is that we are always close to death, which is a seismic conceptual shift in a culture that is in denial of death, where we "go to absurd lengths to keep the almost-dead alive for as long as possible" and "believe in an afterlife that's an eternal holiday for 'I.'"

> We hear about near-Death experiences, perhaps marveling at their mystical elements, forgetting that Life itself is a near-Death experience. Right now.... Death, in the form of impermanence, is always with and within us, from breath to breath, ever now, already eating through whatever veils or gates we may have installed between Life and Death.... Avoiding Death deadens us. Getting intimate with Death enlivens us.[73]

While imparting genuine spiritual wisdom, Masters is not preoccupied with being appointed, or self-appointed, as a modern mystic. Masters makes a poignant statement in relation to NDE claims.

> A NDE may open one's heart and transform one's life for the better, but it generally does not radically decentralize egoity—at least for very long—and may in fact even strengthen it, in sometimes very subtle ways. The certainty that Death is not the end may do more to fuel "I's" craving for immortality than to spur an actual exploration of the nature of "I." This has been unintentionally supported by the glowingly positive pictures conveyed by the majority of NDE reports.[74]

But if Masters's 5-MeO-triggered near-death experience offered any lessons in psychospiritual development, there is no replicable therapeutic model to be found here. While useful as a meditation on mortality, Masters hardly provides a manual of encouragement for future users. If Szára was the Neil Armstrong of DMT, Masters behaves like the last man off the moon.

Experiment at La Rosacita

Experiential journalist and multimedia entheographer Rak Razam's introduction to 5-MeO offers another flight path, at a dramatic remove from Masters's. Four decades after the Year of the Gnome, and the subsequent experiment at La Chorrera, Razam's experiment at La Rosacita proved to be an unexpected sidetrack to a commissioned report on the Peruvian ayahuasca "gringo trail" for *Australian Penthouse*. His documentary film codirected with Tim Parish *Aya: Awakenings* features an extraordinary segment where, on July 7, 2006, Razam smokes 5-MeO with curandero Ron Wheelock in his jungle lodge La Rosacita just outside Iquitos. In the film he's wearing an EEG skullcap fitted by neuroscientist Juan Acosta, described as "a classic mad scientist on the frontiers of consciousness who's traded his castle for a thatched hut and his lab coat for bermuda shorts and beads."[75] The device is apparently used to feed Razam's altered-state brainwaves into a computer for later receptor-site analysis and brain mapping. "Wire me up and fire me in to the mind of God," announces Razam before lying back in the cot. Wearing eye goggles, a data cap, and the world's widest grin, it appears as if he lay astride a transdimensional operating table. He claims to be "vibrationally clean," having participated in a dozen ayahuasca journeys over the previous weeks, "bungee jumping into the Godhead." Razam also performed a preflight, ten-minute alpha meditation intended to bring his "brainwaves down," meaning he was present and without resistance to his pending departure from body and mind. In the style native to the experiential journalist, a few minutes of his experience are depicted in the film, adding a unique whole-world-is-watching feel to the psychonautical endeavor. There possibly hasn't been a more visually promoted tryptamine experience on record. After launch, Razam is held down by Wheelock, as if, without that assistance, his whole vibrating body would rise from the cot.[76]

The film doesn't capture what's going down at the receptor sites of this brazen test pilot, but the filmed episode is visually enhanced by an extraordinary tripping sequence, with Razam applying a detailed voice-over.

> Holy mother of God, I'm melting into *it*. . . . Wave after wave of energy and I'm breaking through an infinite kaleidoscopic matrix of pure unadulterated consciousness. The current of life is streaming through me and it's like a brainwave of God. And I'm surfing it, surfing God's wave. Somewhere within I can feel the broadcast of a pattern signal, a cosmic heartbeat, like the pulse of life from a baby from within the mother. The feeling keeps flowing as I break through layers, pop dimensional membranes, and there is no fear, no holding back. Just pure consciousness, merging with where it came from. The Godhead. The Overmind. Mother. Matrix. Union.

Much of the narrative is transposed from Razam's book, *Aya Awakenings: A Shamanic Odyssey,* documenting the mission and its phases, adopting a style that reads like a hybrid of Leary and Ginsberg.[77] Within twenty seconds, "somewhere within I can feel the broadcast of a pattern signal, a cosmic heartbeat like the pulses of life from a baby within the mother. The feeling keeps flowing as I break through layers and pop dimensional membranes . . ." Over three minutes in, his head jerks back, and Razam releases a long exhalation. "It's like cosmic orgasm, total interface with the Godhead, merging overlapping becoming IT, IT becoming me, full telepathic union— no separation, no fear, all the levels of maya and illusion and noise stripped away and this is IT and IT is all there is and all is love."[78]

In the treatment Razam gives the episode in his book, one of the greatest hero's-journey narratives and boy's own adventures—the lunar space race—is adopted to allegorize the mission. Of his mood before smoking, Razam wrote, "I feel like that first monkey they fired off into outer space back in the 1950s," while at the same time romancing the days when "astronauts were exploring new frontiers and changing the world with their discoveries. And I'm the lucky chimp."[79] And as he comes up, Razam comes across like a proto-hominid who has just caressed the monolith. It sounds like one hundred monkeys are banging away on a cosmic typewriter, an intriguing idea given that Acosta's device holds some resemblance to Leary's ambitious efforts to convert the experience of "neurological unity" into measurable data via the experiential typewriter. Leary was buoyed by the prospect of developing a device with a polygraph to record the brainwaves, circulatory changes, and breathing alterations of psychedelic wayfarers whose experiential and physiological data was to be collated with the aim of forming an experiential language.[80] In his film, Razam doesn't sound another word about Acosta and his neurological data. *Aya* is a medium by which the event is communicated, just as Leary, using the means at his disposal (i.e., his ebullient writing style), transcribed his 1962 DMT experience in place of the analysis of measurable data.[81]

We are a long way from the Newton Center, but *Aya Awakenings* captures experiential language *in situ*. Reviewing the moment, Razam states that he was "expressing pure Ur-language, letting it out of me, heaven and earth pouring through me like molten sound, primal glossolalia pouring out of me like water." And the book clarifies his eureka moment. "I GET IT now, I've locked it in. I know what to DO in this space—you make SOUND, that's how you navigate in here."[82] Besides Razam's gumption to get it on with the Other, the innovation in this exercise is the way the experience is captured through the use of video and sound recording devices, and in postproduction editing, and sound and visual effects engineered by Tim Parish—technologies not available to Leary or the McKennas. "All your you melts away until there's nothing left but IT," he announced as he emerged from the Amazonas of the interior. Subsequent to this episode, Razam needed to summon back and consolidate all of his "I" to build a multimedium entheographic enterprise.[83]

Egos and Energens

Not unlike previous adventurers whose exploits I've introduced, Razam adds to the library holdings on experiential language—here through primal ululations and subsequent interpretations—shaped, not unlike his forebears, by a composite of contextual and conditional factors at, and leading into, the point of contact. Despite their different experiences, Razam is likely to agree with Masters that "reality-unlocking breakthroughs—which are the crown jewels of spiritual experience—do not cut through the Mystery of the Real, but rather only affirm and deepen It. Revelation, infused with a Wonder beyond wonder, outshines all explanation."[84] This seems far from the attitude of outspoken 5-MeO-DMT advocate, and entheologian, Martin Ball, who, if we are to swallow the hubris, has penetrated deeper into the heartland of the Real than any previous explorer and returnee. And in this superhero's journey, Ball has passed "beyond belief," shattered the illusion of religion, and gained a commanding view on Reality. In an article published on *Reality Sandwich* in 2010, Ball stated that "I had come to understand things that others hadn't—even the so-called 'great mystics' and 'masters,' because it was simply too clear to me where their egos were influencing what they were saying and teaching."[85] In *Being Human: An Entheological Guide to God, Evolution and the Fractal Energetic Nature of Reality*,[86] Ball explained how he'd forged a path beyond ego, belief, religion, and meaning, and that entheogens, or what he calls *energens*, and especially 5-MeO, permitted him to experience "the immediate nature of infinity energetically." Subsequently, Ball established the "Entheological Paradigm," a model of reality that he claims assists others to obtain, with the help of 5-MeO, the experience of being pure energy. While Ball claims to have founded a spiritual science with replicable and verifiable techniques, a memo seems to have been missed on the nature of scientific paradigms, which, as notably argued by Thomas Kuhn in *The Structure of Scientific Revolutions*, can be qualified, if somewhat crudely, as quasi-metaphysical systems of belief, maintained by systems of faith and power. In the Entheological Paradigm we are introduced to an attempt to corner the truth through the apparent *paradigmatic* status of its knowledge claims, which aren't actually *claims* to knowledge at all, since Ball is *channeling* a direct line on Reality—or nondual unitary consciousness. We are familiar with this kind of strategy. In his response to prevailing trends in transpersonal psychology, Jorge Ferrer has mounted a challenge to the "exaltation of the epistemic value of individual inner experiences" especially evident among proponents of the "perennial philosophy" like Ken Wilber.[87] While Wilber at least identifies the surface (cultural) manifestations of deep (universal) structures, the integral study of which is central to his defense of the "perennial philosophy," in the Entheological

Paradigm no such valuation of culture exists, because Ball has passed "beyond belief."

With the assistance of 5-MeO, in a matter-of-fact way, Ball claims to have discovered "the genuine truth about the nature of the self and the nature of reality."[88] In a further article on *Reality Sandwich*, Ball swaggered deeper into the conversation, claiming that "I seriously doubt that there are many people on this planet who come anywhere near my experience level with 5-MeO-DMT, and I probably have more experience with the far weaker DMT than most as well." Naming the sacred cow he aimed to slaughter, he added, "I would be genuinely surprised if Terence had as much experience with 5-MeO as I do."[89] Like a rabid terrier, Ball chases down McKenna's "elves," who are mauled as projections of his ego. Terence McKenna's experiences "do not present us with an intrepid explorer discovering new realms," it is argued. "Rather, we are presented with a clear picture of an individual who is unable to recognize himself in the mirror of tryptamine consciousness.... From the perspective of unitary consciousness, Terence appears to have never managed to transcend his ego and therefore appears to have failed to realize the genuinely true potential of the entheogenic medicines he ingested." Ultimately, "Terence brought us deep and abiding confusion."[90] In the final estimation, McKenna "shows us the complete opposite of DMT's true potential." It is a provocative proposition, and there are those who would share similar views. Unfortunately, the case against Terence McKenna turns out to be rather callow and self-aggrandizing. Evaluating McKenna's tone of voice, choice of words, speech patterns, and laughter in three of his public raps, Ball's opinion was that McKenna was "not speaking from his energetic center," and that the machine elves were "all quite clearly *ideas* for Terence, not *truths* he has experienced and felt in his heart."[91] Now McKenna is just the tip of the iceberg, for *all* entity phenomena and visions associated with DMT/5-MeO (e.g., Vivian's encounter above) would be dismissed as illusory according to the Entheological gospel, alongside—and this might be the most telling point—the ongoing significance these encounters and communications hold in the lives of returnees, including those presumably deluded and confused egos producing visionary art and music. But the spiritual chauvinism doesn't end there, for presumably the symbolic and therapeutic resources of all cultural and religious traditions are equally devalued, including those Amazonian traditions where DMT and / or 5-MeO are active compounds used for millennia in brews or snuffs.

If trouncing the ego is a mandatory step in the evolution of consciousness—an objective shared by Ball and McKenna as spokesmen for tryptamines—we must question if those mounting this challenge convincingly accomplish this goal in their own life and practice. If evolving consciousness is the objective, then it seems we have a long struggle ahead, for in a form of narcissism parading as science, "entheology" appears to be the apotheosis of elitism possible within entheogenic experimentation. Awakened to one's own divinity, the user is exalted beyond belief, dispute, reproach . . . and humor too. At one possible terminus, we have a new mystical exceptionalism that is, hypocritically, created in one's own image. While Terence McKenna may have inflated his separate ego in the form of elves, those gnomish pranksters bounce around like party balloons next to the *Hindenburg*esque "Entheological Paradigm."

The Jaguar Process

Among those who advocate the benefits of 5-MeO, but who makes no pretension to the throne in the tryptamine palace, is Ralph Metzner, who even today, more than half a century since his efforts with Leary and the experiential typewriter, maintains his role as "ground control," while also achieving orbit himself. While the means and methods have been modified, the effort to ensure an appropriate balance of personal and environmental conditions for an optimal psychospiritual outcome remains a chief concern. For several decades, Metzner has helped develop therapeutic rituals in which 5-MeO, preferred over DMT, is embraced not only as a means for spiritual transformation, but as a possible treatment for a range of psychiatric, psychosomatic, and immunological disorders. With an overriding concern for healing, this medicine is adopted to further the integration of spiritual, mental, emotional, and physical domains. Such is the view expounded in Metzner's *The Toad and the Jaguar*, where he joins therapists who have been journaling their successes with 5-MeO over the past decades.

In the late 1980s, Metzner traveled to Tucson, Arizona, to harvest the hallucinogenic exudate from *B. alvarius*. Key breakthrough episodes are recounted, such as Metzner's recognition of his connection to a "lattice-like tapestry," an "infinite ever-changing molecular web" regarded as a "matrix of all possibility." Gaining a similar vista to that achieved by Leary back in 1962, albeit now via 5-MeO, and using optimized insufflation techniques, Metzner reported: "A sun of pure white light radiates out from the center of the swirling, pearl-studded crystalline grid."[92] He further recounted a next-level preparation amounting to a form of divine grace.

> Images of decapitation, dismemberment, disembowelment flashed by, in rapid succession, including an image of being run through the chest with a sword—yet there was no fear or horror associated with these images. The following thoughts occurred: "Death comes to all, now it's your turn. This is it, the termination. Resistance is impossible and pointless besides. It's too late, the annihilation has already happened." As I gradually came back to my body, after ten minutes in real time, I felt bathed in pure joy and completely at peace with myself, the world and my death.[93]

This is an extraordinary passage. By marked contrast to Masters's reckless approach, DMT and 5-MeO are "sacraments," the use of which are optimized through "collaborative caution, experienced guidance and respect." The experiences of those undergoing therapy are not evaluated against some kind of legendary mystical standard whereby "visions" amount to little more than hyperspace junk, but are received on their own merits as in the following experience reported by a female participant: "Then there is a bird, a swan, light and large, who flies with me over the Earth, and the Earth is so beautiful. The Earth looks as though set with pearls, dazzlingly beautiful, and I have the thought 'Oh my God, how beautiful it is.' I am overwhelmed by the beauty of the Earth."

Since the 1980s, Metzner has participated in small healing circles in North America and Europe in which a combination of DMT and 5-MeO was used, before 5-MeO was adopted as the preferred medicine, consumed first through inhalation techniques, and later insufflation. Not an enthusiast of the "retinal circus" triggered by DMT, in the earlier period vaporizers were used to smoke 5-MeO, for an effect lasting ten to fifteen minutes. This technique proved far more effective than DMT, which given the difference in strength would require three difficult lungfuls to achieve anything like the same results. 5-MeO snuffs were later adopted in therapy, since that mode of delivery gave longer qualitative results. While one would need to assault the nasal cavity with 50–60 mg of DMT for an effective dose, 5–10 mg of 5-MeO could be inhaled into the nasal passage in one hit, with minimal burning sensation, providing an experience lasting forty-five minutes to an hour. With the snuffing method, a further advantage was the onset of action at five to seven minutes from insufflation, a duration enabling "meditative centering" and decreasing the likelihood of anxiety-triggered dissociation due to the abrupt onset with the inhalation method. Metzner is very clear to sound a warning concerning the precise measurements involved and the need for appropriate preparations, intentions, and context. He recommends absorptive trance states where awareness remains in the body but is simultaneously expanded into extradimensional and infrasonic realms, enabling full memory upon returning.[94]

In his small group healing ceremonies, Metzner has participated in what he calls "the Jaguar process." The phrase is adopted because the rapid onset of the medicine powder when smoked or inhaled was "reminiscent of ancient Mayan mythic images of the open mouth of a jaguar, with the face of a human shaman looking out from within its jaw." Given careful attention to preparation and conditions of use, the Jaguar ceremonies appear to have been a remarkable testament to the therapeutic value of DMT/5-MeO-DMT. In endorsing preparatory meditation and ceremonies involving an experienced sitter, conscious intention, and debriefing circles that protect against "the possibility of possession by a malicious entity or person," Metzner outlines the circumstances by which the type of experience visited upon Masters can be avoided. From his own experience, he also reflects that a "panic state" can develop if onset is resisted. "The shimmering network freezes and congeals. . . . There is dread and terror associated with it and it can develop into a full blown hallucination of a hell-realm. . . . It's a fully developed hell, with demons torturing me, reminiscent of concentration camp accounts or the torture chambers of the Inquisition. It has an historical feel to it, as if I'm a participant observer of collective human history, since I know these are not personal memories from my life."[95]

This description is reminiscent of another of our formative figures, Burroughs, who was clearly so panic-stricken that he kept barbiturate on hand. Like a fire retardant, sedatives were intended to hose down the effect of "Prestonia," enabling the pretention of control, echoing his earlier experience with yagé. By being the commandant of his experience, and defying its effects, Burroughs had doubtlessly contributed to the outcome. Ironically, while the "antidote" was a precaution against dying, its adoption and use may have imprisoned Burroughs in a condition that was conveyed to him through a disturbing sequence of soul-searing "death" images experienced during his "overdose." The desire to command and ride gunshot over the experience is mirrored in a composite of horrors—ovens, torture, compassionless creatures with claws, human sacrifice, genocide, Hiroshima, war—all dramatically emblematic of the absence of freedom, and probably enough to give confirmation to Grof that Burroughs was reliving the agony of birth, with his repeated use of an "antidote" in these crucial moments an unconscious device protecting him from a passage into life. Of course, complex factors are pertinent to this reaction. The substance was relatively unknown, nor did Burroughs have a handle on an effective dose. Not least of all, the literary outlaw was experimenting at the height of the Cold War, with the prospect of perishing in a nuclear conflagration at any moment providing a real, not mythical, backdrop for his "Prestonia" experiments and the Nova Trilogy.

The contrast with Burroughs (and Masters) is striking. The "white-hot metal lattice" so menacing for Burroughs transforms into a "lattice-like tapestry," a source of "primordial pure light," for Metzner. What in the former is an oppressive psychic-badland, where the possibility of physical death was nigh, is in the latter a landscape of "pure awareness," a "radiant void" in which one is potentially exposed to the "truth of the unlimited eternally fresh, fiery present," potentiating a "sense of unbounded joy and sensory delight beyond description." What for Burroughs was an experimental agent, a future divining rod, ultimately a poison, is for Metzner, and those whose experiences he reports, a psychospiritual medicine. This comparison isn't exactly fair since Burroughs was shooting DMT, not insufflating 5-MeO, but you can only imagine how things might have turned out for Burroughs if he'd prepared with hatha yoga asanas and had a circle chanting mantras and channeling "purifying inner-fire energy."[96] He may have likely stopped writing altogether.

Coming Up

By way of their breakthrough experiences, a spectrum of pioneers have made a range of claims about the significance of DMT/5-MeO-DMT. In their own unique ways, the legacy of these emissaries and evangelists is that of the psychedelic hero's journey—where the wayfarer, upon return, introduces the uninitiated to the experience, through improved techniques of use or via intriguing oratories. But while this desire for propagation is common to these and other trailblazers discussed in this book, the commonality ends there since, as their examples demonstrate, the tryptamine breakthrough inaugurates varying and complex patterns of response-ability. In fact, the outcomes are so diverse that one could question if we're discussing the same compound in each case (i.e., 5-MeO-DMT, which has been the chief focus of this chapter). To account for this variation, it must be recognized that in each case, dosage, route of administration, and technique, the psychological state of the user, their background, experience, and intention, and the physical, social, cultural, and historical context are factors combining to shape sometimes dramatically different experiences. Whether one faces the psychological equivalent of a nuclear blast or makes a smooth transit into the cosmic otherworld, whether the event is of the "This is it!" or "What the fuck was that?" pedigree, affording a sensation of divine grace or the suspicion of cosmic crisis, whether it is wonderful or dreadful, affirmative or subversive, perchance one gains access to the Mind of G/d or merges with the Overself, the full spectrum of variables composing "set" and "setting" are pivotal to outcomes.

Whether the breakthrough event impacts well-being or worldview, incites lifeway reevaluations or stimulates the evolution of consciousness, depends very much on how episodes are integrated. If the psychedelic experience is a journey, it does not terminate when the psychonaut returns to base-camp reality, since the real adventure has only just begun. "DMT can't supply enlightenment any more than anything else," offers Art Van D'lay in the *Open Hyperspace Traveler*. "All it does is open up to the user a radically alien perspective." The rest is up to you. "Just like traveling to India, falling in love, surviving a plane crash, etc., these things alone won't transform who you are; they can, however, serve as catalysts toward growth and transformation. You can call it divinity or call it a con, but I choose to see it as a mirror. The experience is nothing more or less than that which I bring to the table. I am both the creator and passenger. It's me scrambled up and thrown back at me."[97] The true merit of the experience depends on subsequent life-path directions that may, for instance, be measured in a variety of behavioral patterns post-event, which is a perspective outlined in James Fadiman's *The Psychedelic Explorer's Guide: Safe, Therapeutic and Sacred Journeys*.[98] While recognizing the value of the application of psychedelics for psychotherapeutic purposes, Fadiman has been a longtime advocate for the "problem-solving" potential of psychedelics among "normal" users, with implications for creative breakthroughs in the realms of science and technological innovation. Remote from the seismic shift addressed among the various spokesmen in this chapter, Fadiman supports subperceptual- or micro-dosing (e.g., 10 μg of LSD), which, as the case studies and wider anecdotal evidence in his book suggest, enhances a range of daily functions and practices performed by users.

Fadiman had been undertaking pioneering research in this area in the 1960s before his project was shut down by the FDA in 1966, along with all other civilian research using psychedelics in the United States. DMT was not among the chemical agents recruited into Fadiman's "problem-solving" study. "We did not have access to DMT, and more than likely, we were not aware of its existence."[99] It is perhaps little wonder that Fadiman's path had not crossed with DMT. The typical rapid onset and comparatively brief duration of DMT (and 5-MeO), along with the comparable magnitude of the "event," places it at considerable variance to the psychopharmacological action of LSD (and mescaline and psilocybin). With the development of vaporizing, insufflation, and blending techniques, with refinements in dosage enabled by the more potent 5-MeO-DMT, and following the advent of customizable methods (e.g., in smoking blends like changa) facilitating "sub-breakthrough" events, in the future researchers may be presented with opportunities to revise approaches in which the full potential of DMT has been disregarded or unrecognized. From my own observations, there is considerable evidence of regular "lower-dose" experimentation among the user population (e.g., taking small lungfuls from a vaporizing device), to clear the mind, for use as a meditational aid, and to improve well-being. Then again, some DMT proponents will deplore gravitation from the profound spiritual benefits and potency of the breakthrough experience.

Another commonality to the pioneers covered in this chapter is that they are *all* men. As with Campbell's monomyth, the psychedelic hero's journey is a masculine process. Even the comprehensive collection of writings by women about drugs, *Sisters of the Extreme,* holds only one account of DMT, that of the pseudonymous Gracie. Her short account of an experience with MDA and DMT, which we have already encountered as part of the mid-1980s psychonautical reports *Notes from Underground* by Gracie and Zarkov, actually precedes most of those covered in this chapter.[100] How might we explain this paucity of high-profile translations of DMT events performed by women? It could simply be that women experiencing breakthroughs with DMT and other tryptamines are less inclined to make an *event* of these events, less interested in making a potential cult of themselves. It could also be that the "breakthrough" events achieved by women are of a different quality . . . less linear and thereby nonamenable to transcription in story-arcs with a beginning and an end; they may be more convulsive than penetrative. In *The Life Cycle of the Human Soul,* Ralph Metzner relates the story of a woman who participated in a "Jaguar" session reporting reliving her own birth, herself giving birth to her child, while simultaneously achieving orgasm, while noting that similar experiences have been reported among those undergoing holotropic breathwork.[101] Clearly, the penetrative breakthrough events related in this chapter are representative of only some of the story.

Perhaps the Hyperspace Lexicon needs to be expanded, or perhaps there are unspeakable events for which no words are suited. This is the territory approached by Diana Reed Slattery in *Xenolinguistics.* While DMT was relatively marginal to the palette of mind alterants with which Reed Slattery downloaded and explored the visible language Glide, it was no walk in the park. After her second DMT experience, she was gobsmacked.

"How could I say that an experience I just had was both patently absurd and more real than real, at the same time?" And yet *Xenolinguistics* is a testament to the psychonautical practice of speaking the unspeakable, which, as far as DMT is concerned, has been the overwhelming province of men.[102] From a historical point of view, an intentional excavation of the field (e.g., a study of personal memoirs and the recording of oral histories) is likely to uncover insights from women born of experiences with DMT. And on this note, I conclude this chapter with the experience of "Sophia," having smoked DMT in a living room in Palo Alto in 1965. Although written by a male—Rick Watson—the account is of an actual event, albeit with the name changed. Sophia was a Cosmic Spider,

> hovering in black space far above the earth, sending out from thousands of spinnerets the transparent neural tubes I had seen, down through the night sky into the psyches of everyone she knew, connecting them all up in a silken mycelial web, their memories and dreams being pumped in superfluid form through her body, she said she could converse with everyone at once ... be there, right inside them, and they in her ... a vast galactic polymer whose strands reached everywhere, and through which you could contact anyone.[103]

CHAPTER 11

Virtual Threshold

Visionary Art and the Liminal Aesthetics of DMT

Navigating the Mundus Imaginalis

In his classic essay "Heaven and Hell," Huxley was sensitive to dramatic variability in the visionary experience occasioned by psychedelics. Mescaline was embraced as a chemical agonist of experience, triggering speculation on the psychoneurological etiology of visionary art, expressing what Eckhart might have called "Is-ness" (*Istigkeit*) at one extreme, and the "horror of infinity" at the other. In his budding neurotheology, Huxley paid more attention to the sublime splendors of existence, as made transparent in the folds of his gray flannel trousers during his debut with mescaline in the spring of 1953. But he was also disposed to identify the negatively transfigured world, as apparent in the "intrinsically appalling" visions of the schizophrenic, and he took interest too in the infernal visions amplified by fear, hatred, anger, and an agonizing attachment to the body during visionary states, which were thought to be operating in the later works of Van Gogh, and in Kafka, Géricault, and Goya.[1]

If Huxley were around today, it is likely that his imagination would be rather alive on the subject of DMT (and ayahuasca), and their effects—aesthetics teeming with magnificent vistas, from the sublime, to the terrifying, to the ridiculous. And yet Huxley's ideas *are* alive, inscribed in the upgraded flight manuals of navigators who, like Alex Grey—among the more experienced wayfarers in the transdimensional realms—offer sagacious advice for those who follow. Displaying his debt, here's Grey speaking to the ontological shock accompanying extremes encountered within the antipodes of the human imagination.

Basically you've got your heaven and your hell. So for me they are representatives of your inner nature. We all have these forces. And we can recognize that they are forces that are operative in the world as well. And I think that in the altered states it's best to be in witness mode and not to sort of sell your soul to some sort of demon or something that you encounter in that situation. You are encountering your own inner domains, and if there is a struggle you should look deeply into this demon that's manifesting or wrathful being and basically see it as a form of a teaching.[2]

In Grey's spiritual anatomy of adverse psychic conditions, with trained intent and guided reflection, exposure to the full range of human experiences potentiated by psychoactives is transformative. Penetrating trouserfolds, human skin, organ tissue, and "the veils" themselves, Grey's X-ray vision has exposed the human body, culture, and evolution in raw, horrific, and sublime detail. His first DMT experience provided a powerful vision of a figure he'd been painting in a dream, a vision realized in the 1993 work *Transfiguration* (see Figure 15), in which a figure hovering over the earth enters a translucent "hypersphere" and undergoes infinite "interconnectedness." "As I inhaled, the material density of my body seemed to dissolve," recalls Grey, "and I 'popped' into the bright world of living geometry and infinite spirit. I noticed strange jewel-like chakra centers within my glowing wire-frame spirit body and spectral colors that were absent from my dream painting. I was in my future painting and was being given an experience of the state so I could better re-create it."[3] Depicting a personal ascension, *Transfiguration* seemed to illuminate Grey's own transformation from agnostic existentialist to radical transcendentalist by way of a series of entheogenic experiences beginning in the mid-1970s when he and Allyson Rymland met under the influence of LSD.

With Grey as a figurehead, mediating transpersonal realms of consciousness in which they have become adroit explorers, visionary artists are the contemporary transposers of a hyperspatial otherworld, access to which has been made increasingly available through DMT and other tryptamines. While this accessibility enables, potentially, anyone to become a visionary artist, the past decade has seen the appearance of envisioned psychonauts who, using a variety of tools at their disposal, have accomplished wide recognition through their skillful transposition of what scholar of Sufism Henry Corbin called the *mundus imaginalis*. Offering insight on this development, Erik Davis explains that the visionary artist "opens up personal expression to a transpersonal dimension, a cosmic plane that uncovers the nature that lies beyond naturalism, and that reveals, not an individual imagination, but a *mundus imaginalis*." Corbin's *mundus imaginalis*, which he used to describe the *alam al-mithal*—the "visionary realm where prophetic experience takes place"—shines a brilliant light on tryptamine hyperspace. As Davis explains, the *mundus imaginalis* "is a realm of the imagination, but a true imagination that has a claim on reality because it mediates between the sensual world and the higher abstract realms of angelic or cosmic intelligences. The *mundus imaginalis* is a place of encounter and transformation."[4]

Offering a distinct rendering of the *mundus imaginalis* projected on countless T-shirt prints and poster designs, Grey's oeuvre—e.g., *Net of Being*—is a favored visual resource for those seeking to translate their own journeys in the imaginal world of DMT hyperspace. In this way, Grey may have performed for the iconography of DMT (its visualization) what McKenna performed for its lexicography (as the voice of DMT). Together with Strassman, who offered a popular Buddhist-inflected theory on pineal function, these three hyperspace emissaries have provided the experient with resources to parse the spice test over the last two decades. The encounters, panoramas, conceptual frameworks, and hyperspace theory of these pioneers have shaped psychonautical heuristics, providing interpretative resources unavailable in earlier years of use when the experience was unprecedented, and was without signposts. Not long ago, there were no websites with effective and safe use guidelines. There was no "entheogenic university" with an accumulated wealth of anonymous user experiences for comparison and contrast. No classifications of entity types encountered in the tryptamine imaginalis housed in online collections like hyperspace bestiaries. No catacomb-like cybergalleries of visionary art. No viral YouTube videos.

In the timeline of DMT use, the further back we go, the greater is the likelihood of the user being unprepared, even utterly overwhelmed, circumstances provoking theophanies of great consequence. With McKenna, and Leary and Hubbard before him, and certainly Burroughs before them, the DMT experience was like a virgin rainforest, untrammeled and unknown, with these pioneers embarking on machete-wielding encounters for which there were few, if any, advance surveys. There were no aesthetic or lexicographical charts, and no flight manuals, just as there were no soundscapes of entheonica. Although few of these figures could have been considered novices, they were jumping off raw nevertheless, which is among the reasons why their experiences were so powerful. McKenna's experience could not be countenanced against anything he knew. He was appalled. Caught inside his eureka moment, he forged a repertoire to meet its strangeness. Although informed by his ongoing studies, even Huxley's writings offered scant intelligence on what McKenna encountered that rainy night in 1965, and Jung neither, since McKenna believed that the "elves" weren't archetypal, measurable, or paradigmatic. McKenna's breakthrough event was then not unlike that of other pioneers whose experiments on a variety of compounds occasioned unprecedented experiences. But while these explorers, like the prodigious Shulgin, were true pioneers, since the breakthrough experience is a profound rupture—an *ontoseismic* event—it remains as significant as ever for present-day experients. "In the Amazon and other places where visionary plants are understood and used, you are conveyed," says McKenna, "into worlds that are appallingly different from ordinary reality. Their vividness cannot be stressed enough. They are more real than real, and that's something that you sense intuitively. They establish an ontological priority."[5]

It was clear that one needn't travel to the Amazon to rupture one's ontological certainty. Disparate and uncertain as they are, the events recounted in the previous chapter bore transformative outcomes for all. These breakthroughs were quintessentially liminal events, exemplifying the user threshold that potentiates significant outcomes for the traveler exposed to visions, beings, information, noetics, and novelty in the virtuality of DMT space, retrieved and perhaps incorporated into their lives. Regardless of whether the experience has an appreciable impact on the lives of users, having journeyed "there and back again," they act as if they are *initiates,* a perception common among diverse returnees, who share trip reports with fellow travelers in private gatherings or personal camping spaces at festivals or through retellings of the adventures of "SWIM" (Someone Who Isn't Me) on webfora. Sometimes returnees choose to be tattooed with DMT's molecular structure, geometric designs, or depictions of beings they've encountered. But if returnees act like initiates, they do so in ways different from traditional initiation rituals, especially as the experience appears marked more by its liminality (in-betweenness) than postliminal outcomes. This chapter, then, explores the liminality of DMT, shedding light on the aesthetics of use, by way of attention to a range of literary, graphic, and sculptural media.

The Virtuality of DMT

As is common to returnee reports, the spice avatar typically departs from his or her ontological routine, enters an in-between state nominally referred to as "hyperspace," and returns to one's mind, body, and routine state. Ritual studies theorists might recognize in this process the phases of "separation," "liminality," and "reaggregation" postulated by comparative folklorist Arnold van Gennep as native to rites of passage in which novices pass across a symbolic threshold transiting to a new status.[6] While transitional, the threshold "space-time" of the DMT experience is not Euclidean, but the virtuality of Nth-dimensional hyperspace. This is not the hyperspace of abstract mathematical formulas, but one that possesses interactive veridicality to the liminar, often since it is the source of explicit visual information. While spectacular, the visions are internal and are subject to great variation, an experience native to a world where the shamanic has become individualized, performance internalized, and trance states dedicated to achieving outcomes for the user consistent with the diversity of life experiences, expectations, and intentions. The properties of the virtual experience are of course dependent on dose, quality, and conditions of use, as well as intention, as the likes of Nick Sand and Ralph Metzner have known too well.

DMT virtualization appears to be characterized by at least three—gnostic, therapeutic, and ludic—modalities of use that often interact to frame the experience. In the first instance, DMT use is closely associated with the deeply personal experience of gnosis, where the experient, as ex-pastor

Gabriel D. Roberts conveyed in Chapter Five, arrives at an awareness of the intrinsic nature of reality (i.e., as it truly is), a truth-bearing destination previously occulted from view. DMT and other tryptamines inaugurate transparencies not atypically involving a realization of disconnection with, or alienation from, one's higher self, nature, and relationships. Enabling such an awakening, DMT is often approached as a sacrament, and in this way it can be likened to the use of psilocybin-containing mushrooms, mescaline, or ayahuasca used in nontraditional contexts, as explained by Wouter Hanegraaff.

> Entheogenic sacraments like ayahuasca are credited with the capacity of breaking mainstream society's spell of mental domination and restoring us from blind and passive consumers unconsciously manipulated by "the system" to our original state of free and autonomous spiritual beings.... They are seen as providing *gnosis:* a salvational knowledge of the true nature of one's self and of the universe, which liberates the individual from domination by the cosmic system.[7]

As an integral component of ayahuasca, but also as an independent agent, DMT carries this liberating potentiality, and should be recognized within the context of what Hanegraaff has identified as "entheogenic esotericism," which takes its place, previously neglected, in the history of Western esotericism.[8]

DMT is also adopted as a tool with an intended therapeutic efficacy. This mode is consistent with neoshamanic practice in which psychotechnologies are deployed with self-therapeutic outcomes. In his research on out-of-body and contact experiences among Australian DMT users, Des Tramacchi documented practices of "self-shamanising" where modern subjects become "their own clients and their own healers," seeking remedies for alienation and "soul loss" compatible with desired liberation from dependence on biomedical solutions.[9] Like ayahuasca neoshamanism, and therefore unlike possession trance and cults of dissociation, the "trance" state obtained with the rapid plunge into DMT hyperspace is an out-of-body state in which one's body is not typically animated. While the DMT breakthrough may provoke "cultural criticism" of the kind associated with the purgative process implicit to ayahuasca neo-shamanism,[10] next to the guided ceremony of the ayahuascan, the DMT-trance ritual is accelerated, hyperindividualized, and private. In the "self-shamanism" of illicit entheogenic practice, the question of accessibility remains. Under a cynical light, we may question whether, for the majority of users, the "shaman" has been replaced by one's "dealer," and a therapeutic community by unscrupulous actors. A perspective sometimes adopted by senior experients has been that DMT chooses the user. Robert Hunter once stated to Terence McKenna that DMT is "self-selecting." That is, "it knows who it wants, for whatever reasons it wants them, and scares the bejezus out of anyone else. Those who ought to have it will find themselves in possession of it."[11]

Finally, since its adoption among small circles of users in the 1960s, DMT has been embraced for recreational purposes, with smoking blends like changa pivotal to this development. The outcomes of optimal blends are apparent at dance festivals where, as opposed to full out-of-body states, users become animated in dance, often under the power of a combination of substances. Here, DMT hyperspace is accessed more for pleasurable effects than for divinatory purpose and curative outcome. While this approach could be dismissed as simply "recreational," an amusement with trivial and inconsequential outcomes, it seems sanguine to follow the lead of Ott, who, circumscribing the modern extramedical use of DMT and other entheogens, preferred the term "ludibund" and its variant "ludible"—deriving from the Latin *ludere,* meaning literally "playful, full of play."[12] Such terminology recognizes that, if not strictly entheogenic, use may be no less serious, especially given that "play" transgresses boundaries (not only that which separates consciousness from unconsciousness, and the material from the spiritual, but lawful behavior from its antithesis). In the age of prohibition in which DMT is classified as a "dangerous drug" with abusive potential, play is suffused with danger. That is, where DMT is forbidden, players are outlaws. But as the history of countercultures attests, from Beats to Bohemians, from Boomers to Burners, those who act ambiguously with regard to the law, who play outside the rules, who test the boundaries, are barometers of innovation, creativity, and cultural change.

Next-Level Experience

The DMT trance is typically convoluted by all operational modes just outlined, which have a shaping influence on the contours of the tryptamine threshold. That DMT inaugurates a passage experience has been impressed upon a great many seasoned travelers, some even identifying levels and phases common to the transit. Having been introduced to DMT in 1987 in Hawaii with Terence holding the pipe, Peter Meyer has classified experiential events according to the following. At Level I, a "pre-hallucinatory experience" is shaped by an "interior flowing of energy/consciousness," which Meyer states may be "extremely intense," producing "positive feeling content." At Level II, vivid, brilliantly colored, geometric visual hallucinations are noted. "Here one is observing a patterned field, basically two-dimensional, although it may have a pulsating quality. One may remember having seen this before." What is then labeled the Transitional Phase (or Level IIB) is the "tunnel or breakthrough experience." Here, the user may see or fly through a tunnel. "A veil may part, a membrane may be rent." At this stage, a breakthrough to "another world," or perhaps a series of breakthroughs, occurs. Alternatively, Meyer suggests that it may be the case that the transition from Level II to Level III is near-instantaneous, with no feeling of transition. Finally, at Level III, the traveler enters three- or higher-dimensional space, involving possible contact with entities. This stage is characterized by one's awareness of being in an "objective" space—that is, a space of at least three dimensions in which objects or entities may be encountered. Sometimes these entities appear to be intelligent beings communicating with the observer. This stage may be frenetic, where events happen at incomprehensible speeds and where one is left bewildered. Alternatively, the cosmic show may be relatively coherent, as an epic picture emerges, not uncommonly involving the creation and evolution of the universe, with an understanding of one's role in the drama. Travel is possible at this level, and one may assume the form and consciousness of a bird. "The limits of this stage, if any, are unknown. There may be transitions to further stages."[13] Parapsychologist David Luke has indeed added a Level IV, what he calls "the white light."[14] As recognized by Luke, the staggered process resembles that outlined by cognitive psychologist Benny Shanon, who gave specific attention to the predominant visual or visionary phenomena in the ayahuasca experience, from "splashes of colour" and "geometric designs," to "interactive scenes" and "scenes of flight," to "Supreme Light."[15]

Others have offered more explicit detail regarding the passage to be negotiated by the experienced user. In the 1960s, with an accumulation of DMT episodes in the hundreds, Nick Sand had an unexpected breakthrough amounting to a form of initiation, as recounted in *The Entheogen Review* in 2001, not long after his release from prison (itself constituting a further level of initiation). In his account, Sand related a classical passage experience preceded by a long approach through a "region of incredible design": "Multi-colored grids flexing and slowly twisting, carnivals of colorful patterns, and little people peering through fences; hieroglyphs of arcane and hauntingly familiar aspects, but not quite decipherable." Since there was no one educating him about how to use this sacrament, nor had he any idea how deep he could travel, the spice pioneer presumed this was all there was to it, and had variations on this bedazzling experience over hundreds of trips. And yet, he felt there was something missing in these encounters, something he did not quite understand, and he was "aching to find the meaning behind it all."[16] Sand later realized he could walk through these "veils," but not without first confronting his rigid psychological structures and boundaries. He became aware that the beautiful patterns were "disguises that protected my limited mind from seeing a deeper reality." He came to realize that the mesmerizing designs were "symbols of psychological states that were in this form because I didn't want to see that truth about myself yet."[17] When Sand attained this realization, the designs disappeared, and "the beyond opened."

> Suddenly, I was walking up a steep road carved into the side of a sheer, jagged wall of grey rock. On my right was the mountain, on my left a cliff that dropped straight down into a huge canyon whose other side was a range of these jagged mountains. I was hiking up this steep mountain to a higher place of knowledge. I had penetrated the veil of superficial distractions of the lower mind, and I was approaching the region of the higher mind—a land of magic and realization. As I trudged along this road I saw a gate—a huge ornate rusty portcullis beside which stood a

small but very nasty looking beast with piercing red eyes, no neck, large fangs, and an obviously very bad temper. This demon or demigod was without doubt the guardian to the gate of higher knowledge. Humbly, I begged permission, "May I please pass?" The guardian choked and snarled, then fixing me with a penetrating stare, nodded unpleasantly while he hauled laboriously on a chain that slowly lifted the gate. As I passed through, everything faded away and I was back sitting with the pipe in my hand. I was totally disappointed that I had gotten through the gate but had not made it to the magic land just beyond. In my ignorance I did not realize that I had passed from level one to level two, and the gatekeeper was my initiation.[18]

Passing through that gate, and during subsequent trips, Sand encountered teachers of varying denominations whose collective wisdom seemed to boil down to the Gurdjieffian gnosis that "there is no 'other,' no subjective/ objective—no duality at all; just convenient structures for teaching our- selves those sacred lessons that we have known, but forgotten."[19]

While Sand had apparently satisfied the requirements of the gatekeeper guarding the route to higher knowledge, David Luke was bounced by what he surmises may have been archetypal guardian deities of the underworld. Luke has told of an experience in which he was cautioned against return- ing to DMT space. Smoking the spice on a secluded beach on the banks of the River Ganges, Luke gained a brief glimpse of what he recognized as the "truly forbidden," but was repelled by a terrifying creature that was all disembodied eyes attached to snake bodies guarding the secret and preventing both further access and recall. "The multitudinous eyes of the being before me suddenly and quite deliberately blocked my curious con- sciousness's further explorations by mesmerizing me with its squirming, rhythmic eyeball hypnosis." Luke had the sensation that he was "intruding upon a cosmic gathering to which I wasn't invited," that he had interloped upon the sacred realm of the dead, the underworld, entry to which was prevented by a powerful guardian spirit. Subsequently, he found similar beings in mythology, such as Azrael—the Islamic Angel of Death—who is considered to possess ten thousand eyes and is "the holy psychopomp who ushers souls into the realm of the dead." Several years later, Luke discovered the ancient Tibetan deity Za (or gza'), who appears with half the body of a snake and is covered in a thousand eyes. From this pattern in mythology, he then discovered more and more "many-eyed apparitions" in trip reports on DMT and other entheogens, and forged the realization that the entity he encountered on the banks of the Ganges "is the archetype of the guardian of the realm of death and the doorway to occult knowledge."[20]

It's a doorway familiar to psychedelic artist and publisher of magazine *The Invisible College* Gwyllm Llwydd, who first smoked DMT in Denver, Colorado, in 1967, although it wasn't until the 1990s that he was compelled to take it seriously. Llwydd's unpublished short story "Gate Keepers" is a tale about a world of beings (the Larvals) kept unconsciously captive in a gravity well. With a deep gnostic bent, the story depicts those bad angels, the Archons, who have "cultivated the gravity well's fields of consciousness for untold millennia," harvesting the emotions, passions, and fears of the Larvals. In the hand of the Archons are the Watchmakers, tasked to keep the Larvals in advanced stages of amnesia, by "fabricating cultural impulses, religions, economic systems and various fads" implanted into Larval consciousness. In this oppressive system, the Gate Keepers are tasked to prevent awakening Larvals from passing through a series of gates leading beyond the gravity well. Over the last "70 cycles," a state of instability has occurred, aided by "wild cards" that seemed to "emerge from the flora," encouraging more and more strident Larvals to seek escape from the well. But even while the Archons counteract with repressive forms of control, incarceration, witch hunts, and the like, eliminating "stray Larval hives causing the imbalance," mutant Larvals bearing molecular keys to the gates pose new threats to the system.

Their plight invested in the visions brought back by avatars, Llwydd's Larvals huddle around a mutant in their midst, one whose efforts to storm the gates have been thwarted repeatedly by the distracting antics of the Gate Keepers. But preparations were being made to go again. "One hit. Another. Then the rush ... Arcing up into crystalline fragments of consciousness, the Larval perceived the great light." While the Gate Keepers had mobilized to police this latest incursion, on this occasion of great moment the mutant Larval bound past them "into its native home, unfettered, in ecstasy." With repeated efforts and improved techniques, the avatar eventually achieves the light, as depicted in Llwydd's work *Beyond the Gate Keepers* (see Figure 16).

> It was almost physical, the buffeting, motion and speed of the jour-
> ney, and before he realized it he exploded into a great chamber, full of
> light, and was startled to behold a vast being sitting before him in what
> seemed to be meditation, with multiple arms not unlike Vishnu though
> the arms were shaped almost like tentacles which as he beheld them
> beckoned to him.[21]

In both story form and visual art we encounter media tasked to convey the DMT experience, with Llwydd mobilizing his own Larval-like DMT events during hundreds of sessions to breathe life into a gnostic-*Matrix* narrative at the heart of which is the theme of *transition*. This is no simple rite of passage or process of individuation, but a gnosis-bearing accomplishment where the breakthrough holds world-saving gravitas—where breaking through amounts to liberation from oppression. I will return to this theme later. For now, we might take a lesson from nanobrain, who sheds new light on the "machine elves of hyperspace," which he claims are little more than "door bitches ... preprogrammed usherettes preventing the DMT-user from accessing the divine show." By contrast, he advised me, "you *are* the show, you've got the backstage pass. You want to go through the curtains."[22]

Gates, Portals, and Passages

Affording access to one's higher self, plunging into the underworld, exposing novitiates to system crises, sowing the seed of dissension, a preparation for the inevitable, liberation from a gated universe, DMT is infused with *potential*, as evident in the archetypally liminal symbols that permeate the experience and user representations: doors, gates, tunnels, time holes, windows on the fourth dimension. Sometimes depicted as spiraling wormholes, other times fabulous archways pulsating in colors not of this world, hyperdimensional polytopes like rotating tesseracts, or fractal checkerboard vortices imbued with countless arcane sigils, thresholds are native to the DMT experience and its art. Among the most common symbols of passage in the breakthrough experience is what many identify as the "chrysanthemum" effect. For McKenna, the "chrysanthemum" appeared in the form of Chinese baroque, which, with enough DMT ingested (i.e., a "third toke"), would give way before the traveler. And then "there's a sound like a saran wrap bread wrapper being crumpled up and thrown away . . . and then there's a defined sense of bursting through something, a membrane." Terence McKenna, of course, became the lead commentator on this threshold-popping moment. In a stunning depiction of the transit, *DMTrmx*, visual-media producers Martin Stebbing and Toke Kim Klinke feature his master's voice: "there's an enormous cheer that goes up as you pass through this membrane."[23]

McKenna often described the subsequent moments possessing a carnival or circus-like quality: a state that defies categories, is unlexicographical, non-Euclidean, grotesque. As he had it, the circus most approximated "the archetype of DMT."[24] If there was a means to rapidly "run away with the circus," DMT was the grease oiling that mechanism. And it was a freak show with its own exotic clowns—for what is a circus without clowns? But no mere three-ring-circus performers, the elf clowns are anomalous ambassadors of defiance, and grotesquely kinky too. SFos's epic passage is consonant. Seconds in, and there were "all sorts of frequency modulations and crescendoed stacatto pops as the trip descended."

> This sound data was quiveringly involved with these visual architectonic dream waters that were beginning to emerge, dripping and slipping amongst themselves, and my being became overwhelmed by vacuous, gravity-like suction experiences which impelled me further in. . . . The sucking experience took over for a while then, driving the morphological acrobatics of spacelove that lay before me. There was something about it that makes me think of a voluptuous alien seductress with big, fat lips pulling me to her body in the weirdest feeling embrace ever. It felt like I was being smeared sensually and lustfully around the space in some sort of vacuum-tube funhouse.[25]

If the transit into the interior of DMT space is, for some, like being pulled through a uterine funhouse, for others the membrane is majestic, and the passage ceremonious. A designer of interactive event-installations evoking passage between these and higher dimensions, Carey Thompson is no stranger to the threshold. The principal work is the DiMethyl Temple. Codesigned by Rob Newell, and with assistance from Victor Olenev and Xavi, as a white facade with a doorway, often opening to a gallery displaying the work of visionary artists, the DiMethyl Temple is described by Thompson as a "functioning portal for people to gain entrance into the multidimension." The Temple was first installed at Burning Man in 2005, the vast, flat, white, alkaline surface of the Black Rock Desert an impressionable blank canvas upon which, even then, some 36,000 people sculpted, painted, and danced themselves into being (see Figure 18).

Cultivating an interactive visionary aesthetic downstream from what Huxley called the "sacramental vision" and what Lawrence Caruana, in his *A Manifesto of Visionary Art*, calls the work of translating the "invisible landscape" into mind-altering imagery, Thompson is connected to a visionary-arts tradition whose remote ancestors include Hieronymus Bosch, William Blake, and Salvador Dalí, and with more recent forebears in the likes of Ernst Fuchs, Robert Venosa, and Alex Grey.[26] While identified with a lineage indebted to Surrealism and Magic Realism, Thompson is a spiritual artivist whose oeuvre is responsive to an accumulation of world crises, not least of all the separation of spirit from matter. Alongside peers like Android Jones, Thompson's work is intentionally activational. It is intended to help catalyze, as he writes, "one's core connection with the source, that which connects us all, to heal the schism between ourselves as humans and the world around us"—a process in which he is himself experienced, with the assistance of plant allies.[27]

Thompson's early work *Diosa Madre Tierra* (Spanish for "Goddess Mother Earth") (see Figure 19) has a provenance bearing resemblance to the creation of Grey's *Transfiguration*. While the work was inspired by an experience with psilocybin-containing mushrooms, Thompson recounts what happened when he completed the circle by smoking a hit of DMT:

My world dissolved into the painting as I fully entered it with my entire being. The fusion of my self with my creation was of oneness and it was a totally new and amazing feeling to be inseparable from a tangible object which came through me. At one point, the imagery DeMaTerialized and a tunnel formed which I was shot through. The face of my beloved partner who had passed away less than a year before appeared as I flew by only to enter into a portal revealing the realm of the spirit. It was if I had physically died and was being given a glimpse of the other side, only to witness the sheer beauty and boundless bliss of that world. I could literally feel and see the remaining vestiges of fear of death fly off of me and the liberation was amazingly profound. I had no idea this was even possible and I felt I had entered into an entirely new form of healing.[28]

The DiMethyl Temple facade emerged as an extension of this interactive alchemy. As Thompson conveys, for those entering the space, "the fearsome monster creating the façade would strip the entrant of their identity, dissolving egoic structures, but also serving as a guardian during the experience within." In 2006, the installation enjoyed prominence at festivals around the world, with a symmetrical design philosophy iterated in sculptures constructed over subsequent years and installed at a variety of events as stargates or portal-pyramid stages for artists like Tipper and the band Beats Antique, whose skills in shaping sonic architecture from varied and sometimes-disparate sources are consistent with the fusional sophistication of the sculptures. These remixtical installations sample iconography and archetypal symbols from world sacred architecture, especially Mayan, Egyptian, and Balinese temple designs. Such sacred templates have held appeal for Thompson since they have commonly connected humans with the heavens, usually in the form of alignments with solar cycles or astral positions. Today, his Temples potentiate an alignment of the inner worlds of event habitués with the outer universe. Just as the portal surface is animated after nightfall with a shifting array of projected hues, each entrant is afforded the opportunity to imbue the blank facade with personal significance, a practice that tends to diverge markedly from the function of temples in the ancient cultures inspiring the appropriations.

I met Thompson in April 2006 at Soulclipse, a festival mounted on the path of the total solar eclipse in the south of Turkey near the city of Antalya. We were a world away from the Black Rock Desert, but it was a solid foundation for the DiMethyl Temple, given that the eclipse was the context for the alignment of the Earth, Sun, and Moon with the bodies of seven thousand souls who had gathered from points around the globe. Explaining his efforts, Thompson is clearly indebted to mystics committed to the restoration of balance in an era of escalating peril. He is positioned among a growing network of artists who "communicate impulses that are coming from some galactic source, and translate them and crystalize them into works of art and music and sound, and through these forms ... catalyze human transformation and social change." Thompson is among the most influential of aesthetes sailing in Terence McKenna's esoteric slipstream, with his painting *Singularity* standing as a benchmark entry on the eschaton.[29]

That work has held prime position inside the DiMethyl Temple, which formed the ritual entrance to the Inner Visions Gallery at Boom 2006, a spectacular gallery-emporium for visionary art. At Boom that year, Thompson's structure was saturated with liminality, with entrants situated between the worlds of the mortal and immortal, the earth and the heavens, the inner and the outer. With the installation redeploying Mayan iconography, participants could also situate themselves in the 2012 zeitgeist six years prior to the galactic jump-off. Furthermore, the DiMethyl Temple was a core component of the Liminal Village, the crowning achievement of Boom's studied interest in initiation, an optimized arena for lectures, panels, workshops, films, and interactive art dedicated to population causes such as "stewardship," "cooperation," "balance," and "sustainable energy." In 2006, the Liminal Village updated the Convention Area, which appeared first at Boom in 2000, becoming the Dynamic Mythologies Tent (note the acronym) in 2002. For Liminal Village creator Naasko Wripple, the idea was inspired by the Shamanarchy Experiments at club Megatripolis in London, as well as the Entheobotony Seminars, Mindstates, Bioneers, and the Prophet's Conference.[30] It was also deeply indebted to the then newly departed McKenna, with promotions for the Dynamic Mythologies Tent adopting lines from his "Alien Dreamtime" performance delivered in San

Francisco in 1993: "We are somehow part of the planetary destiny, atoms of the world soul, and how well we do determines how well the experiment of life on earth does, because we have become the cutting edge of this experiment."

Operating a six-day, twenty-four-hour program in subsequent events, the Liminal Village became a showcase for a spectrum of core concerns among participants, including those integral to the emergent entheocultural network. With McKenna acting as a posthumous guide, and with thousands of people flowing through on a daily basis, the Liminal Village became an intentional space for exchanging coordinates for personal, cultural, and planetary transformation. In 2006, Wripple oversaw the construction of a four hundred square meter bamboo structure (the Omniplex) designed by Balinese architect Amir Rabik. The structure was aligned with the festival according to feng shui principles, was grounded by crystal gridwork, and featured a solid wooden carving of the mythical figure Garuda at its entrance. An entheogenic sensibility permeated the village, drawing huge crowds eager to hear the likes of Daniel Pinchbeck, Graham Hancock, and Shipibo ayahuascero Guillermo Arévalo. They would also view artwork displayed in the adjacent Inner Visions Gallery, which then and subsequently showcased the work of leading visionary artists, including those who have depicted aspects of hyperspace liminality like Martina Hoffmann, Luke Brown, and Amanda Sage.

Held at a lakeside site in the Beira Baixa province of Portugal, and attracting participants from more than a hundred countries, Boom is the gathering ground for a visionary-arts movement in which trance dance has primary appeal. Founded by Diogo Ruivo and Pedro Carvalho in 1997, in an attempt to capture the Goa vibe, the biennial festival has evolved into a sacred site for enthusiasts of psychedelic music, art, and culture. While participants are seated in contemplation in the Liminal Village, over in the Dance Temple, and in other dance venues on-site, thousands grow animated in dance. Such was the case in 2012 when, shepherded by a pair of Quetzal dragons while facing Carey Thompson's "GoD" stage design (see Figure 20), temple-goers became enthusiastic disciples to the advice of Alan Watts: "Sometimes you have to go out of your mind to come to your senses." Around the dancefloor and across the grounds of the event,

317

accessing a palette of sensory enhancements, seekers cruise an interactive art gallery and tech-house of mirrors in which each entrant is an accessory to the spectacle. Light-years from an "art" world in which audiences are witness to aesthetics produced by a few for the many, indigenes of this offworld interzone are encouraged to be cocreators of visionary artifice. At its best, this echo of transformational festival culture offers a living canvas upon which participants are empowered to sculpt themselves into being. No event carries this off better than Burning Man, which in 2006 occasioned the appearance of the Entheon Village, so named by Alex Grey, where visionary painters exhibited banners and performed live works in the many domes and sculptural tents of the Village. The main dome of the Entheon Village, where the Palenque Norte lecture series commenced that year, was originally planned with a giant DMT molecule at its apex.

Tryptamine Liminality

As anthropologist of ritual Victor Turner would have it, *liminality* is society's revelatory mode, and culture's revolving doorway, the variability of which was ultimately reckoned to possess evolutionary functionality. In other words, the liminal realm is pregnant with potential. In between prescribed roles and responsibilities, from the coming-of-age rituals of the Ndembu of Zambia to modern stage theater, liminars (i.e., those in between) access what Turner knew as a "realm of pure possibility."[31] A hyperreflexive threshold in which the obligatory may be converted into the desirable, it was also a realm where tradition and custom may be challenged and subverted: the psychocultural interstices birthing novelty. While Turner did not observe the role of psychopharmacology in his "comparative symbology" of liminality as found in works like *The Ritual Process* and *From Ritual to Theater*, DMT hyperspace is quintessentially liminal. In traditional passage rites, including those associated with coming-of-age, conversion, or initiation, novitiates are exposed, in the fashion outlined by scholar of the Greek Eleusinian and Orphic mysteries Jane Harrison, to the ultimate values of a culture—its *sacra*. Such is accomplished through "what is shown" in rituals of exhibition (i.e., the display of significant objects), "what is done" in rituals of enactment (i.e., dramatic performance), and "what is said" in rituals of instruction (i.e., oral histories).[32] Through these practices hedged off from ordinary life, cultural precepts, esoteric languages, code words, and sacred data are transmitted and carried back into the postliminal world.

These ritual modes by which cultural *sacra* are conveyed hold striking resonance with the DMT experience, which may replicate in bizarre virtuality these universal "rituals" of transmission. First of all, there are the rituals of exhibition. Many hyperspace travelers report being shown objects of great significance. We have already heard from Binkie2000 (in Chapter Nine), who described a liquid light world "infused with pure energy and potential," where information was transmitted via language "made of pure light wave vibrations, thought, sight, smell, touch, taste." Some of the entities that unfolded in that realm held out objects "very close in front of my eyes for me to look at. 'Check this out!' they giggle, 'Look, carefully, SEE what this is, remember it!' 'This is how it all works' they seemed to say. The objects looking like flash drive tickets, seemed to be information storage devices, full of infinite potential."[33] Another telling example, from which a spectacular beneficence ensued, can be found in the following.

> The female being got in my face and communicated to me (not in words) look at what's ON the pedestal! I looked up and saw a diamond shaped object that was made of similar stuff to the walls but infinitely more brilliant, more dazzling, more unspeakably awesome. And as my smile grew and total awe and amazement filled me, this female being began flying around the object at great speed, keeping her eyes fixed on me. She was doing flips and sharp turns and cheering as though she was celebrating the fact that she had the chance to show me. She kept communicating to me, Look at it! Look at it! Isn't this awesome?! This continued, and I kept my eyes on that unbelievable object as the scene began to fade.[34]

As for instances of enactments, of the dramaturgy of the *sacra*, we have already encountered the following story from Nick Sand, worthy of repeating here. Having taken DMT intramuscularly (0.9 mg per kg of body weight) while seated on a Persian carpet amid candles and incense and listening to a recording of Sharan Rani playing a love raga on a sarod, Sand recounts an intimate interlude.

> I was filled with overwhelming feelings of womanly love and sensuality. I looked down and was very surprised to see myself dressed in filmy harem pants and no shirt on. I had a beautiful copper-colored female body—breasts and all. I had many bangles on my arms, and ankle bells on my legs. I looked around and found that I was dancing a seductive love raga to the two musicians facing me playing sarod and tabla. We were performing in the courtyard of a beautiful Indian temple similar to Bubhaneshwar Temple, famed for its erotic sculpture and soaring towers.[35]

The sensation of suddenly being cast into a luscious, exotic, or futuristic role in a period drama for which one hadn't prepared but for which one seems naturally competent is typically accompanied by a perception of arriving at a state of unprecedented full-bodied awareness. This sensation is redolent in the account of Lyle (on DMT & Methoxetamine).

> Then this feeling came over me, a feeling that what I was seeing was an ancient place. While visually it looked sharp and futuristic, I had an overwhelming feeling that it was older than time. This might sound odd, but it reminded me of what I mentally picture as a 1950s soda shop, but much more mystic and magical of course. Like everything is outlined in chrome and it is all flashy and new looking, but it still has the retro feel. It's the best I can describe it but the ancient feeling of where I was at sharply contrasted the futuristic visuals that were occurring. I was still stupefied about what was going on, but I slowly began to realize that what was happening wasn't a bad thing, in fact it was somewhat pleasant, and accepted my fate that this was reality now, or perhaps how it had always been, for all I knew at that point. In that instant of acceptance the energy that was going through my body snapped and cracked and the pulse in my body became a steady surge, it was as if I was finally plugged in to everything. I thought to myself, this is it, this is what every human in history has strived to reach, this place here is the point of existence. While what was going on around me was visually

crazy and it was mentally confounding, I accepted it and I felt it accept me back. Something just felt right about it, I keep calling it the beautiful chaos, and that's just the perfect way to describe it.[36]

And as for the rites of instruction, returnees commonly report exposure to a language that is multisensorial. The first of two exemplary reports is from Meyer's collection. "They were everywhere jabbering in indecipherable tongues, juggling incandescent neon microworlds of dancing beings, and morphing with a zen-like, diaphanous fluidity that remains a primal miracle no matter how often you lay your all too human eyes on it."[37] Richard Gehr offers the final example.

> During my second hit, an invisible horn section mounted a rapid crescendo as my body began to vibrate sympathetically. Ontological warp speed arrived in a startlingly immediate flash as the universe quite literally deconstructed itself in front of my eyes into a complex green and red geometrical grid that artist Alex Grey has rendered as the "Universal Mind Lattice." An impossibly elaborate onrush of candycolored, chaotically presented patterns of pure visual information then ensued as the intergalactic Wagnerian horn section continued to blow a spectacular fanfare. The emotional content was one of genuine awe, a briefly terrifyingly integration of my neurology into the submolecular fabric of the universe.[38]

How might the traveler absorb this torrent of information? A breakthrough experience is commonly reported to be like receiving the complete and expanded encyclopedia of cosmic history, pancultural awareness, and total biographical recall within a seconds-long download, where the user has difficulty holding on to anything solid. Not only is it impossible to stop the roller coaster and report on one's status midride, but the postride debriefing is recondite, as travelers are exposed to the deluge. This amounted to Graham Hancock's experience when first smoking DMT. "It happened unbelievably fast," he recounted. "One second I was outside the wall of colors, mesmerized and menaced by it. The next second...BAM! I was projected through it into some strange, pristine geometrical space on the other side of the wall" where "vast amounts of information have been stored." While the experience was like a strange kind of induction where Hancock was being shown "how we do things here," and where enormous amounts of data were being transferred to him, he didn't have the software installed to interpret it.

> Very often, strings of almost recognizable numbers and letters would appear, but just as frequently I would see sections of script from languages that were completely unknown to me—sometimes expressed in what looked like hieroglyphs, picture writing, or signs. Constantly shifting, sorting, and juggling like a computer program running through a thousand different alphabets in an instant, the lines themselves seemed to come alive at certain moments and to behave in a way that reminded me of small, diligent mechanical ants and spiders. Then the display changed in the blink of an eye, and it wasn't simple monochrome lines anymore, but pairs of colorful writhing snakes wrapped around one another, drawn down to a minute, submicroscopic scale, as though I were being allowed to peer deep into the nucleus of a cell and to witness the dance of DNA—the ultimate "Master of Transformations." What did it all mean? What was I being told here? Why was I being shown this?[39]

In Binkie2000's classic episode, a breakthrough was also reported into a molecular realm alive with a "musical vibratory language" delivered by light beings. But while this language was "completely new," there seemed no need for further interrogation since it also possessed an astonishing familiarity. It was "completely, 100% familiar and reassuring. I seemed to understand them, as it were."[40]

While the precise nature of what is shown, done, and said in DMT hyperspace is notoriously ambiguous, as seen time and again in user reports, the transmissions hold significance to wayfarers. In this virtual realm of the strangely familiar, visitors are offered a direct uplink, not so much to the actual meaning of things seen, done, and heard, but to the inherent feeling of the sacred itself, to which the virtually experienced are exposed, which is felt more than known, or is known because it is felt. This is consistent with SFos's post-spice revelations. While he was "so existentially surpassed by the quality of what I had just been a part of," the conclusion was crystalline. "I definitely felt I had been closer to the core of the real than ever before and that this mystery is front and center to who we are as humans, who we really are. I felt very connected to my universe, very sensitive and strong and in touch with things."[41] And to possess this *feeling* is to know implicitly that this dimensional space-time continuum is not all that there really is. We have arrived at the noetics of the revelatory process itself. Simon Posford described something of this experience in his encounter with entities on his initial voyage. "They were feeding me information, nourishing me, and then they asked, 'What do you want to see?' For some reason, I thought 'time.' I don't know why I thought 'time,' but they replied in a slightly ominous way, 'okay, we're going to show you time!' Although I can't conceive of it in my head now, or transcribe it with such a limited form of language (maybe that's what music is for?), but in that moment, I totally understood time."[42] *Knowing* what time is in such a state is one thing; possessing the capability to convey it is another. As we know, McKenna made his "Timewave" a lifework, and Posford would transpose his own experience in musical compositions.

If the transmissions native to the DMTverse constitute information, the content is esoteric, paragnostic, and potentially subversive. In passage rites found in African cultures, Victor Turner knew that ritual "enfranchises speculation," allowing "a certain freedom to juggle with the factors of existence." But, as he further knew, "this liberty has fairly narrow limits" in societies like the Ndembu, where there were "axiomatic principles of construction, and certain basic building blocks that make up the cosmos and into whose nature no neophyte may inquire."[43] By contrast, offering its users a cache of possibilities, DMT places in the hands of the prepared voyager of consciousness a pneumatic drill potentially powerful enough to crack the foundations of one's cultural and historical awareness. Furthermore, to parse events, the experient is compelled to draw on one's own resources and interpretive methods, themselves often shaped by frames of reference and circulating aesthetics from McKenna, Strassman, Grey, and others, enabling users to navigate their tryptaminality, articulated in an accumulation of expressions constituting a storehouse of knowledge shared among the entheogenic esoteric milieu.

Entheodelic Storytelling

In recent years, the entheoliminal encounter has given shape to cultural expressions among which Graham Hancock's fiction stands paramount. Launching entheo-fiction at a cracking pace, the first novel in a projected trilogy, *Entangled: The Eater of Souls* is epic dark fantasy in which DMT, ayahuasca, mushrooms, ketamine, and other "allies" are integral to a narrative entangled with wormholes, out-of-body states, and the telepathic powers of Neanderthals. Inspired by sessions drinking ayahuasca, *Entangled* was Hancock's first hand at writing fiction, having established himself as an author of alternative history. While demonstrating a continuing passion for alternate histories, *Entangled* shows the author's interest in Strassman's speculations on the role of endogenous DMT, alongside ideas cribbed from quantum physics, the study of NDEs, and time travel. In *Entangled,* a fictional project is conducted at present-day UC Irvine by maverick DMT researcher Dr. John Bannerman, who is on the hunt for "the holy grail of quantum physics.... Proof of the existence of parallel universes and a reliable method for getting volunteers into them and back again in one piece." Bannerman's team introduces DMT to volunteers in a clinical study designed to test for "an alternate system of human perception—a sort of sixth sense that might be harnessed to explore other dimensions of reality." Having received an IV injection of DMT, and meeting with the "machine elves" overseeing switchboards enabling transit to another world where she encounters a spirit guide and eventually astral travels to the last days of the Neanderthals, world-saving heroine Leoni appears to be apprentice to an interdimensional molecular technology.[44] A theme underwriting this style of fiction is that the *break through* experience (enabled by "entheogens") potentiates a *break from* oppression—in this case from ruthlessly aggressive masculine cultures of domination. It is a theme not unfamiliar to readers of fantasy and science fiction, where magical practices and scientific innovations are confabulated to achieve liberating objectives—only now, entheogens (like DMT) are integral to the emancipation.

Hancock's fiction is at the leading edge of what Benton Rooks has called "entheodelic storytelling."[45] Offering a creative variation on the magical potentialities of tryptamines, such storytelling includes Rooks's graphic novel trilogy *Yugaverse: A Graphic Novel Universe,* involving the adventures of Abaraiis, a wizard, who, having smoked 5-MeO-DMT, acquires magical powers to combat the Kaos sorcery masters, the Lizard Kings. Written and illustrated by Mister Strange, *Psychonautica: DMT: A Graphic Novel* offers another digital-mediated form of entheodelic storytelling (see Figure 21). "We are taught to live in fear and that the unknown is evil," Mister Strange writes at the outset of *Psychonautica,* a graphically illustrated tale of self-realization following several experiments with the "elf spice." Documenting the subsequent examination of lifestyle and habit, *Psychonautica* offers a further take on the ontological departure from the known. The story's avatar is "sucked into an airless vacuum devoid of anything familiar." Not unlike the "ontoseismic" event with which we are familiar, the circumstance hastens a state of panic preceding an Odyssean resolution in which Mister Strange's ego faces obliteration in a cosmic battle involving twin serpents, before encountering the "central point of intelligence between this realm and the next." In what appears to be a classic "Level III" experience, and reminiscent to me of Gwyllm Llwydd's entity depicted in *Beyond the Gate Keepers,* Mister Strange finds himself facing "The One."

> Like a renaissance masterpiece encompassing every known permutation and aspect of life on every world and depicting each culture that has ever existed through time had been found floating in the farthest regions of the universe. The Golden City is a living recording of everything. It declared "Look at me, I am The One."

The "central point of intelligence" is an ultimate source of wisdom and higher knowledge that seems to facilitate recognition of cultural conditioning. The "lethal idea" that only wealth can buy happiness is exposed, and a new imperative is transmitted: "It is now our chance to make drastic changes no matter how uncomfortable the consequences."[46]

Whether expressed in personal trip reports or graphic novels, it is common among experienced navigators of these realms to report admittance to an urspace of primary wisdom. While there is great variation, such a "space" is not uncommonly revered as a "vaulted dome," which is received as the ultimate destination to which one arrives following sometimes-epic passage through tunnels and chambers. This vaulted space seems to be regarded as much as an "inner sanctum" (a sanctuary and place of worship) as it is a "control center" (complete with scientific instrumentation and monitoring devices), like the archetypal Wizard's control room behind the curtains, as it is an "elf dome," like the vaulted space of the Big Top in the cosmic circus.

Reports often conflate the spiritual, scientific, and carnivalesque aspects of a sacred panopticon of unfathomable proportions—the point from which all places and times, past/present/future, can be viewed. Even while returnees bemoan the futility of conveying colors, shapes, and patterns, let alone content "seen" in that realm, some make comparative reference to the interior of the dome in the Sheikh Lotfollah Mosque in Isfahan, Iran, which is considered to be a work of Persian Islamic genius. Upon first setting eyes on this marvel, art historian Robert Byron noted that the dome of Sheikh Lotfollah is "inset with a network of lemon-shaped compartments, which decrease in size as they ascend towards the formalised peacock at the apex."[47] And yet this offers nothing on the machinic contour of the space, as in the characterizations of McKenna. "You're at the center of a mountain or something. And you're in a room which aficionados call 'the dome' and people will ask each other 'did you see the dome? Were you there?' It's softly lit, indirectly lit, and the walls—if such they be—are crawling with geometric hallucinations: very brightly colored, very iridescent with deep sheens and very high reflective surfaces. Everything is machine-like and polished and throbbing with energy."[48] In turn, the mosque and the lab offer little insight on the exotic-erotic topsy-turviness of this space.

The "dome" appears to be a virtual space of divine gnosis and potential, which is concentrated in a light source, intense like the sun. In the Hyperspace Lexicon there is a key entry on the "central lightsource," which is said to "overwhelm all other experiences and perceptions." Often *kinesiooptically* perceived, this light is imagined to possess intelligence. "The intensity of the experience is so extreme and lets all other experiences fade to the background that the notion arises of a 'central' light, like central or primal to all experience or existence. In a religious paradigm, the traveler might interpret the Central Light as Buddha, Christ, Krishna or any other radiant and ultimate being in his or her religious paradigm."[49] The "dome" effect appears to be a principal manifestation of the noetic sensation of exposure to universal knowledge, such as that accessed by D. M. Turner in CydelikSpace, which he described as a "storehouse of universal experience" containing "all thoughts which did not occur but could have, and each variation of experience that did not take place."[50] We also have James Oroc's quantum-physics-backed en-light-ening entheogenesis on 5-MeO-DMT, enabling access to "all knowledge in the universe, at once" (i.e., the "Akashic Field").[51] Among the key revelations among experients is that the "knowledge" is nonlocal, which was the point of Daniel Pinchbeck in *Breaking Open the Head*: "There was, in that place, rushing toward me, an overwhelming force of knowledge and sentience.... This was no mental projection. This was not a structure within the brain that the psychoactive had somehow tapped into. It was a nonhuman reality existing at a deeper level than the physical world."[52]

In the opening article of the first issue of *The Nexian*, Hyperspace Fool offered an extraordinary report of a novice DMT event around the turn of the 1990s at a U.S. national Rainbow Gathering in the early afternoon of July 4. In the main meadow, amid 24,000 OMing Rainbow people, having dosed on at least 4 g of dried *cubensis* mushrooms and at least 500 μg of "windowpane" LSD, he was led by a friend to a large Persian rug near the center of the gathering. "Electric shocks were tingling me from head to toe ... and the waves of magnetic force were heavy and mind altering." On the rug were four aged freaks seated in lotus position. "They looked like cosmic gurus in all their regalia. A feeling of intense humility overtook me, and I stood at a respectful distance with my head bowed as my bro exchanged words with them. Without raising my eyes, I could feel them look me over ... and after a pregnant pause, assent that I was acceptable." After positioning himself, he was then handed "a tiny glass chillum full of ash with an orange ball of what could have been some very funky earwax in the center." Then, taking one deep hit with eyes closed, he experienced the universe "created" and "destroyed" nine times over, even before exhaling. There were entities that he met during this and subsequent journeys, including a "hyper-cosmic jester" he called "the Harlequin," who led him down a long hallway referred to as the "Hallways Of Always," claiming that further episodes in this place taught him "that one can travel just about anywhere in time, space, other universes, or whatever from there." Then Hyperspace Fool finally opened his eyes.

Instead of seeing 20k freaks spinning around me, I saw a mass of spirits, and normally invisible entities swarming in and above the din. As hard as this is to imagine, the 20k freaks making as much noise as they possibly could, were the quiet minority of the scene that greeted my startled eyes. I could see various guardian angel type beings that were following specific people around and trying to keep them safe. I could see ghosts and spirits of a wide variety. I could see orders of disembodied entities that were above and invisible to the orders below them. I could see the spirits who watched the spirits who watched the spirits who watched people.

It was clarified that in the upper edge of this scene were "ascended masters, buddhas and other enlightened types. They sat on clouds above the din . . . serene and exuding goodness." But that wasn't all.

Above the clouds and above the Earth itself, I saw a being that may have been larger than the entire Earth. It appeared he was standing out in space, somewhere inside the moon's orbit, and leaning over to observe us. His face took up 85% of the sky. To call him a him is arbitrary, he was a being made completely of high intensity light, of the sort I had seen in the upper upper dimensions. If I had seen him there, I would not have been so shocked. But to see him here, in our world . . . towering over us like a colossus Sentinel. It took my breath away. I gasped after a moment, and then began to feel a mild freak out coming on as he focused his entire attention on ME.

And with attention turned upon him, Hyperspace Fool became a dome-like vessel for information. "It is like some master closet organizer came in, and put a transdimensional shelving system, with rotating coat hangers, and space defying cubbyholes in my head. He packed stuff into my dome until I really could no longer think anymore. When information was overflowing out my ears, he let up."[53]

This is a telling experience on a number of levels. While there is memory of becoming freighted with information, and even fitted-out with a storage system capable of taking the load, it is accompanied by a not-uncommon perception of being incapable of retrieving the freight. While one would need to hitch a ride to an event acutely more high-tech than a Rainbow Gathering to hear it, with his voice flashing in sonic neon within psychedelic electronica, Joe Rogan offers sound bites on the getting of this wisdom that is ultimate and yet as graspable as *unobtainium*. "When you take this stuff, you encounter the most unbelievably beautiful experience, ultimate wisdom. It's like being in front of something that exposes every single aspect of your personality, of your thoughts, everything you've ever said and done, reads right through you, connects you to everything in the world and you're being communicated with."[54] While it is an experience rarely finding form in any medium, we might actually move closer to obtaining it in the work of Android Jones. For example, if we imagine the mind-explosion represented in Jones's work *Forward Escape* to be operating in reverse (i.e., more like an implosion), this work illustrates how an event of this magnitude can be conveyed using digital painting techniques. Jones is known for blending vector graphics and digital painting techniques to fashion zeitgeist-evoking panoramas. Inspired by Tipper's album of the same name, *Forward Escape* (see Figure 22) shows Jones's expert hand as a pandemonium of textures, colors, and shapes cascade from a human skull in concatenations of mounting complexity. As mentioned, the cascades can be reverse-engineered to approximate the divine motherload transmission discussed here.[55]

Another artist warranting attention is Cyb, responsible for a remarkable hyperspice oeuvre, and who, while expressing to me the challenge of capturing fragments of a higher-dimensional experience, has achieved consistently outstanding results. Such can be observed in *Metamorph* (see Figure 23), which appears to offer a window on the transfiguring event transpiring inside the dome of mind itself. Cyb speaks to the vexing task of capture in an approach he calls "digital collaging," where, using Photoshop with various filters, a drawing tablet, and a pressure-sensitive pen, he pieces elements together "layer upon layer, tweaking, merging and changing" as he proceeds. "Trying to capture a single frame from the chaotic whirlwind of an experience is an almost impossible task," he notes. "The complexity and ever shifting nature of the vision, coupled with the rapid dissolving of the event into lost memory, leaves only fragments to build on." Despite carrying only fragments back, Cyb's masterful defragmentation speaks for itself.[56]

I can make only faint brushstrokes in the challenge to communicate the remarkable range of techniques deliberately deployed to evoke the hyperspatial events under consideration. An entire book can, and no doubt will, be devoted to the subject of DMT art. One further artist requires introduction here, one who has been perfecting the use of evocative, computer-generated imagery. Beau Deeley, whose work *Divine Moments of Truth* forms the cover design of this book, has explained to me that while "throughout human history gnostics, oracles, shamans, mystics and visionaries have been responsible for bringing back visions, knowledge and ideas to those unable or unwilling to traverse the depths of inner and outer space," digital-imaging techniques endow artists with "the ability to map and document these realms and then contribute their depictions of these places and concepts directly into our collective cultural repository." Deeley's detailed efforts to faithfully render his entheogenic experiences involve a process of translation commencing with grid patterns drawn on graph paper, evolving into seamless vector patterns mapped on and in 3-D objects and spaces, before 2-D and 3-D fractal software and digital painting techniques are used to shape and enhance the experience. Deeley's *Intentionality: Dimensions of Manifestation* (see Figure 24) is representative of a new phase of work that had its inception with his first ayahuasca experience in 2011, which was then augmented by further ayahuasca and changa ceremonies in 2012. By revisiting the sites of these ceremonies and "becoming attuned to the energy of these places," Deeley was able to complete the work during six weeks in 2014. While the downsized reproduction does little justice to the detail in the original—a problem with most of the artwork reproduced in this book—Deeley clearly possesses an ability to channel the "energy vibrations." As he stated with regard to this work: "Consciousness is a fractal of the universe feeding itself sensations caused by energetic vibrations the frequency of which have sufficiently lowered to be perceptible to the senses which in turn feeds back as new stimuli."[57]

While in recent times we've seen efforts in experiential journalism, entheo-fiction, graphic novels, digital techniques, and more traditional painting styles to render the liminality of the DMT event, others sample from popular culture to illuminate otherwise hopelessly baroque transmissions. In the early period of use, there may have been little else one could turn to (other than world religious and mystical traditions). From the vast library of cultural media, all Oscar Janiger could (much later) compare his 1961 episode on DMT with was John Boorman's 1974 dystopian feature, *Zardoz*. [58] In that film, the hero, Zed—Sean Connery, appearing like a sci-fi gay biker—breaks out of the crystal prison called the Tabernacle and liberates the Eternals. Featuring more layers than an onion, the film was roundly panned by critics upon release. But if you peel away the layers, the story has a ring of pertinence. Zed delivers that which had been denied the decadent Eternals for millennia: death. In a sequence "out of time," Zed receives transmission of the accumulated historical knowledge of the Eternals, and in this supergnosis he is called to bring an "end to eternity." In a statement that holds strong resonance with the effects of DMT: "Now we can say 'yes' to death, but never again 'no,'" announces the Eternal Avalow near the film's conclusion.

DMT and Liminal Being

While elements of ritual transition are evident within DMT trance reports and other artifacts of experience, for a great many tryptamine travelers the goal is the *liminal condition* itself, enabled by venerated alkaloids. This is typically not the liminality native to conventional curative or divinatory rites, nor a traditional rite of passage where neophytes assume a status at the terminus of a symbolic pathway. It appears that DMT and its functional analogues are valued by users for threshold effect more than medicinal outcomes of the kind documented in a range of ethnobotanical contexts, and that are typical to ayahuasca shamanism. Not simply awakening divinity within, *entheoliminality* prolongs the inner divine, a set of practices that, often sans the intended telos, is directed to that which is happening *now* (e.g., being, grace, existence). Such is consistent with the optimization of *liminal being* within psychedelic electronica, where the interventions of DJ/producers are devised to orchestrate not the transformation of being and status but a superliminal state of *being in transit*. In this transitory condition, sensory technologies, visionary arts, and shamanic plants are adopted to shatter social conditioning and augment visionary experiences.[59]

In neoshamanic trance states such as those associated with tryptamines, it is recognized that the work of transformation is ultimately the responsibility of the user. While snuffs and potions containing DMT have been used for centuries in South and Central America, as Rooks points out, with tryptamine technologies "shamanic self-initiation . . . has never been quite so easy."[60] The self-shamanizing rites of the DMT user might then better approximate what Victor Turner reckoned to be the elective, experimental, and subversive—i.e., "liminoidal"—ritual evident in postindustrial cultures that potentiates revolutionary outcomes. As with ayahuasca neoshamanism, DMT use is not prescriptive, but involves a decision on the part of users, who—guided by technical and safe use instructions accessible on various webfora and shared among friends and fellow users—elect to travel illuminating pathways that are highly unique and are personalized according to the fashion of the individual wayfarer. As Julian Palmer states, "each individual must find their own way with this compound and it seems that each person has their own journey with it, which they must discover."[61] But while individuals choose to adopt user practices, the *ludibility* of which may have been enhanced by optimizable smoking blends, user status remains criminalized as a result of what is widely regarded as repressive laws. And since such laws violate cognitive liberty and even religious freedom—as is the implication of embracing substances as "entheogens"—tryptamine liminality is characterized by a range of defiant behaviors, from the clandestine to the revolutionary. In any case, since many DMT users are dissidents in the world in which they were born, are familiar with lifestyles alternative to dominant education, work, health, and leisure practices, and have experimented previously with other entheogens, they already embody a habitus with operational models open to new ways of being human. Deciding to take DMT may then be an artifact of one's lifecourse. Users, such as the many whose lives I have touched upon in this book, will then lay claim to have been "chosen" to take this path, or otherwise to have been prepared for it.

Elective or compelling, the commitment to improve methods and optimize outcomes reveals a highly augmented structure of experience.

It seems we are not far removed from what has been known among psychologists as "edgework," such as voluntary risk-taking in the practice of skydivers, BASE jumpers, and a range of extreme leisure pursuits where the "edge" negotiated is not only that separating life from death, but consciousness from unconsciousness, and sanity from its antithesis.[62] As DMT use grew, the highly sought-after breakthrough event would motivate enthusiasts of extreme sports, martial arts, and mountain climbing—users who are empowered by courting the edge, rugged individualists who seek out next-level kicks, and for whom use may amount to a psychological wilderness experience. Undertaking private vision quests as solo explorers or in small groups, experimentalists will seek to maximize the potential for ontological and metaphysical challenge by smoking DMT in geophysical regions remote from home and dense urban populations. David Anirman wrote of a memorable event on LSD and DMT while climbing to a peak somewhere in the United States in the late 1960s.

> One inhalation of the concentrated smoke, and the world melts into its patterning constituents. A second inhalation, and the body becomes transfixed with a silence so deep and so startling that within it a tear would fall as a torrent. A third inhalation, and sentience visibly radiates itself from everywhere: plants and animals are transfigured to their sacred essence and pebbles sparkle like self-conscious, magical jewels. But the balance is delicate. The vision can detonate along with the nervous system that falters before it.[63]

If there is a power to be converted from the edge experience, a current that can be redirected to the benefit of the edgeworker, it is the profound uncertainty associated with being proximate to the edge. Although shaped by a host of personal variables with manifold outcomes, tryptamines supply a virtual threshold laden with risk. Anirman captures the mood. "I remember one trip when my head disappeared, but not the rest of me, and for an excruciating half hour I lay in smoldering ruins. With DMT's quick uncontrollable rush, I simultaneously expanded and contracted. My body bloated, my head shrank to nothing, and an unshrieked scream disappeared with my vocal cords. Sometime later, after murky contortions through the tarpits of addled time, I re-emerged as a disjointed, amoeba like thing, putting itself back together with psychic pseudopods."[64] As found among edgeworking subcultures where belonging derives from plunging into the unknown, and stature is built from the performance of death-defying feats, it may be that extreme experiences of this nature serve similar ends.

And yet the psychospiritual outcomes of use remain distinct possibilities. There is probably no more telling example of the potency of the unknown than that offered by Robert Masters: a telling, if because terrifying, case of tryptaminality in which that author plunged into an extremely adverse state, ultimately embraced for its "extraordinarily fertile opportunities." Masters's apocalypse of the self was a near-fatal, and later near-suicidal, departure from the mundane. "There seems to be only this unperimetered, amorphous monstrosity all around me, ready to swallow and obliterate and possess me," Masters noted in his diary. "My mind rides the slopes of my previous life like an escaped sled with an accelerating black avalanche a microsecond behind. Suddenly, without premeditation, I go into the terror, no longer fighting or resisting it, no longer attempting to witness it. The Minotaur's face is only inches away. My mind splinters, unraveled by the Minotaur's bleeding howl of recognition."[65]

The archetype of the Minotaur becomes critical to the passage through the darkness, with Masters reflecting that the Minotaur will not "stroll up to the surface and sit still while we paint or sculpt its likeness." No, "if we truly want to bring it to canvas or poetic life, we're going to have to descend—and not just intellectually—to its lair, with no solid guarantee that we will return (or at least return intact)."[66] The archetypal monster, the confrontation with which allegorizes one's facing of the feared unknown, the Minotaur is of key significance for Masters, who confronts his fear of nonbeing, his dread of being other than "I." Masters's confrontation permitted him to turn dread on its head.

> In its very capacity to reveal to us the innate groundlessness both of our world and of the identity through which we attempt to maintain the illusory security of that world, dread can not only scare us scriptless, but can also—if well used—serve our transition from egically governed selfhood to Being-centered selfhood.... As such, it is the dragon guarding the

fabled treasure, the penumbral beastgod protecting the sacred threshold, the amorphous yet suffocatingly palpable demon we must wrestle (or dance) with until it is no longer an "it," but only reclaimed us.[67]

In a passage that will have made Turner pay attention, Masters states that "darkness is universal uterinity, ever pregnant with Being." And how to arrive at a "Being-centered selfhood"? One must take "a leap of almost inconceivable faith, a naked plunge into the 'dark side' of the Unknowable."[68] I guess this is all very well in hindsight. Masters did not choose this path. His was a strategy of survival, a salvage operation following a remarkable feat of recklessness. While his experience could hardly stand as a model to be replicated, Masters admitted from the outset that his was no hero's journey.

Another figure not unaccustomed to the naked plunge into the unknown, nor unfamiliar with the Minotaur, and yet whose experience offers a unique and intentional approach to the phenomenon at hand, is ChaOrder Magician Orryelle Defenestrate-Bascule. If the DMT trance is quintessentially liminal, then what happens when the endogenous compound meets one of the more liminal beings walking the planet? Well, it seems that you get a peacock angel with colors unimaginably iridescent. Our paths first crossed in the mid-1990s when s/he wove a series of Labyrinth installations and interactive performances by hir Metamorphic Ritual Theatre Company, at the Australian outdoor events ConFest and Earthcore. The Labyrinths were designed so that each "initiate" passed through a labia-like gateway into an elaborate maze where they engaged with various mythic characters and eventually met the central Minotaur, who as their shadow-self reflected the way they related to him. He would "slay" them with a struggle or simply an embrace, according to their attitude toward him, then the initiates would ascend a spiral staircase in a mirror chamber before eventually being reborn through the labial gateway.[69] That was back before the refurbishment of Defenestrate-Bascule's physical temple, performed via hermaphroditic mutations leading to a "WoManifest Wedding Ceremony with Self" in 2000. Early experiments entering into the DMT trance while gazing into a peacock tail-feather eye saw Orryelle invoke the peacock angel—Melek Taus. It was later discovered that certain sound frequencies and iridescent colors can produce similar experiences, since they trigger the release of DMT in the brain. Indeed, it is Orryelle's conviction that smoking DMT can not only induce an array of vibrant iridescent colors, but that working intensively with vibrant iridescent colors can "activate DMT in the brain chemistry."[70] The work *Melek Taus and the Path of Venus* is exemplary (see Figure 25). As a detail of a larger canvas found in hir collection *Distillatio*—the final in a quartet of alchemical art books—the work is a distillation of oils, peacock-egg-tempera, gold and copper leaf, peacock feathers, and snakeskin, and is condensed thus:

> Every eight years the orbit of the planet Venus creates a pentagram in the sky, so here we see the love Goddess Venus/Aphrodite overlaid on the pentagrammatical seed-pod of a halved apple. Thus three layers of this sacred geometry are depicted: cosmic, deific expressed in the human form, and plant. The planet Venus as the Morning Star is also represented by Melek Taus, the peacock angel of the Yezzidi, and the similarly-iridescent Quetzalcoatl/Kukulcan ("Feathered Serpent") of the Aztecs and Mayans.[71]

Having worked with black-and-white media until recently, Orryelle discovered that immersing hirself in color facilitated "a kind of hypnogogia—not only a greatly increased awareness and perception of colour and its effects in the physical waking world, but also a delirious array of flickering myriad-hued mandalas when I closed my eyes after a long night at the easel."[72]

Orryelle explained to me the events that hatched *Melek Taus and the Path of Venus*, which was completed in a simple rented dwelling on the edge of a small town in the Australian bush with a panoramic view of the night sky, featuring "Venus central in the vista near the bloodshot horizon." Under those conditions, s/he had discovered that a peafowl egg delivered the perfect media. "As practical alchemy involves the embodiment of spirituality, the enactment and magical materialisation of the quintessential, so this journey thus led me for my final canvas to the acquisition of a peafowl's egg, the real-eyes-ation that I should crack the white shell that contains like a spectral fan unfolding every iridescence in potentia, to make the culminating mixture of tempera." Working night after night with the tempera and pea-cock feathers, transfixed by their iridescence, s/he discovered a color-glazing technique to simulate the peacock tail-feather eye used as a background to the final layer. Orryelle explained that each night s/he would emerge after hours of painting

> to see the spread of stars sparkling in the clear night air, and around each would flicker bands of turquoise, violet and indigo—the sky resplen-dent with layers and layers of peacock eyes, somehow both subtle and spectacular simultaneously. Despite being a result of perceptual alchemy rather than drug-induced, these were not fleeting hallucinations to be banished with a refocusing of the eyes—they would persist even when I tried to make them go away and see what was really there. Eventually I could only realise that they are really there, and how we see things is a matter of how much we tune into the different frequencies and band-widths of colour and light which permeate our multi-hued existence.[73]

Across a spectrum of media, the arts of storytelling lend sense to non-sense, and convert the unknown into meaning. As I discovered following my episode recounted in the Prologue to this book, an entheogenic NDE places one's self in the director's chair, enabled through the act of writing, the medium of the "trip report"—the autoentheography. As Jeffrey Kripal has noted, within the occult and paranormal milieu, authorship renders the impossible possible, a circumstance also apparent within the entheo-genic milieu, where trip decoders and transmission hackers become the composers of their own lives, *writing their way out*.[74] It's a lifelong practice, as shown by the life of Stan Grof, who entitled his autobiography replete with psychoactively charged experiences *When the Impossible Happens*. In the DMT user community at any rate, users the world over write, paint, sculpt, perform their way out of impossible "breakthroughs." Earlier, I mentioned the modes of ritual transmission introduced by Jane Harrison: rituals of display, performance, and instruction. In condensed form, these types of ritual transmit the *sacra* through what is "shown," "done," and "said." All modes are heavily reliant on the five senses. With entheogens, we become witness to a mode of transmission as variable as the individual experient, in which information is received by way of extrasensory impressions, a higher-dimensional event unavailable to the "five senses." We are now inside pure imagination, by which I do not mean, dismissively, that it's "only in your imagination." In other-dimensional space, we may be exposed to an alternate mode of ritual transmission—perhaps something like "what is X'd," the preferred nomenclature of Robert Hunter, for whom all known sense-oriented verbs were inadequate in conveying what he'd "X'd" when taking DMT. Perhaps *what is undone* may better describe the mode of transmission native to that place, than "what is done." Comparing DMT with LSD experiences, Leary appeared to have a handle on this, writing that "the shattering of learned form perception, the collapse of learned structure was much more pronounced" with DMT.[75] A means by which dissolution of perceptual constants is accomplished is synesthesia, where, for instance, that which is "seen" and "heard" are conflated. The received world collapses, too, in the grip of the paranormal, higher dimensions, and extrasensory perceptions that inherited language—already challenged to adequately transcribe five sensory perceptions—fails to convey. As many a mind-begoggled returnee knows, words fail, a vexatious circumstance that, as mentioned in Chapter Seven, sheds light on the *aporrheta* (the "unrepeatables") at Eleusis.

There has been considerable debate about what had transpired inside the Telesterion during the two thousand years of the rites of Eleusis. As is well known among historians, upon pain of death or banishment, initiates were prohibited from uttering what had been transmitted to them during the secret ceremony inside the temple. It seemed to have worked, because we know very little about this secret ceremony and the chemical composition of the *kykeon* drunk by initiates. I've suspected that it may bear fruit to recognize that the "unrepeatables" weren't transmitted outside of the experience not only because of an interdiction, but because language (spoken and written) is incapable of conferring that objective. The unrepeatables were essentially unrepeatable. You simply had to be there to know the score. Anyone in attendance at protean events, from the acid tests to acid house raves, knows this noetic logic. There's an overload of the senses. And no one outside the perimeter, and parameters, of this experience can know it, because they weren't there to sense it, using *all* of the five senses, and more. Of course, in modern times, drug prohibition has inaugurated new injunctions, leading to clandestinity and self-censorship. In fact, due to these injunctions, those outside the experience are more likely to discredit or even censure the vibe than acknowledge its sovereignty. Primary experients will create artifice—chants, music, dance moves—to give expression to its noetic logic, but as the proverbial statement that may have been kicked off by thirteenth-century mystic and poet Rumi goes: the insanity of those who dance is apparent among those who cannot hear the music.

For its habitués, spicespace holds resonance: the sensation of its veridicality, the fundamental inadequacy of language to render it understandable, the suspicion among outsiders of pathology or, at best, "hallucination." But the experience won't be denied. Those who've known hyperspace and its unutterability commune in knowing silence about what they've "seen" there. Mind hives are established for dialogue on the virtues and vicissitudes of tryptaminal virtuality. New brogue is channeled in the effort to mediate it, novel scripts divulge the self awakened to its own divinity, and galleries are erected like halls of mirrors reflecting back to self an awareness of its own disparate authorship. To be self-aware may be the ultimate concern of the entheogenic movement, but it cannot be achieved without removing the barriers to self-discovery. To accomplish this state, one must learn to embrace the unknown.

CHAPTER 12

Entity Mosaic

Creatures from the Trypt

When reviewing a thousand pages of detailed notes taken at the bedside of sixty volunteers who'd received DMT in four hundred sessions over five years, Rick Strassman was taken by the unexpected recurrence of *beings* in approximately half of the accounts. Equally surprising to him was that these Others were multifarious in character and intent. Such diversity is unsurprising given the uncertainty of the lived experience of *otherness* associated with DMT and its functional analogues. From teacher to archon, elf to mantid, therianthrope to tree spirit, this unpredictable mosaic of Others, a veritable bestiary of archetypes, forms the subject of this penultimate chapter.

Writing in *True Hallucinations* of a meeting with a giant insect that "seemed to be observing and sometimes exerting influence to keep us moving gently towards a breakthrough," for Terence McKenna, the Other approximated an omniscient spirit-guide archetype: The Teacher. At La Chorrera in '71, Dennis had become medium to an energy "like the sound of a giant insect," an experience for which DMT had already prepared the brothers. Terence wrote, "because of the bizarre nature of the DMT flash, with its seeming stress upon themes alien, insectile, and interstellar, we were led to speculate that this teacher was somehow a diplomat-anthropologist, come to give us the keys to galactarian citizenship."[1] While Dennis would distance himself from the episode, the benevolent attitude of the Other encountered using tryptamines was the thrust of his brother's lifelong enucleation of the noisy tykes that had first paid him a house call in 1965—those "syntactical homunculi" whose relationship with humans is that "they love us! They care for some reason."[2]

The entity-as-teacher is simply one model complex in the study of the DMT entity phenomenon. Rather than performing roles in the evolution

of species and consciousness, entities are, for other experients, defini-
tively monstrous—beings whose interventions in human affairs are far
from benevolent. Having been aware of malevolent demiurge-like entities
apropos the gnostic tradition, Jim DeKorne was especially keen to warn
of the dangers of entity encounters. "It behooves all psychedelic explorers
to prudently evaluate the kinds of 'allies' they choose to integrate into
their psyches. The higher the level of unification the better; otherwise it is
seductively easy to become entrapped within dimensional resonances of
dubious ultimate value."[3] These specters are known to appear in multiple guises. While allies, such as those of an insectoid nature, are deemed
to exist, their purpose seems ambivalent in the light of reports where
travelers are subject to examination or are experimented upon, devoured
even, by aliens characterized as mantids—which is entirely consistent
with the Western narrative of the daemonic insect.[4] And in case you are
accustomed to believing it's elves all the way down, conveying the report
of one high-dose volunteer who was crushed and raped anally by croc-
odiles, Strassman noted that the episode—while not at all typical of his
volunteers' reports—served nevertheless as a reminder of the potential
dangers of DMT.[5]

Significant Elf Proclivity

In the history of DMT contact reports, the decidedly more innocuous elves
are as common as rats in your barn. While Leary had dropped hints about
"merry erotic energy nests" of "elf-like insects" in *The Psychedelic Review* in
the mid-1960s, it was McKenna, following his entreatment to their antics
in 1965, who later propagated the contact meme throughout underground
culture. Also regarded by McKenna as "gnomes" or "tykes," these entities
encountered in DMT space colored the discourse of psychonaut musicians,
authors, and sculptors during the 1990s and early 2000s. They made an
appearance in Gracie and Zarkov's how-to guide "DMT: How and Why to
Get Off." Taking a hit of DMT on October 9, 1984, Zarkov reported "direct
awareness of an overwhelmingly powerful and knowledgable *presence!*"
Exposed to the "control panel for the entire universe," he became witness
to those working the dials. "A gaggle of elf-like creatures in standard issue

irish elf costumes, complete with hats, looking like they had stepped out of a hallmark cards 'happy saint patrick's day' display, were doing strange things with strange objects that seemed to be a weird hybrid between crystals and machines."[6] Similar creatures appeared before some of Strassman's group. "There were a lot of elves," recalled Karl.

> They were prankish, ornery, maybe four of them appeared at the side of a stretch of interstate highway I travel regularly. They commanded the scene, it was their terrain! They were about my height. They held up placards, showing me these incredibly beautiful, complex, swirling geometric scenes in them. One of them made it impossible for me to move. There was no issue of control; they were totally in control. They wanted me to look! I heard a giggling sound—the elves laughing or talking at high-speed volume, chattering, twittering.[7]

Reported visitations permeate web forums and portals such as the Vaults of Erowid, where one is struck by the uncanny sense of familiarity they evoke. "They kept saying welcome back and words like: the big winner, he has returned, welcome to the end and the beginning, you are The One! As I looked around the room I felt the sense of some huge celebration upon my entry to this place. Bells were ringing, lights flashing."[8]

Vying for attention, forming visible languages, and in command of incomprehensible instrumentation, "machine elves" multiplied like white rabbits during the 1990s, becoming virtual mascots within psychedelic trance and ambient genres. In 1994, Space Tribe's Olli Wisdom celebrated the advent of the Hyper Space Age with the driving "Machine Elf"—released on TIP Records' debut LP *The Yellow Compilation*—featuring Mr. Spock remarking "visual contact firmly established, request permission to land." In 1995, Belgians Mark Poysden and Stefan Osadzinski released their abstract breakbeat album *Bitone* under the name Self Transforming Machine Elves, a name also adopted as the moniker of a techno-chillout duo from Amsterdam. Having made his own ventures into DMT space, Simon Posford (as Hallucinogen) emerged in 1996 with "Gamma Goblins" on debut Twisted Records album *Deranger*. Featuring the twisted laughter of techno-sprites peeking through a spanking rhythm, the legendary track might have been the soundtrack for the hybrid habitués of hyperspace. Over the next few years, a barrage of acts representing a variety of genres identified with the machinic/humanoid mutants in titles like "Self Transforming Machine Creatures of Hyperspace" by trance collaboration Nervasystem & Aether on *The Mama Matrix Most Mysterious* (1999), and dark-trance compilation *Significant Elf Proclivity* released on Ambivalent Records in 2002. By this stage, machinic cyber elves had populated the landscape of psychedelia, mutating the atavistic Tolkienesque archetypes of the earlier generation, and propagating in psychedelic fiction and textile fashion.

Since the avalanche in artist sobriquets and iconographic depictions coincided with the circulation of McKenna's memes in the 1990s (and indeed with the popularization of the internet), it prompts the question: were the elves actually nonlocal entities or mischievous sprites cast loose on the imagination by the psychedelic bard himself? The zeitgeist was sung in countless correspondences, like SFos's classic report from 1995, where McKenna is studiously referenced as one turning in an essay for Transdimensional Studies 101. "For what seemed like centuries I played with the trippy freaky elves and they kept bringing me into atrium after atrium in the antics annex." Having tumbled forward into elfland, SFos notes that "Terence McKenna is apt in calling these entities 'elves.' They are elves/not-elves. They don't appear, they kind of ooze out of the woodwork seductively and before you know it they're there—the whole realm is infested with these creatures like nothing else you could ever imagine. They do sing things that are like 'self-dribbling jeweled basketballs' or whatever you want to call them. They make Faberge egg concoctions."[9]

But while the illustrious antics of "elves" are appropriately appropriated or plagiarized in manifold accounts, in others they appear sans the trumpet call of McKenna. Apparently independent to elf lore, David Luke found himself, eyes closed, "stuffed full of light by what I can only describe as little elves." The experience, replicated in the reports of fellow travelers, drove Luke toward a serious consideration of the ontology of these beings.[10] We may never know with certainty if it was McKenna's cheerleading that prompted a swarm of elves to buzz transdimensional intrepids, but it does appear that, given the circulation of his theories about the Logos and its elven ambassadors, in addition to Gracie and Zarkov's circulars from the Nth dimensions, they were "disproportionately represented" in DMT accounts from the 1980s onward.[11] And yet, this preponderance gave many cause to regard elves with suspicion. They became experiential baubles, like the chintziest ornaments on your Christmas tree. They are even embarrassing to behold, as was the case when Daniel Pinchbeck took mushrooms in Palenque with the desire to be shown something "evoking the cruel and silent Mayan gods," not the horrifyingly cheerful Disney elves that appeared to him instead.[12] But imagining it's all simply benign and bonhomie with the spice folk would be a crude assessment. An anonymous contributor reporting in *The Entheogen Review* in the mid-1990s revealed a sinister side to entities whose actions are to the standard "machine elves of hyperspace" as the furious "infected" in *28 Days Later* are to the shambling zombies of *The Night of the Living Dead*.

> I close my eyes and lean back. I feel and hear a shift as the hyper-express elevator takes me away from my body to my destination and I arrive in a place filled with intense white light where hideous, bodiless, pointed-eared, purple and green entities bound toward me and they laugh, jeer and ridicule me; where these grotesque elf, joker or clown-like caricatures rush at me one at a time and in clusters; where they curl their hideous, clown like mouths and wag their tongues in my face; where I relive every real and imagined humiliation I suffered in childhood; where a great sorrow and disappointment fills me as they come at me faster and faster; where I start to crumble under their onslaught, so I open my eyes but still they come; where I realize I have to face them so I close my eyes and focus on my breathing, and the demonic forces back off and I feel myself coming out of the trip.[13]

By the early 2000s, like the Elves vanishing to Valinor, the elf-predilection receded in psychedelic folklore. Either that, or they were simply overrun by the teeming legions of hyperspace. That said, someone should have forwarded the memo to Cynic frontman Paul Masvidal, who is vocal about them in "Elves Beam Out," a song on the former death-metal band's 2011 EP *Carbon-Based Anatomy*—demonstrating that they may pop up and beam out from the unlikeliest of places.

Entity Phantasmagoria

Placing this elf-collecting exercise aside, given that McKenna's proclamations concerning elves will have been familiar to Strassman's New Mexico
volunteers, it is notable that only a small percentage of the entities reported
in that study were described as elves or elf-like. Regarded as "beings,"
"aliens," "guides," and "helpers," these entities manifested as clowns, reptiles, mantises, bees, spiders, cacti, and stick figures.[14] Based on his own
experience and surveys of Erowid users, Jon Hanna confirms that DMT
space is populated by a multitude of discarnate entities, including "typical
sci-fi extraterrestrials, humanoids, jellyfish, insectoids, clowns/Pierrots,
reptilians, robots, octopods," the cataloging of which he suggests could
lead to a *Bestiarum Vocabulum*, a psychonautical-entity compendium that
charts their form, frequency of appearance, and association with specific
psychedelics.[15]

A classification of supernatural beings encountered by ayahuasca users
was earlier undertaken by Benny Shanon. In *Antipodes of the Mind*, Shanon
lists: mythological beings (such as gnomes, elves, fairies, and monsters of
all kinds); chimeras or hybrids (typically half human, half animal, like mer-
maids); transforming or shapeshifting beings (e.g., human to puma, tiger,
or wolf); extraterrestrials (e.g., accompanied by spacecraft); angels and
celestial beings (usually winged human-like beings that may be transparent or composed of light); semi-divine beings (may appear like Jesus, Buddha, or typically Hindu, Egyptian, or pre-Columbian deities); and demons,
monsters, and beings of death (e.g., the angel of death).[16] David Luke has
subsequently added the category of plant teachers or plant spirits to this
list, and, in the light of their close association with DMT, has suggested
adding insectoid-aliens, especially the praying mantis, to the extraterrestrial category.[17] While falling short of a specific DMT bestiarum, poring
over countless descriptions of DMT beings, Clifford Pickover gathered
more data on the phenomenon. "They are frequently described as elflike,
alien, or angelic—and of indeterminate gender. Some have multiple faces.
Some are made of light. Some seem to materialize from the background
and duplicate themselves. A wide range of beings have been described as
robots, larval beings, alien space insects, androids, machine-elves, clowns,
dwarves, praying-mantis entities, and fairies." Even the insectoidal entities

comprise a unique menagerie, with Pickover finding numerous reports with visions of "lapidary insects," "elflike insects," "cricket creatures," "mechanical insects," "pirate mantids," "mantis beings," "wise mantises," and "mantises in scarlet robes."[18]

An expanding entourage of entities has been recorded at the DMT-Nexus inclusive to the Hyperspace Lexicon.[19] There, explorers lodge unique classificatory systems identifying an ecology of entities: explorers like NGC_2264, whose entities dwell within a hierarchical system, with greater and lesser beings comprising a "super-organism," or "collective intelligence," perhaps even different faces of the same entity. The exquisite detail of NGC_2264's diverse entities contrasts with "machine elves" as a 3-D tarot deck compares with primitive shades etched on a cave wall. There are, for instance, the Strange Visitors who appear to worship "some sort of cosmic arachnoid overlord," and who behave like snobbish inspectors who "revel in and even exaggerate their weirdness and 'otherness,' emphasizing all kinds of bizarre cultural customs and sensibilities." These pretentious "auditors" seem obsessed with aesthetics, scents, and other sensory input, "in particular the smell and 'feel' of crystals and minerals." Then there's the intimidating military force identified as The Legion, described as "an intergalactic Roman Empire or Third Reich." Under the weight of this scenario, the spice avatar is surrounded by "a legion of domineering, faceless soldiers . . . accompanied by a 'warlord-general' wearing something like a cybernetic plague doctor mask, towering, bipedal mecha-like constructs, bio-mechanical monstrosities, and other colossal warmachines." Among various other listed characters is The Triad, a sinister trio who follow our contactee around, but who have a penchant for slipping beyond the periphery of perception. NGC_2264 appears to have encountered The Triad once only, an experience that may have felt like an eternity. "The state they induced in me was utter confusion and terrifying out-of-control dementia, the closest thing I've experienced to full possession." The entities bore "an arcane tome full of unreadable text that radiated an aura of dread and insanity," which was intended for our hyperspace traveler, who recalls an object resembling a stylized corruption of Metatron's Cube. "There were some pages of complex symbological imagery and other mystifying diagrams, but they just mocked the futility of my efforts as I tried to discern their dark meaning."

From such descriptions it is striking how advanced travelers comport themselves like *players* in a role-playing game (RPG). Surveying such a cast of personalized entities, in whose ranks live less sinister beings like The Guide and The Dream Teacher, is indeed like becoming familiar with the characters, rules, and challenging environment of an RPG. Each character possesses distinct sensibilities, aesthetics, motivations, and evolving attitudes toward the avatar with whom they form an ongoing relationship. Not only do risk and uncertainty pervade, collaborative and competitive aspects resonate with an online multiplayer RPG environment. Among the essential actors in NGC_2264's pantheon are The Human Spirits, beings who "typically presented themselves as my peers . . . [who] seemed completely autonomous and independently intelligent." While allies of a sort, these entities are ultimately described as willful and coercive. "It was only after my confrontation with them that they began to show their true nature and regularly attack me (with varying degrees of success)."[20]

The diversity of entities and their mode of appearance was addressed by Tramacchi, who offers a thoughtful study of DMT users and their encounters with the Other. Tramacchi prefers the term "ultradimensional"—in favor of "extraterrestrial" or "alien"—since "aliens" may derive from "worlds separated from ours in more esoteric ways, whether by 'vibration,' 'frequency,' strange 'angles,' or other quirks of physics."[21] He also identified a variety of functions performed by ultradimensional entities. Like Hermes, they may be "psychopomps, who guide the subject through the DMT Umwelt, or they may be psychosurgeons who operate on the subject's visionary body, or they may be fiends who try to devour the visionary."[22] It is not uncommon for longer-term explorers to report encounters with diverse entities over the course of their lives, or during periods of use, with the establishment of ongoing relationships with specific entities or entity-types a common occurrence. Introducing a collection of events experienced over a two-year period, Psychedaniellia provides an excellent example. Psychedaniellia reported her experiences—using DMT, often with a range of other compounds—to Erowid in 2014. "My experiences have ranged from spiritually glowing to mind-boggling to disgusting and terrifying, and entities I have 'met' have had many different qualities," she wrote. "Some have been helpful and affirming of all that I value in life, and others seemed to intend to use me for their own purposes or trick me."[23] Psychedaniellia purposefully avoided listening to Terence McKenna's descriptions of "DMT space" before her experiments. Her candid, open-minded, and humble reports are offered like dream fragments, except that, compared with dreams, the events were received with a striking noetic quality accompanied by profound emotional states (i.e., sense of loss, embarrassment, elation, etc.) and apparently incomparable to anything experienced in waking life or dream states. The reports, of which I provide fragments, offer curious insight on the hyperspace passage rite, although it is true that there may be as many variations of this as there are experients. The passage from novitiate to adept (who decreased usage once integrating the "gift") is strongly evocative of the "self-shamanising" propensity of DMT observed by Tramacchi.

On her first experience, Psychedaniellia encountered "three alien-like beings that were tall and slender. They weren't very detailed; they were seen mainly as silhouettes. One of them came up to me with a round seed-like object in his hands and presented it to me. It had a glowing pinpoint of light, and he seemed to be trying to get me interested in the object." Subsequent encounters included a confronting "mother entity" described as "shapeless; dripping, melting, ugly, terrifying, disgusting," and an "angry spirit" (encountered when doing "DMT on top of LSD and 4-AcO-DiPT") inquiring: "Why do all you humans ignore us? We're all around you, ALL the time, causing so much to happen, yet you credit yourselves for everything!" Later, with "DMT on top of Ketamine," it appears Psychedaniellia was being actively recruited.

> I encountered an entity who seemed to have some sort of high status, business-wise. He asked me if I would like to take on a very important job position in hyperspace, since I was apparently "fit for the position." I felt so bewildered and astonished at the time . . . as if I was thinking . . . "You'd *really* choose *me*?!" . . . I felt like the position was something very serious and important and I didn't think it should be taken lightly. I psychically communicated to the entity that I needed a bit of time to

think, as it seemed like an important position of leadership as the entity had implied. I thought about it for what seemed like a while (but was probably not actually very long), and I decided to respect the offer/position and take it. I communicated this to the entity, but then the experience dissipated.[24]

The very next episode, involving "DMT on top of 4-ho-MiPT," appears to have been a continuation of this scenario. "I met the 'boss' entity, he seemed to be some sort of CEO in hyperspace! (Ridiculous to think about, but that is how it seemed.) He seemed all-knowing and completely ancient. He appeared to be made out of antique wood, and was covered in various compartments such as drawers, doors and windows. During this experience, I felt very honored to meet this entity. It seemed like he imparted some serious knowledge unto me about 'intent manifestation' in the waking life through dream and trance states." It seems that with this and further lessons in "Existence 101," Psychedaniellia was reminded of her "personal mission" to "bring together the world of dreams and the waking state." Subsequent entity events got down to brass tacks. On 30 mg of DMT together with "a few milligrams of 5-MeO-DMT and three nitrous chargers in one big balloon," she felt like she was being "schooled on existence" with a "teacher entity telling us that we were all meant to be intent manifestors."

The collapse of the DMT trance and the waking state appears to have been made manifest in a series of encounters with an orange healing "feminine presence." These nurturing entities possessed "a tremendous healing power," described as being very warm and without an agenda, other than to feed and care for her. In subsequent episodes, these recurring peaceful "female healing entities" appear to have endowed Psychedaniellia with the gift of song.

But then, something told me to sing. So I started singing/channeling a song from or for the spirits. They became interested and came up to me very close. One of them placed a clay jar in front of me and with every note I sang, an entity would place a small glowing (pinpoint of light) object into the jar. I think the objects were mainly lime green or yellow. I gradually transitioned back, but I kept singing the song as I came down.

350

I recorded it on my phone so that I would never forget it. I still sing this song before doing DMT sometimes, as it helps to calm me down and sometimes I can invoke those healing entities with the song.[25]

In a subsequent event, she describes doing just that—i.e., invoking the healing spirits "by singing the beautiful song." When they appeared, "they seemed a bit concerned about my health again (my health had gotten a bit worse and I was constantly having stomach problems). They came up to me and seemed to be offering me healing. Then, before I knew it, one of the entities extended and fused into my stomach area and seemed to actually become a part of me. As I felt nothing but benevolence from these entities, my understanding was that she wanted to be there to help me to get through difficult times ahead, because I was definitely going to need resilience." As a postscript, she writes, "and it's true—the past year has been one of the most difficult times of my life, but I think I'm doing well."

Finally, Psychedaniellia describes an extraordinary event involving DMT "with MDMA." "As soon as I entered the trance state," she recounts, "I felt my mouth filling up with some sort of 'food' but it was textured just like dirt and even tasted like it. . . . It felt like medicine of the earth. . . . I felt an intense flash of insight and knowledge after consuming this food." Described as "food for thought," and as a "profoundly beautiful moment," the flash was received as a sign of her "need to help people to be more in touch with their subconscious mind, their dreams, and their intuitions." Subsequently, she "felt a strong urge to send powerful intent to the whole universe and to all of the people in this world, for them to become more in touch with these parts of themselves in hopes of making the world a better place." For Psychedaniellia, completion of the "passage" appears reliant on the manifesting of intent—in her case the merging of dream state with waking life, and to expound this practice to others. Her reporting of these events on Erowid animated this intent (and my recounting of those experiences here provides further animation).

The entity phenomenon is complex ontological terrain. In later comments about his 1990s trials and DMT entities more generally, Strassman reflected that he was startled most by "their awareness of us." And yet, while entities appeared sentient, their reaction to the presence of the newly arrived is diverse. Often welcoming toward travelers who are expected, and who may be received like royalty or long-lost family members, perhaps even greeted like champions on Cosmic Wheel of Fortune, at other times they are overcome with surprise and shock, not unlike that provoked by the sudden appearance of an alien species, a ghost, or an intruder. And so, while the reception committee is oftentimes warm, welcoming, and celebratory, hostility remains a distinct possibility, especially if player-intrepids make a sudden incursion into "their" world. A fundamental variation in the motivation of these foreign actors is also identified: "either they want to help or they request help."[26] This is an important observation on conduct in the trans-entity DMTverse. Entities may be providers or extractors of knowledge. They come to our aid or demand our servitude. They offer pearls of wisdom or make penetrating inquiries. Whether benefactor or tyrant, mentor or student, ambassador or scientist, missionary or prospector, teacher or archon, the disparate motivations and polar characteristics of DMT entities adds to the uncertain nature of the ecology of DMT space.

At one edge of the scale, one is lavished with gifts in a kind of homecoming ticker-tape parade. McKenna's celebrated observations that the elves were showering him with presents is an experience replicated in the reports of many transdimensional trekkers, whereby the indigenes of DMT space present travelers with amazing objects like Fabergé eggs devised from complex arcane symbology arriving in patterns that are not immediately comprehensible, especially because the gratuities arrive in rapid streams of information. Typically, these objects appear like puzzles to be solved, messages to be translated, hieroglyphs to be interpreted, code to be parsed, salves to be applied, a mystery to be unlocked—all suggestive of the esoteric core of the DMT experience. "They were trying to show me as much as possible," recalled Chris.

> They were communicating in words. They were like clowns or jokers or jesters or imps. There were just so many of them doing their funny little thing. I settled into it. I was incredibly still and I felt like I was in an incredibly peaceful place. Then there was a message telling me that I had been given a gift, that this space was mine and I could go there anytime. I should feel blessed to have form, to live. It went on forever.

There were blue hands, fluttering things, then thousands of things flew out of these blue hands. I thought "What a show!" It was really healing.[27]

But Strassman's group offered contrasting reports on what "they" were up to. Here's Ben:

It started with a sound. It was high-pitched like a tightly taut wire. There were four or five of them. They were on me fast. As crazy as this sounds, they looked like saguaro cactus, very Peruvian in color. They were flexible, fluid, geometrical cacti. Not solid. They weren't benevolent but they weren't non-benevolent. They probed, they really probed. They seemed to know time was limited. They wanted to know what I, this being who had shown up, was doing.... I felt like something was inserted into my left forearm, right here, about three inches below this chain-link tattoo on my wrist. It was long. There were no reassurances with the probe. Simply business.[28]

Among the experienced in Strassman's group, there were various reports of probes, implants, surgery, and "research" conducted by beings whose intentions were unknown, and whose objectives were questionable. This phenomenon is replicated in broader DMT-returnee commentaries. "I began to see my body 'open up' like a 'field of wheat' and it was almost like my body had transformed to a complex garden of aquaculture, where the liquid silky strands of my being were being 'harvested.'" This returnee "felt as if they were analyzing me for some research they did, or some project 'they' were involved in. I didn't feel as if it were hostile but it definitely didn't feel very friendly either.... They appeared to be in total control of my body, and the vast majority of my mind."[29] As Strassman was himself acutely aware, such commentaries are consistent with reports of alien-abduction episodes, such as those documented by psychiatrist John Mack in *Abduction: Human Encounters with Aliens*. Abductees have typically reported feelings of helplessness, becoming trapped, and being experimented upon. Robert Masters condensed the reported findings of:

(a) feeling strange bodily vibrations or paralysis, as a light of unusual brightness, seemingly otherworldly and often circularly shaped, approaches, into which one is helplessly drawn or sucked; (b) finding oneself in an enclosure that appears to contain technical equipment, surrounded by and at the complete mercy of aliens—usually humanoid, but also sometimes reptilian or insect-like—who generally relate to one with clinical detachment; and (c) being on something like an examining or treatment table, and subjected to various physical procedures, especially probings with sophisticated instruments, by the aliens.[30]

Studies of the effects of DMT and other tryptamines have offered insights on the alien-abduction phenomenon. Before taking up entheofiction, and buoyed by his own encounters with entities using ayahuasca and DMT, in his popular book *Supernatural: Meetings with the Ancient Teachers of Mankind,* Graham Hancock amassed a wealth of information pointing to commonalities between specifically *hybrid* creatures: "machine elves," bug-eyed researchers, reptilian creatures, the humanoid ("Grey") aliens appearing in the post–World War II era, the twisted, shape-shifting "fairy" folk endemic to the Celtic fringe of western Europe from medieval through Victorian times, and the human/animal therianthropes. Of particular interest to Hancock, the latter are associated with shamanic visions and initiations as appearing in the painted caves of Upper Paleolithic Europe and in the rock art of the San of southern Africa, especially in the so-called "wounded man" figures—the first alien-abduction reports in recorded history. Pouring over Strassman's volunteer reports, Hancock found that their encounters with typically ambivalent humanoid figures, and the transmission of vital information, are traits replicated not only in UFO abductions like those documented by Mack, and in the antics of fairies in Celtic folklore, but in world shamanic traditions, where altered states of consciousness appear to be the universal techniques for entity propagation.[31]

Tracing the groundbreaking neuropsychological thesis of archaeologist David Lewis-Williams, Hancock holds that the most ancient art of humankind was inspired by humans in states of consciousness altered by ingested psychoactive plants, or through rhythmic dancing, fasting, and sensory deprivation.[32] Such classic shamanic techniques are thereby implicated in the dawning of religion, and are speculated to be the "mysterious X-factor" elevating our ancestors out of the cognitive shadows about forty thousand years ago. For Hancock, Lewis-Williams didn't go far enough in unraveling the mystery of human origins, insistent as he is that the visual—entoptic or phosphene—phenomena depicted in the art of the ancients derives from "hard-wired" neurochemistry. For the likes of Lewis-Williams, the evolution of consciousness can be explained as a product of the evolution of brain structure, and nothing more. But in *Supernatural,* Hancock insists that there is something more, and DMT may provide the answers. By grifting Strassman's proposal that DMT "retunes" the brain's capacity to "pick up" the Other, as one might switch television channels from black-and-white to color programming, we arrive at an extension of the analogy used by Grof to explain how the brain functions not so much as a transmitting mechanism but as a device for receiving information, an idea that can be traced through Huxley back to William James and is pivotal to understanding the phenomenological significance of "entity" encounters and contact experiences.[33] Hancock has been among the most enthusiastic promulgators of the brain's role as a receiving device—even apparitions of the "Virgin Mary" that are the famed legacy of saints, the visions of prophets, and other outcomes of religious ecstasy can be explained from this thesis.

In developing his views, Hancock took cues from ufologist Jacques Vallée. In *Passport to Magonia,* Vallée connected the dots between aliens (i.e., UFOs) and fairies: creatures small in stature, with big black eyes, dwelling outside space and time, abducting humans, and motivated by interspecies breeding. Vallée commenced a line of research holding that the UFO phenomena were not extraterrestrials, but multidimensionals.[34] Following from Evans-Wentz's *The Fairy Faith,* Vallée speculated that aliens were basically high-tech fairies for the twentieth century. Personal exposure to DMT, as well as Strassman's speculations on the DMT-induced etiology of contact phenomena, gave Hancock pause to evolve a comparative-research program in the multidimensional-entity phenomenon (while, at the same time, ignoring Terence McKenna's contributions to this field). Throwing painted rocks at "established science," Hancock develops the view that an independent "intelligence" lies behind this phenomenon.

These non-physical entities seem to have mastered a "technology," and I use the word advisedly, that enables them to enter our material world and to manifest in it a quasi-physical, "shape-shifting," sometimes therianthropic, sometimes large-headed and small-bodied humanoid form— but always evanescent, ephemeral, somehow luminous, almost but not quite transparent.[35]

In the previous chapter we met with the disembodied eyes staring down David Luke. Drawing on his own experience and studies of the entity phenomenon, Luke's speculations on the recorded appearance of serpents with "disembodied eyes" in a variety of shamanic and cultural contexts might add weight to Hancock's views on the existence of a phenomenon that is independent of the experient. As Luke wrote, "one such being that commonly appears to naive DMT users is an entity consisting of multiple entwined serpents covered in multitudinous eyes, often forming a Fibonacci-spiral-like geometrical shape. Obscure references to a similar mythological entity, sometimes identified as 'the angel of death,' also exist in various cultural cosmologies, possibly indicating the trans-cultural nature of this entity." Luke does not obsess over a particular cause. Such data pose challenging questions, he would later declare, "as to whether the entity is culturally mediated . . . or a culture-free universal feature of DMT activation (naturally or artificially) in the brain, with possible incorporeal origins."[36] While not placing all his chips either way, Luke acknowledges the ontological value of shamanic entity experiences. For him, the multi-dimensional phenomena and omnidirectional visions commonly reported by those experienced with DMT and other tryptamines, as well as by those who have encountered NDEs—including those who are congenitally blind—cannot be adequately accounted for by models insisting that shamanic "visions," and indeed the origins of religion, are founded in optical (or "entoptical") hallucinations, as in the neuropsychological-shamanistic theory of Paleolithic rock art. Competing models, such as those where the phenomenology of altered states of consciousness is investigated on their own terms—as in Charles Tart's "state-specific science"—are hard-won, given the entrenchment of materialist-reductionist scientific models. For Luke, for whom entity encounters in all their forms are broadly paranormal phenomena, the nature of which can be approached, investigated, and replicated through the instrument of DMT, the solution is to improve experimental research designs.[37]

Encounters on the Borderlands
of the Possible

Entity contact in the DMTverse has been a heated subject within psychedelic studies and among users, with skirmishes flaring in cyberspace over the past twenty years. Author of McKenna's Timewave Zero software, Peter Meyer has proposed that entity encounters are common to what he classified as a Level III experience. According to Meyer, as reported in articles published on his website, the common experience of these nonphysical entities flies in the face of "physicalism," which has seen enchantment banished from the universe. Meyer was adamant that "these entities have intersubjective validity—lots of people agree about them, or at least, that they exist. And lots more would be able to report that they exist if DMT were legal." Hyperspace, and the DMT entities found within it, "constitute a fundamental challenge to those philosophers who espouse physicalism in any form."[38] In the 1990s, Meyer became something of a hyperspace quantity surveyor, gathering evidence in the form of trip reports, the weight and numbers of which he believed would establish "that the world experienced with the help of DMT is as real as your back yard (and maybe even more so)."[39]

For two decades, Meyer collected DMT trip reports—340 in total—with 226 (66.5 percent) reports stated to include testimonials of contact with a variety of sentient, independently existing beings.[40] Forming an extraordinary range of entity experiences, this collection was curated in support of an earlier report, "Apparent Communication with Discarnate Entities Related to DMT," offering speculation of the kind that has become customary to those familiar with disembodied personalities in hyperspace. The report is among the earliest attempts to elucidate DMT and its subjective effects. Preoccupied with finding an explanation for the entities so commonly reported by DMT users, Meyer proffered a list of hypotheses for the entity experience on DMT.

1. There are no alien entities at all; it's merely subjective hallucination.
2. DMT provides access to a parallel or higher dimension inhabited by independently existing intelligent entities.
3. DMT allows awareness of processes at a cellular or even atomic level.

It might even be an awareness of quantum mechanical processes at the atomic or subatomic level.

4. As a neurotransmitter, DMT causes the older reptilian parts of the brain to dominate consciousness, resulting in a state of awareness that appears totally alien.

5. Psychedelic tryptamines are the biochemical means by which we may contact the creator(s).

6. DMT provides access to the world of the dead, and entities are the souls, or personalities, of the departed.

7. DMT entities are beings who have mastered the art of time travel and can communicate with humans but without materializing.

8. The entities are probes from an extraterrestrial or an extradimensional species, sent out to make contact with organisms such as ourselves who are able to manipulate their nervous systems in a way that allows communication to take place.[41]

Of these hypotheses, Meyer himself favored (2) (entities communicate with humans in hyperspace) and (6) (entities are souls of the dead), subsequently ranging into deeper speculation, expanding on and combining these views.

It is possible that this physical world is actually an incubator of souls, in the sense that, just as the womb is an incubator of our physical body, our life in this world enables the development of a mental body which can persist beyond the dissolution of the physical one; and that just as birth is a transition from the womb to a higher-dimensional and vastly more complex world, so death (if the mental body is sufficiently developed) is a transition from the world of physical life to the higher-dimensional and vastly more complex world of the DMT entities.[42]

It is a theme with a pedigree, as spiritualist proponents of the "fourth dimension" maintained variations of this idea in the nineteenth century. Are DMT-triggered entities souls of the dead, or even our future disembodied selves, communicating with us from the beyond? Does DMT enable those so affected to glimpse aspects of consciousness that have left this mortal coil? Does exogenous DMT prepare one for the transition? What could be the role of endogenous DMT in this process?

Meyer has been something of a scholar-diplomat representing those experienced in the hyperdimensional realms and who've reported on its inhabitants. And he has also acted as a defendant—for instance, responding to the deprecations of Martin Ball, who dismisses entity contact as illusory, a projection of ego. Using the testimonies of independently existing intelligent beings in his collected reports, Meyer has countered allegations that the entities, and indeed the worlds experienced, are simply ego projections. What we need, Meyer suggests, is not "shallow pop psychology," or more "physicalism," but more research. "Just smoke 20–50 mg of pure DMT. The people who do this, and who go beyond the 2-dimensional 'chrysanthemum pattern' to come face-to-face with the entities, are the true *gnostics* of our age."[43]

In more recent times, "physicalism" appears to have grown in sophistication. Former editor of *Psychedelic Illumination Magazine,* and publisher of *Trip Magazine* and *DoseNation.com,* James L. Kent has argued that the entities experienced by users of DMT and other psychedelics are not disincarnate nor autonomous, but informational processes deriving from the same brain organs and neural circuitry as dreams. Kent's *Psychedelic Information Theory: Shamanism in the Age of Reason* offers a Multi-State Theory in which psychedelic experience, including the perception of elves, is explained not in terms of spirituality or metaphysics, but through a Control Interrupt Model, which posits that "all hallucination begins with a high-frequency periodic interruption of multisensory frame stability that could be described as a wave interference pattern."[44] This neurotheological model grew from an earlier essay, "The Case against DMT Elves," penned partly in response to the strident proclamations of Pickover, who, in prolific internet postings and in books like *Sex, Drugs, Einstein, and Elves: Sushi, Psychedelics, Parallel Universes, and the Quest for Transcendence,* had championed the existence of DMT elves and other entities, even calling for the establishment of a "DMT machine-elf research center."[45]

In Kent's complex neuro-reductionist model of hallucination, DMT elves and other discarnate entities are "psychedelic information" or "spirit information" that humans "disambiguate" from a nonlinear experience and "integrate" and translate into linear systems—i.e., beliefs, culture, religion. "The content of the hallucination is not as important as the process by which the subject takes that content and shapes it into lasting memories, beliefs, and behaviors; this is the process of encoding psychedelic information into synaptic networks."[46] This rationalist systems theory approach permits Kent to recognize the value and significance of the information itself, without needing to identify its roots in phenomena that can be neither measured nor verified. Kent's guiding term appears to be "hallucinogenesis," which is a neuroscience-informed theory that intentionally cleaves away from the unscientific embarrassments of "entheogenesis." In this system, elves, other entities, and, indeed, mystical experiences are not dismissed; they simply become psychedelic information. At the center of the psychedelic-information process is "the pharmacological action of a small number of molecules hitting a tiny subset of neural receptors for a relatively short duration of time. The ongoing information process generated by this small pharmacological interaction goes far beyond the normal range of what we expect drugs to accomplish."[47] Kent's commitment to banish enchantment from the world has been challenged by those for whom DMT has confirmed the realization that consciousness lies beyond the brain. Julian Palmer, for instance, takes issue with hardheaded information theory. "James Kent appears to assume a paradigm in which all information arises within the closed system that is the human mind/body brain. This view conflicts with the reports from thousands of people who say that the information they receive is very coherent, and actually is very clearly from outside that apparent circuit." Ultimately, according to Palmer, Kent just hasn't smoked enough DMT.[48]

Apparently removed from the phenomenal experience of tryptamine use, some commentators confidently act as experts on entity encounters and DMT. One such expert, Scott A. McGreal, explains in his column on *Psychology Today* that those attracting a crowd of entities are simply "high in absorption." By this, McGreal means a "readiness to experience deep attentional involvement in which a person experiences a heightened sense of the reality of the object of their attention." Enhanced by previous experience with psychedelics, "absorption" is thought to lead those afflicted to become open to unconventional beliefs and ideas, and is a chief explanation for the perceived "reality" of entity encounters, along with belief in a litany of paranormal experiences.[49] While it's a position from which one could cast doubt on the validity of Strassman's research (along with much contactee discourse), explaining away encounters as a by-product of perception discredits their ontological status. Might not attention-seeking entities seek out those with a natural capacity to "absorb"? In any case, a high number (about half) of Strassman's high-dose volunteers met with entities, indicative of an experiential prevalence that David Luke suggests is "genuinely induced by the drug—not just a psychological priming effect."[50]

While such approaches demonstrate a reluctance to recognize paranormal phenomena on their own terms, others have attempted to devise methods to monitor and read the presence of entities. In response to a proposal by M. A. Rodriguez to experimentally prove or disprove the existence of entities by requesting that they answer puzzles unknown to the DMT traveler, Luke pointed out that such methods of (dis)proving the existence of entities are as inherently flawed as attempts made by parapsychologists to (in)validate the existence of discarnate entities considered to be spirits of the dead—like those ostensibly communicated with via trance mediums. "It remains a possibility," explains Luke, "that any information provided by ostensibly discarnate entities may actually be due to the 'super' psi of the receiver (e.g. the medium or DMT explorer) receiving the information directly from an earthly incarnate source."[51]

Ambassadors of DMT Endogenicity and "Alien Worlds"

It was a sweltering afternoon in July of 2013. The lecture theater at the Royal Naval College, Greenwich—the venue for London's second Breaking Convention conference—was packed to the rafters as Andrew Gallimore, a biochemist from Cambridge University whose impressions of Terence McKenna were accurate enough to bring the house down, introduced his "Building Alien Worlds" thesis on DMT as an "ancestral neuromodulator," expanded later that year in the *Journal of Scientific Exploration*.[52] Gallimore ran with one of several key themes identified by researchers publishing in the same journal five years earlier. Those researchers had studied reports of DMT users claiming contact with "alien worlds," where the occupants thereof were apparently more real than the consensus world.[53] Clearly enthusiastic about these "alien worlds," Gallimore was not invoking "aliens" buzzing through our skies or "Greys" living among us, but worlds alien to or otherwise different from the "consensus world" represented in our brains. Integral to this alien world is the strange feeling of familiarity DMT users perceive despite its extremely bizarre nature—A familiarity most evident in the cheers of "elves" welcoming users home. For Gallimore, such a reception could be expected if DMT is an "ancestral neuromodulator," and if humans hold a deep background familiarity with this alien home.

Gallimore speculates that the modern practice of ingesting exogenous DMT stimulates an ancient brain function, lost in the mists of time. While the human brain may have once secreted DMT endogenously in psyche-delic concentrations, that function has now apparently been lost. But at high doses, today, that function can be reconstituted. The thesis relies on an understanding of the structural equivalence of the DMT molecule to the endogenous neuromodulator serotonin, which, as Gallimore explains, "has evolved to hold the brain's thalamocortical system in a state in which the consensus world is built. When serotonin is replaced by DMT, the thalamocortical system shifts into an equivalent state, but one in which an apparently alien world is built."[54] Among Gallimore's chief propositions is that the human brain once cycled between serotonin and DMT secretion, possibly with a diurnal rhythm. While serotonin may have been secreted during waking (daytime) hours, when it was integral to the evolution of the brain's consensus world–building ability, DMT may have been secreted during REM sleep (i.e., nighttime), when the brain's "alien world" building capabilities evolved. If this was the case,

> the brain underwent a parallel neural evolution, in which two entirely separate world-building capabilities were developed. Perhaps, how-ever, in order to cement the human species more firmly in the consensus world, the DMT secreting ability of the brain was gradually lost and only serotonin remained. As a consequence, all knowledge of the other reality was eventually forgotten. It is possible that dreaming is a vestigial function from the time when DMT was secreted during sleep.

If this were true, for Gallimore it explains why the exogenous introduction of DMT has the effect it does—i.e., its powerful sense of familiarity and veridicality. "DMT may allow the expression of intrinsic thalamocortical activation patterns that developed in a world that is not so much alien, but from which we have become alienated, allowing us a brief but astonishing glimpse at a long-forgotten hyperdimensional heritage."[55]

Like any sweeping model of reality, Gallimore's proposition does not arrive sans difficulties. His speculations appear to rely upon a rather ideal DMT state. In this model, sheer diversity of experience is replaced with an overconsensualized "alien world" model explained by deep brain function. And by deep, Gallimore means evolutionary. Not unlike Kent's proposal, the model sidesteps the need to verify if these are external "freestanding" realities independent to the observer, since from his point of view, there is no consciousness external to "the informational structure that has a neural representation in the brain."[56] The proposition is therefore essentially lodged in support of a neurobiological basis of reality. While seeking to "progress beyond the confines of materialist dogma," the approach displays a persistent dualism in which the world ("consensus" or "alien") is a projection of neuronal structures. This is a position at odds with the insights of a great many hyperspace travelers whose experiences have been addressed in this book. That said, the proposal that DMT is less a drug than an "ancestral neuromodulator," with its exogenous use awakening an ancient function in the brain, is a head-turner, because it implies that DMT has an identity functionally different from that of other "psychedelics," with which it has long been classified.

While the "alien world" presented here is essentially perceived to be the heritage from which modern humans have become alienated, for others, the "alien world" is quite literally all around us (and yet, from which we're still alienated). Another speaker at Breaking Convention 2013, Graham Hancock, has been vocal in his claims that DMT mediates communication with a world beyond. In the light of his research on entities, ancient artists, and the origins of religion, he is today among the most popular and vocal proponents of the implications of the endogenous status of DMT, embraced as a kind of "missing link" connecting shamanic initiates, abductees, contactees, and prophecy throughout history.

The veridical authenticity of entities is a status to which they are raised throughout his epic, *Supernatural.*

> By whatever name we know them—spirits, fairies, aliens—it really is almost as though the beings we are dealing with have been changing and developing alongside us for thousands of years, and that they therefore cannot simply be mass delusions, as scientists would like us to believe, but must have a definite, independent reality outside the human brain.[57]

Hancock turns to DNA to explain this mystery, and is drawn ultimately to DMT's apparent capacity to enable access to "specific information recorded billions of years previously."[58] In doing so, he invokes Jeremy Narby's proposal in his book *The Cosmic Serpent: DNA and the Origins of Knowledge* that DNA encodes intelligent messages that are decoded in altered states of consciousness (i.e., using ayahuasca). Furthermore, Hancock is indebted to the work of discoverer of the double helix, Francis Crick, who in *Life Itself: Its Origin and Nature,* speculated that DNA is too complex to have evolved by chance, but originated in an alien civilization with advanced engineering technologies. This was Crick's theory of "directed panspermia,"[59] which, as Hancock recognizes, echoes ayahuasca-inspired mythologies found among peoples of the Amazonas.

Hancock's meditation on the role of DMT in the brain—enabling its mechanism as a receiver—is very clearly reliant on Strassman's formulations in *DMT: The Spirit Molecule,* later elaborated in *Inner Paths to Outer Space,* a multiauthored collaboration headed by Strassman.[60] Drawing on archaeological sources and the history of religion, psychopharmacologist Ede Frecska's contributions on DMT's status as an "endohallucinogen" are of primary interest here. A critic of the neuroscientific paradigm, and at the forefront of research into the somato-physiological function of DMT, Frecska patched together a rough thesis on the role of DMT in the history of the divine encounter. In his speculations, DMT is considered to be the source of "paleocontact," by which he means spiritual illuminations, transformative experiences, cosmic dramas, and even civilization-forming moments that have derived from encounters with divine beings. Among the chief examples are the Anunnaki, the Sumerian gods reported to be "coming from outer space, modifying humans, inseminating women, and transferring significant information."[61] The most significant developmental steps in ancient history are stated to be based on divine encounters like these, and Frecska turns to endogenous DMT release to uncover the mysteries of creation myths and ancient legends (i.e., contact narratives) replicated throughout human cultures and evident in spontaneous alternative states of consciousness in the contemporary world, notably because these encounters are replicated in the exogenous DMT experience itself. Extending Hancock's popular distillations, in a rolling snowball of loose suppositions where the "spirit molecule" assumes a life of its own, ancient gods, like the Anunnaki, or the ghosts of 'Ain Ghazal, are reckoned to have been real beings. Frecska concludes that humans had "come into contact with a spiritual intelligence that appears to antedate space-time as we know it," with gods emerging "intrapsychically in the form of spiritual experience through nonlocal, extradimensional connections within the multiverse."[62]

The possible role of endogenous DMT released in NDEs, in religious ecstasy, or by means of ritual techniques like fasting and prayer is at the core of Rick Strassman's own speculative research trajectory. While in his earlier work Strassman looked to Buddhism (and specifically the *Tibetan Book of the Dead*), along with theories of dark matter and parallel universes, to render the world as experienced by DMT users sensible, in his recent book *DMT and the Soul of Prophecy: A New Science of Spiritual Revelation in the Hebrew Bible*, he turns to the Hebrew Bible, and specifically the prophetic state, for answers.[63] Jammed with speculation, among the book's chief propositions is that his high-dose DMT recipients and noted biblical prophets (who may have been flooded with DMT during times of crisis and sleep deprivation) have something in common: they are gifted with the grace of God. Moreover, the former are unaware of this divine relationship, largely due to the absence of an equivalent holy book to articulate their revelations. Strassman appears to have found a way out of the darkness. A transit point is conveyed via the report of Saul in *DMT: The Spirit Molecule*. Saul's high-dose DMT revelation, briefly recounted in Chapter Five, is revisited in the opening pages of *DMT and the Soul of Prophecy* (where Saul is renamed Leo), an experience favorably compared with the prophetic vision of Ezekiel, who, exiled from Judea in mid-sixth century BCE Babylonia, had an encounter with God and four chayot (living things) surrounded on four sides by great wheels. Passages are paraphrased from the book of Ezekiel. "As for the appearance of the living things, their appearance was like fiery coals, burning like the appearance of torches.... There was a brilliance to the fire, and from the fire went forth lightning.... Then I heard the sound of their wings like the sound of great waters ... the sound of the words like the sound of a company."[64]

Born into a Jewish family, Strassman returned to his roots after completing his pivotal 1990s research by studying the books of the Hebrew Bible, learning Hebrew, and making himself familiar with the interpretative models of medieval Jewish philosophers. Comparing the perception of visions, voices, extreme emotions, and somatic sensations across data sets, he found that prophetic states have profound phenomenological similarities with the data gathered from his DMT volunteers, proposing that "elevated endogenous DMT may mediate the features of the prophetic experience that it shares with the experimental DMT effect."[65]

While comparing prophets and trippers, using his original categories—e.g., somatic effects, emotions, perception, cognition, and volition—a further category is added: relatedness. Not far from Frecska's focus on "divine encounters," Strassman is concerned with interactions between God, intermediaries, and other "beings" (a word he prefers over "entities"), and those apprehending them—a prophetic state that may enable healing, protection, and the communication of vital information. An "interactive-relational" process is found implicit in the reports of volunteers from his 1990s trials, where spoken word, telepathy, and visual symbols were the means by which a variety of beings communicated with subjects who'd been given DMT. Revising earlier conclusions, the recognition of DMT relationships gave Strassman pause to reflect on the inadequacy of the Buddhist "unitive-mystical" model he had earlier embraced. This development is consistent with a deviation from Buddhism precipitated by Strassman's expulsion from his Zen Buddhist community, which reacted strongly to an article he published in 1996 in *Tricycle: The Buddhist Review*, where he relayed the story of volunteer Elena, who, having been injected with DMT, reported that "I met a living buddha!" His suggestion that dedicated Buddhist practitioners with little success in their meditation "might benefit from a carefully timed, prepared, supervised, and followed-up psychedelic session to accelerate their practice" apparently didn't sit well with the lamas, nor were they pleased with the imputation, as crooked as it was, that enlightenment could be found at the end of a needle.[66] Strassman also lamented that the Zen Buddhist model could recognize only the essentially *empty* nature of the DMT world and the *illusory* character of its occupants.

It was an unsatisfying situation, since Strassman, as covered in Chapter Five, had already abandoned a strict psychoanalytic model, accepting the authenticity of his volunteers' reports. Another model seemed necessary, one sympathetic to the ontological veracity of the experience, and he found this model in the Old Testament, where he also discovered God, or more accurately YHVH (the Hebrew word for God). Essentially, Strassman found striking resemblances between God (and intermediary beings such as angels) and those beings encountered by some of the volunteers in his DMT trials, confirming for him the understanding that the Hebrew God is "a God who uses the brain as an agent rather than a God produced as an epiphenomenon of brain physiology." That is, this comparative study confirms a "theoneurological" approach, which, as a counterpoint to the dominant neurotheological model in which the brain *generates* spiritual experience, asserts that "the brain is the agent through which God communicates with humans." God is back.[67]

Yet, Strassman's mission is not simply hailing the glory of God, but helping others to find Him too, aided by a study of the metaphysical systems of Hebrew scholars. So while he observed a resemblance between prophetic states and the psychedelic states of his volunteers, there is a gulf separating them, especially as the former possess messages with greater depth, complexity, and profundity. The beings with which his volunteers were familiar tended to communicate information that, rather than offering metaphysical guidelines, was more aesthetic and imaginative in character. Here's a phenomenological account of how this difference might come about.

If endogenous DMT were involved in the workings of the imaginative faculty in prophecy, it is in the service of transmitting God's influence to the experient. The divine overflow bestows perceptible form to fundamentally imperceptible information by using the imagination to generate more or less recognizable objects that are intended to convey that information. Then the intellect more or less accurately interprets and communicates the message that the imaginative contents represent. After administering DMT in a research setting, the same putative elevation of brain levels of the compound may exist as in the prophetic state. However, in this case, DMT is stimulating the imagination "from below," as it were, and not "from above." In addition, it is not affecting the rational faculty in any significant manner. The relative paucity of the DMT state's message may then reflect a difference in what catalyzes elevated brain DMT levels. Divine efflux stimulates the imagination—perhaps through DMT—as well as the intellect, whereas DMT only activates the imagination.

Strassman calls for a renaissance in the divine overflow, eliciting "true prophecy" from the DMT experience through its judicious use. "I encourage those who take psychedelic drugs for spiritual purposes to turn to the Hebrew Bible for guidance in strengthening their rational faculty in order to infuse the relatively message-poor but imagination-rich drug state with additional meaning."[68]

A high-dose injection of DMT is, therefore, not enough. To "comprehend the scope of God's creation," and thus the DMT experience, users ought to bury their heads in the Bible. By immersing oneself in scripture, the user will "draw closer to Him—that is, approach prophecy—through love for and awe of His creating and sustaining this unfathomably complex universe."[69] Strassman probably couldn't have chosen a more ambitious mission. History may prove otherwise, but selling the Bible to DMT users, praying to YHVH, taking DMT on the Sabbath, and, what's more, building the foundations for a Jewish DMT church, seem to me as challenging as marketing leprosy. Strassman is not unaware of the challenge, informing me that "the Hebrew Bible suffers from thousands of years of abuse, as well as being used as an instrument of abuse for thousands of years, and is a particularly difficult topic to bring into discussions about clinical research with psychedelics."[70] Grave problems with fundamentalist interpretations of the source text aside, Strassman is motivated by a text that he claims is more compatible with the worldview of the majority of DMT users—which, unlike the *Bhagavad Gita* and the Buddhist sutras, is "right beneath our noses." "I don't think we have to reinvent the wheel," he explained, "but we do have to return to our origins a little bit more intently, critically and passionately."[71]

DMT users in the wider entheogenic community are no strangers to a variety of alternative spiritual and animist traditions, which, in addition to popular cultural resources like science fiction and role-playing games, comprise a repertoire of semantic hooks and metaphysical tools for the traveler-players of hyperspace. If not animated by shamanism, which Strassman dismisses with surprisingly little discussion, advocates typically find appeal in occult and esoteric religious traditions that are likewise right beneath our noses, and long existing in opposition to, or alongside, the world's dominant theological systems. Indeed, the entity phenomenon may itself represent a telling variation of the contemporary pluralization of "intermediary beings" otherwise reckoned to be transformative and empowering sources of metaphysical knowledge in the history of Western esotericism.[72]

Continued study of DMT and the wider entheogenic community is likely to uncover a considerable wealth of textual, visual, and sonic language that, while far short of a DMT holy book, would illustrate that an experiential language *is* in formation. That DMT remains a controlled "drug" is doubtlessly implicated in the absence of a metaphysical system or, indeed, church of DMT. It also explains the paucity of official research on the entity phenomenon—research that could, for instance, compare tryptamine entity phenomena with the practice of channeling, or "articulated revelation," that Wouter Hanegraaff deemed to be the first major trend in New Age esotericism. How might psychedelic-inspired channeling events compare with other trance-induced states, which occasion a host of teachers, guides, and other entities, such as "sacred masters, spirit guides, angels, extraterrestrials, various historical personalities (Jesus, Paul, etc.), God/the 'Ultimate Source,' gods and goddesses of antiquity, and the collective unconscious or Universal Mind, but also 'group entities,' incarnate or discarnate animals (dolphins, whales), nature spirits or 'devas,' gnomes, fairies, plants, and finally the 'higher self' of the channel"?[73] We have very little in the way of a formal response, since, under the paradigm of prohibition, such inquiry has been forestalled, and the absence of psychedelic-induced "articulated revelations" in studies of Western esotericism simply echoes the politics of knowledge in the age of prohibition.[74]

However we regard his strategy, Strassman seems committed to stirring the hornet's nest. The proposal of taking DMT to "access more cogent and highly articulated imaginal experiences of scripture" may goad rabbinical ire.[75] And yet, if a lungful of DMT could breathe life into scripture, Strassman's approach might strengthen Judaism—the position he adopts. Key inquiries motivate evaluation of the message content in his volunteers' accounts. Is the interpretation of DMT experience "consistent with the ethos pervading the Hebrew Bible"? Does it conform to the practice of the Golden Rule and to the "abolition of idolatry"?[76] If interpretation does not conform to the ethos of the Old Testament as a guiding principle, the implication is that it is equivalent to "false prophecy," a position likely to fuel acrimony within the wider soul-sailing community. With Strassman buried deep in the Old Testament, insights formulated in the wider research underground are disregarded. Take, for instance, Meyer's conclusions that contactees are the "true gnostics of our age." Or Terence McKenna's perception that hyperspace travelers are accessing the Logos. Are the syncretic visionary works of Alex Grey representative of idolatry and "false prophecy"? That Strassman's own interpretative speculations, and in particular his formulations on the pineal gland, have saturated the DMT-using community is worthy of consideration, or should that now be identified as "false prophecy," given that it lends so heavily from belief in reincarnation? In fact, as the book you're reading has demonstrated, a rippling suite of memes have circulated, through which DMT returnees know and interpret the entity phenomenon.

Among Strassman's chief concerns is the absence of evidence for meaningful relationships with beings among DMT users, as revealed in his data from twenty years earlier. There's the trouble. The early-1990s UNM research was a clinical study designed chiefly to monitor immediate effects, and was not designed to evaluate the impact of DMT in the lives of volunteers post-trials. There were a small number of follow-up interviews and casual impressions obtained, and from these Strassman found "most did think they had grown in some ways, especially in response to their high-dose encounters with the spirit molecule."[77] Rather than raking over raw data from two decades ago to buttress another theological model, I suspect that what is required are careful approaches that evaluate user practices over a period of years. Given the continuing prohibitory research climate, we appear to be some distance from an experimental study that might, for example, offer comparative evaluation of the short- and long-term effects of DMT (and 5-MeO) of differing provenance (e.g., synthesized and extracted), comparing the effects of varying botanical sources and administration techniques over large samples of volunteers, with attention to common themes, not the least entities, along with the full range of artistic expression and metaphysical interpretation. While yielding no hard clinical controlled data as such, researchers have to this point collected useful qualitative and phenomenological data through surveying users. While such data gathering seems to have been most commonly performed among quite random communities of anonymous users online, Des Tramacchi's study used interviews and surveyed users networked within the Australian entheo-community.

Tramacchi's interlocutors reported a spectrum of effects, of which I can only offer a partial summary. At one extreme there appeared to be a preoccupation with "death and dismemberment." Accounts he collected included "visions of landscapes covered in blood, vomit, and skeletal remains; encounters with skeletal entities; encounters with tutelary spirits; and the modification of the subject's internal organs through surgical interventions performed by Spirits."[78] In another pattern, interlocutors appear to have become concerned with achieving "deeper connections with the Earth," not uncommonly following communications with "Earthspirits, or Earth-energies" during their DMT trance, which was thought to be "potentially therapeutic for both the individual and the planet."[79] We seem to have returned to the hellish and heavenly realms identified by Huxley and by Grey. On the one hand, then, we have a palpable atmosphere of decay and senescence present in user reports and artistic expressions—an enveloping shadowland not unlike that depicted in the screenplay of Noé's perverse epic *Enter the Void*—and on the other, there are outcomes consistent with the "ecodelic" thesis of Richard Doyle in *Darwin's Pharmacy*, where ayahuasca, DMT, and other substances are inspiring language and evolving consciousness to the benefit of the noösphere. Tramacchi's study demonstrates that a carefully designed ethnography can offer useful insights on diverse trends and patterns among those networked in a community of use—a community whose lifestyle embrace of entheogens might illustrate, given further attention to sustained entheography, metaphysical resources brought to and enlivening the DMT experience. Whether the near-future climate will grow more promising for the support of clinical and entheographic research projects of this nature is yet to be seen.

To return to the vexatious entities, the debate on DMT entities opens up the Pandora's box of the brain/mind problem. Strassman has stated that "no data yet exists regarding endogenous DMT activity in non-drug-induced altered mental states such as dreams, near-death, or any type of spiritual experience."[80] And yet the ideas he and others like Hancock and Frecska have presented are predicated on a prediction, prophetic or otherwise, that the human brain can produce tryptamine in DMT-flash concentrations. What emerges is an enigmatic x-theory in which spontaneous DMT release could explain the universal litany of "contact" and NDE phenomena— gods, spirits, apparitions, fairies, UFOs, and alien abductions that have been reported throughout history. This cloud of speculation led Strassman, in his earlier research phase, to regard the pineal gland as the source of endogenous DMT, a position now buoyed by the discovery of DMT in the pineal gland of rats. The comparative weight of historical, cultural, and archaeological evidence, say these proponents of the role of endogenous DMT in religion, myth, and consciousness, supports Strassman's theoneurological perspective, hitched as it is to his missional interpretation of the Hebrew Bible. Such drives us a long distance from Andrew Gallimore, whose "alien worlds" thesis allows for a pineal capable of producing DMT, but only in the remote past.

Perinatal Resonance

Before closing this chapter, there is another angle to cut on the entity phenomenon and the role of DMT in consciousness, using a lens informed by the insights of Stanislav Grof. Many returnee reports convey a mood of abject peril, with contactees articulating an unparalleled rupture, a dramatic circumstance overseen by the entities encountered. One has often burst through a membrane into an alien environment where "they" have the experient under observation, or are conducting unsolicited surgical experiments on one's body. Here, the experient may be subjected to "research" involving implants or extractions. At the same time, many will meet with an uncanny sense of familiarity. The experience is foremost an ordeal (similar to alien-abduction narratives), but it may also (again, not unlike abductions) turn out to be quite wonderful. Sunyata offers an exemplary report.

> Suddenly, I'm in front of a giant swirling disc, with coloured moving patterns, the "chrysanthemum" that McKenna talked about, and I'm pushed into it. It feels almost too intense and I got the impression that I was definitely heading down the rabbit hole this time, am I dying? I have little time to contemplate this, cause fluid starts coming out of every part of my body, feet, arms, head, ass and heart are all pouring out some liquid substance which is somehow me, I can no longer feel my body. I have the impression of lying in a hospital bed, with doctors watching over me, monitoring my condition, discussing excitedly. Then my consciousness slips, which bothers me today, because something extraordinary must have happened while I was unconscious.[81]

A similar narrative was evident in Strassman's study. "Volunteers find themselves on a bed or in a landing bay, research environment, or high-technology room," Strassman observed. He constructs a composite situation.

> The highly intelligent beings of this "other" world are interested in the subject, seemingly ready for his or her arrival and wasting no time in "getting to work." There might be one particular being clearly in charge, directing the others. Volunteers frequently comment about the emotional quality of the relationships: loving, caring, or professionally detached... . Their "business" appeared to be testing, examining, probing, and even modifying the volunteer's mind and body. Sometimes testing came first, and after results were satisfactory, further interactions took place. They also communicated with the volunteers, attempting to convey information by gestures, telepathy, or visual imagery. The purpose of contact was

uncertain, but several subjects felt a benevolent attempt on the beings' part to improve us individually or as a race.[82]

Among Strassman's volunteers, there were common reports of interventional activities that, as he noted, strongly resembled alien abductions. It is not an unimportant aside that the context of the research—i.e., a government medical facility where volunteers received intravenous injections and were being monitored by scientists—may have shaped the nature of the contact events. Dmitri offers a striking example.

> I felt like I was in an alien laboratory, in a hospital bed like this, but it was over there. A sort of landing bay, or recovery area. There were beings. I was trying to get a handle on what was going on. I was being carted around. It didn't look alien, but their sense of purpose was. . . . There was one main creature, and he seemed to be behind it all, overseeing everything. The others were orderlies, or dis-orderlies. They activated a sexual circuit, and I was flushed with an amazing orgasmic energy. A goofy chart popped up like an X-ray in a cartoon, and a yellow illumination indicated that the corresponding system, or series of systems, were fine. They were checking my instruments, testing things.[83]

Dmitri was careful to add that the experience was not like any UFO abduction he'd heard about. He was not terrorized. "These beings were friendly. I had a bond with one of them. It was about to say something to me or me to it, but we couldn't quite connect. It was almost a sexual bond, but not sex like intercourse, but a total body communication. I was filled with feelings of love for them. Their work definitely had something to do with my presence. Exactly what remains a mystery."[84]

While Dmitri offers but one interpretation, a picture emerges from a great many experiences—including many contactees not confined to a hospital bed monitored by scientists—that cannot be easily dismissed. Some contactees may be reliving their own birth. Simply put, the "entities" may be a resonance of one's memories of obstetricians, midwives, nurses, and other medical staff, as well as, notably, one's own mother: "I had a bond with one of them." Some cases appear to shine brilliant light on this interpretation. Take, for instance, Jeremiah. During the first few minutes of his nonblind high-dose injection, Jeremiah burst out with: "Whoa!" "Wow!" "Incredible!"

> It was a nursery. A high-tech nursery with a single Gumby, three feet tall, attending me. I felt like an infant. Not a human infant, but an infant relative to the intelligences represented by the Gumby. It was aware of me, but not particularly concerned. Sort of a detached concern, like a parent would feel looking into a playpen at his one-year-old lying there. As I went into it, I heard a sound: hmmm. Then I heard two to three male voices talking. I heard one of them say, "He's arrived."[85]

The perinatal interpretation is consistent with Grofian psychotherapy, in which it is also figured that entities may be an echo of past lives, carried in one's DNA. Such accounts—some traumatic, others resolved—are given meaning through Grof's theory of perinatal resonance, where the often deeply traumatic experiences of birth are potentially replayed throughout one's life and otherwise made manifest in a variety of episodes, personality traits, and cultural forms, as, for instance, detailed in Grof's study of H. R. Giger,[86] whose artwork masterfully portrays the hopelessly anguished predicament of the fetus trapped in uterine contractions. Stanislav and Christina Grof's founding understanding is that "holotropic" therapy enables individuals to relive and process that primal trauma. The Grofs have shown that psychedelics and breathwork are useful in facilitating therapeutic outcomes through "rebirthing" practices.

While Grof, from an early stage of his research, was disinterested in the role of DMT in therapy, its effects shed light on the process. This is a view taken by Robert Masters, who not only saw the parallels between his traumatic experiences and alien-abduction narratives, but offered speculation on how his own difficult birth might have contributed to his traumatic experience in the months following his 5-MeO event. There is a dream Masters recalled during that period. "I awaken, laying on my belly with my knees tucked under me. My head feels huge, my body tiny. I'm in the birth canal, but with no feeling. I am drugged. Ten minutes pass and I don't move. The feeling of no-feeling pervades me. At last, some writhing, some lateral movement of my hips. My head is too big to move. Now, more movement.

A tiny bit of sound. Then I explode, crying hard. No tears."[87] The marathon episode advances into dark, primal states of confinement, in which Masters becomes trapped in a cosmic no-way-out scenario. And since he knew the Grofs understood that extreme forms of fear of death and loss of control are associated with birth memories, Masters turns to his traumatic natal abduction to make sense of it all. "Because the fetus is completely confined during the birth process and has no way of expressing the extreme emotions and sensations involved," the Grofs state, "the memory of the event remains psychologically undigested and unassimilated. Much of our later self-definition and our attitudes toward the world are heavily contaminated by this constant reminder of the vulnerability, inadequacy, and weakness that we experienced at birth."[88] Masters has cause to reflect on his own birth—a not-atypical experience for someone born in 1947. "Drugs, forceps, supine subservient mother, doctors treating labor like an operation, newborn a rag doll held upside down and slapped and measured, then wrapped up in hospital blankets rather than in motherlove and skin-to-skin contact." Drawing the connection between the kind of birthing practice represented by his own birth and alien-abduction reports like those documented by Mack, he identifies the primal signature of the traumatic birth.

(a) overly bright light, often somewhat circular at first (the vaginal "gate"), toward which one is literally pulled or drawn (not only through the expulsive force of contractions, but perhaps also through artificial induction or the use of forceps); (b) arrival in an "alien" environment, the delivery room (one's umbilical link to the earthly—one's mother—having maybe been prematurely severed); (c) being surrounded and stood over by "non-mother," emotionally-removed, masked and capped beings (of whom mostly only the eyes and forehead are seen—hence the myth of prominently-eyed aliens); (d) being treated like a piece of meat; and (e) being subjected to very painful or distressingly intrusive procedures (poked, stretched, probed, suctioned, circumcised, and so on).[89]

Pulling this together in an attempt to make sense of his own experience, Masters sees the alien-abduction phenomenon as strongly suggestive of birthing practices. Part of his reasoning for this was the consonance of the reports of many of Strassman's research subjects with those claiming to be alien abductees. He also recognized that Strassman speculated that endogenous DMT may be naturally released during stressful life-cycle episodes, including birth. It is the case that, especially if the mother is not anesthetized, "the massive flooding of stress hormones over the mother's and fetus's pineal glands may be enough to override the pineal defense system and set in motion DMT release."[90] Strassman speculated that with heavy anesthetics or delivery by Cesarean section, the newborn is unlikely to have received a primal "high-dose DMT session," which could have significant implications in later life in the event of exposure to unexpected and traumatic events. In highly unexpected and stressful life situations—perhaps even stimulated by the introduction of DMT or a high-dose analogue, as was the case with Masters—if individuals had their primal perinatal event anesthetized, later dramatic life (and death) episodes may prove disorienting and frightening. As Strassman admitted, the area is underresearched.

As a contrast to Masters's epic rebirthing trauma, another of Strassman's volunteers, Sean, offers possible evidence of a classical rebirth experience—i.e., a therapeutic reliving of birth.

> I immediately saw a bright yellow-white light directly in front of me. . . . There are no symbols in my language that can begin to describe that sense of pure being, oneness, and ecstasy. There was a great sense of stillness and ecstasy. I have no idea how long I was in this confluence of pure energy, or whatever/however I might describe it. Finally I felt myself tumbling gently and sliding backward away from this Light, sliding down a ramp. I could see myself doing this, a naked, thin, luminescent childlike being that glowed with a warm, yellow light. My head was enlarged, and my body was that of a four-year-old child. Waves of the Light touched me as my body receded from it. I was almost dizzy with happiness as the slide down the ramp finally ended.[91]

Another volunteer, Rex, then offers detail on a first-contact breakthrough narrative, progressing from a state of alarm to reassurance. At first, the beings were present and they were experimenting on him. "I saw a sinister face, but then one of them somehow tried to begin reassuring me. Then the space opened up around me. There were creatures and machinery. . . .

There was a female. I felt like I was dying, then she appeared and reassured me. She accompanied me during the viewing of the machinery and the creatures. When I was with her I had a deep feeling of relaxation and tranquility."[92] Could it be that in this and other cases like it, DMT was enabling experients the opportunity to relive their birth and postnatal moments?

Finally, while Terence McKenna spent much of his career meditating on the heavy shadows cast from the future, he would occasionally alight on the primal condition one's condition is in at birth. With DMT, "there's an impression of transition . . . being propelled by some kind of muscle behind you that is pushing you. I mean, yes, birth canal, yes yes of course. . . . Think of the fetus in the womb at the moment of transition. . . . The walls are closing in. It's being crushed and strangled. Gone are the endless amniotic oceans of a few months before: the weightlessness, the effortless delivery of food through the umbilical cord. Suddenly, it's just boundaries and agony and crushing pressure." Shedding more light on this situation, in his exchange with Grateful Dead's Robert Hunter, McKenna alluded to a poignant past event-memory associated with a composite of DMT breakthroughs that had "the vibe of a pediatric ward." While the room is high-tech, there are closets jammed with teddy bears, and the wallpaper is patterned with "dancing bears and mice in tutus." In this candid exchange, he ruminated upon those wondrous objects that had been offered to him by the "tykes" in the DMT encounter. Perhaps they were, he admitted, simply toys: "no more than plastic geometric shapes strung on a rope and hung over an infant's bassinet for its amusement and to teach it spatial and color coordination." But then, he contended that the maternity ward metaphor goes deeper.

There is a feeling of arrival, of anxious doctors, and a sense of enormous decompression and relief. Come to think of it, decompression is a good metaphor for how DMT makes me feel, it is as if I had returned at last to my natural medium of existence, having left a zone of constriction and pressurized limitation, hence I feel inflated in every sense in that place. And then there is the language lesson that they always insist on giving me and insist is the entire point of our little meetings.[93]

There is a further level to this rebirthing episode that bears mention, since the experience with tryptamines appears to have incited the notion of humanity necessarily being born out of history into the next level, cosmic time, hyperspace, where "all of magical humanity is awaiting us and cheering us on, lending their weight." The DMT event afforded insight on the idea that life itself is like a womb, that humans are in "some kind of metamorphic stage like the pupa of a butterfly."[94] It does seem possible that, with Terence McKenna, primary rebirth experiences triggered by tryptamines gave birth to a quavering makeshift thesis on the end of time as we know it (informed by Jung, Whitehead, and the rapidly accumulating crises of history). The seemingly endless variations of the "Timewave" story appeared to be mutually satisfying for all: therapy for McKenna, and entertainment for his audiences.

Whether triggering birth memories (including memories of the primary "aliens" encountered by newborns), permitting a therapeutic rebirth experience, facilitating a review of past lives and newborn development, or giving birth to post-historical fantasies—these are among the many potential strands unraveling from the thick braided rope that is DMT.

Smoke and Mirrors

As this chapter has canvassed, a host of speculators have exerted considerable effort to establish the cause of DMT entities—who they are, what they are, where they come from. Do they come from the future? Are entities a product of the past? And if so, is it the deep evolutionary past, "memories" from past lives, newborn contact, or early development? Apologists and contactees from a variety of disciplines have forged interpretations, with disciplinary background and epistemological assumptions shaping the character of their inquiries. The inquiry on DMT entities is only in its infancy, but I suspect that our likelihood of establishing their true identity is as futile as nailing the nature of spirits, angels—or, for that matter, God—once and for all. Various commentators have, in their own ways, stated as much. They have averred that the identity of the DMT entities is of lesser import than how they function. Dennis McKenna has, for instance, argued that the cause of DMT—e.g., the human mind, the birthing process, past lives, nature, technology, another dimension, God—is unimportant next to its message, its potential to trigger novel ideas and to spark evolution.

It's a position that echoes not only Strassman's reasons for studying pro-phetic scripture, but Dennis's brother's thoughts regarding the UFO. Rather than explaining its cause or revealing its mystery—the chief preoccupation among ufologists—Terence called for an examination of the meaning and function of the UFO phenomenon. The position was inherited from William James, who in his Gifford Lectures, later published as *The Varieties of Religious Experience*, directed attention away from obsessions with the origins of religion in a supreme being or a neurological function, focusing instead on the psychological consequences of religion. That it is not the origins of the teachers, but the fruits of their teachings, that are of significance is a view also approximating the approach of Nick Sand. Even if the "entities" are products of our minds, this is no reason to dismiss them as simply ego projections. The teachings are of intrinsic value for Sand, who does not fixate on the physical appearance of the variety of beings he encountered, beings that did not appear like anything or anyone he'd ever seen, but were nevertheless bizarrely familiar to him. "I think that this is significant, in that the lesson is one of personal responsibility. These are our creatures created by the infinitely capable creative force to teach us about ourselves. They are mirrors that help us to do the difficult job of looking at ourselves, and remembering who we are."[95] We are perhaps not remote from the conclu-sion reached by Des Tramacchi, for whom the "others" encountered with DMT are a composite of our other-self, an expression of the self-othering vital to the modern practice of reversing soul-loss.

> The great reputation of DMT rests on its ability to give rise to encounters with the *other than self*, even if in psychological terms we interpret this to mean *our own other*. Even within ourselves we are not alone. This is existentially vital because any Self needs an Other in order to be itself. ... *This* is the key to DMT's great attraction: that it may heal us of our existential wounds by confronting us with an absolute autonomous will. It is a shamanic medicine for a modern form of soul-loss illness: alien-ation. It is not enough that we experience the external other, the other waits within as well.[96]

But the nature of who we are (and who we are not) is no simple assess-ment. Perhaps this is why a figure prevalent among the mosaic of beings encountered in the DMT state is that of the trickster, who in various guises confuses, shape-shifts, and subjects one to the grand cosmic joke. The trickster figure demonstrates that entities are not always pure in intention. They do not always tell the truth. Their information may be specious and controversial. Indeed, elves, jesters, and many other DMT entity forms lie somewhere between friend and foe, the familiar and the strange, good and evil. These hyperspace harlequins hold a notorious capacity to stir the pot, to turn the world inside out, to shake one from one's comfort zone, to cause a rupture, an *othering*, that in most cases converts to the benefit of the contactee in search of their identity. Given the mosaic of entities and the accompanying mosaic of ideas adopted to explain them, it seems judicious to avoid concluding statements. That said, it would seem fitting that the DMT molecule itself appears to be animated with the purpose of the trickster, fueling, as it has, controversy over the role of the brain and the meaning of consciousness that is unlikely to be put to rest anytime soon.

CHAPTER 13

The Many-Sided Mystery
of DMT

In a story published in the *Saturday Evening Post* in 1958, Aldous Huxley wrote of the revolutionary implications for the then-emergent availability of "physiologically costless, or nearly costless, stimulators of the mystical faculties" that pose relatively few physical overheads to the user. "That famous 'revival of religion,' about which so many people have been talking for so long," he enthused, "will not come about as the result of evangelistic mass meetings or the television appearances of photogenic clergymen."

> It will come about as the result of biochemical discoveries that will make it possible for large numbers of men and women to achieve a radical self-transcendence and a deeper understanding of the nature of things. And this revival of religion will be at the same time a revolution. From being an activity mainly concerned with symbols, religion will be transformed into an activity concerned mainly with experience and intuition—an everyday mysticism underlying and giving significance to everyday rationality, everyday tasks and duties, everyday human relationships.[1]

Huxley presaged the legacy of LSD that, over the next decade, fueled a revolution. And while anyone could point out that fifty years of prohibition hardly constitutes a revolution, the cultural impact of psychedelia is legion. If Huxley were writing today about tryptamines, and notably DMT, he could note that the biochemical discoveries of the present—i.e., mounting data on its neurochemisty—amount to a recognition that "everyday mysticism" is potentiated, or at least modulated, by the human brain, which is not far from his intuition that divinity is a genuine human trait, not contrived from without, but a chemically mediated faculty within.

DMT is a quintessential compound in the human chemistry of divinity, which even today remains enigmatic. A curious compound that compels one to grow curiouser at every juncture in its unmasking, the mystery of DMT is its source of appeal—a law of attraction that, in the interwoven sequence of events documented in this book, has also attracted the heavy-handedness of "the law." But there is a luster to the shadows. It could be said that among the chief "successes" of prohibition is that edicts criminalizing the use of DMT and other tryptamine derivatives amount to signs that blink in neon beseeching generations of experimentalists to "Try this!" And try it they have, in practices expanding as techniques of synthesis and delivery evolved, as botanical sources were identified and methods of extraction optimized; and as virtual reality enabled a cultural proliferation expressed in experiential languages, synesthetic artifice, and repertoires of communication borrowed from esoteric traditions and science fiction. In the entheogenic cultural movement, what is officially a "crime" may be an act of creativity. It is, after all, impossible to keep a cap on human nature.

This book has explored the many-sided mystery that is DMT. In the sixty years since its psychopharmacology was discovered by Stephen Szára, N,N-dimethyltryptamine became a powerful cultural enigma. Inciting fear or evoking hope, suffused with danger or charged with gnosis, this is a most controversial compound, with those who wish to prohibit or liberate it, restrict availability or augment effect, contesting its meaning. Rejected as "the nightmare hallucinogen" or celebrated as "the spirit molecule," a substance with no recognized value to science, or a neurotransmitter essential to normal human brain functioning and physiology, scheduled as a dangerous drug, or the X-factor in the evolution of consciousness, DMT is an enigma that has repeatedly defied circumscription. As neurobiologists, psychopharmacologists, psychiatrists, religionists, parapsychologists, dimensionologists, entheologians, backyard alchemists, and many others jostle for the truth over the subject of entities, we are presented with a veritable kaleidoscope of meaning. "Psychotomimetic" or "psychedelic," "psychotogen" or "entheogen," a trip to "the Ovens" or a "metaphysical reality pill," a cornucopia of signifiers illustrate not only the disputed legacy of DMT, but that it is a tipping point in the struggle to obtain the measure on consciousness. While lawmakers sweep it under the cultural rug, where it shares crowded space with a forbidden pharmacopoeia, speculation about "the brain's own psychedelic" fuels a controversy that shows little sign of abating.

When prohibitionists criminalized a compound scheduled alongside opiates and cocaine as a danger to human health, they were at the same time choking research that could lead to truth claims challenging those currently enshrined as law. So far as DMT is concerned, the only noteworthy project undertaken behind the iron curtain of prohibition in the last fifty years is the research of Rick Strassman, responsible for promulgating the popular notion of the "spirit molecule," and enshrining into entheogenic folklore the proposition that the pineal gland (the "seat of the soul") is the brain's site of DMT synthesis, the bridge between matter (brain) and spirit (mind). We saw how Strassman's paradigm rattling research effectively slipped through the defenses of federal bodies, and we have seen how the ongoing black-holing of research on the subjective effects of DMT in healthy humans has created an official knowledge vacuum. But we saw, too, that an independent, experimental, and virtualized underground has mobilized in the void, flourishing under the power of home-baked conceptual frameworks, notably that which recognizes DMT and its tryptamine relatives as "entheogens"—an idea emboldened by the tryptamine's celebrated endogenicity and speculations concerning its role in normal consciousness and visual perception. Referring to current research endeavors, Strassman enthuses that "the enzyme that finalizes the synthesis of endogenous DMT (and the gene that codes for it) is active in the retina." If the very idea of a "psychedelic pineal" is daunting from an epistemological standpoint, then what are we to make of the possibility that, as he speculates, "a 'hallucinogen' mediates our visual and conscious worlds"?[2]

Terror drug or instrument of gnosis, possessing no redeeming qualities or expressing the soul, a horror show or a therapeutic sacrament, a dangerous drug or essential to normal consciousness, in the decades since its action was first evaluated in humans, we have formed a deeply ambivalent relationship with DMT and its analogues. Here is a compound of many faces, its multifaceted nature due in no small part to its variable exogenous and endogenous characteristics. At one naive extreme, it is simply an illicit product of underground drug laboratories. At another unproven extreme, it is synthesized in psychedelic quantities in the natural laboratory of the pineal gland. This ambivalence is in some ways consequential to the extremes reported by users. Enchantment or ordeal, beneficence or dread, heavenly or hellish, the spectrum of experience simply echoes extremes evident within the human psyche. This variability appealed to scientists in the pre-prohibition era, in which the labels "psychotogen" and "psychedelic" were born, in which DMT's nightmarish or transcendental parameters were discovered, and from which it was understood that a complex of personal factors, environmental conditions, dose, and techniques of use were integral to outcomes. It is a variability that animates the cornucopia of entities with which users are familiar, including the concentrated ambivalence embodied by those hyperspatial punks, the machine elves.

This variability has been expressed in the history, or indeed histories— and overwhelmingly *his*-stories—documented in this book. These are stories signaling the sentiment of the quest, with that old chalice the "Holy Grail," or just "the grail," repeatedly invoked to denote the objective. We have been privy to a concatenation of grail-like quests, each inflected by a unique challenge and motivation, each occasioning a distinct order of sacrifice, risk taking, and innovation. For the first bioassayist, Stephen Szára, *it* was a chemical key that could open and lock the door on psychosis, a discovery that in the 1950s was believed to be within reach—as obtainable as a Nobel Prize. For William Burroughs, *it* (i.e., yagé) was the "final fix," the ultimate high that could put a permanent edge on pain—worth trekking into the remote jungles of the Amazon. For alchemical midwife Nick Sand, *it* was the antidote to nuclear apocalypse—furnished in his mother's bathtub in Brooklyn. For Leary, *it* was the gateway to the psychedelic (r) evolution—the path to an "experiential language." For Rick Watson and his cohort, *it* was point break on the wave of cultural experimentation. For hyperspace evangelist Terence McKenna, *it* was "the key" to mystery, the higher dimensions—even death itself. For Dennis McKenna, *it* was a synergistic key to unlock the mystery of ayahuasca—the planetary medicine. For Alex Grey, *it* was "infinite connectedness." For Rick Strassman *it* was the "spirit molecule"—the bridge between spirit and matter, life and death. For Nen, *it* was a "teacher plant"—the connection with the

Dreamtime. And on it goes. Each questing and ingesting legate passes their gift to subsequent wayfarers who, heir to this caravan of holiness, strike new ground, sometimes professing discoveries at great variance with one another. For Rabbi Bakst, for instance, *it* is *"Messianic* DMT," the "Living Liquid" (*Mayim Chayim*), the road to the higher-dimensional Tree of Knowledge foretold by Hebrew prophets and dependent on appropriate meditation and devotional techniques. And yet, for others, the Tree of Knowledge can be grown, harvested, and smoked. For others still, the trees and their alkaloids can be mixed, decocted, infused to almost endless variations, with the grail malleable and customizable.

A persistent theme throughout these empirical accomplishments is one of becoming an initiate, of achieving direct access to the Other, a gnosis transcribed using the language, for example, of quantum physics, neurochemistry, sacred geometry, the Kabbalah, shamanism. Among key interpreters and those who follow in their wake, the clash with profound alterity implicit to the DMT event is converted into artifice, ideology, and paradigms erected in the here and now. The "this is it" rapture of the tryptamine experience may have an affirmational or shattering effect on tradition. One development stands out among these *initiations*. The growth in the understanding of the neuropharmacology of DMT and other tryptamines is consistent with a development of a reverence for molecular process, a respect for botanical sources, and the natural world, which, through personal experience, is understood to possess authority. Perhaps the most tangible evidence of this reverentiality is its aesthetic footprint. Schooled in mystery, architects of the sacred adopt advanced means of perception to mediate the unspeakable. Radical self-expressionists, punk logicians, cognitive libertarians, technoccultists, and "war correspondents," who, as Diana Reed Slattery remarks, "report from the battlefield of the War on Drugs,"[3] transpose and perform the contours of hyperspace through text, sculpture, paint, digital media, film, music, spoken word, and other media that I have likely neglected in this book.

While cartographers of hyperspace may dispute its parameters, and some lament the absence of a "church of DMT," the ontoseismic event explored in this book is a liminal rupture that, under appropriate conditions, *renders the Other familiar to the self,* a private quest from which life-changing insights, personal transformation, and fellowship flower. If the achievements documented in these pages are symptomatic of the quest—scientific, spiritual, aesthetic, or otherwise—then this document has itself been a quest, with *the grail* of this book being awareness and, ultimately, the freedom to determine one's own mental processes, as research continues to shine a light in the darkness. While a humble step in that direction, a great distance must yet be covered, as further details emerge of the events that have been documented, and the many that have not.

ENDNOTES

Prologue

1. "A serene and magical state which is largely independent of what drug is used—if any drug at all—and might be called a 'peak experience,' in the terminology of the psychiatrist, Abe Maslow. It cannot be repeated at will with a repetition of the experiment. Plus-four is that one-of-a-kind, mystical or even religious experience which will never be forgotten. It tends to bring about a deep change of perspective of life-direction in the person who is graced with it." Alexander Shulgin and Ann Shulgin, *PiHKAL: A Chemical Love Story* (Berkeley, CA: Transform Press, 1991), xxv.

Chapter 1

1. Terence McKenna, *Food of the Gods: The Search for the Original Tree of Knowledge* (New York: Bantam Books, 1992), 258.
2. This book is not a manual for DMT production or use. Consuming DMT and other tryptamines is a serious undertaking compounded by federal and international laws prohibiting possession. For a valuable educational manual outlining the safe and responsible use of entheogens, including DMT, see Enoon et al., eds., *Open Hyperspace Traveler: A Course Handbook for the Safe and Responsible Management of Psychoactives*, An Entheogenic University/DMT-Nexus production, 2014, www.oht.me. For minimizing risks and maximizing outcomes in the psychedelic experience, see Rick Strassman, "Preparing for the Journey," in Rick Strassman, Slawek Wojtowicz, Luis Eduardo Luna, and Ede Frecska, *Inner Paths to Outer Space: Journeys to Alien Worlds through Psychedelics and Other Spiritual Technologies* (Rochester, VT: Park Street Press, 2008), 268–298. Also see Ralph Metzner, *Allies for Awakening: Guidelines for Productive and Safe Experiences with Entheogens* (Berkeley, CA: Green Earth Foundation and Regent Press, 2015).
3. As reported in Matt Sledge and Ryan Grim, "If You Haven't Heard of DMT Yet, You Might Soon," *Huffington Post*, December 9, 2013, www.huffington-post.com/2013/12/09/dmt-use_n_4412633.html.
4. Adam R. Winstock, Stephen Kaar, and Rohan Borschmann, "Dimethyltryptamine (DMT): Prevalence, User Characteristics and Abuse Liability in a Large Global Sample," *Journal of Psychopharmacology* 28, no. 1 (2013): 49, 53.

5. Normally, DMT is ineffective when taken orally (unless in very high doses), because monoamine oxidase (MAO) enzymes will rapidly break it down before it can have any effect in the brain. With ayahuasca—the brew in which the vine *Banisteriopsis caapi* is decocted with DMT boiled from admixture plants—a mechanism has evolved in which ß-carboline alkaloids present in *B. caapi* act to inhibit MAO, thus protecting the passage of DMT into the brain.

6. For LSD, see Martin A. Lee and Bruce Shlain, *Acid Dreams: The Complete Social History of LSD: The CIA, the Sixties, and Beyond* (New York: Grove Press, 1992; first published 1985), and Jay Stevens, *Storming Heaven: LSD and the American Dream*, 2nd ed. (London: Paladin, 1989). For MDMA, see Simon Reynolds, *Generation Ecstasy: Into the World of Techno and Rave Culture*, 2nd ed. (New York: Routledge, 1999). For LSD and MDMA, see Tom Shroder, *Acid Test: LSD, Ecstasy, and the Power to Heal* (New York: Blue Rider, 2014). For psilocybin, see Andy Letcher, *Shroom: A Cultural History of the Magic Mushroom* (London: Faber and Faber, 2006).

7. Dominique Fontanilla, Molly Johannessen, Abdol R. Hajipour, Nicholas V. Cozzi, Meyer B. Jackson, and Arnold E. Ruoho, "The Hallucinogen *N,N*-Dimethyltryptamine (DMT) Is an Endogenous Sigma-1 Receptor Regulator," *Science* 323, no. 5916 (2009): 934–937.

8. Zevic Mishor, Dennis J. McKenna, and J. C. Callaway, "DMT and Human Consciousness," in *Altering Consciousness: Multidisciplinary Perspectives* (*Volume 2: Biological and Psychological Perspectives*), eds. Etzel Cardeña and Michael Winkelman (Santa Barbara, CA: Praeger, 2011), 104.

9. For a useful and accessible breakdown on the chemistry, botany, and pharmacology of tryptamines, see Dennis J. McKenna and Jordi Riba, "New World Tryptamine Hallucinogens and the Neuroscience of Ayahuasca," *Current Topics in Behavioral Neurosciences* (Epub, February 6, 2015).

10. Julius Axelrod, "Enzymatic Formation of Psychotomimetic Metabolites from Normally Occurring Compounds," *Science* 134, no. 3475 (1961): 343. For an overview of the history of these discoveries, see Mishor, D. McKenna, and Callaway, "DMT and Human Consciousness."

11. M. A. Thompson, E. Moon, U. J. Kim, J. Xu, M. J. Siciliano, and R. M. Weinshilboum, "Human Indolethylamine *N*-methyltransferase: cDNA Cloning and Expression, Gene Cloning, and Chromosomal Localization," *Genomics* 61 (1999): 285–297; N. V. Cozzi, T. A. Mavlyutov, M. A. Thompson, and A. E. Ruoho, "Indolethylamine *N*-methyltransferase Expression in Primate Nervous Tissue," *Society for Neuroscience Abstracts* 37, no. 840.19 (2011).

12. Steven A. Barker, Jimo Borjigin, Izabela Lomnicka, and Rick Strassman, "LC/MS/MS Analysis of the Endogenous Dimethyltryptamine Hallu-

cinogens, Their Precursors, and Major Metabolites in Rat Pineal Gland Microdialysate," *Biomedical Chromatography* 27, no. 12 (2013): 1690–1700.

13. See, for example, Ede Frecska, Attila Szabo, Michael J. Winkelman, Luis E. Luna, and Dennis J. McKenna, "A Possibly Sigma-1 Receptor Mediated Role of Dimethyltryptamine in Tissue Protection, Regeneration, and Immunity," *Journal of Neural Transmission* 120 (2013): 1295–1303.

14. Cosmic Oneness, "Alex Grey's Sacred Art," *Psychedelic Adventure.net*, 2008, www.psychedelicadventure.net/2008/09/alex-greys-sacred-art.html.

15. Christopher Cott and Adam Rock, "Phenomenology of N,N-Dimethyltryptamine Use: A Thematic Analysis," *Journal of Scientific Exploration* 22, no. 3 (2008): 367.

16. Report #115 in Peter Meyer's collection "340 DMT Trip Reports Attesting to Contact with Apparently Independently-Existing Intelligent Entities within What Seems to Be an Alternate Reality," www.serendipity.li/dmt /340_dmt_trip_reports.htm#115.

17. Jeremy Bigwood and Jonathan Ott, "DMT: The Fifteen Minute Trip," *Head* 2, no. 4 (1977): 56–69.

18. "Why Is DMT Illegal if It Occurs Naturally in Everyones Brain," uploaded to YouTube March 28, 2008, www.youtube.com/watch?v=GhEj314cmLw.

19. L. Servillo, A. Giovane, M. L. Balestrieri, R. Casale, D. Cautela, and D. Castaldo, "*Citrus* Genus Plants Contain Nmethylated Tryptamine Derivatives and Their 5hydroxylated Forms," *Journal of Agricultural and Food Chemistry* 61, no. 21 (2013): 5156–5162; Morris Crowley, "Citrus Growers Manufacture Huge Amounts of DMT," *The Nexian*, June 13, 2014, http://the-nexian.me/home/knowledge/112-citrus-growers-manufacture-huge-amounts-of-dmt.

20. Arianne Cohen, "Walking on Sunshine," *Elle*, November 2013: 302–305; Abby Aguirre, "The New Power Trip: Inside the World of Ayahuasca," *Marie Claire*, February 18, 2014, www.marieclaire.com/world-reports /ayahuasca-new-power-trip.

21. The street term "spice" is used throughout this book, although it should be mentioned that, other than having a loose association with altered higher-dimensional states and pungent aromatics, the effects and outcomes of DMT are discordant with those of the drug melange (or "spice"), the essential commodity in Frank Herbert's *Dune* series, which, according to Paul Stamets, was influenced by Herbert's experience with psilocybin mushrooms (Paul E. Stamets, *Mycelium Running: How Mushrooms Can Help Save the World*, Berkeley, CA: Ten Speed Press, 2005). The prescience-enhancing property of melange makes safe and accurate interstellar travel possible. It also possesses fatally addictive properties, which is at dramatic

odds with properties of DMT (and psilocybin), which are not known to cause physical dependence.

22. Enoon et al., *Open Hyperspace Traveler.*

23. Linda Doherty, "Teen Trippers Trying Dangerous 'Natural' Drug," *Sydney Morning Herald,* May 2, 1998.

24. Daniel Pinchbeck, *Breaking Open the Head: A Psychedelic Journey into the Heart of Contemporary Shamanism* (Portland, OR: Broadway, 2002).

25. Vanessa Grigoriadis, "Daniel Pinchbeck and the New Psychedelic Elite," *Rolling Stone,* September 7, 2006, www.vanessagrigoriadis.com/pinchbeck .html.

26. Peter De Conceicao, "The DMT Molecule: A Tryst with Spirits, Elves and Aliens," *Examiner.com,* August 6, 2009, www.examiner.com/article/the -dmt-molecule-a-tryst-with-spirits-elves-and-aliens.

27. Russell Brand, *BrandX* S01E13, FX Networks, November 30, 2012, http:// vimeo.com/54643690#.

28. Dexthepole, "What a DMT Trip Is Like," uploaded to YouTube January 11, 2010, www.youtube.com/watch?v=xRr6klXmalI.

29. John Barclay, "Interviews with People Who Just Smoked DMT," *VICE* magazine online, March 21, 2012, www.vice.com/read/interviews-with -people-who-just-smoked-dmt.

30. "DMT: A Psychedelic New Drug," episode of *Drugs, Inc.,* National Geographic Channel (2012).

31. "DMT: The Psychedelic Drug 'Produced in Your Brain,'" *The Feed,* SBS 2, November 10, 2013, www.sbs.com.au/news/article/2013/11/08/dmt -drug-produced-our-brain.

32. "Dimethyltryptamine (DMT)," *Cracked.com,* October 26, 2011, www .cracked.com/funny-2450-dimethyltryptamine-dmt.

33. "Dorian Yates—into the Shadow," interview on *London Real,* uploaded to YouTube March 29, 2013, www.youtube.com/watch?v=fNqR-Ifj7xQ.

34. Michele Ross, interviewed by Amber Lyon, "Neuroscientist Describes Her DMT Trip," *Reset.me,* uploaded to YouTube June 15, 2014, www.youtube .com/watch?v=yqtvuzcL84M&feature=youtube.

Chapter 2

1. Stephen Szára, "The Comparison of the Psychotic Effect of Tryptamine Derivatives with the Effects of Mescaline and LSD-25 in Self-Experiments," in *Psychotropic Drugs: Proceedings of the International Symposium on Psychotropic Drugs, Milan 1957,* eds. Silvio Garattini and Vittorio Ghetti (Amsterdam: Elsevier, 1957), 462.

2. While DMT was synthesized first in 1931 by Canadian chemist Richard

H. F. Manske, the compound was filed away, its psychoactive properties unknown. Unaware that he was identifying the same compound, in 1946, Brazilian industrial chemist Oswaldo Gonçalves de Lima published findings on his extraction of an alkaloid he called *nigerina* (or "nigerine") from the root bark of *Mimosa hostilis* (now *Mimosa tenuiflora*), a known ingredient of the inebriating beverage from northeastern Brazil *vinho da jurema*. While this was the first discovery of DMT as a natural product, since "nigerine" (subsequently identified as DMT) was among several alkaloids identified in *M. hostilis*, Gonçalves de Lima could not isolate which among them were psychoactive. O. Gonçalves de Lima, "Observações sôbre o 'Vinho da Jurema' Utilizado pelos Índios Pancarú de Tacaratú (Pernambuco)," *Arquivos do Instituto de Pesquisas Agronómicas* 4 (1946): 45–80.

3. Abram Hoffer, Humphry Osmond, and John R. Smythies, "Schizophrenia: A New Approach II," *Journal of Mental Science* 100 (1954): 29–45.

4. Stephen Szára, "DMT at Fifty," *Neuropsychopharmacologia Hungarica* 9, no. 4 (2007): 202.

5. M. S. Fish, N. M. Johnson, and E. C. Horning, "Piptadenia Alkaloids. Indole Bases of P. Peregrina (L.) Benth. and Related Species," *Journal of the American Chemical Society* 77 (1955): 5892–5895; Stephen Szára, "Hallucinogenic Effects and Metabolism of Tryptamine Derivatives in Man," *Federation Proceedings* 20 (1961): 885–888. The intoxicating effects of *cohoba* had been reported since the time of Columbus's second voyage to the Americas, 1493–1496. S. H. Wassén, "Anthropological Survey of the Use of South American Snuffs," in *Ethnopharmacologic Search for Psychoactive Drugs*, Public Health Service Publication No. 1645, eds. D. H. Efron, B. Holmstedt, and N. S. Kline (Washington, DC: U.S. Government Printing Office, 1967), 233–289.

6. Stephen Szára, "The Social Chemistry of Discovery: The DMT Story," *Social Pharmacology* 3 (1989): 238.

7. Szára, "The Comparison of the Psychotic Effect," 462.

8. Szára, "The Social Chemistry of Discovery," 238.

9. Stephen Szára, "Dimethyltryptamine: Its Metabolism in Man: The Relation of Its Psychotic Effect to the Serotonin Metabolism," *Experientia* 12 (1956): 411–441; Szára, "The Comparison of the Psychotic Effect," 462.

10. A. Sai-Halász, G. Brunecker, and S. Szára, "Dimethyltryptamin: Ein Neues Psychoticum," *Journal Psychiatria et Neurologia* (Basel, Switzerland), 135 (1958): 285–301. However, as argued by Ott, "Lewin would surely have categorized the entheogenic tryptamines as *Phantastica* (as he did *péyotl*, the fly-agaric and *yajé*) or as *Excitantia* (as he had categorized *paricá* or *Anadenanthera* snuff)." See Jonathan Ott, *Pharmacotheon: Entheogenic Drugs, Their*

Plant Sources and History (Kennewick, WA: Natural Products Co., 1996; first published 1993), 84.

11. See W. J. Turner and S. Merlis, "Effects of Some Indolealkylamines on Man," *Archives of Neurology and Psychiatry* 81, no. 1 (1959): 121–129. For MKUltra, see Lee and Shlain, *Acid Dreams*. Also see Ott, *Pharmacotheon*, 54.

12. Partly underwritten by funding that, unknown to Wasson, was provided by a CIA front foundation.

13. Albert Hofmann beat him to it, when in the late 1950s he isolated and named the active compounds psilocybin and psilocin from self-experiments with *Psilocybe mexicana*.

14. John Marks, *The Search for the Manchurian Candidate: The CIA and Mind Control* (New York: Times Books, 1979), 83.

15. For an overview of the history of these and subsequent discoveries, see Mishor, D. McKenna, and Callaway, "DMT and Human Consciousness."

16. While 5-MeO-DMT and other short-acting entheogenic tryptamines remained legal in the United States, as Ott (*Pharmacotheon*, 187) indicates, they became subject to classification as illegal DMT analogues under the Controlled Substances Analogue Enforcement Act of 1986. In 2011, 5-MeO-DMT was added to Schedule I.

17. Terence McKenna, "Alchemical Youth at the Edge of the World," presented at Camden Centre, London, June 15, 1992, http://deoxy.org/t_camden.htm.

18. For research conducted in Germany in the 1970s, see P. GerBickel, A. Dittrich, and J. Schoepf, "Altered States of Consciousness Induced by N,N-dimethyltryptamine (DMT)," *Pharmakopsychiatry Neuropsychopharmakol* 9, no. 5 (1976): 220–225.

19. William S. Burroughs. *Junkie: Confessions of an Unredeemed Drug Addict* (New York: Ace Books, 1953).

20. In 1923 Colombian chemist Guillermo Fischer Cárdenas had in fact isolated an alkaloid in yagé he named *telepatina*, which was later identified as the harmala alkaloid harmine. The origins of this curious mythology may lie in the written accounts of Rafael Zerda Bayón, who traveled in the upper Putumayo River region in 1915, reporting the apparent telepathic function of ayahuasca visions (see Ott, *Pharmacotheon*, 233).

21. In Spruce's "Notes of a Botanist on the Amazon and Andes," unpublished until 1908, the effects were conveyed (in the summary of Schultes) as "a narcosis characterized by frighteningly realistic colored visual hallucinations and a feeling of extreme and reckless bravery." See Richard E. Schultes, "The Identity of the Malpighiaceous Narcotics of South America," *Botanical Museum Leaflets* 18, no. 1 (1957): 4.

22. Appendix 5, "From Burroughs' March 1956 '*Yagé* Article' Manuscript," in

William S. Burroughs and Allen Ginsberg, *The Yagé Letters: Redux,* ed. with an Introduction by Oliver Harris (San Francisco: City Lights Books, 2006; first published 1963), 91.

23. Appendix 4, passages from draft of "Burroughs' January 1956 '*Yagé* Article' Manuscript," in Burroughs and Ginsberg, *Yagé Letters: Redux,* 88. One wonders if this were a similar résumé submitted to the Office of Strategic Services (OSS), which Burroughs had attempted to join in 1942.

24. Appendix 5, "From Burroughs' March 1956 '*Yagé* Article' Manuscript," in Burroughs and Ginsberg, *Yagé Letters: Redux,* 92.

25. William S. Burroughs, "Letter from a Master Addict to Dangerous Drugs," *British Journal of Addiction to Alcohol and Other Drugs* 53, no. 2 (August 3, 1957): 119–132, www.cs.cmu.edu/afs/cs.cmu.edu/user/ehn/Web/release/BurroughsLetter.html.

26. William S. Burroughs, *Queer* (New York: Penguin, 1985), xxii.

27. Burroughs to Ginsberg, May 15, 1952, in William S. Burroughs, *The Letters of William S. Burroughs, 1945–1959,* ed. Oliver Harris (New York: Penguin, 1994), 125.

28. The material in *Queer* was intended as part of a work eventually published in three parts (including what became *Naked Lunch* and *The Yagé Letters*), all illustrative of the formative influence that yagé, and the Amazonas, had on Burroughs.

29. Burroughs, *Queer,* 49.

30. Ibid., 76, 50.

31. Burroughs and Ginsberg, *Yagé Letters: Redux.*

32. As Burroughs scholar Oliver Harris has explained in his Introduction to the *Redux* version, with an "epistolary" form *staged* as "letters" from Burroughs to Ginsberg, *The Yagé Letters* is as convoluted in the history of its production as it is in its hybrid content.

33. Schultes had himself followed Richard Spruce, who in 1854 observed the preparation and use of the snuff *yopo* among the Guahibo of the Orinoco basin, commenting that it was used by all the tribes of the upper tributaries.

34. Burroughs, *The Letters,* 155.

35. John Lardas, *The Bop Apocalypse: The Religious Visions of Kerouac, Ginsberg, and Burroughs* (Urbana: University of Illinois Press, 2001), 182.

36. Burroughs, *The Letters,* 171, 179–180.

37. Letter to Ginsberg, July 10, 1953, in Burroughs, *The Letters,* 184.

38. Letter to Ginsberg, from Lima, Peru, July 10, 1953, in Burroughs and Ginsberg, *Yagé Letters: Redux,* 50.

39. Oliver Harris, Introduction to Burroughs and Ginsberg, *Yagé Letters: Redux,* xxiv.

40. Richard M. Doyle, *Darwin's Pharmacy: Sex, Plants, and the Evolution of the Noösphere* (Seattle: University of Washington Press, 2011), 98.
41. Joanna Harrop, "The *Yagé* Aesthetic of William Burroughs: The Publication and Development of His Work 1953–1965," PhD thesis, Queen Mary, University of London, 2010, 162. Recognizing the significance of nonaddictive psychoactives in Burroughs's experimental work, Harrop makes an important distinction between his use of nonaddictive substances (i.e., yagé, DMT, mescaline, and psilocybin) and the substances of addiction (principally opiates) that predominate in commentary on the life and works of Burroughs, with many commentators conflating these diverse groups of substances and their effects in a monopolizing narrative of "addiction." The approach offers further refutation of the "junk paradigm" by which Burroughs's oeuvre has so often been characterized—see Oliver Harris, *William Burroughs and the Secret of Fascination* (Carbondale: Southern Illinois University Press, 2006).
42. Based on a letter to Ginsberg on July 16, 1953, in Burroughs, *The Letters*, 182.
43. William S. Burroughs, *Naked Lunch: The Restored Text* (London: Fourth Estate, 2010; first published 1959), 91. In a parenthesized passage, Burroughs confirms that this text describing The Interzone's Meet Café was written in a state of yagé intoxication. Like the text above, it is a passage from "The Composite City" entry of *The Yagé Letters* derived from a letter to Ginsberg sent from Lima, Peru, July 10, 1953.
44. Harrop, "The *Yagé* Aesthetic," 155.
45. Although there are reported incidences in which ß-carbolines appear to possess independent hallucinogenic properties similar to those of DMT. See Stephan V. Beyer, *Singing to the Plants: A Guide to Mestizo Shamanism in the Upper Amazon* (Albuquerque: University of New Mexico Press, 2009), 216.
46. Burroughs, *Naked Lunch: The Restored Text*, 31.
47. Burroughs, *The Letters*, 171.
48. Appendix 5, "From Burroughs' March 1956 '*Yagé* Article' Manuscript," in Burroughs and Ginsberg, *Yagé Letters: Redux*, 97; Harris, Introduction, Burroughs and Ginsberg, *Yagé Letters: Redux*, xxii. It would not be until the late 1960s that the role of the admixtures, and the presence of DMT in them, were identified by students of Schultes. A. H. Der Marderosian, H. V. Pinkley, and M. F. Dobbins, "Native Use and Occurrence of *N,N*-dimethyltryptamine in the Leaves of *Banisteriopsis rusbyana*," *American Journal of Pharmacy* 140 (1968): 137–147; Homer V. Pinkley, "Plant Admixtures to Ayahuasca, the South American Hallucinogenic Drink," *Lloydia* 32 (1969): 305–314.
49. Tim Leary, *High Priest* (Berkeley, CA: Ronin, 1995; first published 1968), 218.

50. Appendix 5, "From Burroughs' March 1956 'Yagé Article' Manuscript," in Burroughs and Ginsberg, *Yagé Letters: Redux*, 99.

51. This is also a point made by Dennis McKenna: "I doubt [Burroughs] would have suspected that the active principle of Yaje was his 'nightmare drug,' DMT!" Personal communication, March 6, 2015.

52. The naming of the synthesized product, "Prestonia," seems to have been influenced by mistaken and unsupported claims, stemming from a misreading of Richard Spruce's notes, that *Prestonia amazonica* was a source of yagé, and even a source of DMT. American chemists Hochstein and Paradies had in fact claimed to have identified *Prestonia amazonica* as a source of DMT, and the constituent brew. F. A. Hochstein and A. M. Paradies, "Alkaloids of Banisteria caapi and Prestonia amazonicum," *Journal of the American Chemical Society* 79, no. 21 (1957): 5735–5736. Such claims were subsequently countered by Richard E. Schultes and Robert F. Raffauf, "Prestonia: An Amazon Narcotic or Not?" *Botanical Museum Leaflets* 19, no. 5 (1960): 109–122. Alternately, and most unlikely, Burroughs was hitting extracted alkaloids from *Prestonia amazonica*, which has not been identified as a source of DMT. If this were true, it would make for a fascinating historical revision.

53. Barry Miles, *Call Me Burroughs: A Life* (New York: Hachette Book Group, 2014), 371, 372, 390.

54. From letter to Brion Gysin, April 8, 1961, in William S. Burroughs, *Rub Out the Words: The Letters of William S. Burroughs 1959–1974*, ed. with an Introduction by Bill Morgan (New York: Penguin, 2012), 70.

55. Harrop, "The *Yagé* Aesthetic," 199.

56. Burroughs to Gysin, April 18, 1961, File C-37, BP NYPL, in Harrop, "The *Yagé* Aesthetic," 201.

57. Harrop, "The *Yagé* Aesthetic," 204 ("Untitled material enclosed with letter, Burroughs to Gysin 20 April 1961, BP NYPL").

58. William S. Burroughs, "Comments on the Night before Thinking," *Evergreen Review*, September–October 1961. This article derived from a document "Overdose of Synthesized Prestonia" enclosed with letter to Gysin on April 27, 1961, filed in the William S. Burroughs Papers held at the New York Public Library.

59. From letter to Gysin, April 8, 1961, Burroughs, *Rub Out the Words*, 70.

60. From letter to Gysin, May 8, 1961, Burroughs, *Rub Out the Words*, 75.

61. Burroughs, "Letter from a Master Addict to Dangerous Drugs," 129.

62. From letter to Gysin, April 8, 1961, Burroughs, *Rub Out the Words*, 70.

63. Ted Morgan, *Literary Outlaw: The Life and Times of William S. Burroughs* (New York: W. W. Norton, 1988), 370.

64. William S. Burroughs, "Points of Distinction between Sedative and Con-sciousness-Expanding Drugs," in *LSD: The Consciousness-Expanding Drug*, ed. David Solomon (New York: G. P. Putnam's Sons, Berkley Medallion, 1964).

65. Harrop, "The *Yagé* Aesthetic," 212.

66. William S. Burroughs, *Nova Express: The Restored Text* (New York: Grove Press, 2013; first published 1964), 92.

67. William S. Burroughs, letter to Leary, Cargo U.S. Consulate Tangier, Morocco, May 6, 1961, http://deoxy.org/h_wbdmt.htm.

68. Tim Leary, "Programmed Communication during Experiences with DMT (Dimethyltryptamine)," *Psychedelic Review* no. 8 (1966): 84.

69. James Oroc, *Tryptamine Palace: 5-MeO-DMT and the Sonoran Desert Toad* (Rochester, VT: Park Street Press, 2009), 307.

70. Leary, "Programmed Communication," 84.

71. Anthony France, "Mind-Busting Jungle Drug Hits the UK," *The Sun*, July 10, 2010. The article also referred to ex-Royal Marine Bruce Parry's "agonis-ing DMT trip in the Amazon," which had been shown on the BBC program *Tribe* in 2008. Parry had taken ayahuasca and reported a "humbling" and ultimately beneficial experience.

72. See Stevens, *Storming Heaven*, 180.

73. The trailer, for instance, refers to "DMT," not "DMT-19."

74. Lee and Shlain, *Acid Dreams*, 32–34.

75. Rick Watson, personal communication, February 28, 2015.

76. Ibid.

77. Rick Watson, "DMT, or, Spider Woman Comes to Town" (unpublished short story, April 16–17, 1993).

78. Ibid.

79. Stephen Szára, "A Scientist Looks at the Hippies," an unpublished report to the Supervisor, Psychopharmacology Section, National Institute of Mental Health, Clinical Psychopharmacology Laboratory, St. Elizabeth's Hospital, Washington, DC, 1968. Partially reproduced in Cheryl Pellerin, *Trips: How Hallucinogens Work in Your Brain* (New York: Seven Stories Press, 1998).

80. Stephen Szára, "Are Hallucinogens Psychoheuristic?" *NIDA Research Mono-graphs* 146 (1994): 40, 38–39.

Chapter 3

1. Oscar Janiger, interviewed by David Jay Brown and Rebecca McClen Novick, *Mavericks of the Mind* (Santa Cruz, CA: MAPS, 2010; first published 1993), 250.

2. Stevens, *Storming Heaven*, 114.

3. Leary, "Programmed Communication," 84.

4. Alan Watts, "Psychedelics and Religious Experience," *California Law Review* 56, no. 1 (1968): 76.
5. Lee and Shlain, *Acid Dreams*, 44.
6. Todd Brendan Fahey, "The Original Captain Trips," *High Times*, November 1991.
7. In Todd Brendan Fahey's *Wisdom's Maw: The Acid Novel* (Vancouver, Canada: Far Gone Books, 1996), Hubbard is painted as a CIA man through and through, in support of the author's not-uncommon thesis that the CIA and FBI attempted to disorient dissent by manufacturing and circulating LSD, which then slipped from their control by the mid-1960s, at which time they nuked the experiment with a new prohibition. Interviewed by R. U. Sirius, Fahey stated, "I'm flat out positive that Hubbard was CIA. The kind of access he had to Sandoz, to the Army, to Senators, State Attorney Generals . . . he had to have been CIA." R. U. Sirius interviews Todd Brendan Fahey, "It's Alright Maw: I'm Only Bleeding," *Mondo 2000*, November 1997: 67–69.
8. Janiger, in Lee and Shlain, *Acid Dreams*, 51.
9. Stevens, *Storming Heaven*, 114.
10. Ibid., 141.
11. Alfred M. Hubbard, "REPORT: D.M.T. EXPERIENCE (1961): An Experience with DMT (ID 78447)," *Erowid.org*, April 30, 2009, www.erowid.org/exp/78447.
12. The report indicates that Hubbard experimented with DMT in Ontario earlier in 1961. There may be a record of Hubbard using DMT before 1961, but such has not come to light.
13. Tim Leary, "The Religious Experience: Its Production and Interpretation," *Psychedelic Review* 1, no. 3 (1964): 324, 342, 326.
14. Ram Dass and Ralph Metzner (with Gary Bravo), *Birth of a Psychedelic Culture: Conversations about Leary, the Harvard Experiments, Millbrook and the Sixties* (Santa Fe, NM: Synergetic Press, 2010), 71.
15. Leary, "Programmed Communication." DMT and other tryptamine derivatives had been introduced in the inaugural issue of *The Psychedelic Review*. In a survey of psychedelic drugs, Ralph Metzner had earlier reported that in doses of 1 mg per kg, DMT was "similar to LSD or mescaline, but with a shorter duration of effect." Ralph Metzner, "The Pharmacology of Psychedelic Drugs I: Chemical and Biochemical Aspects," *Psychedelic Review* 1, no. 1 (1963): 73.
16. When Leary ("Programmed Communication," 84) wrote that "we were eager to see if the fabled 'terror-drug' would fit the set-setting theory," fitting the phrase within quotation marks he may well have actually started the meme he attributed to Burroughs. In Bigwood and Ott's article in *Head*

magazine (1977), the authors note that if it weren't for Leary and his colleagues, "the terror drug would have been excluded from the Psychedelic Age." By the time of Strassman's research, the phrase "terror drug" appears synonymous with Burroughs's experience. See Rick Strassman, *DMT: The Spirit Molecule: A Doctor's Revolutionary Research into the Biology of Near-Death and Mystical Experiences* (Rochester, VT: Park Street Press, 2001), 47.

17. Leary, "Programmed Communication," 84.

18. Robert E. L. Masters and Jean Houston, *The Varieties of Psychedelic Experience* (Rochester, VT: Park Street Press, 2000; first published 1966), 163.

19. Leary, "Programmed Communication," 85.

20. Ibid., 86.

21. Ibid., 87.

22. Ibid.

23. Tim Leary, Richard Alpert, and Ralph Metzner, *The Psychedelic Experience: A Manual Based on the Tibetan Book of the Dead* (Sacramento, CA: Citadel Press, 1964).

24. Tim Leary, "The Experiential Typewriter," *Psychedelic Review* no. 7 (1966): 70–85.

25. Leary, "Programmed Communication," 90.

26. Ibid.

27. The experiential typewriter was a primitive predecessor to Leary's concept of "Tele-thought." See Jennifer Ulrich, "Transmissions from the Timothy Leary Papers: Experiments in Teletype to Tele-Thought," NYPL Archives, April 18, 2013, www.nypl.org/blog/2013/04/18/timothy-leary-papers -experiments-teletype-tele-thought.

28. Leary, "Programmed Communication," 89.

29. Leary, *High Priest*, 215–216.

30. Ibid., 228.

31. Burroughs, *Nova Express*, 4.

32. Doyle, *Darwin's Pharmacy*, 186.

33. Leary, "Programmed Communication," 90–91.

34. Ibid., 87.

35. The first thing to distinguish between the contexts of use is that Burroughs's "overdose" was on approximately 100 mg, nearly double Leary's hit.

36. Leary, "Programmed Communication," 86.

37. Tim Leary, "Playboy Interview: Timothy Leary," *Playboy* 13, no. 9 (September 1966): 93–112, 250–251, 254–256.

38. Bigwood and Ott, "DMT: The Fifteen Minute Trip."

39. Humphry Osmond once had to talk down Hubbard, high on psilocybin, from shooting Leary. Fahey, "The Original Captain Trips."

40. Ott, *Pharmacotheon*, 186.

41. Leary, "Programmed Communication," 83.

42. Don Lattin, *The Harvard Psychedelic Club: How Timothy Leary, Ram Dass, Huston Smith, and Andrew Weil Killed the Fifties and Ushered in a New Age for America* (New York: HarperOne, 2010).

43. Tom Wolfe, *The Electric Kool-Aid Acid Test* (London: Black Swan, 1993; first published 1968), 101. Associated with an "everlasting paranoia," the experience seemed to carve a deep scar into Sandy, who, back on the West Coast, wigs out and finds himself in a Monterey jail.

44. Lee and Shlain, *Acid Dreams*, 102.

45. Stevens, *Storming Heaven*, 324.

46. In Ken Babbs and Paul Perry, *On the Bus: The Complete Guide to the Legendary Trip of Ken Kesey and the Merry Pranksters and the Birth of the Counterculture* (New York: Thunder's Mouth Press, 1990), 101.

47. Ibid., 102.

48. Ibid., 103.

49. R. U. Sirius, *Timothy Leary's Trip Thru Time* (Santa Cruz, CA: Futique Trust, 2013), 40.

50. R. U. Sirius, personal communication, February 2, 2015.

51. Wolfe, *The Electric Kool-Aid Acid Test*, 163.

52. Hunter S. Thompson, *Hell's Angels* (London: Penguin Books, 1967), 221, 223.

53. Wolfe, *The Electric Kool-Aid Acid Test*, 163.

54. Lyrics from "We're the Fugs," on The Fugs, *Virgin Fugs*, 1967. Full references for all audio recordings are listed in the Discography.

55. Ed Sanders, personal communication, March 1, 2015.

56. The 13th Floor Elevators, *The Psychedelic Sounds of The 13th Floor Elevators*, August 1966.

57. Paul Drummond, *Eye Mind: The Saga of Roky Erickson and the 13th Floor Elevators, The Pioneers of Psychedelic Sound* (Los Angeles: Process Media, 2007), 117.

58. Joe Nick Patoski, "The Roky Erickson," posted on "Notes and Musings," June 17, 2010, http://joenickp.blogspot.com/2010/06/roky-erickson-1975.html (originally published in 1975 by Patoski et al. in *Not Fade Away: The Texas Music Magazine* 1, no. 1). See also Jonathan Taylor, David Arnson, and Jon Hanna, "DMT and Music," in *DMT Underground: A Compendium of Unauthorized Research*, ed. Jon Hanna, forthcoming (draft chapter).

59. "Lenny Bruce Describes Smoking DMT in UCLA Lecture, 1966," posted on *Dangerous Minds*, March 1, 2014, http://dangerousminds.net/comments/lenny_bruce_describes_smoking_dmt_in_ucla_lecture_1966.

60. Paul Krassner, "See the Sacred Word and Win $100," *High Times*, February 1981.

61. In Michael Hollingshead, *The Man Who Turned on the World* (New York: Abelard-Schuman, 1974), Chapter 5.

62. Ibid.

63. Ibid.

64. Joe Bageant, "Ghosts of Tim Leary and Hunter Thompson," 2007, www .joebageant.com/joe/2007/05/ghosts_of_tim_l.html. The account was related at the time of a bizarre series of public debates Leary staged with fellow ex-con Liddy that were documented in *Return Engagement* (directed by Alan Rudolph, 1983).

65. ∞Ayes, "Moving into the Sacred World of DMT," *The Entheogen Review* 10, no. 1 (2001): 38. Circumstantial evidence suggests that "∞Ayes" was a pseudonym used by Nick Sand, and the articles under that pen name are widely credited to Sand.

66. Jon Hanna, Tania Manning, and Diana Reed Slattery, "Interview with Nick Sand" (unreleased), Mind States, May 6, 2012. As Ott (*Pharmacotheon*) has conveyed, by the late 1960s there were other pioneers who advertised how-to guides in underground publications, including the mysterious R. E. Brown of Austin, Texas, who was involved in the synthesis of DMT and DET. R. E. Brown, *The Psychedelic Guide to Preparation of the Eucharist* (Austin, TX: Linga Sharira Incense Co., 1968); and Mary Jane Superweed, *The D. M. T. Guide: Drug Manufacturing for Fun and Profit* (San Francisco: Stone Kingdom Syndicate, 1969).

67. From *The Substance: Albert Hofmann's LSD* (directed by Martin Witz, 2011).

68. Jon Hanna, personal communication, February 2, 2015.

69. Stewart Tendler and David May, *The Brotherhood of Eternal Love* (London: Cyan Books, 2007; first published 1984), 79.

70. Hanna, Manning, and Slattery, "Interview with Nick Sand."

71. Jon Hanna, personal communication, February 2, 2015.

72. Tim Scully, "Meeting Owsley and Smoking DMT," unpublished document, March 21, 2015.

73. Ibid.

74. Tendler and May, *The Brotherhood of Eternal Love*, 59–60.

75. Jon Hanna, personal communication, February 2, 2015.

76. Watson, "DMT, or, Spider Woman Comes to Town."

77. Ibid.

78. Ibid.

79. Ralph Metzner, personal communication, May 29, 2014.

80. Ott, *Pharmacotheon*, 188.

81. Szára, "A Scientist Looks at the Hippies."

82. ∞Ayes, "Just a Wee Bit More about DMT," *The Entheogen Review* 10, no. 2 (2001): 51.

83. Jon Hanna, "Erowid Character Vaults: Nick Sand Extended Biography," *Erowid.org,* November 5, 2009, www.erowid.org/culture/characters/sand _nick/sand_nick_biography1.shtml.

84. Nick Sand, "Reflections on Imprisonment and Liberation as Aspects of Consciousness," presented at Mind States II conference, May 27, 2001, www.matrixmasters.net/archive/NickSand/037-NickSand2001.mp3.

85. Nick Sand, interview by Daniel Williams on *The Opium Den Talk Show,* 2009, www.theopiumden.net/chapters/audio/interviews/41909/nsands.mp3.

86. ∞Ayes, "Just a Wee Bit More about DMT," 54.

87. Ibid., 51.

88. Ibid.

89. Hanna, "Erowid Character Vaults: Nick Sand."

90. ∞Ayes, "Just a Wee Bit More about DMT," 56.

91. Ibid., 53.

92. Ibid.

93. Ibid., 56.

94. Sand, interview by Daniel Williams.

95. email from Bear Stanley, August 29, 1997, in the possession of Jon Hanna (personal communication).

96. Dennis McNally, *A Long Strange Trip: The Inside History of the Grateful Dead* (New York: Broadway Books, 2002), 83.

97. Blair Jackson, *Grateful Dead: The Music Never Stopped* (New York: Delilah Communications, 1983).

98. David Gans, *Conversations with the Dead: The Grateful Dead Interview Book* (New York: Citadel Underground, 1991), 304.

99. The admission is from an email dialogue Hunter had with Terence McKenna in 1996 on www.levity.com/orfeo. It is a record of communication about the frontiers of DMT experimentation somewhat reminiscent of the exchange between Burroughs and Ginsberg more than forty years prior, only here the dialogue was made immediately transparent by way of the internet.

100. Tim Leary, "The Second Fine Art: Neo-Symbolic Communication of Experience," *Psychedelic Review* no. 8 (1966), 10.

101. Nicholas Schou, *Orange Sunshine* (New York: St. Martin's Press, 2010), 227.

102. In Taylor, Arnson, and Hanna, "DMT and Music."

103. Iggy Pop quoted at *Deoxy.org,* http://deoxy.org/h_iggy.htm. For further discussion of Iggy Pop's use of DMT, see Taylor, Arnson, and Hanna, "DMT and Music."

104. Ott, *Pharmacotheon,* 164.

Chapter 4

1. Dennis J. McKenna, *The Brotherhood of the Screaming Abyss: My Life with Terence McKenna* (St. Cloud, MN: Polaris, 2012), 156.
2. Terence McKenna, "Under the Teaching Tree," presented at Ojai Foundation, 1993; Terence McKenna, "Understanding and the Imagination in the Light of Nature," presented in Los Angeles, October 17, 1987.
3. Rick Watson, personal communication, February 28, 2015.
4. Terence McKenna, "Psychedelics Before and After History," presented at San Francisco's California Institute of Integral Studies, October 2, 1987.
5. T. McKenna, "Understanding and the Imagination in the Light of Nature."
6. In Richard Gehr, "Omega Man: A Profile of Terence McKenna," *Village Voice*, April 5, 1992, www.levity.com/rubric/mckenna.html.
7. Ibid.
8. Terence McKenna, "Shamanism, Alchemy, and the 20th Century," presented in Mannheim, Germany, 1996.
9. Terence McKenna, *True Hallucinations: Being an Account of the Author's Extraordinary Adventures in the Devil's Paradise* (San Francisco: Harper, 1993), 77.
10. D. McKenna, *The Brotherhood*, 158.
11. Dennis J. McKenna, "Ayahuasca and Human Destiny," *Journal of Psychoactive Drugs* 37, no. 2 (2005): 231–234.
12. Richard E. Schultes, "Virola as an Orally Administered Hallucinogen," *Botanical Museum Leaflets* 22, no. 6 (June 25, 1969): 229–240.
13. Wade Davis, *One River: Explorations and Discoveries in the Amazon Rainforest* (New York: Simon & Schuster, 1996), 474.
14. Richard E. Schultes, "A New Narcotic Snuff from the Northwest Amazon," *Botanical Museum Leaflets* 16, no. 9 (1954): 241–260; Davis, *One River*, 473.
15. Davis, *One River*, 476.
16. Alexander Price, "Immanentizing the Eschaton: An Interview with Dennis McKenna," *Reality Sandwich*, 2009, https://realitysandwich.com/13139/interview_dennis_mckenna/. While it had been proposed that the DMT was rendered orally active by the MAO-inhibiting effects of ß-carboline alkaloids (see Schultes, "Virola as an Orally Administered Hallucinogen"; Richard E. Schultes and Tony Swain, "De Plantis Toxicariis e Mundo Novo Tropicale Commentationes. XIII. Further Notes on Virola as an Orally Administered Hallucinogen," *Journal of Psychedelic Drugs* 8, no. 4, 1976: 317–324; and Richard E. Schultes, "Evolution of the Identification of the Myristicaceous Hallucinogens of South America," *Journal of Ethnopharmacology* 1, no. 3, 1979: 211–239), a proposal earlier mooted for the activity of snuffs (see B. Holmstedt and J. E. Lindgren, "Chemical Constituents and Pharmacology of South American Snuffs," in *Ethnopharmacologic Search*

for Psychoactive Drugs, eds. Efron et al., 1967, 339–373), Dennis and eth-nobotanist colleagues would later determine that the oral activity of the *Virola* pellets was unlikely to have resulted from the potentiation of the tryptamines via inhibition of MAO by ß-carbolines, but from the combined effect of the MAO-inhibitory activity of their constituent tryptamines. See D. J. McKenna, G. H. N. Towers, and F. S. Abbott, "Monoamine Oxidase Inhibitors in South American Hallucinogenic Plants. Part 2: Constituents of Orally Active Myristicaceous Hallucinogens," *Journal of Ethnopharmacology* 12, no. 2 (1984): 179–211. By the 1980s, Dennis had assumed a pivotal role in determining the synergetic pharmacology of ayahuasca, and the princi-pal role of DMT in this mechanism. See D. McKenna, Towers, and Abbott, "Monoamine Oxidase Inhibitors in South American Hallucinogenic Plants," 195–223; and D. J. McKenna, L. E. Luna, and G. H. N. Towers, "Biodynamic Constituents in Ayahuasca Admixture Plants: An Uninvestigated Folk Phar-macopoeia," in *Ethnobotany: Evolution of a Discipline*, eds. S. von Reis and R. E. Schultes (Portland, OR: Dioscorides Press, 1995).

17. Terence McKenna and Dennis McKenna, *The Invisible Landscape: Mind, Hal-lucinogens and the I Ching* (New York: HarperOne, 1993; first published 1975).

18. Wouter J. Hanegraaff, "'And End History. And Go to the Stars': Terence McKenna and 2012," in *Religion and Retributive Logic: Essays in Honour of Professor Garry W. Trompf*, eds. Carole M. Cusack and Christopher Hartney (Leiden, Netherlands: Brill, 2010), 296.

19. T. McKenna, *True Hallucinations*, 72.

20. Ibid., 6.

21. Ibid., 71.

22. While it took them a while to recognize it, given psilocybin is "almost the same compound" as DMT, and "only different enough to be orally active," it was in fact "the 'perfect orally active form of DMT' that we sought, and found, at LC." Dennis McKenna, personal communication, March 1, 2015.

23. D. McKenna, *The Brotherhood*, 236.

24. Ibid., 237.

25. Ibid., 252.

26. T. McKenna, *True Hallucinations*, 93.

27. Michael J. Harner, "The Sound of Rushing Water," *Natural History* 77, no. 6 (1973): 28–33.

28. Terence McKenna, "Mind and Time, Spirit and Matter," presented in Santa Fe, New Mexico, May 26–27, 1990, http://deoxy.org/timemind.htm.

29. T. McKenna, *True Hallucinations*, 60. I am reminded here of what is consid-ered to be among the primary experiences of the medium Jane Roberts, most noted for channeling the entity Seth. Roberts describes her initial

experience: "It was as if the physical world were really tissue-paper thin, hiding infinite dimensions of reality, and I was suddenly flung through tissue paper with a huge ripping sound" (Jane Roberts, *The Seth Material*, New York: New Awareness Network, 1970, 11). The equivalence between these episodes, especially the resonant audiology, is uncanny.

30. T. McKenna, *True Hallucinations*, 67.
31. D. McKenna, *The Brotherhood*, 245.
32. Jeffrey J. Kripal, *Mutants and Mystics: Science Fiction, Superhero Comics, and the Paranormal* (Chicago: University of Chicago Press, 2011), 147.
33. T. McKenna, *True Hallucinations*, 61.
34. Ibid., 68.
35. Ibid., 53, 81.
36. Ibid., 120.
37. Ibid., 95.
38. For "Timewave Zero," see McKenna and McKenna, *The Invisible Landscape*, Part Two, 119–205; and Terence McKenna, "New Maps of Hyperspace," in Terence McKenna, *The Archaic Revival: Speculations on Psychedelic Mushrooms, the Amazon, Virtual Reality, UFOs, Evolution, Shamanism, the Rebirth of the Goddess, and the End of History* (San Francisco: Harper, 1991), 90–102.
39. In Price, "Immanentizing the Eschaton."
40. D. McKenna, *The Brotherhood*, 246.
41. Rick Watson, personal communication, February 26, 2015.
42. In Nevill Drury, "Sacred Plants and Mystic Realities," in T. McKenna, *The Archaic Revival*, 239.
43. Terence McKenna, "DMT, Mathematical Dimensions, Syntax and Death" (from presentation, n.d.), uploaded to YouTube August 28, 2013, www.youtube.com/watch?v=VuEXBBaFAbw.
44. T. McKenna, "Understanding and the Imagination in the Light of Nature."
45. McKenna and McKenna, *The Invisible Landscape*, 15.
46. A sample from Funkopath, "Skwirm," on 12-inch *Skwirm*, 1997.
47. Terence McKenna, "Linking the Past, Present and the Future of Psychedelics," presented at The Bridge Psychedelic Conference, Stanford University, Stanford, California, February 2–3, 1991.
48. Jerome Rothenberg, ed., *Maria Sabina: Selections* (Berkeley: University of California Press, 2003), 49.
49. T. McKenna, Ojai Foundation.
50. Terence McKenna, "Among Ayahuasquera," in *Gateway to Inner Space: Sacred Plants, Mysticism and Psychotherapy,* ed. Christian Ratsch (Dorset, UK: Prism Press, 1991; first published 1989), 203, 198.

51. Dennis McKenna, personal communication, March 1, 2015.

52. T. McKenna, "Among Ayahuasquera," 206.

53. From a 1992 spoken-word performance backed by The Shamen, www .deoxy.org/t_re-evo.htm. This performance also provided inspiration for The Shamen's *Re: Evolution*, 1993.

54. Jonathan Ott, *Ayahuasca Analogues: Pangaean Entheogens* (Occidental, CA: Jonathan Ott Books, 1994), 12; T. McKenna, *Food of the Gods*, 112.

55. Maxine Rochlin and Morgan Harris (directors), *The Alchemical Dream: Rebirth of the Great Work*, Mystic Fire Productions, 2008. Originally titled *Coincidencia Oppositorum: The Unity of Opposites*.

56. T. McKenna, "Among Ayahuasquera," 192.

57. Michael Harner, *The Way of the Shaman: A Guide to Power and Healing* (San Francisco: Harper and Row, 1980).

58. T. McKenna, *Food of the Gods*, 98.

59. Terence McKenna, "DMT," (from presentation, n.d.), www.youtube.com /watch?v=pVXvLLOaI7Q.

60. T. McKenna, "DMT, Mathematical Dimensions."

61. J. B. S. Haldane, *Possible Worlds and Other Essays* (New York: Harper and Brothers, 1928), 286.

62. John Horgan, *Rational Mysticism: Spirituality Meets Science in the Search for Enlightenment* (New York: Mariner, 2003); William Rowlandson, "Nourished by Dreams, Visions and William James: The Radical Philosophies of Borges and Terence McKenna," *Paranthropology* 1 (2012): 46–60.

63. Horgan, *Rational Mysticism*, 192.

64. Rowlandson, "Nourished by Dreams," 47.

65. Ibid., 48.

66. D. McKenna, *The Brotherhood*, 71.

67. Terence McKenna, "A Conversation over Saucers," *Revision: The Journal of Consciousness and Change* 11, no. 3 (Winter 1989): 26, 27. Reproduced in McKenna, *The Archiac Revival*, 58–70.

68. D. McKenna, *The Brotherhood*, 128.

69. Carl Jung, *Flying Saucers: A Modern Myth of Things Seen in the Skies* (London: Routledge & Kegan Paul, 1959).

70. Terence McKenna, "Aliens and Archetypes," *Thinking Allowed with Jeffery Mishlove*, PBS TV, 1990.

71. T. McKenna, "Psychedelics Before and After History."

72. Terence McKenna, "Psychedelics and a Free Society," presented at Esalen Institute, Big Sur, California, 1984.

73. Although, as Dennis writes (in *The Brotherhood*, 147), his brother had already acquired this gift by the time he'd entered UC Berkeley in 1966,

when, under the influence of cannabis, he could "keep a group seated on the floor in his bedroom spellbound for hours."

74. Terence McKenna, "Rap Dancing into the 3rd Millennium," presented at Starwood XIV Festival, Brushwood Folklore Center, Sherman, New York, July 19–24, 1994.

75. Terence McKenna, "Tryptamine Hallucinogens and Consciousness," presented at Lilly/Goswami Conference on Consciousness and Quantum Physics at the Esalen Institute, Big Sur, California, December 1983, in T. McKenna, *The Archaic Revival*, 34–47, www.youtube.com/watch?v=RU-fyMZ5uZL0.

76. Ibid.

77. See the most comprehensive bibliography at www.terencemckenna.com.

78. Jeffrey Kripal, *Esalen: America and the Religion of No Religion* (Chicago: University of Chicago Press, 2007), 374.

79. T. McKenna, "Tryptamine Hallucinogens and Consciousness."

80. Kripal, *Esalen*, 510–511, note 33.

81. Christopher Partridge, *The Re-Enchantment of the West: Alternative Spiritualities, Sacralization, Popular Culture and Occulture, Vol. 2* (London: T&T Clark International, 2006), 117.

82. See Hans Thomas Hakl, *Eranos: An Alternative Intellectual History of the Twentieth Century* (Montreal: McGill-Queens University Press, 2013); Wouter J. Hanegraaff, "Entheogenic Esotericism," in *Contemporary Esotericism (Gnostica)*, eds. Egil Asprem and Kennet Granholm (Durham, UK: Acumen, 2013), 404.

83. T. McKenna, "Rap Dancing into the 3rd Millennium."

84. Wouter J. Hanegraaff, *New Age Religion and Western Culture: Esotericism in the Mirror of Secular Thought* (New York: State University of New York Press, 1998).

85. Hanegraaff, "'And End History. And Go to the Stars,'" 293; Hanegraaff, "Entheogenic Esotericism," 404.

86. T. McKenna, "Tryptamine Hallucinogens and Consciousness," 45.

87. Ibid., 44.

88. Colin Campbell, "The Cult, the Cultic Milieu and Secularization," in *The Cultic Milieu: Oppositional Subcultures in an Age of Globalization*, eds. Jeffrey Kaplan and Heléne Lööw (Walnut Creek, CA: AltaMira Press, 2002; first published 1972), 12–25.

89. Egil Asprem, "Intermediary Beings," in *The Occult World*, ed. Christopher Partridge (New York: Routledge, 2015), 648.

90. T. McKenna, "Mind and Time, Spirit and Matter."

91. T. McKenna, "Under the Teaching Tree."

92. T. McKenna, "Tryptamine Hallucinogens and Consciousness," 45.

93. In Daniel Moler, *Machine Elves 101* (*Or, Why Terence McKenna Matters*) (New York: Reality Sandwich, 2012).

Chapter 5

1. Hunter S. Thompson, *Fear and Loathing in Las Vegas: A Savage Journey to the Heart of the American Dream* (New York: Random House, 1971), 46.

2. Strassman, *DMT: The Spirit Molecule*, 83.

3. Strassman and colleagues studied the neuroendocrine, autonomic, and cardiovascular effects of, and perhaps most importantly the subjective reactions to, DMT under controlled settings. Rick J. Strassman and Clifford R. Qualls, "Dose-Response Study of N,N-Dimethyltryptamine in Humans. I. Neuroendocrine, Autonomic, and Cardiovascular Effects," *Archives of General Psychiatry* 51, no. 2 (1994): 85–97; Rick J. Strassman, Clifford R. Qualls, Eberhard H. Uhlenhuth, and Robert Kellner, "Dose-Response Study of N,N-Dimethyltryptamine in Humans. II. Subjective Effects and Preliminary Results of a New Rating Scale," *Archives of General Psychiatry* 51, no. 2 (1994): 98–108. They also reported on tolerance developing to the physiological but not to the psychological effects of repeated doses of DMT: Rick J. Strassman, Clifford R. Qualls, and Laura M. Berg, "Differential Tolerance to Biological and Subjective Effects of Four Closely Spaced Doses of N,N-Dimethyltryptamine in Humans," *Biological Psychiatry* 39 (1996): 784–795.

4. Also see Rick Strassman, "Human Hallucinogenic Drug Research in the United States: A Present-Day Case History and Review of the Process," *Journal of Psychoactive Drugs* 23 (1991): 29–38.

5. For a review of this research, see Steven A. Barker, Ethan H. McIlhenny, and Rick Strassman, "A Critical Review of Reports of Endogenous Psychedelic N,N-Dimethyltryptamines in Humans, 1955–2010," *Drug Test Analysis* 4 (2012): 617–635. This review suggests that compelling mass spectral evidence exists confirming the presence of DMT and its close relatives in certain human biological fluids.

6. Axelrod, "Enzymatic Formation of Psychotomimetic Metabolites from Normally Occurring Compounds."

7. Steven A. Barker, John A. Monti, and Samuel T. Christian, "N,N-Dimethyltryptamine: An Endogenous Hallucinogen," *International Review of Neurobiology* 22 (1981): 83–110.

8. J. C. Callaway, "A Proposed Mechanism for the Visions of Dream Sleep," *Medical Hypotheses* 26, no. 2 (1988): 119–124.

9. Rick Strassman, "DMT: The Brain's Own Psychedelic," in Strassman, Wojtowicz, Luna, and Frecska, *Inner Paths to Outer Space*, 42.

10. Strassman, *DMT: The Spirit Molecule,* 49.
11. Rick Strassman, *DMT and the Soul of Prophecy: A New Science of Spiritual Revelation in the Hebrew Bible* (Rochester, VT: Park Street Press, 2014), 30.
12. Strassman, "DMT: The Brain's Own Psychedelic," 42.
13. Strassman, *DMT: The Spirit Molecule,* 313.
14. Ibid., 54.
15. Rick Strassman (interviewed by Martin W. Ball), "Voyaging to DMT Space with Dr. Rick Strassman, M.D.," *Reality Sandwich,* July 18, 2008, http://reality-sandwich.com/5697/voyaging_dmt_space_with_dr_rick_strassman_md.
16. Rick Strassman and Marc Galanter, "The Abhidharma: A Cross-Cultural Model for the Psychiatric Application of Medication," *International Journal of Social Psychiatry* 26 (1980): 293–299.
17. Strassman, *DMT: The Spirit Molecule,* 60.
18. Ibid., xvii, 76.
19. Strassman, "DMT: The Brain's Own Psychedelic," 40.
20. Rick Strassman, "The Pineal Gland: Current Evidence for Its Role in Consciousness," *Psychedelic Monographs and Essays* 5 (1991): 188, 182.
21. D. M. Turner, *The Essential Psychedelic Guide* (San Francisco: Panther Press, 1994), 67.
22. Serena Roney-Dougal, "The Pineal Gland: Psychic and Psychedelic Powerhouse," *Paranthropology: Journal of Anthropological Approaches to the Paranormal* 2, no. 2 (2011): 29. For a comprehensive review of research investigating the pineal as a possible site for the production of DMT, 5-MeO-DMT, and bufotenin, see David Luke, "Psychoactive Substances and Paranormal Phenomena: A Comprehensive Review," *International Journal of Transpersonal Studies* 31 (2012): 101–103.
23. Strassman, *DMT: The Spirit Molecule,* 75.
24. Helena P. Blavatsky, *The Secret Doctrine: The Synthesis of Science, Religion and Philosophy. Vol. II* (*Anthropogenesis*) (London: Theosophical Publishing Company, 1888), 267.
25. Anthony Peake, *The Infinite Mindfield: The Quest to Find the Gateway to Higher Consciousness* (London: Watkins, 2013).
26. Helena P. Blavatsky, "Dialogue on the Mysteries of the After Life [Part 2]," *Lucifer* 3 (January 15, 1889): 407–417.
27. "Pineal Gland Activation Secrets with Justin Verrengia," January 2, 2014, www.youtube.com/watch?v=QkF5Ngro3VY; Iona Miller, "Pineal Gland, DMT and Altered State of Consciousness," *Journal of Consciousness Exploration and Research* 4, no. 2 (March 4, 2013): 217; Brad Olsen, *Modern Esoteric: Beyond Our Senses* (San Francisco: CCC, 2014), 278.

28. Anna Hunt, "Top 8 Supplements to Boost Your Pineal Gland Function," *Waking Times*, November 16, 2014. http://www.wakingtimes.com/2014/11/16/top-8-supplements-boost-pineal-gland-function/.

29. Olsen, *Modern Esoteric*, 285.

30. Kimah, "Interview with Ananda on Dark Room Retreat Alchemy," www.akasha.de/~aton/DR.html.

31. Tony Wright and Graham Gynn, *Left in the Dark: The Biological Origins of the Fall from Grace* (Lulu, 2007), 124, xiii.

32. Dieter Broers (director), *Solar Revolution*, Screen Addiction, 2012.

33. Chance Gardner (director), "Episode 5: Navigating the Afterlife," *Magical Egypt: A Symbolist Tour*, CustomFlix, 2005.

34. "The Real You," *Adventure Time*, season 2, episode 15, Cartoon Network (original air date: February 14, 2011). I thank David Luke, who alerted me to this segment, reciting it word for word at the afterparty to London's Breaking Convention 2013, www.youtube.com/watch?v=rE9Cwa5EDDw.

35. Blair MacKenzie Blake, *IJYNX* (Brisbane, Australia: Daily Grail. 2003).

36. Blair MacKenzie Blake, "DMT and Magick: An Occultist Ponders the Neurochemical Basis of Magick and the Paranormal," in *Dark Lore Vol. II* (Brisbane, Australia: Daily Grail, 2008).

37. Blair MacKenzie Blake, "Crowley, DMT and Magick," *Sub Rosa* 2 (2005): 26, 25.

38. Ibid., 27.

39. Joel David Bakst, *The Jerusalem Stone of Consciousness: DMT, Kabbalah and the Pineal Gland* (Manitou Springs, CO: City of Luz, 2013), vii, xii, xi.

40. Ibid., xii.

41. Natalie Jacobs, "The Psychedelic Rabbi," *San Diego Jewish Journal*, February 2014, http://sdjewishjournal.com/sdjj/february-2014/the-psychedelic-rabbi-2/.

42. Bakst, *The Jerusalem Stone of Consciousness*, xvi.

43. Jacobs, "The Psychedelic Rabbi."

44. Gabriel D. Roberts, "Episode 134 Gabriel D. Roberts—Losing My Religion," *Project Archivist* podcast, November 15, 2014, www.projectarchivist.com/?tag=gabriel-d-roberts.

45. Ott, *Pharmacotheon*, 60.

46. Gabriel D. Roberts, *The Quest for Gnosis* (CreateSpace, 2014); Gabriel D. Roberts, "Blasting Off with Dr. DMT," *VICE*, April 2, 2014, www.vice.com/read/blasting-off-with-dr-dmt.

47. Roberts, "Losing My Religion."

48. Dr. Future, "Sorcery and Drugs in Opening the Last Days Spirit Portal," presented at Last Days Conference, Nashville, 2010. Dr. Future was inter-

viewed on *Nowhere to Run* radio with Chris White in 2010, www.youtube .com/watch?v=5tZtw0xuO4w#t=5480.

49. H. P. Lovecraft, "From Beyond," *The Fantasy Fan* 1, no. 10 (1934): 147–151.

50. Stuart Gordon (director), *From Beyond*, MGM, 1986.

51. Jim DeKorne, *Psychedelic Shamanism: The Cultivation, Preparation, and Shamanic Use of Psychotropic Plants* (Port Townsend, WA: Breakout Productions, 1994), 103, 104.

52. Rick Strassman, "Chapter 13, Contact through the Veil: 1," excerpted from *DMT: The Spirit Molecule* reprinted in *The Entheogen Review* 9, no. 2 (2000): 4–12.

53. ∞Ayes, "Moving into the Sacred World of DMT," 38.

54. Ibid., 32.

55. Strassman, *DMT: The Spirit Molecule*, 189.

56. ∞Ayes, "Just a Wee Bit More about DMT," 52.

57. ∞Ayes, "Moving into the Sacred World of DMT," 32, 35, 38, 39.

58. Ibid., 36.

59. ∞Ayes, "Just a Wee Bit More about DMT," 53.

60. ∞Ayes, "Moving into the Sacred World of DMT," 32–33.

61. Ibid., 37.

62. Strassman, *DMT: The Spirit Molecule*, 163, 190.

63. Ibid., 235.

64. Ibid., 304.

65. Rick Strassman, "Sitting for Sessions: Dharma and DMT Research," *Tricycle: The Buddhist Review*, Fall 1996: 81–88.

66. Strassman, *DMT: The Spirit Molecule*, 343, 344. In the opening of Strassman's *DMT and the Soul of Prophecy* (p. 1), where "Saul" is renamed "Leo," the experience is favorably compared with the prophetic vision of Ezekiel, among many such visions in the Hebrew Bible. See Chapter Twelve.

67. Strassman, *DMT: The Spirit Molecule*, 154.

68. Daniel Appel, "Can the Roots of Spiritual Experience Be Found in Brain Chemistry?" October 30, 2013, https://ultraculture.org/blog/2013/10/30 /spiritual-experience-brain-chemistry.

69. Rick Strassman (interviewed by Graham Hancock), in Graham Hancock, *Supernatural: Meetings with the Ancient Teachers of Mankind* (London: Arrow Books, 2005), 751–752.

70. Strassman, *DMT and the Soul of Prophecy*, 4.

71. Barker, Borjigin, Lomnicka, and Strassman, "LC/MS/MS Analysis of the Endogenous Dimethyltryptamine Hallucinogens." This article followed on the heels of research showing that INMT (indolethylamine N-methyltransferase)—the enzyme responsible for synthesizing DMT—was found in the central nervous system of primates, including the

pineal gland, motor neurons, spinal cord, and retina. Cozzi, Mavlyutov, Thompson, and Ruoho, "Indolethylamine N-methyltransferase Expression in Primate Nervous Tissue." This had itself followed from the late 1990s' discovery of the human gene that codes for INMT: Thompson, Moon, Kim, Xu, Siciliano, and Weinshilboum, "Human Indolethylamine N-Methyltransferase."

Chapter 6

1. Rick Strassman, "Interview with Rick Strassman," *The Nexian*, no. 2 (2014), 33.
2. David Nickles, "Criminals and Researchers: Perspectives on the Necessity of Underground Research," *The Nexian*, no. 2 (2014): 45.
3. Ibid., 40.
4. Ott, *Pharmacotheon*, 58, 77, 59.
5. Ibid., 60. Wasson's account of his consumption of *Psilocybe*-containing mushrooms and the ritual of the *velada* with curandera María Sabina in Huautla de Jiménez, Oaxaca, Mexico, on June 29/30, 1955, was reported in *LIFE* magazine in 1957. Robert G. Wasson, "Seeking the Magic Mushroom," *LIFE* 49, no. 19 (May 13, 1957): 100–102, 109–120.
6. Carl A. P. Ruck, Jeremy Bigwood, Danny Staples, Jonathan Ott, and R. Gordon Wasson, "Entheogens," *Journal of Psychedelic Drugs* 11, nos. 1–2 (1979): 145–146.
7. Hanegraaff, "Entheogenic Esotericism," 392, 393.
8. Wouter J. Hanegraaff, "Ayahuasca Groups and Networks in the Netherlands: A Challenge to the Study of Contemporary Religion," in *The Internationalization of Ayahuasca*, eds. Beatriz C. Labate and Henrik Jungaberle (Zürich, Switzerland: LIT, 2011), 85–103.
9. Thomas B. Roberts, ed., *Spiritual Growth with Entheogens: Psychoactive Sacramentals and Human Transformation* (Rochester, VT: Park Street Press, 2012; first published 2001).
10. Huston Smith, *Cleansing the Doors of Perception: The Religious Significance of Entheogenic Plants and Chemicals* (New York: Tarcher, 2000), xvi–xvii.
11. Stanislav Grof, *LSD: Doorway to the Numinous: The Groundbreaking Psychedelic Research into Realms of the Human Unconscious* (Rochester, VT: Park Street Press, 2009; first published 1975); Thomas B. Roberts, *The Psychedelic Future of the Mind: How Entheogens Are Enhancing Cognition, Boosting Intelligence, and Raising Values* (Rochester, VT: Park Street Press, 2013); Jim Fadiman, *The Psychedelic Explorer's Guide: Safe, Therapeutic, and Sacred Journeys* (Rochester, VT: Park Street Press, 2011).
12. See, for example, "The Potential Religious Relevance of Entheogens," a special section of *Zygon: Journal of Religion and Science* 49, no. 3 (September 2014).

13. Roland R. Griffiths, William A. Richards, Una D. McCann, and Robert Jesse, "Psilocybin Can Occasion Mystical-Type Experiences Having Substantial and Sustained Personal Meaning and Spiritual Significance," *Psychopharmacology* 187 (2006): 268–283; William A. Richards, "Here and Now: Discovering the Sacred with Entheogens," *Zygon: Journal of Religion and Science* 49, no. 3 (September 2014): 653.

14. Dennis McKenna, personal communication, June 8, 2015.

15. Shulgin and Shulgin, *PiHKAL;* Alexander Shulgin and Ann Shulgin, *TiHKAL: The Continuation* (Berkeley, CA: Transform Press, 1997).

16. Ott, *Pharmacotheon,* 187.

17. Gracie and Zarkov, "Three Beta-Carboline Containing Plants as Potentiators of Synthetic DMT and Other Indole Psychedelics," Note 7 in *Notes from Underground: A Gracie and Zarkov Reader,* 1985, www.erowid.org/library/books_online/notes_from_underground.pdf. A comprehensive compendium of homegrown experimentation can be found in *Some Simple Tryptamines* (Austin, TX: A Better Days Publication, 2007; first published 2002) by Keeper Trout, also responsible for the *Trout's Notes* series compiling summaries of chemical, botanical, pharmacological, and ethnobotanical data on psychoactive plants, http://troutsnotes.com.

18. Jonathan Ott, "Pharmahuasca: Human Pharmacology of Oral DMT Plus Harmine," *Journal of Psychoactive Drugs* 31, no. 2 (1999): 176.

19. MAOs (monoamine oxidases) are enzymes that normally neutralize the psychoactive effects of tryptamines.

20. Holmstedt and Lindgren, "Chemical Constituents and Pharmacology of South American Snuffs"; Stig Agurell, Bo Holmstedt, and Jan-Erik Lindgren, "Alkaloid Content of *Banisteriopsis rusbyana,*" *American Journal of Pharmacy* 140, no. 5 (1968): 148–151.

21. McKenna, Towers, and Abbott, "Monoamine Oxidase Inhibitors in South American Hallucinogenic Plants," 195–223; Jeremy Bigwood in Ott, *Pharmacotheon,* 227; Gracie and Zarkov, "Three Beta-Carboline Containing Plants"; Ott, *Ayahuasca Analogues.*

22. Ott, "Pharmahuasca," 173.

23. Jon Hanna and Jonathan Taylor, "Is DMT Everywhere? The Short, Intense Trip of *N,N*-Dimethyltryptamine" (unpublished document).

24. Jim DeKorne, "Entheogen: What's in a Word?" *The Entheogen Review* 1, no. 2 (1992): 2.

25. Ibid.

26. Jim DeKorne, "Smokable DMT from Plants: Part 1," *The Entheogen Review,* Winter 1993.

27. Jim DeKorne, "Phalaris Update," *The Entheogen Review,* Fall 1994.

28. DeKorne, *Psychedelic Shamanism*, 81.

29. Turner, *The Essential Psychedelic Guide*, 77, 78.

30. For "ayahuasca borealis," see Ott, *Pharmacotheon*, 245. For "anahuasca," see Ott, *Ayahuasca Analogues*, and Jonathan Ott, *The Age of Entheogens and the Angels' Dictionary* (Kennewick, WA: Natural Products Co., 1995).

31. Ott, "Pharmahuasca," 174.

32. Noman, "DMT for the Masses," *The Entheogen Review* 15, no. 3 (2006): 91–92.

33. nen888, "Trying to Improve Acacia Information," posted to DMT-Nexus June 28, 2011, www.dmt-nexus.me/forum/default.aspx?g=posts&t=23472.

34. Fred Turner, *From Counterculture to Cyberculture: Stewart Brand, the Whole Earth Network, and the Rise of Digital Utopianism* (Chicago: University of Chicago Press, 2006).

35. Doyle, *Darwin's Pharmacy*, 16, 17.

36. Dark Nebula & Scatterbrain, "Geometric Patterns," on *Psionic Earth*, 2004.

37. Shulgin and Shulgin, *TiHKAL*, 263–264.

38. While I have received secondhand reports of successful extractions claiming 0.5 percent DMT from the phyllodes and bark of *A. pycnantha,* there appears to be little evidence for this.

39. Neil Pike, personal communication, December 8, 2014.

40. While in the 1970s Pike was made aware of DMT from reading Wolfe's *The Electric Kool-Aid Acid Test* and Leary's writings, he was unexpectedly introduced to its effects in the rainforested backwoods of Australia. He recalls the afternoon at a rented farmhouse near Nimbin in the late 1970s during a "psychedelic kirtan" jam circle. The song he recalls was George Harrison's "It's All Too Much." He was playing guitar and it was customary to have a nonmusician hold a ganja joint to the mouths of musicians, "allowing them to imbibe without losing the vibe." On this occasion the vibe was inflected with a new sensation. "As I exhaled, the smoke formed into wondrous colourful curlicues . . . a smokey 3-D persian carpet that shimmered and lingered in front of me as the haze dissolved. A strong psychedelic rush rose up my spine." Pike sucked in a few more deep puffs and "strummed determinedly as I clung on for dear life. Long experience in playing music on psychedelics had taught me that if you keep strumming through the first rush, you can often ride the whole thing to new and interesting places." With their extended jam lasting fifteen minutes, Pike and fellow musicians arrived at a place frequented regularly over subsequent decades. Neil Pike, "The First Time I Smoked DMT," 2015, www.paganlovecult.com/philos/first_dmt.html.

41. A report in the 1990 CSIRO publication *Plants for Medicines*, using findings in J. S. Fitzgerald and A. A. Sioumis, "Alkaloids of the Australian Legumi-

nosae. V. The Occurrence of Methylated Tryptamines in Acacia maidenii F. Muell," *Australian Journal of Chemistry* 18 (1965): 433–434.

42. "Extracting DMT from *Acacia maidenii*," *Erowid.org*, www.erowid.org /plants/acacia/acacia_extract1.shtml. "Extraction from *Acacia maidenii* Bark," *The Entheogen Review* 5, no. 1 (1996): 6–7.

43. "Extracting DMT from *Acacia maidenii.*"

44. Nen, personal communication, July 25, 2014.

45. Nen interviewed by Rak Razam, "The DreaMTime Invasion: DMT and the Origins of Religion, with Nen," podcast on *In a Perfect World*, 2013, http:// in-a-perfect-world.podomatic.com/entry/2013-07-07T03_05_22-07_00.

46. jamie and nen888 (with additional research by dreamer042 and *The Nexian* editorial staff), "Entheogenic Tryptamines, Past and Present: Folkways of Resilience," *The Nexian*, no. 2 (2014): 9.

47. nen888, "Entheogenic Effects of NMT (Monomethyl-tryptamine)," posted to DMT-Nexus, July 1, 2011, www.dmt-nexus.me/forum/default.aspx -?g=posts&t=23544.

48. Nen, "Entheogenic Effects of NMT from Acacia," presented at Entheogenesis Australis conference, December 2011.

49. Vince Cakic, Jacob Potkonyak, and Alex Marshall, "Dimethyltryptamine (DMT): Subjective Effects and Patterns of Use among Australian Recreational Users," *Drug and Alcohol Dependence* 111, nos. 1–2 (2010): 30–37.

50. E., Australia, "Urgent Report on the Australian *Acacia* Situation," *The Entheogen Review* 5, no. 4 (1996): 10.

51. Nen and David Nickles, "When DMT Equals Killing the Environment," posted to DMT-Nexus, October 1, 2014, http://the-nexian.me/home /knowledge/131-when-dmt-equals-killing-the-environment.

52. Nen, personal communication, July 25, 2014.

53. Nen, personal communication, December 2, 2014.

54. Nen, personal communication, July 25, 2014.

55. jamie, "Phalaris Teachers: Temperate Sources of Tryptamine Gnosis," *The Nexian*, no. 2 (2014): 67.

56. Ibid., 65.

57. Robin Rodd, "Snuff Synergy: Preparation, Use and Pharmacology of *Yopo* and *Banisteriopsis Caapi* among the Piaroa of Southern Venezuela," *Journal of Psychoactive Drugs* 34, no. 3 (2002): 273–279.

58. Torsten Wiedemann, personal communication, June 2, 2013.

59. Kate Hamilton, "The Freakiest Trip," *Sydney Morning Herald* (*Good Weekend*), March 29, 2003, 42–45.

60. Floyd Davis, "Don't Mention the Plants," n.d., www.rainbowdreaming .org/the_plants.html.

61. Floyd Davis, Skeeta Power, Mango Frangipanni, and Nina Rae, *Illuminated Adventures* (Mullumbimby, NSW, Australia: Psychedelia Australis, 1998).
62. Julian Palmer, *Articulations: On the Utilisation and Meanings of Psychedelics* (Thornbury, Victoria, Australia: Anastomosis Books, 2014), 58, 49, 45, 84.
63. From chocobeastie, "Changa: A Smoking Blend Containing Ayahuasca and Other Herbs," posted to DMT-Nexus February 9, 2011, www.dmt-nexus .me/forum/default.aspx?g=posts&t=19331. The post formed the basis for an article later published in the *EGA Journal.*
64. Ray Thorpe, personal communication, December 19, 2014.
65. Ray Thorpe, personal communication, January 5, 2015.
66. Julian Palmer, personal communication, April 26, 2013.
67. Olympus Mon, "The Art of Changa," *The Nexian,* no. 2 (2014): 48.
68. Ibid., 49.
69. Palmer, *Articulations,* 109.
70. Julian Palmer, personal communication, January 13, 2015.
71. Julian Palmer, personal communication, April 26, 2013.
72. Ibid.
73. Ibid.
74. M. L. Pochettino, A. R. Cortella, and M. Ruiz, "Hallucinogenic Snuff from Northwestern Argentina: Microscopical Identification of *Anadenanthera colubrina* var. *cebil* (Fabaceae) in Powdered Archaeological Material," *Economic Botany* 53, no. 2 (1999): 127–132.
75. Davis, "Don't Mention the Plants."
76. Ray Thorpe, personal communication, December 19, 2014.
77. Ken W. Tupper and Beatriz C. Labate, "Plants, Psychoactive Substances and the International Narcotics Control Board: The Control of Nature and the Nature of Control," *Human Rights and Drugs* 2, no. 1 (2012): 17–28.
78. Jon Hanna, "Got Changa?" *Erowid Extracts* 15 (November 2008): 18–19, www.erowid.org/chemicals/dmt/dmt_article1.shtml.
79. www.psytranceismyreligion.com is now offline.
80. Smith, *Cleansing the Doors of Perception,* xvi–xvii.
81. Erik Davis, "Boom Festival 2008," *Dose Nation,* 2008, www.dosenation .com/listing.php?id=5045.
82. DeKorne, "Smokable DMT from Plants: Part 1," 1.
83. Nen, personal communication, December 2, 2014.
84. Chen Cho Dorge, "Changa: The Evolution of Ayahuasca," *Reality Sandwich,* 2010, www.realitysandwich.com/changa_evolution_ayahuasca. The article was originally posted on Dorge's website, www.changa.esotericpharma.org.
85. Jorge Ferrer, *Revisioning Transpersonal Theory: A Participatory Vision of Human Spirituality* (Albany: State University of New York Press, 2002), 37, 38.

86. Daniel Mirante, "Notes on the Western Paradigm of Ayahuasca," blog post April 23, 2010, www.ayahuasca.com/ayahuasca-overviews/a-response-to -the-reality-sandwich-article-changa-the-evolution-of-ayahuasca-or-notes -on-the-western-paradigm-of-ayahuasca/.

87. Marlene Dobkin de Rios, "Drug Tourism in the Amazon," *Anthropology of Consciousness* 5, no. 1 (1994): 16–19; Marlene Dobkin de Rios, "Mea Culpa: Drug Tourism and the Anthropologist's Responsibility," *Anthropology News,* October 2006: 20.

88. carpedmt, comment on "Notes on the Western Paradigm of Ayahuasca," May 24, 2010.

89. Julian Palmer, personal communication, November 13, 2014.

90. jamie and nen888, "Entheogenic Tryptamines," 7, 10, 5.

91. Morris Crowley, "Agrostis: Tryptamines in the Crucible of Civilization," *The Nexian,* April 4, 2014, http://the-nexian.me/home/knowledge/86-agrostis -tryptamines-in-the-crucible-of-civilization.

92. David S. Flattery and Martin Schwartz, *Haoma and Harmaline: The Botanical Identity of the Indo-Iranian Sacred Hallucinogen "Soma" and Its Legacy in Religion, Language and Middle Eastern Folklore* (Berkeley: University of California Press, 1989).

93. Little has been validated concerning the purported history of *Acacia* use among Australian indigenous populations for the purpose of obtaining altered states of consciousness. While Nen has worked with indigenous communities in NSW and in the Northern Territory since the mid-1990s, learning about "sacred plants" and their applications, he is not at liberty to divulge secret knowledge transmitted in ceremony and initiation that cannot be communicated "outside of direct transmission." Nen, personal communication, July 25, 2014.

94. Nen interviewed by Rak Razam, "The DreaMTime Invasion."

95. jamie and nen888, "Entheogenic Tryptamines," 8, 10.

96. Nickles, "Criminals and Researchers," 44.

Chapter 7

1. Christopher Partridge, *The Re-Enchantment of the West: Alternative Spiritualities, Sacralization, Popular Culture and Occulture, Vol. 1* (London: T&T Clark International, 2004).

2. See Graham St John, *Global Tribe: Technology, Spirituality and Psytrance* (Sheffield, UK: Equinox, 2012).

3. The Infinity Project, "Stimuli," on *Feeling Weird,* 1995.

4. Blue Lunar Monkey, "Hikuri Om," on *Shamanic State,* 2006.

5. From Daksinamurti, *Shanti Jatra II: Shamans and Healers,* 2012.

6. Sideform, "Santo Daime," on *Santo Daime,* 2011.

7. Merkaba, "Hooked on Jungle," on *Awaken,* 2010.

8. 1200 Mics, *1200 Micrograms,* 2002.

9. Although not an album track list, the idea of listing entheogenic favorites queued up as track names may have had its origins thirty-five years earlier in the song "Hashish" from the musical Hair, which began Off-Broadway in 1967. A few persistent favorites can be identified.

   Hashish, cocaine, marijuana

   Opium, LSD, DMT

   STP, BLT, A&P, IRT

   APC, Alcohol

   Cigarettes, shoe polish, cough syrup, peyote

   Equinol, dexamil, camposine, Chemadrine

   Thorazine, trilophon, dexedrine, benzedrine, methedrine

   S-E-X and Y-O-U, Wow!

10. Braincell, "Psychoactive Plants," on *Transformation of Reality,* 2007.

11. Tron's "Amasonic," on *Divine Inventions,* 2008.

12. Dark Nebula & Scatterbrain, "Geometric Patterns," on *Psionic Earth,* 2004.

13. Ekoplex, *Discovering the Ancient,* 2012; Fragletrollet, "Shamanizer," on *Shamanisma,* 2008; Merkaba, "Icaro," on *Language of Light,* 2012.

14. SiLo and Humerous, "New Path," on *New Path,* 2014.

15. From Darpan and Bhakta's New Age / ambient album *Temple of Glowing Sound,* 2006.

16. Via Axis, "Tryptamine Dimensions," on *Expressions of One,* 2011.

17. 1200 Mics, "DMT," on *1200 Micrograms,* 2002.

18. Dark Nebula, "Book of Stones," on *The 8th Sphere,* 2003.

19. "Plants and Animals" by Patchbay and Ital on the debut album from Brazilian Patchbay, *Southern Cross,* 2012, from the film *DMT: The Spirit Molecule.*

20. Terence McKenna, sampled by The Irresistible Force (Morris Gould) on chill track "Mountain High" from debut album *Flying High,* 1992. This is among the first McKenna/DMT samples.

21. Eat Static, "Prana," *Abduction,* 1993.

22. Liquid on Safi, "Shamanic Madness," on *13 Moon* (compiled by Cosmic Sun), 2006.

23. *Alien Dreamtime* was a multimedia event at the Transmission Theater, San Francisco, February 26–27, 1993.

24. Merkaba's "Primal Earthly Pledge," on *Language of Light,* 2012.

25. Morpheus from Astral Projection's "Back from Hell," on *Psytisfaction,* 2004.

26. 9West, "Wake Up," on *Nuance,* 2006.

27. From Streamers's "Power and Light," on *Goa Trance Vol. 19,* 2012.

28. 1200 Mics, "DMT," on *1200 Micrograms*, 2002.

29. Atma, "The Exorcism of the Spirit," on *Map of Goa Vol. 2*, 2006.

30. Entheogenic, "Ground Luminosity," on *Spontaneous Illumination*, 2003. Ott's 2005 remix of "Ground Luminosity" (Entheogenic, *Dialogue of the Speakers*) finishes the sentence: "against which all other creative efforts are measured."

31. Coming Soon, "Ayahuasca," on *Become One*, 2013.

32. Blue Lunar Monkey's "Mysterious Xperience," on *Beyond 2012*, 2008.

33. Hujaboy, "Liquifried," on *Planetary Service*, 2009.

34. From "Freakstuff," on *A Spark of Light*, 2009, by Brazilian Arthur Magno (a.k.a. Fractal Flame).

35. Mood Deluxe, "Stealthy Fungus," on *Divine Inventions*, 2008.

36. Polyphonia vs. Zik, "Fucking Dimensions," on *Shockwave Machine*, 2007; Mister Black, "DMT Molecule" (compiled by Demoniac Insomniac, on *Anahata*, 2009.

37. Fobi vs Mr. Madness, "On the Spot," on *Welcome to Freakdom*, 2012.

38. Quantize, "Dymethyltryptamine," on *Borderline*, 2009.

39. Wizack Twizack, "Join My Cult," on *MystaGogue: Beyond the Boundaries of Logic and Comprehension*, 2011.

40. Milosz Zielinski, personal communication, April 14, 2014.

41. Spirit Molecule's "Psychedelic Journey," on *Lysergic State*, 2012.

42. Therange Freak, "Dreamland," on *How the Moon Was Made*, 2012.

43. Exoplanet, "Dimethyltryptamine," on *Metasophia*, 2009.

44. Sonic Entity, "Spirit Molecule," on *Goa Vol. 46*, 2013; Dr. Hoffman, "Spirit Molecules," on *Paperworks*, 2013.

45. Xikwri Neyrra, "Knockin' on Matrix Door," on Goa Gil's compilation *Shri Maharaj*, 2011.

46. Wizack Twizack, "Spirit Molecule," on *Space No More*, 2010.

47. Hux Flux, "Finite Automata," on *Circle Sine Sound*, 2015.

48. Mitch Schultz (director), *DMT: The Spirit Molecule*, Spectral Alchemy, Synthetic Pictures, 2010.

49. Hypnoise, "Demetrium" (compiled by Boom Shankar and Alexsoph), on *Transmissions*, 2012. Mueli first related this story in *The Entheogen Review*: C. M., "DMT Entities," *The Entheogen Review* 2, no. 4 (1993): 3.

50. From the expired website: DMTRMX, www.dmtrmx.com.

Chapter 8

1. Raja Ram, personal communication, November 13, 2010.

2. Raja Ram, personal communication, November 16, 2010.

3. Here and below, Nik Sequenci, personal communication, February 3, 2012.

4. Here and below, Martin Glover, personal communication, June 4, 2015.

5. Johann Bley, personal communication, June 10, 2015.

6. DMT, "DMT," on *Dragonfly Classix*, 1998; Hallucinogen, "LSD," on *Twisted*, 1995.

7. Celtic Cross, *Hicksville*, 1998; Killing Joke, *Pandemonium*, 1994; Crowded House, *Together Alone*, 1993; The String Cheese Incident, *Untying the Not*, 2003.

8. Dub Trees, *Nature Never Did Betray the Heart That Loved Her*, 2000; *Butterfly Dawn*, LSD—Liquid Sound Design, 2003.

9. Zeff, who dubbed MDMA "Adam" (its earliest street name), introduced MDMA as a therapeutic technique to thousands of clients both directly and indirectly (by influencing other therapists). See Myron J. Stolaroff, *The Secret Chief Revealed: Conversations with Leo Zeff, Pioneer in the Underground Psychedelic Therapy Movement* (Santa Cruz, CA: MAPS, 2004). Significantly, Zeff was introduced to MDMA in 1977 by chemist Alexander Shulgin, who had newly synthesized it in 1976 (see Shulgin and Shulgin, *PiHKAL*, 73), exposing his "low-calorie martini" to many friends and researchers. As a disseminator of the recipes, experimental methods, and phenomenological effects of these and other compounds, Shulgin was to Zeff as McKenna was to Sequenci. Common to all these relationships is the absence of a profit motive.

10. Miki Wisdom, personal communication, November 13, 2011.

11. Raja Ram, personal communication, November 16, 2010.

12. Simon Posford interviewed by Alex Grey in the first issue of *CoSM* (*Chapel of Sacred Mirrors*) magazine, 2005: 18.

13. David Jay Brown, "Shpongle and Psychedelics: An Interview with Simon Posford," November 2011, http://mavericksofthemind.com/simon-posford.

14. Raja Ram, personal communication, November 13, 2010.

15. Nik Sequenci, personal communication, February 3, 2012.

16. Posford, interviewed by Alex Grey, 18.

17. Experimental Audio Research, *Mesmerised*, 1994.

18. Spectrum, *Forever Alien*, 1997. Paul Lester, "Temples, Hookworms and the New Generation of Psychedelic Adventurers," *The Guardian*, September 27, 2013, Music section, www.theguardian.com/music/2013/sep/26/temples-hookworms-new-generation-psychedelia.

19. Time Machines, *Time Machines*, 1998. From the release notes at www.discogs.com/Time-Machines-Time-Machines/release/59116. The track exists alongside three others on the EP stated to be inspired by "experimental new psychedelic drugs" that band members had been sent by "international chemists for their investigation and inspiration in their recreational work." Those accompanying tracks are "7-Methoxy-β-Carboline:

(Telepathine)," "2,5-Dimethoxy-4-Ethyl-Amphetamine: (DOET / Hecate)," and "4-Indolol,3-[2-(Dimethylamino)Ethyl], Phosphate Ester: (Psilocybin)."

20. Insectoid, *New Vistas / Shamantec Images,* 1996.

21. Aldous Huxley, *Moksha: Aldous Huxley's Classic Writings on Psychedelics and Visionary Experience,* eds. Michael Horowitz and Cynthia Palmer (Rochester, VT: Park Street Press, 1982), 62.

22. Insectoid, *Groovology of the Metaverse,* 1998.

23. Nick Spacetree, personal communication, July 25, 2014.

24. Later, as Nick Matrix, Space Tree collaborated with Vietnam veteran and Castaneda freak Skai Talon (as 3rd Attention) pursuing an acaciated perspective in the composition of "Realms of the Lesser Light" (*Psychedelic Krembo—Selected Tunes—Part 1,* 1996). Unreleased and newly mastered Space Tree material is scheduled for release as *Space Tree* in 2015.

25. Simon Ghahary, personal communication, May 6, 2015.

26. Space Tribe, "Cicadas on DMT," on *Ultrasonic Heartbeat,* 1996; Insectoid, *Groovology of the Metaverse,* 1998.

27. Brown, "Shpongle and Psychedelics."

28. Robin Graat, personal communication, October 29, 2014.

29. Gaiana, "Deep Blue Skies," on *Blue Sangoma Sounds,* 2014.

30. Psilly, "Boom Festival 2010," 2010, www.fleshprism.com / category / outside -insights (accessed July 13, 2011, page no longer live).

31. In Taylor, Arnson, and Hanna, "DMT and Music."

32. Run DMT, *Union of Opposites,* 2012; NiT GriT, "Dimethyltryptamine," on *Synthetic Heaven,* 2010; NiT GriT, "The Awakening," on *The Awakening,* 2010.

33. Natty Morrison, "NiT GriT—*Synthetic Heaven* EP Review," *The Untz,* July 6, 2010, www.theuntz.com / news / nit-grit-synthetic-heaven-ep-review /.

34. Mimosa, *Hostilis,* 2008.

35. Experimental Sound Project, "Chacruna Dub," on *Dub Dimensions,* 2011.

36. Ben Zen, "Dimethyltryptamine," on *Audio Astronaut,* 2014.

37. Shauna O'Donnell, "Interview with Alistar V of D.M.T.," *Muen Magazine,* January 17, 2011, www.muenmagazine.net / 2011 / 01 / interview-with-alistar -v-of-d-m-t /.

38. Gareth Grundy, "Flying Lotus and the Power of Dreams," *The Guardian,* May 16, 2010, www.theguardian.com / music / 2010 / may / 16 / flying-lotus -cosmogramma-interview.

39. Sturgill Simpson, *Metamodern Sounds in Country Music,* 2014.

40. Akasha Project, www.akashaproject.de / htmlen / practice_molecamb.html.

41. Nik Sequenci, personal communication, February 3, 2012.

Chapter 9

1. T. McKenna, "Mind and Time, Spirit and Matter."

2. In Rupert Sheldrake, Terence McKenna, and Ralph Abraham, *Chaos, Creativity and Cosmic Consciousness* (Rinebeck, NY: Monkfish, 2001; first published 1992), 47.

3. Aldous Huxley, *The Doors of Perception and Heaven and Hell* (New York: Harper Perennial, 2009; first published 1955), 84.

4. Ibid., 83–84.

5. Rob Dickins, "Reimagining the World: A Psychedelic Psychogeography," *Psychedelic Press UK*, September 19, 2013, http://psypressuk.com/2013/09/19/4638.

6. Terence McKenna, "Alien Love," in T. McKenna, *The Archaic Revival*, 1991: 75.

7. Tim Leary and Richard Alpert, "Foreword" to Alan Watts, *The Joyous Cosmology: Adventures in the Chemistry of Consciousness* (New York: Pantheon Books, 1962), ix–xv.

8. Leary, "Programmed Communication."

9. Doyle, *Darwin's Pharmacy;* Diana Reed Slattery, *Xenolinguistics: Psychedelics and Language at the Edge of the Unspeakable* (Berkeley, CA: Evolver Editions, 2015).

10. Leary and Alpert, "Foreword" to Watts, *The Joyous Cosmology*, xiii.

11. In Strassman, *DMT: The Spirit Molecule*, 46.

12. See Graham St John, "Aliens Are Us: Cosmic Liminality, Remixticism and Alienation in Psytrance," *Journal of Religion and Popular Culture* 25, no. 2 (2013): 186–204.

13. Tim Leary, *Exo-Psychology: A Manual on the Use of the Nervous System According to the Instructions of the Manufacturers* (Los Angeles: Starseed/Peace Press, 1977).

14. Terence McKenna, "New Maps of Hyperspace," originally a lecture at the Berkeley Institute for the Study of Consciousness, 1984; first published in *Magical Blend*, no. 22 (April 1989); and reprinted in T. McKenna, *The Archaic Revival*, 102, 101.

15. T. McKenna, "Mind and Time, Spirit and Matter."

16. T. McKenna, "New Maps of Hyperspace," 94.

17. Hyperspace grew complicated as mathematicians and physicists strove to propose theories recognizing the significance of higher dimensions. Thus, while hyperspace originally referred to "the fourth dimension" or fourth spatial dimension, subsequent to Einstein's special theory of relativity wherein time is recognized as the fourth dimension (a theory that came to own the concept of "the fourth dimension"), hyperspace became known as "the fifth dimension." Subsequent to developments in quantum physics,

we have seen the likes of string theory, ten-dimensional superstring theory, bosonic string theory (which requires the space-time continuum to have twenty-six dimensions), and speculation concerning parallel dimensions reignited in M-theory, all of which, as Michio Kaku has conveyed in his popular books *Hyperspace* and *Parallel Worlds,* express the reality that the laws of nature become simpler and more elegant when expressed in higher dimensions.

18. Stephen M. Phillips, "A Short History of the Fourth Dimension," n.d., www.smphillips.8m.com / a-short-history-of-the-fourth-dimension.html.

19. P. D. Ouspensky, *Tertium Organum: The Third Canon of Thought, a Key to the Enigmas of the World,* trans. Nicholas Bessaraboff and Claude Bragdon (Rochester, NY: Manas Press, 1920), 193. First published in Russian in 1912.

20. Ouspensky, *Tertium Organum,* 162.

21. Ibid., 47.

22. Gary Lachman, *The Secret History of Consciousness* (Great Barrington, MA: Lindisfarne Books, 2003), 48.

23. Ibid., 49.

24. Reed Slattery, *Xenolinguistics,* 9.

25. Margaret Wertheim, *The Pearly Gates of Cyberspace: A History of Space from Dante to the Internet* (New York: W. W. Norton, 1999).

26. Turner, *From Counterculture to Cyberculture,* 141–174.

27. John Markoff, *What the Dormouse Said: How the 60s Counterculture Shaped the Personal Computer Industry* (New York: Penguin, 2005).

28. Teafaerie, "Virtuality," *Teatime: Psychedelic Musings from the Center of the Universe,* May 31, 2012, www.erowid.org / columns / teafaerie / 2012 / 05 / 31 / virtuality.

29. Rak Razam interviewed by Magenta Imagination Healer, "Back to the Garden: Awakening to the Shamanic Paradigm," *Reality Sandwich,* 2014, http:// realitysandwich.com / 214776 / rak_razam_garden /.

30. Roy Ascott, *Telematic Embrace: Visionary Theories of Art, Technology, and Consciousness,* ed. Edward A. Shanken (Berkeley: University of California Press, 2003), 365.

31. D. McKenna, *Brotherhood,* 123.

32. ∞Ayes, "Just a Wee Bit More about DMT," 52.

33. Sten Odenwald, "Who Invented Hyperspace? Hyperspace in Science Fiction," *Astronomy Café,* 1995, www.astronomycafe.net / anthol / scifi2.html.

34. Strassman, *DMT: The Spirit Molecule,* 212.

35. Ibid., 215.

36. Ibid.

37. Kripal, *Mutants and Mystics,* 2.

38. Report #66 from a list of reports originally compiled by "Pup" and later among those collected by Peter Meyer, "340 DMT Trip Reports," www.serendipity.li/dmt/340_dmt_trip_reports.htm#66.

39. Gracie and Zarkov, "DMT: How and Why to Get Off," Note 3 in *Notes from Underground: A Gracie and Zarkov Reader*, December 1984 (revised August 1985), www.erowid.org/library/books_online/notes_from_underground.pdf.

40. As vaporizing techniques evolved, convection vaporization (where a stream of hot air passes through and around the product) became preferable to conduction vaporization (where a hot surface conducts heat directly to the product). For aficionados like the Teafaerie, like "spaceships," electronic vaporizers injected with DMT that has been first dissolved in ethanol and then mixed with 40 percent glycerin and 60 percent propylene provide "hyperdrive potency" at 1 g per 2.5 mL. Teafaerie, "How to Build a Better Spaceship," *Teatime: Psychedelic Musings from the Center of the Universe*, May 29, 2014, www.erowid.org/columns/teafaerie/2014/05/.

41. Gracie and Zarkov, "DMT: How and Why to Get Off," 4.

42. Curiously, the section on Gracie and Zarkov did not see print in the original version of *Cyberia* published by Flamingo in 1994, but is available online at www.lycaeum.org/~sputnik/GandZ/GandZ.html. When twenty years after the book's publication I queried Rushkoff about this omission, he was apparently unaware that this entire section had been omitted by Flamingo in the original work as intended. The following passage has therefore been unavailable to readers of *Cyberia*: "The growing numbers of normal-seeming Americans who are enjoying DMT on a regular basis attests, at least, to the fact that even the most extremely disorienting DMT adventures need not hamper one's ability to lead a 'productive' life."

43. Douglas Rushkoff, *Cyberia: Life in the Trenches of Hyperspace* (London: Flamingo, 1994), 15.

44. Ibid., 18.

45. Terence McKenna, "The Psychedelic Society," presented at Esalen Institute, Big Sur, California, 1984 (reproduced in Charles S. Grob, *Hallucinogens: A Reader*, New York: Tarcher/Putnam, 2002, 42).

46. P. D. Ouspensky, *A New Model of the Universe* (New York: Alfred A. Knopf, 1931), 342.

47. T. McKenna, "Tryptamine Hallucinogens and Consciousness," 44.

48. Ibid., 38.

49. T. McKenna, "A Conversation over Saucers."

50. Terence McKenna in Sukie Miller, "Interview: Terence McKenna," *Omni* 15, no. 7 (1993): 69–92.

51. Terence McKenna, "Mind, Molecules and Magic," presented at Esalen Institute, Big Sur, California, June 1984.

52. "Gracie's 'Visible Language' Contact Experience: An Experience with DMT and MDA (ID 1859)," *Erowid.org*, June 15, 2000, www.erowid.org /exp/1859.

53. Binkie2000, "Visiting Hyperspace—Light Journey: An Experience with DMT (ID 85120)," *Erowid.org*, July 19, 2010, www.erowid.org/exp/85120.

54. T. McKenna, in Sheldrake, McKenna, and Abraham, *Chaos, Creativity and Cosmic Consciousness*, 5.

55. Terence McKenna, in Rupert Sheldrake, Terence McKenna, and Ralph Abraham, *The Evolutionary Mind: Conversations on Science, Imagination and Spirit* (Rinebeck, NY: Monkfish, 2005; first published 1998), 48.

56. Ibid., 53.

57. Ralph Abraham, in Sheldrake, McKenna, and Abraham, *The Evolutionary Mind*, 24–26.

58. Turner, *The Essential Psychedelic Guide*, 126.

59. Des Tramacchi, "Vapours and Visions: Religious Dimensions of DMT Use," PhD thesis, School of History, Philosophy, Religion and Classics, University of Queensland, Brisbane, Australia, 26–30; Clifford A. Pickover, *Surfing through Hyperspace: Understanding Higher Universes in Six Easy Lessons* (Oxford, UK: Oxford University Press, 2001), 90.

60. From Strassman (interviewed by Ball), "Voyaging to DMT Space with Dr. Rick Strassman, M.D."

61. Hyperspace Lexicon, https://wiki.dmt-nexus.me/Hyperspace_lexicon.

62. Ken Adams (director), *Imaginatrix: The Terence McKenna Experience*, Magic Carpet Media, 2014.

63. Terence McKenna, *Orfeo: A Dialog between Robert Hunter and Terence McKenna*, 1996, www.levity.com/orfeo.

64. DeKorne, *Psychedelic Shamanism*, 64.

65. T. McKenna in dialogue with Robert Hunter, 1996.

Chapter 10

1. Joseph Campbell, *The Hero with a Thousand Faces*, 3rd ed. (Novato, CA: New World Library, 2008; first published 1949), 30.

2. D. McKenna and J. Riba, "New World Tryptamine Hallucinogens and the Neuroscience of Ayahuasca." While this chapter addresses 5-MeO-DMT (5-methoxy-*N,N*-dimethyltryptamine) as well as DMT (*N,N*-dimethyltryptamine) breakthrough events, these compounds should not be confused. While both are short-acting hallucinogens, 5-MeO-DMT, often abbreviated here as "5-MeO," is a different chemical than DMT, and is active in much

lower doses (e.g., as little as 2 mg). See Erowid Crew, "5-MeO-DMT Is Not 'DMT': Differentiation Is Wise," *Erowid Extracts* 17 (November 2009), 16, www.erowid.org/chemicals/5meo_dmt/5meo_dmt_article1.shtml.

3. Stanislav Grof, *When the Impossible Happens: Adventures in Non-Ordinary Reality* (Boulder, CO: Sounds True, 2006), 255.

4. Ibid., 255–256.

5. See Stanislav Grof, *Realms of the Human Unconscious: Observations from LSD Research* (New York: Viking Press, 1975).

6. Hyperspace Lexicon.

7. Pinchbeck, *Breaking Open the Head*, 242.

8. Clifford A. Pickover, *Sex, Drugs, Einstein, and Elves: Sushi, Psychedelics, Parallel Universes, and the Quest for Transcendence* (Petaluma, CA: Smart Publications, 2005), 91.

9. Hyperspace Lexicon.

10. DeKorne, "Smokable DMT from Plants: Part 1," 2.

11. DeKorne, *Psychedelic Shamanism*, 69.

12. Ibid., 100.

13. Robert A. Masters, *Darkness Shining Wild: An Odyssey to the Heart of Hell and Beyond* (Surrey, BC, Canada: Tehmenos Press, 2005; 2nd ed. 2009), 136.

14. Grant Morrison interviewed in Suicidegirls.com, February 27, 2005, https://suicidegirls.com/girls/anderswolleck/blog/2679166/grant-morrison/.

15. Stephen Gaskin, *Haight Ashbury Flashbacks: Amazing Dope Tales of the Sixties* (Berkeley, CA: Ronin Books, 1980).

16. Hubbard, "REPORT: D.M.T. EXPERIENCE: An Experience with DMT."

17. Peter Meyer, "Apparent Communication with Discarnate Entities Related to DMT," in *Psychedelic Monographs and Essays Volume 6*, ed. Thomas Lyttle (Boynton Beach, FL: P M & E, 1993), 29–69; reproduced on Erowid, www.erowid.org/chemicals/dmt/dmt_writings2.shtml.

18. "Terence McKenna on Art Bell," April 1, 1999, www.jacobsm.com/deoxy/deoxy.org/tmab_4-1-99.htm; T. McKenna, "DMT, Mathematical Dimensions."

19. Shpongle, *Nothing Lasts . . . But Nothing Is Lost*, 2005.

20. Rushkoff, *Cyberia*, 129.

21. Erik Davis, "Return Trip," *Aeon*, November 2, 2012, http://aeon.co/magazine/psychology/erik-davis-psychedelics/.

22. Horgan, *Rational Mysticism*, 191.

23. T. McKenna, "Tryptamine Hallucinogens and Consciousness," 34–47.

24. In Shulgin and Shulgin, *TiHKAL*, 417.

25. ∞Ayes, "Just a Wee Bit More about DMT," 56.

26. Strassman, *DMT: The Spirit Molecule*, 221.

27. Shpongle, "A New Way to Say Hooray," on *Tales of the Inexpressible*, 2001.

The sample was also used on Tim Freke's ambient "Hooray in a New Way (The Elves of Hyper Space)," on *Megatripolis*, 1996.

28. T. McKenna, *True Hallucinations*, 7.

29. There is no evidence to indicate that Grimble Gromble, the gnome in Pink Floyd's "The Gnome" (on *The Piper at the Gates of Dawn*, 1967), was a DMT-inspired visitation, although Barrett was a persistent user of LSD. The original whispered line is "Hooray, another way for gnomes to say . . . Ooh my."

30. Walter E. Evans-Wentz, *The Fairy Faith in Celtic Countries* (New York: Citadel Press, 1990; first published 1911).

31. Terence McKenna, "Elven Ramblings," (from presentation, n.d.), www.youtube.com/watch?v=wUhXnQBy7RY.

32. Ibid.

33. Ibid.

34. T. McKenna, "Mind and Time, Spirit and Matter."

35. Sacha Defesche, "The 2012 Phenomenon: A Historical and Typological Approach to a Modern Apocalyptic Mythology," MA thesis, University of Amsterdam, 2007; Norman Cohn, *The Pursuit of the Millennium: Revolutionary Millenarians and Mystical Anarchists of the Middle Ages* (Oxford, UK: Oxford University Press, 1957).

36. T. McKenna, "Alchemical Youth at the Edge of the World."

37. T. McKenna, in Sheldrake, McKenna, and Abraham, *The Evolutionary Mind*, 62.

38. Terence appeared to grow cynical about the date, and those who ardently attached themselves to it (Dennis dismissed the idea). See Richard Metzger, "Timewave Zero: Did Terence McKenna *Really* Believe in All That 2012 Prophecy Stuff?" *Dangerous Minds*, June 6, 2012. http://dangerousminds.net/comments/timewave_zero_did_terence_mckenna_really_believe_in_all_that_2012_prophecy.

39. Turner drowned in a few inches of water in a bathtub (likely high on ketamine) on New Year's Eve 1996, his final meeting with the "water spirit." In *The Essential Psychedelic Guide*, Turner documents his gravitation toward rivers, waterfalls, beaches, and other sites of flowing water as optimum locations for journeying. DMT was regarded as the chief "water spirit plant."

40. D. M. Turner, interviewed by Elizabeth Gips at *Tripzine*, www.tripzine.com/listing.php?id=dmturnergips.

41. Turner, *The Essential Psychedelic Guide*, 122.

42. Turner, interviewed by Gips.

43. D. M. Turner, "Entity Contacts: Exploring Hyperspace," *The Entheogen Review*, Winter Solstice 1995: 4–7.

44. Ibid.

45. Turner, *The Essential Psychedelic Guide*, 126.

46. Ibid., 127, 128, 141.

47. Ibid., 74.

48. Turner, interviewed by Gips.

49. Turner, *The Essential Psychedelic Guide*, 123.

50. Thomas Lyttle, "Toad Licking Blues," in *You Are Being Lied To*, ed. Russ Kick (New York: Disinformation Co., 2001), 241–244.

51. Michael Valentine Smith, *Psychedelic Chemistry*, 4th ed., corrected and expanded (San Francisco: Rip Off Press, 1976); see Ott, *Pharmacotheon*, 182.

52. Wade Davis and Andrew T. Weil, "Identity of a New World Psychoactive Toad," *Ancient Mesoamerica* 3 (1992): 51–59.

53. Ott, *Pharmacotheon*, 182.

54. Oroc, *Tryptamine Palace*, 178, 66, 229, 5.

55. Ibid., 114, 112, 113, 114.

56. Ibid., 118.

57. Erik Davis, "Remixing the Matrix: An Interview with Paul D. Miller, a.k.a. DJ Spooky," *Trip Magazine*, Spring 2003.

58. www.dmtsite.com.

59. Oroc, *Tryptamine Palace*, 169, 177.

60. Ibid., 178, 177.

61. Ibid., 197.

62. Turner, *The Essential Psychedelic Guide*, 131.

63. Oroc, *Tryptamine Palace*, 199.

64. Masters, *Darkness Shining Wild*, 14, 17.

65. Ibid., 2, 18.

66. Ibid., 97.

67. Ibid., 19, 47, 153, 22.

68. Oroc, *Tryptamine Palace*, 174, 194.

69. Masters, *Darkness Shining Wild*, 74.

70. Huxley, *Heaven and Hell*, 135.

71. Masters, *Darkness Shining Wild*, 66, 8.

72. Ibid., 36.

73. Ibid., 194, 110, 113, 110.

74. Ibid., 60.

75. Rak Razam and Tim Parish (directors), *Aya: Awakenings*, Icaro Foundation, 2013.

76. For the unedited video of the experiment at La Rosacita, as featured on *Aya: Awakenings*, see https://vimeo.com/83370532.

77. Rak Razam, *Aya Awakenings: A Shamanic Odyssey* (Berkeley, CA: North

Atlantic Books, 2013). The book was previously published as *Aya: A Shamanic Odyssey* (Icaro Publishing, 2009).

78. Ibid., 115, 116.

79. Ibid., 113.

80. Leary, "The Experiential Typewriter," 82.

81. In the book, Juan Acosta explains to Razam that his data set was unusable. "You went in too deep, too high and strong a frequency. All that convulsing won't be good for a clear reading." Razam, *Aya: A Shamanic Odyssey*, 123.

82. Ibid., 117.

83. In 2015, Acosta and Razam formed Terra Incognita, an NGO to further explore EEG tryptamine pathways, as well as language, and to bring back maps of hyperspace: www.terra-incognita-project.org.

84. Masters, *Darkness Shining Wild*, 159.

85. Martin Ball, "Energy, Ego, and Entheogens: The Reality of Human Liberation from Illusion," *Reality Sandwich*, October 19, 2010, www.realitysandwich .com/energy_ego_and_entheogens.

86. Martin Ball, *Being Human: An Entheological Guide to God, Evolution and the Fractal Energetic Nature of Reality* (Ashland, OR: Kyandara, 2009).

87. Ferrer, *Revisioning Transpersonal Psychology*, 23.

88. Ball, "Energy, Ego, and Entheogens."

89. Martin Ball, "Terence on DMT: An Entheological Analysis of McKenna's Experiences in the Tryptamine Mirror of the Self," *Reality Sandwich*, 2010, http://realitysandwich.com/51650/terence_dmt/.

90. Ibid.

91. While these articles attracted heavy criticism on the original *Reality Sandwich* comments forum, this response did not survive a website upgrade. The articles were subsequently reprinted in Martin Ball, *The Entheological Paradigm: Essays on the DMT and 5-MeO-DMT Experience . . . And the Meaning of It All* (Ashland, OR: Kyandara, 2011). Ball failed to respond to his many critics on the *Reality Sandwich* forum or in his book.

92. Ralph Metzner, *The Toad and the Jaguar: A Field Report of Underground Research on a Visionary Medicine: Bufo Alvarius and 5-methoxy-dimethyltryptamine* (Berkeley, CA: Green Earth Foundation and Regent Press, 2013), 34–35.

93. Ibid., 39.

94. Ibid., 66, 38, 68–69.

95. Ibid., 43, 57, 50.

96. Ibid., 34, 60.

97. Art Van D'lay, in Enoon et al., *Open Hyperspace Traveler*.

98. Fadiman, *The Psychedelic Explorer's Guide*.

99. James Fadiman, personal communication, March 3, 2015.

100. Cynthia Palmer and Michael Horowitz, *Sisters of the Extreme: Women Writing on the Drug Experience* (Rochester, VT: Park Street Press, 2000), 280–282.

101. Ralph Metzner, *The Life Cycle of the Human Soul: Incarnation; Conception; Birth; Death; Hereafter; Reincarnation* (Berkeley, CA: Regent Press, 2011), 27.

102. Reed Slattery, *Xenolinguistics*, 119.

103. Watson, "DMT, or, Spider Woman Comes to Town."

Chapter 11

1. Huxley, *The Doors of Perception and Heaven and Hell*, 134–136.

2. From Alex Grey, interviewed by Cameron Steel on *Contact Talk Radio*, 2002.

3. Alex Grey, *Transfigurations* (Rochester, VT: Inner Traditions, 2001), 150.

4. Erik Davis, "The New Eye: Visionary Art and Tradition," *COSM: Journal of Visionary Culture* IV (2006): 59–62.

5. Terence McKenna, "Alien Love," presented at Shared Visions, Berkeley, California, 1983; originally published in *Magical Blend* no. 17 (1987); in T. McKenna, *The Archaic Revival*, 78.

6. Arnold van Gennep, *The Rites of Passage* (London: Routledge & Kegan Paul, 1960; first published 1909).

7. Hanegraaff, "Ayahuasca Groups and Networks in the Netherlands," 88.

8. Hanegraaff, "Entheogenic Esotericism," 392–409.

9. Tramacchi, "Vapours and Visions," 29.

10. Alex K. Gearin, "Good Mother Nature: Ayahuasca Neoshamanism as Cultural Critique in Australia," in *The World Ayahuasca Diaspora: Reinventions and Controversies*, eds. Beatriz Labate, Clancy Cavnar, and Alex Gearin (Farnham, UK: Ashgate, 2016, forthcoming).

11. Robert Hunter, *Orfeo: A Dialog between Robert Hunter and Terence McKenna*, 1996, www.levity.com/orfeo.

12. Ott, *Pharmacotheon*, 16.

13. Meyer, "Apparent Communication with Discarnate Entities Related to DMT."

14. David Luke, "Discarnate Entities and Dimethyltryptamine (DMT): Psychopharmacology, Phenomenology and Ontology," *Journal of the Society for Psychical Research* 75, no. 1 (2011): 33.

15. Benny Shanon, *Antipodes of the Mind: Charting the Phenomenology of the Ayahuasca Experience* (Oxford, UK: Oxford University Press, 2002), 293.

16. ∞Ayes, "Just a Wee Bit More about DMT," 54.

17. Ibid.

18. Ibid., 55.

19. Ibid., 52.

20. David Luke, "Disembodied Eyes Revisited. An Investigation into the

Ontology of Entheogenic Entity Encounters," *The Entheogen Review* 17, no. 1 (2008): 2, 7.

21. From Gwyllm Llwydd's unpublished short story "Gate Keepers," 2015.

22. nanobrain, personal communication, April 1, 2012.

23. Martin Stebbing and Toke Kim Klinke, *DMTrmx*, 2013, https://vimeo.com/37633048.

24. T. McKenna, "Rap Dancing into the 3rd Millennium."

25. SFos, "The Elven Antics Annex: An Experience with DMT (ID 1841)," *Erowid.org*, June 14, 2000, www.erowid.org/exp/1841.

26. Lawrence Caruana, *A Manifesto of Visionary Art* (Paris: Recluse, 2001).

27. www.galactivation.com.

28. Carey Thompson, "DeMaTerialized," *Visionary Review*, Fall 2007, http://visionaryrevue.com/webtext4/thompson.html.

29. For *Singularity*, see www.galactivation.com/gallery/paintings/.

30. Naasko Wripple, "The Liminal Village," in *Boom Book* (Lisbon, Portugal: Good Mood Productions, 2007), 77.

31. From Turner's seminal paper, originally published in 1957, "Betwixt and Between: The Liminal Period in *Rites de Passage*," in Victor Turner, *The Forest of Symbols: Aspects of Ndembu Ritual* (Ithaca, NY: Cornell University Press, 1967), 93–111.

32. Jane Harrison, *Prolegomena to the Study of Greek Religion* (Charleston, SC: Nabu Press, 2010; first published 1903).

33. Binkie2000, "Visiting Hyperspace."

34. universal shaman, "Mother Spirit Awaits: An Experience with DMT (ID 30919)," *Erowid.org*, September 28, 2004, www.erowid.org/exp/30919.

35. ∞Ayes, "Moving into the Sacred World of DMT," 33.

36. Lyle. "The Beautiful Chaos: An Experience with DMT & Methoxetamine (ID 96444)". Erowid.org. Oct 10, 2012. erowid.org/exp/96444.

37. Report #66 from Meyer's collection ("340 DMT Trip Reports"), www.serendipity.li/dmt/340_dmt_trip_reports.htm#66.

38. Gehr, "Omega Man: A Profile of Terence McKenna."

39. Hancock, *Supernatural*, 517–518.

40. Binkie2000, "Visiting Hyperspace."

41. SFos, "The Elven Antics Annex."

42. Brown, "Shpongle and Psychedelics."

43. Turner, "Betwixt and Between," 106.

44. Graham Hancock, *Entangled: The Eater of Souls* (London: Arrow, 2011), 117.

45. Benton Rooks, "Beyond the Machine Elves: On DMT Culture, Visionary Plants and Entheodelic Storytelling," *Reality Sandwich*, 2014, http://

realitysandwich.com/216190/beyond-the-machine-elves-on-dmt-culture
-visionary-plants-and-entheodelic-storytelling.

46. Mister Strange, *Psychonautica: DMT: A Graphic Novel*, 2012, www
.misterstrange.com.

47. Robert Byron, *The Road to Oxiana* (London: Pimlico, 2004; first published
1937), 178.

48. T. McKenna, "Rap Dancing into the 3rd Millennium."

49. Hyperspace Lexicon.

50. Turner, *The Essential Psychedelic Guide*, 127.

51. Oroc, *The Tryptamine Palace*, 197.

52. Pinchbeck, *Breaking Open the Head*, 240.

53. Hyperspace Fool, "Beyond: A Trip Report," *The Nexian*, no. 1 (2014): 9.

54. Joe Rogan, sampled in Extrinsic, "Psychedelic Liberation," on *The LSD
Connection*, 2011.

55. This YouTube video shows *Forward Escape* created using time-lapse: www
.youtube.com/watch?v=8cDudlTKxbY.

56. See Cyb's gallery at the DMT-Nexus: www.dmt-nexus.me/art/art_cyb
.html; Cyb, personal communication, February 23, 2015.

57. Beau Deeley, personal communication, March 2 and 6, 2015.

58. Oscar Janiger in Brown and Novick, *Mavericks of the Mind*, 250.

59. Graham St John, "Liminal Being: Electronic Dance Music Cultures, Ritualization and the Case of Psytrance," in *The Sage Handbook of Popular Music*,
eds. Andy Bennett and Steve Waksman (London: Sage, 2015), 243–260.

60. Rooks, "Beyond the Machine Elves."

61. Palmer, *Articulations*, 39–40.

62. Stephen Lyng, "Edgework: A Social Psychological Analysis of Voluntary
Risk Taking," *American Journal of Sociology* 95, no. 4 (1990): 876–921.

63. David Anirman, *Sky Cloud Mountain* (Bloomington, IN: iUniverse, 1979),
15.

64. Ibid.

65. Masters, *Darkness Shining Wild*, 4.

66. Ibid., 124.

67. Ibid., 87.

68. Ibid., 95, 89.

69. The Metamorphic Ritual Theatre Company's Labyrinth, www.crossroads
.wild.net.au/lab.htm.

70. Orryelle Defenestrate-Bascule, personal communication, February 27, 2015.

71. Orryelle Defenestrate-Bascule, *Distillatio* (London: Fulgur, 2015).

72. Orryelle Defenestrate-Bascule, personal communication, February 27, 2015.

73. Ibid.

74. Jeffrey Kripal, *Authors of the Impossible: The Paranormal and the Sacred* (Chicago: University of Chicago Press, 2010), 25.

75. Leary, "Programmed Communication," 86.

Chapter 12

1. T. McKenna, *True Hallucinations*, 142.

2. T. McKenna, "Rap Dancing into the 3rd Millennium."

3. DeKorne, *Psychedelic Shamanism*, 100.

4. Adam Dodd, "The Daemonic Insect: *Mantis religiosa*," in *Animals as Religious Subjects: Transdisciplinary Perspectives*, eds. David Clough, Celia Deane-Drummond, and Becky Artinian-Kaiser (London: Bloomsbury T&T Clark, 2013), 103–124.

5. Strassman, *DMT: The Spirit Molecule*, 263.

6. In Gracie and Zarkov, "DMT: How and Why to Get Off."

7. Karl, in Strassman, *DMT: The Spirit Molecule*, 188.

8. C. G., "The People Behind the Curtain: An Experience with DMT (ID 1839)," *Erowid.org*, June 14, 2000, www.erowid.org/exp/1839.

9. SFos, "The Elven Antics Annex."

10. Luke, "Discarnate Entities and Dimethyltryptamine," 36; David Luke, "So Long as You've Got Your Elf: Death, DMT and Discarnate Entities," in *Daimonic Imagination: Uncanny Intelligence*, eds. Angela Voss and William Rowlandson (Cambridge, UK: Cambridge Scholars Publishing, 2013), 282–291.

11. Tramacchi, "Vapours and Visions," 95.

12. Pinchbeck, *Breaking Open the Head*, 215.

13. Anonymous Canada, "DMT Entities," *The Entheogen Review*, Summer Solstice 1995, 6.

14. Strassman, *DMT: The Spirit Molecule*, 185.

15. Jon Hanna, "Aliens, Insectoids, and Elves! Oh, My!" *Erowid.org*, 2012, www.erowid.org/chemicals/dmt/dmt_article3.shtml.

16. Shanon, *Antipodes of the Mind*.

17. Luke, "Discarnate Entities and Dimethyltryptamine," 35.

18. Pickover, *Sex, Drugs, Einstein, and Elves*, 93.

19. Hyperspace Lexicon.

20. NGC_2264's classification, at Hyperspace Lexicon.

21. Tramacchi, "Vapours and Visions," 127.

22. Ibid., 108.

23. Psychedaniellia, "Hierarchies of Hyperspace A Collection: An Experience with DMT, 4-HO-MiPT, 4-AcO-DiPT, LSD, DPT, Ketamine, Methoxetamine, 5-MeO-DMT, Nitrous Oxide and MDMA (ID 101485)," *Erowid.org*, May 16, 2014, www.erowid.org/exp/101485.

24. Ibid.

25. Ibid.

26. Rick Strassman, "The Varieties of the DMT Experience," in Strassman, Wojtowicz, Luna, and Frecska, *Inner Paths to Outer Space*, 6.

27. Chris, in *Strassman, DMT: The Spirit Molecule*, 192.

28. Ibid., 198.

29. Report #229 from Meyer's list at www.serendipity.li/dmt/340_dmt_trip _reports.htm#229.

30. John Mack, *Abduction: Human Encounters with Aliens* (New York: Simon & Schuster, 1994); Masters, *Darkness Shining Wild*, 73.

31. Hancock, *Supernatural*.

32. David J. Lewis-Williams, *A Cosmos in Stone: Interpreting Religion and Society through Rock Art* (Walnut Creek, CA: Altamira Press, 2002).

33. See Stanislav Grof, *Beyond the Brain: Birth, Death, and Transcendence in Psychotherapy* (New York: State University of New York Press, 1986), 22.

34. Jacques Vallée, *Passport to Magonia: From Folklore to Flying Saucers* (Chicago: Henry Regnery, 1969).

35. Hancock, *Supernatural*, 483.

36. Luke, "Discarnate Entities and Dimethyltryptamine," 38.

37. David Luke, "Rock Art or Rorschach: Is There More to Entoptics Than Meets the Eye?" *Time and Mind: The Journal of Archaeology, Consciousness and Culture* 3, no. 1 (2010): 9–28; Charles Tart, "States of Consciousness and State-Specific Sciences," *Science* 176 (1972): 1203–1210.

38. Peter Meyer, "Physicalism: A False View of the World," July 2008, www .serendipity.li/dmt/physicalism.htm.

39. Peter Meyer, "Physicalism: A Pernicious World View," 2012, www .serendipity.li/dmt/physicalism_2.htm.

40. Peter Meyer, "340 DMT Trip Reports," www.serendipity.li/dmt/340_dmt _trip_reports.htm.

41. Meyer, "Apparent Communication with Discarnate Entities Related to DMT."

42. Meyer, "Physicalism: A False View of the World."

43. Peter Meyer, "A Reply to Martin Ball's 'Terence on DMT,'" 2010, www .serendipity.li/dmt/reply_to_ball.htm.

44. James L. Kent, *Psychedelic Information Theory: Shamanism in the Age of Reason* (Seattle: PIT Press, 2010), 190.

45. James L. Kent, "The Case against DMT Elves," *Tripzine*, May 4, 2004, http:// tripzine.com/listing.php?id=dmt_pickover; Pickover, *Sex, Drugs, Einstein, and Elves*, 229.

46. Kent, *Psychedelic Information Theory*, 15, 23.

47. Ibid., 25–26.

48. Julian Palmer, "Trying to Explain Away DMT: An Analysis of 'The Case against DMT Elves,'" n.d., www.julianpalmerism.com/jameskent.html.

49. Scott A. McGreal, "DMT, Aliens, and Reality—Part 2," *Psychology Today*, October 4, 2012, www.psychologytoday.com/blog/unique-everybody -else/201210/dmt-aliens-and-reality-part-2.

50. David Luke, personal communication, October 5, 2014.

51. Marko A. Rodriguez, "A Methodology for Studying Various Interpretations of the N,N-dimethyltryptamine-Induced Alternate Reality," *Journal of Scientific Exploration* 21, no. 1 (2007): 67–84; Luke, "Discarnate Entities and Dimethyltryptamine," 37.

52. Andrew R. Gallimore, "Building Alien Worlds—The Neuropsychological and Evolutionary Implications of the Astonishing Psychoactive Effects of N,N-Dimethyltryptamine (DMT)," *Journal of Scientific Exploration* 27, no. 3 (2013), 455–503.

53. Cott and Rock, "Phenomenology of N,N-Dimethyltryptamine Use."

54. Gallimore, "Building Alien Worlds," 455.

55. Ibid., 493, 498.

56. Ibid., 483, 459.

57. Hancock, *Supernatural*, 499.

58. Ibid., 561.

59. Jeremy Narby, *The Cosmic Serpent: DNA and the Origins of Knowledge* (New York: Tarcher/Putnam, 1998); Francis Crick, *Life Itself: Its Origin and Nature* (New York: Touchstone, Simon & Schuster, 1982).

60. Strassman, Wojtowicz, Luna, and Frecska, *Inner Paths to Outer Space*.

61. Ede Frecska, "Close Encounters of the Ancient Kind and Spontaneous DMT Release," in Strassman, Wojtowicz, Luna, and Frecska, *Inner Paths to Outer Space*, 249.

62. Ibid., 249, 252.

63. Strassman, *DMT and the Soul of Prophecy*.

64. From the book of Ezekiel, in Strassman, *DMT and the Soul of Prophecy*, 1.

65. Ibid., 258.

66. Strassman, "Sitting for Sessions."

67. Strassman, *DMT and the Soul of Prophecy*, 16, 4.

68. Ibid., 259, 293.

69. Ibid., 286.

70. Rick Strassman, personal communication, December 2, 2014.

71. Strassman (interviewed by Ball), "Voyaging to DMT Space with Dr. Rick Strassman, M.D."

72. Asprem, "Intermediary Beings."

73. Hanegraaff, *New Age Religion and Western Culture*, 23, note 2.

74. While comparative phenomenological studies are lacking, for a comprehensive survey of studies of psychoactive substances and paranormal phenomena, see Luke, "Psychoactive Substances and Paranormal Phenomena."

75. Strassman, *DMT and the Soul of Prophecy*, 290.

76. Ibid., 295.

77. Strassman, *DMT: The Spirit Molecule*, 267.

78. Tramacchi, "Vapours and Visions," 93.

79. Ibid., 73.

80. Strassman, *DMT and the Soul of Prophecy*, 14.

81. Sunyata, "Speaking in Tounges: An Experience with DMT (ID 39857)," *Erowid.org*, January 28, 2005, www.erowid.org/exp/39857.

82. Strassman, *DMT: The Spirit Molecule*, 199.

83. Dmitri, in Strassman, *DMT: The Spirit Molecule*, 76.

84. Ibid.

85. Jeremiah, in Strassman, *DMT: The Spirit Molecule*, 193.

86. Stanislav Grof, *HR GIGER and the Zeitgeist of the Twentieth Century* (Solothurn, Switzerland: Nachtschatten Verlag AG, 2014).

87. Masters, *Darkness Shining Wild*, 72.

88. Christina Grof and Stanislav Grof, *The Stormy Search for the Self: A Guide to Personal Growth through Transformative Crisis* (Los Angeles: Tarcher, 1990), 149.

89. Masters, *Darkness Shining Wild*, 73.

90. Strassman, *DMT: The Spirit Molecule*, 75.

91. Sean, in Strassman, *DMT: The Spirit Molecule*, 244.

92. Rex, in Strassman, *DMT: The Spirit Molecule*, 208.

93. Terence McKenna, *Orfeo: A Dialog between Robert Hunter and Terence McKenna*.

94. T. McKenna, "Rap Dancing into the 3rd Millennium."

95. ∞Ayes, "Just a Wee Bit More about DMT," 56.

96. Tramacchi, "Vapours and Visions," 155–156.

Chapter 13

1. Aldous Huxley, "Drugs That Shape Men's Minds," *Saturday Evening Post*, October 18, 1958.

2. Rick Strassman, personal communication, December 2, 2014.

3. Reed Slattery, *Xenolinguistics*, 10.

REFERENCES

∞Ayes. "Moving into the Sacred World of DMT." *The Entheogen Review* 10, no. 1 (2001): 32–39.

∞Ayes. "Just a Wee Bit More about DMT." *The Entheogen Review* 10, no. 2 (2001): 51–56.

Aguirre, Abby. "The New Power Trip: Inside the World of Ayahuasca." *Marie Claire*, February 18, 2014. www.marieclaire.com/world-reports/ayahuasca -new-power-trip.

Agurell, Stig, Bo Holmstedt, and Jan-Erik Lindgren. "Alkaloid Content of *Banisteriopsis rusbyana*." *American Journal of Pharmacy* 140, no. 5 (1968): 148–151.

Anirman, David. *Sky Cloud Mountain*. Bloomington, IN: iUniverse, 1979.

Anonymous Canada. "DMT Entities." *The Entheogen Review*, Summer Solstice 1995: 6.

Appel, Daniel. "Can the Roots of Spiritual Experience Be Found in Brain Chemistry?" October 30, 2013. https://ultraculture.org/blog/2013/10/30/spiritual -experience-brain-chemistry.

Asprem, Egil. "Intermediary Beings." In *The Occult World*, edited by Christopher Partridge. New York: Routledge, 2015.

Ascott, Roy. *Telematic Embrace: Visionary Theories of Art, Technology, and Consciousness*. Edited by Edward A. Shanken. Berkeley: University of California Press, 2003.

Axelrod, Julius. "Enzymatic Formation of Psychotomimetic Metabolites from Normally Occurring Compounds." *Science* 134, no. 3475 (1961): 343.

Babbs, Ken, and Paul Perry. *On the Bus: The Complete Guide to the Legendary Trip of Ken Kesey and the Merry Pranksters and the Birth of the Counterculture*. New York: Thunder's Mouth Press, 1990.

Bageant, Joe. "Ghosts of Tim Leary and Hunter Thompson." 2007. Accessed May 2, 2013. www.joebageant.com/joe/2007/05/ghosts_of_tim_l.html.

Bakst, Joel David. *The Jerusalem Stone of Consciousness: DMT, Kabbalah and the Pineal Gland*. Manitou Springs, CO: City of Luz, 2013.

Ball, Martin W. "Voyaging to DMT Space with Dr. Rick Strassman, M.D." *Reality Sandwich*, July 18, 2008. http://realitysandwich.com/5697/voyaging_dmt _space_with_dr_rick_strassman_md.

Ball, Martin. *Being Human: An Entheological Guide to God, Evolution and the Fractal Energetic Nature of Reality*. Ashland, OR: Kyandara, 2009.

Ball, Martin. "Terence on DMT: An Entheological Analysis of McKenna's Experiences in the Tryptamine Mirror of the Self." *Reality Sandwich,* 2010. http://realitysandwich.com/51650/terence_dmt/.

Ball, Martin. "Energy, Ego, and Entheogens: The Reality of Human Liberation from Illusion." *Reality Sandwich,* October 19, 2010. www.realitysandwich.com/energy_ego_and_entheogens.

Ball, Martin. *The Entheological Paradigm: Essays on the DMT and 5-MeO-DMT Experience . . . And the Meaning of It All.* Ashland, OR: Kyandara, 2011.

Barclay, John. "Interviews with People Who Just Smoked DMT," *VICE* magazine online, March 21, 2012. www.vice.com/read/interviews-with-people-who-just-smoked-dmt.

Barker, Steven A., Jimo Borjigin, Izabela Lomnicka, and Rick Strassman. "LC/MS/MS Analysis of the Endogenous Dimethyltryptamine Hallucinogens, Their Precursors, and Major Metabolites in Rat Pineal Gland Microdialysate." *Biomedical Chromatography* 27, no. 12 (2013): 1690–1700.

Barker, Steven A., Ethan H. McIlhenny, and Rick Strassman. "A Critical Review of Reports of Endogenous Psychedelic N,N-Dimethyltryptamines in Humans, 1955–2010." *Drug Test Analysis* 4 (2012): 617–635.

Barker, Steven A., John A. Monti, and Samuel T. Christian. "N, N-Dimethyltryptamine: An Endogenous Hallucinogen." *International Review of Neurobiology* 22 (1981): 83–110.

Beyer, Stephan V. *Singing to the Plants: A Guide to Mestizo Shamanism in the Upper Amazon.* Albuquerque: University of New Mexico Press, 2009.

Bigwood, Jeremy, and Jonathan Ott. "DMT: The Fifteen Minute Trip." *Head* 2, no. 4 (1977): 56–69.

Binkie2000. "Visiting Hyperspace—Light Journey: An Experience with DMT (ID 85120)." *Erowid.org.* July 19, 2010. www.erowid.org/exp/85120.

Blavatsky, Helena P. *The Secret Doctrine: The Synthesis of Science, Religion and Philosophy. Vol. II (Anthropogenesis).* London: Theosophical Publishing Company, 1888.

Blavatsky, Helena P. "Dialogue on the Mysteries of the After Life [Part 2]." *Lucifer* 3 (January 15, 1889): 407–417.

Brand, Russell. *BrandX* S01E13. FX Networks. November 30, 2012. http://vimeo.com/54643690#.

Brown, David Jay. "Shpongle and Psychedelics: An Interview with Simon Posford." November 2011. http://mavericksofthemind.com/simon-posford.

Brown, David Jay, and Rebecca McClen Novick. *Mavericks of the Mind.* Santa Cruz, CA: MAPS, 2010. First published 1993.

Brown, R. E. *The Psychedelic Guide to Preparation of the Eucharist.* Austin, TX: Linga Sharira Incense Co., 1968.

Burroughs, William S. *Junkie: Confessions of an Unredeemed Drug Addict.* New York: Ace Books, 1953.

Burroughs, William S. "Letter from a Master Addict to Dangerous Drugs." *British Journal of Addiction to Alcohol and Other Drugs* 53, no. 2 (August 3, 1957): 119–132. www.cs.cmu.edu/afs/cs.cmu.edu/user/ehn/Web/release /BurroughsLetter.html.

Burroughs, William S. Letter to Leary. Cargo U.S. Consulate Tangier, Morocco, May 6, 1961. http://deoxy.org/h_wbdmt.htm.

Burroughs, William S. "Comments on the Night before Thinking." *Evergreen Review,* September–October 1961.

Burroughs, William S. "Points of Distinction between Sedative and Consciousness-Expanding Drugs." In *LSD: The Consciousness-Expanding Drug,* edited by David Solomon. New York: G. P. Putnam's Sons, Berkley Medallion, 1964.

Burroughs, William S. *Queer.* New York: Penguin, 1985.

Burroughs, William S. *The Letters of William S. Burroughs, 1945–1959.* Edited by Oliver Harris. New York: Penguin, 1994.

Burroughs, William S. *Naked Lunch: The Restored Text.* London: Fourth Estate, 2010. First published 1959.

Burroughs, William S. *Rub Out the Words: The Letters of William S. Burroughs 1959–1974.* Edited with an Introduction by Bill Morgan. New York: Penguin, 2012.

Burroughs, William S. *Nova Express: The Restored Text.* New York: Grove Press, 2013. First published 1964.

Burroughs, William S., and Allen Ginsberg. *The Yagé Letters: Redux.* Edited with an Introduction by Oliver Harris. San Francisco: City Lights Books, 2006. First published 1963.

Byron, Robert. *The Road to Oxiana.* London: Pimlico, 2004. First published 1937.

Cakic, Vince, Jacob Potkonyak, and Alex Marshall. "Dimethyltryptamine (DMT): Subjective Effects and Patterns of Use among Australian Recreational Users." *Drug and Alcohol Dependence* 111, nos. 1–2 (2010): 30–37.

Callaway, J. C. "A Proposed Mechanism for the Visions of Dream Sleep." *Medical Hypotheses* 26, no. 2 (1988): 119–124.

Campbell, Colin. "The Cult, the Cultic Milieu and Secularization." In *The Cultic Milieu: Oppositional Subcultures in an Age of Globalization,* edited by Jeffrey Kaplan and Heléne Lööw, 12–25. Walnut Creek, CA: AltaMira Press, 2002. First published 1972.

Campbell, Joseph. *The Hero with a Thousand Faces.* 3rd ed. Novato, CA: New World Library, 2008. First published 1949.

Caruana, Lawrence. *A Manifesto of Visionary Art.* Paris: Recluse, 2001.

C. G. "The People Behind the Curtain: An Experience with DMT (ID 1839)." *Erowid.org.* June 14, 2000. www.erowid.org/exp/1839.

chocobeastie. "Changa: A Smoking Blend Containing Ayahuasca and Other Herbs." Posted to DMT-Nexus February 9, 2011. Accessed February 3, 2012. www.dmt-nexus.me/forum/default.aspx?g=posts&t=19331.

C. M. "DMT Entities." *The Entheogen Review* 2, no. 4 (1993): 3–4.

Cohen, Arianne. "Walking on Sunshine." *Elle*, November 2013: 302–305.

Cohn, Norman. *The Pursuit of the Millennium: Revolutionary Millenarians and Mystical Anarchists of the Middle Ages.* Oxford, UK: Oxford University Press, 1957.

Cosmic Oneness. "Alex Grey's Sacred Art." *Psychedelic Adventure.net*, 2008. Accessed June 3, 2010. www.psychedelicadventure.net/2008/09/alex-greys -sacred-art.html.

Cott, Christopher, and Adam Rock. "Phenomenology of N,N-Dimethyltryptamine Use: A Thematic Analysis." *Journal of Scientific Exploration* 22, no. 3 (2008): 359–370.

Cozzi, N. V., T. A. Mavlyutov, M. A. Thompson, and A. E. Ruoho. "Indolethylamine N-methyltransferase Expression in Primate Nervous Tissue." *Society for Neuroscience Abstracts*, 37, no. 840.19 (2011).

Crick, Francis. *Life Itself: Its Origin and Nature.* New York: Touchstone, Simon & Schuster, 1982.

Crowley, Morris. "Agrostis: Tryptamines in the Crucible of Civilization." *The Nexian*, April 4, 2014. http://the-nexian.me/home/knowledge/86-agrostis-tryptamines-in-the -crucible-of-civilization.

Crowley, Morris. "Citrus Growers Manufacture Huge Amounts of DMT." *The Nexian*, June 13, 2014. http://the-nexian.me/home/knowledge/112-citrus -growers-manufacture-huge-amounts-of-dmt.

Dass, Ram, and Ralph Metzner (with Gary Bravo). *Birth of a Psychedelic Culture: Conversations about Leary, the Harvard Experiments, Millbrook and the Sixties.* Santa Fe, NM: Synergetic Press, 2010.

Davis, Erik. "Remixing the Matrix: An Interview with Paul D. Miller, a.k.a. DJ Spooky." *Trip Magazine*, Spring 2003.

Davis, Erik. "The New Eye: Visionary Art and Tradition," *COSM: Journal of Visionary Culture* IV (2006): 59–62.

Davis, Erik. "Boom Festival 2008." *Dose Nation*, 2008. www.dosenation.com /listing.php?id=5045.

Davis, Erik. "Return Trip." *Aeon*, November 2, 2012. http://aeon.co/magazine /psychology/erik-davis-psychedelics/.

Davis, Floyd. "Don't Mention the Plants." n.d. Accessed November 4, 2014. www.rainbowdreaming.org/the_plants.html.

Davis, Floyd, Skeeta Power, Mango Frangipanni, and Nina Rae. *Illuminated Adventures.* Mullumbimby, NSW, Australia: Psychedelia Australis, 1998.

Davis, Wade. *One River: Explorations and Discoveries in the Amazon Rainforest.* New York: Simon & Schuster, 1996.

Davis, Wade, and Andrew T. Weil. "Identity of a New World Psychoactive Toad." *Ancient Mesoamerica* 3 (1992): 51–59.

De Conceicao, Peter. "The DMT Molecule: A Tryst with Spirits, Elves and Aliens." *Examiner.com,* August 6, 2009. https://groups.google.com/forum/#!topic/sixties-l/iaFIdup6sHs.

Defenestrate-Bascule, Orryelle. *Distillatio.* London: Fulgur, 2015.

Defesche, Sacha. "The 2012 Phenomenon: A Historical and Typological Approach to a Modern Apocalyptic Mythology." MA thesis, University of Amsterdam, 2007.

DeKorne, Jim. "Entheogen: What's in a Word?" *The Entheogen Review* 1, no. 2 (1992): 2.

DeKorne, Jim. "Smokable DMT from Plants: Part 1." *The Entheogen Review,* Winter 1993: 1.

DeKorne, Jim. *Psychedelic Shamanism: The Cultivation, Preparation, and Shamanic Use of Psychotropic Plants.* Port Townsend, WA: Breakout Productions, 1994.

DeKorne, Jim. "Phalaris Update." *The Entheogen Review,* Fall 1994.

de Rios, Marlene Dobkin. "Drug Tourism in the Amazon." *Anthropology of Consciousness* 5, no. 1 (1994): 16–19.

de Rios, Marlene Dobkin. "Mea Culpa: Drug Tourism and the Anthropologist's Responsibility." *Anthropology News* (October 2006): 20.

Der Marderosian, A. H., H. V. Pinkley, and M. F. Dobbins. "Native Use and Occurrence of *N,N*-dimethyltryptamine in the Leaves of *Banisteriopsis rusbyana.*" *American Journal of Pharmacy* 140 (1968): 137–147.

Dexthepole. "What a DMT Trip Is Like." Uploaded to YouTube January 11, 2010. www.youtube.com/watch?v=xRr6klXmalI.

Dickins, Rob. "Reimagining the World: A Psychedelic Psychogeography." *Psychedelic Press UK,* September 19, 2013. http://psypressuk.com/2013/09/19/4638.

"Dimethyltryptamine (DMT)." *Cracked.com,* October 26, 2011. www.cracked.com/funny-2450-dimethyltryptamine-dmt.

"DMT: The Psychedelic Drug 'Produced in Your Brain.'" *The Feed,* SBS 2, November 10, 2013. www.sbs.com.au/news/article/2013/11/08/dmt-drug-produced-our-brain.

"DMT: A Psychedelic New Drug." Episode of *Drugs, Inc.* National Geographic Channel, 2012.

Dodd, Adam. "The Daemonic Insect: *Mantis religiosa.*" In *Animals as Religious Subjects: Transdisciplinary Perspectives,* edited by David Clough, Celia Deane-Drummond, and Becky Artinian-Kaiser, 103–124. London: Bloomsbury T&T Clark, 2013.

Doherty, Linda. "Teen Trippers Trying Dangerous 'Natural' Drug." *Sydney Morning Herald*, May 2, 1998.

Dorge, Chen Cho. "Changa: The Evolution of Ayahuasca." *Reality Sandwich*, 2010. Accessed March 9, 2012. www.realitysandwich.com/changa_evolution _ayahuasca.

Doyle, Richard M. *Darwin's Pharmacy: Sex, Plants, and the Evolution of the Noösphere*. Seattle: University of Washington Press, 2011.

Dr. Future, interviewed on *Nowhere to Run* radio with Chris White, 2010. Uploaded to YouTube December 28, 2010. Accessed May 13, 2014. www .youtube.com/watch?v=5tZtw0xuO4w#t=5480.

Dr. Future. "Sorcery and Drugs in Opening the Last Days Spirit Portal." Presented at Last Days Conference, Nashville, 2010.

Drummond, Paul. *Eye Mind: The Saga of Roky Erickson and the 13th Floor Elevators, The Pioneers of Psychedelic Sound*. Los Angeles: Process Media, 2007.

E., Australia. "Urgent Report on the Australian *Acacia* Situation." *The Entheogen Review* 5, no. 4 (1996): 10.

Enoon et al., eds. *Open Hyperspace Traveler: A Course Handbook for the Safe and Responsible Management of Psychoactives*. An Entheogenic University/DMT-Nexus production, 2014. Accessed November 26, 2014. www.oht.me.

Erowid Crew. "5-MeO-DMT Is Not 'DMT': Differentiation Is Wise." *Erowid Extracts* 17 (November 2009): 16. www.erowid.org/chemicals/5meo_dmt /5meo_dmt_article1.shtml.

Evans-Wentz, Walter E. *The Fairy Faith in Celtic Countries*. New York: Citadel Press, 1990. First published 1911.

"Extracting DMT from *Acacia maidenii*," *Erowid.org*, www.erowid.org/plants /acacia/acacia_extract1.shtml.

"Extraction from *Acacia maidenii* Bark." *The Entheogen Review* 5, no. 1 (1996): 6–7.

Fadiman, Jim. *The Psychedelic Explorer's Guide: Safe, Therapeutic, and Sacred Journeys*. Rochester, VT: Park Street Press, 2011.

Fahey, Todd Brendan. "The Original Captain Trips." *High Times*, November 1991.

Fahey, Todd Brendan. *Wisdom's Maw: The Acid Novel*. Vancouver, Canada: Far Gone Books, 1996.

Ferrer, Jorge. *Revisioning Transpersonal Theory: A Participatory Vision of Human Spirituality*. Albany: State University of New York Press, 2002.

Fish, M. S., N. M. Johnson, and E. C. Horning. "Piptadenia Alkaloids. Indole Bases of P. Peregrina (L.) Benth. and Related Species." *Journal of the American Chemical Society* 77 (1955): 5892–5895.

Fitzgerald, J. S., and A. A. Sioumis. "Alkaloids of the Australian Leguminosae. V. The Occurrence of Methylated Tryptamines in Acacia maidenii F. Muell." *Australian Journal of Chemistry* 18 (1965): 433–434.

Flattery, David S., and Martin Schwartz. *Haoma and Harmaline: The Botanical Identity of the Indo-Iranian Sacred Hallucinogen "Soma" and Its Legacy in Religion, Language and Middle Eastern Folklore.* Berkeley: University of California Press, 1989.

Fontanilla, Dominique, Molly Johannessen, Abdol R. Hajipour, Nicholas V. Cozzi, Meyer B. Jackson, and Arnold E. Ruoho. "The Hallucinogen *N,N*-Dimethyltryptamine (DMT) Is an Endogenous Sigma-1 Receptor Regulator." *Science* 323, no. 5916 (2009): 934–937.

France, Anthony. "Mind-Busting Jungle Drug Hits the UK." *The Sun*, July 10, 2010.

Frecska, Ede, Attila Szabo, Michael J. Winkelman, Luis E. Luna, and Dennis J. McKenna. "A Possibly Sigma-1 Receptor Mediated Role of Dimethyltryptamine in Tissue Protection, Regeneration, and Immunity." *Journal of Neural Transmission* 120 (2013): 1295–1303.

Gallimore, Andrew R. "Building Alien Worlds—The Neuropsychological and Evolutionary Implications of the Astonishing Psychoactive Effects of N,N-Dimethyltryptamine (DMT)." *Journal of Scientific Exploration* 27, no. 3 (2013): 455–503.

Gans, David. *Conversations with the Dead: The Grateful Dead Interview Book.* New York: Citadel Underground, 1991.

Gaskin, Stephen. *Haight Ashbury Flashbacks: Amazing Dope Tales of the Sixties.* Berkeley, CA: Ronin Books, 1980.

Gearin, Alex K. "Good Mother Nature: Ayahuasca Neoshamanism as Cultural Critique in Australia." In *The World Ayahuasca Diaspora: Reinventions and Controversies,* edited by Beatriz Labate, Clancy Cavnar, and Alex Gearin. Farnham, UK: Ashgate, 2016 (forthcoming).

Gehr, Richard. "Omega Man: A Profile of Terence McKenna." *Village Voice,* April 5, 1992. www.levity.com/rubric/mckenna.html.

GerBickel, P., A. Dittrich, and J. Schoepf. "Altered States of Consciousness Induced by *N,N*-dimethyltryptamine (DMT)." *Pharmakopsychiatry Neuropsychopharmakol* 9, no. 5 (1976): 220–225.

Gips, Elizabeth. Interview with D. M. Turner. *Tripzine.* Posted on May 1, 2001. www.tripzine.com/listing.php?id=dmturnergips.

Gonçalves de Lima, O. "Observações sôbre o 'Vinho da Jurema' Utilizado pelos Índios Pancarú de Tacaratú (Pernambuco)." *Arquivos do Instituto de Pesquisas Agronómicas* 4 (1946): 45–80.

Gracie and Zarkov, *Notes from Underground: A Gracie and Zarkov Reader* (1983–1985). www.erowid.org/library/books_online/notes_from_underground.pdf.

"Gracie's 'Visible Language' Contact Experience: An Experience with DMT and MDA (ID 1859)," *Erowid.org.* June 15, 2000. www.erowid.org/exp/1859.

Grey, Alex. *Transfigurations.* Rochester, VT: Inner Traditions, 2001.

Grey, Alex. Interviews Simon Posford, *CoSM (Chapel of Sacred Mirrors)* 1 (2005): 18.

Griffiths, Roland R., William A. Richards, Una D. McCann, and Robert Jesse. "Psilocybin Can Occasion Mystical-Type Experiences Having Substantial and Sustained Personal Meaning and Spiritual Significance." *Psychopharmacology* 187 (2006): 268–283.

Grigoriadis, Vanessa. "Daniel Pinchbeck and the New Psychedelic Elite." *Rolling Stone,* September 7, 2006. www.vanessagrigoriadis.com/pinchbeck.html.

Grof, Christina, and Stanislav Grof. *The Stormy Search for the Self: A Guide to Personal Growth Through Transformative Crisis.* Los Angeles: Tarcher, 1990.

Grof, Stanislav. *Realms of the Human Unconscious: Observations from LSD Research.* New York: Viking Press, 1975.

Grof, Stanislav. *Beyond the Brain: Birth, Death, and Transcendence in Psychotherapy.* New York: State University of New York Press, 1986.

Grof, Stanislav. *When the Impossible Happens: Adventures in Non-Ordinary Reality.* Boulder, CO: Sounds True, 2006.

Grof, Stanislav. *LSD: Doorway to the Numinous: The Groundbreaking Psychedelic Research into Realms of the Human Unconscious.* Rochester, VT: Park Street Press, 2009. First published 1975.

Grof, Stanislav. *HR GIGER and the Zeitgeist of the Twentieth Century.* Solothurn, Switzerland: Nachtschatten Verlag AG, 2014.

Grundy, Gareth. "Flying Lotus and the Power of Dreams," *The Guardian,* May 16, 2010.www.theguardian.com/music/2010/may/16/flying-lotus-cosmogramma-interview.

Hakl, Hans Thomas. *Eranos: An Alternative Intellectual History of the Twentieth Century.* Montreal: McGill Queens University Press, 2013.

Haldane, J. B. S. *Possible Worlds and Other Essays.* New York: Harper and Brothers, 1928.

Hamilton, Kate. "The Freakiest Trip." *Sydney Morning Herald* (*Good Weekend*), March 29, 2003: 42–45.

Hancock, Graham. *Supernatural: Meetings with the Ancient Teachers of Mankind.* London: Arrow Books, 2005.

Hancock, Graham. *Entangled: The Eater of Souls.* London: Arrow, 2011.

Hanegraaff, Wouter J. *New Age Religion and Western Culture: Esotericism in the Mirror of Secular Thought.* New York: State University of New York Press, 1998.

Hanegraaff, Wouter J. "'And End History. And Go to the Stars': Terence McKenna and 2012." In *Religion and Retributive Logic: Essays in Honour of Professor Garry W. Trompf,* edited by Carole M. Cusack and Christopher Hartney, 291–312. Leiden, Netherlands: Brill, 2010.

Hanegraaff, Wouter J. "Ayahuasca Groups and Networks in the Netherlands: A Challenge to the Study of Contemporary Religion." In *The Internationaliza-*

tion of Ayahuasca, edited by Beatriz C. Labate and Henrik Jungaberle, 85–103. Zürich, Switzerland: LIT, 2011.

Hanegraaff, Wouter J. "Entheogenic Esotericism." In *Contemporary Esotericism* (*Gnostica*), edited by Egil Asprem and Kennet Granholm, 392–409. Durham, UK: Acumen, 2013.

Hanna, Jon. "Got Changa?" *Erowid Extracts* 15 (November 2008): 18–19. Accessed October 20, 2013. www.erowid.org/chemicals/dmt/dmt_article1.shtml.

Hanna, Jon. "Erowid Character Vaults: Nick Sand Extended Biography." *Erowid.org.* November 5, 2009. Accessed September 22, 2014. www.erowid .org/culture/characters/sand_nick/sand_nick_biography1.shtml.

Hanna, Jon. "Aliens, Insectoids, and Elves! Oh, My!" *Erowid.org.* 2012. www .erowid.org/chemicals/dmt/dmt_article3.shtml.

Hanna, Jon, and Jonathan Taylor. "Is DMT Everywhere? The Short, Intense Trip of *N,N*-Dimethyltryptamine." Unpublished document.

Harner, Michael J. "The Sound of Rushing Water." *Natural History* 77, no. 6 (1973): 28–33.

Harner, Michael. *The Way of the Shaman: A Guide to Power and Healing.* San Francisco: Harper and Row, 1980.

Harris, Oliver. *William Burroughs and the Secret of Fascination.* Carbondale: Southern Illinois University Press, 2006.

Harrison, Jane. *Prolegomena to the Study of Greek Religion.* Charleston, SC: Nabu Press, 2010. First published 1903.

Harrop, Joanna. "The *Yagé* Aesthetic of William Burroughs: The Publication and Development of His Work 1953–1965." PhD thesis, Queen Mary, University of London, 2010.

Hochstein, F. A., and A. M. Paradies. "Alkaloids of Banisteria caapi and Prestonia amazonicum." *Journal of the American Chemical Society* 79, no. 21 (1957): 5735–5736.

Hoffer, Abram, Humphry Osmond, and John R. Smythies. "Schizophrenia: A New Approach II." *Journal of Mental Science* 100 (1954): 29–45.

Hollingshead, Michael. *The Man Who Turned on the World.* New York: Abelard-Schuman, 1974. Accessed April 20, 2013. www.psychedelic-library.org /hollings.htm.

Holmstedt, B., and J. E. Lindgren. "Chemical Constituents and Pharmacology of South American Snuffs." In *Ethnopharmacologic Search for Psychoactive Drugs,* Public Health Service Publication No. 1645, edited by D. H. Efron, B. Holmstedt, and N. S. Kline, 339–373. Washington, DC: U.S. Government Printing Office, 1967.

Horgan, John. *Rational Mysticism: Spirituality Meets Science in the Search for Enlightenment.* New York: Mariner, 2003.

Hubbard, Alfred M. "REPORT: D.M.T. EXPERIENCE (1961): An Experience with DMT (ID 78447)." *Erowid.org*. April 30, 2009. www.erowid.org/exp /78447.

Hunt, Anna. "Top 8 Supplements to Boost Your Pineal Gland Function." *Waking Times*, November 16, 2014. Accessed July 10, 2015. http://www.wakingtimes .com/2014/11/16/top-8-supplements-boost-pineal-gland-function/.

Hunter, Robert, and Terence McKenna. *Orfeo: A Dialog between Robert Hunter and Terence McKenna*. 1996–1997. Accessed March 30, 2013. www.levity.com/orfeo.

Huxley, Aldous. "Drugs That Shape Men's Minds." *Saturday Evening Post*, October 18, 1958.

Huxley, Aldous. *Moksha: Aldous Huxley's Classic Writings on Psychedelics and Visionary Experience*. Edited by Michael Horowitz and Cynthia Palmer. Rochester, VT: Park Street Press, 1982.

Huxley, Aldous. *The Doors of Perception and Heaven and Hell*. New York: Harper Perennial, 2009. First published 1955.

Hyperspace Fool. "Beyond: A Trip Report." *The Nexian* no. 1 (2014): 4–10.

Hyperspace Lexicon. https://wiki.dmt-nexus.me/Hyperspace_lexicon.

Jackson, Blair. *Grateful Dead: The Music Never Stopped*. New York: Delilah Communications, 1983.

Jacobs, Natalie. "The Psychedelic Rabbi." *San Diego Jewish Journal*, February 2014) http://sdjewishjournal.com/sdjj/february-2014/the-psychedelic-rabbi-2/.

jamie. "Phalaris Teachers: Temperate Sources of Tryptamine Gnosis." *The Nexian* no. 2 (2014): 63–68.

jamie and nen888 (with additional research by dreamer042 and *The Nexian* editorial staff). "Entheogenic Tryptamines, Past and Present: Folkways of Resilience." *The Nexian* no. 2 (2014): 5–12.

Jung, Carl. *Flying Saucers: A Modern Myth of Things Seen in the Skies*. London: Routledge & Kegan Paul, 1959.

Kaku, Michio. *Hyperspace: A Scientific Odyssey through Parallel Universes, Time Warps, and the 10th Dimension*. New York: Doubleday, 1994.

Kaku, Michio. *Parallel Worlds: A Journey through Creation, Higher Dimensions, and the Future of the Cosmos*. New York: Doubleday, 2005.

Kent, James L. "The Case against DMT Elves." *Tripzine*, May 4, 2004. http:// tripzine.com/listing.php?id=dmt_pickover.

Kent, James L. *Psychedelic Information Theory: Shamanism in the Age of Reason*. Seattle: PIT Press, 2010.

Kimah. "Interview with Ananda on Dark Room Retreat Alchemy." Accessed October 11, 2013. www.akasha.de/~aton/DR.html.

Krassner, Paul. "See the Sacred Word and Win $100." *High Times*, February 1981.

Kripal, Jeffrey. *Esalen: America and the Religion of No Religion.* Chicago: University of Chicago Press, 2007.

Kripal, Jeffrey. *Authors of the Impossible: The Paranormal and the Sacred.* Chicago: University of Chicago Press, 2010.

Kripal, Jeffrey J. *Mutants and Mystics: Science Fiction, Superhero Comics, and the Paranormal.* Chicago: University of Chicago Press, 2011.

Lachman, Gary. *The Secret History of Consciousness.* Great Barrington, MA: Lindisfarne Books, 2003.

Lardas, John. *The Bop Apocalypse: The Religious Visions of Kerouac, Ginsberg, and Burroughs.* Urbana: University of Illinois Press, 2001.

Lattin, Don. *The Harvard Psychedelic Club: How Timothy Leary, Ram Dass, Huston Smith, and Andrew Weil Killed the Fifties and Ushered in a New Age for America.* New York: HarperOne, 2010.

Leary, Tim. "The Religious Experience: Its Production and Interpretation." *Psychedelic Review* 1, no. 3 (1964): 324–346.

Leary, Tim. "The Experiential Typewriter." *Psychedelic Review* no. 7 (1966): 70–85.

Leary, Tim. "The Second Fine Art: Neo-Symbolic Communication of Experience." *Psychedelic Review* no. 8 (1966): 9–32.

Leary, Tim. "Programmed Communications during Experiences with DMT (Dimethyltryptamine)." *Psychedelic Review* no. 8 (1966): 83–85.

Leary, Tim. "Playboy Interview: Timothy Leary." *Playboy* 13, no. 9 (September 1966): 93–112, 250–251, 254–256.

Leary, Tim. *Exo-Psychology: A Manual on the Use of the Nervous System According to the Instructions of the Manufacturers.* Los Angeles: Starseed/Peace Press, 1977.

Leary, Tim. *High Priest.* Berkeley, CA: Ronin, 1995. First published 1968.

Leary, Tim, and Richard Alpert. "Foreword" to Alan Watts, *The Joyous Cosmology: Adventures in the Chemistry of Consciousness,* ix–xv. New York: Pantheon Books, 1962.

Leary, Tim, Ralph Metzner, and Richard Alpert. *The Psychedelic Experience: A Manual Based on the Tibetan Book of the Dead.* Sacramento, CA: Citadel Press, 1964.

Lee, Martin A., and Bruce Shlain. *Acid Dreams: The Complete Social History of LSD: The CIA, the Sixties, and Beyond.* New York: Grove Press, 1992. First published 1985.

"Lenny Bruce Describes Smoking DMT in UCLA Lecture, 1966." Posted on *Dangerous Minds,* March 1, 2014. Accessed March 15, 2015. http://dangerousminds.net/comments/lenny_bruce_describes_smoking_dmt_in_ucla_lecture_1966.

Lester, Paul. "Temples, Hookworms and the New Generation of Psychedelic Adventurers." *The Guardian,* September 27, 2013. www.theguardian.com/music/2013/sep/26/temples-hookworms-new-generation-psychedelia.

Letcher, Andy. *Shroom: A Cultural History of the Magic Mushroom.* London: Faber and Faber, 2006.

Lewis-Williams, David J. *A Cosmos in Stone: Interpreting Religion and Society through Rock Art.* Walnut Creek, CA: Altamira Press, 2002.

Llwydd, Gwyllm. "Gate Keepers." Unpublished short story, 2015.

London Real. "Dorian Yates—Into the Shadow." Interview. Uploaded to YouTube March 29, 2013. www.youtube.com/watch?v=fNqR-Ifj7xQ.

Lovecraft, H. P. "From Beyond." *The Fantasy Fan* 1, no. 10 (1934): 147–151.

Luke, David. "Disembodied Eyes Revisited. An Investigation into the Ontology of Entheogenic Entity Encounters." *The Entheogen Review* 17, no. 1 (2008): 1–9, 38–40.

Luke, David. "Rock Art or Rorschach: Is There More to Entoptics Than Meets the Eye?" *Time and Mind: The Journal of Archaeology, Consciousness and Culture* 3, no. 1 (2010): 9–28.

Luke, David. "Discarnate Entities and Dimethyltryptamine (DMT): Psychopharmacology, Phenomenology and Ontology." *Journal of the Society for Psychical Research* 75, no. 1 (2011): 26–42.

Luke, David. "Psychoactive Substances and Paranormal Phenomena: A Comprehensive Review." *International Journal of Transpersonal Studies* 31 (2012): 97–156.

Luke, David. "So Long as You've Got Your Elf: Death, DMT and Discarnate Entities." In *Daimonic Imagination: Uncanny Intelligence,* edited by Angela Voss and William Rowlandson, 282–291. Cambridge, UK: Cambridge Scholars Publishing, 2013.

Lyng, Stephen. "Edgework: A Social Psychological Analysis of Voluntary Risk Taking." *American Journal of Sociology* 95, no. 4 (1990): 876–921.

Lyttle, Thomas. "Toad Licking Blues." In *You Are Being Lied To,* edited by Russ Kick, 241–244. New York: Disinformation Co., 2001.

Mack, John. *Abduction: Human Encounters with Aliens.* New York: Simon & Schuster, 1994.

MacKenzie Blake, Blair. *IJYNX,* Brisbane, Australia: Daily Grail, 2003.

MacKenzie Blake, Blair. "Crowley, DMT and Magick." *Sub Rosa* 2 (2005): 22–30.

MacKenzie Blake, Blair. "DMT and Magick: An Occultist Ponders the Neurochemical Basis of Magick and the Paranormal." *Dark Lore Vol. II.* Brisbane, Australia: Daily Grail, 2008.

Magenta Imagination Healer. Interview with Rak Razam. "Back to the Garden: Awakening to the Shamanic Paradigm." *Reality Sandwich,* 2014. http://realitysandwich.com/214776/rak_razam_garden/.

Markoff, John. *What the Dormouse Said: How the 60s Counterculture Shaped the Personal Computer Industry.* New York: Penguin, 2005.

Marks, John. *The Search for the Manchurian Candidate: The CIA and Mind Control.* New York: Times Books, 1979.

Masters, Robert A. *Darkness Shining Wild: An Odyssey to the Heart of Hell and Beyond.* Surrey, BC, Canada: Tehmenos Press, 2009. First published 2005.

Masters, Robert E. L., and Jean Houston. *The Varieties of Psychedelic Experience.* Rochester, VT: Park Street Press, 2000. First published 1966.

McGreal, Scott A. "DMT, Aliens, and Reality—Part 2." *Psychology Today,* October 4, 2012. www.psychologytoday.com/blog/unique-everybody-else/201210/dmt-aliens-and-reality-part-2.

McKenna, Dennis J. "Ayahuasca and Human Destiny." *Journal of Psychoactive Drugs* 37, no. 2 (2005): 231–234.

McKenna, Dennis J. *The Brotherhood of the Screaming Abyss: My Life with Terence McKenna.* St. Cloud, MN: Polaris, 2012.

McKenna, D. J., L. E. Luna, and G. H. N. Towers. "Biodynamic Constituents in Ayahuasca Admixture Plants: An Uninvestigated Folk Pharmacopoeia." In *Ethnobotany: Evolution of a Discipline,* edited by S. von Reis and R. E. Schultes. Portland, OR: Dioscorides Press, 1995.

McKenna, Dennis J., and Jordi Riba. "New World Tryptamine Hallucinogens and the Neuroscience of Ayahuasca." *Current Topics in Behavioral Neurosciences.* Epub, February 6, 2015.

McKenna, D. J., G. H. N. Towers, and F. S. Abbott. "Monoamine Oxidase Inhibitors in South American Hallucinogenic Plants: Tryptamine and ß Carboline Constituents of Ayahuasca." *Journal of Ethnopharmacology* 10, no. 2 (1984): 195–223.

McKenna, D. J., G. H. N. Towers, and F. S. Abbott. "Monoamine Oxidase Inhibitors in South American Hallucinogenic Plants. Part 2: Constituents of Orally Active Myristicaceous Hallucinogens." *Journal of Ethnopharmacology* 12, no. 2 (1984): 179–211.

McKenna, Terence. "Elven Ramblings." (from presentation, n.d.). Uploaded to YouTube May 18, 2009. www.youtube.com/watch?v=wUhXnQBy7RY.

McKenna, Terence. "DMT." (from presentation, n.d.). Uploaded to YouTube November 17, 2009. www.youtube.com/watch?v=pVXvLLOaI7Q.

McKenna, Terence, "DMT, Mathematical Dimensions, Syntax and Death." (from presentation, n.d.). Uploaded to YouTube August 28, 2013. www.youtube.com/watch?v=VuEXBBaFAbw.

McKenna, Terence. "Alien Love." Presented at Shared Visions, Berkeley, California, 1983. Originally published in *Magical Blend* no. 17 (1987). In T. McKenna, *The Archaic Revival,* 72–89.

McKenna, Terence. "Tryptamine Hallucinogens and Consciousness." Presented at Lilly/Goswami Conference on Consciousness and Quantum Physics at the Esalen Institute, Big Sur, California, December 1983. In T. McKenna, *The Archaic Revival*, 34–47. www.youtube.com/watch?v=RUfyMZ5uZL0.

McKenna, Terence. "Mind, Molecules and Magic." Presented at Esalen Institute, Big Sur, California, June 1984.

McKenna, Terence. "Psychedelics and a Free Society." Presented at Esalen Institute, Big Sur, California, 1984.

McKenna, Terence. "Psychedelics Before and After History." Presented at San Francisco's California Institute of Integral Studies, October 2, 1987.

McKenna, Terence. "Understanding and the Imagination in the Light of Nature." Presented in Los Angeles, October 17, 1987.

McKenna, Terence. "A Conversation over Saucers." *Revision: The Journal of Consciousness and Change* 11, no. 3 (Winter 1989): 23–30. Reproduced in McKenna, *The Archaic Revival*, 58–70.

McKenna, Terence. "Mind and Time, Spirit and Matter." Presented in Santa Fe, New Mexico, May 26–27, 1990, http://deoxy.org/timemind.htm.

McKenna, Terence. "Aliens and Archetypes." *Thinking Allowed with Jeffery Mishlove*. PBS TV, 1990.

McKenna, Terence. "Linking the Past, Present and the Future of Psychedelics." Presented at The Bridge Psychedelic Conference, Stanford University, Stanford, California, February 2–3, 1991.

McKenna, Terence. *The Archaic Revival: Speculations on Psychedelic Mushrooms, the Amazon, Virtual Reality, UFOs, Evolution, Shamanism, the Rebirth of the Goddess, and the End of History*. San Francisco: Harper, 1991.

McKenna, Terence. "Among Ayahuasquera." In *Gateway to Inner Space: Sacred Plants, Mysticism and Psychotherapy*, edited by Christian Ratsch, 179–212. Dorset, UK: Prism Press, 1991. First published 1989.

McKenna, Terence. *Food of the Gods: The Search for the Original Tree of Knowledge*. New York: Bantam Books, 1992.

McKenna, Terence. "Alchemical Youth at the Edge of the World." Presented at Camden Centre, London, June 15, 1992. Accessed September 1, 2013. http://deoxy.org/t_camden.htm.

McKenna, Terence. *True Hallucinations: Being an Account of the Author's Extraordinary Adventures in the Devil's Paradise*. San Francisco: Harper, 1993.

McKenna, Terence. "Under the Teaching Tree." Presented at Ojai Foundation, 1993.

McKenna, Terence. "Rap Dancing into the 3rd Millennium." Presented at Starwood XIV Festival, Brushwood Folklore Center, Sherman, New York, July 19–24, 1994.

McKenna, Terence. "Shamanism, Alchemy, and the 20th Century." Presented in Mannheim, Germany, 1996.

McKenna, Terence. "Terence McKenna on Art Bell," April 1, 1999. www .jacobsm.com/deoxy/deoxy.org/tmab_4-1-99.htm.

McKenna, Terence. "The Psychedelic Society." Presented at Esalen Institute, Big Sur, California, 1984. Reproduced in *Hallucinogens: A Reader*, edited by Charles S. Grob, 38–46. New York: Tarcher/Putnam, 2002.

McKenna, Terence, and Dennis McKenna. *The Invisible Landscape: Mind, Hallucinogens and the I Ching*. New York: HarperOne, 1993. First published 1975.

McNally, Dennis. *A Long Strange Trip: The Inside History of the Grateful Dead*. New York: Broadway Books, 2002.

Metzger, Richard. "Timewave Zero: Did Terence McKenna *Really* Believe in All That 2012 Prophecy Stuff?" *Dangerous Minds,* June 6, 2012. http:// dangerousminds.net/comments/timewave_zero_did_terence_mckenna _really _believe_in_all_that_2012_prophecy.

Metzner, Ralph. "The Pharmacology of Psychedelic Drugs I: Chemical and Biochemical Aspects." *Psychedelic Review* 1, no. 1 (1963): 69–115.

Metzner, Ralph. *The Life Cycle of the Human Soul: Incarnation; Conception; Birth; Death; Hereafter; Reincarnation*. Berkeley, CA: Regent Press, 2011.

Metzner, Ralph. *The Toad and the Jaguar: A Field Report of Underground Research on a Visionary Medicine: Bufo Alvarius and 5-methoxy-dimethyltriptamine*. Berkeley, CA: Green Earth Foundation and Regent Press, 2013.

Metzner, Ralph. *Allies for Awakening: Guidelines for Productive and Safe Experiences with Entheogens*. Berkeley, CA: Green Earth Foundation and Regent Press, 2015.

Meyer, Peter. "340 DMT Trip Reports Attesting to Contact with Apparently Independently-Existing Intelligent Entities within What Seems to Be an Alternate Reality." Accessed October 26, 2014. www.serendipity.li/dmt/340 _dmt_trip_reports.htm.

Meyer, Peter. "Apparent Communication with Discarnate Entities Related to DMT." In *Psychedelic Monographs and Essays Volume 6*, edited by Thomas Lyttle, 29–69. Boynton Beach, FL: P M & E, 1993. Reproduced on Erowid, www.erowid.org/chemicals/dmt/dmt_writings2.shtml.

Meyer, Peter. "Physicalism: A False View of the World." July 2008. www .serendipity.li/dmt/physicalism.htm.

Meyer, Peter. "A Reply to Martin Ball's 'Terence on DMT.'" 2010. www .serendipity.li/dmt/reply_to_ball.htm.

Meyer, Peter. "Physicalism: A Pernicious World View." 2012. www.serendipity .li/dmt/physicalism_2.htm.

Miles, Barry. *Call Me Burroughs: A Life*. New York: Hachette Book Group, 2014.

Miller, Iona. "Pineal Gland, DMT and Altered State of Consciousness." *Journal of Consciousness Exploration and Research* 4, no. 2 (March 4, 2013): 214–233.

Miller, Sukie. "Interview: Terence McKenna." *Omni* 15, no. 7 (1993): 69–92.

Mirante, Daniel. "Notes on the Western Paradigm of Ayahuasca." Blog post, April 23, 2010. www.ayahuasca.com/ayahuasca-overviews/a-response-to -the-reality-sandwich-article-changa-the-evolution-of-ayahuasca-or-notes -on-the-western-paradigm-of-ayahuasca/.

Mishor, Zevic, Dennis J. McKenna, and J. C. Callaway. "DMT and Human Consciousness." In *Altering Consciousness: Multidisciplinary Perspectives* (*Volume 2: Biological and Psychological Perspectives*), edited by Etzel Cardeña and Michael Winkelman, 85–119. Santa Barbara, CA: Praeger, 2011.

Mister Strange. *Psychonautica: DMT: A Graphic Novel*, 2012. www.misterstrange .com.

Moler, Daniel. *Machine Elves 101* (*Or, Why Terence McKenna Matters*). New York: Reality Sandwich, 2012.

Morgan, Ted. *Literary Outlaw: The Life and Times of William S. Burroughs*. New York: W. W. Norton, 1988.

Morrison, Grant. Interviewed in Suicidegirls.com, February 27, 2005. https:// suicidegirls.com/girls/anderswolleck/blog/2679166/grant-morrison/.

Morrison, Natty. "NiT GriT—*Synthetic Heaven* EP Review." *The Untz*, July 6, 2010. www.theuntz.com/news/nit-grit-synthetic-heaven-ep-review/.

Narby, Jeremy. *The Cosmic Serpent: DNA and the Origins of Knowledge*. New York: Tarcher/Putnam, 1998.

Nen. "Entheogenic Effects of NMT from Acacia." Presented at Entheogenesis Australis conference, December 2011.

Nen and David Nickles. "When DMT Equals Killing the Environment." Posted to DMT-Nexus October 1, 2014. Accessed October 7, 2014. http://the-nexian .me/home/knowledge/131-when-dmt-equals-killing-the-environment.

nen888. "Trying to Improve Acacia Information." Posted to DMT-Nexus June 28, 2011. www.dmt-nexus.me/forum/default.aspx?g=posts&t=23472.

nen888. "Entheogenic Effects of NMT (Monomethyl-tryptamine)." Posted to DMT-Nexus July 1, 2011. Accessed October 27, 2014. www.dmt-nexus.me /forum/default.aspx?g=posts&t=23544.

Nickles, David. "Criminals and Researchers: Perspectives on the Necessity of Underground Research." *The Nexian* no. 2 (2014): 37–47.

Noman. "DMT for the Masses." *The Entheogen Review* 15, no. 3 (2006): 91–92.

Odenwald, Sten. "Who Invented Hyperspace? Hyperspace in Science Fiction." *Astronomy Café*, 1995. www.astronomycafe.net/anthol/scifi2.html.

O'Donnell, Shauna. "Interview with Alistar V of D.M.T." *Muen Magazine*, January 17, 2011. www.muenmagazine.net/2011/01/interview-with-alistar -v-of-d-m-t/.

Olsen, Brad. *Modern Esoteric: Beyond Our Senses*. San Francisco: CCC, 2014.

Olympus Mon. "The Art of Changa." *The Nexian* no. 2 (2014): 48–53.

Oroc, James. *Tryptamine Palace: 5-MeO-DMT and the Sonoran Desert Toad.* Rochester, VT: Park Street Press, 2009.

Ott, Jonathan. *Ayahuasca Analogues: Pangaean Entheogens.* Occidental, CA: Jonathan Ott Books, 1994.

Ott, Jonathan. *Pharmacotheon: Entheogenic Drugs, Their Plant Sources and History.* Kennewick, WA: Natural Products Co., 1996. First published 1993.

Ott, Jonathan. *The Age of Entheogens and the Angels' Dictionary.* Kennewick, WA: Natural Products Co., 1995.

Ott, Jonathan. "Pharmahuasca: Human Pharmacology of Oral DMT Plus Harmine." *Journal of Psychoactive Drugs* 31, no. 2 (1999): 171–177.

Ouspensky, P. D. *Tertium Organum: The Third Canon of Thought, a Key to the Enigmas of the World.* Translated by Nicholas Bessaraboff and Claude Bragdon. Rochester, NY: Manas Press, 1920. First published in Russian in 1912.

Ouspensky, P. D. *A New Model of the Universe.* New York: Alfred A. Knopf, 1931.

Palmer, Cynthia, and Michael Horowitz. *Sisters of the Extreme: Women Writing on the Drug Experience.* Rochester, VT: Park Street Press, 2000.

Palmer, Julian. "Trying to Explain Away DMT: An Analysis of 'The Case against DMT Elves.'" n.d. www.julianpalmerism.com/jameskent.html.

Palmer, Julian. *Articulations: On the Utilisation and Meanings of Psychedelics.* Thornbury, Victoria, Australia: Anastomosis Books, 2014.

Partridge, Christopher. *The Re-Enchantment of the West: Alternative Spiritualities, Sacralization, Popular Culture and Occulture, Vol. 1.* London: T&T Clark International, 2004.

Partridge, Christopher. *The Re-Enchantment of the West: Alternative Spiritualities, Sacralization, Popular Culture and Occulture, Vol. 2.* London: T&T Clark International, 2006.

Patoski, Joe Nick. "The Roky Erickson." Posted on "Notes and Musings," June 17, 2010.http://joenickp.blogspot.com/2010/06/roky-erickson-1975.html.

Peake, Anthony. *The Infinite Mindfield: The Quest to Find the Gateway to Higher Consciousness.* London: Watkins, 2013.

Pellerin, Cheryl. *Trips: How Hallucinogens Work in Your Brain.* New York: Seven Stories Press, 1998.

Phillips, Stephen M. "A Short History of the Fourth Dimension." n.d. www.smphillips.8m.com/a-short-history-of-the-fourth-dimension.html.

Pickover, Clifford A. *Surfing through Hyperspace: Understanding Higher Universes in Six Easy Lessons.* Oxford, UK: Oxford University Press, 2001.

Pickover, Clifford A. *Sex, Drugs, Einstein, and Elves: Sushi, Psychedelics, Parallel Universes, and the Quest for Transcendence.* Petaluma, CA: Smart Publications, 2005.

Pike, Neil. "The First Time I Smoked DMT." 2015. www.paganlovecult.com /philos/first_dmt.html.

Pinchbeck, Daniel. *Breaking Open the Head: A Psychedelic Journey into the Heart of Contemporary Shamanism.* Portland, OR: Broadway, 2002.

"Pineal Gland Activation Secrets with Justin Verrengia." Uploaded to YouTube January 2, 2014. Accessed February 13, 2014. www.youtube.com/watch ?v=QkF5Ngro3VY.

Pinkley, Homer V. "Plant Admixtures to Ayahuasca, the South American Hallucinogenic Drink." *Lloydia* 32 (1969): 305–314.

Pochettino, M. L., A. R. Cortella, and M. Ruiz. "Hallucinogenic Snuff from Northwestern Argentina: Microscopical Identification of *Anadenanthera colubrina* var. *cebil* (Fabaceae) in Powdered Archaeological Material." *Economic Botany* 53, no. 2 (1999): 127–132.

"The Potential Religious Relevance of Entheogens." Special section of *Zygon: Journal of Religion and Science* 49, no. 3 (September 2014).

Price, Alexander. "Immanentizing the Eschaton: An Interview with Dennis McKenna." *Reality Sandwich,* 2009. Accessed December 11, 2014. https:// realitysandwich.com/13139/interview_dennis_mckenna/.

Psilly. "Boom Festival 2010." 2010. Accessed July 13, 2011. www.fleshprism .com/category/outsideinsights (page no longer live).

Psychedaniellia. "Hierarchies of Hyperspace A Collection: An Experience with DMT, 4-HO-MiPT, 4-AcO-DiPT, LSD, DPT, Ketamine, Methoxetamine, 5-MeO-DMT, Nitrous Oxide and MDMA (ID 101485)." *Erowid.org.* May 16, 2014. www.erowid.org/exp/101485.

Razam, Rak. *Aya Awakenings: A Shamanic Odyssey,* Berkeley, CA: North Atlantic Books, 2013.

Razam, Rak. "The DreaMTime Invasion: DMT and the Origins of Religion, with Nen." Podcast on *In a Perfect World,* 2013. Accessed December 1, 2013. http:// in-a-perfect-world.podomatic.com/entry/2013-07-07T03_05_22-07_00.

"The Real You." *Adventure Time,* season 2, episode 15, Cartoon Network (original air date: February 14, 2011). www.youtube.com/watch?v=rE9Cwa5EDDw.

Michele Ross, interviewed by Amber Lyon. "Neuroscientist Describes Her DMT Trip." *Reset.me.* Uploaded to YouTube June 15, 2014. www.youtube .com/watch?v=yqtvuzcL84M&feature=youtube.

Reynolds, Simon. *Generation Ecstasy: Into the World of Techno and Rave Culture.* 2nd ed. New York: Routledge, 1999.

Richards, William A. "Here and Now: Discovering the Sacred with Entheogens." *Zygon: Journal of Religion and Science* 49, no. 3 (September 2014): 652–665.

Roberts, Gabriel D. *The Quest for Gnosis.* CreateSpace, 2014.

Roberts, Gabriel D. "Blasting Off with Dr. DMT." *VICE*, April 2, 2014. Accessed November 26, 2014. www.vice.com/read/blasting-off-with-dr-dmt.

Roberts, Gabriel D. "Episode 134 Gabriel D. Roberts—Losing My Religion." *Project Archivist* podcast, November 15, 2014. Accessed November 26, 2014. www.projectarchivist.com/?tag=gabriel-d-roberts.

Roberts, Jane. *The Seth Material.* New York: New Awareness Network, 1970.

Roberts, Thomas B., ed. *Spiritual Growth with Entheogens: Psychoactive Sacramentals and Human Transformation.* Rochester, VT: Park Street Press, 2012. First published 2001.

Roberts, Thomas B. *The Psychedelic Future of the Mind: How Entheogens Are Enhancing Cognition, Boosting Intelligence, and Raising Values.* Rochester, VT: Park Street Press, 2013.

Rodd, Robin. "Snuff Synergy: Preparation, Use and Pharmacology of *Yopo* and *Banisteriopsis caapi* among the Piaroa of Southern Venezuela." *Journal of Psychoactive Drugs* 34, no. 3 (2002): 273–279.

Rodriguez, Marko A. "A Methodology for Studying Various Interpretations of the N,N-dimethyltryptamine-Induced Alternate Reality." *Journal of Scientific Exploration* 21, no. 1 (2007): 67–84.

Roney-Dougal, Serena. "The Pineal Gland: Psychic and Psychedelic Powerhouse." *Paranthropology: Journal of Anthropological Approaches to the Paranormal* 2, no. 2 (2011): 24–35.

Rooks, Benton. "Beyond the Machine Elves: On DMT Culture, Visionary Plants and Entheodelic Storytelling." *Reality Sandwich,* 2014. http://realitysandwich .com/216190/beyond-the-machine-elves-on-dmt-culture-visionary-plants -and-entheodelic-storytelling.

Rothenberg, Jerome, ed. *Maria Sabina: Selections.* Berkeley: University of California Press, 2003.

Rowlandson, William. "Nourished by Dreams, Visions and William James: The Radical Philosophies of Borges and Terence McKenna." *Paranthropology* 1 (2012): 46–60.

Ruck, Carl A. P., Jeremy Bigwood, Danny Staples, Jonathan Ott, and R. Gordon Wasson. "Entheogens." *Journal of Psychedelic Drugs* 11, nos. 1–2 (1979): 145–146.

Rushkoff, Douglas. *Cyberia: Life in the Trenches of Hyperspace.* London: Flamingo, 1994.

Sai-Halász, A., G. Brunecker, and S. Szára. "Dimethyltryptamin: Ein Neues Psychoticum." *Journal Psychiatria et Neurologia* (Basel, Switzerland), 135 (1958): 285–301.

Sand, Nick. "Reflections on Imprisonment and Liberation as Aspects of Consciousness." Presented at Mind States II conference, May 27, 2001. Accessed

May 24, 2014. www.matrixmasters.net/archive/NickSand/037-NickSand 2001.mp3.

Sand, Nick. Interview by Daniel Williams on *The Opium Den Talk Show,* 2009. Accessed May 18, 2014. www.theopiumden.net/chapters/audio/interviews /41909/nsands.mp3.

Schou, Nicholas. *Orange Sunshine.* New York: St. Martin's Press, 2010.

Schultes, Richard E. "A New Narcotic Snuff from the Northwest Amazon." *Botanical Museum Leaflets* 16, no. 9 (1954): 241–260.

Schultes, Richard E. "The Identity of the Malpighiaceous Narcotics of South America." *Botanical Museum Leaflets* 18, no. 1 (1957): 1–56.

Schultes, Richard E. "Virola as an Orally Administered Hallucinogen." *Botanical Museum Leaflets* 22, no. 6 (June 25, 1969): 229–240.

Schultes, Richard E. "Evolution of the Identification of the Myristicaceous Hallucinogens of South America." *Journal of Ethnopharmacology* 1, no. 3 (1979): 211–239.

Schultes, Richard E., and Robert F. Raffauf. "Prestonia: An Amazon Narcotic or Not?" *Botanical Museum Leaflets* 19, no. 5 (1960): 109–122.

Schultes, Richard E., and Tony Swain. "De Plantis Toxicariis e Mundo Novo Tropicale Commentationes. XIII. Further Notes on Virola as an Orally Administered Hallucinogen." *Journal of Psychedelic Drugs* 8, no. 4 (1976): 317–324.

Scully, Tim. "Meeting Owsley and Smoking DMT." Unpublished document, March 21, 2015.

Servillo, L., A. Giovane, M. L. Balestrieri, R. Casale, D. Cautela, and D. Castaldo. "*Citrus* Genus Plants Contain Nmethylated Tryptamine Derivatives and Their 5hydroxylated Forms." *Journal of Agricultural and Food Chemistry* 61, no. 21 (2013): 5156–5162.

SFos. "The Elven Antics Annex: An Experience with DMT (ID 1841)." *Erowid .org.* June 14, 2000. www.erowid.org/exp/1841.

Shanon, Benny. *Antipodes of the Mind: Charting the Phenomenology of the Ayahuasca Experience.* Oxford, UK: Oxford University Press, 2002.

Sheldrake, Rupert, Terence McKenna, and Ralph Abraham. *Chaos, Creativity and Cosmic Consciousness.* Rinebeck, NY: Monkfish, 2001. First published 1992.

Sheldrake, Rupert, Terence McKenna, and Ralph Abraham. *The Evolutionary Mind: Conversations on Science, Imagination and Spirit.* Rinebeck, NY: Monkfish, 2005. First published 1998.

Shroder, Tom. *Acid Test: LSD, Ecstasy, and the Power to Heal.* New York: Blue Rider, 2014.

Shulgin, Alexander, and Ann Shulgin. *PiHKAL: A Chemical Love Story.* Berkeley, CA: Transform Press, 1991.

Shulgin, Alexander, and Ann Shulgin. *TiHKAL: The Continuation.* Berkeley, CA: Transform Press, 1997.

Sirius, R. U., interviews Todd Brendan Fahey. "It's Alright Maw: I'm Only Bleeding." *Mondo 2000*, November 1997: 67–69.

Sirius, R. U. *Timothy Leary's Trip Thru Time*. Santa Cruz, CA: Futique Trust, 2013.

Slattery, Diana Reed. *Xenolinguistics: Psychedelics and Language at the Edge of the Unspeakable*. Berkeley, CA: Evolver Editions, 2015.

Sledge, Matt, and Ryan Grim. "If You Haven't Heard of DMT Yet, You Might Soon." *Huffington Post*, December 9, 2013. www.huffingtonpost .com/2013/12/09/dmt-use_n_4412633.html.

Smith, Huston. *Cleansing the Doors of Perception: The Religious Significance of Entheogenic Plants and Chemicals*. New York: Tarcher, 2000.

Smith, Michael Valentine. *Psychedelic Chemistry*. 4th ed., corrected and expanded. San Francisco: Rip Off Press, 1976.

Stamets, Paul E. *Mycelium Running: How Mushrooms Can Help Save the World*. Berkeley, CA: Ten Speed Press, 2005.

Stebbing, Martin, and Toke Kim Klinke. *DMTrmx*, 2013. https://vimeo.com /37633048.

Steel, Cameron. Interviews Alex Grey. *Contact Talk Radio*, 2002.

Stevens, Jay. *Storming Heaven: LSD and the American Dream*. 2nd ed. London: Paladin, 1989.

St John, Graham. *Global Tribe: Technology, Spirituality and Psytrance*. Sheffield, UK: Equinox, 2012.

St John, Graham. "Aliens Are Us: Cosmic Liminality, Remixticism and *Alien*ation in Psytrance." *Journal of Religion and Popular Culture* 25, no. 2 (2013): 186–204.

St John, Graham. "Liminal Being: Electronic Dance Music Cultures, Ritualization and the Case of Psytrance." In *The Sage Handbook of Popular Music*, edited by Andy Bennett and Steve Waksman, 243–260. London: Sage, 2015.

Stolaroff, Myron J. *The Secret Chief Revealed: Conversations with Leo Zeff, Pioneer in the Underground Psychedelic Therapy Movement*. Santa Cruz, CA: MAPS, 2004.

Strassman, Rick. "The Pineal Gland: Current Evidence for Its Role in Consciousness." *Psychedelic Monographs and Essays* 5 (1991): 167–205.

Strassman, Rick. "Human Hallucinogenic Drug Research in the United States: A Present-Day Case History and Review of the Process." *Journal of Psychoactive Drugs* 23 (1991): 29–38.

Strassman, Rick. "Sitting for Sessions: Dharma and DMT Research." *Tricycle: The Buddhist Review*, Fall 1996: 81–88.

Strassman, Rick. "Chapter 13, Contact through the Veil: 1." Excerpted from *DMT: The Spirit Molecule* reprinted in *The Entheogen Review* 9, no. 2 (2000): 4–12.

Strassman, Rick. *DMT: The Spirit Molecule: A Doctor's Revolutionary Research into the Biology of Near-Death and Mystical Experiences*. Rochester, VT: Park Street Press, 2001.

Strassman, Rick (interviewed by Graham Hancock). In Graham Hancock, *Supernatural: Meetings with the Ancient Teachers of Mankind*, 743–756. London: Arrow, 2005.

Strassman, Rick. *DMT and the Soul of Prophecy: A New Science of Spiritual Revelation in the Hebrew Bible*. Rochester, VT: Park Street Press, 2014.

Strassman, Rick. "Interview with Rick Strassman." *The Nexian* no. 2 (2014): 27–35.

Strassman, Rick, and Marc Galanter. "The Abhidharma: A Cross-Cultural Model for the Psychiatric Application of Medication." *International Journal of Social Psychiatry* 26 (1980): 293–299.

Strassman, Rick J., and Clifford R. Qualls. "Dose-Response Study of N,N-Dimethyltryptamine in Humans. I. Neuroendocrine, Autonomic, and Cardiovascular Effects." *Archives of General Psychiatry* 51, no. 2 (1994): 85–97.

Strassman, Rick J., Clifford R. Qualls, and Laura M. Berg. "Differential Tolerance to Biological and Subjective Effects of Four Closely Spaced Doses of N,N-Dimethyltryptamine in Humans." *Biological Psychiatry* 39 (1996): 784–795.

Strassman, Rick J., Clifford R. Qualls, Eberhard H. Uhlenhuth, and Robert Kellner. "Dose-Response Study of N,N-Dimethyltryptamine in Humans. II. Subjective Effects and Preliminary Results of a New Rating Scale." *Archives of General Psychiatry* 51, no. 2 (1994): 98–108.

Strassman, Rick, with Slawek Wojtowicz, Luis Eduardo Luna, and Ede Frecska. *Inner Paths to Outer Space: Journeys to Alien Worlds through Psychedelics and Other Spiritual Technologies*. Rochester, VT: Park Street Press, 2008.

Sunyata. "Speaking in Tounges: An Experience with DMT (ID 39857)." *Erowid. org*. January 28, 2005. www.erowid.org/exp/39857.

Superweed, Mary Jane. *The D. M. T. Guide: Drug Manufacturing for Fun and Profit*. San Francisco: Stone Kingdom Syndicate, 1969.

Szára, Stephen. "Dimethyltryptamine: Its Metabolism in Man: The Relation of Its Psychotic Effect to the Serotonin Metabolism." *Experientia* 12 (1956): 411–441.

Szára, Stephen. "The Comparison of the Psychotic Effect of Tryptamine Derivatives with the Effects of Mescaline and LSD-25 in Self-Experiments." In *Psychotropic Drugs: Proceedings of the International Symposium on Psychotropic Drugs, Milan 1957*, edited by Silvio Garattini and Vittorio Ghetti, 460–467. Amsterdam: Elsevier, 1957.

Szára, Stephen. "Hallucinogenic Effects and Metabolism of Tryptamine Derivatives in Man." *Federation Proceedings* 20 (1961): 885–888.

Szára, Stephen. "The Social Chemistry of Discovery: The DMT Story." *Social Pharmacology* 3 (1989): 237–248.

Szára, Stephen. "Are Hallucinogens Psychoheuristic?" *NIDA Research Monographs* 146 (1994): 33–51.

Szára, Stephen. "DMT at Fifty." *Neuropsychopharmacologia Hungarica* 9, no. 4 (2007): 201–205.

Tart, Charles. "States of Consciousness and State-Specific Sciences." *Science* 176 (1972): 1203–1210.

Taylor, Jonathan, David Arnson, and Jon Hanna. "DMT and Music." In *DMT Underground: A Compendium of Unauthorized Research,* edited by Jon Hanna. Forthcoming (draft chapter).

Teafaerie. "Virtuality." *Teatime: Psychedelic Musings from the Center of the Universe.* May 31, 2012. www.erowid.org/columns/teafaerie/2012/05/31/virtuality.

Teafaerie. "How to Build a Better Spaceship." *Teatime: Psychedelic Musings from the Center of the Universe.* May 29, 2014. www.erowid.org/columns/teafaerie /2014/05/.

Tendler, Stewart, and David May. *The Brotherhood of Eternal Love.* London: Cyan Books, 2007. First published 1984.

Thompson, Carey. "DeMaTerialized." *Visionary Review,* Fall 2007. http://vision -aryrevue.com/webtext4/thompson.html.

Thompson, Hunter S. *Hell's Angels.* London: Penguin Books, 1967.

Thompson, Hunter S. *Fear and Loathing in Las Vegas: A Savage Journey to the Heart of the American Dream.* New York: Random House, 1971.

Thompson, M. A., E. Moon, U. J. Kim, J. Xu, M. J. Siciliano, and R. M. Weinshilboum. "Human Indolethylamine N-methyltransferase: cDNA Cloning and Expression, Gene Cloning, and Chromosomal Localization," *Genomics* 61 (1999): 285–297.

Tramacchi, Des. "Vapours and Visions: Religious Dimensions of DMT Use." PhD thesis, School of History, Philosophy, Religion and Classics, University of Queensland, Brisbane, Australia, 2006.

Trout, Keeper. *Some Simple Tryptamines.* 2nd ed. Austin, TX: A Better Days Publication, 2007. First published 2002.

Tupper, Ken W., and Beatriz C. Labate. "Plants, Psychoactive Substances and the International Narcotics Control Board: The Control of Nature and the Nature of Control." *Human Rights and Drugs* 2, no. 1 (2012): 17–28.

Turner, D. M. *The Essential Psychedelic Guide.* San Francisco: Panther Press, 1994.

Turner, D. M. "Entity Contacts: Exploring Hyperspace." *The Entheogen Review,* Winter Solstice 1995: 4–7.

Turner, Fred. *From Counterculture to Cyberculture: Stewart Brand, the Whole Earth Network, and the Rise of Digital Utopianism.* Chicago: University of Chicago Press, 2006.

Turner, Victor. "Betwixt and Between: The Liminal Period in *Rites de Passage.*" In Victor Turner's *The Forest of Symbols: Aspects of Ndembu Ritual,* 93–111. Ithaca, NY: Cornell University Press, 1967. Turner's paper was first published in 1957.

Turner, W. J., and S. Merlis. "Effects of Some Indolealkylamines on Man." *Archives of Neurology and Psychiatry* 81, no. 1 (1959): 121–129.

Ulrich, Jennifer. "Transmissions from the Timothy Leary Papers: Experiments in Teletype to Tele-Thought." NYPL Archives, April 18, 2013. www.nypl.org /blog/2013/04/18/timothy-leary-papers-experiments-teletype-tele-thought.

universal shaman. "Mother Spirit Awaits: An Experience with DMT (ID 30919)." *Erowid.org.* September 28, 2004. www.erowid.org/exp/30919.

Vallée, Jacques. *Passport to Magonia: From Folklore to Flying Saucers.* Chicago: Henry Regnery, 1969.

van Gennep, Arnold. *The Rites of Passage.* London: Routledge & Kegan Paul, 1960. First published 1909.

Wassén, S. H. "Anthropological Survey of the Use of South American Snuffs." In *Ethnopharmacologic Search for Psychoactive Drugs,* Public Health Service Publication No. 1645, edited by D. H. Efron, B. Holmstedt, and N. S. Kline, 233–289. Washington, DC: U.S. Government Printing Office, 1967.

Wasson, Robert G. "Seeking the Magic Mushroom." *LIFE* 49, no. 19 (May 13, 1957): 100–102, 109–120.

Watson, Rick. "DMT, or, Spider Woman Comes to Town." Unpublished short story, April 16–17, 1993.

Watts, Alan. *The Joyous Cosmology: Adventures in the Chemistry of Consciousness.* New York: Pantheon Books, 1962.

Watts, Alan. "Psychedelics and Religious Experience." *California Law Review* 56, no. 1 (1968): 74–85.

Wertheim, Margaret. *The Pearly Gates of Cyberspace: A History of Space from Dante to the Internet.* New York: W. W. Norton, 1999.

"Why Is DMT Illegal if It Occurs Naturally in Everyones Brain." Uploaded to YouTube March 28, 2008. www.youtube.com/watch?v=GhEj314cmLw.

Winstock, Adam R., Stephen Kaar, and Rohan Borschmann. "Dimethyltryptamine (DMT): Prevalence, User Characteristics and Abuse Liability in a Large Global Sample." *Journal of Psychopharmacology* 28, no. 1 (2013): 49–54.

Wolfe, Tom. *The Electric Kool-Aid Acid Test.* London: Black Swan, 1993. First published 1968.

Wright, Tony, and Graham Gynn. *Left in the Dark: The Biological Origins of the Fall from Grace.* Lulu, 2007.

Wripple, Naasko. "The Liminal Village." In *Boom Book,* 74–104. Lisbon, Portugal: Good Mood Productions, 2007.

1200 Mics. *1200 Micrograms.* TIP World. 2002. TIPWCD21. CD, Album.

13th Floor Elevators, The. *The Psychedelic Sounds of The 13th Floor Elevators.* International Artists. August 1966. IA-LP-1. Vinyl, LP, Album, Mono.

9West. "Wake Up." *Nuance* (compiled by Emok and Banel). Iboga Records. 2006. IBOGACD43. CD, Comp.

Astral Projection. "Back from Hell." *Psytisfaction.* Phonokol. 2004. 2299-2. CD, Comp.

Atma. "The Exorcism of the Spirit." *Map of Goa Vol.* 2. Yellow Sunshine Explosion. 2006. YSE 127-2. 2×CD, Comp.

Ben Zen. "Dimethyltryptamine." *Audio Astronaut.* 2014. Mixtape.

Blue Lunar Monkey. "Hikuri Om." *Shamanic State.* AP Records. 2006. AP146. CD, Comp, Mixed.

Blue Lunar Monkey. "Mysterious Xperience." *Beyond 2012.* Synergetic Records. 2008. SYNDIGI002. 10×File, WAV, Album.

Braincell. "Psychoactive Plants." *Transformation of Reality.* Glowing Flame Records. 2007. GFRCD09. CD, Album.

Butterfly Dawn. LSD—Liquid Sound Design. 2003. bflcd64. CD, Comp.

Celtic Cross. *Hicksville.* Dragonfly Records. 1998. BFLCD 31. CD, Album.

Coming Soon. "Ayahuasca." *Become One.* Spin Twist Records. 2013. SPN1DIGI119. 4×File, MP3, EP, 320.

Crowded House. *Together Alone.* Capitol Records. 1993. CDP 724382704829. CD, Album.

Dark Nebula. "Book of Stones." *The 8th Sphere.* Digital Psionics. 2003. DPSICD06. CD, Album.

Dark Nebula & Scatterbrain. "Geometric Patterns." *Psionic Earth.* Digital Psionics. 2004. DPSICD08. CD, Comp.

Darpan and Bhakta. *Temple of Glowing Sound.* My Master Music. 2006. 2×CD, Album.

DMT. "DMT." *Dragonfly Classix.* Dragonfly Records. 1998. BFLCD 28. 2×CD, Comp.

Dr. Hoffman. "Spirit Molecules." *Paperworks.* SICK. 2013. CD, Album.

Dub Trees. *Nature Never Did Betray the Heart That Loved Her.* LSD—Liquid Sound Design. 2000. BFLCD 42. CD, Album.

Eat Static. "Prana." *Abduction.* Planet Dog. 1993. BARK CD 001. CD, Album.

Ekoplex. "Aya." *Discovering the Ancient*. Omnitropic. 2012. OMNI 007. 9×File, WAV, Album, Mixed.

Entheogenic. "Ground Luminosity." *Spontaneous Illumination*. C.O.R.N. Recordings. 2003. CORNCD01. CD, Album.

Exoplanet. "Dimethyltryptamine." *Metasophia*. Proton Particles. 2009. PSI0904. File, MP3.

Experimental Audio Research. "D.M.T. Symphony (Overture to an Inhabited Zone)." *Mesmerised*. Sympathy for the Record Industry. 1994. SFTRI279. LP, CD, Album.

Experimental Sound Project (ESP). "Chacruna Dub." *Dub Dimensions*. Ajnavision Records. 2011. AJNA003CD. CD, Comp.

Extrinsic. "Psychedelic Liberation." *The LSD Connection*. Yo Soy Records. 2011. 8×File, FLAC, Comp.

Fobi vs Mr. Madness. "On the Spot." *Welcome to Freakdom*. Free Radical Records. 2012. FRRCD008. 2×CD, Comp.

Fractal Flame. "Freakstuff." *A Spark of Light*. FX System. 2009. MP3.

Fragletrollet. "Shamanizer." *Shamanisma*. Space Baby Records. 2008. SBCD001. 2×CD, Comp.

Fugs, The. *Virgin Fugs*. ESP-Disk. 1967. ESP 1028. Vinyl, LP, Album.

Funkopath. "Skwirm." *Skwirm*. 21-3 Records. 1997. TO3 005. Vinyl, 12-inch.

Gaiana. "Deep Blue Skies." *Blue Sangoma Sounds*. Blue Hour Sounds. 2014. BHSCD011. 2×CD, Comp.

Hallucinogen. "LSD." *Twisted*. Twisted Records. 1995. bflcd 15. CD, Album.

Hujaboy. "Liquifried." *Planetary Service* (compiled by DJ Insanix and Neuromotor). Mechanik Records. 2009. MECH007. CD, Comp.

Hux Flux. "Finite Automata." *Circle Sine Sound*. Z-Plane Records. 2015. ZPLCD01. CD, Album.

Hypnoise. "Demetrium." *Transmissions* (compiled by Boom Shankar and Alexsoph). BMSS Records. BMSS2CD007. 2012. 2×CD, Comp.

Infinity Project, The. "Stimuli." *Feeling Weird*. TIP Records. 1995. TIPCD3. CD, Album.

Insectoid. *Groovology of the Metaverse*. WMS Records. 1998. WMS LP 02. CD, Album.

Insectoid. *New Vistas / Shamantec Images*. Kavator Records. 1996. KAV 01. Vinyl, 12-inch.

Irresistible Force, The. "Mountain High." *Flying High*. Rising High Records. 1992. RSN CD5. CD, Album.

Killing Joke. *Pandemonium*. Butterfly Records. 1994. BFLCD9. CD, Album.

Liquid on Safi. "Shamanic Madness." *13 Moon* (compiled by Cosmic Sun). Spliff Music. 2006. SP1CD017. CD, Comp.

Merkaba. "Hooked on Jungle." *Awaken*. Zenon Records. 2010. ZENCD024. CD, Album.

Merkaba. "Icaro." *Language of Light*. Merkaba Music. 2012. 7×File, FLAC, Album.

Merkaba. "Primal Earthly Pledge." *Language of Light*. Merkaba Music. 2012. 7×File, FLAC, Album.

Mimosa. *Hostilis*. Muti Music. 2008. Muti023. 7×File, WAV, EP.

Mister Black. "DMT Molecule." *Anahata* (compiled by Demoniac Insomniac). Active Meditation Music. 2009. AMM001. 11×File, WAV, Comp.

Mood Deluxe. "Stealthy Fungus." *Divine Inventions*. Liquid Records. 2008. LRCD007. CD, Comp.

NiT GriT. "The Awakening." *The Awakening*. 2010. EP.

NiT GriT. "Dimethyltryptamine." *Synthetic Heaven*. 2010. EP.

Not My Cup of Tea. Demon Tea. 2001. DMT CD07. CD, Comp.

Oozie Goodness—The Eye Opening Elixir. Demon Tea. 1998. DMT CD02. CD, Comp.

Ott. "Ground Luminosity (Ott's New Yoghurt Loom Mix)." Entheogenic's *Dialogue of the Speakers*. Chillcode Music. 2005. CHILLCD003. CD, Album.

Para Halu. "Adrenochrome." *Shanti Jatra II: Shamans and Healers* (compiled by Daksinamurti). Shanti Jatra. 2012. SJMCD002. CD, Comp.

Patchbay and Ital. "Plants and Animals." *Southern Cross* (by Patchbay). Mosaico Records. 2012. MSCRCD001. CD, Album.

Pink Floyd. "The Gnome." *The Piper at the Gates of Dawn*. Columbia. 1967. SX 6157. Vinyl, LP, Album, Mono.

Polyphonia vs. Zik. "Fucking Dimensions." *Shockwave Machine*. Tremors Underground Productions. 2007. TUP07-02. CD, Comp.

Psychedelic Krembo—Selected Tunes—Part 1. Krembro Records. 1996. 519636. CD, Comp.

Quantize. "Dymethyltryptamine." *Borderline* (compiled by DJ Osho). Echoes Records. 2009. ECHOCD-IL006. CD, Comp.

Run DMT. *Union of Opposites*. Play Me Records. 2012. PLAY069. 12×File, MP3, 320.

Shamen, The, with Terence McKenna. *Re: Evolution*. One Little Indian. 1993. 118TP 12. 12-inch, Single.

Shpongle. *Are You Shpongled?* Twisted Records. 1998. TWSCD4. CD, Album.

Shpongle. *Divine Moments of Truth*. Twisted Records. 2000. TWSC14. CD, Single.

Shpongle. "The God Particle." *The God Particle*. Twisted Records. 2011. TWSDL43. 2×File, MP3, EP, 320.

Shpongle. *Ineffable Mysteries from Shpongleland*. Twisted Records. 2009. TWSCD36. CD, Album.

Shpongle. *Nothing Lasts . . . But Nothing Is Lost*. Twisted Records. 2005. TWSCD28. CD, Album.

Shpongle. *Tales of the Inexpressible.* Twisted Records. 2001. TWSCD13. CD, Album.

Sideform. "Santo Daime." *Santo Diame.* TesseracTstudio. 2011. TESD0013. 3×File, Single, MP3, 320.

SiLo and Humerous. "New Path." *New Path.* Iono Music. 2014. INM1DIGI137. 3×File, MP3, 320.

Sonic Entity. "Spirit Molecule." *Goa Vol. 46* (compiled by DJ ShaMane). Yellow Sunshine Explosion. 2013. MillYSE 304-CD. 2×CD, Comp.

Space Tribe. "Cicadas on DMT." *Ultrasonic Heartbeat.* Spirit Zone Recordings. 1996. SPIRITZONE016. Vinyl, 12-inch.

Spirit Molecule. "Psychedelic Journey." *Lysergic State.* Impact Music Records. 2012. IMPACTD003. 3×File, MP3, 320.

Streamers. "Power and Light." *Goa Trance Vol. 19* (compiled by DJ Tulla). Yellow Sunshine Explosion. 2012. MillYSE 277-CD. 2×CD, Comp.

String Cheese Incident, The. *Untying the Not.* SCI Fidelity Records. 2003. SCI 1015. CD, Album.

Sturgill Simpson. *Metamodern Sounds in Country Music.* High Top Mountain Records. 2014. HTM002. CD, Album.

Therange Freak. "Dreamland." *How the Moon Was Made.* Space Baby Records. 2012. SBCD010. CD, Comp.

Tim Freke Feat with Terence McKenna. "Hooray in a New Way (The Elves of Hyper Space)." *Megatripolis.* Funky Peace Productions 2000 Ltd. 1996. Funky PCD1. 2×CD, Comp.

Time Machines. *Time Machines.* Eskaton. Eskaton 010. 1998. CD, Album.

Tron. "Amasonic." *Divine Inventions.* Liquid Records. 2008. LRCD007. CD, Comp.

Via Axis. "Tryptamine Dimensions." *Expressions of One.* Ovnimoon Records. 2011. OVNICD016. CD, Album.

Wizack Twizack. "Join My Cult." *MystaGogue: Beyond the Boundaries of Logic and Comprehension* (compiled by Overdream). Skygravity Records. 2011. CD, Comp.

Wizack Twizack. "Spirit Molecule." *Space No More.* AntiShanti Records. 2010. ASHRCD002. CD, Album.

Xikwri Neyrra. "Knockin' on Matrix Door." *Shri Maharaj* (mixed by Goa Gil). Avatar Records. 2011. AVA066. CD, Comp.

FILMOGRAPHY

Adams, Ken, dir. *Imaginatrix: The Terence McKenna Experience.* Magic Carpet Media, 2014.

Boorman, John, dir. *Zardoz.* John Boorman Productions, 1974.

Broers, Dieter, dir. *Solar Revolution.* Screen Addiction, 2012.

Cronenberg, David, dir. *Naked Lunch.* Film Trustees, Ltd., 1991.

Erickson, Blair, dir. *Banshee Chapter.* Sunchaser Entertainment, 2013.

Gardner, Chance, dir. *Magical Egypt: A Symbolist Tour.* "Episode 5: Navigating the Afterlife." CustomFlix, 2005.

Gelb, David, dir. *The Lazarus Effect.* Blumhouse Productions, 2015.

Gordon, Stuart, dir. *From Beyond.* MGM, 1986.

Jung, David, dir. *The Possession of Michael King.* Gold Circle Films, Quickfire Films, 2014.

Kubrick, Stanley, dir. *2001: A Space Odyssey.* MGM, 1968.

Kubrick, Stanley, dir. *The Shining.* Warner Bros., 1980.

Noé, Gaspar, dir. *Enter the Void.* Fidélité Films, Wild Bunch, BUF, 2009.

Razam, Rak, and Tim Parish. dirs. *Aya: Awakenings.* Icaro Foundation, 2013.

Rochlin, Maxine, and Morgan Harris, dirs. *The Alchemical Dream: Rebirth of the Great Work.* Mystic Fire Productions, 2008.

Rudolph, Alan, dir. *Return Engagement,* 1983.

Russell, Ken, dir. *Altered States.* Warner Bros., 1980.

Schultz, Mitch, dir. *DMT: The Spirit Molecule.* Spectral Alchemy, Synthetic Pictures, 2010.

Witz, Martin, dir. *The Substance: Albert Hofmann's LSD.* Ventura Film, 2011.

Zemeckis, Robert, dir. *Contact.* Warner Bros., 1997.

INDEX

"Sorcery and Drugs in Opening the Last
    Days Spirit Portal" (Dr. Future),
    131–132
soul
    death and reincarnation of, 119–120
    expression of, as effect, 6, 46, 50–51
    pineal gland as seat of, 120, 121, 143
sounds
    audio rupture/threshold popping,
        91–92, 214, 313
    buzzing energy fields, 91, 92, 93, 214
    for DMT release in brain, 335–336
    for hyperspace navigation, 289
    miscellaneous, 49
    speed, 243–244
    voices, 49, 52–53, 85–86, 91, 209, 229, 269
space exploration, 230–232, 288
Spacemen 3, 211
space-time reorientations, 6, 15, 25–26, 71,
    185–186, 228, 235–236
Space Tree, 159, 212–213
Spacetree, Nick (Nen), 159, 161–165, 175,
    180, 212–213
Space Tribe, 207–208, 214, 343
spatial entheogens, 162–163
Spectrum, 211
Spirit Molecule, 196–197
Spooky (DJ), 280
Spruce, Richard, 21
Stanford Research Institute (SRI), 38–40,
    45, 83
Stanley, Owsley "Bear," 68–70, 72, 76–78,
    84, 101
Star Sound Orchestra, 219–220
Stebbing, Martin, 313
storytelling, 311–312, 324–325
Strange Visitors (entities), 347
Strassman, Rick, 114, 121, 147, 217, 218.
    See also University of New Mexico
    DMT research
String Cheese Incident, The, 206
Stropharia cubensis, 90
Structure of Scientific Revolutions, The
    (Kuhn), 290
Subotnick, Morton, 211
Sub Rosa (magazine), 127
Sumerian mythology, 364–365

Sun, The (newspaper), 34
Supernatural (Hancock), 354–355, 364
Surfing through Hyperspace (Pickover), 254
Swain, Fred, 49, 51
Sydney Morning Herald (newspaper), 166
synesthesia, 6, 30–31, 92, 192, 338
synthesized DMT, 29–34, 68–70
Syrian rue (Peganum harmala), 153, 156,
    162, 169, 274
Szára, Stephen, 15–17, 19, 40, 73, 230, 386

T
Taino Indians, 16
Tapper, Dennis, 197–198
taste, 70
tattoo art, 195
teacher plants, 9, 176, 180, 237–238
Teafaerie, 237–238
Teilhard de Chardin, Pierre, 251
Tekou Maru II (ship), 223
telepathine, 20, 23, 28
"10X changa" (smoking blend), 171
teonanácatl, 18–19, 150
terror, as effect
    experiences and descriptions, 43, 45,
        48–49, 66, 135, 267
    overdoses and, 29, 283–287
    resistance provoking, 294
Tertium Organum (Ouspensky), 234–236
"That Worlds May Live" (Bond), 242
"Theogony" (Hesiod), 199
theoneurology. See religious/spiritual
    experiences
Therange Freak, 197
therapy. See healing
Thinking Allowed with Jeffery Mishlove
    (television show), 106
third eye, 121–122, 128
13th Floor Elevators, 63, 211
Thompson, Carey
    art style and purpose, 314
    DiMethyl Temple, 314–316, insert
    Diosa Madre Tierra, 314–315, insert
    GoD stage design, 317, insert
    Singularity, 316
Thompson, Hunter S., 61, 115, 185
Thorpe, Ray, 169, 173

ABOUT THE AUTHOR

GRAHAM ST JOHN, PHD, is an Australian cultural anthropologist specializing in entheogens, dance music cultures, and neotribes. He has authored several books, including *Global Tribe: Technology, Spirituality and Psytrance* (Equinox, 2012), and *Technomad: Global Raving Countercultures* (Equinox, 2009) and has been awarded postdoctoral Fellowships in Australia, United States, Canada, and Switzerland, where he recently began researching the global Burning Man diaspora in Europe. A frequent speaker at conferences and transformational festivals, he is the founding Executive Editor of *Dancecult: Journal of Electronic Dance Music Culture.*

About North Atlantic Books

North Atlantic Books (NAB) is an independent, nonprofit publisher committed to a bold exploration of the relationships between mind, body, spirit, and nature. Founded in 1974, NAB aims to nurture a holistic view of the arts, sciences, humanities, and healing. To make a donation or to learn more about our books, authors, events, and newsletter, please visit www.northatlanticbooks.com.

North Atlantic Books is the publishing arm of the Society for the Study of Native Arts and Sciences, a 501(c)(3) nonprofit educational organization that promotes cross-cultural perspectives linking scientific, social, and artistic fields. To learn how you can support us, please visit our website.